War in an Age of Revolution,

This volume investigates a critical moment in the hist............ ...... It ....
historians of the early modern and modern eras to speak to one another across
the great historiographical divide that has traditionally separated them. The central
questions in the volume have to do with the historical place of revolutionary warfare
on both sides of the Atlantic – the degree to which such warfare extended practices
common in the eighteenth century or introduced fundamentally new forms of
warfare. Among the topics covered in the volume are the global dimensions of
warfare, logistics, universal military service and the mobilization of noncombatants,
occupation, and the impact of war on civilian life in both Europe and North
America.

Roger Chickering is Professor of History at the BMW Center for German and
European Studies, Georgetown University. His recent publications include *The
Great War and Urban Life in Germany: Freiburg, 1914–1918* (2007) and *A World at
Total War: Global Conflict and the Politics of Destruction, 1937–1945* (2005), coedited
with Stig Förster and Bernd Grenier.

Stig Förster is Professor of General Modern History at the University of Bern and
has also taught at the University of Augsburg and held research fellowships at the
German Historical Institutes in London and Washington, D.C. His most recent
publications include *Der doppelte Militarismus. Die deutsche Heeresrüstungspolitik zwischen Status-quo-Sicherung und Aggression, 1890–1913* (1985) and *Die mächtigen Diener
der East India Company. Ursachen und Hintergrunde der britischen Expansionspolitik in
Südasien, 1793–1819* (1992).

PUBLICATIONS OF THE GERMAN HISTORICAL INSTITUTE

Edited by Hartmut Berghoff
with the assistance of David Lazar

The German Historical Institute is a center for advanced study and research whose purpose is to provide a permanent basis for scholarly cooperation among historians from the Federal Republic of Germany and the United States. The Institute conducts, promotes, and supports research into both American and German political, social, economic, and cultural history; into transatlantic migration, especially in the nineteenth and twentieth centuries; and into the history of international relations, with special emphasis on the roles played by the United States and Germany.

Recent books in the series:

Cathryn Carson, *Heisenberg in the Atomic Age: Science and the Public Sphere*

Michaela Hoenicke Moore, *Know Your Enemy: The American Debate on Nazism*

Matthias Schulz and Thomas A. Schwartz, editors, *The Strained Alliance: U.S.-European Relations from Nixon to Carter*

Suzanne L. Marchand, *German Orientalism in the Age of Empire: Religion, Race, and Scholarship*

Manfred Berg and Bernd Schaefer, editors, *Historical Justice in International Perspective: How Societies Are Trying to Right the Wrongs of the Past*

Carole Fink and Bernd Schaefer, editors, *Ostpolitik, 1969–1974: European and Global Responses*

Nathan Stoltzfus and Henry Friedlander, editors, *Nazi Crimes and the Law*

Joachim Radkau, *Nature and Power: A Global History of the Environment*

Andreas W. Daum, *Kennedy in Berlin*

Jonathan R. Zatlin, *The Currency of Socialism: Money and Political Culture in East Germany*

War in an Age of Revolution, 1775–1815

Edited by

ROGER CHICKERING
Georgetown University

STIG FÖRSTER
Universität Bern, Historisches Institut

GERMAN HISTORICAL INSTITUTE
Washington, D.C.
and

 CAMBRIDGE
UNIVERSITY PRESS

CAMBRIDGE UNIVERSITY PRESS
Cambridge, New York, Melbourne, Madrid, Cape Town,
Singapore, São Paulo, Delhi, Mexico City

Cambridge University Press
The Edinburgh Building, Cambridge CB2 8RU, UK

Published in the United States of America by Cambridge University Press, New York

www.cambridge.org
Information on this title: www.cambridge.org/9781107692657

First published 2010
First paperback edition 2013

A catalogue record for this publication is available from the British Library

Library of Congress Cataloguing in Publication Data
War in an age of revolution, 1775–1815 / edited by Roger Chickering, Stig Förster.
p.   cm. – (Publications of the German Historical Institute)
Includes bibliographical references and index.
ISBN 978-0-521-89996-3 (hbk.)
1. Military art and science – History – 18th century.   2. Military art and science –
History – 19th century.   3. Revolutions – History – 18th century.   4. Revolutions –
History – 19th century.   5. Europe – History, Military – 1789–1815.   6. United
States – History – Revolution, 1775–1783.   7. United States – History – War of 1812.
8. War and society – Europe – History.   9. War and society – North America – History.
I. Chickering, Roger, 1942–   II. Förster, Stig.
U39.W36   2009
355.0209´033–dc22   2009044094

ISBN 978-1-107-69265-7 Paperback

Contents

Contributors

Katherine B. Aaslestad, Department of History, West Virginia University

Jeremy Black, Department of History, University of Exeter

T. H. Breen, Department of History, Northwestern University

Marion Breunig, Historical Seminar, University of Heidelberg

Michael Broers, Lady Margaret Hall, University of Oxford

Roger Chickering, Department of History, Georgetown University

Donatus Düsterhaus, "War Experiences" Research Group, University of Tübingen (2005–8); University Library, University of Heidelberg

Mary A. Favret, Department of English, Indiana University

Alan Forrest, Department of History, University of York

Stig Förster, Historical Institute, University of Bern

Azar Gat, Department of Political Sciences, Tel Aviv University

Karen Hagemann, Department of History, University of North Carolina at Chapel Hill

Beatrice Heuser, School of Politics and International Relations, University of Reading

Günther Kronenbitter, Department of History, University of Augsburg

Wolfgang Kruse, Historical Institute, Fern Universität Hagen

Jörg Nagler, Historical Institute, University of Jena

Timothy J. Shannon, Department of History, Gettysburg College

Ute Planert, Historical Seminar, University of Wuppertal

John Lawrence Tone, School of History, Technology, and Society, Georgia Institute of Technology

Dierk Walter, Theory and History of Violence Research Unit, Hamburg Institute for Social Research

Matthew C. Ward, Department of History, University of Dundee

A Tale of Two Tales

Grand Narratives of War in the Age of Revolution

ROGER CHICKERING

Historians of warfare in the modern era do not talk a lot to their colleagues who study the early modern period. This problem betrays a more general lack of communication among scholars who regard one another across the late-eighteenth-century divide. It is also due to the curricular segregation that survives at colleges and universities in Europe and North America. In the field of military history, however, the problem is particularly complicated. It has been exacerbated by the two different master narratives that have, for the past half century, organized the history of Western warfare in the early modern and modern eras. Despite remarkable congruities, each narrative has shaped its epoch into a coherent unit more effectively than it has addressed the connections between the two. The issues of narrative articulation are not peripheral. They have to do in the broadest sense with the military significance of the revolutionary transition in the Atlantic world at the end of the eighteenth century. At issue is not only the conduct of operations on the battlefield but also the changing role of warfare in the history of society, politics, and culture.

The master narrative that currently presides over the history of warfare in early modern Europe is that of the "military revolution." Michael Roberts christened this concept in his inaugural lecture at Queen's University in Belfast in January 1955.[1] In an intellectual exercise that was as elegant as it was breathtaking, Roberts related all the major dimensions of military and political development in the early modern era to a single technological innovation. The introduction of firearms into European armies during the middle decades of the sixteenth century was, he argued, a revolutionary act. It quickly resulted in far-reaching tactical changes in European land forces,

---

[1] Michael Roberts, "The Military Revolution, 1560–1660," in *Essays in Swedish History* (Minneapolis, 1967), 195–225.

once Maurice of Nassau introduced volley fire at the end of the same century and the armies of Gustavus Adolphus demonstrated several decades later how effectively this tactic could be exploited in offensive operations. Tactical innovation thereafter molded strategy, encouraging battles among ever-larger armies of highly trained musketeers. By the middle of the seventeenth century, the imperatives of raising, drilling, feeding, and supplying great bodies of soldiers had recommended the creation of standing armies. This organizational innovation was the principal marker of early modern absolutism, the centralization and expansion of royal bureaucracies, which in turn became the channels through which the militarization of society fed in the eighteenth century. Tactical innovations were thus, Roberts wrote, "the efficient cause of changes which were really revolutionary. Between 1560 and 1660 a great and permanent transformation came over the European world."[2]

One sign of Roberts's influence has been the vibrant debate that his lecture provoked.[3] It has not been difficult to challenge either the timing or the causal links among some of the developments that he had sought to unite in a single analytical edifice. The most important of his critics has been Geoffrey Parker. Parker has argued that one of the central features of the military revolution, the expansion of European armies, owed less to infantry firearms than to artillery; and he has insisted that the development of artillery was primarily a response to new designs in fortification that were introduced during the sixteenth century.[4] The hallmark of these innovations, the so-called *trace italienne*, enhanced dramatically the defensibility of fortresses and thus multiplied the challenges that faced besieging armies. Although the introduction of this independent variable seemed like a blemish on Roberts's grand design, Parker captured a consensus of opinion at the end of the debate when he endorsed, in its basic contours, the idea of a military revolution in the early modern era. All the criticism of Roberts had, he conceded, failed "to dent the basic thesis: the scale of warfare in early modern Europe was revolutionized, and this had important and wide-ranging consequences."[5] As if to document the vitality of Roberts's revolutionary model, military

---

2 Ibid., 217.
3 See Michael Duffy, ed., *The Military Revolution and the State, 1500–1800* (Exeter, U.K., 1980); Clifford J. Rogers, ed., *The Military Revolution Debate: Readings on the Military Transformation of Early Modern Europe* (Boulder, Colorado, 1995); Jeremy Black, ed., *War in the Early Modern World* (Boulder, Colorado, 1999).
4 Geoffrey Parker, "The 'Military Revolution,' 1560–1660 – A Myth?" *Journal of Modern History* 48 (1976): 195–214; see also Parker, *The Military Revolution: Military Innovation and the Rise of the West, 1500–1800* (Cambridge, U.K., 1988).
5 Parker, "Military Revolution," 214.

analysts have more recently claimed it as a guide to thinking about what they are calling "revolutions in military affairs," or RMAs.[6]

The master narrative of military history in the early modern epoch begins in any case with tactical change induced by technology. By contrast, the narrative of war in the modern era commences amid political upheaval.[7] The wars that began in Europe in 1792 represent, as David Bell argues, "The First Total War" – an altogether new sort of warfare, "the cataclysmic intensification of the fighting," in which understandings of war lurched toward an apocalyptic and redemptive vision of a "final, cleansing paroxysm of violence."[8] The emphasis in Bell's gripping account falls on the culture of war, but it comports with arguments long advanced by military historians about the conduct of operations. Russell Weigley summarized these arguments in the early 1990s, when he wrote that the levée en masse "was the first forging of the thunderbolt of a new kind of war – the total war of nations pitting against each other all their resources and passion."[9] From this perspective, the French Revolution laid the moral and ideological foundations of total war, as it blurred the distinctions between combatants and noncombatants. The nation's defense claimed the participation of everyone, whether as soldiers in the field or as providers of material and moral support at home. This principle henceforth established the basic patterns of military history for the next two centuries, as warfare intensified and expanded radically in scope. The unleashing of nationalism translated into the unprecedented intensity of battlefield operations, which were driven by passions that made soldiers both more mobile and implacable in their pursuit of victory. Popular hatreds were mobilized, so the same passions encouraged the radicalization of war aims and the discrediting of moderation, diplomatic compromise, and the restraints that had once been set on war by custom, law, and humanity. At the same time, the ideologization of warfare drove the exponential expansion of European armies, just as it extended dramatically the geographical scope of their operations.

In this reading, the technological revolution of the nineteenth century was the complement of the ideological revolution of the late eighteenth century. Industrialization made total war materially possible. It provided

6 MacGregor Knox and Williamson Murray, eds., *The Dynamics of Military Revolution, 1300–2050* (Cambridge, U.K., 2001).

7 Roger Chickering, "Total War: Use and Abuse of a Concept," in *Anticipating Total War: The German and American Experiences, 1871–1914*, ed. Manfred Boemeke, Roger Chickering, and Stig Förster (Cambridge, U.K., 1999), 13–28.

8 David A. Bell, *The First Total War: Napoleon's Europe and the Birth of Warfare as We Know It* (Boston, 2007), 9, 316.

9 Russell F. Weigley, *The Age of Battles: The Quest for Decisive Warfare from Breitenfeld to Waterloo* (Bloomington, Indiana, 1991), 290.

the means to equip, transport, and coordinate vast armies, which came
to number in the millions of men, as well as to inflict military violence
systematically on the producers of war's material instruments: the civilians
who had, thanks to the modern logic of combat, become no less critical than
soldiers to the prosecution of war. These developments reached a frightful
climax in the two great industrial conflicts of the twentieth century, the
"century of total war."[10] Hiroshima and Auschwitz became its icons – the
one a symbol of the technological virtuosity that threatened total military
destruction, and the other a symbol of popular hatreds that had totalized
the definition of *enemy*.

Both of these grand narratives, the one based on military revolution, the
other on total war, have been more effective in identifying beginnings than
endings. The concept of total war was born in the twentieth century, amid
two world wars and in anticipation of a third, which was supposed to be
an apocalyptic conflict that would bring the grand narrative to the kind
of culmination envisaged by Dr. Strangelove. It has yet to happen. In the
meantime, the idea of total war has provided little guidance to the hot wars
of the late twentieth and early twenty-first centuries; and sixty years after
the fact, historians are drawing the hopeful conclusion that the era of total
war ended in 1945.

The end of the early modern military revolution carries less immediate
practical implications, but it is arguably of greater historiographical significance, insofar as it bears immediately on the narrative beginning of total
war. Michael Roberts himself complicated this issue by denying it, arguing
instead that total war was the direct issue or a phase of the military revolution: "By 1660 the modern art of war had come to birth. Mass armies, strict
discipline, the control of the state, the submergence of the individual, had
already arrived." "The road lay open, broad and straight," he concluded,
"to the abyss of the twentieth century."[11] Parker was more circumspect,
not to say coy. He dated the "culmination" of the military revolution in the
middle decades of the eighteenth century. Thereafter, he argued, the quick-
ening pace of innovation, the appearance of light-infantry and light-cavalry
units, the introduction of divisional organization, and the development of
standardized mobile artillery all marked a qualitative leap. The events of
the century's last decade then represented "a further revolution in military
manpower." But the cumulative impact of changes since the mid-eighteenth
century was unambiguous. "The scale of warfare," Parker wrote, was, by

---

10 Raymond Aron, *The Century of Total War* (Boston, 1955).
11 Roberts, "Military Revolution," 217–18.

1800, "so totally transformed that it might be said that another 'military revolution' had occurred."[12]

Parker's cautious use of the word *totally* in this connection indicated that he was alive to the narrative problems that lurked in his own argument, but his suggestion that the modern era in military history began forty years before the French Revolution, within the womb of the ancien régime, did not resolve the issues that have dogged the effort to relate the two military revolutions to each other. A central problem has been the divergent perspectives that the two narratives have encouraged on war and society in the eighteenth century. In the narrative of military revolution, the eighteenth century witnessed the climax of the story, the culmination of centuries of military expansion, the growing pervasiveness of warfare – as well as military organization and values – in European politics and society. It was an age of nearly uninterrupted warfare, experiments in conscription, crippling financial burdens on society, and the supremacy of military culture.[13]

This characterization of the eighteenth century perturbs the narrative of total war. In this narrative, the eighteenth century represents instead the well-ordered terminus a quo of total war. It stands as the classical age in which warfare was both limited in scope and, as Bell's account has shown, frequent enough to count as a routine undertaking in the eyes of men who thought about the place of war in society and politics.[14] Wars were fought in the Age of Reason for the sake of calculated dynastic ambition by small, professional armies according to generally accepted rules of engagement and conventions that reflected the mores of the aristocratic officer class. Most of the armed forces were recruited by force or guile from the nonproductive sectors of society. They were held together by little more than draconian discipline, which restricted the mobility of soldiers to the range in which their officers could immediately supervise and supply them. As a consequence, civilians were largely spared the military depredations that had plagued the seventeenth century.

This picture of warfare in the eighteenth century defies the ideas of Michael Roberts, which accentuate the military continuities across the era of the French Revolution. In the narrative of total war, by contrast, the French Revolution involved much more than an expansion in the scale of warfare; it was foremost a revolution in attitudes. It was, as one historian

---

12 Parker, "Military Revolution," 153.
13 See Quincy Wright, *A Study of War* (Chicago, 1964), 647–9; André Corvisier, *Armies and Societies in Europe, 1494–1789* (Bloomington, Indiana, 1979); Otto Büsch, *Military System and Social Life in Old Regime Prussia, 1713–1807* (Atlantic Highlands, New Jersey, 1996).
14 Bell, *First Total War*, 21–51.

has observed, "a *political-ideological* revolution that remade warfare from top to bottom."[15] "By enlisting mass emotions," to quote Russell Weigley again, the nation-in-arms ruptured the "restraints upon the violence of war by stoking the fires of hatred among peoples."[16] Soldiers inspired by patriotic élan were the key to this more intensive kind of warfare. The fact that they were highly motivated had far-reaching tactical and strategic consequences. On the battlefield, these patriotic warriors constituted a "terrible mass." Untethered from rote drill, they fought effectively as skirmishers, maneuvered in flexible formations, attacked in column with cold steel, and pursued their defeated enemies in a way that armies schooled in the old regime could not. Because they could be trusted not to desert, these new soldiers represented a much more formidable strategic force; they could maneuver more rapidly from battlefield to battlefield. They could live off the land, liberated from constant oversight and the ponderous supply trains that shackled their antagonists. The logistics of the new war thus had consequences much like those of the levée en masse; wherever French troops marched, whether in France or abroad, civilians were drawn – willing or not – directly into the prosecution of war as suppliers of field armies.

This analysis of the French Revolution's military repercussions is not disinterested. It owes a great deal to the language of the revolutionaries themselves, as well as to the commentaries of Gerhard von Scharnhorst, Carl von Clausewitz, and other observers outside France, who subsequently sought to make sense of their own military misfortunes at the hands of the French.[17] This analysis has also become increasingly problematic, thanks in part to work that Roberts inspired on war and society in the early modern era and in part to careful scholarship on the armies of the Revolutionary era themselves. It thus seems pertinent again to pose the question of just how the revolutionary upheavals of the late eighteenth century revolutionized warfare. How were revolutionary armies different from both their forebears and their antagonists? And in what ways was the impact of war on civilian society transformed?

These questions can also be reformulated in light of the provocation that Michael Roberts issued a half century ago. One can argue that the two

---

15 MacGregor Knox, "Mass Politics and Nationalism as Military Revolution: The French Revolution and After," in Knox and Murray, *Dynamics*, 58 (italics in original).
16 Weigley, *Age of Battles*, 279.
17 See Jean-Paul Bertaud, *The Army of the French Revolution: From Citizen-Soldiers to Instrument of Power* (Princeton, New Jersey, 1988), 102–3, 154–5; see also Wolfgang Kruse, *Die Erfindung des modernen Militarismus: Krieg, Militär und bürgerliche Gesellschaft im politischen Diskurs der Französischen Revolution 1789–1799* (Munich, 2003); Azar Gat, *The Origins of Military Thought from the Enlightenment to Clausewitz* (Oxford, 1989), 99–214; Peter Paret, *Yorck and the Era of Prussian Reform, 1807–1815* (Princeton, New Jersey, 1966).

grand narratives of military history do not in fact collide in the Revolutionary era. In this alternate reading, the transition in European warfare from the eighteenth to the nineteenth century was marked less by rupture than by continuity, the playing out of dynamics that were already evident in the ancien régime, the testing of ideas long articulated and institutions long anticipated. In this light, the principal innovations that the armies of the Revolutionary era were supposed to embody turn out to be ambivalent, if not illusory. The changes that accompanied war in the age of revolution can thus be understood better as part of a single narrative.

To be sure, one basic innovation of the Revolutionary era seems to remain beyond dispute. The French armies that were raised during the Revolutionary era do appear to have been more representative of the general populace than their predecessors of the earlier eighteenth century had been. The proposition that the armies of Revolutionary France represented a broadly based citizen army can appeal to a distinguished tradition of scholarship.[18] The more recent analysis of Samuel Scott, which confirms this conclusion, suggests that the construction of a French national army in the 1790s was marked by the departure of foreign units and by greater rates of recruitment from the south and west of France – areas that were more remote from the country's vulnerable frontiers. Principally, though, the emerging revolutionary army saw a marked decline in the proportion of urban artisans and a corresponding increase in the poor rural classes, peasants and day laborers, among the recruits of the early 1790s.[19] The significance of this modulation is not, however, self-evident; nor does it suggest radically new reasons for enlistment. Scott himself notes that both rural and urban recruits tended to be poor, and that many of them were persuaded to enlist by economic necessity. In other words, they followed a familiar inducement, which had for centuries driven recruitment in the French royal army and in professional armies elsewhere in Europe, at least to the west of Russia.[20]

In the narrative of total war, the case for a revolutionary transformation at the end of the eighteenth century turns primarily on the question of motivation. The fact that tens of thousands of young men volunteered for military service in the early years of the French Revolution is extraordinary. But it is another question how, if at all, the ideological enthusiasm that

---

18 Albert Souboul, *Les soldats de l'an II* (Paris, 1959); André Corvisier, *L'armée française de la fin du XVIIme siècle au ministère du Choiseul* (Paris, 1964).

19 Samuel F. Scott, *The Response of the Royal Army to the French Revolution: The Role and Development of the Line Army, 1787–1793* (Oxford, 1978), 186–90.

20 Corvisier, *Armies*, 131–6; see also M. S. Anderson, *War and Society in Europe and the Old Regime, 1618–1789* (Montreal, 1988), 120–4.

moved them to join the colors thereafter animated a new kind of soldier. Recent scholarship has illuminated the complexities of combat motivation; it has also thrown doubts on the influence of ideology on behavior under fire.[21] It has thus drawn into question one of the principal claims about differences between the revolutionary armies and their opponents. Desertion, the classic marker of ill-motivated troops, was no less common among the volunteer armies of the Revolution than among the professional armies of the eighteenth century.[22] Rates of desertion in the French armies fell only with the amalgamations in 1793–4, whose purpose and effect were to bring more discipline to units of volunteers – in other words, to make them fight more like the professionals against whom they took the field.

Both before and after the amalgamations, motivation appears to have pivoted on the small combat group – on the discipline, authority, respect, sense of honor, and collective pride that prevailed in units of soldiers from the regimental level down. Group dynamics in these units have always been complicated. Ideology and discipline were but two of the components in an implicit contract that regulated relations among troops and officers – even in the armies of the eighteenth century. "Soldiers may have enlisted under what amounted to absolute terms of service," remarks Dennis Showalter in his study of Frederick the Great's army. "In practice they had very solid ideas of their implied rights."[23] Scott notes of the French royal army that regimental loyalties "increased cohesion among the soldiers and between them and their immediate superiors, the NCO's."[24] The political education that revolutionary governments promoted among French troops in the early 1790s bore massively on questions of small-group cohesion, but the impact was equivocal.[25] Rewriting the contract in the new language of natural rights (to say nothing of voting) could undermine as well as strengthen discipline in the ranks.[26] In his study of the revolutionary Armée du Nord, John Lynn has admittedly reached different conclusions. He identifies the squad or *ordinaire* as the most important primary group, and he argues that the revolutionary ideal of fraternity enhanced discipline and cohesion, "tightening bonds and defining the relationship between men as familial,

21 Anthony Kellett, *Combat Motivation: The Behavior of Soldiers in Battle* (Boston, 1982), 327.
22 Bertaud, *Army*, 260.
23 Dennis Showalter, *The Wars of Frederick the Great* (London, 1996), 6. See also Christopher Duffy, *The Military Experience in the Age of Reason* (New York, 1988), 129–36; Sascha Möbius, "Die Kommunikation zwischen preußischen Soldaten und Offizieren im Siebenjährigen Krieg zwischen Gewalt und Konsens," *Militärgeschichtliche Zeitschrift* 63 (2004): 325–53.
24 Scott, *Response*, 35.
25 Alan Forrest, *The Soldiers of the French Revolution* (Durham, North Carolina, 1990), 89–124.
26 Bertaud, *Army*, 261–2.

based on affection, support, and a strong degree of selflessness."[27] This conclusion would rest more secure, however, in the company of empirical comparison with other armies of Revolutionary France, as well as with their predecessors.[28]

The question of soldiers' motivation has also been linked to the introduction of new, more flexible tactical formations in the revolutionary armies, whose infantry could, unlike their predecessors, fight in line, column, or as *tirailleurs*. As evidence of high motivation in the Armée du Nord, Lynn appeals to "the tactical reliance upon the élan of troops massed in spirited bayonet assaults and the initiative of individuals dispersed as skirmishers."[29] The origins and significance of this "flexible tactical system of surprising variety" have been at issue for more than a century, since Jean Colin first drew attention to its roots in the old regime.[30] The scholarship of Robert Quimby has left no doubt, however, that the flexible *ordre mixte* was a child of the eighteenth century, that it incubated in the minds of Jacques-Antoine Hippolyte de Guibert and his forebears decades before the French Revolution, and that it lay at the foundation of field regulations that were introduced into the royal French army in 1791 – at a time when the army was still, in most basic respects, an institution of the ancien régime.[31]

Finally, a revolution in the motivation of soldiers also figures in the transformation of logistics that is said to have brought a massive increase in the burdens imposed by revolutionary armies on civilians. Because the new soldiers of the Revolution believed in their cause, they could be trusted to live off the land in small groups. They no longer required the elaborate system of magazines and supply trains that large field armies had required, lest the bulk of the soldiery desert. However, innovations brought by the Revolution to logistics have also been the subject of controversy, thanks largely to the work of Martin van Creveld who has blamed Clausewitz for distorting basic continuities that survived the Revolution. Armies lived off the land before the French Revolution as well as after it. "Eighteenth century armies," van Creveld insists, "lived as their predecessors had always done, and as their successors were destined to do until – and including – the first weeks of World War I; that is, by taking the bulk of their needs

27 John A. Lynn, *The Bayonets of the Republic: Motivation and Tactics in the Army of Revolutionary France, 1791–94* (Urbana, Illinois, 1984), 173.
28 See Bertaud, *Army*, 240.   29 Lynn, *Bayonets*, 178.
30 Jean Colin, *L'éducation militaire de Napoléon* (Paris, 1901); see also A. M. J. Hyatt, "The Origins of Napoleonic Warfare: A Survey of Interpretations," *Military Affairs* 30 (1966–67): 177–85.
31 Robert S. Quimby, *The Background of Napoleonic Warfare: The Theory of Military Tactics in Eighteenth-Century France* (New York, 1968).

away from the country."[32] The depredations that the armies of the French Revolution visited on areas through which they marched thus continued an age-old tradition of the *chevauchée* against vulnerable civilians.[33]

These judgments are difficult to square with the proposition that modern warfare began precipitously at the end of the eighteenth century. So are other continuities that historians have traced between the armies of the French Revolution and their predecessors. Still, it would be idle to argue that no fundamental change took place in European warfare in the 1790s. At issue are the nature, dimensions, and causes of the transformation. The narrative of total war has emphasized the dramatic escalation in the intensity of war, which accompanied the ideological transformation of the soldiery and the civilians who supported them. Nationalism, in this logic, "injected into war a ferocity that far outstripped the religious fanaticism of the preceding century."[34] This proposition is doubtful at best and impossible to demonstrate in any case. The whole argument for the intensification of war by revolution rests on shaky assumptions about both the practical impact of ideology on the battlefield and the institutional dynamics in the armies of the old regime (to say nothing of cloudy understandings of *intensity*).

An alternative reading of the late eighteenth century is plausible, but it requires rethinking both the governing narratives. It is based on the proposition that the most revolutionary feature of the new French armies was their size.[35] The most important changes in warfare were hence due to the sheer force of numbers. Bigger armies continued, however, to win.[36] The achievement of the revolutionary governments was to create the institutions to recruit and support vast armies, although here again, particularly in the case of conscription, the French could draw amply on precedents from the eighteenth century. The military relevance of ideology lay principally in its contribution to these numbers. Whatever its impact on the motivation of soldiers in the field, patriotism encouraged them to enlist in the first place; hence it made possible the building of armies that dwarfed their opponents on the battlefield. Desertion remained a fact of life in these new armies, but great pools of manpower made it a less critical problem than it had been in smaller, professional armies. At the same time, numerical superiority recommended the employment of shock tactics in the knowledge that losses

---

32 Martin van Creveld, *Supplying War: Logistics from Wallenstein to Patton* (Cambridge, U.K., 1977), 33.
33 Mark Grimsley and Clifford J. Rogers, eds., *Civilians in the Path of War* (Lincoln, Nebraska, 2002).
34 Williamson Murray and MacGregor Knox, "Thinking about Revolutions in Warfare," in Murray and Knox, *Dynamics*, 8.
35 T. C. W. Blanning, *The French Revolutionary Wars, 1787–1802* (London, 1996), 116–28.
36 See Gunther E. Rothenberg, *The Art of Warfare in the Age of Napoleon* (London, 1977), 247–55.

could be replaced. These tactics, which featured attack in columns, had the added advantage of requiring minimal training of recruits. Finally, these new armies were so large that they mandated parceling and the adoption of divisional organization; there was no other practical way to move them. Even divided, however, the armies generated enormous logistical requirements, which demanded that soldiers draw resources on a new scale, if not a new model, from the lands through which they marched.

In this reading, the continuities deserve more emphasis than the ruptures; and the two narratives are joined. The French Revolution can be situated in the same master narrative as the military revolution of the early modern era. In the modern and early modern eras, the common narrative theme is the dramatic increase in the size of armies and their weight in civilian society and culture. The French Revolution represents less a break with developments in the eighteenth century than their extension. The Revolution originated in the financial crisis of the ancien régime, which was itself occasioned by the costs of the military revolution. Thanks to the passions that the French Revolution liberated, its armies then expanded exponentially, linked by civic values as well as compulsion, to the populations that sustained them. If this argument is valid, Michael Roberts was right. The armies of Revolutionary France represented a pivot, but as Roberts put it in 1956, "the armies of the Great Elector are linked infrangibly with those of Moltke and Schlieffen."[37]

As the following essays make abundantly clear, the validity of this argument remains at issue. The essays are a prequel to a series of volumes that have, over the past decade, taken up the problem of total war from the mid-nineteenth to the mid-twentieth century.[38] They grew out of five conferences that surveyed the growing purview of warfare from the American Civil War to the end of the Second World War. A sense of discomfort reigned at these conferences, however, for the participants had to employ an understanding of total war that was worked out only with difficulty and was never fully accepted. One of the difficulties was that conventional understandings of total war rested on narrative assumptions about war in the early modern era, which we had not studied.

---

37 Roberts, "Military Revolution," 217.
38 Stig Förster and Jörg Nagler, eds., *On the Road to Total War: The American Civil War and the German Wars of Unification, 1861–1871* (Cambridge, UK 1997); Manfred Boemeke, Roger Chickering, and Stig Förster, eds., *Anticipating Total War: The German and American Experiences, 1871–1914* (Cambridge, UK 1999); Roger Chickering and Stig Förster, eds., *Great War, Total War: Combat and Mobilization on the Western Front, 1914–1918* (Cambridge, UK 2000); Roger Chickering and Stig Förster, eds., *The Shadows of Total War: Europe, East Asia, and the United States, 1919–1939* (Cambridge, UK 2003); Roger Chickering, Stig Förster, and Bernd Greiner, eds., *The World at Total War: Global Conflict and the Politics of Destruction, 1937–1945* (Cambridge, UK 2005).

We therefore resolved at the end of the conference on World War II to address this narrative problem in a final conference, at which we would turn to the late eighteenth century in search of developments that anticipated or laid the foundations of the great, comprehensive industrial wars of the twentieth century. Sensitive, however, to the risks of anachronism and teleological thinking, we attempted to limit our use of the term *total war* to the extent possible at this last conference. We tried to balance the elements of change and continuity in the era that began with the American Revolution and concluded with the defeat of Napoleon in 1815. We discovered, however, that our enterprise was significantly complicated not only by the collision of two grand historical narratives. We also confronted another historiographical divide, which has itself been encouraged by the structure of university curricula on both sides of the Atlantic. Despite growing interest in "Atlantic history," scholars of war in Europe and North America have not communicated well with one another.[39] The American Revolution has occupied at best a marginal place in the grand narratives of military history. The limited size of the forces that were involved in this conflict makes it hard to square with Roberts's thesis, which is riveted to European history and makes no claims to comprehend events in North America. In the narrative of total war, which does claim to comprehend the American Revolution, developments in North America are relevant; this revolution figures as an arena for experiments in skirmishing tactics by highly motivated citizen-soldiers. The American Revolution thus offers a premonition of the titanic developments that followed shortly in Europe. America remains, however, a sideshow, and the military relationship between the revolutionary wars on either side of the Atlantic – whether this relationship was causal, metaphorical, or coincidental – remains to be illuminated.

The essays that follow explore this relationship, as well as questions of continuity and rupture in military affairs during a pivotal era that German historians are now calling the "Sattelzeit."[40] The initial section of the volume is devoted to interpretive issues that occupied contemporary observers no less than they do historians today. Azar Gat revisits the military revolution to argue that military developments be analyzed in a broader framework of European modernization, in which lines of causation were more complex than the contentions of Michael Roberts or Geoffrey Parker have allowed. Gat also argues that "social mobilization" and the "participatory

---

39 The foundational text is Robert R. Palmer, *The Age of the Democratic Revolution: A Political History of Europe and America, 1760–1800*, 2 vols. (Princeton, New Jersey, 1959–64).

40 Otto Brunner, Werner Conze, and Reinhart Koselleck, eds., *Geschichtliche Grundbegriffe. Historisches Lexikon zur politisch-sozialen Sprache in Deutschland*, 8 vols. (Stuttgart, 1972–97), 1:xv.

civic-national modern state" – two topoi that are commonly invoked to explain the revolutionary changes of the late eighteenth century – were already central to the modernization of states in the old regime. Beatrice Heuser's essay treats the French writer Guibert, whose vision of "peoples' war" was said to have influenced both George Washington and Napoleon. Heuser urges caution, however, in drawing lines between the French theorist, whose writings of the 1770s did seem remarkably prescient by the end of the eighteenth century, and the kinds of conflict that became known as total war in the twentieth. Ute Planert pleads for still more circumspection. In a survey of military institutions and practices of the eighteenth century, particularly as these related to compulsory military service and the relationship of military and civil society, she concludes that the "wars of the French Revolution arose less as a revolutionary caesura than as a stage in an evolutionary process."

Dierk Walter's survey of developments in the Kingdom of Prussia insists, in contrast, that aspects of the military reforms in this land did in fact represent revolutionary change. This conclusion attaches not to tactical or organizational reforms in the Prussian army, for which models had been well established, but instead to the breaking of the aristocratic monopoly on the officer corps and the Prussians' decision to adopt a thoroughgoing form of compulsory short-term military service. In addition, Walter writes, the kind of "people's war" that was envisaged in the Landsturmverordnung of 1813 represented as "close an approximation of total war as a pre-industrial society could achieve." This conclusion corresponds to the perceptions of Friedrich von Gentz, the conservative publicist who lived through these dramatic events as a confidante to Clemens von Metternich. In his essay, Günter Kronenbitter analyzes Gentz's writings on war in the era of "this awful revolution," which Gentz associated with the name of Bonaparte. Although he had little knowledge of military affairs, Gentz was well attuned to their revolutionary impact on international politics. They required, as Kronenbitter shows, a revolutionary recasting of international relations, an international system in which political stability, fortified by "legal and moral balance," would prevent war in order to prevent revolution. Stig Förster's essay completes this section with an analysis of the global dimensions of the revolutionary wars of the Sattelzeit. These conflicts did not represent the "first world war." This distinction belongs instead, he argues, to the Seven Years' War. But the wars of the revolutionary era carried more profound implications. They "involved political and social revolution. These were civil and international wars at the same time." The reasons had less to do, however, with revolutionary changes in the art of warfare than with the global expansion of the European powers in the eighteenth century.

The volume's remaining essays are grouped under the two rubrics that have guided most analyses of revolutionary transformation in warfare during this era. The one group analyzes changes on the battlefield, the other treats the broader intersections of war and society in the revolutionary period. Timothy Shannon begins by analyzing the military practices of Native Americans during the Sixty Years' War, which raged intermittently between 1754 and 1814 in North America, as white settlers pushed ever further into territories inhabited by Native Americans. Shannon shows that each side necessarily adopted the methods of the other and that the product was a greater reliance on "the skulking way of war" – an "indigenous version of *la petite guerre*" – by both. In the process, both sides embraced a kind of "racialized militancy" that anticipated the wars of a later era, insofar as it increasingly made civilians the targets of military action, although Shannon emphasizes that this variety of total war "appears to have been something that was done to Indians, rather than something they practiced." Matthew Ward then analyzes the role of colonial militias in the War of American Independence. He emphasizes that, by virtue both of custom and training, these organizations preferred *la petite guerre* and were, as a consequence, the objects of suspicion and complaint among the leaders of both the American and British regular armies. The American leaders, however, effectively coordinated the actions of their regular and irregular forces, turning the militias into a major factor in the military success of the American Revolution.

John Tone's essay provides a bridge between North America and Europe, as it analyzes the significance of *la petite guerre* as a method of resisting Napoleonic armies on the Iberian Peninsula. Although Tone emphasizes their variety in the peninsular campaign, irregular forces attracted the disdain of regular officers, whether British or French, much as they had in North America. In the Spanish case, however, they provided a welcome complement to the British regular troops. Tone also insists, however, that the term *total war* is inappropriate to understanding warfare in this part of the world in the early nineteenth century. The guerilla war against the French involved too small a portion of the Spanish population and too insignificant a share of its resources. Jeremy Black's observations on naval warfare in the era of revolution provide another bridge between North America and Europe (and beyond). Black takes note of a paradox: although the era produced no revolutionary changes in naval technologies, it witnessed what was, in some respects, the most "total" naval warfare in history. "The length of large-scale, deep-sea naval conflict then," he writes, "has never been matched since, the nearest equivalent being the American-Japanese war in the Pacific during World War Two." Navies also figured large in the logistics of land war in America and Europe. In this connection, Alan Forrest emphasizes that success on the battlefields of revolutionary Europe depended on the skill and efficiency with which soldiers could be transported, supplied, and provided with medical care, and that the mass armies of the French Revolution confronted civilian politicians with immense administrative challenges, for which the old armies of the ancien régime offered little precedent. The French success in meeting these logistical challenges thus itself represented a revolutionary achievement of sorts.

The final group of essays considers the broader dimensions of warfare, its impact on civilian life and its social and cultural institutions. T. H. Breen's essay analyzes the infrastructure of mobilization in the American colonies on the eve of the Revolutionary War, as well as the networks of local committees, known collectively as the Association, that monitored trade with Britain. Breen also demonstrates the growing militancy, discipline, and polarization that attended their efforts, as tensions with the mother country approached war and political mobilization turned military. Jörg Nagler then explores the pervasive implications of war for the institution of slavery in North America, as the British encouraged insurrections among the slave populations of the American colonies. The object was both to enhance British manpower with contingents of grateful liberated slaves and to compel the colonialists to commit resources to the prevention and suppression of slave rebellions. Wolfgang Kruse analyzes the complex domestic implications of the levée en masse in revolutionary France and the debates over raising an army for "revolutionary civil war," in which the bounds between foreign and domestic, state and society, military and civilian, ultimately disappeared. "The claims of the revolutionary state on its citizens," Kruse concludes, "became total."

If the essays of Breen, Nagler, and Kruse suggest that the exemptions of civilian affairs from the claims of war disappeared early in the revolutionary era, the essays of Michael Broers, Marion Breunig, and Katherine Aalestad address the practical impact of new forms of warfare on civilian life. Broers's analysis of events on the Italian Peninsula recounts the staggering burdens of French occupation, particularly once it was geared to the demands of Napoleon's great armies. Occupation now meant "conscription and taxation on a scale hitherto unimaginable for the communities of the hinterlands," as the peoples of Italy found themselves slated "to become the fodder of the Napoleonic war machine." Broers also shows how these

burdens resulted in popular mobilization, both in service of the French and
in a series of popular rebellions against French rule, which flared around the
peninsula. Marion Breunig recounts the burdens that major urban centers
in North America bore during the War of 1812. Here the British pursued
a strategy that was geared to an era of popular government. As one British
officer put it, by compelling people "to experience the real hardships and
miseries of warfare, you will soon compel the[ir] representatives to a vote
of peace." Breunig's essay shows how the inhabitants of Washington and
Baltimore experienced early on the sort of warfare against cities that William
Tecumseh Sherman, Giulio Douhet, and others subsequently brought to
virtuosity. Hamburg, Copenhagen, and Amsterdam were also major urban
areas that felt the burdens of war, although, as Katherine Aalestad demonstrates in her essay on northern Europe, their afflictions were of a different
order than those suffered in Washington and Baltimore. The Napoleonic
Wars did not admit neutrality, so Denmark, Holland, and the city-states of
North Germany found themselves herded into the continental system, the
coercive regime of material support that encompassed the occupied European continent. The results were pervasive. If they did not constitute total
war, they did bring war "into the harbors, warehouses, marketplaces, and
homes" and ensured, as Aalestad writes, "that the home front became a war
zone."

The final group of essays address cultural dimensions of the revolutionary wars. Donatus Düsterhaus examines the reaction of religious bodies to
French expansion. His investigation focuses on the experience of Protestant, Catholic, and Jewish communities in Alsace during the early 1790s.
All were affected, although the region's Protestants, who numbered among
the most enthusiastic advocates of the Revolution, were the least discom-
fited by the new regime's hostility to organized religion – at least until the
fall of the monarchy. The antireligious animus was radicalized in any event
by the outbreak of war in 1792 and the prospect that counterrevolutionary
armies would invade Alsace. In these circumstances, Düsterhaus speaks of a
"double war experience," the fact that Alsatians contended not only with
the immediate demands of supporting French armies with men and money
but also with an assault on their deepest beliefs. Karen Hagemann addresses
another dimension of popular mobilization in revolutionary war. Beginning
with the levée en masse, mobilization accompanied the articulation of modern gender roles, the division of communities into the men who fought and
the women who supported them. After a comparative analysis of literary
and visual representations of this division in France and Prussia, she concludes that, despite the different political outcomes in the two countries,

universal military service anchored "the construction of hegemonic concepts of nineteenth-century masculinities." Finally, Mary Favret exploits literary sources to investigate the impact of global war in Britain. Although most people were affected from a distance, the impact of war – in the form of taxation, repression, and shortages – was pervasive here, too. The work of British writers suggests, as Favret observes, that "the routines and habits of everyday life" were "engaged at almost every turn with the conduct of global war."

This observation captures a consensus that links the studies in this volume. In Europe at least, the transformation of the battlefield appears to have been primarily a function of larger armies, but the impact of war on civilian life registered more fundamental changes. Any attempt to weigh the continuities in military history across the eighteenth and nineteenth centuries – or to judge the similarities in the European and North American experiences of war – must thus acknowledge that popular mobilization for war became general during this era. Warfare ceased in principle to exempt anyone. Not only did armies become much larger; their impact on civilian society also became much more pervasive and disruptive. To call this phenomenon total war in the age of revolutionary war is, as several of the authors have noted, to indulge in hyperbole. But family resemblances were at least recognizable.

PART I

Perspectives on a Military History of the Revolutionary Era

1

What Constituted the Military Revolution of the Early Modern Period?

AZAR GAT

Europe experienced a so-called military revolution. Firearms transformed both field and siege warfare. Armies greatly expanded and became more permanent; they were increasingly paid for, administered, and commanded by central state authorities that grew progressively more powerful. Similar processes affected navies, with which the Europeans gained mastery over the seas. All of the foregoing are widely agreed upon. Yet the time frame of the revolution and the causal relationship between its various elements remain in dispute. Undertaking a thorough revision of the concept of the military revolution, this chapter argues that, rather than being rooted predominantly in military developments, the military revolution should be understood within the framework of Europe's overall, centuries-long process of modernization.

HOW REVOLUTIONARY WAS THE MILITARY REVOLUTION?

The concept of the military revolution was first introduced by Michael Roberts. He was a historian of northern Europe, so it is not surprising perhaps that he traced the crucial phase of the process to that region during its period of greatness (1560–1660). His reasoning, especially concerning the causes of the process, is unilinear and improbable.[1] He has suggested that the creation of standing armies resulted simply from tactical reasons, as the combination of shot and pike in the infantry formation necessitated more complex drilling and, consequently, longer service. He has further maintained that a more ambitious strategy, made possible by tactically more flexible

---

1 Michael Roberts, "The Military Revolution, 1560–1660" (1955), reprinted in C. Rogers, ed., *The Military Revolution Debate* (Boulder, Colorado, 1995), 13–36.

This essay draws upon the author's *War in Human Civilization* (New York, 2006). The previously published portions are used with the permission of Oxford University Press.

21

armies during the Thirty Years' War (1618–48), called for larger forces. In a similar one-directional vein – with the military as the cause – he has argued that both processes strengthened central states authorities, with all the ensuing political and social consequences. Rather than specifically address each of these arguments, I deal with them more generally in what follows.

It was Geoffrey Parker who developed the military revolution concept more fully and made it his own. A leading student of military developments in the Spanish Empire, Parker has pointed out that the processes described by Roberts had, in fact, been well under way in the Spanish army from early in the sixteenth century. Mapping the general scope of the change, Parker has written: "Between 1530 and 1710 there was a ten-fold increase both in the total numbers of armed forces paid by the major European states and in the total numbers involved in the major European battles."[2] The former increased from a few tens of thousands to hundreds of thousands, while the latter increased from many thousands to many tens of thousands on each side – during a period when Europe's population as a whole grew by only about 50 percent. The record in absolute numbers was naturally held by Europe's greatest powers. The Spanish Empire paid for 150,000 soldiers in the 1550s, 200,000 in the 1590s, and 300,000 in the 1630s. France, which succeeded Spain as Europe's mightiest power in the seventeenth century, paid for 50,000 soldiers in the 1550s, 150,000 in the 1630s, and 400,000 in the 1700s.[3] In both cases, the actual numbers of men in service were somewhat lower.[4]

As Parker's reckonings show, Roberts's time frame for the military revolution not only starts too late but also ends too early. Whereas Parker has concentrated on pushing the beginning of the revolution back in time, Jeremy Black has called attention to the period 1660–1720, when the European armies continued to grow while also becoming more permanent.[5] One may add that, although France did not match its exhaustive 1700s record during most of the eighteenth century, other armies continued to expand. Not only Europe's largest army but also the armies of each of the great

---

2 Geoffrey Parker, "'The Military Revolution, 1560–1660'–A Myth?" (1976), reprinted in Rogers, *Military Revolution Debate*, 37–55, esp. 43.

3 Ibid., 44.

4 John Hale, *War and Society in Renaissance Europe, 1450–1620* (London, 1985), 61–3; David Parrott, *Richelieu's Army: War, Government and Society in France, 1624–1642* (Cambridge, U.K. 2001), 164–222; John Lynn, "Recalculating French Army Growth during the Grand Siècle, 1610–1715" (1994), reprinted in Rogers, *Military Revolution*, 117–48; A. Corvisier, ed., *Histoire militaire de la France*, vol. 1, *Des origines à 1715*, ed. P. Contamine (Paris, 1992), 361–6.

5 Jeremy Black, *A Military Revolution? Military Change and European Society, 1550–1800* (London, 1991); and "A Military Revolution? A 1660–1792 Perspective," in Rogers, *Military Revolution Debate*, 95–116.

powers grew to hundreds of thousands in wartime. Furthermore, why stop in the eighteenth century, as the debaters have done? By the last years of that century, the French Revolutionary armies comprised three-quarters of a million men, to say nothing of the armies of millions that came after industrialization. And returning to the beginning of the process, a historian of late-medieval Europe has extended the time frame of the military revolution back into that period.[6] Long-serving paid troops became common during the Hundred Years' War, and the foundations of permanent state armies, such as the French *compaignies d'ordonnance*, were laid down toward the end of that war.

Thus, the so-called military revolution extended over quite a number of centuries. It is suggested here that it paralleled and was closely related to Europe's wider, sweeping transformation during those same centuries; indeed, that it formed an "aspect" of early modernization.[7] What, then, constituted the revolution, and how did it interact with Europe's general transformation? As Parker has indicated, a major element of the military revolution that also contributed to the rise in the size of armies was the revival and proliferation of infantry. Half as expensive as cavalry, infantry accounted for most of the armies' growth in absolute terms. Here, too, the process had been in full swing well before and irrespective of the advent of infantry firearms, which entered into general use only around 1500. It was most prominently manifested in the crushing victories of both the English longbow and the Swiss pike formations over the knightly cavalry in the fourteenth and fifteenth centuries. Indeed, although the introduction of firearms into field warfare is widely believed to have caused the demise of cavalry, it actually revived it. Because of the matchlock's slow rate of fire – about one shot per minute – harquebusiers and musketeers during the sixteenth and seventeenth centuries required the protection of spearmen. This combination of shot and pike was cumbersome and decreased infantry's tactical flexibility, mobility, and shock effect in comparison to the earlier, irresistible Swiss phalanx. It thus contributed to infantry's growing tendency to seek protection behind field fortifications. Supplementing its

---

6 Clifford Rogers, "The Military Revolutions of the Hundred Years War," in Rogers, *Military Revolution Debate*, 55–94.

7 As it has been recognized that the change was, in effect, more protracted than originally defined, Jeremy Black has suggested that it is better understood as a transition rather than a revolution. Black, "A Military Revolution." Rogers has reasonably proposed that the process corresponded to the evolutionary model of punctuated equilibrium, whereby periods of slower change alternated with bursts of heightened growth. In my view, once it is realized that at issue is, in effect, the massive transformation associated with modernity in general in the span of a few centuries, the designation *revolution* or *transition* becomes merely semantic.

shock weapons with pistols, cavalry again became the principal offensive arm in the open field, which it would remain for another two centuries in and outside Europe. While the cheaper and more versatile infantry proliferated and increasingly adopted firearms, cavalry continued to make up a large share of armies, usually between one-quarter and one-half, sometimes more.[8]

Thus, the rise of infantry can account only partly for armies' growing size and adoption of more regular service. While infantry grew in number and in relative share, cavalry, too, increased. Armies grew overall. According to Parker, what mainly accounts for the growth is another major element of the military revolution, the advent of firearm fortifications.

By the fifteenth century, Western Europe had taken the lead in the development of the gun, for, as Kenneth Chase brilliantly explains, firearms proved to be more useful for the Europeans than for Eurasian state societies that bordered on the steppe. Those societies' main security problem were horse nomads, who had no walled settlements to be breached and against whom infantry was ineffective because they would not be pinned down.[9] By the middle of the fifteenth century, European wrought-iron guns, using "corned" powder and firing stone balls, became potent enough to render

8 Parker, "Military Revolution," 44; Frank Tallett, *War and Society in Early-Modern Europe* (London, 1992), 28–31; M. E. Mallett and J. R. Hale, *The Military Organization of a Renaissance State: Venice c. 1400 to 1617* (Cambridge, U.K., 1984), 126, 137–8, 375. The ebbs and flows of the process are highlighted by Simon Adams, "Tactics or Politics? 'The Military Revolution' and the Hapsburg Hegemony, 1525–1648," in *Tools of War: Instruments, Ideas, and Institutions of Warfare, 1445–1871*, ed. John Lynn (Urbana, Illinois, 1990), 36; James Wood, *The King's Army: Warfare, Soldiers, and Society during the Wars of Religion in France, 1562–1576* (Cambridge, U.K., 1996), esp. 127–33, 144–52; Parrott, *Richelieu's Army*, 60–1; and Lynn, *Giant of the Grand Siècle*, 527–30. In the Swedish and Russian armies of the early eighteenth century, cavalry still accounted for close to one half of the forces. See Carol Stevens, "Evaluating Peter's Army: The Impact of Internal Organization," in *The Military and Society in Russia, 1450–1917*, ed. E. Lohr and M. Poe (Leiden, 2002), 153–4. For an explanation, see Jeremy Black, introduction to *War in the Early Modern World* (London, 1999), 18.

9 For the spread of firearms: Joseph Needham, Ho Ping-Yü, Lu Gwei-Djen, and Wang Ling, *Science and Civilization in China*, vol. 5, pt. 7, *Military Technology: The Gunpowder Epic* (Cambridge, U.K., 1986), 39–51, 365–9, is monumental and exhaustive; Kenneth Chase, *Firearms: A Global History to 1700* (New York, 2003) is illuminating and transforms the discussion on the subject; Thomas Allsen, "The Circulation of Military Technology in the Mongolian Empire," in *Warfare in Inner Asian History (500–1800)*, ed. Nicola Di Cosmo, (Leiden, 2002), 265–93, emphasizes the Mongol role; Carlo Cipolla's pioneering *Guns and Sails in the Early Phase of European Exploration, 1400–1700* (London, 1965) still has value; Bert Hall, *Weapons and Warfare in Renaissance Europe: Gunpowder Technology and Tactics* (Baltimore, 1997) is the most informed on the first centuries in Europe; David Ayalon, *Gunpowder and Firearms in the Mamluk Kingdom* (1956; reprint, London, 1978); Djurdjica Petrović, "Fire-arms in the Balkans on the Eve and after the Ottoman Conquests of the Fourteenth and Fifteenth Centuries," in *War, Technology and Society in the Middle East*, ed. V. Parry and M. Yapp (London, 1975) , 164–94; Kelly DeVries, "Gunpowder Weapons at the Siege of Constantinople, 1453," in *War and Society in the Eastern Mediterranean, 7th–15th Centuries*, ed. Y. Lev (Leiden, 1997), 343–62; Iqtidar Alam Khan, "Early Use of Cannon and Musket in India: AD 1442–1526," in *Warfare and Weaponry in South Asia, 1000–1800*, ed. J. Gommans and D. Kolff (New Delhi, 2001), 321–36; Jos Gommans, *Mughal Warfare* (London, 2002), 144–62.

tall, walled fortifications ineffective. By the end of the century, King Charles VIII of France's siege guns – cast from bronze; mounted on mobile, wheeled carriages; and shooting iron balls – opened the gates of every fortified city that the king encountered during his invasion of Italy (1494–5).

Yet contrary to popularly held perceptions, the supremacy of the siege gun over the castle was brief and transitory. Artillery fortifications were developed as the answer to siege artillery. In Italy, a new type of low-lying perturbing angular stronghold, the bastion, provided a broad platform from which guns could keep the enemy at a distance and sweep the ditch with flanking cross fire.[10] From the 1520s on, the balance between besieger and besieged was restored to pretty much what it had been before the advent of the gun. The siege again became a slow and laborious process, as it had been throughout history. At least in Europe, where the new technologies and techniques became available to both sides in each theater of war into which they spread, improvements of the attack and defense of fortified places pretty much canceled each other out.

How, then, did the revolutionary advent of the new forms of fortification and siege craft relate to the growth of armies, as Parker believes it did? Parker has rightly pointed out that the new style of fortifications that spread from Italy to the rest of Western Europe (where it was known as *trace italienne*) was so successful that it came to dominate warfare. Places fortified in the new style proliferated and became almost impregnable to gun power. Unless aided by tactical surprise or by treason, sieges spanned many months and, in a few cases, even years.[11] Battles became rare. Armies engaged primarily in sieges and raids. All this is undisputed. However, according to Parker, the multiplication of fortresses required more garrison troops than before. Furthermore, because fortresses grew larger and could dominate areas stretching hundreds of meters beyond their walls with their gunfire, larger forces were needed to surround and besiege their perimeters. This explanation for the growth of European armies has been incorporated into many history books, yet some scholars disagree. Examining the data, John Lynn has concluded that the new fortresses did not require larger numbers of troops to defend or attack and hence were not the reason for the growth of

10 John Hale, "The Early Development of the Bastion: an Italian Chronology, c. 1450–c. 1534," reprinted in his *Renaissance War Studies* (London, 1983), 1–29; Simon Pepper and Nicholas Adams, *Firearms and Fortifications: Military Architecture and Siege Warfare in Sixteenth Century Siena* (Chicago, 1986); Christopher Duffy, *Siege Warfare: The Fortress in the Early Modern World, 1494–1660* (London, 1979).

11 Parker, *The Army of Flanders and the Spanish Road, 1567–1659* (Cambridge, U.K., 1972), 5–12; "The Military Revolution"; *The Military Revolution: Military Innovation and the Rise of the West, 1500–1800* (Cambridge, U.K., 1989), 13–14, which cites a list of examples; as does Charles Oman, *A History of the Art of War in the Sixteenth Century* (London, 1937), 544–5.

the European armies.[12] Indeed, one may add, the fortress obviously cannot explain the inflation in the size of navies, which occurred along with the growth of the armies as an integral part of the military revolution.[13]

I concur with Lynn and wish to expand the argument further. As I indicated previously, I hold that, apart from the brief transition period between 1450 and 1520, the introduction of the gun into both siege craft and fortifications, while profoundly transforming them, nonetheless fundamentally changed neither the balance between them nor between siege and field warfare, as compared to earlier periods. Throughout history, sieges were slow and laborious, taking many months and years to complete successfully. In regions where fortified cities and fortresses abounded, warfare essentially revolved around sieges. Armies often concentrated on one selected prize during each annual campaign, as they would do in early modern Europe.

Examples are so much the stuff of history as to make the citing of them somewhat trivial. They start with the campaigns of subjugation conducted by the empires of the ancient Near East and those of preunification China. Although the Roman legions are renowned for their battlefield performance, experts are well aware that siege work was just as significant, if not more so, in Rome's centuries-long expansion in Italy. Similarly, Hannibal's War is remembered for the crushing battles of the Trebbia (218 BC), Trasimene (217 BC), Cannae (216 BC), and Zama (202 BC). But it was in the grinding and protracted attrition of siege warfare, year after year, that Hannibal was defeated. Concentrating on one great objective at a time, the Romans took Syracuse (212 BC) after a two-year siege, Capua (211 BC) after another two years of siege, and Tarentum (209 BC) after the city was betrayed to them; and these were only the largest cities. Carthage itself fell to Rome in the Third Punic War, after a siege that lasted no fewer than three years (149–146 BC) – even though the Roman army was the master of such operations. Siege work dominated Rome's protracted pacification of Spain and subjugation of all the other lands of the Mediterranean. And apart from incessant raiding and a few large-scale invasions, Rome's centuries-long conflict with Parthia and Sassanian Persia revolved around siege operations.

---

12 John Lynn, "The *trace italienne* and the Growth of Armies: The French Case," in Rogers, *Military Revolution*, 117–48.

13 As Parker himself, in fact, holds. See, e.g., "The Military Revolution," 43. Parker, *Military Revolution*, 24, claims that wherever in Europe the new fortifications appeared, there was a parallel growth in the size of armies. But rather than representing cause and effect, this correlate merely demonstrates that the politically, economically, and militarily most advanced powers were ahead in applying all the elements of the military revolution.

It is equally well recognized that in medieval Europe itself, before the advent of the gun, warfare was dominated by the existence of a dense network of fortified strongholds, both baronial and royal, that exercised a similar effect on warfare as in the early modern period. Battles were rare, and apart from raiding, warfare predominantly consisted of more or less sustained efforts to take a key fortified stronghold in annul campaigns. It was this pattern that characterized the French kings' military drive to reduce the English Angevin empire in France, the Hundred Years' War, and the struggles between Christians and Muslims in both Spain and the Holy Land.[14]

All of the above constituted protracted struggles of attrition – often dragging on for years, decades, and centuries – as was the case in northern Italy, the Low Countries, and the Rhineland. Those were the regions of the most intense warfare in the sixteenth and seventeenth centuries and where, in consequence, the new firearm fortifications proliferated. Parker has argued that firearm fortifications were larger than the older ones, but it was, in fact, the European towns and cities themselves that greatly expanded during the late Middle Ages and early modern period. Consequently, their fortified area expanded as well. (Indeed, it took long before medieval cities filled up the perimeter of their ruined Roman walls, where such existed.) Preartillery fortifications had been as extensive as early modern ones in the large cities of the ancient Near East, classical antiquity, Byzantium, Islam, and China. Ur's walls stretched for nine kilometers in the middle of the third millennium BC; classical Athens's long walls, for thirty-five; Carthage's triple lines of fortifications, for thirty-four; Syracuse's, for twenty-seven; those of the Tang capital Changan, for thirty-five; and those of Ming Nanking, for thirty-nine. These, of course, were the giants of cities, but premodern city fortifications regularly stretched for kilometers, sometimes in double and triple lines, and were as long and as elaborate as any city fortifications in the early modern period.

Thus, although Parker is correct in claiming that the perimeter of the siege had to be enlarged in the early modern period to distance the besiegers a few hundred meters from the fortress's ramparts and gunfire, this extension was not as significant as he reckons. In sieges of large premodern cities, the besiegers already held lines that stretched for many kilometers and even tens of kilometers. In each of the great Roman sieges mentioned here, the

---

14 On this well-recognized theme, see more specifically Richard Jones, "Fortifications and Sieges in Western Europe, c. 800–1450," in *Medieval Warfare: A History*, ed. M. Keen (Oxford, 1999), 163–85; Jim Bradbury, *The Medieval Siege* (Woodbridge, Virginia, 1992). Parker himself, *Military Revolution*, 7, is well aware that medieval warfare was precisely of that nature.

Roman armies that numbered in the tens of thousands erected long double lines of fortifications facing both the besieged city and outside relief armies. Investing Alesia, the great Gallic stronghold (52 BC), Julius Caesar's eight legions (theoretically close to eighty thousand men, including the *auxilia*) constructed an inner ring of some seventeen kilometers and an outer one of twenty-two. Moreover, it should be noted that, even if the perimeter of the siege was enlarged because of firearm fortifications, this did not necessarily place a greater demand for troops on the besieger; for firearms meant that armies also adopted a shallower formation than earlier, both on the battlefield and in manning lines of investment.

In addition, Parker has claimed that the new massive fortifications were highly expensive. They allegedly consumed such great resources that, despite the continuous growth in military manpower, field armies never grew sufficiently to overcome the tangled web of fortifications. Consequently, wars dragged on and became inherently indecisive. Again Parker's claim has been echoed by many historians, who cite the impressive-sounding sums of money spent on individual fortifications but do not set those figures in the context of the powers' total military expenditures. In actuality, statistics derived from a variety of separate cases throughout Europe consistently reveal that fortifications consumed a fairly small portion of the total military expenditure. Venice, which heavily fortified both its Italian terra firma territory and overseas empire, spent only about 5 to 10 percent of its total defense expenditures on fortifications during the sixteenth and early seventeenth centuries. The data from Spain suggest a similar figure, probably closer to 5 percent than 10. When a sophisticated and exceptionally expensive fortress-building program was carried out in France for Louis XIV by Marshal Vauban, the cost in the peak years (1682–83) reached only about 17 percent of the total military expenditure.[15]

15 Parker, *Army of Flanders*, 5–12; and *Military Revolution*, 12. Among those who have adopted his thesis are John Hale (see below); M. S. Anderson, *War and Society in Europe of the Old Regime, 1618–1789* (London, 1988), 88, 140–1; and *The Origins of the Modern European State System, 1494–1618* (London, 1998), 9–10, 22; Adams, "Tactics or Politics," 36; Tallett, *War and Society*, 10, 38, 51, 168–9; James Tracy, *Emperor Charles V, Impresario of War: Campaign Strategy, International Finance and Domestic Politics* (Cambridge, U.K., 2002), 30. However, interestingly enough, all these scholars to some degree have known otherwise. Thus, although attributing the expansion of armies and the spiraling costs of war to firearms and artillery fortifications, Hale's meticulous calculations for Venice tell a wholly different story. See Mallett and Hale, *Military Organization*, 409, 432–3, 436–7, 440–1, 444–5, 468–9, 470–2, 478, 480, 483–4, 487; Hale, *War and Society in Renaissance Europe*, 1985, 46–7, 234–5. For Spain, see I. A. A. Thompson, *War and Government in Habsburg Spain, 1560–1620* (London, 1976), 34, 69–71, 288–93; and "'Money, Money, and Yet More Money!' Finance, the Fiscal-State and the Military Revolution: Spain, 1500–1650," in Rogers, *Military Revolution*, 273–98, esp. 276–82. Parker, "In Defense of *The Military Revolution*," ibid., 253, has replied that most of the money for fortifications was spent by the Spanish Empire in Flanders, Italy, and North Africa rather than in mainland Spain. However, the same also applied to all the other military expenses

In his correspondence with me, Parker has argued that these relatively modest sums are misleading because much of the cost of fortifications was borne by local authorities and local subjects and did not register in state budgets. That was, however, also true of other major items of military expenditure, such as the costs of billeting and feeding troops, nonstipendiary military service, and corvée labor. Local contributions thus probably did not significantly change the share of expenditure allocated to fortifications in total military expenditure. Moreover, part of the cost of war, including fortifications, had always been paid locally. There was no fundamental change here in the early modern period that can account for the military revolution. If anything, the change went in the opposite direction, as we shall see.

Indeed, massive fortifications had always constituted a major aspect of warfare. Furthermore, in contrast to the prevailing assumption, a number of specialized studies on the subject have demonstrated (to little avail) that the new style of fortifications was by no means more expensive than the old one. The new broad and low-lying ramparts were constructed of earth and rubble dug up from the ditches, and thus absorbed artillery fire better than stone or bricks. Therefore, they were built in much less time and with greater ease than the older stone fortifications. Masonry or bricks were occasionally used, but only for outer facing, to protect the earth from rapid erosion by the elements. In the majority of cases, as in earlier times, the local population was conscripted as unskilled labor to carry out most of the construction; they were supplemented by a small number of paid artisans.[16] The main

---

(above all troops), which probably leaves the ratio much the same. Indeed, the previously mentioned Italian figures support Thompson's conclusions, as do the figures for France cited by Lynn, "The *trace italienne.*" Also compare the figures in Lynn, *Giant of the Grand Siècle,* 592, to French overall military and general expenditure in Richard Bonney, "France, 1494–1815," in *The Rise of the Fiscal State in Europe, c. 1200–1815,* ed. R. Bonney (Oxford, 1999), 143.

16 Judith Hook, "Fortifications and the End of the Sienese State," *History* 62 (1977): 372–87, accentuates earlier cursory claims that the cost of the new fortifications was prohibitive; strangely, however, her article has close to nothing by way of figures, economic analysis, and estimated costs in relation to Siena's overall budget. While admitting that the city was already in bad financial condition for other reasons (375–6), she provides no evidence that the new fortifications contributed to its decline. Indeed, the costs she does cite for the fortification of Siena's dependent towns: four thousand ducats for Montalcino, four thousand for Chiusi, two thousand for Lucignano (379, 381), although not insignificant, were far from prohibitive, and were partly borne by the locals; by way of comparison, the upkeep of the Spanish garrison cost Siena close to four thousand ducats in 1551 alone (375), and one naval galley cost six thousand ducats to build, and the same sum to maintain each year (see *infra* note 28). Furthermore, Hook is well aware that most of the workforce was conscripted with little cost to the state (376–8, 383–4). Indeed, frequently cited in support of the claim that the new Italian fortifications were hugely expensive, Pepper and Adams's admirable study of Siena, *Firearms and Fortifications,* 30–4, 163, 171, in fact strongly claims the opposite. Duffy, *Siege Warfare,* 91–3, mainly refers to the Dutch even-lighter earth fortifications, which were the most numerous; see also John Childs, *Armies and Warfare in Europe, 1648–1789* (Manchester, U.K., 1982), 135. David Eltis, *The Military*

economic problem with the new style of fortifications, unnoted by scholars, was actually the revolutionary nature of the change: older fortifications had to be built anew within a few decades or even years, concentrating the financial outlay in each region of Europe that was reached by the change to a brief period of time. All the same, while military expenditure, including that allocated to fortifications, dramatically rose overall during early modernity, the new fortifications apparently continued to account for much the same share of that expenditure as had preartillery fortifications in older times, when the 10 percent figure seems to keep turning up in the rare surviving records.[17]

But if artillery fortifications in themselves were not more expensive than earlier fortifications, were they not actually made more expensive by the cost of the artillery that was mounted on them and the powder and shot they stored? In all countries, the vast majority of land guns and associated ammunition were deployed in fortified places rather than with the field armies. Still, although widely assumed by scholars to have represented a huge financial outlay, artillery, too, is consistently shown by separate data from the various powers throughout the early modern period to have constituted as modest a share as fortifications of the European states' overall military expenditure, probably around 4 to 8 percent. John Hale, for example, believes that artillery and other firearms greatly increased the cost of war, but by his own figures, artillery constituted only 8 percent of French military expenditure in 1482 (Corvisier estimates 6 to 8 percent in 1500).[18] Hale presumably ascribes that fairly modest share to the early date, but, given that the French army itself was still relatively small, and its artillery the most advanced in Europe and cast from expensive bronze, percentages should

---

Revolution in Sixteenth Century Europe (London, 1995), 29, esp. chap. 4, realizes but somehow does not fully assimilate the fact that the new earth fortifications neither were more expensive nor took longer to build than their predecessors. For the cost of Venice's old-style fifteenth-century fortifications, see Mallett and Hale, *Military Organization*, 87–94; and for the decades old-style fortifications often took to complete, see James Tracy, ed., *City Walls: The Urban Enceinte in Global Perspective* (Cambridge, U.K., 2000), 71. Hale, *War and Society*, 207–8, rightly points out that conscript labor was not without its indirect costs. And yet much of its employment took place off-season or during leisure time and made use of the unemployed.

17 Data for premodern times is extremely poor. In Athens, fortifications amounted to about 10 percent of military expenditure. See Raymond Goldsmith, *Premodern Financial Systems: A Historical Comparative Study* (Cambridge, U.K., 1987), 261n60. For some medieval prices, see Bradbury, *Medieval Siege*, 69, 74, 131–2. During his long crusade to the Holy Land (1248–54), King Louis IX of France spent the huge sum of more than 1 million silver livres, of which about 100,000 were spent on massive fortifications: HF, t. 21, 512–515, cited in J. Prawer, *Histoire du Royaume Latin de Jérusalem* (Paris, 1975), 2:353n73.

18 Hale, *War and Society*, 46–7; Corvisier and Contamine, *Histoire militaire*, 1:245. The idea that artillery and gunpowder were exceedingly costly is repeated by Anderson, *State System*, 19–20, again presenting sums out of context of overall military expenditure; also Tallett, *War and Society*, 169, but see his conclusion at *infra* note 31.

not be supposed to have increased in later times (when cheap cast-iron guns became the standard). In another study, Hale cites the impressive sums of money that Venice spent on gunpowder, but, according to his own figures, they, too, amounted to a low percentage of the overall defense budget.[19] Similarly, in 1538 France spent some 36,000 *livres tournois* on saltpeter, the most expensive component of gunpowder, when its overall annual defense expenditure was around 1 million *livres*.[20] According to I. A. A. Thompson, artillery constituted only 4 to 5 percent of Spain's military expenditure in the sixteenth and early seventeenth centuries.[21] In mid-seventeenth century Russia, the strong but largely imported (and therefore expensive) artillery arm is calculated to have constituted less than 10 percent of the army's budget.[22] Finally, going beyond artillery, handheld firearms were not fundamentally more costly than the highly expensive defensive and offensive cold steel arms and crossbows of medieval times.

These data bear on other significant questions. For example, contrary to myth, the magnates' independent power did not decline because of the siege gun that destroyed their castles or because of the costs incurred in remodeling their castles according to the new style or because of the cost involved in maintaining their own artillery and other firearms. Both magnates and city-states acquired artillery and constructed bastion fortifications.[23] Their problem – which revealed itself well before the advent of gunpowder – was not in their inability to adopt the new technologies, which they did, but in being too small to withstand the new large, increasingly bureaucratic-financial national-territorial states.

The cost of fortifications, artillery, and firearms is indicative of the structure of the military budgets in general: although financially significant, military hardware and capital goods constituted only a minority of the powers'

---

19 Mallett and Hale, *Military Organization*, 401–2, 461–501.

20 *Histoire militaire*, 1:247; Bonney, "France, 1494–1815," 139. All this also puts into better perspective Fernand Braudel's staggering figures for gunpowder costs in his *Civilization and Capitalism 15th–18th Century*, vol. 1, *The Structure of Everyday Life* (1979; Berkeley, California, 1992), 395; his calculations of Venice's overall capital investment in gunpowder stock, even if valid, are misleading, for it is the annual replacement cost that counts.

21 Thompson, "Money, Money," 279; and *War and Government in Habsburg Spain*, 290–3, 296.

22 Richard Hellie, "The Cost of Muscovite Military Defense and Expansion," in Lohr and Poe, *Military and Society in Russia*, 41–66, esp. 65; see also J. Kotilaine, "In Defense of the Realm: Russian Arms Trade and Production in the Seventeenth and Early Eighteenth Century," in ibid., 67–95.

23 Well noted by Thompson, "Money, Money," 278, 280, and forcefully, despite their inconsistencies regarding the relative cost of the new fortifications and firearms. See Hale, *War and Society*, 248–9; Tallett, *War and Society*, 188–93, 205. For the Italian city-states' artillery, which was among the most advanced in Europe, see Mallett and Hale, *Military Organization*, 81–7; Hale, *War and Society*, 156; Pepper and Adams, *Firearms and Fortifications*, 12–13. Condottieri too possessed their own artillery. All this again contradicts Braudel, *Civilization and Capitalism*, 1:393.

overall military expenditure. Navies, the most capital-intensive armed service, are a striking demonstration of this general rule. Even in Venice, the
foremost Italian maritime power, the army cost more than the navy throughout the sixteenth century, sometimes twice as much.[24] In the leading naval
power of the first half of the seventeenth century, the Dutch Republic,
which like Venice was also obliged to maintain a large army, the army cost
more than twice as much as the navy.[25] Even in Britain, the leading naval
power of the eighteenth century and an island, expenditures on the army
and navy ran neck and neck.[26] More significantly, the price of the warships
themselves accounted for only a minor share of the navies' overall budget.
Lumber, the main raw material, was inexpensive and was still locally plentiful for use by all the powers, at least in the sixteenth century (that would
no longer be the case in the seventeenth century). As for the workforce
employed in naval construction, as expensive at it was per capita, it was
much smaller in size than the manpower engaged in the armed forces.[27]
In the mid-sixteenth century, the annual upkeep of a galley, the standard
oared warship of the Mediterranean, "equaled the cost of its original construction, about 6000 ducats"; foodstuffs cost twice as much as hardware in
the provisions.[28] Indeed, it is because pay and provisions cost navies more
than ships that the Ottomans were able to respond to their loss of some
two hundred galleys in the Battle of Lepanto (1571) by a massive rebuild-
ing program and to recover the lost matériel, if not the manpower, in less
than a year.[29] The expenditure on sailing warships during the seventeenth
and eighteenth centuries followed the same pattern, even though each ship

24 Mallett and Hale, *Military Organization*, 462; Jean-Claude Hocquet, "Venice," in Bonney, *Fiscal
    State*, 384.
25 Marjolein 't Hart, "The United Provinces, 1579–1806," in Bonney, ed., *Fiscal State*, 312.
26 John Brewer's calculations in *The Sinews of Power: War, Money and the English State, 1688–1783*
    (London, 1989), 31, strike the balance more toward the army, whereas those presented by David
    French, *The British Way in Warfare, 1688–2000* (London, 1990), 59, suggest an average ratio of 4 to
    6 in favor of the navy.
27 Cf. the calculations offered for the Venetian arsenal, one of the most developed and better docu-
    mented in Europe, by Robert Davis, *Shipbuilders of the Venetian Arsenal: Workers and Workplace in
    the Preindustrial City* (Baltimore, 1991), 28, to the data in Mallett and Hale, *Military Organization*,
    494–501. Also see Frederic Lane, "Naval Action and Fleet Organization, 1499–1502," in *Renaissance
    Venice*, ed. J. Hale (London, 1973), 146–73, esp. 159–62; and *infra* note 29 for the Ottomans.
28 Braudel, *The Mediterranean and the Mediterranean World*, 841, and the documentary evidence there;
    see also the details in Thompson, *War and Government in Habsburg Spain*, 168, 171, 173, 175, 289,
    294nn, 300–2. Although lacking the costs of building and ammunition, the Ottoman document
    published by C. H. Imber, "The Cost of Naval Warfare: The Accounts of Hayreddin Barbarossa's
    Herceg Novi Campaign in 1539," *Archivum Ottomanicum* 4 (1972): 203–16, appears to point in the
    same direction. See also the *infra* note 29.
29 Palmira Brummett, *Ottoman Seapower and Levantine Diplomacy in the Age of Discovery* (Albany, New
    York, 1994), 96, 218n30; Colin Imber, "The Reconstruction of the Ottoman Fleet after the Battle
    of Lepanto, 1571–2," in *Studies in Ottoman History and Law* (Istanbul, 1996), 85–101.

carried up to one hundred heavy guns, more than any field army: the cost of maintaining a sailing warship for one year was roughly the same as the price of building one.[30]

The simple fact behind all these statistics has been noted by only a few scholars: although hardware of all sorts was expensive, pay and provisions for soldiers and mariners constituted by far the largest items in states' military expenditures.[31] In the early modern period, hardware became crucial for victory and required an advanced and sophisticated technological and social infrastructure to produce and deploy effectively. Nonetheless, paying and providing for the growing and increasingly more permanent manpower employed in armies and, in smaller numbers, in navies constituted the principal cost of the military revolution. Indeed, to the extent that warfare became static and indecisive, it was not because fortifications were so expensive but, on the contrary, because, as was the case earlier in history, they were so much cheaper than troops that they were a better value. "It was much cheaper in the long run to invest capital in a fortress and then to maintain within it a small garrison than to meet the crippling recurrent burden of large numbers of troops."[32]

Let us now put aside the effect of fortifications and pass on to a more general point: any explanation for the huge increase in the military manpower and expenditures of the European states during early modernity that is based on growing needs or necessities, whether resulting from fortifications or from any other factor, is fundamentally misconstrued. To be sure, high levels of conflict increase resource mobilization and allocation for war. Yet when embroiled in struggles for high stakes – often the highest – and locked into arms races, antagonists typically strive to mobilize as large a force as they are possibly able to, often pushing the limits of their capabilities. Their reciprocal need to outweigh one another is expressed in greater investment, most notably in larger armed forces, irrespective of whether fortifications play a significant role. This has been the case throughout history whenever

---

30 Brewer, *Sinews of Power*, 34–7.
31 Clearly noted by Childs, *Armies and Warfare*, 62. Having emphasized the huge expense on fortifications and artillery, Tallett, *War and Society*, 170–1, arrives at the same conclusion, which is similarly implicit in Mallett and Hale, *Military Organization*, 494–501, and Tracy, *Charles V*, and explicit in Hellie, "Costs of Muscovite Military Defense."
32 Pepper and Adams, *Firearms and Fortifications*, 30–1; also see Tallett, *War and Society*, 171–2: "Given the relative cheapness of forts compared to armies"; Mallett and Hale, *Military Organization*, 92. Hook, "Fortifications," 387, followed by Adams, "Tactics or Politics," 37, cites this as the contemporary rationale but wrongly believes it was erroneous. Gábor Ágoston, "The Cost of the Ottoman Fortress System in Hungary in the Sixteenth and Seventeenth Centuries," in *Ottomans, Hungarians, and Habsburgs in Central Europe: The Military Confines in the Era of Ottoman Conquest*, ed. Géza Dávid and Pál Fodor (Leiden, 2000), 195–228, actually deals with the high cost of the troops stationed at the fortresses in this frontline province rather than with the cost of the fortresses themselves.

conflict levels were high. Early modernity was not unique in this respect.[33] However, whereas needs are unbounded, resources are not. If early modern European armies, navies, and war expenditure grew continuously, it was not because of needs – of whatever nature and however pressing – but because the powers were able to mobilize greater resources than before, which led to the escalation of arms races. Although supply and demand are closely related, it is chiefly on the supply side – Europe's overall resources and the states' ability to tap them – that one should concentrate.

Indeed, it is widely recognized that growing resource mobilization for war and the rise of the central state in Europe were closely linked and mutually reinforcing processes. Parker, too, has emphasized this factor in the best and most balanced of his several formulations of the military revolution thesis.[34] "War made the state, and the state made war."[35] From the thirteenth century, many European rulers increasingly succeeded in obtaining the reluctant consent of representative assemblies to the imposition of taxes that were intended to cover for the high costs of state wars. For in contrast to the endemic small-scale warfare that was salient in the politically fragmented Europe of the High Middle Ages, state wars posed a real economic problem: they had to be paid for directly. Large states meant distant wars, distance meant time, and time meant money. Prolonged campaigning far away from home required both special and costly logistical arrangements and pay for long-serving warriors rather than reliance on local part-timers. With fortifications, too, the truly significant change in terms of their economic burden was that they were now increasingly built by the state rather than by local barons. Although still largely constructed by local corvée labor, they nevertheless involved money allocations from a central purse, which presupposed resource circulation to and from the state. A spiraling, centuries-long process was set in motion, whereby money voted for the state to pay for troops increased central state power and gradually gave it monopoly over legitimate force, making warfare all the more a state affair

---

33 This has been noted by Eltis, *Military Revolution*, 32.
34 Parker "Military Revolution," 45–9; already but unilinearily in Roberts, "Military Revolution," 20–3.
35 Tilly, ed., *The Formation of National States in Western Europe* (Princeton, New Jersey, 1975), 42. The literature on this subject is vast, but see esp. Tilly, "War Making and State Making as Organized Crime," in *Bringing the State Back In*, ed. P. Evans, D. Rueschemeyer, and T. Skocpol (Cambridge, U.K., 1985), 169–91; Michael Mann, *States, War and Capitalism* (Oxford, 1988); Brian Downing, *The Military Revolution and Political Change: Origins of Democracy and Autocracy in Early Modern Europe* (Princeton, New Jersey, 1992); Bruce Porter, *War and the Rise of the State* (New York, 1994); Thomas Ertman, *Birth of the Leviathan: Building States and Regimes in Medieval and Early Modern Europe* (Cambridge, U.K., 1997); Martin van Creveld, *The Rise and Decline of the State* (Cambridge, U.K., 1999).

and, in turn, further increasing the state's powers of taxation, administration, and command. The "tax state" gradually superseded the feudal "domain state" as paid soldiers replaced feudal troop levies.[36]

But, again, how does the European experience stand in a global perspective? How does the new, early modern European state compare with other large-scale centralized states in history? What constituted a novelty in Western Europe was hardly a novelty in other regions and times. The new European state was actually less centralized and bureaucratic than, for example, imperial Rome or imperial China during their golden ages. While highlighting the rise of the early modern state, scholars have also become much more aware of its power limitations. The state had to compromise with local power, privileges, and institutions, which resisted the diminishment of their independence and status. These compromises, which resulted in tax exemptions and uneven tax burdens, caused serious inefficiencies in the state's money-raising system. In particular, the state compromised with the aristocracy, which shed some of its old privileges but gained others in return. The so-called absolutist state was actually a heterogeneous composite of territories and privileges, wherein the aristocracy was incorporated as the upper office-holding stratum of the state's structure.[37] Thus, because the state was unable to subdue local aristocratic power, the penetration of state administration was limited; and because state administration was limited, the state depended on the aristocracy to serve as an intermediate agent of government. In the military field, too, the state delegated the recruitment, administration, and even part of the financing of troops to local dignitaries, commissioned as colonels. Similar processes affected navies, which in the sixteenth century still predominantly relied on privately owned ships commissioned or requisitioned for a campaign.

Let us now examine the growth of large-scale standing armies, that central element of the military revolution, from a comparative perspective. As already noted, large states' size generally favored standing armies. The European experience presents no special case. Distance was a key factor.[38] European armies grew increasingly permanent largely because the new large states fought protracted wars in remote theaters of operations. Even though

---

36 The concepts were coined by Joseph Schumpeter, "The Crisis of the Tax State," *International Economic Papers* 4 (1918; 1954): 5–38. Bonney's two edited volumes – *Economic Systems* and *The Rise of the Fiscal State* – include the most comprehensive and authoritative recent studies.

37 More or less suggested, in a Marxist vein, by Perry Anderson, *Lineages of the Absolutist State* (London, 1974), but more persuasively developed by Hillay Zmora, *Monarchy, Aristocracy and the State in Europe, 1300–1800* (London, 2001).

38 Cf. Braudel, *Mediterranean and the Mediterranean World*, 355–94; Parker, *Army of Flanders*, 21 and passim; and *The Grand Strategy of Philip II* (New Haven, Connecticut, 1998), chap. 2.

the much cheaper militias were greatly encouraged by rulers, they invariably remained insignificant, for their active employment consistently floundered on their unwillingness to serve for long periods of time and far away from their home territories.[39]

Historically, 1 percent of the population constituted the upper sustainable limit of purely professional troops that had to be paid regularly. The Roman principate's ratio, as fixed by Augustus, of some 250,000 to 300,000 regular soldiers to an imperial population of more than 40 million, exemplifies this golden rule. As the later empire was obliged to substantially increase that number, it found itself locked in an economic-military vicious circle. In this respect, too, the new European states do not appear to have diverged much from historical standards.[40] Because of rising agricultural productivity, especially in northern Europe, the early modern states were more densely populated than the lands of antiquity. Gibbon noted that Louis XIV of France possessed an army that was as large as that of imperial Rome, even though France (ancient Gaul) was only one province of the ancient Roman Empire.[41] However, at 20 million, France's population was four times greater than that of Roman Gaul and about half as large as that of the entire Roman Empire. Furthermore, Louis XIV's increase of the number of French troops to a peak of 350,000 to 400,000, or nearly 2 percent of the population, during his later wars around 1700, was as unsustainable as the increase in the number of Roman troops to as much as double Augustus's ratio during the wars of the triumviri, the civil wars of the third century, and the late empire. The exceptionally large French army was kept for only a few years under dire military circumstances and contributed to France's defeat through exhaustion. In peacetime, it was reduced to about 150,000 men, less than 1 percent of the country's population.

Earlier, the Spanish Empire, with a European population of some 12–13 million, surpassed the 1 percent mark in 1555 and the 2 percent mark in the 1630s. However, even though this increase was partly financed by the flow

---

39 Cross-European surveys are offered in André Corvisier, *Armies and Societies in Europe, 1494–1789* (Bloomington, Indiana, 1979), 28–36, 52–60, 131–2; Childs, *Armies and Warfare*, 59–60; Hale, *War and Society*, 198–208; Tallett, *War and Society*, 83–5; Anderson, *War and Society*, 18–21, 90–4. For some studies of individual countries, see Mallett and Hale, *Military Organization: Venice*, 78–80, 350–66; Thompson, *War and Government: Spain*, 126–45; (by contrast, during the Reconquista, which had taken place close to home in the Iberian Peninsula itself, civic militias played a prominent role; see Theresa Vann, "Reconstructing a 'Society Organized for War,'" in *Crusaders, Condottieri, and Canon: Medieval Warfare in Societies around the Mediterranean*, ed. D. Kagay and L. Villalon (Leiden, 2003), 389–416); Lynn, *Giant of the Grand Siècle*, 371–93.

40 Already noted at the time by Adam Smith, *The Wealth of Nations*, bk. 5, chap. 1, pt. 1, the low percentage has been sensed by Hale, *War and Society*, 75, 105, and, more clearly, by Tallett, *War and Society*, 217–18.

41 Edward Gibbon, *The Decline and Fall of the Roman Empire* (London, 1993), 1:23–4.

of bullion from Spain's American possessions, which by the late sixteenth century accounted for nearly a quarter of the state's income,[42] such troop levels were unsustainable and precipitated Spain's bankruptcy and decline from power. The Dutch, with a European population of about 1.5 million, were exceptional in their ability to sustain an army of 50,000 – 3 percent of the population – along with a powerful navy during the 1630s; but they, too, overtaxed themselves when Louis XIV's wars forced them to maintain as many as 100,000 men under arms with a European population that still numbered less than 2 million. Seventeenth-century Sweden under Gustavus Adolphus and his successors, with a population of less than 1.5 million in Sweden and Finland proper and perhaps double as many when the empire is counted, kept armies that occasionally exceeded 100,000; at its peak, the army comprised 180,000 men, or 6 percent of the population. But Sweden was able to do so only by living in and off foreign territories through exceptionally effective looting and extortion of its neighbors in the Baltic and Central Europe. In addition, Sweden was heavily subsidized by France during the Thirty Years' War. Once it lost the military preeminence that made these measures possible, Sweden rapidly shrank to its natural size.[43] Frederick II's Prussia, which, with a population of about 5 million, had 250,000 soldiers under arms during the Seven Years' War (1756–63) and more than 150,000 in peacetime, employed similar methods.[44] In addition, Prussia was more efficiently run than its neighbors and was wholly dedicated to its army. Like Charles XII's Sweden, it revived the principle of keeping some of its soldiers on a semiprofessional basis by releasing them for long agricultural leaves during parts of the year (the canton system). It also received heavy subsidies from its British ally during the Seven Years' War. Its extreme concentration on the military elicited Count Mirabeau's famous remark that Prussia was an army that possessed a state rather than the other way around.

Britain, with a home population of 9 million at the advent of the eighteenth century (and which began to grow rapidly in the later part

42 Earl Hamilton, *American Treasure and the Price of Revolution in Spain, 1501–1650* (New York, 1965), 34; Thompson, *War and Government*, 68–9, 288; Juan Gelabert, "Castile, 1504–1808," in Bonney, *Fiscal State*, 213.
43 Sven Lundkvist, "The Experience of Empire: Sweden as a Great Power," and Sven-Erik Aström, "The Swedish Economy and Sweden's Role as a Great Power, 1632–1697," both in *Sweden's Age of Greatness, 1632–1718*, ed. Michael Roberts (London, 1973), 20–57, 58–101; Michael Roberts, *The Swedish Imperial Experience* (Cambridge, U.K., 1979), chap. 2. The problem is well summarized by Porter, *War and the Rise of the State*, 92. Robert Frost's excellent *The Northern Wars: War, State and Society in Northeastern Europe, 1558–1721* (Harlow, U.K., 2000), is now the most comprehensive on Sweden, Poland, and Russia.
44 See ibid., 115.

of the century), expanded its army and navy to more than 100,000 men, or
1 percent of its population, during its first major European involvement,
the Nine Years' War (1689–97). It came close to two hundred thousand
(2 percent) during the Seven Years' War and the American Revolutionary War. However, these were peak war numbers, and Britain's peacetime
establishment was less than half as large. In contrast, its navy and army
were engaged globally, and their provision was particularly costly. Moreover, Britain's wartime subsidies to its allies amounted to between one-fifth
and one-quarter of its entire defense expenditure. During the Seven Years'
War, for example, it paid for one hundred thousand allied (mostly Prussian)
troops. Costs and manpower figures continued to spiral upward during the
Napoleonic Wars, when Britain was able to match the might of Revolutionary and imperial France with the proceeds of burgeoning industrialization.
In 1809, for example, Britain employed some 375,000 men in its army
and navy. This figure comprised more than 2 percent of its population of
12 million and its 5 million subjects in Ireland. Subsidies to its continental allies during the final campaigns of the Napoleonic Wars (1812–15)
comprised the same proportion of Britain's much larger defense expenditure as previously, this time paying for nearly half a million allied troops,
mostly Russian, Prussian, and Austrian.[45] However, these again were peak
war-effort years that could not be and were not sustained indefinitely.

Thus, on the face of it, the much discussed steep rise in the size of the
European armies during early modernity, while very real to be sure, barely
seems to represent an increase over historical levels of mobilization of standing armies in large states. When examined in broader, comparative terms,
it was not in fact such a novelty. Indeed, here, as in general, the European
case involves an optical distortion. Some changes that seem revolutionary
in early modern Europe because of that civilization's peculiar ascent from
low levels of political concentration, urbanism, and commercialism within
only a few centuries were incremental in other civilizations that, not having experienced such severe regression as the European Dark Ages, had
maintained greater cultural and political continuity.

Much the same applies to the advent of firearms, whose transforming
effect on society and state, in Europe as well as elsewhere in Eurasia – at
least before the eighteenth century – is often much exaggerated. As Chase
has shown so well, firearms proved the most useful for the people of West-
Central Europe because geography dictated that pitched battles and sieges,

45 Brewer, *Sinews of Power*, 30–2; Christopher Hall, *British Strategy in the Napoleonic War, 1803–15*
(Manchester, U.K., 1992), 1, 11, 15–16; Bonney, "Struggle for Great Power Status," 380–4, 387.

rather than the elusive light horsemen of the steppe, constituted their main military challenge. Fighting against Europeans in the Balkans, the Ottomans adopted firearms no less successfully. All the same, other economic, social, and political developments – such as the revival of urbanism and the money economy – had been mainly responsible for the transformation of the European state system from around 1200. And in the Ottoman Empire, as well as in other civilizations of Eurasia where firearms replaced older weapons and reshaped battle tactics and siege craft, the already-developed state armies otherwise exhibited few changes. Although they incorporated artillery and infantry firearms, there was little fundamental change in army and state structure, organization, and social composition between the Ottomans and their Turkic and Iranian predecessors or Mamluk and Safavid contemporaries; between Mughal India and the earlier Delhi sultanate; and between the Ming or Manchu (Ching) and their predecessors in China. Nor were any of these powers inferior to Europe in military might, to say the least. The Ottoman Empire, the only one of them that bordered on Europe, exerted heavy military pressure on it for centuries. Thus, in historical terms, the much-used concept of gunpowder empires has far less to it than is commonly assumed.

The introduction of firearms was undoubtedly a historical landmark. Firearms transformed field and siege warfare, and they were indispensable for keeping up militarily within the sedentary zone. The Mamluks succumbed to the Ottomans (1516–17) because they had fallen behind in the adoption of firearms. The Iranian Safavids were able to escape a similar fate only because their light horsemen adjusted their tactics and proved too mobile to pin down in the vast and arid terrain of their homeland and the frontier territories that separated them from the Ottomans. The Delhi sultanate's fall in 1526 to Babur, founder of the Mughal Empire, was due in large part to the latter's superior use of firearms. After the Portuguese introduced the gun into Japan in 1543, the warlord Oda Nobunaga employed muskets decisively in the Battle of Nagashimo (1575), and gun power continued to rise in significance during the civil wars that led to unification. To cite Chase again, because Japan, as Western Europe, was sheltered from the steppe nomads, firearms proved more useful in its internal wars than they did anywhere else in East Asia. How decisively they contributed to Japan's unification, which, like the European new monarchies, had been long in the making, is, however, an open question.[46] To conclude this brief survey: where there

---

46 Chase, *Firearms*, is a scholarly landmark on the causes of the differential spread of firearms in Eurasia. His chapter on Japan, which extensively uses Japanese sources, is particularly useful (the same is true for his chapters on China). See also Delmer Brown, "The Impact of Firearms on Japanese

was no decisive imbalance in the possession of firearms, the effect of firearms on military affairs, and through them, on society and state − in Europe and elsewhere − was not so revolutionary. As scholars have recognized, gunpowder exercised a far more revolutionary effect at sea, in combination with that second element of Francis Bacon's trio of modernity: ocean navigation.[47]

MASTERY OF THE SEAS, MARKET REGIMES, AND WAR

The establishment of a European trading system after 1500 that, for the first time in history, encompassed the entire globe constituted the single most important factor in the shaping of modernity and was the true engine of the so-called European miracle. It transformed European society, economy, and state. Markets grew to play an unprecedented role, granting some European states greater resources and, hence, greater power than other states, while making Europe as a whole increasingly wealthier and more powerful in relation to other parts of the world. Ultimately, the global trading system stimulated industrialization and a quantum leap in wealth and power. Although challenged by some recent scholarship, this picture, which originated with Adam Smith and Karl Marx, remains broadly valid.[48]

Warfare, 1543–98," *Far Eastern Quarterly* 7 (1948): 236–53. Noel Perrin, *Giving Up the Gun: Japan's Reversion to the Sword, 1543–1879* (Boulder, Colorado, 1979), is criticized as scholarly dubious. I disagree with Chase's assessments on one point. Although he notes (*Firearms*, 175–86) that large infantry armies and increasingly larger daimyo domains were growing to dominate Japanese warfare and politics well before the introduction of firearms, and though he concedes that firearms became widely available to all sides, he credits them with hastening unification. Parker, too, who in *Military Revolution*, 140–5 (esp. 140), carefully avoided such a claim, embraces it in his "In Defense of *The Military Revolution*," 338.

47 In this I agree with Braudel, *Civilization and Capitalism*, 1:385, 397.
48 Among the proponents of this view are Adam Smith, *The Wealth of Nations*, bk. 4, chap. 7; Karl Marx and Friedrich Engels, *Manifesto of the Communist Party*; Karl Marx, *The Capital*, chap. 31; Braudel, *Civilization and Capitalism*, ii; *Wheels of Commerce*, 601; Immanuel Wallerstein, *The Modern World System I: Capitalist Agriculture and the Origins of the European World-Economy in the Sixteenth Century* (New York, 1974); Andre Frank, *World Accumulation, 1492–1789* (New York, 1978). Recent research has rightly emphasized Europe's internal economic growth, but the two developments were obviously mutually reinforcing. According to Patrick O'Brien, "European Economic Development: The Contribution of the Periphery," *Economic History Review* 35 (1982): 1–18, Europe's global commercial activities were marginal to its economic activity, constituting only 25 percent of its trade even as late as 1790; also (somewhat more positively), see "European Industrialization: From the Voyages of Discovery to the Industrial Revolution', in *The European Discovery of the World and Its Economic Effects on Pre-Industrial Society, 1500–1800*, ed. H. Pohl (Stuttgart, 1990), 154–77. However, see the decidedly positive assessment of Neils Steensgaard, "Commodities, Bullion and Services in Intercontinental Transactions before 1750," ibid., 9–23 (and the data compiled by Frank, 105–6, 215–9, 225, 232–3). As O'Brien himself acknowledges, it is often the marginal economic advantage that counts. Indeed, while Kenneth Pomeranz, *The Great Divergence: China, Europe, and the Making of the Modern World Economy* (Princeton, New Jersey,

The military aspects of Europe's expansion have been thoroughly covered by scholars. During the first two centuries of their presence in South and East Asia, the Europeans were far too weak to challenge the mighty but continentally oriented empires on whose margins they were more or less tolerated. Their heavily armed sailing ships, however, mastered the seas and much of their trade.[49] By sheer historical coincidence, guns were now making the sailing ship, traditionally a vessel for trade, a superior warship to the oared galley that had dominated sea warfare in the narrow seas. But although gun power was a significant contributing factor to the Europeans' new global success, other factors were more decisive in deciding which Europeans would reap the advantages of that success. Although the preindustrial European economy remained predominantly agrarian, mastery of markets of global scale and a growing manufacturing sector that prospered by virtue of that mastery became a significant source of wealth, a more liquid form of wealth than previously known. The emergence of a global trading system thus became the primary catalyst for the formation of capitalism in Europe. Indeed, the sheer unprecedented scale of the global trading system transformed power relations between and within European societies more than the predominance of any commercial power had in the past. The states that won out in the contest for domination over global trade secured the resources that made them strong in the European power struggle. And it was the traders' states that were best equipped to win the global trade contest.[50] Wealth and power were becoming increasingly interchangeable. Consequently, to survive, power had to serve the interests of the producing and trading economy, and the more it did so, the more power was generated. Any shackles put on social wealth creation by the state's political and military elite only undermined the power of that elite in competition with other states. For the first time in history, parasitic warrior states and warrior elites were falling behind economically productive states and elites in terms of power. Economic performance was becoming the key to power, and

---

2000), undermines many assumptions regarding the differences between Western Europe and the other great civilizations of Eurasia, he emphasizes the crucial marginal advantage accorded by the Europeans' global position with great sophistication and much nuance. The same spirit and same conclusion are found in Janet Abu-Lughod, *Before European Hegemony: The World System A.D. 1250–1350* (New York, 1989), 363. Finally, Maddison, *World Economy* (Paris, 2001), 93 , shows that in the case of the leading British economy, extra-European trade was not marginal at all but constituted about half the country's overall trade by 1774.

49 Cipolla's pioneering *Guns and Sails* is still of some value; Robert Gardiner, ed., *Cogs, Cravels and Galleons: The Sailing Ship, 1000–1650* (London, 1994), covers the technical side; Bailey Diffie and George Winius, *Foundations of the Portuguese Empire*, is a good overview; see also Parker, *Military Revolution*, chap. 3.

50 This has more or less been suggested by Wallerstein, *Modern World*-System (New York, 1974).

the capitalist trading and manufacturing economy increasingly spearheaded economic performance.

Let us return to the military revolution. It has been argued here that in historical, comparative terms there seems to have been no radical novelty in the size of the new standing European armies. Yet if armies and navies together grew somewhat larger in comparison to those of other large states and if hardware such as guns marginally increased the cost of war, there were three main sources for such possible growth. First, growth in agricultural productivity per capita since antiquity appears to have marginally increased Europe's surpluses. Second, there was the income that came from extra-European activities, such as the flow of American bullion into the Spanish treasury (a mixed blessing that deepened Spain's economic retardation as a rentier state) and earnings from trading and manufacturing that were mostly reaped by the Dutch and English. Third, the early modern state developed deficit financing to historically unprecedented levels. These three sources were intricately intertwined, and the European states varied in the efficiency with which they tapped them and, hence, in their success in the great powers' struggle.

States differed in their taxing ability. The larger the state, the greater were its aggregate tax revenues, yet there were also disadvantages to size in early modern Europe. As we have already noted, the new, territorially composite and absolutist European state, with its regional and class privileges, probably taxed less efficiently than, for example, the Roman Empire had. The main tax burden in imperial Spain lay on Castile, and all attempts to equalize it throughout the empire met with very limited success and precipitated rebellions in the Low Countries, Catalonia, Naples, Sicily, and Portugal. In France, provincial privileges, defended by local assemblies, were almost equally entrenched. And in the eighteenth century, the territorially composite Austrian Empire faced even greater taxing difficulties than France. Smaller and more homogeneous states, such as England, the Dutch Republic, and Prussia, were ultimately able to tax more evenly. But England, too, lost its American colonies when it tried to spread the burden of taxation onto its imperial periphery.

Mastery over global trade and a prosperous manufacturing sector were other factors that enhanced taxation efficiency in various ways. Indeed, their indirect benefits transcended their direct contributions to national wealth. A comparison of the national wealth of Britain and France during their eighteenth-century struggle indicates that, because France's population was about three times greater than Britain's and agriculture was still the largest sector of the economy, the French economy was more than double the size of Britain's.[51] And yet it is agreed that Britain won the naval-military contest by virtue of its superior financial capabilities. The more liquid financial resources of Britain's far more commercialized economy were the key to its success.[52]

Borrowing in the present meant mortgaging the future. It constituted a more or less successful investment in that future and, like any leveraged investment, was a high-risk and high-gain one. A Darwinian race for credit grew to dominate the arms race between the powers. All of them pushed borrowing to the limit and beyond, building up massive debts. The Spanish debt in 1623 spiraled to ten years of royal receipts.[53] Powers like Spain, whose credit status deteriorated, ultimately lost out in the race. In the case of France, the hopeless financial tangle that resulted from borrowing for military purposes famously brought down the monarchy and the ancien régime. France fell victim to the crisis even though in absolute terms its debt only amounted to some 60 percent of Britain's; in relative terms, its debt burden was smaller still, for it equaled just more than half of France's gross national product, whereas Britain's debt was almost twice its gross national product.[54] Indeed, the British national debt leaped upward with every war during the eighteenth century, rocketing to a staggering twenty times its average annual tax income after the American War of Independence or about twice its annual gross national product. Between half and two-thirds of Britain's tax income were spent annually on (low) interest payments to service the debt, which paid for 30 to 40 percent of its spending during the wars. Importantly, about 20 percent of the debt represented foreign investment.[55] Britain was the ultimate winner in the leveraged race only because victories gave it a colonial empire and commanding position over global trade, which in turn also boosted its home economy in a period of substantial economic expansion. Wealth paid for war, and war laid the foundation for greater wealth creation. It was the wealthy and economically more efficient that won out in that race.

Scholars have debated whether the waste of war proved economically beneficial in the final analysis owing to the spin-off effects of large state investment in metallurgy, mining, shipbuilding, and supply on developing

51 Peter Mathias and Patrick O'Brien, "Taxation in England and France, 1715–1810: A Comparison of the Social and Economic Incidence of Taxes Collected for the Central Governments," *Journal of European Economic History* 5 (1976), 601–50; Bonney, "Struggle for Great Power Status," 336–8.

52 Brewer, *Sinews of War*, 180–3.

53 Geoffrey Parker, "War and Economic Change: The Economic Costs of the Dutch Revolt," in *War and Economic Development*, ed. J. Winter (Cambridge, U.K., 1975), 57.

54 Bonney, "Struggle of Great Power Status," 345.

55 Dickson, *Financial Revolution*, 10, 304–37 (esp. 320); Brewer, *Sinews of Power*, 30, 114–7.

economies.[56] But more significant perhaps, war formed an integral part of a historical process in which more productive market economies triumphed over traditional economic–political regimes. The European and global penetration of the market economy was made possible and was much quickened by the close interaction of economic leadership and military superiority. If this was so, then early modern war carried a huge dividend in terms of economic development. Indeed, because of the strong connection between wealth and power, states were just as concerned with increasing their economic productivity to stay competitive against other states in the pursuit of power as they were in exerting their power to secure economic advantage. To make themselves more productive, they undertook economic, social, and political reforms.[57] War thus played a central role in propelling forward the process of modernization in general.

BACON'S TRIO OF MODERNITY AND THE MILITARY REVOLUTION

It is time to return to the much-debated concept of the military revolution to consider how it is to be understood. A definition of its time span and constitutive elements only makes sense by viewing it as an interacting component, an aspect, of the West's overall – continuous and sweeping – transformation rather than in narrower military terms. This transformation began around 1200, as the revival and growth of urbanism, the money economy, and large-scale centralized country-states generated increasingly larger, more centralized, and more permanent state armies, with infantry playing a more prominent role. All these were greatly boosted from the late fifteenth century by the wide-reaching effects of Bacon's trio that launched modernity: gunpowder, the printing press, and ocean navigation. The introduction of firearms, while transforming both siege and field warfare, quickly resulted in restored equilibriums – barely different from those that had prevailed earlier – between fortifications and siege craft as between infantry and cavalry. The staggering growth in the size of the European armies, as compared to mobilization levels during the earlier period of Europe's medieval fragmentation, was indeed revolutionary in European terms. However, mainly attributed to the process of state centralization in Europe, the new large permanent armies were far less revolutionary

---

56 Werner Sombart, *Krieg und Kapitalismus* (Munich, 1913); John Nef, *War and Human Progress: An Essay on the Rise of Industrial Civilization* (London, 1950); and more briefly, see Hale, *War and Society*, chap. 8; Tallett, *War and Society*, 216–32.

57 Already noted by John Hall, "States and Societies: The Miracle in Comparative Perspective," in *Europe and the Rise of Capitalism*, ed. J. Baechler, J. Hall, and M. Mann (Oxford, 1988), 36; Linda Weiss and John Hobson, *State and Economic Development* (Cambridge, U.K., 1995), 89–90.

when measured in historical and comparative terms. For quite a while, the early modern European experience represented no significant increase over sustainable mobilization levels achieved by well-organized large bureaucratic states through history – up to 1 percent of the population. It was only the interaction of these developments with Bacon's two other modern innovations that was to make the European experience truly pathbreaking – in comparison to the past and to the record of Asia's great civilization centers of the time.

Indeed, by the eighteenth century, the Europeans had pulled ahead of all the other civilizations of Eurasia in terms of power and wealth. As already mentioned, at least initially, empires throughout Eurasia incorporated firearms within traditional social and institutional frameworks – in the Ottoman case, hardly less thoroughly than the Europeans. As late as 1683, the Ottoman army was still capable of besieging Vienna, a century and a half after it had done so for the first time. Yet this was the swan song of Ottoman military might. Even during the heyday of the Ottoman Empire, there had never been a real threat of it conquering Central and Western Europe. Its power could not be extended farther than the Danube Plain, where its armies could be supplied by river, and where its sipahi feudal cavalry was able to graze its horses, enjoyed tactical superiority, and was not too far away to return back home after its obligatory summer campaigning season.[58] After 1683, however, military superiority, hitherto enjoyed by the Ottomans, increasingly shifted to the Europeans, and the Ottoman frontiers in Europe began to roll back.

The unfolding effects of Bacon's trio were responsible for this change in the balance of power. First, as long as matchlock harquebusiers and musketeers needed the protection of pikemen in the face of cavalry and in hand-to-hand fighting, the tactical flexibility and offensive role of infantry were severely hindered. However, with the development of the bayonet that was fixed to the muzzle of the musket, the pike could be abolished. At about the same time, the flintlock replaced the matchlock, again increasing the musket's reliability and effectiveness.[59] Only now did infantry, comprising solely musketeers, become the queen of the battlefield, in Europe and overseas. Because for geopolitical reasons European infantry had traditionally

---

58 See G. Veinstein, "Some Views on Provisioning in the Hungarian Campaigns of Suleiman the Magnificent," in *État et société dans l'empire Ottoman, XVIe-XVIIIe siècles* (Aldershot, U.K., 1994), chap. 7; Caroline Finkel, *The Administration of Warfare: The Ottoman Campaign in Hungary, 1593–1606* (Vienna, 1988); Rhoads Murphey, *Ottoman Warfare, 1500–1700* (New Brunswick, New Jersey, 1999), 20–5, 65–6, 85–103, and passim. Oman, *Art of War*, bk. 7, can still be read with profit.

59 Black, *A Military Revolution?* and "A Military Revolution?"; Chase, *Firearms*.

been superior to others, Europe was the main beneficiary of that change. Thus, the Ottomans' elite Janissary infantry now proved too small a force, whereas their large mass of cavalry – including, at last, the horse archer – became obsoletet.[60]

It was, however, Europe's mastery of the seas (aided by its naval gun power) that proved the decisive factor in its development, creating the first global trading system and precipitating the rise of capitalism in Europe. And whereas firearms could largely be assimilated into traditional societies, a highly developed market economy could not. By the eighteenth century, even before industrialization, Europeans had grown perhaps as much as twice as rich as their contemporaries in Asia, in per capita terms.[61] Not only did this growth provide Europe with the resources and financial institutions necessary to maintain progressively larger and more permanent armies and navies, but also the expansion of the market economy transformed European society and politics. The old military-agrarian extractive elite was gradually drawn into the market and/or had to share power with the rising commercial bourgeoisie. Autocratic power that initially benefited from and reinforced these processes sooner or later everywhere had to become attuned to the interests of these economically and socially powerful classes, incorporate them into the state, or hand over power to them. With the aid of print communications, there emerged an increasingly participatory civic-national modern state, where state power became impersonal, public resources were separated from the private wealth of leaders and subjected to closer scrutiny, and the rule of law prevented arbitrary state action. No longer did autocratic rule, patrimonial political power, constitute the main avenue to wealth. Hitherto subservient to extractory political power, wealth creation increasingly dominated it, thereby generating yet greater power.

---

60 Halil Inalcik, "The Socio-Political Effects of the Diffusion of Firearms in the Middle East," and V. Parry, "La manière de combattre," both in Parry and Yapp, *War, Technology and Society*, 195–217 and 218–56. Chase, *Firearms*. It should be noted that the Ottomans were at least partly adapting: in the seventeenth century, the number of Ottoman infantry increased while that of cavalry decreased. See M. Yapp, "The Modernization of Middle Eastern Armies in the Nineteenth Century: A Comparative View," in ibid., 344; Murphey, *Ottoman Warfare*, 16. Ottoman use of field artillery in the seventeenth century was also more advanced than previously thought. See Murphey, 109–12; Gábor Ágoston, "Ottoman Artillery and European Military Technology in the Fifteenth and Seventeenth Centuries," *Acta Orientalia Academiae Scietiarum Hungaricae* 47 (1994): 15–48.

61 Arguing that the East Asian civilizations did not fall behind Europe until industrialization, Pomeranz, *Great Divergence*, does not pay sufficient attention to Bacon's trio. Paul Bairoch, "European Gross National Product, 1800–1975," *Journal of European Economic History* 5 (1976): 287, roughly estimates that European per capita product was about 20 percent higher than Asia's in 1800. However, Maddison, *World Economy*, 28, 42, 44, 47, 49, 90, 126, 264, criticizing both Pomeranz and Bairoch, calculates that Europe overtook Asia in per capita wealth from 1400 and continuously widened its lead to twice the Asian per capita product by the eve of industrialization (thrice in the Netherlands and Britain).

While decreasing despotic power, these developments greatly enhanced states' infrastructural power by, inter alia, deepening social mobilization. Furthermore, as greater public legitimacy was conferred on the regime, as its social support base was widened, and as lawful and peaceful means for changing government became available, violent usurpation decreased and domestic political stability increased. These again reflected the old virtues of mixed polities as defined by Aristotle and his disciples. European states increasingly freed themselves from both specters of regicide and imbecile hereditary rulers that haunted traditional autocratic states and regularly threw them into periods of chaos or inaction.

Indeed, by the eighteenth century, not only the Ottomans but also other Asian empires found themselves falling behind Europe in wealth and power, as well as experiencing domestic-dynastic decline. In India, the decline and disintegration of the mighty Mughal Empire in the early eighteenth century made it possible for the British East Indian Company, a statelike efficient capitalist organization, to take over as the new overlords. Utilizing its great wealth (largely derived from India itself) to hire native troops, the company also built on the newly developed superiority of European-style musket-bayonet infantry and field artillery over the semifeudal cavalry that constituted the mainstay of Indian social and military power. In the late eighteenth and early nineteenth centuries, Indian states responded by successfully emulating the Europeans, hiring European officers, adopting and manufacturing advanced artillery, and raising modern infantry armies. Nonetheless, all resistance attempts ultimately failed, for although the Indian sepoy could be made into no less effective infantry than the European serf-peasant, the Indian states did not enjoy the monopoly over armed force and the degree of social cohesiveness that had been achieved in Europe by the eighteenth century.[62] In China, Manchu dynastic decline was to come only a century after the Mughal decline, and Europeans were powerless to make inroads into that country until well into the nineteenth century. All the same,

---

62 On this I am in agreement with D. H. A. Kolff, "The End of an Ancien Regime: Colonial War in India, 1798–1818," in *Imperialism and War: Essays on Colonial Wars in Asia and Africa*, ed. J. De Moor and H. Wesseling (Leiden, 1989), 22–49, and *Naukar, Rajput and Sepoy: The Ethnohistory of the Military Labour Market in Hindustan, 1450–1850* (Cambridge, U.K., 1990); Jos Gommans, "Warhorse and Gunpowder in India *c.* 1000–1850," in Black, *War in the Early Modern World*, 105–27, esp. 118–19; and "Indian Warfare and Afghan Innovation during the Eighteenth Century," in Gommans and Kolff, *Warfare and Weaponry in South Asia*, 365–86; and *Mughal Warfare*, 74, 166, 204; Bruce Lenman, "The Transition to European Military Ascendancy in India, 1600–1800," in Lynn, *Tools of War*, 100–30; John Lynn, "Victories of the Conquered: The Native Character of the Sepoy," in *Battle: A History of Combat and Culture* (Boulder, Colorado, 2003), 145–77. Although failing to consider the power advantage accorded by eighteenth-century European social-political organization, Pomeranz, *Great Divide*, 4, 18–20, 201–6, emphasizes the role of the European great commercial corporations and their effective use of force in alliance with their respective states.

although industrialization during that century is rightly cited as the crucial advance that made China (and Japan) impotent vis-à-vis Western power, preindustrial national European armies of the Napoleonic era were already far superior to any outside Europe. The Mamluk and Ottoman forces proved no match for Napoleon's expeditionary army during his 1798–9 campaign in the Levant. Only China's huge size, as well as distance and problems of power projection, sheltered it (and Japan) from European intervention for a short while longer.

To recapitulate, the so-called military revolution that was to give Europe global ascendancy emanated neither from muskets and drill nor from artillery fortifications – nor, indeed, from any other tactical development in itself. Rather, the revolution was one element of Europe's general, centuries-long process of modernization, boosted by the unfolding and interacting effects of all the three elements of Bacon's trio of modernity, which transformed European economy, society, and state, and with them the military and war.

2

Guibert

Prophet of Total War?

BEATRICE HEUSER

"Le 'Dieu de la guerre' est près de se révéler, car nous avons entendu son prophète" – "The god of war is about to reveal himself, as we have heard his prophet." Thus wrote the French strategist Jean Colin in his book on the military education of Napoleon, and the prophet he had in mind was Jacques Antoine Hippolyte, Count de Guibert, a prolific writer of the eighteenth century.[1] Indeed, the connection between Guibert and Napoleon is supported by historical evidence. Napoleon was made to read Guibert's works at the military school he attended, and he apparently admired Guibert greatly. He later called Guibert's principal work, *Essai général de tactique* ("A General Essay on Tactics"), "a book fit to educate great men." He took it on campaign with him and bestowed a pension on Guibert's widow "in consideration of the works of M. de Guibert and of the advantages which the French Army has drawn from them."[2] George Washington is also reported to have read Guibert and to have said, "The works of M. de Guibert are my companions of war."[3]

The influence of Guibert's writings on the warfare of the French Revolution, however, was at best indirect. To be sure, his *Essai général de tactique* was so widely read and so frequently and thoroughly studied that several authors wrote entire books as commentaries on his views – usually to take him to task over his views with regard to marching in columns, his preferred length for the bayonet, or the deep order or the shallow order for

---

1 Jean Lambert Alphonse Colin, *L'education militaire de Napoléon* (Paris, 1901), quoted in Matti Lauerma, *Jacques-Antoine-Hippolyte de Guibert (1743–1790)* (Helsinki, 1989), 25.
2 Lucien Poirier, *Les voix de la stratégie* (Paris, 1985), 124.
3 So Guibert's widow claimed in the first posthumous edition of the *Essai*: see Jean-Paul Charnay, "Portraits de Guibert," in *Guibert ou le soldat philosophe*, ed. Centre d'Études et de Recherché sur les Strategies et les Conflicts (Paris, 1981), 16.

shooting volleys.[4] But Guibert was not among the authors of the great *Encyclopédie*, even though the *encyclopédistes* writing on military matters had read and referred to his *Essai*. As Kathleen Hardesty Doig has found, the *encyclopédistes* were fairly conservative where military technology, doctrine, and concepts of recruitment and training were concerned.[5] Guibert, in his earlier writings, was more revolutionary than they were when it came to his ideas about the need for citizens to identify with and defend their country as citizen-soldiers.

On the sociopolitical front, however, the *encyclopédistes* and philosophes were more radical than Guibert. Some philosophes, most notably Voltaire, hoped to abolish warfare altogether and did not think that the creation of mass armies would be helpful for this purpose. When he was in his thirties, Guibert distanced himself from the position of the philosophes, professing his belief that war was an eternal human phenomenon but could be made rarer and less bloody if waged in the way he advocated.[6] When the Revolution erupted, the revolutionaries, while borrowing here and there from his ideas, regarded Guibert as not radical enough, associating him with the monarchy's failed reforms. Guibert therefore cannot be said directly to have played a part in the thinking of the great actors of the Revolution, the Dantons, Robespierres, or Carnots. And yet some of the ideas he set out in his *Essai général de tactique*, especially on the need for all citizens to defend their country, seem to have found their echo in revolutionary rhetoric and practice, above all, that of total mobilization, the levée en masse.

One believer in Guibert's prophetic gifts was the French anthropologist Roger Callois. Commenting on the way of war of the French Revolution, he argued that it is a misperception and misrepresentation to think of the levée en masse as a "desperate expedient" or "that the tactics of the armies of the Year II were only a function of the inexperience of the generals and the soldiers":

A reading of Guibert shows that both fit a doctrine which was already 20 years old, worked out by one of the most admired theoreticians of the century, and doubtless the object of impassioned discussions.... In advance [of its time], [the doctrine] analyzed the conditions of a new form of recruitment, it developed a new strategy, it sketched the mindset of the future combatant. It foresaw the violence of war,

---

4 Anon. [Marquis de Silva], *Remarques sur quelques articles de l'Essai général de tactique* (Turin, 1773); Le G[énéral Charles Emmanuel de] de W[arner]y, *Remarques sur l'Essai général de tactique de Guibert* (Warsaw, 1781); see also the works of Francois-Jean Mésnil-Durand.
5 Kathleen Hardesty Doig, "War in the Reform Programme of the Encyclopedie," *War and Society* 6, no. 1 (May 1988): 1–9.
6 *Défense du systême de guerre moderne, ou Réfutation complette du systême de M. de M[énil] D[urand] par l'auteur de l'Essai général de tactique*, 2 vols. (Neuchâtel, 1779).

the mobility of troops, the disdain for conventions, the boldness of maneuvers, the conscription of recruits, the frequency and the fierceness of battles, the[ir] decisive character.[7]

And for Lucien Poirier, the Fifth Republic general turned philosopher of strategy, there was no doubt that "thirty years in advance, [Guibert] announced the furies of nationalism."[8] The Gaullist politician and intellectual Léo Hamon commented on Guibert's later writings that they reflected the fear with which he had discovered the slippery slope leading to the apocalyptic conflicts of later times.[9]

There is thus broad agreement that Guibert was indeed the prophet of French Revolutionary and Napoleonic warfare.[10] If one identifies its seeds in this era, one should then ask to what extent Guibert was also the prophet of total war.

THE YOUNG GUIBERT

Jacques-Antoine Hippolyte de Guibert was born in 1743 as the only son of Jean-Bénôit Guibert, a member of the minor nobility and an officer in the French army. The boy was only thirteen when his father first took him on campaign at the outbreak of the Seven Years' War. Jacques-Antoine was to witness that war in its entirety, fighting on the side of the French against the Prussians under Frederick the Great. In the course of the war, the adolescent rose to the rank of captain, while his father became a brigadier. Together, they took part in several battles, including those at Rossbach and Minden, which Frederick famously won. Against the backdrop of these experiences, which he must have discussed in great detail with his father or have heard his father discuss with other officers, the young Guibert became a great admirer of Frederick, as he reckoned that Frederick had revolutionized warfare.[11] And yet he recognized shortcomings even in Frederick's conduct of warfare and dreamed of even more intensive, comprehensive, and decisive campaigns.

Guibert wrote down his thoughts on the subject of the art of war and society in his two-volume *Essai général de tactique* when he was in his early twenties, toward the end of several years of independent study in Paris,

---

7 Roger Caillois, *Bellone ou la perte de la guerre* (Brussels, 1963), 84, 101, quoted in *Guibert ou le soldat philosophe*, 115.
8 Poirier, *Les voix*, 139.
9 Léo Hamon, "Guibert devant la politique," in *Guibert ou le soldat philosophe*, 164.
10 See also Guglielmo Ferrero, *Aventure: Bonaparte en Italie, 1796–1797* (Paris, 1936), 85–6, quoted in *Guibert ou le soldat philosophe*, 112.
11 *Défense du systême de guerre moderne*, 2:228.

where he had followed his father, who had been employed at the Ministry of War. The *Essai* thus deals with much more than what we today would call tactics. He included a great tour d'horizon of France's relations with many other countries as well as a most impressive sketch of a utopian state. Like Kant's later ideal nonaggressive republic, Guibert's ideal state would have no territorial ambitions and wage only defensive wars. It would be open to commerce and the arts, and it would thus serve in every possible way as an example to other countries. Kant, it is worth emphasizing, wrote his *Zum Ewigen Frieden* only in 1795, a quarter of a century after Guibert; we have here a classic example of ideas that were in the air, engendered at much the same time in different places by the reading of Montesquieu, Voltaire, and others.

As Guibert took some of his basic ideas on the *ius ad bellum* from Montesquieu, it is imperative to outline these briefly. Montesquieu's De *l'esprit des lois* (1748) was frowned upon by French patriots because of its approval of the British system, just as Guibert was criticized thirty years later for his admiration for Frederick the Great. Unlike Voltaire, Montesquieu accepted war as an inherent part of human relations and saw it as justified above all in the case of self-defense.[12] The types of states Montesquieu admired most – democracies, oligarchies, and constitutional monarchies – were those he thought most likely to wage only defensive wars. In books nine and ten of De *l'esprit des lois*, he reflected upon the relationship of the law with the defensive use of force, and he opined, "The spirit of monarchy is war and aggrandizement; the spirit of the republic is peace and moderation."[13] He refined this argument by pointing to dictates of size. A monarchy of middling size would be inclined to surround itself by fortresses à la Vauban to strengthen its defenses. (Despotic regimes, however, would not dare build fortresses on their own territory, as they would trust no guardian of such a fortress to be loyal to them.)[14] A smallish state, by contrast, might be tempted to wage a preventive war for fear that a neighbor might grow to become a threat.[15] A democracy would contradict its own ideals of liberty if it ever waged aggressive wars with the aim of lasting conquest (as opposed to an offensive campaign aimed at neutralizing a neighboring territory for a limited time), let alone the enslavement a conquered people.[16] We will see several of these views taken up by Guibert in his *Essai général de tactique*.

Writing after the Seven Years' War, from which France emerged with dishonor, Guibert vented his dissatisfaction with the customs of waging war in his age, which he blamed in part for France's defeat. Here his description

12 Montesquieu: *De l'esprit des lois* (Paris, 1990), 1:273.
13 Ibid., 1:267.   14 Ibid., 1:265–9.
15 Ibid., 1:273–4.   16 Ibid., 1:274–7.

of warfare under the ancien régime: "Today, all of Europe is civilized," he proclaimed.

Wars have become less cruel. Outside combat, blood is no longer shed. Towns are no longer destroyed. The countryside is no longer ravaged. The vanquished people are only asked to pay some form of tribute, often less exacting than the taxes that they pay to their sovereign. Spared by their conqueror, their fate does not become worse [after a defeat]. All the states of Europe govern themselves, more or less, according to the same laws and according to the same principles. As a result, necessarily, the nations take less interest in wars. The quarrel, whatever it is, isn't theirs. They regard it simply as that of the government. Therefore, the support for this quarrel is left to mercenaries, and the military is regarded as a cumbersome group of people and cannot count itself among the other groups within society. As a result, patriotism is extinct, and bravery is weakening as if by an epidemic.[17]

For this reason, the majority of military thinkers under the ancien régime were, Guibert contended, working within limited parameters. They usually had the practical knowledge of experienced soldiers, and their interests were limited to organizational and operational matters, such as the recruitment of troops, training and discipline, patterns of deploying troops and composing armies (infantry, cavalry, artillery), logistics, and other truly tactical considerations (e.g., how to besiege a fortified place and how to fortify places to withstand sieges, or how to cross rivers without becoming excessively vulnerable to enemy attacks).

These are the main subjects addressed in the military writings of Henry Lloyd, Frederick the Great, Maurice de Saxe, Jean de Folard (whom Guibert despised wholeheartedly),[18] and most of their contemporaries. They operated in a political context in which the political aims of commanding princes were as clear as they were simple: the self-preservation of ruling dynasties and the defense or aggrandizement of their lands, as we read in the political testament of Frederick the Great.[19] Jean-Jacques Rousseau put it similarly: "The business of kings or of those who discharge their duties has only two aims: extend their domination abroad and to render it more absolute internally."[20] As war aims were thus fairly straightforward in this period, when religion featured much less than at any time since antiquity, and when all princes essentially wanted to uphold the existing social order, hardly any military thinker considered the possibility of extending wars, of making

17 Jacques-Antoine-Hippolyte de Guibert, "Essai général de tactique," in Guibert, *Stratégiques*, ed. Jean-Paul Charnay and Martine Burgos (Paris, 1977), 187–8.
18 *Défense du systême de guerre moderne*, 1.
19 "Das Politische Testament Friedrichs des Grossen." (1768), in: Die Politischen Testament der Hohenzollern, ed. Richard Dietrich (Cologne, 1986), 650.
20 Jean-Jacques Rousseau, "Jugement sur la paix perpetuelle" (Neuchâtel, 1782), para. 1175, http://oll. libertyfund.org/index.php?option=com_staticxt&staticfile=show.php&title=710&search=extend+their+domination&layout=html#a_2011872.

them more decisive, more brutal, or more far reaching. They thought and wrote about how to make battles technically more efficient and armies more disciplined, how to deploy forces more effectively, not how to revolutionize warfare as such.

Count Guibert was the crucial exception to this rule that the eighteenth century produced limited thinking about limited wars. He paired military experience and the quest for a more decisive victory with a politico-philosophical approach.

In the *Essai général de tactique*, the young Guibert set out his reflections on the wars of his age that he had witnessed or read about against the background of the societies he knew.

Now that all the peoples of Europe are, so to speak, mixed . . . because of the similarity of the principles of their governments, by . . . their morals, by politics, travel, literature, the national prejudices which used to separate them no longer exist. . . . Today indeed all the nations of Europe model themselves on one another. . . . Today all the troops of Europe have, with small differences, the same constitutions, which is to say . . . constitutions . . . which are based neither on honor nor on patriotism.[21]

It was not only the ways of conducting war and the military constitutions that determined the nature of warfare under the ancien régime. Guibert also identified deep structural patterns in macroeconomics and demographics, which played crucial roles. "Today," wrote Guibert,

the States have neither treasure, nor a population surplus. Their expenditure in peace is already beyond their income. Still, they wage war against each other. One goes to war with armies which one can neither [afford to] recruit, nor pay. Victor or vanquished, both are almost equally exhausted [at the end of a war]. The mass of the national debt increases. Credit decreases. Money is lacking. The fleets do not find sailors; armies lack soldiers. The ministers, on one side and on the other, feel that it is time to negotiate. Peace is concluded. Some colonies or provinces change hands. Often the source of the quarrels has not dried up, and each side sits on the rubble, busy paying his debts and keeping his armies alert.[22]

In Guibert's description of the situation in the eighteenth century, we see where Clausewitz drew his inspiration for his passages on civil-military relations:[23] Guibert described eighteenth-century Europe as full of

tyrannical, ignorant or weak governments; the strengths of nations stifled by their vices; individual interests prevailing over the public good [common wealth]; morals, that supplement of laws which is so often more effective than them, neglected or

21 Guibert, "Essai général de tactique," 186–7.   22 Ibid., 137–8.
23 Carl von Clausewitz, Vom Kriege, 19th ed., ed. Werner Hahlweg (Bonn, 1991), 967.

corrupted; . . . the expenses of governments greater than their incomes; taxes higher than the means of those who have to pay them; the population scattered and sparse; the most important skills neglected for the sake of frivolous arts; luxury blindly undermining all states; and governments finally indifferent to the fates of the people, and the peoples, in return, indifferent to the successes of governments.[24]

We hear here echoes of Tacitus and Suetonius deploring Rome's abandonment of the republican virtues that made it the greatest power in the known world. And, indeed, Guibert was setting eighteenth-century Europe in contrast to republican Rome, the Rome whose citizens had conquered many kingdoms and whose pride in their citizenship made them feel superior to the kings they defeated.[25] Guibert did not come down entirely against the royal order of France. He described France, his fatherland, as composed of the king and the three estates of citizens. This was not merely paying lip service to the monarchy to get past the censors: Guibert felt obliged to publish the *Essai général de tactique* abroad – in London in 1772 and in Leiden a year later – for fear of censorship. At the very least, we have here a clear shift from the old loyalty to the king only – *regnalism*, as defined by Susan Reynolds[26] – to a new reverence for the entire polity, the country and its citizens. He thus dedicated the *Essai* to his *patrie*, not his king, even though he saw his king as father of his fatherland.

Yet this patriotism was mixed with a universalist, humanist approach, as he defined his patriotism as free from pride as well as from hatred or disdain for other peoples. "I can thus be useful for my fellow citizens, while not displeasing foreigners. I can write for France, and be read by the rest of Europe."[27] (This attitude can still be found in his writings a decade later, when he contended: "I am not writing only for France; I am addressing also those foreign armies who practice what we discuss.")[28]

What, then, was it that Guibert wanted for France? A new military rooted in a new society, a military able to deal with enemies decisively. "Imagine," he wrote,

that a people will arise in Europe that combines the virtues of austerity and a national militia with a fixed plan for expansion, that it does not lose sight of this system, that, knowing how to make war at little expense and to live off its victories, it would not be forced to put down its arms for reasons of economy. One would see that people subjugate its neighbors, and overthrow our weak constitutions, just as the fierce north wind bends the slender reeds. . . . Between these peoples, whose

---

24 Guibert, "Essai général de tactique," 135   25 Ibid., 135.
26 Susan Reynolds: *Fiefs and Vassals: The Medieval Evidence Reinterpreted* (Oxford, U.K., 1994).
27 Ibid., 132.
28 Guibert, *Défense du système de guerre moderne*, 4.

quarrels are perpetuated by their weakness [i.e., they cannot fight to the finish], one day there might still be more decisive wars, which will shake up empires.[29]

It is impossible to read this passage without thinking of the levée en masse during the French Revolution and of the Napoleonic achievements. It is as if Napoleon had consciously set out to be Aquilon, the fierce north wind, that swept across Europe bending the slender reeds of the old monarchies.

What would be the strategy of Guibert's ideal state? He imagined it to be defensive in a Montesquieuian sense: it would wish for peace and fight only defensive wars. Here, Guibert injected a strong dose of mercantilism. The overarching policy of the government of his ideal state would be to engender prosperity on every level through internal growth of production turned into riches through trade. It would open its ports, let its commerce flow, and trade with as many other countries as possible. That, in turn, dictated this state's foreign and defense policy. To secure copious and free trade, the state's arms had to be feared but "never its ambitions." The state "would not fear that [foreigners] visit its arsenals, its ports, . . . its troops" because it would have nothing to hide.[30] To the contrary, "the view of its resources would make [others] wish for its friendship, and fear its arms."[31] Negotiations between the states of his new world would be conducted in good faith, while in the actual world of his times, "It is the weakness of our governments which puts into their negotiations so much obliquity and bad faith. It is that which foments the divisions between the peoples, which . . . corrupts reciprocally the officials of all [state] administrations."[32] The motto of Guibert's ideal state would be "Liberty, Security, Protection."

This state, vigilant to avenge its injuries, will politically be the ally of no people; but it will be the friend of all. It will bring them, without cease, words of peace. It will be, if it can, the mediator in all its quarrels, not because of its interests, not in order to profit from its mediation, not because of any chimerical balance of power calculations. . . . It will propose its arbitration, because peace is a good, and [the state] knows its price; because war interrupts the communications which should exist between the peoples, and it harms also neighboring countries. . . . [This state] would say to its neighbors: "O peoples! O my brothers! Why are you tearing each other apart? What false politics are separating you? Nations are not born as enemies. They are the branches of the same family. Come benefit from the spectacle of my prosperity. . . . I do not fear that my neighbors become happy and powerful – the more they do, the more they will cherish calm. It is from public happiness that universal peace will be born."[33]

29 Guibert, "Essai général de tactique," 138.   30 Ibid., 148
31 Ibid., 149.   32 Ibid., 145.
33 Ibid., 149–50.

The reader is left to wonder who, in Guibert's view, stood in the way of attaining this utopia – and cannot quite shake off the feeling that it is the selfish, the incompetent, the uncaring monarch and his supporters. Indeed, later in the *Essai*, Guibert expressed doubts that one individual alone could rule over a country without making it suffer from his whims.[34] But then there was the enlightened Frederick the Great, who served as the inspiration for Guibert's vision of a vigorous prince who would bring about "that great revolution" of rekindled patriotism, virtue, and morale – a revolution, in short, in state, society, and strategy.[35]

It was thus the Roman spirit, not Roman tactics, that should be copied, according to Guibert. This in his view was where Maurice of Nassau and Gustavus Adolphus of Sweden (and indeed Folard,[36] still considered the greatest teacher of the art of war in France at the time) went wrong. Technology had changed, Guibert noted, and it was pointless to try to copy Roman and Greek battle formations – phalanxes and all the rest – when you had firepower. Was it not pointless, for example, to have more than three lines of troops with firearms, as any further line could not fire? Rather than advocate a slaving copying of the ancients where tactics were concerned, Guibert, in the *Essai*, called for imaginative innovation and explored a variety of tactical approaches.

If the Roman republic offered a useful model for the modern day, it was, above all, Guibert thought, in civil-military relations. Like Machiavelli before him, he wanted a return to the Roman system of organizing citizens to defend their own country, of mobilizing the population. That would reduce the cost of waging war by reducing dependence on foreign mercenaries – which Guibert viewed as expensive and unenthusiastic about the country they fought for. Citizen armies, driven by patriotism, would be, Guibert believed, "invincible."[37]

In this view, Guibert was as much the successor of Machiavelli as of the French philosophical discourse into which he had been born. Perhaps the single most important area in which French thinkers – including Guibert – began to distinguish themselves from other European military thinkers was the subject of the recruitment of soldiers and their relationship with state and society.

Recall that in the fifteenth century, the French royal state under Charles VII was the first in Europe to develop the political postulate that only the

34 Ibid., 143.   35 Ibid., 150.
36 Jean-Charles Chevalier de Folard, *Nouvelles découvertes sur la guerre, dans une dissertation sur Polybe* (Paris, 1724).
37 Guibert, "Essai général de tactique," 135.

crown, only the central government of the budding state, only the king, had the right to have an army and, further, that this army should be a standing army ready for action all year. Centralizing and monopolizing the right to a standing army was perhaps the most crucial step on the way to the assertion of the authority of the monarch in France. It was that monopoly that enabled one of Charles VII's successors, Louis XIV, to claim to be the state, a claim the great Francophone philosophers of statehood would have endorsed.[38]

This meant that France abandoned limited, seasonal military service by the peasantry, who by definition could not provide a standing army, for the professional army that came to be associated with the monarchic state system and absolutism. Against this stood the spirit of the Enlightenment and its ideas about statehood and society, which were rooted in classical models and the idea of a social contract. Periodic revivals of Roman republican ideals – in the Swiss cantons during the thirteenth and fourteenth centuries, in the writings of Machiavelli around 1500, and under the Nassaus in the sixteenth century and Gustavus Adolphus in the seventeenth – had linked premodern practices of military service owed to one's lord and neoclassical calls for the defense of the res publica by all citizens, and thus for universal male military service. The thinkers of the French Enlightenment also made this connection, and here was the origin of the dramatic link made between the citizen-soldier, the levée en masse, and the French revolutionary ideals of equality and universality.

Under the ancien régime, France had both a professional army and a militia, whose members, scattered all over the country, had to perform two to six years' seasonal military service. In peacetime, this service consisted only of annual exercises of eight to fifteen days. In 1775, the French militia was changed into a simple reservoir of recruits for the main professional army. Wars under the ancien régime were fought mainly by professional – in part mercenary – soldiers, as was true for most parts of Europe. This meant that the armies of the eighteenth century, like those that fought the Hundred Years' War and the Thirty Years' War, consisted of soldiers from many different countries. Within the individual armies, they were usually grouped together by country of origin; and yet these groups were rarely homogeneous ethnically. The wars of the eighteenth century were not national wars, fought with the nations' armies: they were princes' wars, fought with the princes' armies.

38 Above all François Hotman and Jean Bodin: see Julian Harold Franklin, *Jean Bodin and the Rise of Abolutist Theory* (Cambridge, U.K. 1973).

Guibert, by contrast, wanted to develop an army of citizen–soldiers. He thus advocated a certain degree of militarization of society. He wanted to see the education of youngsters in a martial spirit and of the entire society in a spirit of rigor, discipline, and patriotism.[39] This would make a really fierce war possible, he wrote enthusiastically in his *Essai*, the sort of war that could be fought to the finish. And this is what, as a young man writing in his twenties, he regarded as desirable: a truly decisive war that mobilized the entire citizenry, not the lukewarm affairs of his day.

The world of limited battles and indecisive warfare so deprecated by Guibert was to be profoundly shaken by the introduction of new values, values for which the people of France were prepared to fight not only against their own government, their monarchy, but also against all other countries. The French Revolution, with its ideals of liberty, equality, and fraternity, was the fierce northerly wind that swept away the luxury and the indulgence and the peace of this relatively calm age. The young Guibert, like many thinkers of his time, had craved this change. But he was not thinking about the bloodshed, the pain, and the destruction that those who set the revolutionary fire to the rococo palaces of France would unleash. The twentieth century French strategist Lucien Poirier has called the young Guibert the sorcerer's apprentice who conjured up these devastating flames in a society built entirely of very dry wood, with the tinder of social grievances everywhere: "The *Essai* appears very ambiguous to us today," he noted:

Nothing allows us to say that [Guibert] preferred offensive war to the defensive, which is moreover more in keeping with the project of happiness and the political system he asked for. But his remarks about an offensive strategy, the axiom of a decisive battle calling, by mental continuity, for a war of annihilation, the references to the nation in arms which packed off the rules of the game [of war] into the museum of history, all this allows a polarised reading: that of a strategy ... of annihilation.[40]

And this was the reading of his text that the Convention, Carnot, and Saint-Just preferred, as well as Napoleon, with his quest for the decisive battle.

THE MATURE GUIBERT

As with Clausewitz, we find that Guibert changed his views about war over time and, as with Clausewitz, particularly on the issue of limited or absolute

---

39 Guibert, "Essai général de tactique," 188.   40 Poirier, *Les voix*, 289, 292.

war. Only Guibert saw this distinction a good half century before Clausewitz had his sudden revelation on the subject.[41] Unlike Clausewitz, Guibert had since his youth understood the existence of both of these forms of war. And what is most amazing is that Guibert understood this distinction before the French Revolution had created the levée en masse. In fact, Guibert predicted a form of war almost twenty years before it was practiced in Europe; indeed, as we have seen, his ideas contributed to its creation.

Guibert had gone through alternating periods of success and disappointment in the decades between his service in the Seven Years' War and the storming of the Bastille. In 1769, after completing the *Essai* but before its publication in 1772, he saw active service again in France's short campaign to subdue the newly acquired Corsica. In 1773, he embarked on a self-financed tour of Central Europe, mainly to study the military systems of Prussia and the Habsburg Empire.[42]

After that, Guibert had a roller-coaster career, marked by peaks of fame and influence and deep valleys of depression and self-imposed exile from the world on his family estate. Through his father, who had risen to the rank of lieutenant general but served mainly as an administrator in Paris, Guibert, still nominally an officer with an infantry regiment, periodically became involved in military administration himself. He rose to the rank of brigadier at the age of thirty-eight, but he never rose as far as his father had. He had two periods in influential positions at the side of ministers. These were Count Saint-Germain (minister of war from 1775 to 1777), Marshal de Ségur, Count Brienne as minister of war and archbishop of Toulouse, Loménie de Brienne (older brother of Count Brienne) as minister of finances, whom he advised on a cost-effective restructuring of the French military forces in 1787–8, and on the creation of a war council to coordinate decision making. In each case, Guibert was involved in fundamental reforms of the French military, which were very much in the spirit of his views and writings.[43] He was also seen as very influential by jealous competitors, who turned into political enemies when Guibert became principal rapporteur of the War Council. They not only spread venomous criticism about him but also attacked him fiercely to his face.[44] In 1779, during a lull between his two periods of government service, Guibert

---

41 See Beatrice Heuser, *Reading Clausewitz* (London, 2002), 33–41.
42 Lauerma, *Guibert*, 116–17.
43 As Lauerma shows convincingly in *Guibert*, 98, 175–211.
44 Samuel Anderson Covington, "The Comité Militaire and the Legislative Reform of the French Army, 1789–1791" (Ph.D. diss., University of Arkansas, 1976), 1–17.

published his *Défense du système de guerre modern*, to which we shall return shortly, encapsulating much of the advice he had been giving his ministers.

At the outbreak of the French Revolution, the Military Committee that succeeded the War Council overthrew practically all the reforms Guibert's council had instigated.[45] In March 1789, Guibert unsuccessfully tried to have himself elected to the estates general. On July 14, 1789, Louis XIV closed down the War Council, and Guibert's involvement came to an end. Frustrated, Guibert sat down to write a new book on civil-military relations. *De la force publique considérée par tous ses rapports* was published in 1790; shortly after it appeared, Guibert was seized by the fatal illness that carried him off at the age of forty-six.

Taken together, the *Défense* and *De la force publique* make clear that Guibert the nobleman had changed his mind about the role and constitution of the armed forces in the years since writing the *Essai*. By the time he was writing *De la force publique*, the sorcerer's apprentice had thrown away his matches, smelling the first smoke rising up where the sparks had caught. With visions of conflagration in mind, Guibert sought, as Jean Klein has noted, to contain the fury of the forces of human nature that his own earlier writing had contributed to unleashing, the "laws of nature" he had so light-heartedly invoked in his *Essai*.[46] The *Défense* and *De la force publique* are, in Klein's words, "an appeal for moderation" prompted by his vision of imminent conflagration.[47] Once again, Guibert was cast in the role of prophet.

In the *Défense*, Guibert took leave of advocating a militia that would be raised ad hoc as principal means of the defense of France. Instead, he now argued for the creation of an even larger standing army, ideally a professional army of two hundred thousand men. A militia might supplement this force,[48] but, in an age of what Guibert regarded as high-technology warfare, mobilizing and training one would take too long to be of much use if the country were attacked. Interestingly, Guibert continued to hope that his country's armed forces would serve only to defend it. He argued at length that war had become very rare in the course of the eighteenth century and less bloody and cruel than in previous ages – but now he wanted to keep it that way! The best deterrent to enemy attack, he was now convinced, was a large professional army.[49]

---

45 Ibid., 18–27.
46 Guibert, "Essai général de tactique," 149; Jean Klein, "Guibert et les relations internationals," in *Guibert ou le soldat philosophe*, 171.
47 Klein, "Guibert et les relations internationals," 173.
48 Guibert, *Défense*, 2:238. 49 Ibid., 2:271–2.

Domestic political reasons also figured in Guibert's change of mind about the desirability of a citizen army. He stated blandly in the *Défense* that republics were not the best political system for all countries and argued that France was best served with a monarchy.[50] (To escape French censorship, Guibert had the book published in Neuchâtel, Switzerland, which was under Prussian rule at the time. Again, this statement therefore cannot be interpreted as a bow in the direction of the French crown, but at best a nod to Frederick the Great. There is nothing to indicate, however, that this was not Guibert's sincere opinion at the time and until the end of his life.) He devoted some space to the argument whether a large standing army was a prop to a tyranny. It was not, he decided, but rather a check on tyrannical tendencies as well as the greatest support for a legitimate government.[51] He had clearly abandoned his great faith in the soldier-citizen and was rapidly moving into the camp of the champions of law and order who feared the consequences of putting a weapon into every peasant's hands.

Ten years later, when he was writing *De la force publique*, Guibert sent a letter to the National Assembly under the pseudonym Abbé Raynal, warning against the passions that the appeal to the whole nation and universal military conscription would unleash. He pleaded urgently for the re-creation of a professional army and against unleashing the forces of human nature.[52]

While he was a supporter of the ideals of liberty inherent in the French Revolution, and of the transfer of a good portion of sovereignty from the king to the National Assembly and the provincial assemblies, Guibert was not and had never been in favor of eliminating the monarchy altogether.[53] More important for our purposes, he no longer regarded the limitations on war under the anciens régimes as decadent and had come to regard them in a thoroughly positive light. In *De la force publique*, which contained complete passages also found in his letter to the National Assembly, he displayed conservative inclinations and took a moderate position on political reform.[54] Where earlier he had been the advocate of a citizen army, of the type of army that would be created under the French Revolution, he now praised professional armies. He seems to have taken some of the criticism leveled against his *Essai* to heart, particularly by General de Warnery, who

---

50 Ibid., 2:221–3.   51 Ibid., 2:220–1.

52 "Lettre à l'Assemblée nationale publiée sous le nom dee l'abbé Raynal" (Dec. 10, 1789), in Guibert, *Stratégiques*, 667–75.

53 Guibert, *Projet de discours d'un citoyen aux trois orders de l'Assemblee de Berry* (n.p., 789).

54 Guibert, "De la force publique," in *Stratégiques*, 589.

had written at length to refute the idea of the possibility of a citizen army.[55] Guibert partly took up the general's arguments and added stimulating considerations of his own. In the view of the mature Guibert, the soldier and the civilian citizen were two opposites who have little in common:

So that training and discipline may prevail in the army, the army has to make them its occupation, its habit, and its glory. But the principles which are at the basis of discipline, and the dispositions which make up the military spirit, are necessarily and naturally in opposition with all the principles of the spirit of the [civilian] citizen. Soldiers have to be hungry for war, citizens must love peace. Equality and liberty are the rights of the citizen. Subordination and passive obedience are the duties of the solder. Soldiers cannot have the same tribunals, nor the same punishments [e.g., for murder] . . . as citizens. Soldiers have to have an esprit de corps and a professional feeling. Citizens should only have public and national feelings. In the present state of Europe and of military art, to want a citizen army is to aim to bring very disparate principles and elements together.[56]

It was with these arguments that Guibert advocated a professional army: "we need men who will commit themselves by a voluntary contract of some years or months."[57] Some further reasons that he gives are again still of relevance today, particularly for those countries like Germany that still have conscription. Guibert, back in 1790, pointed out that a militia, a conscript army, an army of citizens, could not easily operate outside its own country: "Outside one's frontiers is not even enough. Today, the hostilities between the great peoples, through commercial relationships and through the colonies, can have as their theatre all parts of the world."[58] He went on to argue:

If the task at hand is only to defend one's fields, one's house, one's family, every man becomes soldier or at least a combatant. Every man can, animated by these great interests, give his life or take a life. But in a vast empire, can you persuade all inhabitants that all the provinces of that empire should be equally valuable to them? Can you make the people from the South of France defend Flanders or Alsace, or those of the inner provinces of France defend the shores of the Mediterranean or of Gascony?[59]

Indeed, it is arguments along these lines that have in recent years persuaded France and most other NATO members to abandon conscription for all-volunteer professional armed forces.

Discipline was another problem that Guibert saw with militias. How could you make the masses obey properly – how could you bring them

55 Le G. de W[arner]y, *Remarques sur l'Essai général de tactique de Guibert*, 189–93.
56 Guibert, "De la force publique," 574.   57 Ibid., 574.
58 Ibid., 573–4.   59 Ibid., 612–13.

to act like a well-trained professional force? What the young man in his twenties had thought so desirable – the bloody war fought with the total mobilization of the population – horrified the mature Guibert of forty-six. During the eighteenth century, civilians usually experienced war indirectly, through increased taxation. Creating vast citizen armies, Guibert warned, would not only make warfare more expensive but also make citizens direct participants in warfare and envelop them in all its horrors:

Even those that are defeated, even those whose countries become the theatres [of war], hardly experience disastrous calamities. Blood is only shed by the armies, and generosity and humanitarian feelings halt further blows, once one side has won. One always respects the life and often also the property of prisoners. One exchanges them or trades them for a small ransom. One never puts fire to or ravages the country. The population works and sows in the middle of the [military] camps. And discipline glories in the preservation of what does not need to be destroyed.

But if the nations themselves will be involved in the war, all that will change. The inhabitants of a country having become soldiers will be treated as enemies. The fear of having them against you, the fear of leaving them behind will make you destroy them. At least one will seek to confound them and intimidate them by ravages and desolation. Think back to the barbarism of ancient wars, to those wars where the fanaticism and the spirit of taking sides has armed the people. That is what you will give birth to once again.[60]

Having given this warning, the mature Guibert went on to praise the happy, bygone age of limited war.[61]

In what again sounds today like a very modern argument, Guibert called for a small, well-trained, well-equipped, and highly mobile army. Already in his *Essai* of twenty years earlier he had criticized the tendency of the governments of his time to go for quantity rather than for quality and expressed his conviction that this quantity was achieved at the expense of mobility and really good training. This was one of the points that Guibert admired about Frederick the Great, the only ruler, in Guibert's view, who understood the importance of training (drill) and, through new tactics of maneuver (which others failed to develop). Guibert understood that Frederick won only by outmaneuvering his enemies. Of Frederick's army itself, Guibert thought little, initially dismissing it as "a motley crowd of stipendiaries, vagabonds, foreigners."[62] But in *De la force publique*, Guibert calls for just the sort of army Frederick had commanded.

At the same time, the mature Guibert recognized that a standing army would, through the sheer power it commanded, always pose a threat to

---

60 Ibid., 613–14.   61 Ibid.
62 Guibert, "Essai general de tactique," 162.

civilized society. Once again, he was prophetic in his insight, as the history of civil-military relations in France from Napoleon to de Gaulle or the experiences of any number of other countries attests. He argued in *De la force publique* that the public force, the civilian government, has to be particularly careful to assert its own predominance over the standing professional army, which "could become dangerous for public freedom, if all the forces of the nation are not the brake and the counterweight to it."[63]

CONCLUSION

To take up the question posed at the beginning of this essay, did Guibert's thinking presage total war? There are many definitions of this term. After burrowing deeply into the subject, Stig Förster and Jörg Nagler have defined total war as follows: "total war, at least theoretically, consists of total mobilization of all the nation's resources by a highly organized and centralized state for a military conflict with unlimited war aims (such as complete destruction of the home front, extermination and genocide)."[64] The term *total war* has been used in two separate fashions. It was first used by two Frenchmen, Alphonse Séché, who wrote about the "totalization of the national strength" during the First World War,[65] and Léon Daudet, who called that war a "total war."[66] They both referred mainly to the total mobilization of populations and the economies on both sides in that conflict. (This is usually the meaning associated with *total war* in the English-language literature on the subject as well.) Leaving the economic dimension aside, mobilization on this scale can be associated less with Napoleon than with the Revolutionary levée en masse of 1793. Such a mobilization was very much in keeping with Guibert's thinking as a young man in his *Essai*.

As popularized by Erich von Ludendorff in 1935, the term *total war* added a crucial aspect to the idea of a total mobilization of economy and population: total war would include a fight to the finish. The objective of such a war would be nothing less than the total enslavement or, better still, extermination of the enemy's population, while trying to "breed" more "Aryans."[67]

---

63 Guibert, "De la force publique," 590.
64 Stig Förster and Jörg Nagler, "Introduction," in *On the Road to Total War: The American Civil War and the German Wars of Unification, 1861–1871* (Cambridge, U.K. 1997), 11.
65 Alphonse Seché, *Les guerres d'enfer* (Paris, 1915), 124.
66 Léon Daudet, *La guerre totale* (Paris, 1918), 8–9.
67 Erich von Ludendorff, *Der Totale Krieg* (Munich, 1935), translated by A.S. Rappoport as *The Nation at War* (London, 1936).

This genocidal dimension of total war, encompassed in Förster and Nagler's definition of the term, is nowhere to be found in Guibert's writings. It could have crept in via his reading of the ancients or the discussion of their practices by Montesquieu, but it did not. The total mobilization of the population of a social entity – from tribe to city to kingdom – can be found in many historical periods and in many places. The Melians did their utmost to fend off the Athenians, and the Romans rallied around with a societywide war effort to withstand the onslaught of the Celts and other invaders.

Genocidal persecutions had also been known long before Raphael Lemkin coined the term in 1944. They were known to the ancients in the total destruction of Carthage; to the Dark Ages in the devastating raids of the Huns and, later, the Magyars; to medieval Europeans in the merciless persecution of heretics and non-Christians, including their children, as in the case of the Albigensians, and in anti-Jewish pogroms; and to early modern people through the ravages of the Thirty Years' War, most famously with the sack of Magdeburg, which Guibert alluded to in his *Défense*. This is how Montesquieu wrote about war aims, or what a state might intend to do with a conquered country:

A State which has conquered another treats it in one of the following ways: the former continues to govern the latter according to the latter's laws, and does not [even] take for itself the exercise of political and civil; or [the conqueror] gives [the conquered] a new political and civil government; or [the conqueror] destroys the society, and disperses it among others; or, finally, it exterminates all the [conquered] citizens. The first fashion is the one that conforms to the law of nations that we follow today; the fourth corresponds furthest with the law of nations of the Romans; I leave it to others to judge to what degree we have become better. Here we have to render homage to our modern times, to the reason which is present, to the religion of today, to our philosophy, to our morals.[68]

Clearly, then, the "extermination of all the citizens" of the conquered state was something known to the philosophers of the Enlightenment from classical antiquity but was seen by Montesquieu as incompatible with the ideals and values of his times. Even the enslavement of a conquered population was acceptable to Montesquieu only as a temporary expedient toward reestablishing the security of one's own state's security. He saw it as "contrary to nature" that such slavery should be "eternal."[69] Total war in the genocidal sense in which the term was defined by Ludendorff and practiced by the National Socialists against the Jews, the Roma, and the Slavs was thus

---

68 Montesquieu, *L'esprit*, 1:274–5.   69 Ibid., 1:275.

an idea with which Montesquieu and, at the very least through reading him, Guibert were familiar. And yet this is clearly a line of thought completely absent from Guibert's writings. It clearly did not fit into either his or Montesquieu's system of values and ideals. Nor did the extermination of the aristocratic class that was espoused as a political and social aim by the French Revolution fit the world as they wanted it; they were not at the origin of totalitarian democracy any more than they were at the origin of total genocidal war.[70]

To conclude, then, the young Guibert prophesied and wished for something like the levée en masse, the total mobilization of one's own side in a defensive war but not for total war à la Ludendorff with the aim of annihilating an enemy nation. The older Guibert, by contrast, disassociated himself even from the former. The latter's works were rarely read beyond his own life span and are quite at odds with what happened in the French Revolutionary and Napoleonic Wars; the older Guibert was more a counterrevolutionary than anything else. Had he not died from natural causes in 1790, one wonders whether he might not have died soon after under the guillotine.

70 J. L. Talmon, *The Origins of Totalitarian Democracy: Political Theory and Practice during the French Revolution and Beyond* (London, 1952).

3

Innovation or Evolution?

The French Wars in Military History

UTE PLANERT

Political and military historians commonly regard the wars of the French Revolution and the Napoleonic era as a caesura in world history. These wars, they argue, brought about a fundamental change not only in the realm of politics but also in the nature of warfare. Pointing to the "nationalization of the war and the militarization of national feelings" in this period, historians have cited a number of elements that are, they argue, characteristic of total warfare.[1] These include the importance of ideology, unlimited war aims that tend toward annihilation of the enemy, the development of unlimited destructive potential, the geographical expanse of military operations, the abandonment of moral and legal conventions, the deployment of mass armies, and the mobilization of civilian populations and economies for purposes of war.[2] Correspondingly, most historians agree that the path toward total warfare began at the end of the eighteenth century and the beginning of the nineteenth.[3] Roger Chickering has called

1 Geoffrey Best, *War and Society in Revolutionary Europe 1770–1870*, 2nd ed. (Phoenix Mill, U.K., 1998), 65.
2 See Stig Förster and Jörg Nagler, eds., *On the Road to Total War: The American Civil War and the German Wars of Unification, 1861–1871* (Cambridge, U.K., 1997); Manfred F. Boemeke, Roger Chickering, and Stig Förster eds., *Anticipating Total War: The German and American Experiences, 1871–1914* (Cambridge, U.K., 1999); Roger Chickering and Stig Förster, eds., *Great War, Total War: Combat and Mobilization on the Western Front, 1914–1918* (Cambridge, U.K., 2000); Roger Chickering and Stig Förster, eds., *The Shadows of Total War: Europe, East Asia, and the United States, 1919–1939* (Cambridge, U.K., 2003); Roger Chickering, Stig Förster, and Bernd Greiner, eds., *A World at Total War: Global Conflict and the Politics of Destruction, 1937–1945* (Cambridge, U.K., 2005). Stig Förster gives an overview of these conferences in "Das Zeitalter des totalen Krieges 1861–1945: Konzeptionelle Überlegungen für einen historischen Strukturvergleich," *Mittelweg 36*, no. 8 (1999): 12–29. See also Ian F. W. Beckett, "Total War," in *War, Peace, and Social Change in Twentieth-Century Europe*, ed. Clive Emsley, Arthur Marwick, and Wendy Simpson (Milton Keynes, U.K., 1989); Thomas Powers and Ruthven Tremain, *Total War: What It Is, How It Got That Way* (New York, 1988).
3 See, e.g., Eric Hobsbawm, *The Age of Revolutions* (London, 1962); Michael Howard, *War in European History* (Oxford, 1976); Daniel Pick, *War Machine: The Rationalization of Slaughter in the Modern Age* (New Haven, Connecticut, 1993); Wolfgang Kruse, *Die Erfindung des modernen Militarismus:*

this consensus among historians the "master narrative" of modern military
history.[4]

Carl von Clausewitz figures as the main authority for this view. He
coined the term *absolute war* to describe developments that began during the
French Revolution.[5] But the Prussian military theorist's authority cannot
be claimed in attempting to draw a line from absolute war in the age of
Napoleon to total war in the twentieth century. Clausewitz himself doubted
whether "all wars will henceforth have this great character," and he did not
presume to judge whether "all future wars in Europe will always be waged
with the full power of the state and hence only for the major interests
of the people, or whether a separation between governments and peoples
will gradually emerge again."[6] For Clausewitz the contemporary witness,
the future was open. It is thus worthwhile to recall the ambiguity of the
historical situation that he faced.

This chapter focuses on lines of tradition that connected the wars of the
Revolutionary and Napoleonic era to those waged in the early modern era.
Claiming that military destruction took on new dimensions at the end of the
eighteenth century requires setting a standard by the "tamed Bellona" of the
earlier decades of the century, not the Thirty Years' War or the subsequent
depredations of Louis XIV.[7] In fact, the quest for limited warfare in the
eighteenth century represented more the exception than the rule. Johannes
Burkhardt has argued that the "lack of peace in early modern times" was
based on a complex theory of state building,[8] and recent scholarship on
nationalism has characterized modern states as the fruits of war.[9] From
this perspective, the wars of the French Revolution fit in a long European

Krieg, Militär und bürgerliche Gesellschaft im politischen Diskurs der Französischen Revolution, 1789–1799
(Munich, 2002); D. Moran and A. Waldron, eds., *The People in Arms: Military Myth and National
Mobilization since the French Revolution* (Cambridge, U.K., 2003) ; Dieter Langewiesche, "Zum Wandel
von Krieg und Kriegslegitimation in der Neuzeit," *Journal of Modern European History* 1 (2004):
5–27.

4 Roger Chickering, "Total War: The Use and Abuse of a Concept," in Boemeke et al., *Anticipating
Total War*, 13–28; Roger Chickering, "Militärgeschichte als Totalgeschichte im Zeitalter des totalen
Krieges," in *Was ist Militärgeschichte?* ed. Thomas Kühne and Benjamin Ziemann (Paderborn, 2000),
301–14.

5 Carl von Clausewitz, *Vom Kriege*, 19th ed., ed. Werner Halweg (Bonn, 1980), 211, 970–2.

6 Ibid., 972–3.

7 Johannes Kunisch, "Von der gezähmten zur entfesselten Bellona: Die Umwertung des Krieges im
Zeitalter der Revolutions- und Freiheitskriege," in *Fürst – Gesellschaft – Krieg: Studien zur bellizistischen
Disposition des absoluten Fürstenstaates* (Cologne, 1992), 203–26.

8 Johannes Burkhardt, "Die Friedlosigkeit der Frühen Neuzeit. Grundlegung einer Theorie der
Bellizität Europas," *Zeitschrift für Historische Forschung* 24 (1997): 509–74.

9 Dieter Langewiesche, "Nation, Nationalismus, Nationalstaat in der europäischen Geschichte seit dem
Mittelalter," in *Föderative Nation: Deutschlandkonzepte von der Reformation bis zum Ersten Weltkrieg*, ed.
Dieter Langewiesche and Georg Schmidt, (Munich, 2000), 9–30.

tradition of state building by war that led from the early modern era to the nineteenth century.[10]

This chapter will thus argue that the wars of the French Revolution arose less as a revolutionary caesura than as a stage in an evolutionary process. The chapter focuses on questions of compulsory military service and the relationship between the military and the civilian population. In both cases, it contends, the master narrative of modern military history should be qualified because it takes insufficient note of lines of continuity to early modern times, overlooks differences between the French Revolutionary and the Napoleonic Wars themselves, and encourages a mistaken picture of developments during the nineteenth century.

The interaction of nationalism, citizenship, and war on the European continent first became evident in the aftermath of the French Revolution. But these connections had been discussed long before. In France, the Comte de Guibert reflected on the nationalization of war, as did the partisans of the Holy Roman Empire during the Seven Years' War.[11] At the same time, the increase of military power; the more frequent deployment of light troops and artillery; and the introduction of smaller, structured subdivisions of armies during the eighteenth century furnished the practical basis of Revolutionary and Napoleonic warfare.[12] Although the armies that fought between 1792 and 1815 were much larger than their precursors, none of the tactics or technologies they employed were new.[13]

The wars of the French Revolution were admittedly legitimized on fundamentally new grounds. The revolutionaries fought for the victory of the revolution, at first within the state, then against the enemy states of the ancien régime.[14] With Napoleon's seizure of power, however, the legitimization of war by revolution came to an end. The *Grand Empire* justified its wars in the interests of the *grande nation*. These interests closely resembled those of the French monarchy in the eighteenth century, be it mercantile and colonial rivalry with England or securing France's supposedly natural frontiers.

Napoleon also instituted important changes in the levying of troops. France did indeed give birth to revolutionary citizen armies in 1792 when

10 Langewiesche, "Zum Wandel," 20–1.
11 On Guibert, see Beatrice Heuser, "Guibert: Prophet of Total War?" in this volume.
12 Peter Wilson, "European Warfare 1450–1815," in *War in the Early Modern World*, ed. Jeremy Black (London, 1999), 177–206; Volkmar Regling, "Grundzüge der Landkriegsführung zur Zeit des Absolutismus und im 19. Jahrhundert," *Handbuch zur deutschen Militärgeschichte 1648–1939*, 6 vols. (Munich, 1964–79), 6:11–426.
13 Peter Browning, *The Changing Nature of Warfare: The Development of Land Warfare from 1792 to 1945* (Cambridge, U.K., 2002), 50.
14 Ibid., 22–3.

it employed volunteer units.[15] The standing armies of the absolute monarchs were replaced by a new armed force of *soldats citoyen*.[16] The Jacobins' levée en masse in 1793 represented an attempt to mobilize a whole country for war, and it led to the first stages of a state-supervised war economy.[17] The foreign military threat enabled the Jacobin regime to raise an army of eight hundred thousand. The regime was not able, however, to convince the rural population of the need for mass conscription. Fewer than half the peasants who were liable for military service reported for duty.[18] In the early 1790s, two hundred thousand men fled military service annually.[19] Resistance to recruitment became a major weapon of counterrevolution in France.[20]

Compulsory service was formally introduced only in 1798, on the eve of the War of the Second Coalition. The Directory, which introduced the measure, exempted only breadwinners, priests, students, and government officials from conscription.[21] Under Napoleon, however, the principle of universal conscription was further compromised. After 1802, the propertied classes were allowed to hire substitutes, while notables received preferment. Their sons went to the newly founded military schools for officers. These young men soon dominated the officer corps, as well as the military and civil administration. Others joined the ceremonial *gardes d'honneur*, hence avoiding the greater imposition of regular military service.[22]

Given the numerous possibilities for exemption enjoyed by propertied citizens as well as by certain regions and occupational groups that were regarded as important to the economy and public administration, the rank and file of the Napoleonic army increasingly comprised the lower strata of society. At the same time, Napoleon reduced the number of conscripts after 1800. Veterans, who served twelve-year terms, increasingly took the place of

---

15 Jean-Paul Bertaud, *Valmy, la démocratie en armes* (Paris, 1989); Thomas Hippler, "Service militaire et intégration nationale pendant la Révolution française," *Annales Historiques de la Révolution Française* 3 (2002): 1–16.

16 Wolfgang Kruse, "Bürger und Soldaten. Die Entstehung des modernen Militarismus in der Französischen Revolution," in *Der Bürger als Soldat: Die Militarisierung europäischer Gesellschaften im langen 19. Jahrhundert: Ein internationaer Vergleich*, ed. Christian Jansen (Essen, 2004), 47–67; Wolfgang Kruse, *Die Erfindung des modernen Militarismus: Krieg, Militär und bürgerliche Gesellschaft im politischen Diskurs der französischen Revolution, 1789–1799* (Munich, 2003).

17 Howard G. Brown, *War, Revolution, and the Bureaucratic State: Politics and Army Administration in France, 1791–1799* (Oxford, 1995), 207–34.

18 Geoffrey Wawro, *Warfare and Society in Europe, 1792–1914* (London, 2000), 2–3.

19 Ibid., 3.

20 Alan Forrest, *Conscripts and Deserters: The Army and French Society during the Revolution and Empire* (New York, 1989).

21 Charles J. Esdaile, *The Wars of Napoleon* (London, 1995), 49.

22 Gilbert Ziebura, *Frankreich 1789–1870: Entstehung einer bürgerlichen Gesellschaftsformation* (Frankfurt, 1979), 96; Esdaile, *Wars*, 55–6.

recruits, so the Napoleonic army underwent <u>intensive professionalization</u>. In this way, the empire created an army that resembled the professional armies of the ancien régime.[23] In the wake of French expansion, however, regiments were increasingly raised among the inhabitants of occupied lands. As the proportion of foreigners in the Napoleonic army rose, the pressure of conscription in the heart of the empire declined. The Grande Armée was drawn from the populations of Belgium, Poland, Italy, Switzerland, Ireland, and the German states.[24]

Clausewitz failed to recognize these changes. He equated Napoleon with the French Revolution. He therefore referred to the "Revolution's twenty years of victory" and identified the Napoleonic army with the revolutionary armed forces.[25] Yet even as the illustrious reformer argued that war under Napoleon approached its "true nature" with the deployment of the "whole people,"[26] Napoleonic France was in fact "the very antithesis of a Nation-in-Arms."[27]

Many of the changes instituted by the French had been anticipated in the eighteenth century. After mid-century, the idea of coupling political participation to the commitment to "die for the fatherland" surfaced in the political journalism of the Holy Roman Empire.[28] There was also an intense debate about the "foolish chimera" of "eternal peace."[29] For patriotic reasons, commentators rejected standing professional armies and called for the revival of traditional militias.[30]

The age of pure mercenary armies had come to an end in the Holy Roman Empire long before the French Revolution. Militia systems had been deployed in addition to regular armies since the sixteenth century. These bodies were used for defensive warfare alone, however, and they generally proved inferior to mercenary troops. They had thus fallen out of use in most parts of the Holy Roman Empire by the beginning of the

---

23 Alan Forrest, *Napoleon's Men: The Soldiers of the Revolution and Empire* (London, 2002).
24 Esdaile, *Wars*, 52–6.   25 Clausewitz, *Vom Kriege*, 997.
26 Ibid., 972.   27 Esdaile, *Wars*, 38.
28 Thomas Abbt, "Vom Tode für das Vaterland" (1761), in *Aufklärung und Kriegserfahrung: Klassische Zeitzeugen zum Siebenjährigen Krieg*, ed. Johannes Kunisch (Frankfurt, 1996), 589–650; cf. Johannes Kunisch and Herfried Münkler, eds., *Die Wiedergeburt des Krieges aus dem Geist der Revolution: Studien zum bellizistischen Diskurs des ausgehenden 18. und beginnenden 19. Jahrhunderts.* (Berlin, 1999).
29 Johann Valentin Embser, *Die Abgötterei unseres philosophischen Jahrhunderts. Erster Abgott: Ewiger Friede* (Mannheim, 1779), 8.
30 Justus Möser, "Von der Nationalerziehung der alten Deutschen," *Patriotische Phantasien*, 4 vols. (Berlin, 1786), 4:13–18; Joseph von Sonnenfels, "Über die Liebe des Vaterlands," in *Gesammelte Schriften*, 10 vols. (Vienna, 1783–7), 7:190–225. See also Ute Planert, "Wann beginnt der 'moderne' deutsche Nationalismus? Plädoyer für eine nationale Sattelzeit," in *Die Politik der Nation: Deutscher Nationalismus in Krieg und Krisen, 1760–1960*, ed. Jörg Echternkamp and Sven O. Müller (Munich, 2002), 25–59.

eighteenth century.[31] In the course of that century, the great continental powers also discarded the idea of relying primarily on mercenary armies. Not least to save money, monarchs increasingly drafted their own subjects into military service. A large conscript army was introduced in Russia after 1700. Prussia made military service compulsory for subjects in 1733, when the kingdom introduced the cantonal system (*Kantonreglement*). Even though many exemptions applied in practice and the major part of the army still consisted of volunteers, the idea of compulsory military service for all male residents was introduced.[32] Austria and a number of smaller states in the Holy Roman Empire followed the Prussian example in the last third of the century.[33] In some south German territories, remnants of the militia system survived. The interest in militias took on greater cogency once French Revolutionary troops threatened the Rhine border. Long before Frederick William III invoked Prussian patriotism during the Wars of Liberation, states along the Rhine appealed to loyalty to the Holy Roman Empire in mobilizing their subjects for militia service.[34]

In German-speaking Europe, efforts to arm the people were most successful in border regions where frequent conflicts with France provided the impetus for residents to defend themselves. Outside these immediately threatened areas, attempts to organize militias found little resonance despite the pamphlets and sermons that members of the educated middle classes wrote to promote militia service as an "institution of national education" that embodied "Hermann's warlike spirit."[35] During the War of the Second Coalition (1799–1802), the attempt was made in some parts of Austria to call subjects to arms, but militiamen could not be raised in sufficient numbers. Meanwhile, it had become clear that home guards were inferior

31 Helmut Schnitter, "Die überlieferte Defensionspflicht: Vorformen der allgemeinen Wehrpflicht in Deutschland," in *Die Wehrpflicht: Entstehung, Erscheinungsformen und politisch-militärische Wirkung*, ed. Roland G. Foerster (Munich, 1994), 29–37; Helmut Schnitter, *Volk und Landesdefension: Volksaufgebote, Defensionswerke, Landmilizen in den deutschen Territorien vom 15. bis zum 18. Jahrhundert* (East Berlin, 1977); Gerhard Oestreich, "Zur Heeresverfassung der deutschen Territorien von 1500–1800: Ein Versuch vergleichender Betrachtung," in *Geist und Gestalt des frühmodernen Staates: Ausgewählte Aufsätze* (Berlin, 1969), 290–310.

32 Otto Büsch, *Militärsystem und Sozialleben im alten Preussen 1713–1807: Die Anfänge der sozialen Militarisierung der preussisch-deutschen Gesellschaft* (Berlin, 1962); Rainer Wohlfeil, *Vom Stehenden Heer des Absolutismus zur allgemeinen Wehrpflicht, 1789–1814* (Munich, 1979).

33 Johann Christoph Allmeyer-Beck and Erich Lessing, *Das Heer unter dem Doppeladler: Habsburgs Armeen 1718–1848* (Munich, 1981); Karl Stiefel, *Baden 1648–1952*, 2 vols. (Karlsruhe, 1978).

34 Otto Heinl, *Heereswesen und Volksbewaffnung in Vorderösterreich im Zeitalter Josefs II. und der Revolutionskriege* (Freiburg, 1941); Reinhold Lenz, *Volksbewaffnung und Staatsidee in Österreich, 1792–1797* (Vienna, 1926).

35 Wohlfeil, *Vom Stehenden Heer*, 59; Eberhard Friedrich Georgi to Johann Christoph Schwab, Sept. 12, 1794, cited in Erwin Hölzle, *Das Alte Recht und die Revolution: Eine politische Geschichte Württembergs in der Revolutionszeit 1789–1805* (Munich, 1931), 121.

to French troops. French occupation of the Habsburg provinces soon put an end to the renewed deployment of militias.[36]

After the collapse of the Holy Roman Empire, popular discontent over militia service went hand in hand with a widespread unwillingness to serve in regular armies, whether with or against Napoleon. The alliance of Baden, Württemberg, Bavaria, and other states of southern and central Germany with Napoleonic France had far-reaching military implications for the subjects of those states. By joining the Confederation of the Rhine, Napoleon's German allies were obliged to provide troops. The impact of this obligation was particularly jarring in the former ecclesiastical territories, the territories ruled by the lower nobility, and former free cities that were caught up in the Napoleonic restructuring of Central Europe. Unlike the great territorial states, where cantonal and militia systems had existed, these principalities had not previously imposed military service on their subjects.

Conscription was imposed throughout the Confederation of the Rhine. As need grew, a steadily increasing proportion of liable conscripts was called to arms. As in France, civic elites, such as priests and civil servants, were exempted from military service. Except in Württemberg, where different rules were drafted in 1809, the sons of the propertied classes were allowed to avoid military service by hiring substitutes.

Military service had not been popular in most German states – Prussia was an exception to the rule.[37] In the newly reorganized territories of the south, attempting to levy troops could set off a revolt if the population felt no political allegiance to the state or if taking up arms would entail a clash of confessional loyalties. Popular uprisings against conscription in Mergentheim, Nellenburg, Fürstenberg, and other towns had precedents in earlier rebellions against the attempts by occupying powers to levy troops, such as Sendlingen's "Deadly Christmas" (*Mordweihnacht*) of 1705 and the "Bobbin War" (*Klöppelkrieg*) of 1798 in Luxembourg.[38] In the early years of the Confederation of the Rhine, popular resistance to military service was

36 Ute Planert, *Leben mit dem Krieg: Baden, Württemberg und Bayern zwischen Französischer Revolution und Wiener Kongress* (Habilitationsschrift, University of Tübingen, 2003), 304–22; Ute Planert, *Der Mythos vom Befreiungskrieg. Frankreichs Kriege und der deutsche Süden. Alltag – Wahrnehmung – Deutung 1792–1841* (Paderborn, 2007).

37 Ute Frevert, *Die kasernierte Nation: Militärdienst und Zivilgesellschaft in Deutschland* (Munich, 2001), 141.

38 Richard van Dülmen, "Bäuerlicher Protest und patriotische Bewegung: Der Volksaufstand in Bayern von 1705/6," *Zeitschrift für bayerische Landesgeschichte* 45 (1982): 331–61; Christoph Probst, *Lieber bayrisch sterben: Der bayrische Volksaufstand der Jahre 1705 und 1706*, 2d ed. (Munich, 1980); Gilbert Trausch, "Die Luxemburger Bauernaufstände aus dem Jahre 1798: Der 'Klöppelkrieg,' seine Interpretation und sein Nachleben in der Geschichte des Grossherzogtums Luxemburg," *Rheinische Vierteljahresblätter* 48 (1984): 161–237; Horst Carl, *Okkupation und Regionalismus: Die preussischen Westprovinzen im Siebenjährigen Krieg* (Mainz, 1993), 8.

not directed against France, however, but toward new German sovereigns and their representatives. The unrest remained limited and was usually suppressed with little difficulty by military force.[39] Consequently, individuals developed tactics to avoid military service, including hastily arranged marriage, feigned illness, bribery, and desertion. In the end, military recruitment required massive pressure from the state. The techniques employed by the authorities to force unwilling people to serve included the confiscation of property, revocation of civil rights, arrest of parents, and the drafting of neighbors and relatives.[40]

Despite the change of alliances in 1813, the number of liable men who fled military service in the states of the confederation grew over the course of the Wars of Liberation. In Waldshut, where the number of desertions can be reconstructed by year, more recruits deserted in 1814 than during Napoleon's Russian campaign. In the district of Rottweil in Württemberg, nearly a third of the men who were liable for military service disappeared before the levying of troops began in 1815.[41] Badenese authorities complained of "frequent desertions" by "individuals who are scared of war" and who enjoyed the support of their families and friends.[42] But avoidance of military service during the Wars of Liberation was not limited to southern Germany alone.[43] In the Kingdom of Westphalia, where young soldiers were sent off to Spain and Russia, the number of desertions had fallen after 1806 but then rose again to surpass the pre-1806 figures in 1813; they then stayed at the same high level until 1815.[44] Desertion had less to do with political alliance than with geography: the chances a solider might desert grew as the distance between his home and the theater of war decreased and his prospects for a safe return increased.

The fundamental hostility toward military service persisted even after the end of the Napoleonic Wars in the onetime member states of the Confederation of the Rhine. The reigning monarchs insisted on raising their

---

39 Ute Planert, "Militär, Krieg und zivile Gesellschaft. Rekrutierungsverweigerung im Süden des Alten Reiches," in *Krieg und Umbruch in Mitteleuropa um 1800. Erfahrungsgeschichte(n) auf dem Weg in eine neue Zeit*, ed. Ute Planert (Paderborn, 2009), 111–36; Tobias Kies, "Rosenkranzrevolution und Rekrutierungsverweigerung. Reaktionen auf den Umbruch ländlicher Lebenswelt 1800–1815," in Planert, *Krieg und Umbruch*, 137–56.

40 Planert, "Leben," 326–99.   41 Ibid., 391.

42 Ibid., 385.

43 Michael Sikora, "Desertion und nationale Mobilmachung: Militärische Verweigerung 1792–1815," in *Armeen und ihre Deserteure: Vernachlässigte Kapitel einer Militärgeschichte der Neuzeit*, ed. Ulrich Bröckling and Michael Sikora (Göttingen, 1998), 112–40.

44 Winfried Speitkamp, "Sozialer und politischer Protest im napoleonischen Deutschland," *100 Jahre Historische Kommission für Hessen* (Marburg, 1997), 713–30; Winfried Speitkamp, *Restauration als Transformation: Untersuchungen zur kurhessischen Verfassungsgeschichte 1813–1830* (Darmstadt, 1986), 82.

own armies, not least to make manifest the power status conferred on them by the Congress of Vienna. In Baden, the middle classes, who were now represented in the diet, branded peacetime military service an "evil thing" and a "burden."[45] In Württemberg, the military was blamed for the country's degeneration into a "coercive state" (*Zwangsanstalt*).[46]

There is no evidence in the parliamentary debates on military matters in the south German states during the first half of the nineteenth century that citizenship and patriotism were coming to be associated with military service. Patriotism was thought to be manifested not in joining the army but in demonstrating public spirit in the local community.[47] The great challenge for the monarchies was to adapt military service to the requirements of civil society and an expanding economy. Corporate exemptions had in theory been eliminated, although the nobility still enjoyed privileges enshrined in law. The representatives in Baden's lower house nonetheless insisted that the right to send substitutes to the army was the only thing that made "military service bearable."[48] The liberal middle classes did not wish to grant the state the right to intrude into a citizen's life unless the citizen were entitled to "pursue one's self-chosen occupation by sacrificing a part of his own property."[49] This principle reflected the social composition of the Badenese diet; it applied to citizens who were able to pay for substitutes. Corporate privileges were replaced by the privileges of wealth.

The Badenese government itself held "compulsory service in the regular army to be a great sacrifice" that entailed "various, highly irksome conditions and pressing hardships," for which the soldier was sufficiently compensated "neither by his pay nor by the glory and honour of his social status."[50] In deference to this view, the former states of the Confederation of the Rhine did not introduce universal conscription after the end of the Napoleonic era. They relied instead on a sort of "regular home-guard system."[51] Except for Prussia, most German states introduced compulsory military service only when they joined the North German Confederation after 1866 or during the war against France in 1870–1.[52]

Only to a limited degree, therefore, can one invoke compulsory military service as an indicator of total warfare during the era of the French

---

45 Frevert, *Kasernierte Nation*, 138.
46 Paul Sauer, *Das württembergische Heer in der Zeit des Deutschen und des Norddeutschen Bundes* (Stuttgart, 1958), 13.
47 Paul Nolte, *Gemeindebürgertum und Liberalismus in Baden: Tradition, Radikalismus, Republik* (Göttingen, 1994), 211
48 Cited in Frevert, *Kasernierte Nation*, 138.   49 Ibid.
50 Ibid., 389.   51 Ibid., 146.
52 Ibid., 191.

Revolution. Revolutionary France instituted universal service for only a short time, and Napoleon's army consisted primarily of veterans, who were joined by increasing numbers of troops from allied states. It was in desperation that Napoleon called up the sons of the wealthy and educated for service during his brief return. The Bourbon monarchy repealed the measure, although the regime reestablished universal conscription some years later. Yet again, the propertied classes could buy their way out of serving. It was only during the Franco-Prussian War of 1870–1 that universal compulsory military service was effectively introduced.[53]

The French experience reflected long-standing patterns common in Europe. Austria, for instance, briefly introduced a limited militia in 1808–9. The experiment was unsuccessful, however, so the Austrian government returned to a mixed system of a line army and cantonal recruits. Exemptions were reduced during wartime, but nobles, civil servants, doctors, students, and wealthy peasants all remained exempt until at least 1827.[54] Only in 1868, after the defeat of the Austrian army at Königgrätz, did universal compulsory military service replace the old system of limited conscription in the Habsburg monarchy.[55]

Prussia alone adopted the idea of universal compulsory military service from Revolutionary France. Contrary to the hopes of some Prussian reformers, however, the promises of civic participation as the counterpart to military service remained mere rhetoric. The only practical connection between the two turned out to be the requirement that candidates for public employment had to have completed military service. This measure reflected Prussia's constant search for ways to increase troop levies; in that respect, it was much like the introduction of the cantonal system in the eighteenth century. Prussia also was the only European state to retain universal military service without exemption or substitution after 1815. Short-term military service for all able-bodied men and the revision of the military penal code laid the foundation for the interpenetration of the military and civil realms during the decades that followed but did not help promote citizenship.[56]

---

53 Siegfried Fiedler, *Grundriss der Militär- und Kriegsgeschichte*, vol. 2, *Das Zeitalter der Französischen Revolution und Napoleons* (Munich, 1976), 51.
54 Robert A. Kann, *Geschichte des Habsburgerreiches, 1526–1918*, 2nd ed. (Vienna, 1982), 222–3.
55 Hochedlinger, "Rekrutierung – Militarisierung – Modernisierung," in *Landwehr gegen Napoleon: Österreichs erste Miliz und der Nationalkrieg von 1809*, ed. Ernst Zehetbauer (Vienna, 1999); Rainer Wohlfeil, *Spanien und die deutsche Erhebung* (Wiesbaden, 1965), 165–203; Charles W. Ingrao, *The Habsburg Monarchy, 1618–1815* (Cambridge, 1994), 234–5.
56 Büsch, *Militärsystem*; Rudolf Ibbeken, *Preussen 1807–1813: Staat und Volk als Idee und Wirklichkeit* (Cologne, 1970); Dierk Walter, *Preussische Heeresreformen 1807–1870: Militärische Innovation und der Mythos der "Roonschen Reform"* (Paderborn, 2003).

That "so very military state" did not serve as a model for the former member states of the Confederation of the Rhine.[57] In those states, regular armies and civil society were regarded as separate spheres.[58] Troops of the line remained the central component of royal armies, as the numbers of conscripts were significantly reduced after 1815.[59] In 1848–9, the revolutionaries learned how great the power of monarchs over their armies remained.[60] There was no southern German *Sonderweg,* as Ute Frevert has maintained.[61] It was, rather, Prussia that pursued a special path of its own.

Elsewhere on the continent, the old-line army survived into the nineteenth century in combination with limited forms of conscription that, as before the French Revolution, relied on the lower strata of society. Truly universal compulsory military service was introduced on the European continent only during the last third of the nineteenth century. If compulsory military service is the key element in total war, the wars of the Revolutionary and Napoleonic era do not mark the beginning of the age of total warfare. The Prussian example and the French interlude were exceptions to the general pattern.

The same proposition governed the relationship between the military and the civilian population. Clausewitz's often-quoted phrase "war of extermination for the sake of political existence" represented an extreme position that related to possible war aims; it did not refer to the abolition of distinctions between combatants and noncombatants that subsequently characterized total war. The first hints of this abolition came during the war in Spain, where guerrilla resistance after the defeat of the Spanish army made it difficult for the French occupiers to distinguish between civilians and fighters. This war witnessed acts of utmost cruelty on both sides. The French command, however, had not planned in advance to attack the civilian population. Regular French troops usually observed the rules of war, which prohibited violence against noncombatants.[62] It was the guerrillas who, lacking other instruments of power, turned this conflict into an unlimited war. The French army's response started a spiral of extreme violence on both sides, and soon the conventions of war were abandoned.[63]

---

57 Cited in Frevert, *Kasernierte Nation,* 138.   58 Langewiesche, *Wandel,* 23.
59 Wilson, *European Warfare,* 203.
60 Dieter Langewiesche, "Die Rolle des Militärs in den europäischen Revolutionen von 1848," in *Europa 1848: Revolution und Reform,* ed. Dieter Dowe, Heinz-Gerhard Haupt, and Dieter Langewiesche (Bonn, 1998), 915–32; Christian Jansen, "Die Militarisierung der bürgerlichen Gesellschaft im 19. Jahrhundert," in Jansen, *Der Bürger als Soldat,* 9–23.
61 Frevert, *Kasernierte Nation,* 133.   62 Best, *War and Society,* 176.
63 Gerhard Schulz, "Die Irregulären: Guerilla, Partisanen und die Wandlungen des Krieges seit dem 18. Jahrhundert. Eine Einführung," in *Partisanen und Volkskrieg: Zur Revolutionierung des Krieges im 20. Jahrhundert,* ed. Gerhard Schulz (Göttingen, 1985), 9–35.

Acts of violence against civilians occurred as a result of the dynamics of antiguerrilla warfare, not from a planned strategy of extermination.

Outside Spain, too, civilians assuredly suffered the burdens of war. But the demands for money, food, supplies, and billeting imposed during the Revolutionary wars were nothing new, nor were the complaints against such demands heard throughout southern Germany and many other areas. The Revolutionary and Napoleonic armies observed traditions that extended back into the early modern era. Mobilizing resources in enemy territories was a practice familiar from the Thirty Years' War. Wallenstein was a master at it.[64] The Swedish army recouped much of its military and administrative costs by exploiting the resources of the territories it occupied during that war.[65] Military administration was rationalized and systematized during the seventeenth and eighteenth centuries to exploit conquered lands more effectively, particularly those that were slated for annexation. Indeed, parts of present-day Belgium became, "a field of experimentation for French occupation politics."[66]

Efforts to rationalize the exploitation of conquered lands and to prohibit uncontrolled plundering were limited, however, despite the arguments of legal scholars in favor of making the "art of war" more humane.[67] In this respect, it is instructive to compare the French occupation of Prussia's western provinces during the Seven Years' War and of southern Germany four decades later. There were striking similarities in the measures undertaken to support the armies, in the sanctions to suppress civilian resistance, and in the efforts of soldiers to enrich themselves by taking money, natural produce, livestock, hostages, or bribes from civilians.[68] The differences in the conduct of the troops during these occupations can be attributed to the structural conditions of warfare in the two periods. During the long occupation of Prussian territory in the course of the Seven Years' War, the French eventually pursued a systematic mobilization of resources and negotiated contracts with local representatives for regular contributions.

---

64 Moriz Ritter, "Das Kontributionssystem Wallensteins," *Historische Zeitschrift* 90 (1903): 194–249.
65 Kersten Krüger, "Dänische und schwedische Kriegsfinanzierung im Dreissigjährigen Krieg bis 1635," in *Krieg und Politik 1618–1648: Europäische Probleme und Perspektiven*, ed. Konrad Repgen (Munich, 1988), 275–98; Helmut Backhaus, *Reichsterritorium und schwedische Provinz: Vorpommern unter Karls XI: Vormündern, 1660–1672* (Göttingen, 1969); Beate-Christine Fiedler, *Die Verwaltung der Herzogtümer Bremen und Verden in der Schwedenzeit 1652–1712: Organisation und Wesen der Verwaltung* (Stade, 1987).
66 Carl, *Okkupation*, 6; Hubert van Houtte, *Les occupations étrangeres en Belgique sous l'ancien régime*, 3 vols. (Ghent, 1930).
67 Johann Jakob Moser, *Grund-Säze des jetzt üblichen Völcker-Rechts in Kriegs-Zeiten* (Tübingen, 1752).
68 Carl, *Okkupation*, 171–232; Planert, "Leben mit dem Krieg," 111–259. These methods were used in the Prussian and Austrian armies, too. Cf. Horst Carl, "Invasion und Okkupation im Siebenjährigen Krieg," in *Krieg und Frieden: Militär und Gesellschaft in der Frühen Neuzeit*, ed. Bernhard R. Kroener and Ralf Pröve (Paderborn, 1996), 331–48.

When the French first invaded, however, and again when they left, chaos prevailed. General Claude-Louis Saint-Germain's account of the French withdrawal from Prussia in 1757–8 disproved contemporary ideas about the pacification of warfare. "It is scarcely possible to recount the disorders that have set in," he wrote. "The land has been covered for miles around by our soldiers, who have pillaged, murdered, raped, wrecked, and committed every imaginable atrocity."[69]

Much as in the Seven Years' War, it was the breakdown of military infrastructure and the shortage of supplies rather than ideological fervor that spurred plundering during the wars of the French Revolution. Military discipline routinely collapsed under such circumstances as soldiers tried to relieve their privation on their own. Infrastructural shortcomings also contributed, in tandem with official policy, to corruption among officers. The Bourbon army was based on extended private economies at the regimental and company levels. With the toleration of the state, members of the overstaffed officer corps recouped their investments from resources in enemy territories, much as occupied territories subsidized the royal army.[70] During the Revolutionary wars, the search for personal enrichment was encouraged by the Directory, which expected that the armies would not only support themselves but also provide financial support for the bankrupt republic.[71]

Military riots against civilian populations were common in the mid- and late eighteenth century, particularly during short-term or ill-coordinated military operations such as invasions and retreats. In the cases of the French occupation of Prussia in the middle of the century and the French conquest of the Rhineland at the end, continuous occupation accompanied a rationalization of methods, and the situation of the civilian populations became more bearable.[72] The same applies to French indirect rule in the Confederation of the Rhine.[73]

During the Seven Years' War, violence against the civilian population was usually inaugurated by the so-called light troops. These units were not centrally supplied but were expected to care for their own quarters

---

69 Cited in Carl, "Invasion," 331–2.   70 Ibid., 336–7.

71 T. C. W. Blanning, "Die französischen Revolutionsarmeen in Deutschland: Der Feldzug von 1796," in *Deutschland und Europa in der Neuzeit: Festschrift für Karl Otmar Freiherr von Aretin*, ed. Ralph Melville (Stuttgart, 1988), 1:489–504.

72 Carl, "Invasion"; Carl, *Okkupation*; T. W. C. Blanning, *The French Revolution in Germany* (Oxford, 1983); T. W. C. Blannning, *The French Revolutionary Wars, 1787–1802* (London, 1996); Uwe Andrea, *Die Rheinländer, die Revolution und der Krieg, 1794–1798* (Essen, 1994); Michael Rowe, *From Reich to State: The Rhineland in the Revolutionary Age, 1780–1830* (Cambridge, 2003).

73 Helmut Berding, *Napoleonische Herrschafts- und Gesellschaftspolitik im Königreich Westfalen 1807–1813* (Göttingen, 1983); Walter Demel, *Vom aufgeklärten Reformstaat zum bürokratischen Staatsabsolutismus* (Munich, 1993).

and rations. Consequently, plunder was an unspoken assumption of official policy. For many volunteers, the prospect of enrichment was an inducement to enlist in these units. With Russian Cossacks and Austrian Pandurs as their models, the French and other armies deployed light troops during the Seven Years' War.[74] The "small wars" in which these troops engaged led increasingly to the circumvention of conventions that had provided for the protection of civilians in war.[75]

If the small wars of the mid-eighteenth century anticipated the revolutionary warfare of the 1790s, there were, conversely, still elements of limited warfare in evidence during the wars of the French Revolution. The behavior of revolutionary troops toward civilians varied considerably. There were (frequent) instances of violence and plundering but also attempts to maintain friendly relations, notably by providing assistance at harvest time. In southern Germany, the relationship between the military and the civilian population depended above all on the units with which residents had to deal.[76] The behavior of elite troops and professional soldiers who had served in the royal army resembled the eighteenth-century ideal of pacified warfare. These troops observed an ethos of limited war and disapproved of harm done to civilians. Civilians, in turn, found contact bearable with troops who were well equipped, supplied, and led. In general, elements of the main armies did not riot; problems grew out of smaller units of marauders or recently deployed soldiers who had received little military training.[77]

Through the seventeenth century, the prospect of plunder in enemy territories had fostered the cohesion of mercenary armies. Plunder remained a motivating force during the cabinet wars of the eighteenth century but primarily among the higher ranks. With the democratization of warfare during the Revolutionary wars, the lower ranks, too, sought to participate. At the same time, however, the professionalization of soldiers reduced the likelihood of plunder and violence against civilians. This principle was clear during the Napoleonic era, when the French army underwent renewed professionalization. The armies of 1796 were much less disciplined than Napoleon's troops, whose logistics were also better organized and more efficient. Requisitions remained, but the consolidation of the French state and the new recruitment system eased the burdens on residents of occupied territories. In fact, even the logistical and organizational reforms introduced

74 Carl, "Invasion," 341.
75 Johannes Kunisch, *Der kleine Krieg: Studien zum Heerwesen des Absolutismus* (Wiesbaden, 1973).
76 Planert, "Leben mit dem Krieg," 128.   77 Ibid., 125–36.

by Carnot in 1793–4 led, little by little, to a reduction in the violence against civilians. So did rationalized exploitation of resources. In the "inner empire," the requisitions now took place on the basis of contract and agreement.[78]

The French Revolution and the territorial changes that accompanied it marked the beginning of modern European political history. The Holy Roman Empire disappeared along with its most loyal pillars – the petty principalities, the lands of the lower nobility, the free cities, and the ecclesiastical territories. From the perspective of military history, however, the French Revolution was less of a caesura. There were important lines of continuity linking early modern and revolutionary warfare. The Revolutionary era was different from the twentieth century insofar as entire societies were not permanently mobilized for war. Several regions and social classes were able to evade war, even within societies that were otherwise involved. It was still possible to hire substitutes or to escape into the mountains. To be sure, armies were larger during the Revolutionary era than before, as were the burdens on the civilian populations that supplied them. However, the principle that troops supported themselves in enemy territory was hardly new and had been applied extensively before – even under the "tamed Bellona" of the eighteenth century

Economic and colonial issues were central to the global warfare of the Revolutionary era – Napoleon's continental system is one indication – but the same issues had been at the center of the clashes between England and France a half century earlier. Nor was the systematic broadening of recruitment in European armies an invention of the Revolution. Several European states had begun to institute compulsory military service to mobilize the lower strata of society during the eighteenth century. Moreover, the levée en masse and the imposition of compulsory universal military service were episodic phenomena. In most states that provided conscripted soldiers to the Grande Armée, members of the upper and middle classes remained exempt from military service. Except in Prussia, it was not until the last third of the nineteenth century that the nations of Europe introduced compulsory universal military service.

The French Revolution did not abolish professional armies.[79] Nor was it revolutionary strategists or Napoleon who invented shock tactics as an instrument of warfare. French military theorists had begun to devise column operations in the mid-eighteenth century to overcome the offensive

---

78 See Michael Broers, *Europe under Napoleon, 1799–1815* (London, 1996).
79 Regling, "Grundzüge," 188–91.

limitations of linear formations.[80] During the last years of the ancien régime, Guibert envisaged operations that would culminate in decisive battles.[81] The deployment of the mass armies of the Revolution, which could afford to risk higher casualties, made it possible to test these ideas in practice. The Napoleonic Wars ultimately resulted in the deaths of 20 percent of French men born between 1790 and 1795. The figure for the First World War was 25 percent.[82] In this sense at least, the wars of the Revolutionary era did point toward total war.

Even the role of ideological and national sentiments was limited in the Revolutionary era. Continuing resistance in the Vendée and other rural regions showed that revolutionary zeal was not shared by the entire French population. In the German-speaking countries, the mobilization of patriotism varied among regions and social classes. In Prussia, the center of opposition to Napoleon, national enthusiasm was evident principally in the urban centers, where loyalty to the Prussian monarchy, Protestantism, and communications networks encouraged the spread of nationalist ideas. In rural areas, within Catholic regions, and among ethnic minorities, the situation differed considerably.[83] In the onetime member states of the Confederation of the Rhine, the Wars of Liberation stimulated national sentiments only among an educated minority. The residents of those states had come into contact with troops from not only France but also from several other countries, and they tended to judge the soldiers less by nationality than by behavior.[84]

After the Congress of Vienna, the European states returned to limited warfare. The French wars are thus better analyzed within the framework of evolutionary change than as the beginning of total war. Their principal innovations were not military but political. The French wars corresponded to the battle of competing political ideologies. With the survival of the revolution or Europe's dynasties at stake, neither party was able to compromise. This ideological conflict underlay the quest for decisive warfare, which distinguished the French wars from their predecessors in the late seventeenth and eighteenth centuries.

---

80 Fiedler, *Grundriss*, 99–133.   81 Regling, "Grundzüge," 147.
82 Geoffrey Parker, ed., *The Cambridge Illustrated History of Warfare* (Cambridge, U.K., 1995), 208.
83 Karen Hagemann, "*Mannlicher Muth und deutsche Ehre*": *Nation, Krieg und Geschlecht in der Zeit der antinapoleonischen Kriege Preussens* (Paderborn, 2002).
84 Ute Planert, "Conscription, Economic Exploitation and Religion in Napoleonic Germany," in *Napoleon and His Empire: Europe, 1804–1814*, ed. Philip G. Dwyer and Alan Forrest (London, 2007), 133–48.

4

Reluctant Reformers, Observant Disciples

The Prussian Military Reforms, 1807–1814

DIERK WALTER

The defeat of the Prussian army at Jena and Auerstädt in 1806 triggered the Prussian reforms that laid the foundations for the state's recovery and its remarkable expansion during the nineteenth century. The core element of the reforms was the reorganization of the military. This chapter analyzes three dimensions of the military reforms– recruitment and the organization of the army, plans for insurrectionary warfare, and tactics and doctrine. The analysis takes up four sets of questions. First, how revolutionary were these reforms? Did they represent a radical break with the past? Second, how modern were they? Were the innovations of enduring importance? Third, to what extent did the reforms help to bring about people's war in Prussia? Did they involve an entire society materially and morally in the war effort? Fourth, how relevant are these reforms to concept of total war?[1]

THE ROAD TO UNIVERSAL CONSCRIPTION

When Prussia went to war in 1806, it fielded an army that was based almost exclusively on the twin pillars of the landed gentry and the peasantry. East Elbian landowners officered the army. Together with large contingents of "foreigners" – mostly non-Prussian Germans – East Elbian smallholders and serfs formed the rank and file of the army. Soldiers served in theory for life; in practice, they usually served for twenty years or until they were invalided out. The troops were subject to brutal discipline and corporal

---

1 On the concept of total war, see the introductory essays in Stig Förster and Jörg Nagler, eds., *On the Road to Total War: The American Civil War and the German Wars of Unification, 1861–1871* (Cambridge, U.K., 1997); Manfred Boemeke, Roger Chickering, and Stig Förster, eds., *Anticipating Total War: The German and American Experiences, 1871–1914* (Cambridge, U.K., 1999); Roger Chickering and Stig Förster, eds., *Great War, Total War: Combat and Mobilization on the Western Front, 1914–1918* (Cambridge, U.K., 2000); and Roger Chickering and Stig Förster, eds., *The Shadows of Total War: Europe, East Asia, and the United States, 1919–1939* (Cambridge, U.K., 2003).

punishment. The aristocratic officer corps, by contrast, enjoyed social privileges, including virtual exemption from prosecution before civilian courts
even for nonmilitary crimes. For all practical purposes, the army existed
separated from civilian society. Under the so-called cantonal system (*Kantonsystem*), professionals, the inhabitants of several large cities, and workers in
Prussia's proto-industrial sector were exempt from military service.[2] Prussia
exemplified the military system of the ancien régime. The subjects' primary
duty in peacetime was to be productive and to contribute to the wealth and
welfare of the country; in wartime, they were to keep quiet when the king
lost a battle, as the authorities informed the citizens of Berlin after the defeat
at Jena.

In 1813, after six years of humiliating peace under French hegemony,
Prussia returned to war with an army that was based on universal conscription and consisted entirely of Prussian nationals. Service was for a
term of three years or the duration of the war. The officer corps relied
heavily on commoners, especially in the lower echelons. Town dwellers,
including the sons of wealthy and educated citizens, served in the ranks
together with members of the rural population. A minimum of social privilege was afforded to the well-to-do, primarily the right to choose their unit
if they volunteered before being drafted. Corporal punishment for enlisted
men had been abolished. Officers could be tried for crimes before civilian
courts. Some organizational oddities notwithstanding, Prussia's army was
now an army of citizens who were equal before the law.[3] The burden of
conscription fell on the entire population: 6 percent of the inhabitants of
the monarchy's East Elbian core provinces served during the Wars of Liberation.[4] That figure was not surpassed in any major European state before
World War I.

What were the preconditions for this remarkable transformation in such
a short period? The obvious answer is the French challenge. Before 1806,
France provided the model of a national army. It was based on the levée
en masse, which was nearly blind to social distinctions, and relied on the

---

2 Curt Jany, *Geschichte der Preussischen Armee vom 15. Jahrhundert bis 1914*, 2nd ed., 4 vols. (Osnabrück,
   1967), 3:191–2; Ottomar Freiherr von der Osten-Sacken und von Rhein, *Preussens Heer von seinen
   Anfängen bis zur Gegenwart*, 3 vols. (Berlin, 1911), 3:302; Grosser Generalstab, ed., *Das Preussische Heer
   der Befreiungskriege*, 2 vols. (Berlin, 1912), 1:67–8.
3 See Heinz G. Nitschke, *Die Preussischen Militärreformen 1807–1813* (Berlin, 1983); James J. Shanahan,
   Prussian Military Reforms 1786–1813 (New York, 1945); Rainer Wohlfeil, "Vom stehenden Heer des
   Absolutismus zur Allgemeinen Wehrpflicht (1789–1814)," in *Handbuch zur deutschen Militaergeschichte*,
   ed. Hans Meier-Welcker, 7 vols. (Munich, 1964), vol. 1, section 2; Max Lehmann, *Scharnhorst*, 2 vols.
   (Leipzig, 1886–7).
4 Jany, *Geschichte*, 4:94.

patriotic zeal and initiative of the citizen-soldier rather than on brutal discipline and slavish subordination. After 1806, the Prussian state and army confronted the challenges of recovering from defeat and throwing off the French yoke; and this pressure provided the principal motivation for copying the French model. Nevertheless, six years of intensive discussions among the king, the military reformers, and the civilian government passed before universal conscription was introduced in the spring of 1813.

Years before the battle of Jena, progressive field officers such as Gerhard von Scharnhorst had advocated creating a national army by abolishing foreign recruitment; aristocratic privilege; corporal punishment; and, above all, the exemptions afforded by the *Kantonsystem*. But as the organization of the army reflected the stratification of East Elbian society, such changes had revolutionary implications and were thus deemed impractical before the shock of 1806.[5] Ultimately, the absolute power of the Hohenzollern monarchy rested on the loyalty of the *Junker* officers, the subordination of the peasant-soldiers and foreign mercenaries, and the wealth generated by the exempted classes. Patriotic spirit was not only unnecessary for this system to work; it was also unwanted.[6]

The crushing defeat of 1806 was pivotal in clearing away these obstacles. The abysmal performance of the old army, which melted away in the aftermath of Jena, compelled the king and the officer corps to agree to radical reforms. To remove the disgrace of having failed the country and to regain the confidence of the king, the officer corps was prepared to purge most of its senior members, including one hundred generals.[7] As a consequence, junior officers like Scharnhorst and Hermann von Boyen who were firm advocates of reform were promoted to key positions.

The realization that military reform was overdue was not in itself sufficient to implement the key elements. Some reforms were easy to achieve, such as the revision of the military penal code, the opening of the officer corps to commoners, the introduction of promotion by merit, and the abolition of foreign recruiting. All these elements were basically in place by 1808. The creation of a national army based on universal conscription,

---

5 Otto Büsch, *Militärsystem und Sozialleben im alten Preußen 1713–1807: Die Anfaenge der sozialen Militarisierung der preußisch-deutschen Gesellschaft* (Berlin, 1962).

6 Colmar Freiherr von der Goltz, *Rossbach und Jena: Studien über die Zustände und das geistige Leben in der Preussischen Armee während der Übergangszeit vom XVIII. zum XIX. Jahrhundert* (Berlin, 1883), 102–73; Heribert Händel, *Der Gedanke der allgemeinen Wehrpflicht in der Wehrverfassung des Königreiches Preussen bis 1819: Insbesondere ein Beitrag zur Frage des Einflusses der Französischen Revolution auf die Scharnhorst-Boyensche Reformgesetzgebung nach 1807* (Berlin, 1962); Helmut Schnitter, *Militärwesen und Militärpublizistik: Die militärische Zeitschriftenpublizistik in der Geschichte des bürgerlichen Militärwesens in Deutschland* (Berlin, 1967), 35–45.

7 Reinhard Höhn, *Scharnhorsts Vermächtnis*, 2nd ed. (Frankfurt, 1972), 254–6; Wohlfeil, "Heer," 137–9.

by contrast, faced three additional obstacles: the ongoing disagreement between the king and the army reformers about the importance of overhauling the recruiting system; the civilian resistance to requiring military service of the exempted classes; and, most importantly, French hegemony in Prussia, which had deprived the monarchy of half its territory and imposed crippling economic demands. The Convention of Paris (1808) also imposed strict limits on Prussia's army and prohibited the formation of any reserve or militia force.[8]

French supremacy nonetheless provided the impetus for the reform of Prussia's recruiting system. The king, the army reformers, and the civilian government realized they would have to compromise with one another if the country was to overcome its enforced subordination to France. To make the reform acceptable, a complex military system was created that concealed military service obligation behind a purportedly separate army for the hitherto exempted classes. That army was the Prussian Landwehr. A militia that would supplement the standing army in wartime, it retained ties to the localities and was officered, in theory, by the wealthy and educated.

The establishment of Landwehr was initially a successful compromise measure. It tapped the national manpower pool more effectively than the previous recruiting system had, and it had something to satisfy all interested parties. The military reformers could claim that they had, in a roundabout way, achieved universal conscription and an army of citizen-soldiers. The king had kept his beloved regular army free of dilution by ill-trained citizen-soldiers. The wealthy and educated classes had the privilege of serving in a separate organization in which they were not subjected to the exacting discipline faced by regular troops and through which they could help defend their country in wartime. By limiting the previously exempted classes' service to wartime, the Landwehr satisfied cameralists in the state administration, who regarded military service by the productive classes as detrimental to the state's prosperity. And perhaps most importantly, after its distinguished service in the Wars of Liberation, the Landwehr became the focus of patriotic feelings and provided citizens to whom the regular army offered little attraction with the opportunity to participate in the defense of their fatherland.

The necessary complement to universal service was a short peacetime service. Many were to serve for a few years, whereas in the old army, a few had served for many years. Short-term service was itself a by-product of

---

8 Historische Abtheilung des Generalstabes, *Die Reorganisation der Preussischen Armee nach dem Tilsiter Frieden*, 2 vols. (Berlin, 1854–66), 1:194–5.

enforced disarmament after Tilsit. The famous *Krümper* – supernumerary enlistees – became a convenient means to provide a degree of basic military training to a much larger number of recruits than were actually under the colors at any given time. A certain percentage of the rank and file in every regular company was discharged each month, making room for new recruits or, more commonly, for veterans of the pre-Jena army, who could thus be kept close at hand. Here again, French hegemony had the unintended effect of spurring weaker states to develop new means to reassert their autonomy. The use of the *Krümper* allowed the creation of a large reserve of soldiers with some basic military training – a pool that was not tied to specific regiments or *Kantone* (recruiting districts). This innovation represented a permanent breach in the *Kantonsystem* and paved the way for a national army based upon universal conscription.[9]

In 1814–15, however, the new military system was converted into something quite different. The Landwehr lost its status as a separate entity and became instead a reserve pool for the regular army. Conscripts thus trained in the line for three years and then passed into the reserves for two more years, before finally moving into the Landwehr. During their obligatory fourteen years of service, members of the Landwehr participated in weekend exercises and annual maneuvers. Instead of wartime service in a militia, citizen-soldiers now faced peacetime service in the regular army. This shift signaled the success of the strategy of camouflaging the introduction of universal conscription during the Wars of Liberation by making the Landwehr seem to be a separate army for the previously exempted classes. After 1815, the transformed Landwehr benefited from the glory that the citizen-soldiers had earned in 1813–14 on the battlefields of Germany and northern France. The Landwehr became a popular component of the military, and it made universal conscription acceptable in much of the country.

Prussia was not the only state in Europe that met the challenge of the French levée en masse by expanding the basis of recruitment. It was, however, the only state that extended the innovation to peacetime service. While all the major European powers, including France, returned to systems of selective service with generous exemptions after 1815, Prussia moved to universal peacetime conscription. Admittedly, the implementation was not as universal as the law provided, and it became less so as the century progressed. Still, although the Prussian army called up only a small portion of each age cohort for peacetime service, selection was by lot or date of

---

9 Dierk Walter, *Preussische Heeresreformen 1807–1870: Militärische Innovation und der Mythos der "Roonschen Reform"* (Paderborn, 2003), 253–7, 322–4.

birth, not by social class. The universality of conscription, the equality of all citizens before the law, was upheld. Although the educated and well to do enjoyed minimal privileges – above all, the right to shortened service of one year and accelerated promotion to the officer corps of the Landwehr – no class was exempt from service as a matter of principle. Even in this imperfect form, universal conscription tied army and society together in a way unthinkable under the ancién regime. It made the defense of the state the concern of the entire male population.

Prussia thus proved itself a belated but adept disciple of the French Revolution. Whereas Carnot gave France the largely unorganized levée en masse in response to war, Scharnhorst and Boyen gave Prussia a more effective (and repressive) system of universal conscription in peacetime. Both systems tapped the state's manpower pool more thoroughly than ever before, but Prussia's did so with much more planning, preparation, and control from above. It was, at the core, an authoritarian version of revolutionary mass mobilization.[10]

Although imposed from above, Prussia's military reforms were a step toward people's war. Prussian citizens flocked to the colors in the spring of 1813 to throw off the French yoke. Many did not wait to be called up for service. The nationalist literature of the nineteenth and early twentieth centuries exaggerated the pan-German nationalism of the uprising of 1813, the outburst of patriotic feelings, and the popular willingness to accept sacrifice to achieve victory, but all these elements were present.[11] In the Wars of Liberation, the Prussian people accepted their share of responsibility for the defense of the fatherland. Never again would they keep quiet when the king lost a battle, nor would any king ask them to do so.

Insofar as the universal service obligation marked the advent of people's war in Prussia, it also represented a first step on the road to total war. State and society were mobilized for warfare in 1813–14 on a scale that would not be surpassed until the world wars of the twentieth century. Still, in a proto-industrial society fighting a comparatively short war with a regular army mostly on foreign soil, the disruption of economic and social life was marginal. In fact, the French occupation and forced contributions to

---

10 Walter, *Heeresreformen*, chaps. 5–6. On the Landwehr, see also Dorothea Schmidt, *Die preussische Landwehr: Ein Beitrag zur Geschichte der allgemeinen Wehrpflicht in Preussen zwischen 1813 und 1830* (Berlin, 1981); Dennis E. Showalter, "The Prussian Landwehr and Its Critics," *Central European History* 4 (1971): 3–33.

11 Hans-Ulrich Wehler, *Deutsche Gesellschaftsgeschichte*, 5 vols. (Munich, 1987–2008), 1:522–30; Thomas Nipperdey, *Deutsche Geschichte 1800–1866: Buergerwelt und starker Staat* (Munich, 1983), 83–5; Rudolf Ibbeken, *Preussen 1807–1813: Staat und Volk als Idee und Wirklichkeit* (Cologne, 1970), 373–439.

the French war effort before 1813 had a greater socioeconomic impact on Prussia than the mobilization for the wars of 1813–14 did. Nevertheless, many Prussian officials and citizens alike believed that the human and material resources of the core provinces were being pushed to their limits in 1814.[12]

By the same token, the time had not yet come for wars waged against entire societies or in the name of extreme war aims. The allies waged war against Napoleon, not the French people; and their victory over France left the social and (in 1814) political structure of the country largely intact. Still, warfare was now an issue of the people, so the first steps had been taken toward the confrontation of entire societies in the wars of the twentieth century.

The military system that evolved in Prussia between 1807 and 1814 was modern enough to enable Prussia to fight a people's war that approached the dimensions of the late nineteenth century. The recruitment system and military organization that emerged from the Scharnhorst-Boyen reforms survived, with modifications such as the so-called Roon reforms of 1859–60, until the end of the monarchy in 1918.[13] In fact, its principal elements – universal conscription, territorial recruiting, and short-term active service followed by extended service in the reserves – survived until the end of the Cold War in the West German army. Some elements of the reform – opening the officer corps to commoners, for example, and basing promotions on merit – were so modern that they were scarcely acceptable to contemporaries. They were revoked or allowed to fall into abeyance after the Wars of Liberation, only to be reintroduced decades later.

It is hard to exaggerate the revolutionary character of the Prussian military reforms. They broke with a century-old tradition of limiting officer commissions to the nobility and promoting officers by seniority – a practice that survived in the British and American armies much longer. Although Prussian authorities attempted to reduce the proportion of commoners in the officer corps during the nineteenth century – successfully for a while – they could no longer exclude them entirely. It took creative pretexts to keep them out of the most exclusive units. Commoners were concentrated in the less desirable regiments and the technical branches until the creation

---

12 Boyen to Gneisenau, Berlin, June 16, 1815, in *Das Leben des Feldmarschalls Grafen Neidhardt von Gneisenau*, ed. Gerhard Heinrich Pertz and Hans Delbrück, 5 vols. (Berlin, Reimer, 1864–80), 4:534–5.
13 Walter, *Heeresreformen*, chaps. 7–8.

of mass armies in the late nineteenth century dashed residual hopes for an officer corps exclusively of *Junker*.[14]

Short-term service, too, was a revolutionary principle. There was a striking difference between the professional soldier, who grew old serving the colors, and the citizen-soldier who served for two or three years at a young age. The rank and file of the old army had in effect been a social formation largely detached from civil society. The new army comprised a large part of the male population, and conscripts returned to civic life after their active service and military socialization. Short-term service wedded army and society.

Contrary to the Hohenzollern legend, the *Kantonsystem* of the ancien régime did not constitute a de facto system of universal conscription. The invocation of the duty of all Prussian subjects to serve the king in the defense of the fatherland in the service regulations of the eighteenth century was merely a literary trope. The obligation to serve was neither universal nor egalitarian; it was empty of the ideals that made universal conscription a crucial factor in the development of modern civil society. The *Kantonsystem* was merely a means to bring order to a recruiting market that had become disruptively violent and chaotic. To the Hohenzollern kings, universal military service obligation sounded suspiciously like a militia, which Frederick William I had abhorred and abolished. The Prussian ideal before 1806 was an army of professionals whose loyalty was to their king and their officers, not their country. The national army of citizen-soldiers represented a radical departure from this ideal, and in abolishing practices such as corporal punishment, it made a clear distinction between the citizen-soldier and the professional mercenary.[15]

In other respects, too, the new army was fundamentally different from the old. The principle of territorial recruiting, for example, bore only a superficial resemblance to the *Kantonsystem* of recruitment, arguments about the continuities in Prussian military organization notwithstanding. The *Kantone* did not cover the entire kingdom, and the system was riddled with exemptions. By contrast, the regimental recruiting districts of the new army spanned the breadth of the kingdom and made every male inhabitant liable to service.

14 Manfred Messerschmidt, "Das preussisch-deutsche Offizierkorps 1850–1890," in *Das deutsche Offizierkorps 1860–1960*, ed. Hanns Hubert Hofmann (Boppard am Rhein, 1980), 21–38; Karl Demeter, *Das Deutsche Offizierkorps in Gesellschaft und Staat 1650–1945*, 2nd ed. (Frankfurt, 1962).
15 Gerhard Papke, "Von der Miliz zum Stehenden Heer: Wehrwesen im Absolutismus," in Meier-Welcker, *Handbuch*, 1:202–7, 218–22, 264–76; Emil Obermann, *Soldaten – Bürger – Militaristen: Militär und Demokratie in Deutschland* (Stuttgart, 1958); Kurt Jany, "Die Kantonverfassung des altpreussischen Heeres," in *Moderne Preussische Geschichte 1648–1947: Eine Anthologie*, ed. Otto Büsch and Wolfgang Neugebauer, 3 vols. (Berlin, 1981), 2: 76–809; Hans Delbrück, *Geschichte der Kriegskunst*, 4 vols. (Hamburg, 2003), 1:507–8; 4:319–20.

Despite its successes, the new military system failed to achieve some of goals it was designed to fulfill. Elements remained that, from a twenty-first century perspective, were not modern. While the new army was in many respects an army of the people, it remained the army of the king and could in some circumstances be used against the people. The regular army remained the core of the military system, and neither its structure nor its purpose changed. The Prussian army continued to be dominated by the nobility, especially in peacetime, when the Landwehr was inactive. The army still rested on subordination and strict discipline. These characteristics reflected the structure of the state; despite the political and social reforms of the Napoleonic era, power ultimately continued to rest in the hands of the king and the *Junker*. In fact, introduction of universal conscription made the army more egalitarian than the state. In asking Prussians to die for their country but withholding the vote from them, the monarchy seemed to have failed to fulfill its part of the bargain. Universal suffrage was the complement of universal conscription, but Prussia extended the franchise to all of its male citizens only long after having imposed obligatory military service on them. This fact spoke volumes about the nature of the Prussian state and society.[16]

PEOPLE'S WAR À OUTRANCE

Ancien régime Prussia was not the most likely state to employ irregular forces in guerilla warfare. Yet circumstances were desperate enough between 1808 and 1811 that Frederick William III was ready to contemplate it. His army had shrunk to the size of a single army corps; in early 1810, it comprised twenty thousand men, or 8 percent of the forces that had fought at Jena in 1806.[17] The French occupiers blocked regular rearmament and imposed crippling payments after the Treaty of Tilsit (1807). Hence the king had few choices if he was unwilling to accept Prussia's dependent status.

The insurrections against French forces in the Vendée (1793–6), Spain (1808), and the Tyrol (1809) suggested a course of action to the Prussians.[18] In those insurrections, rural populations had risen more or less sponta- neously in the name of dynastic loyalties and in defense of their ways of life. The Prussian reformers associated with Scharnhorst, particularly August

---

16 Friedrich Meinecke, *Das Leben des Generalfeldmarschalls Hermann von Boyen*, 2 vols. (Stuttgart, 1896–9), 2:389–91; Ernst-Rudolf Huber, *Deutsche Verfassungsgeschichte seit 1789*, 8 vols. (Stuttgart, 1957–99), 1:224–5; Wohlfeil, "Heer," 187–8.

17 Generalstab, *Reorganisation*, 2:156–71.

18 Walter Laqueur, *Guerilla Warfare: A Historical and Critical Study* (New Brunswick, New Jersey, 2004), chap. 1.

Graf Neidhardt von Gneisenau, attempted to orchestrate a similar uprising – in advance and from above. They envisioned full-scale guerrilla war against the French occupation forces. According to Gneisenau, Prussia faced extinction. The country's military forces were barely sufficient to preserve a semblance of honor. People's war would enable the state to survive, he argued, for the Spanish example had shown that a conventional occupation force could not defeat a popular uprising.

The proposals that Scharnhorst and Gneisenau put forth addressed primarily the technical details of organizing an insurrection. They sought to ensure cooperation between the irregular forces and the army, deeming such cooperation indispensible to a war of liberation. Every able-bodied man above the age of sixteen was to be armed, with pikes if firearms were not available, and enlisted in a militia. The militias would then support the regular army and fight guerrilla campaigns against the enemy's soft targets. In the occupied provinces, civil administration was to shut down to deprive the enemy of support. The army reformers thus envisioned a combination of civil disobedience and armed resistance; both were designed to make the cost of occupation unbearable for the enemy.

The reformers went beyond envisioning a new form of warfare. They also had to address the crucial question of how Prussian subjects could be motivated to rise in arms in defense of their country after centuries of being told that the king's wars were none of their business. They came up with a carrot-and-stick response. The stick was the threat of punishment, which could range from dispossession of property, loss of nobility, and permanent disqualification from holding public office. The carrot was less tangible. It amounted to vague intimations that Prussians would be granted the right to political participation in exchange for sharing in the responsibility of defending the fatherland.

This promise reflected the reformers' romantic political convictions and their idealistic worldview, but they were in fact not in a position to make good on it. Frederick William III remained skeptical about the reformers' proposals. He agreed that even the most desperate attempt to regain Prussia's freedom was better than permanent subjugation, but he doubted whether his subjects, accustomed to authoritarian rule, could initiate or sustain an uprising in the face of enemy reprisals without firm guidance from above. As a result of his reservations, nothing came initially of the plans for national insurrection.[19]

---

19 Rudolf Vaupel, ed., *Die Reorganisation des Preussischen Staates unter Stein und Hardenberg*, 2 vols. (Leipzig, 1938), 2:549–52, 554–7, 561–3, 574; Pertz and Delbrück, *Gneisenau*, 2:112–42.

The ground had nonetheless been laid for one of the most extraordinary components of the Prussian military reforms. On April 21, 1813, as the fight to expel the French was well under way, Frederick William III yielded to Gneisenau's pressure and issued the Landsturmverordnung,[20] a proclamation calling on his subjects to undertake people's war à outrance. Every Prussian subject, regardless of sex or age, was made responsible for the defense of the fatherland. The French invasion was to be met by total civilian and military resistance. Women and children would serve in auxiliary roles. All able-bodied men between the ages of fifteen to sixty who were not serving in the regular army or Landwehr were to serve in the Landsturm. This body was to be organized by the population itself; officers were to be elected from the ranks of local landowners, civil servants, foresters, and schoolteachers. Not only military authorities but also district or county Landsturm leaders could call units into action. Because most Prussian civilians did not own firearms, Landsturm members were to be armed with pikes, pitchforks, maces, sabers, axes, and scythes. The Landsturm was supposed to fight a guerrilla campaign in support of the regular army; to deny the enemy the use of the occupied country and its resources; and to pin down enemy troops in the rear, outside the main areas of operations.

The Landsturmverordnung contained elaborate provisions regarding organization and modes of resistance. In occupied cities, all cooperation with the enemy was forbidden, all administration was to cease functioning, and citizens were called upon to accept some civil disorder rather than support the enemy by forming home guards. Districts that were about to fall to the enemy could be evacuated, on the proviso that they first be made uninhabitable – food supplies and other resources were to be destroyed and all transportation infrastructure dismantled. Above all, the Landsturm was to function as a guerrilla force. Uniforms, flags, or other means of identification were prohibited. Landsturm members were to pose as village folk. The Landsturmverordnung prescribed attacks by night. Enemy soldiers were to be killed and stripped of their arms and kit. To avoid detection, Landsturm units were permitted to kill any prisoners they took.

In invoking the example of Spanish guerrilla fighters, the Landsturmverordnung went far beyond the traditional rules of warfare. Those rules, as Prussian officials were well aware, held that civilians who were found bearing arms without a recognized uniform or equivalent means of identification did not enjoy the rights of combatants and risked summary execution. The

---

20 Egon von Frauenholz, *Das Heerwesen des XIX. Jahrhunderts* (Munich, 1941), 161–71.

Landsturmverordnung accordingly threatened reprisals should the French authorities not treat captured Landsturmmänner as legitimate combatants.

The Landsturm never became a significant military factor, primarily because most of the fighting during the Wars of Liberation took place beyond Prussian territory. It would be hard, however, to overstate the historical significance of the Landsturmverordnung. Seven years after Jena, it called on Prussians to fight a full-scale people's war on their own initiative. It attested to the fundamental changes that had quickly taken place at the core of the Prussian military system. There was no little irony in the fact that the Prussian king ordered his subjects to be self-reliant defenders of the country and that he attempted to bring about a popular rising by royal decree. The Prussian state never came so close to waging total war, to removing the limits on warfare and mobilizing the entire population. The spring of 1813 witnessed the high tide of people's war in Prussia.

It passed quickly. The Landsturmverordnung had been in force for only three months before a broad coalition of conservative officers, civil servants, and bourgeois notables convinced the king that he had gone too far.[21] Armed mobs roaming the countryside without control from above were as much a threat to the monarchy as to the foreign occupiers. In a revised decree of July 17, 1813, the Landsturm was put on a short leash. In the countryside, it was drastically reduced in size, lost its autonomous organization, and was converted into a reserve force of the Landwehr. In the cities, it was abolished in favor of home guards subordinate to the Landwehr. The scorched-earth provisions of the original proclamation were toned down or revoked.[22] People's war was to be controlled by the authorities.

ORGANIZATION, TACTICS, DOCTRINE

During the reform era, the Prussian regular army adopted important innovations in organization, tactics, and doctrine. Modeled after the French *corps d'armée*, permanent combined units of all arms were introduced. These units were initially established at the brigade level because the Convention of Paris had restricted the size of the army. Later regulations made provision for these units to be deployed in depth in battle. This innovation represented a significant improvement over the shallow linear formations that the old army had preferred. Moreover, a battalion of light infantry – fusiliers – was added to

---

21 Pertz and Delbrück, *Gneisenau*, 3:136–41, 684–9; Meinecke, *Boyen*, 1: 288–300; Friedrich Nippold, ed., *Erinnerungen aus dem Leben des General-Feldmarschalls Hermann von Boyen*, 3 vols. (Leipzig, 1889–90), 3:49–50, 72–80.
22 Frauenholz, *Heerwesen*, 172–5.

each two-battalion line regiment. Light infantry training was made manda-
tory for the entire army, and the third rank of all line battalions was to be
proficient in skirmishing. This change reflected the practices of the French
armies, which had advanced behind *voltigeurs* (skirmishers) whose sniping
disrupted and demoralized the enemy prior to the clash of regular units.
Finally, the Prussian infantry adopted the *Angriffskolonne* (attack column) as
a standard formation: a battalion's eight platoons would be arrayed in dense
order, four deep but only two wide. Here again, the Prussians emulated
the French, who had employed the highly mobile column rather than the
cumbersome line to spearhead shock attacks by throwing densely packed
masses of men against weak points of the enemy's front.

The Prussian army was quick to institutionalize these changes. The forces
that went to war in 1813 were up to date in the tactics and doctrine of the
era and thus met the French on equal terms. One of the reasons for the
speed of reform was that none of the organizational or tactical innovations
was fundamentally new. The members of the Prussian officer corps had
been aware of the new ideas and practices before 1806, but bureaucratic
sluggishness and military traditionalism had impeded the implementation of
reforms. Self-contained divisions or corps of all arms, light infantry tactics,
and attack in columns had all been discussed throughout Europe since
the middle of the eighteenth century and hesitantly introduced in some
countries before the French Revolution. The efficiency with which the
French armies employed these new tools after 1792 then provided a major
incentive for other powers to follow suit.[23]

And they did so, enjoying the latecomer's advantage. They avoided difficulties that had troubled the French armies in adopting new practices and
tactics; instead, the latecomers could adopt the final product. The Prussians
were in fact such good students that they failed to recognize that some of
the French innovations were of limited value if adopted uncritically. The
Prussian army had traditionally relied on close-order musketry drill, which
had been designed to increase the rate of fire. The use of attack columns
was developed for French armies that were composed of raw recruits whose
training had been brief and rudimentary. Adding the column to the Prussian army's tactical repertoire would have been useful as a complement to
the line, if both formations had been employed flexibly. Relying on the

---

23 Geoffrey Best, *War and Society in Revolutionary Europe, 1770–1870* (Leicester, 1982), 63–188; Hew
Strachan, *European Armies and the Conduct of War* (London, 1983), 23–59; Larry H. Addington, *The
Patterns of War since the Eighteenth Century* (Bloomington, Indiana, 1984), 21–38; Reinhard Sauter-
meister, *Die taktische Reform der preussischen Armee nach 1806* (Ph.D. diss., University of Tübingen,
1935).

column alone, however, meant throwing away skills in which the Prussian army excelled in favor of others in which it did not. The column was also a dead end. It became axiomatic during the Napoleonic Wars that the column always defeated the line – despite the counterexample of the success of the British line against the French column in Spain. The column thereafter survived into an age in which it was no longer practicable. Once more effective firearms became widely available in the mid-nineteenth century, the massed attack column became a liability. Yet Prussian infantry regulations relied on the shock attack with the bayonet, not on firepower, even after the breech-loading rifle was introduced in the 1840s.

There was, therefore, nothing revolutionary about the organizational and tactical changes in the Prussian army between 1807 and 1813. These innovations were state of the art, and Prussia was catching up. The modernity of these innovations was also ambiguous. Some reforms, such as the permanent combined commands of all arms and the light infantry tactics, have remained relevant to the present. A NATO division today does not differ in its basic organizational principles from the Prussian brigade that was established during the Wars of Liberation, and the rifleman in the field today is an identifiable descendant of the French voltigeur and Prussian fusilier. All these phenomena represent stark contrasts to the huge, unwieldy firing lines of drilled automatons that Frederick II fielded. In this respect, the Prussian military reforms did herald the advent of modern tactics. Yet other elements of the Prussian reforms, such as the attack column, proved in the long run to be dead ends. In none of these fields, however, was the Prussian army the originator; it was instead an observant pupil.

CONCLUSION

If the tactical innovations of 1807–13 were not revolutionary, those in the fields of recruitment and insurrectionary warfare were. There was a dramatic break between the lifetime-service professional army of peasants and foreign mercenaries before 1806 – a body that was detached from civil society – and the short-service army of conscripts after 1813. In adopting compulsory universal military service, Prussia crossed a threshold, and there was no turning back. Once male subjects were liable to military service and made personally responsible for the security of the fatherland – not through contract, but by virtue of citizenship – they acquired, in principle, the right to participate in decisions about the country's destiny. Universal conscription, together with its necessary complement, the political and social reforms of 1807–13, made the eventual grant of a constitution and of universal male suffrage inevitable, although it took an additional thirty years to achieve.

With universal conscription, Prussia entered the era of nationalism and embarked on the road to modernity. Thereafter, the people, rather than monarchs and estates, had the final say about the fate of the country. Popular consent ultimately determined the political aims for which the army fought. Politicians who cared about their futures henceforth had to take this fact into account. The people could be tricked, fooled, bribed, or threatened into fighting a war they did not want – or into not fighting one they did want – but they could not be ignored, and they would not keep quiet when a battle was lost.

This was people's war. The universal conscription army was an army of the people; it fought on behalf of the people; and it was ultimately answerable to the people. A new relationship developed between army and society – a relationship that should not, however, be idealized. If universal conscription gave the people more control over the army, it also gave the army more control over the people. Having a majority of male citizens undergoing military socialization at a formative age gave the army unprecedented influence over civil society. The term *militarism* describes this situation, which made it possible over the decades to imbue society with military customs and values. This was also a result of the Scharnhorst-Boyen reforms. In their effort to turn the army into "the school of the nation *for war*," the military reformers made it the school of the nation in a more general sense.[24]

People's war, in the form of guerrilla war conducted by an entire people, was as close an approximation of total war as a preindustrial society could achieve. The Prussian attempt at people's war, incongruously ordered from above by the crown, amounted to little more than brief, localized gestures. Whether such a war could have been waged at all is open to speculation. Still, in the spring of 1813, the Prussian people – not just the urban middle classes – were politically mobilized, as men flocked to join the regulars and Landwehr to take revenge on their French oppressors. The Landsturmverordnung remains an indication of how far the Prussian government, including the king, had traveled along the road to people's war.

---

24 "Die Haupt-Bildungsschule der ganzen Nation für den Krieg": Gesetz ueber die Verpflichtung zum Kriegsdienst, Berlin, September 3, 1814, sec. 4, in Frauenholz, *Heerwesen*, 181–4.

5

The First World War

Global Dimensions of Warfare in the Age of Revolutions, 1775–1815

STIG FÖRSTER

World War I was not the first world war. Global warfare accompanied European expansion almost from its beginning. From the sixteenth century on, European armed forces fought one another, as well as indigenous peoples, on practically every sea and continent. These encounters were encouraged by the early modern military revolution in Europe, which usually gave European armies a decisive advantage over non-Europeans and enabled European navies to rule the waves worldwide.[1] Above all, European expansion itself created an ever more extensive and close-knit global network of trade, cultural exchange, and political and commercial interest. As rivalries grew among the European powers and as indigenous peoples resisted the alien intruders, military power became the basis of European ambitions overseas. Consequently, wars between Europeans and non-Europeans became common. So did wars between European powers outside Europe, where they often enjoyed the support of indigenous peoples. Overseas wars occasionally culminated in large-scale global conflict, particularly when they became entwined in conflicts in Europe. Warfare thus developed a global dimension in the early modern era.

Geoffrey Parker has argued that the Dutch war of independence against Spain was the first world war in history.[2] He exaggerates. That war was admittedly fought in Asia, the Americas, Africa and on the seas as well as in Europe. In Europe, however, several major powers stood aloof, while elsewhere indigenous participation was limited. Likewise, despite their horrors, the Thirty Years' War (1618–48), the War of the Spanish Succession

---

1 Geoffrey Parker, *The Military Revolution: Military Innovation and the Rise of the West, 1500–1800* (Cambridge, U.K., 1988). See also Wolfgang Reinhard, *Geschichte der europäischen Expansion*, 4 vols. (Stuttgart, 1983–90); Philip D. Curtin, *The World and the West: The European Challenge and the Overseas Response in the Age of Empire* (Cambridge, U.K., 2000).
2 Geoffrey Parker, *Spain and the Netherlands, 1559–1569* (London, 1979), 61.

(1701–14), and the War of the Austrian Succession (1740–8) were not world wars. Although they were fought in part overseas, they, too, remained largely European affairs.

Parker's argument thus raises questions about the meaning of *world war*. The term was in use by the late nineteenth century. Count Alfred Waldersee, the chief of the German General Staff, confided to his diary in 1887 that he expected the next major European conflict to develop into a world war.[3] After the turn of the century, several other German officers made similar remarks. On June 6, 1914, Chancellor Theobald von Bethmann Hollweg observed, "We are drifting towards a world war."[4] When war became unavoidable in the summer of 1914, Helmuth von Moltke, chief of the General Staff, told his adjutant on July 31, 1914: "This war will develop into a world war."[5] It was thus fitting that this war soon became known in Germany as *der Weltkrieg*, "the world war." Still, no one defined the term. Contemporaries used it simply to refer to the size and global dimensions of the war then being fought.

Even today, a precise definition of *world war* is lacking. Many historians use the term without reflection. One modern encyclopedia, though, has offered a useful description. According to this definition, a world war is a conflict that involves most of the countries on the planet, so military action takes place on all the seas and on all the inhabited continents.[6] But there is more to it. World wars are not just global conflagrations. The key lies in their basic structural characteristics. In a world war, local and regional conflicts of all kinds merge into a comprehensive struggle between coalitions and other parties. Peoples on all continents are drawn in. Fighting for their own interests, non-European powers play major roles. Without them, there is no world war. But while European expansion provided a global network as the basis for world wars, major European wars always stood at the core. In general, the conflict among all the great powers, whether inside or outside Europe, lies at the center of world wars, interconnects local and regional conflicts, generates new conflicts at the periphery, and ultimately decides the outcome.

In this light, the Seven Years' War (1756–63) may perhaps qualify as the first world war. All the great powers took part. In Europe, Russia intervened

---

3 Alfred Graf von Waldersee, diary entry, Jan. 1, 1887, Geheimes Staatsarchiv Berlin, I. HA Re 92, Waldersee, A.I., Nr. 14, 1887–8.

4 Cited in Klaus Hildebrand, *Das vergangene Reich: Deutsche Aussenpolitik von Bismarck bis Hitler* (Stuttgart, 1995), 300.

5 Notes of Major von Haeften, Bundesarchiv-Militärarchiv, Freiburg i. Br., N 35/1, Hans von Haeften Papers.

6 *Meyers Enzyklopädisches Lexikon*, 25 vols. (Mannheim, 1971–9), 25:192.

for the first time as a great power, while Prussia not only survived – against all odds – but also managed to establish itself in the exclusive club of major powers. Fighting took place in much of Europe, North America, the Caribbean, West Africa, and India. Overseas powers also participated. The conflict was known in North America as the French and Indian War for good reason. In India, the Nawab of Bengal and several lesser indigenous powers were involved. In a sideshow to the general war, the British East India Company routed its French counterpart and thus began its ascendancy in Bengal. But the role of non-European powers in this war was limited in comparison to events a few decades later. The German historian Theodor Schieder was justified in calling this conflict an "Anglo-French World War."[7] It was mainly a global European war that was fought for both a realignment of power on the old continent and colonial conquest overseas.

At the end of the eighteenth century, however, world war took on more modern features, as the character of warfare changed in the Western world. Whereas the Seven Years' War witnessed the beginnings of nationalism, militarism, and people's armies, the War of American Independence (1775–83) and the French Wars (1792–1815), as the British call them, went much further.[8] They involved political and social revolution. These were civil and international wars at the same time. They implicated most, if not all the great powers as well as many non-European powers. These developments culminated in the French Wars, which unambiguously constituted a world war.[9]

The connection between world war and revolution is the theme of this essay. Did revolution breed world war? Or did the two emerge in parallel or by coincidence?

Like most wars in the eighteenth century, the American War of Independence was not limited to a single theater. It spread to several continents. Fighting took place in the Caribbean, western Africa, and the Mediterranean in addition to North America. It developed into a major naval war as well. In India, the British under Warren Hastings fought an unlikely coalition of the Maratha princes, the nizam of Hyderabad, and Haidar Ali of Mysore. They also held out against fierce French attacks in the Indian Ocean. The continent of Europe, by contrast, remained largely unaffected. Only France and Spain formally entered the contest. All the other powers were content to defend their commercial interests by armed neutrality.

---

7 Theodor Schieder, *Friedrich der Grosse: Ein Königtum der Widersprüche* (Frankfurt, 1983), 202.
8 M. S. Anderson, *War and Society in Europe of the Old Regime, 1618–1789* (London, 1988), 157–204.
9 Paul Fregosi, *Dreams of Empire: Napoleon and the First World War, 1792–1815* (London, 1989); A. D. Harvey, *Collision of Empires: Britain in Three World Wars, 1793–1945* (London, 1992), 3–201.

For this reason, the American Revolutionary War cannot be characterized as a world war. Despite all the revolutionary fervor displayed by Americans in their quest for independence, the war remained a conventional
eighteenth-century conflict in many respects. As usual, colonial powers
used the opportunity to enlarge their empires at the expense of their European rivals or indigenous states and peoples. The governments of France
and Spain attempted to gain revenge for their defeat in the Seven Years'
War and to recover their losses. The war thus remained an affair of ancien
régimes. The American revolutionaries lacked the military power to export
their new ideas to other parts of the world by force. In the end, they could
congratulate themselves for having held their own against difficult odds,
albeit with help from outside. But America was not yet a great power.

In 1789, by contrast, it was one of the greatest powers on earth that
experienced revolution. Although historians have subsequently debated his
claims, Carl von Clausewitz was convinced that the wars that began in 1792
were revolutionary. As he later wrote:

Suddenly war again became the business of the people – a people of thirty millions,
all of whom considered themselves to be citizens.... The people became a participant in war; instead of governments and armies as heretofore, the full weight of
the nation was thrown into the balance. The resources and efforts now available for
use surpassed all conventional limits; nothing now impeded the vigor with which
war could be waged, and consequently the opponents of France faced the utmost
peril.[10]

Clausewitz was not entirely wrong. After 1792, war took on a new character,
not least because the armies mobilized were larger than ever before in
Europe. As entire nations were drawn into support of war and as war itself
developed into a comprehensive public affair, the dimensions and intensity
of warfare grew dramatically.[11]

During twenty-three years of almost continuous fighting, most of
Europe became a battle zone. Several million men became combatants,
and losses were high. According to George Lefebvre, France alone lost
more than 1 million men between 1800 and 1815.[12] The Russian campaign cost Napoleon more than 400,000 men, while the Russians lost at
least 250,000.[13] The magnitude of civilian losses is unknown, but it is safe

---

10 Carl von Clausewitz, *On War*, trans. and ed. Michael Howard and Peter Paret (Princeton, New
   Jersey, 1989), 592.
11 On the increased scale and destructiveness of warfare in this period, see David A. Bell, *The First
   Total War: Napoleon's Europe and the Birth of Warfare as We Know It* (Boston, 2007). On Bell's place in
   the historiography of war, see Roger Chickering's introduction to this volume.
12 Georges Lefebvre, *Napoleon* (Stuttgart, 1989), 214.
13 Hugh Seton-Watson, *The Russian Empire, 1801–1917* (Oxford, 1988), 142.

to conclude that more than a million people lost their lives in the Russian campaign alone. In other large battles, the casualty figures amounted to tens of thousands. At Waterloo, both sides lost more than fifty thousand men.[14] Losses from injury, illness, exhaustion, and hunger were even higher. Including the civilian dead, in all likelihood more than 5 million people died in Europe because of these wars. These were catastrophic losses, although they were not unprecedented. During the Thirty Years' War, some five million people perished in Germany alone.[15] These losses were indeed catastrophic, but, contrary to Clausewitz, they were not unprecedented.

Nor was the change in the character of warfare as radical as Clausewitz assumed. Well before 1789, military reformers inside and outside of France, such as Moritz of Saxony, Jean-Jacques Rousseau, and Jacques Guibert, proposed that local militias be mobilized in the event of war. They envisaged defensive warfare; the revolutionaries in France transformed militias into an offensive weapon. There was in any case a strong element of continuity in the emergence of people's war at the end of the eighteenth century.[16] The French revolutionaries not only made use of older ideas but also had a recent example. In combination with the regular Continental Army, the American revolutionaries had used the traditional British institution of militias in their fight for independence. In fact, people's war first took place in North America.[17] It bespoke the well-advanced state of worldwide communications that this concept of warfare quickly spread across the Atlantic Ocean. For this reason, among others, Robert R. Palmer was justified decades ago in speaking of an "Atlantic Revolution."[18]

Caution is due, however, in analyzing the revolutionary significance of the French Wars. In many respects, they do not constituted a break with the past. Nonetheless, their dynamics were innovative. After 1792, warfare became more extensive, rapid, and ruthless. Huge armies swept across Europe, taking new ideas with them, smashing long-established traditions, and transforming the continent.

---

14 See Russel. F. Weigley, *The Age of Battles: The Quest for Decisive Warfare from Breitenfeld to Waterloo* (Bloomington, Indiana, 1991), 279–539.
15 Ronald G. Asch, *The Thirty Years War: The Holy Roman Empire and Europe, 1618–1648* (London, 1997), 185.
16 Samuel Krähenbühl, "'Volkskrieg' oder 'Krieg der Staatsbürger'? Das Militärsystem der Französischen Revolution" (Lizentiatsarbeit [master's thesis] University of Bern, 2004).
17 Russell F. Weigley, *History of the United States Army*, 2nd ed. (Bloomington, Indiana, 1984), 29–95.
18 Robert R. Palmer, "The World Revolution in the West, 1763–1801," *Political Science Quarterly* 69 (1954): 1–14; Palmer, "La 'Revolution atlantique' – Vingts ans après," in *Die Französische Revolution: Zufälliges oder notwendiges Ereignis?* ed. Eberhart Schmitt and Rolf Reichard, 3 vols. (Munich, 1983), 1:89–104.

Tim Blanning has attributed the origins of war in 1792, as well as the French declaration of war on Britain in 1793, largely to the domestic politics of Revolutionary France.[19] One of these domestic issues originated overseas. Revolutionary ideas had spread to France's most valuable colonial possession, Saint-Domingue (Haiti), and provoked a revolutionary uprising there in 1791. The eventual outcome was the liberation of slaves and independence for Saint-Domingue in 1804. These events represented the most successful slave uprising in history.[20] Its effects were immediately felt on French markets, because French consumers depended on imports of sugar, rum, and coffee from Saint-Domingue. The collapse of sugar imports was particularly hard and resulted in protest riots in France, which put an already-weakened regime under intense pressure. In these circumstances, the agitation of warmongers in the Legislative Assembly, such as the Girondist deputy Jacques-Pierre Brissot, had wide resonance.[21] From the beginning, therefore, the French Wars were not just European affairs, and revolution overseas helped bring them about.

Britain first fought these wars on a global scale. Although confronting the French and their allies overseas was a long British strategic tradition, once Britain went to war with France in 1793 there was a long debate within the government about how to proceed. The minister of war, Henry Dundas, favored a strategy of conquering the enemy's overseas colonies. He explained his reasoning:

I am sure that country [France] will always be the natural enemy of this, and if it is in our power we ought to use our best exertions to annihilate their naval power. . . . We are a small spot in the Ocean without territorial consequences, and our own power and dignity as well as the safety of Europe, rests [*sic*] on our being the paramount commercial and naval power of the world.[22]

Dundas met with strong opposition, however. Supported by Edmund Burke, William Windham, the secretary at war, called for counterrevolutionary intervention in France. The foreign secretary, Lord Grenville, pleaded instead for conventional coalition warfare against France on the European continent. William Pitt, who was a fine administrator of domestic

---

19 T. C. W. Blanning, *The Origins of the French Revolutionary Wars* (London, 1986).
20 Herbert Schottelius, "Die politische Emanzipation von Haiti und Santo Domingo," in *Die Unabhängigkeitsbewegungen in Lateinamerika, 1788–1826*, ed. Inge Buisson and Herbert Schottelius (Stuttgart, 1980), 133–50; Günther Fuchs and Hans Henseke, *Das französische Kolonialreich* (Berlin, 1988), 49–56; David Geggus, "The Haitian Revolution," in *Caribbean Slave Society and Economy*, ed. Hilary Beckles and Verene Shepherd (London, 1991), 402–19.
21 Albert Soboul, *Die Grosse Französische Revolution*, 2 vols. (Frankfurt, 1973), 1:203–11.
22 Dundas to Earl Spencer, Aug. 1799, cited in Piers Mackesy, *War without Victory: The Downfall of Pitt, 1799–1802* (Oxford, 1984), 13.

politics but a poor strategist, was unable to decide among the alternatives. As a result, Britain pursued all these strategies at the same time – with dire consequences.[23] Until 1795, all British interventions on the European continent ended in dismal failure.

Against this background, Dundas seized the opportunity to intervene in the uprising in Saint-Domingue, hoping in the process to conquer most of the French islands in the Caribbean. He even hoped to invade Spanish America. Instead, as a result of disease and logistical failures, the British forces in the region met with a disaster that cost thousands of lives. By 1798, they had been forced to withdraw from most positions, including Saint-Domingue, and Dundas had to postpone his ambitious plans.[24] Nevertheless, there were successes elsewhere. In 1795, British forces occupied the Dutch colonies on the Cape of Good Hope and Ceylon, helping to secure access to India. Dundas's more far-reaching plans to invade Manila in the Spanish Philippines were not implemented, however.

By 1798, Britain had added a global dimension to the European war, albeit with limited results. Dundas's strategy was directed primarily against Britain's colonial rivals, but it was rooted in tradition. The revolution in France provided only the occasion, which Dundas hoped to exploit for imperial ends. The revolutionaries in France were in no position to strike overseas. In fact, they inadvertently aided Dundas's plans by occupying the Netherlands and forcing Spain to become their ally, thus providing the British with an opportunity to attack the colonial possessions of additional rivals. The resulting campaigns represented, however, a continuation of conventional colonial warfare. They did not yet constitute a world war.

In 1798, developments took a new turn. In the spring, the Directory in Paris, acting again on domestic political calculations, allowed General Bonaparte to invade Egypt with a large force. For the first time since the beginning of the revolutionary wars, an important country overseas that was not the possession of a European power came under attack. This development triggered the War of the Second Coalition, as Austria, Russia, and Britain joined forces against France. In his capacity as caliph, Sultan Selim III, the official ruler of Egypt, declared jihad on the French. The Ottoman Empire was the first non-European major power to enter the

---

23 J. Steven Watson, *The Reign of George III, 1760–1815* (Oxford, 1960), 363; Edward Ingram, *Commitment to Empire: Prophecies of the Great Game in Asia, 1797–1800* (Oxford, 1981), 21–114; Ian R. Christie, *Wars and Revolution: Britain, 1760–1815* (London, 1982), 216–20; Peter Jupp, *Lord Grenville, 1759–1834* (Oxford, 1985), 152–5.

24 Michael Wagner, "Zwischen Kolonialexpansion und gegenrevolutionärer Solidarität: Die englische Intervention auf Saint-Domingue, 1793–1798," in *Britische Übersee-Expansion und britisches Empire vor 1840,* ed. Jürgen Osterhammel (Bochum, 1987), 120–53.

contest. By 1812, it had fought first the French and then Britain and Russia.
It also waged war within its own territories, against Serbs, Romanians, and
Arabs. In 1805, Egypt was lost to the Albanian usurper Mehmet Ali. On the
Arabian Peninsula, Ottoman forces fought an uprising among the Wahhabi.
The fighting here, in which Mehmet Ali's forces also intervened, began in
1804 and lasted until 1814. The French invasion of Egypt thus inflamed
large parts of the Middle East.[25]

It is unlikely that Napoleon intended to march his army from Egypt to
India. The feat would have been extremely difficult, if not impossible.[26] As
late as February 1799, he wrote a letter to Tipu Sultan, the ruler of the
southern Indian state of Mysore and a traditional ally of France. Napoleon
made vague promises and asked for information about the situation on the
subcontinent.[27] The news of the French occupation of Egypt was itself
enough to sound alarms in London. Not least among those worried about
the safety of British possessions on the subcontinent was Dundas, who was
also the minister responsible for British India. He and the directors of the
East India Company had agreed to keep India out of the war so as to
not disturb business and to keep the company's finances in good order.
To the surprise and disappointment of the directors, Dundas now changed
course. Additional troops were sent to India, and the new governor-general,
Richard Wellesley, was authorized to wage preemptive war against Mysore
to deprive the French of an ally.

But Wellesley had his own plans. Even before the French set out for
Egypt, he had intended to expand British power at the expense of the
Indian states. In the end, he believed, Britain should be paramount in India.
He hoped military success in India would make him a hero and launch
him on a brilliant political career on his return home. His lieutenants, who
dreamed of prize money and promotions, were eager to carry out these
plans. War against Mysore was therefore welcome to most of the men on
the spot. Once they disposed of Tipu Sultan in 1799, they craved more.
They brought the nizam of Hyderabad under British control the same
year. Foreign mercenaries in the nizam's army, most of whom were French,
were expelled. Over the next few years, in defiance of orders from London,

25 Ingram, *Commitment*, 195–387; Alan Palmer, *The Decline and Fall of the Ottoman Empire* (London, 1992), 61–93.
26 Blanning, *Origins*, 57–8; Jean Tulard, *Napoleon: The Myth of the Saviour* (London, 1984), 66–7; S. P. Sen, *The French in India, 1763–1816* (Calcutta, 1958), 554–9.
27 Bonaparte to Tipu Sultan, Pluvoise 7, 7, in *The Despatches, Minutes, and Correspondence of the Marquess Wellesley, K.G., During his Administration in India*, ed. Montgomery Martin, 5 vols. (London, 1836–7), 1:686–7.

Wellesley waged war against the Maratha Confederation, the last of the great Indian powers. He justified the action by citing the French threat, although he himself did not believe in it. When he left India in 1805, two-thirds of the subcontinent was under direct or indirect British rule. Because central India remained destabilized, the men on the spot demanded a continuation of the policy of conquest, but for the time being they were frustrated. Under orders from London, Lord Minto, who became governor-general in 1807, concentrated instead on operations outside of India. In December 1810, British forces occupied the Île de France (later called Mauritius), the French stronghold in the Indian Ocean. Less than a year later, Java fell to the British.[28] Only in 1817, however, did the war of expansion resume on the Indian mainland.[29]

For much of the time, the French played the role of welcome pretext for the self-interested intrigues of British men on the spot. Otherwise, French troops never made it to India during the world war. Their failure was not due to a lack of effort. While in Egypt, Napoleon was realistic enough not to attempt an invasion of India, but once he took power in Paris and his armies swept across Europe, he began to consider an assault on British possessions in South Asia. In 1801–2, during the negotiations for the Treaty of Amiens, he tried in vain to cajole the British delegation into giving him a foothold in India.[30] A few years later, in 1807, when his armies were fighting in Poland, he concluded the Convention of Finckenstein with Shah Fath Ali of Persia. With this accord, France gained a Persian base for an attack on India in return for a Franco-Persian alliance against Russia. Napoleon even sent General Gardane with a large staff to Tehran to prepare the operation. By the end of 1807, however, Napoleon had entered negotiations with Russia in Tilsit. The resulting peace with Russia in Europe was more important to the French emperor than Asian adventures. Hence, Napoleon abandoned the Persian idea; in return, the czar allowed Napoleon to dismember Prussia. Persia, which had fought Russia in the Caucasus since 1801, lost all French support. The shah later turned to Britain but received scant help. In the Peace of Gulistan (1813), Persia was forced to cede all its provinces north of the Caucasus as well as control over the Caspian Sea to Russia.[31] Napoleon

---

28 Sen, *French*, 591–6; Shiri Ram Bakshi, *British Diplomacy and Administration in India, 1807–1813* (New Delhi, 1971), 67–82.
29 Stig Förster, *Die mächtigen Diener der East India Company: Ursachen und Hintergründe der britischen Expansionspolitik in Südasien, 1793–1819* (Stuttgart, 1992).
30 Ibid., 197–8.
31 Henri Prentout, *L'Ile de France sous Decaen, 1803–1810: Essay sur la politique coloniale du premier empire et la rivalité de la France et L'Angleterre dans les Indes Orientales* (Paris, 1901), 455–8; Muriel Atkin, *Russia and Iran, 1780–1828* (Minneapolis, 1980), 91–144.

dreamed on about an invasion of India, but events in Europe, especially the uprising in Spain, prevented an attempt to realize the idea.[32]

Napoleon's design in India was to attack the East India Company and thereby disrupt the financial markets in London, which would in turn force Britain out of the European war. The French emperor failed, but the British men on the spot achieved part of his design on their own. The wars that their expansionist policy required brought the company close to financial ruin. As a result, Parliament deprived the company of its trade monopoly with India in 1813, initiating the demise of Britain's most famous and successful chartered company. The City was unperturbed, for India was by now open to free trade. Even as the war continued, free-trade imperialism thus gained momentum. It was to dominate Britain's overseas policy in the nineteenth century.[33]

Free-trade imperialism was also the leitmotif of British ambitions in Spanish America. British merchants had been complaining since the 1730s of the rigid conditions for trade in that part of the world. Policy makers began to consider wresting South America from Spain. Conquest of these vast lands was out of the question, however, so British plans focused on supporting independence movements in the hope of gaining economic advantages from states that were newly independent of Spain.[34] When Spain became an ally of France in 1796, some British leaders saw a chance to put these plans into practice. Dundas in particular pushed for action. In 1799, he made his ideas about the future of the Spanish Empire clear to Wellesley:

> The conduct of Spain to this country deserves no favor from us, and the exhausted state in which it appears with regard to every sentiment and feeling that ought to operate on a great monarchy, leaves little ground to hope that it can long maintain its rank among the nations of Europe; and the natural conclusion from all this which at first presents itself is that Great Britain ought to make use of the means in its hands to overturn the power of Spain in South America.[35]

Dundas added that if Britain did not act soon, the United States would take advantage of the situation in South America.[36] On July 22, 1800,

---

32 Förster, *Diener*, 272–5.

33 John Gallagher and Ronald Robinson, "The Imperialism of Free Trade," *Economic History Review* 6 (1953): 1–15. See also Förster, *Diener*, 244–7, 259–69.

34 Vincent T. Harlow, *The Founding of the Second British Empire, 1763–1793*, 2 vols. (London, 1952–64), 2:615–48.

35 Dundas to the Earl of Mornington (Richard Wellesley), Oct. 10, 1799, in *Two Views of British India: The Private Correspondence of Mr. Dundas and Lord Wellesley, 1798–1801*, ed. Edward Ingram (Bath, 1969), 188–9.

36 Ibid. See also Förster, *Diener*, 193–5.

he presented a long memorandum to Pitt's cabinet, proposing combined attacks on Cuba and the South American mainland.[37] As usual, Grenville and Windham opposed Dundas's overseas strategy, while Pitt remained undecided. Consequently, nothing came of Dundas's proposal.[38]

New plans emerged several years later. In 1804, the London merchant William Jacob submitted wide-ranging proposals for British intervention in Spanish America. Support for independence movements, he argued, would eventually lead to the creation of new states that would be open to trade. The agrarian economies of South America would provide lucrative markets for British industrial exports and would provide Britain with cheap raw materials and foodstuffs. In 1808, Sir Arthur Wellesley, the future Duke of Wellington and the younger brother of the former governor-general of India, submitted a similar memorandum to the government. By that time, British authorities had begun to lend cautious support to insurgents in Spanish America such as Francesco Miranda. In the summer of 1806, Admiral Sir Home Popham took matters into his own hands and occupied Buenos Aires without authorization, disrupting a careful strategy that had been worked out in London. Although Popham was recalled and court-martialed, London did send reinforcements, turning the Plata region into a theater of the world war. The British invasion of the Plata region quickly failed, however, in the face of fierce local resistance.[39]

The Spanish uprising against French rule, which began in spring of 1808, altered the situation fundamentally. Spain became an ally, so British ambitions in South America had to be postponed.[40] After the war, however, when Spain was too weak to hold its American empire, Britain did establish an informal empire in South America.

In 1812, fighting began in North America. As in the case of Argentina, economic considerations were the pretext for war. Popham had boasted that his action would open South America to British trade. In the United States, there was considerable enmity against the British, whose countermeasures against Napoleon's continental blockade had allegedly disrupted U.S. trade with Europe – as if the French had not shared responsibility for the disruptions. In fact, shipping interests in the United States opposed war against Britain, but warmongers in Congress, who hoped to complete the liberation of North America from British rule, carried the day. When war broke out, it was fought along the Great Lakes and the eastern coast of the United States; fighting later took place outside of New Orleans. British

37 British Library, London, Melville Papers, Add. Mss. 40 102.
38 Mackesy, *War*, 125–7; Harlow, *Founding*, 2:653–4.
39 Watson, *Reign*, 453–4.   40 Harlow, *Founding*, 2:654–61.

forces burned government buildings in Washington, D.C., and besieged Baltimore. There was much destruction along the Great Lakes. American volunteers and militiamen fought against not only British soldiers, but also volunteers from British America, some of whom came from the French-speaking population. Under Tecumseh, the Shawnee tried for the last time to defend their existence as a people by joining the British, but they met disaster.[41]

The War of 1812, as the Americans came to call it, was but a sideshow to the global conflict, which was reaching its culmination at this time. Although it was a branch of a larger war, the War of 1812 had its own origins and agenda. In this respect, however, it was typical of the network of wars that raged around the globe. The war between Britain and the United States, the war between Persia and Russia, the wars of the Ottoman Empire – each had its own causes but was closely connected to the larger contest among Europe's great powers. The British wars against the Indian powers were triggered by the French invasion of Egypt and then developed their own logic. British intrigues in Spanish America were possible only in the context of general war. At the center stood the great war in Europe, which lasted for more than two decades and implicated all the great powers, as well as many lesser ones. This was a world war.

Early in 1797, a French frigate was battered by British ships of the line in the Arabian Sea. It was by luck alone that the French managed to escape to the Mysorean harbor of Mangalore. The French captain, a man named Ripaud, introduced himself there as an official ambassador who had been sent from the Île de France to offer Tipu Sultan an alliance. Tipu was delighted and greeted Ripaud with honors in the capital, Srirangapatna. He even allowed the French to set up a Jacobin Club, of which Tipu himself became a member. Henceforth, the French in Mysore addressed him as Citoyen Tipou. In the club's founding declaration, members vowed to fight all tyrants – with the exception of Tipu Sultan.

Ripaud was an impostor. There were no French troops on the Île de France waiting to land in India in support of Mysore. Tipu, however, could not resist the temptation to dispatch an emissary to that island to present plans for common military operations to expel the British from India. The surprised French governor Malartic had nothing to offer. He therefore issued a public call for volunteers. He also hoped the get rid of unruly elements on his troubled islands, where slaveholding planters were on the verge of civil war with Jacobin sympathizers. Only ninety-nine men

---

41 Watson, *Reign*, 475–80; Fregosi, *Dreams*, 327–42; J. Mackay Hitsman, *The Incredible War of 1812: A Military History* (Toronto, 1965); Donald R. Hickey, *The War of 1812: A Forgotten Conflict* (Urbana, Illinois, 1989).

answered the call and were shipped to Mangalore. British spies got hold of Malartic's call for volunteers and sent a copy to Calcutta. Wellesley, who had just arrived there, had a pretext to take action against Tipu. News of the French invasion of Egypt provided another. Tipu's embassy to the Île de France and Napoleon's landing in Egypt had nothing to do with each other, but it was easy for Wellesley to allege a connection. Tipu had made a fatal mistake.[42]

The ruler of Mysore harbored no sympathy for the ideas of the French Revolution. Citoyen Tipou probably did not even understand what they were about. Nor was there a social basis for revolution in Mysore. Not even the bitterest among Tipu's British enemies argued that the despot of Srirangapatna had turned into a Jacobin. Tipu merely followed the traditional wisdom of regarding the enemy of his enemy as his friend. He was, in fact, desperate to find allies. In 1792, he had lost a war against the British, the nizam, and the Maratha. The defeat not only had cost him half his territory but also badly weakened the once-mighty Mysore. In this situation, only French support could save him. He was thus ready to play his part in the ongoing global conflict, but his strategy had little to do with the French Revolution. Wellesley and Dundas favored a preemptive strike against Mysore for a variety of reasons, but halting the spread of revolutionary principles on the subcontinent was not among them.

The story of Tipu's end was typical of the pattern of the world war on the periphery. Several indigenous powers were drawn into the conflict. As their rulers tried desperately to find allies, they looked to the Europeans. But few people in Asia or Africa were at all interested in European ideological debates, let alone revolution. When Shah Fath Ali of Persia sought an alliance with Napoleon, he merely sought a strong partner to fend off the Russians. He was just as prepared to ask the British for help. The Mamelukes of Egypt and the Ottoman Empire fought for their survival. In this struggle, it mattered little whether the enemy was a revolutionary power like France or a conservative one like Russia. European attitudes toward the Orient were straightforward, too. The French did not intend to export revolutionary ideas to India, Persia, or even Egypt. Napoleon sought little more than glory, power, and wealth.[43] In this respect, the differences between French and British expansionists were minor. The British did not fight for ideological reasons. Plans to modernize India along the European

---

42 Rosalie Prince Gates, "Tipu Sultan of Mysore and the Revolutionary Governments of France, 1793–1799," *Bengal, Past and Present* 83 (1964): 7–19; Mohibbul Hasan Khan, *History of Tipu Sultan*, 2nd ed. (Calcutta, 1971), 287–90; Förster, *Diener*, 137–44.
43 See Tulard, *Myth*, 65–73.

model developed only later.[44] In their military dimensions, too, the wars in Asia and Africa remained conventional. There was little innovation in the British forces in Asia. Military reforms in the Indian armies followed European models of the eighteenth century. Only the French army in Egypt had revolutionary roots. But as a general proposition, there was no people's war in Africa or Asia.[45]

This proposition did not hold in the Western world. In Europe, the new armies of the French Revolution and Napoleon brought new ideas and reforms wherever they went. "In the beginning was Napoleon," as Thomas Nipperdey declares at the opening of his history of nineteenth-century Germany.[46] The French Wars changed the face of Europe. The independence movement in Spanish America, too, was influenced by the ideas of the French Revolution, as well as by the example of the American Revolution.[47] The War of 1812 in North America was, in some respects, an attempt to complete the victory of that revolution. People's war and revolution thus played important roles in the Western Hemisphere, but they were not the factor that brought about the first world war in history.

Britain was the strongest power overseas. It therefore played a key role in the globalization of warfare. A world war would in fact have been unthinkable without British participation, but the British did not fight revolutionary wars. Apart from the ill-fated strategy of Windham and Burke, they did not even fight ideologically motivated antirevolutionary wars. British economic interests overseas were admittedly connected to another revolution that was under way at the time, namely the industrial revolution, which intensified the drive for free trade and increased British demand for raw materials such as cotton.[48] British aspirations in Spanish America were guided in part by these new economic considerations. But this fact explains neither British expansionist policy in India nor the war against the United States. Moreover, industrialists were not yet leaders of the British economy. British "gentlemanly capitalism" was still in the hands of merchants and financiers – the old elites of the City – who shared power with landed interests.[49]

---

44 Eric Stokes, *The English Utilitarians and India* (Oxford, 1959).

45 Gayl D. Ness and William Stahl, "Western Imperialist Armies in Asia," *Comparative Studies in Society and History* 19 (1977): 2–29; Dirk H. A. Koff, "The End of an Ancien Regime. Colonial War in India, 1798–1818," in *Imperialism and War: Essays on Colonial Wars in Asia and Africa*, ed. J. A. de Moor and H. L. Wesseling (Leiden, 1989), 22–49.

46 Thomas Nipperdey, *Deutsche Geschichte 1800–1866: Bürgerwelt und starker Staat* (Munich, 1983), 11.

47 Inge Buisson, "Die Unabhängigkeitsbewegungen in Iberoamerika," in Buisson and Schottelius, *Unabhängigkeitsbewegungen*, 9–117.

48 Michael M. Edwards, *The Growth of the British Cotton Trade, 1780–1815* (Manchester, U.K., 1967).

49 J. Cain and A. G. Hopkins, *British Imperialism*, 2 vols. (London, 1993), 1:53–104.

In these political and economic circumstances, Britain conducted its war largely according to eighteenth-century traditions.

The fact that the French Wars turned into a world war was due not to revolutionary changes in warfare but to European expansion, which served as the catalyst for global war as most parts of the world became interconnected. Even under these circumstances, however, world war was not inevitable. Had the fighting in Europe ended in 1797 with the Peace of Campo Formio, France would have been left with a great victory on the Continent and Britain would have made scattered gains overseas – an outcome much like those of other major wars during the eighteenth century. The war continued beyond 1797, however, and reached new dimensions when the French invaded Egypt and introduced a momentum that could not be halted. The continuous expansion of the fighting itself provides the best explanation for why the French Wars evolved into a world war and could not end in compromise. Revolutionary and Napoleonic France could not compromise. Primarily for domestic reasons, the internal dynamic of French politics, war became an end in itself. This dynamic initiated war in 1792, prolonged it in 1798, and became the basis of Napoleon's rule. Moreover, revolutionary changes to state and society provided France with the power and resources to fight larger and longer wars than ever before. In this sense, revolutionary warfare did indeed produce the first world war.

Like the world wars of the twentieth century, this world war could end ultimately only in the complete defeat of the force that drove it. As total victory was the sole resolution of this calamity, it is not that surprising that all world wars in history tended toward total war.

6

"The Most Terrible World War"

Friedrich Gentz and the Lessons of Revolutionary War

GÜNTHER KRONENBITTER

To call the French Revolution a turning point in European history is to state the obvious. Those who experienced these years of profound, rapid, and unforeseen change in France were convinced that they were witnessing a radical break with the past. Observers at home and abroad, supporters and detractors of the Revolution alike, agreed that events in France represented a fundamental departure. When citizens seized the Bastille on July 14, 1789, the event instantly became a symbol of heroism and the power of the people. The *vainqueurs de la Bastille* were celebrated as champions of liberty, and bricks from the demolished fortress became coveted souvenirs. Popular accounts and images of the storming of Bastille portrayed the event as one of the defining moments of French and European history.[1]

Through the first half of the twentieth century, most historians regarded the French Revolution as a watershed in modern history. It is not hard to see why. The French Revolution provided a major stimulus to the development of modern political thought and political movements in Europe. There had been different models of political order and visions of progress in the Enlightenment, but the events in France forced the European public – the well-educated cultural and social elites who set the tone of public opinion – to side with either the revolutionaries or their opponents. Politics as drama – and the people, not the princes as main actors – drew the attention of Europe. The notion of a radical reshaping of the social and economic order took root. The division of the political spectrum into left and right originated in the revolutionary assemblies in Paris. Nineteenth-century liberals, democrats, and socialists in Europe identified with different stages

---

1 For the history and historiography of the French Revolution, see Pierre Nora, ed., *Les lieux de mémoire*, vol. 1, *La République* (Paris, 1986); François Furet and Mona Ozouf, eds., *Kritisches Wörterbuch der Französischen Revolution*, 2 vols. (Frankfurt, 1996); Annie Jourdan, *La Révolution, une exception française?* (Paris, 2004).

of the revolutionary process, while European conservatives saw themselves as the heirs to the Revolution's opponents.

Champions of the French Revolution saw the radical change of political and social structures as the implementation of Enlightenment philosophy. Those who abhorred revolutionary turmoil, by contrast, painted the standard-bearers of change as hypocrites. Talk about philosophical principles, critics of the Revolution charged, was intended to fool the public; under the cloak of high-minded programs lurked ambition, a thirst for power, and greed. Radical counterrevolutionary writers invoked conspiracy theories, too, to explain the breakdown of the ancien régime. But on both sides of the ideological divide, contemporaries agreed on a clear-cut distinction between the old and the new order in politics and society. And even when historians began to question these one-dimensional approaches, the proposition survived that the French Revolution represented a radical break with the past. There were few dissenting voices in the nineteenth century. One was Alexis de Tocqueville, who pointed out that the ancien régime had paved the way to administrative centralization and the destruction of the traditional political and social order.

Tocqueville's point has been adopted by historians who see the rise of the state, with its enormous accumulation of power, as the most striking historical process in modern Europe.[2] From this perspective, the French Revolution looks more like an important episode in a long process than like the beginning of a new historical era. In addition, historians have questioned the modernizing effects of the Revolution on societies and economies. The impact of the French Revolution on religion has been reconsidered in recent decades as well, as historians have focused on the vitality of religious life in the nineteenth century. Had it not been for the new interest in political culture and *lieux de mémoire*, the French revolutionaries' – and counterrevolutionaries' – self-perceptions as actors in a great historical drama might have been dismissed as false consciousness. But the so-called cultural turn in historical studies has made historians aware again of the importance of the French Revolution as a generator of meaning. Nevertheless, the older view that the Revolution was a solid "block" and a radical break with the past has not survived.[3]

2 See, e.g., Wolfgang Reinhard, *Die Geschichte der Staatsgewalt: Eine vergleichende Verfassungsgeschichte Europas von den Anfängen bis zur Gegenwart* (Munich, 1999).
3 See, e.g., Gary Kates, ed., *The French Revolution: Recent Debates and New Controversies*, 2nd ed. (New York, 2006); Lynn Hunt, *Politics, Culture, and Class in the French Revolution* (Berkeley, California, 1986).

Violence had a central role in the revolutionary drama. Ritualized violence and public acts of vengeance were basic features of revolutionary uprisings, civil war, and the Terror. The dynamics of revolution were also closely interconnected with war. Military historians have emphasized the radical innovation brought about by the Revolution. As Clausewitz put it, war "again became the affair of the people as a whole, and took on an entirely different character, or rather approached its true character, its absolute perfection" in the course of the Revolution.[4] A stable European peace proved to be unattainable for more than two decades, until the Congress of Vienna laid the foundations for a new international order. Paul W. Schroeder has called this transformation of European international politics a revolution, because "more real change occurred in the arena of international politics than can be demonstrated in other areas of politics and society from other more celebrated revolutions."[5] In the end, Schroeder attributes the increased effectiveness of peaceful conflict management to a learning process among those who were in charge of foreign policy. I apply Schroeder's assumption here to a case study of conservatism and international politics in early-nineteenth-century Europe. The focus will be on Friedrich Gentz, a political publicist who was Metternich's adviser and ghostwriter.

Gentz was born in 1762.[6] His father was a high-ranking Prussian civil servant and a member of Berlin's Huguenot elite. As a student at the Joachimsthalsche Gymnasium in Berlin and the University of Königsberg, Gentz was brought up in the intellectual climate of the German Enlightenment. He became acquainted with Immanuel Kant in Königsberg and was regarded as a follower of Kant when he returned to Berlin. Gentz joined the Prussian civil service and married a woman from another Huguenot family, the sister of the architect Friedrich Gilly. Like many officials in state and ecclesiastical administration, Gentz had literary ambitions. Eventually, he began to publish in the most prestigious journal in northern Germany, the *Berlinische Monatshefte*. His first articles echoed the standard lines of Enlightenment discourse.[7] Natural rights and the social contract were the central themes of

---

4 Carl von Clausewitz, *On War*, ed. and trans. Michael Howard and Peter Paret (Princeton, New Jersey, 1976), 593.
5 Paul W. Schroeder, *The Transformation of European Politics, 1763–1848* (Oxford, 1994), 8.
6 For Gentz's biography, see Paul R. Sweet, *Friedrich von Gentz: Defender of the Old Order* (reprint; Westport, Connecticut, 1970); Golo Mann, *Friedrich von Gentz: Geschichte eines europäischen Staatsmannes* (Zurich, 1947); Jakob Baxa, *Friedrich von Gentz* (Vienna, 1965).
7 For Gentz's publications, memoranda, letters, and diaries, see Graf Anton Prokesch-Osten, ed., *Aus dem Nachlasse Friedrichs von Gentz*, 2 vols. (Vienna, 1867–8); Clemens von Klinkowström, ed., *Aus der alten Registratur der Staatskanzlei: Briefe politischen Inhalts von und an Friedrich von Gentz aus den Jahren 1799–1827* (Vienna, 1870); Comte [Anton] Prokesch-Osten, ed., *Dépêches inédites du Chevalier de*

his first article, which was published in April 1791. In it, he defended the French Revolution against the criticism of Justus Möser, a prominent conservative thinker in Germany. For Möser, who combined anti-absolutist and evolutionist views with a harsh antirationalism, reform and tradition were complementary. The French National Assembly's much-lauded decision to abolish the remnants of feudalism looked to him like a massive attack on property rights, and he condemned the new French constitution and the Declaration of the Rights of Man.[8] Gentz had no patience for Möser's arguments. In a letter from December 1790, he called the French Revolution "the first practical triumph of philosophy. . . . It is our hope and comfort in the face of the multitude of old evils under which mankind sighs."[9] Natural rights theory was his intellectual weapon of choice when it came to defending the Revolution.[10]

Gentz was hardly alone in holding a positive view of the French Revolution in 1790–1. Many members of his generation and sociocultural milieu cheered the revolutionaries. As events progressed, however, their enthusiasm for the Revolution gave way to hostility. Gentz was at the forefront of this shift in opinion. It did take the most dramatic steps in the escalation of the revolutionary process – the execution of Louis XVI and the Terror – to change his mind. Influenced by his friend Wilhelm von Humboldt, Gentz opportunistically switched sides in 1791 and aligned himself with the Prussian government's antirevolutionary stance. When he first read Edmund Burke's *Reflections on the Revolution in France* (1790), he had disapproved of the antirevolutionary thrust of Burke's rhetoric. Soon, however, he began to admire Burke's polemic, although he could not yet endorse Burke's praise of tradition as the backbone of orderly progress. The publication of Gentz's translation of Burke's *Reflections* in 1793 made the author and translator household names in Germany. Conservatives in the nineteenth century were reared on Burke, and Gentz's version of the text made the *Reflections*

Gentz aux hospodars de Valachie: Pour servir à l'histoire de la politique européenne (1813 à 1828), 3 vols. (Paris, 1876–7); Graf Anton Prokesch-Osten, ed., *Zur Geschichte der orientalischen Frage: Briefe aus dem Nachlasse Friedrichs von Gentz 1823–1829* (Vienna, 1877); Graf Anton Prokesch-Osten, ed., *Aus dem Nachlasse des Grafen Prokesch-Osten, k.k. österreichischer Botschafter und Feldzeugmeister. Briefwechsel mit Herrn von Gentz und Fürsten Metternich*, 2 vols. (Vienna, 1881); Richard Fürst Metternich-Winneburg, ed., *Oesterreichs Teilnahme an den Befreiungskriegen: Ein Beitrag zur Geschichte der Jahre 1813 bis 1815 nach Aufzeichnungen von Friedrich von Gentz nebst einem Anhang, "Briefwechsel zwischen den Fürsten Schwarzenberg und Metternich"* (Vienna, 1887); Friedrich Gentz, *Gesammelte Schriften*, 12 vols., ed. Günther Kronenbitter (Hildesheim, 1997–2004).

8 Karl L. Welker, *Rechtsgeschichte als Rechtspolitik: Justus Möser als Jurist und Staatsmann*, 2 vols. (Osnabrück, 1996), 1:364–423.
9 Gentz to Garve, Dec. 5, 1790, in Gentz, *Gesammelte Schriften*, vol. 11, bk. 1:178–9.
10 Ibid., 7:7–33.

popular in Germany. Gentz adapted Burke's text to the intellectual habits and aesthetic expectations of the German public, employing a style of writing that had been honed during the German Enlightenment to convey antirevolutionary zeal.[11]

Even after he broke with Kant and his circle in 1795, Gentz did not abandon natural rights theory. To the dismay of Kant's disciples, Gentz used the language of natural rights to discredit pro-revolutionary arguments that were rooted in Kantian discourse. As an intellectual renegade, he tried to beat the friends of Revolutionary France with their own intellectual weapons and to prove that armed resistance to revolutionary oppression, as in the Vendée, was justified. Kant's followers were appalled and accused him of opportunism. They rejected Gentz's claim that he remained true to the premises of natural rights theory, and they did not appreciate the way in which Gentz integrated the Scottish school's concepts of evolutionary progress into his political theory. According to Gentz, natural rights theory stipulated only that political order be compatible with the rule of law; it could not provide the basis for judging existing constitutions. An analysis of existing political structures or processes had to take into account other realms of knowledge, too. Where natural rights theory was inadequate, empiricism was necessary. The Scottish Enlightenment and German popular philosophy offered an analysis of the dynamics of historical development distinct from the historicism that prevailed in other conservative quarters.[12] Later, in the first two decades of the nineteenth century, Gentz came to support Adam Müller and Friedrich Schlegel, two high-profile representatives of political romanticism. In the end, though, he never entirely endorsed their arguments, and he retained a remarkable preference for rationalist and – when it came to public and international law – positivistic thinking.[13]

Nevertheless, Gentz's empirical and historical analyses of political order prepared him to reflect subsequently on international affairs. In the age of Napoleon, the French Revolution seemed less relevant to this obsessive observer of European affairs. In 1804, Gentz wrote to a friend that "to hinder the demise of Europe's independence as a result of this awful

---

11 Frieda Braune, *Edmund Burke in Deutschland. Ein Beitrag zur Geschichte historisch-politischen Denkens* (Heidelberg, 1917); Hermann Klenner, "Burke, Gentz und die Geburt des bürgerlichen Konservatismus," in *Edmund Burke. Friedrich Gentz. Über die Französische Revolution. Betrachtungen und Abhandlungen*, ed. Hermann Klenner (Berlin, 1991), 697–759.

12 Günther Kronenbitter, "Gegengift: Friedrich Gentz und die Französische Revolution," in *Von 'Obscuranten' und 'Eudämonisten': Gegenaufklärerische, konservative und antirevolutionäre Publizisten im späten 18. Jahrhundert*, ed. Christoph Weiß (St. Ingbert, 1997), 579–608.

13 Günther Kronenbitter, *Wort und Macht. Friedrich Gentz als politischer Schriftsteller* (Berlin, 1994), 82–94.

revolution – that is for now and forever my final task."[14] In the *Historisches Journal*, a review that he edited and filled almost single-handedly in 1799–1800, he analyzed French expansionism and questions of war and peace. In one article, he wrote of Kant's treatise on perpetual peace in a condescending way and ignored Kant's arguments. He discussed but rejected other models of international order as well. Among these was Johann Gottlieb Fichte's concept of autarky as a way to foster peace. According to Gentz, a state's isolation destroyed the basis of its economic progress. In his understanding, the rise of civilization depended on certain human traits. Curiosity and competitiveness drove human beings to take risks and to work hard. In the end, ingenuity and cultural refinement were impossible without restless strife. Therefore, he reasoned, human aggression and progress were related. Because war and violent upheaval could become destructive, the role of politics was to contain violence and make it compatible with economic and cultural progress.[15]

Between the lines, however, Gentz advocated war as a way to restore Europe's balance of power. Prussia had left the first coalition in 1795. Gentz's message in the *Historisches Journal* was not lost on those who supported Prussian neutrality. He called for a coalition to destroy Napoleon's hegemony, but his motives were not above question. This mid-level Prussian official spent money lavishly. Usually in debt, he relied on advances on his publications and on financial help from anti-Napoleonic circles, including British agents. After 1799, he ran afoul of the Prussian government. He got into trouble when he attacked French expansionism in 1801 because the government in Berlin wanted to keep Prussia out of the war. Prussia's neutrality and Gentz's partisanship did not sit well together.[16] When the Austrians asked him to become the mouthpiece for Vienna's anti-Napoleonic policy, Gentz left Berlin. In Vienna, however, his advice and skills as a writer were in demand only in times of confrontation with Napoleon. He was thus delighted when war broke out between Austria and France in 1805, and he tied to persuade the Prussian government to join the crusade against Napoleon. His efforts were in vain, however. After Napoleon's victories at Ulm and Austerlitz, French troops occupied Vienna. Gentz escaped to Bohemia.

In his Bohemian "exile," Gentz soon became involved again in secret diplomacy and intrigues. As Austria's new foreign minister, Johann Graf Stadion, prepared for another war with France, Gentz entered the fray. He

---

14 Gentz to Brinckmann, Dec. 18, 1804, in Gentz, *Gesammelte Schriften*, vol. 11, bk. 2:251.
15 Ibid., 5:632–43; 7:185–6.
16 Kronenbitter, *Wort und Macht*, 258–64, 284–9, 304–9.

supported attempts to form a circle of anti-Napoleonic intellectuals in Dresden. Adam Müller, Heinrich von Kleist, Ernst von Pfuel, and a few others, most of them connected to the romantic movement, undertook a propaganda campaign in support of the Austrian war effort. Stadion styled war against Napoleon as a campaign to free the Germans from the French yoke. Given the multinational character of the Habsburg monarchy, this strategy looked risky, but Stadion persisted. The Austrian army was too weak to beat the French, so appealing to German nationalism looked like a way to rally Napoleon's German allies to the Austrian cause. In connection with this effort, Gentz wrote the official Austrian war manifesto in 1809. But neither this proclamation nor the Dresdeners' attempts at agitation made a difference. The propaganda campaign produced little more than scattered volunteer corps for the war effort. In the Tyrolean rebellion, the only uprising of any significance in 1809, old-fashioned loyalties and local traditions, not German nationalism, motivated the insurgents.

This lesson was not lost on Gentz; his flirtation with German nationalism was over.[17] Several months after the war of 1809, he joined with Stadion's successor, Clemens Graf Metternich.[18] Metternich, who had previously been ambassador to Paris, wanted a prolonged period of peace with Napoleon. Eventually, Gentz put his anti-Napoleonic fervor aside and accepted Metternich's view of international politics. Another defeat by the French would spell the end of the Habsburg monarchy. The best strategy for the time being, then, would be to seek tolerable relations with Napoleon. By 1812, Gentz had become Metternich's confidant, adviser, and ghostwriter. He watched Austria's foreign policy closely and contributed to Metternich's diplomacy, writing memoranda and drafting notes and newspaper articles.

Metternich demonstrated his talent for diplomacy when he won Napoleon's consent to Austria's neutrality in 1813. Without flouting a treaty commitment, the Habsburg monarchy then broke with France. It switched sides but made sure that most of the German states and princes would not be punished for collaborating with Napoleon. The coalition of

---

17 For the circle in Dresden and the war of 1809, see Otto W. Johnston, *Der deutsche Nationalmythos: Ursprung eines politischen Programms* (Stuttgart, 1990), 77–104; Gerhard Schulz, "Von der Verfassung der Deutschen: Kleist und die literarische Patriotismus nach 1806," *Kleist-Jahrbuch* (1993): 56–74; Klaus Müller-Saget, "Heinrich von Kleist: 'Über die Rettung von Österreich'. Eine Wiederentdeckung," *Kleist-Jahrbuch* (1994): 3–48; Helmut Rumpler, *Österreichische Geschichte 1804–1914: Eine Chance für Mitteleuropa. Bürgerliche Emanzipation und Staatsverfall in der Habsburgermonarchie* (Vienna, 1997), 75–104; James Allen Vann, "Habsburg Policy and the Austrian War of 1809," *Central European History* 7 (1974): 291–310.

18 For Metternich's biography and papers, see Heinrich Ritter von Srbik, *Metternich: Der Staatsmann und der Mensch*, 3 vols. (Munich, 1954–7); Richard Fürst Metternich-Winneburg, ed., *Aus Metternich's nachgelassenen Papieren*, 8 vols. (Vienna, 1880–4).

1813–14 was not about revenge but about the reestablishment of a stable international order. Metternich did more to bring about this outcome than anyone but Castlereagh.

In 1814, Gentz was appointed to the prestigious and financially rewarding position of secretary of the congress in Vienna, and he was to hold the same position at the subsequent congresses in Aix-la-Chapelle, Troppau, Laibach, and Verona. The years of congress diplomacy marked the height of Gentz's career. In his letters, he sometimes ridiculed congress diplomacy as a blend of vanity fair and boring negotiations, but he appreciated the close cooperation among the great powers. Therefore, like Metternich, he lamented the demise of consensus in the early the 1820s. The Eastern Question strained Austria's relations with Russia, and Austrian intervention in Italy complicated cooperation with Britain. The international order established in 1814–15 put Austria in a pivotal position, and Metternich, assisted by Gentz, tried to preserve it for as long as possible. The Quadruple Alliance, the Holy Alliance, dominance in Italy, and a strong position within the German confederation strengthened the Habsburg monarchy's place in European politics. It is little wonder that Metternich and Gentz defended the principles of great-power politics established in those years.[19]

Nationalism in Italy and Germany threatened Austria's position more than independence movements in the Ottoman Empire, the Iberian Peninsula, or Latin America did. The territorial integrity of the Habsburg monarchy was at stake in both Italy and Germany. In Italy, Austria intervened militarily when it seemed necessary; the German Confederation made armed repression both impossible and unnecessary. The confederation functioned as an instrument to keep liberal and nationalist groups in check. However, intervention in Italy and support for reaction in Germany, both undertaken in defense of the political order in Europe, tarnished the reputation of the German Confederation and the international system in the long run. By identifying a specific form of conservatism with order and stability in international affairs, Austrian policy put the Vienna system at risk. The outbreak of revolution in Paris and Brussels in 1830, just two years before Gentz's death, was an indication that maintaining peace in Europe was becoming incompatible with preserving the political status quo. Metternich's antirevolutionary zeal tempted him to propose armed intervention, but he acquiesced in the new realities once he became aware of Austria's isolation.

19 Rumpler, *Österreichische Geschichte 1804–1914*, 105–214; Paul W. Schroeder, *Metternich's Diplomacy at Its Zenith, 1820–1823* (Austin, Texas, 1962); Srbik, *Metternich*, 1:556–695; Günther Kronenbitter, "Kutschbock oder Trittbrett: Österreichs Platz im Staatensystem Europas von 1815 bis 1848," in *Europäische Dimensionen österreichischer Geschichte*, ed. Ernst Bruckmüller (Vienna, 2002), 106–16.

Instead of stabilizing Europe, he realized, intervention might lead to war. When Metternich shied away from interventionist policies, he paid tribute to the most important lesson that he learned from his experience with Napoleon. War among the great powers had to be avoided at almost all cost.

Austria had less to win and much more to lose than any other great power from a return to the international politics of the eighteenth century. The Habsburg monarchy could ill afford – literally – another great war. With nationalism a rising force in European politics, the multiethnic empire could hardly gain from expansion, and Austria was no longer in a position to stand alone in an international crisis. Ever loyal to his master, Gentz supported Metternich in his policies to maintain the status quo. He shared Metternich's view that international politics was too complicated for the uninitiated. He considered natural rights theory inadequate for judging international affairs. He believed that a sound assessment of high politics required expertise in the unwritten rules of diplomacy as well as a wealth of information, much of it confidential. Traditions and treaties were more important than abstract principles.[20] Gentz's elitist notion of statecraft reflected his rejection of idealistic approaches to politics in general and international relations in particular. He believed that liberal university professors and political publicists were ignorant of international relations. Even writers who served Austria's propaganda efforts struck him as idealistic and unworldly.

He found political romanticism useful in the fight against nationalist and liberal ideas, but when Müller and Schlegel called for a revival of the *res publica christiana* as an alternative to the struggle for power among nation states, neither he nor Metternich could agree. Both believed that the Catholic Church was to serve the interests of the state, not the other way around. The experience of revolution had discredited the secularization pursued by Emperor Joseph II. Gentz regarded an attack on the church as an assault on the stability of state and society. Anticlericalism was widespread among those who challenged the established post-Vienna system in Italy. In Germany, the liberal-nationalist academic groups praised Luther and the Reformation, which prompted Gentz, a Protestant, to sympathize to a degree with the fervent Catholicism of converts like Müller and Schlegel. He and Metternich insisted, however, that political decisions not be based on theocratic concepts of order. Neither man took serious the religious rhetoric with which the Holy Alliance's treaty of 1815 was imbued. They wanted only to appeal to the czar's proclivity for religious talk. Gentz and, to a greater degree, Metternich were thinking in eighteenth-century categories

20 Gentz, *Gesammelte Schriften*, 3:2–3.

and a rationalist discourse of politics. Their conservatism was preromantic, and it focused on the modern state, not on notions of a *res publica christiana* or a *societas civilis*.[21]

At first glance, Gentz's perspective on international relations continued to be dominated by prerevolutionary categories even after 1815. How did he assimilate the lessons of revolutionary war? To answer this question, it is necessary to examine his analysis of the revolutionary wars. With no knowledge of military topics, he neglected organizational, operational, and strategic issues in favor of the political context of war. But his analysis revealed an understanding of the changes that the Revolution brought to French military forces. By the standards of eighteenth-century great-power politics, the Revolution undermined the basis of France's position in international affairs. Strong leadership was impossible amid the turmoil; the prestige of the ruling dynasty was shattered; the financial and administrative order collapsed; and the military was shaken by the purge of the officer corps and the breakdown of discipline in the ranks. Little wonder that the cabinets of the great powers ceased to respect French military might and feared only the spread of revolutionary ideas. When war broke out in 1792, the governments in Austria and Prussia cracked down on supporters of the French Revolution. They were then taken by surprise when their own military campaign in France failed.

Gentz grasped early the new realities of power politics. He realized that the revolutionary regime in France could draw on almost unlimited financial and manpower resources, at least in the short run. The revolutionaries could disregard the property rights of the old privileged classes. Seizing the property of emigrants and the Catholic Church provided the government in Paris with enormous revenues for the war effort. More important, the country's new rulers did not scruple to ruin the monetary system. The levée en masse and, later, general conscription ensured that France did not lack soldiers. But Gentz also recognized that there was more to the French power than money and troops. The patriotic enthusiasm of the soldiers provided the armies with a fighting spirit unmatched in the armies of the coalition. In his study of the origins and characteristics of the war against the French Revolution, which was first published in 1801, Gentz located three

---

21 Jakob Baxa, *Adam Müllers Lebenszeugnisse*, 2 vols. (Munich, 1966), 1:1186, 2:389–95; Gentz, *Gesammelte Schriften*, vol. 11, bk. /4:410; Prokesch-Osten, *Aus dem Nachlasse Friedrichs von Gentz*, 1:289–301; Metternich-Winneburg, *Aus Metternich's nachgelassenen Papieren*, 1:1–272; Panajotis Kondylis, *Konservativismus: Geschichtlicher Gehalt und Untergang* (Stuttgart, 1986), 16; Günther Kronenbitter, "Friedrich von Gentz und Metternich," in *Konservativismus in Österreich. Strömungen, Ideen, Personen und Vereinigungen von den Anfängen bis heute*, ed. Robert Rill and Ulrich E. Zellenberg (Graz, 1999), 71–87; Srbik, *Metternich*, 1:321–414.

sources for this enthusiasm. At the beginning of the war, soldiers had been motivated by their attachment to revolutionary ideals. Then the defense of the French Republic, and finally the love of glory and heroism boosted the troops' morale.

In an age of economic, social, and political disorder, the army attracted talent and sheltered ambitious officers from the Terror. Under the Directory, the military became independent of civilian control and eventually seized power. Enthusiasm, vigorous leadership, and ruthlessness were, in Gentz's view, its defining characteristics. Thanks to vast financial resources and an almost unlimited reservoir of soldiers, the French could exploit a totally new concept of warfare. Aggressive strategies and sweeping offensive operations on an unprecedented scale ensured French victories. Without the Revolution, Gentz told his readers, this military innovation would not have been possible.[22]

Gentz understood the competitive advantages that the French government enjoyed. But the French needed more than a military revolution to conquer most of Europe. First of all, the cabinets of the great powers failed to recognize that the war against Revolutionary France was a struggle of "armed opinions."[23] Instead of coordinating their propaganda to the war effort, the allies "forgot about the revolution."[24] The coalition forces were inferior in numbers, underfinanced, and led by officers whose careers were based on seniority rather than merit. Hobbled by these shortcomings, they could not practice the new forms of warfare. More important was the lack of agreement among the coalition partners. Gentz was convinced that the lack of military and diplomatic cooperation was due to the way the coalition had been formed. One by one, the powers had joined the fray out of necessity. Because the coalition's members were insufficiently committed to a common cause, traditional rivalries and differing agendas plagued its war efforts. The only solution, Gentz believed, was an offensive campaign.[25]

This belief became Gentz's mantra. Offensive war against France was justified; unanimity and commitment to the common cause were essential to the success of coalition warfare. His hopes for skillful statecraft from the European cabinets were dashed, however, in 1805–6 and again in 1809. In the introductory chapter to his *Fragments on the Balance of Power in Europe*, which appeared in the aftermath of Austerlitz, Gentz harangued Germany's weak-willed political elites. Because the princes and

---

22 Gentz, *Gesammelte Schriften*, 1:183–278.   23 Ibid., 286.
24 Ibid.
25 Ibid., 278–333. For Gentz and Clausewitz, see Kronenbitter, *Wort und Macht*, 317–18.

their advisers could not form a coalition to free Germany and Europe from Napoleon's tyranny, the German people would have to take the initiative in liberating their country of their country.[26] This appeal to the people remained an isolated episode, however. Gentz trusted governments more than the people. When the introduction to the *Fragments* was republished together with a text by the writer August von Kotzebue in an anti-French tract in 1813, it was part of a propaganda campaign launched by the Russians on behalf of a new coalition against Napoleon. Prussia had already switched sides, but the princes in the Confederation of the Rhine still honored their treaty obligations to Napoleon. In Austria, which had been allied to France since 1810, Metternich was embarking on a cautious policy of disengagement. A popular crusade against Napoleon was no longer a part of this policy.[27]

In Gentz's view, international politics belonged in the hands of the ruling elites alone. He made this view clear in 1817, when students and professors celebrated Luther and the Wars of Liberation at the Wartburg. They claimed that, without the volunteers of 1813, it would have been impossible to free Germany from the yoke of Napoleon. Gentz disagreed. He argued that Napoleon could have been overthrown "with regular troops alone, without any volunteers, without arming the people." Without political guidance from the monarchs and the cabinets of Europe and without the courage of regular troops, all the volunteers and militias of Europe could not have prevailed against Napoleon.[28] "Peoples, youth, and volunteers contributed hardly anything," he wrote. "The princes, ministers, and standing armies did all the great and glorious work themselves, especially the wondrous unity among the courts, which had been secretly prepared well in advance."[29] Gentz's criticism of the nationalist interpretation of the Wars of Liberation was calculated to tarnish his opponents' reputations, but he was also convinced that wise statecraft had in fact played the decisive part in the liberation of Europe. The politics of coalition warfare in 1813–14 and the peace settlement of 1814–15 demonstrated the importance of consensus and cooperation among the powers. To promote stability and peace in Europe, diplomacy had to disregard nationalism and observe the principles of international politics.[30]

---

26 Gentz, *Gesammelte Schriften*, 4:xvi–liv.   27 Kronenbitter, *Wort und Macht*, 266–8.
28 Gentz, *Gesammelte Schriften*, vol. 8, bk. /3:43–4.
29 Cited in Brendan Simms, *The Struggle for Mastery in Germany, 1779–1850* (London, 1998), 121.
30 For Gentz's defence of the peace treaty with France in 1815, see *Gesammelte Schriften*, vol. 8, bk. /2:412–14; Jost Dülffer, "Joseph Görres und Friedrich Gentz – Modelle der Friedenssicherung in Deutschland seit der Französischen Revolution," in *Deutschland in Europa. Kontinuität und Bruch*, ed. Jost Dülffer, Bernd Martin, and Günter Wollstein (Frankfurt, 1990), 52–72.

Gentz addressed questions of constitutional change when he first became interested in international affairs in the late 1790s. As he shifted his focus, he drew arguments and metaphors from this earlier work. His defense of interventionist policies was a case in point. In 1801, he justified the coalition's war against France as an act of political self-defense. He invoked an analogy between civil society and the international system. Private ownership did not allow for the unrestricted use of property; the state had the right and obligation to interfere with property rights as soon as the security and well-being of others were at stake. International law was similarly governed by a set of restrictions on sovereignty. To be sure, the differences between the realms of law and politics did not escape Gentz's attention. In international affairs, there was no arbiter to settle disputes and enforce a settlement. In the absence of a legislator, the only foundations of international law were, according to Gentz, treaties among sovereign states. But economic, cultural, and political relations among the European states had become so broadly encompassing and so important to the welfare of all states that major changes in one country inevitably affected others. Even in the absence of general principles to justify intervention, common sense offered guidance. As soon as a government began to destroy the foundations of economic and social order, intervention was appropriate.[31]

As in his writings on constitutional matters, Gentz interwove strands of several philosophical and political discourses in his reflections on international affairs. His views on international law and cultural and economic progress were linked to his analysis of international relations. An eclectic approach made it easier for him to adjust his arguments to his political preferences. On occasion, it was difficult to criticize the diplomacy of the late eighteenth century without getting into trouble. In 1801, he published a treatise on Europe's political situation before and after the French Revolution. These remarks represented a refutation of *De l'état de la France à la fin de l'an VIII* by A. M. Blanc de la Nautte, Count d'Hauterive, who had claimed that the rise of Russia and Prussia to great-power status on the continent and British dominance overseas had undermined the international system established in 1648. He thus justified the expansion of France as a way to redress those imbalances. In attempting to refute Hauterive's argument, Gentz had to address the partitions of Poland, spectacular examples of brutal expansionism in eighteenth-century Europe. At the risk of having his book confiscated, he denounced the policies of Russia, Austria, and Prussia as

31 Ibid., 1:16–23.

acts of violence and abuses of diplomacy.[32] Five years later, he repeated his verdict.[33]

As he reviewed the high politics of the eighteenth century, Gentz was struck by the dilemma of international relations theory. The balance of power was central to both theory and practice. It lent legitimacy to blatant expansionism; together with the concept of compensation, it encouraged perceptions that made ruthless power politics and endless strife more likely. Instead of stability, balance-of-power politics fostered instability. These observations provoked criticism from several quarters. A number of writers, including Kant and Fichte, pleaded for a confederation of European states. Gentz did not believe that perpetual peace could ever be more than an illusion; he even questioned its desirability. Without war, he argued, it might be harder to channel human aggression into a form of violence that could be contained by rules and regulations.[34] The revolutionaries had aimed for an alliance of nations but instead brought about the "most terrible world war."[35] The only way to restore peace and stability, Gentz wrote in 1800, was to accept the reality that the international order could not be enforced like laws within a state. He thus offered a tentative vindication of balance-of-power politics, but he also called on European statesmen to reconcile the principles of domestic and international politics. The rule of law and the search for peaceful resolution of international conflicts should become the norm. This process would take time, and developments like the French Revolution threatened to wreck it, but Gentz hoped for a better international order than that of prerevolutionary Europe.[36]

After the breakdown of international order in 1792 revealed the defects of eighteenth-century high politics, intellectuals and political leaders contemplated new ideas.[37] Some saw the geopolitical shifts caused by the Revolutionary and Napoleonic wars as starting points for further territorial consolidation – a conclusion that made sense in the context of balance-of-power thinking. British and Russian leaders pondered such an approach to a European settlement in 1804–5. Metternich and Gentz entertained

---

32 Ibid., 1:89, 133–4. For the difficulties he had to get his text past the censor, see Kronenbitter, *Wort und Macht*, 145–9.
33 Gentz, *Gesammelte Schriften*, 4:21.
34 Ibid., 5:668; Kronenbitter, *Wort und Macht*, 308–9.
35 Gentz, *Gesammelte Schriften*, 5:680.
36 Ibid., 5:648–55; Kronenbitter, *Wort und Macht*, 306–7.
37 Heinz Gollwitzer, *Europabild und Europagedanke. Beiträge zur deutschen Geistesgeschichte des 18. und 19. Jahrhunderts* (München, 1951), 119–217; Rudolf Vierhaus, "Überstaat und Staatenbund. Wirklichkeit und Ideen internationaler Ordnung im Zeitalter der Französischen Revolution und Napoleons," *Archiv für Kulturgeschichte* 43 (1961): 329–54.

similar thoughts in light of Napoleon's victories in 1805 and 1809.[38] The peace settlement of 1814–15 provided for the territorial consolidation of the German states, and it strengthened the Netherlands and Sardinia as counterweights to renewed French expansionism. At the same time, visions of a European union abounded. The Holy Alliance was one, but Gentz rejected the romanticism that underlay it. In his refutation of the Abbé de Pradt's *L'Europe après le Congrès d'Aix-la-Chapelle*, he claimed that the Holy Alliance rested on the signatories' moral commitment to uphold the international order. But he regarded the treaties of 1814–15 and the Quadruple Alliance of 1815 as the core of this order. It provided a system of protection against future aggressors, which was better geared than the international system of the eighteenth century to keeping the peace, particularly because it was marked by a new spirit of consensus and cooperation among the rulers.[39]

Gentz put forward this argument, although, as de Pradt had observed, Britain and Russia were far stronger than the other great powers and that this inequality was incompatible with the balance of power. Gentz conceded that power was distributed unequally in Europe, but he noted that there had always been dominant powers. This fact was the reason why the weaker states built coalitions. The superior position of Britain and Russia in the international system did not mean the loss of the other powers' independence. Because the anti-Napoleonic coalition had been transformed into an effective defense of the status quo and the independence of all European states, peace and stability enjoyed more reliable protection than it had before.[40] The European system of states worked because it relied on British and Russian self-restraint in European affairs, if not in other regions of the world.

Gentz's views on the European state system after 1815 lend credence to Schroeder's claim that the post-Vienna international order did not rest on eighteenth-century-style balance-of-power politics.[41] The disparities in power and security among the great powers did not wreck the international order. Schroeder has demonstrated that crisis management in Europe after 1814 was not shaped by a balance-of-power system, if that term implies a system "in which the power possessed and exercised by states within the system is checked and balanced by the power of others."[42] Schroeder's thesis

38 Gollwitzer, *Europabild*, 224–5; Kronenbitter, *Wort und Macht*, 272–3.
39 Gentz, *Gesammelte Schriften*, vol. 8, bk. /3:143–4.
40 Ibid., 95–6, 138–43.
41 Paul W. Schroeder, "Did the Vienna Settlement Rest on a Balance of Power?" in *Systems, Stability, and Statecraft: Essays on the International History of Modern Europe* (New York, 2004), 37–57.
42 Ibid., 38.

has not gone unchallenged, but it corresponds to contemporary perceptions, certainly to Gentz's.[43] Long before he wrote his critique of de Pradt's book, Gentz attacked false notions of balance of power. In the *Fragments on the Balance of Power in Europe*, he wrote:

What is usually termed a balance of power is that constitution that exists among neighboring states that are more or less connected with each other, by virtue of which none of them can violate the independence or the essential rights of another without effective resistance from some quarter and consequent danger to itself. Many misconceptions have arisen as a result of the similarity to physical objects upon which the term was based. It has been supposed that those who saw in the balance of power the basis of an association of states were aiming at the most complete equality, or equalization, of power possible, and were demanding that the various states of an area that is politically united should be most precisely measured, weighed and rounded off, one against the other, in respect of size, population, wealth, resources, etc.[44]

Given his conservative understanding of constitutional theory, Gentz lamented this distorted view of international relations. It was the result of

the same confusion of ideas to which, in the field of internal state relations, we owe all the frivolous and airy theories of *civil equality* and all the unsuccessful practical attempts to carry them out. All the citizens in every well-ordered state, and all the states in every well-ordered community of nations, should be equal in law or *equal before the law*, but by no means *equal in rights*. True equality, the only kind attainable by legitimate means, consists in both cases only in this, that the smallest as well as the greatest is assured of its right, and cannot be compelled or harmed by unlawful authority.[45]

Without an executive or judicial power, the international system could protect the weaker powers only by collective action against aggressors. In this analysis of international order, his concept of economic and cultural progress figured large:

An extensive social union was formed among the states in this part of the world, of which the essential and characteristic aim was the preservation and mutual guarantee of the well-won rights of each of its members. From the time when this noble purpose was recognized in all its clarity, there also gradually developed the vital and everlasting conditions on which its achievement depended. Men became aware that there were certain basic rules in the relationship between the strength of each individual part and the whole, without whose constant influence order

---

43 "Paul Schroeder's International System. Essays in Celebration of The Transformation of European Politics, 1763–1848," *International History Review* 16 (1994): 661–880; Peter Krüger and Paul W. Schroeder, eds., *The Transformation of European Politics, 1763–1848* (Münster, 2002).
44 Cited in Chris Brown, Terry Nardin, and Nicholas Rengger, eds., *International Relations in Political Thought: Texts from the Ancient Greeks to the First World War* (Cambridge, U.K., 2002), 307.
45 Ibid., 308.

could not be assured. . . . not *how much power* one or the other possesses; but only whether he possesses it in such a way and under such limitations that he cannot with impunity deprive one of the rest of its own power – this is the question that must be decided in order to pass judgment at any given moment on the relation between individual parts or on the general proficiency of the edifice.[46]

When Gentz wrote the *Fragments* in 1806, it required a leap of imagination to believe that such an international system might emerge in the foreseeable future. In 1814–15, however, the coalition powers began to show self-restraint. Schroeder is correct when he characterizes the Vienna settlement as "a legal and moral balance, an *équilibre des droits*."[47] "The Vienna equilibrium," he writes, "represented ideally a balance between what each state needed or claimed to need in order to fulfil its proper role and function within the European family and what that family as a whole considered necessary and proper. The redistribution was intended to produce a genuinely equal and fair balance in legal rights. Every state was to have its rights and territories recognized and sanctioned internationally."[48] This new concept of international order represented a break with the past, at least in Gentz's understanding. The legal and moral balance reinforced political stability and vice versa.[49]

Gentz was not an advocate of what used to be called realism. Although security concerns ranked high on his agenda and he adhered to the idea of counterweights, the experience of the Revolutionary and Napoleonic wars suggested that in a system of independent states, decision makers had to recognize the moral and legal conditions of peace and stability. A cautious conservative who sympathized with the Scottish school of national economy, Gentz never lost hope in the progress of civilization. Given a secure peace among the powers, the economic and cultural advance of Europe could proceed. However, the complexity of the international system required safeguards against the return of turmoil. The Concert of Europe reduced the destructive potential of balance-of-power politics: "The principle of balance [*équilibre*] or, for better saying, of counterweights formed by particular alliances, principle which had controlled, and too often also disturbed and bloodied Europe during three centuries, is succeeded by a principle of general union, joining together the totality of the States by

---

46 Ibid., 309–10. 47 Schroeder, *Vienna Settlement?* 49.
48 Ibid., 50.
49 Jost Dülffer, "Friedrich Gentz – Kampf gegen die Revolution und für das europäische Gleichgewicht," in *Kriegsbereitschaft und Friedensordnung in Deutschland 1800–1814*, ed. Jost Dülffer (Münster, 1995), 39–56; Gollwitzer, *Europabild*, 158–65, 230–2; Helmut Rumpler, "'Justitia Regnorum Fundamentum' (Friedrich Gentz und die Idee des Rechts in der internationalen Politik)," in *Polgárodás Közép-Európaban*, ed. Éva Somogyi (Budapest, 1991), 143–54.

a federative bond [*lien fédératif*], under the direction of the five principal Powers."[50]

Metternich and Gentz wanted to use the Concert of Europe to conservative ends. They saw domestic tranquillity and international stability as inseparable, and they favored intervention and the coordinated repression of liberal and nationalist movements. This design proved unsustainable in the long run. The antirevolutionary consensus among the great powers, the basis of the conservative Vienna system, did not survive the early 1820s, when British and Austrian assessments of international politics were drifting apart. But these disagreements did not bring about the demise of the international order that had been founded in 1814–15. Respect for the vital interests of all the European powers, a preference for peaceful crisis management, and a commitment to the survival of lesser powers survived in the cabinets of Europe, even though intervention in Belgium, France, and Poland threatened to push Europe into war. In his last articles, which were published in 1831, Gentz called for the peaceful coexistence of different constitutional systems in Europe. He realized that peace alone could stabilize the body politic. To avoid war was the most effective way to prevent revolution.[51] Gentz never forgot the lessons of revolutionary war. However, two decades after his death, in the era of Napoleon III and Bismarck, a new consensus emerged: war could prevent revolution.

---

50 Prokesch-Osten, *Dépêches inédites*, 1:354.
51 Gentz, *Gesammelte Schriften*, vol. 8, bk. 5:172–216; Prokesch-Osten, *Aus dem Nachlasse Friedrichs von Gentz*, 1:265; Kronenbitter, *Wort und Macht*, 199–203.

PART II

The Growing Dimensions of Battle

7

The Native American Way of War in the Age of Revolutions, 1754–1814

TIMOTHY J. SHANNON

The most famous lacrosse ball in history landed inside the gate of Fort Michilimackinac at noontime on June 2, 1763. Earlier that morning, a large number of Ojibwa and Sauk men had gathered on the cleared grounds outside of the fort's palisades to play the game, while their women visited with the post's traders and soldiers. The scene was so commonplace that the fort's commander, Captain George Etherington, and a fellow officer stood outside the open gate among other spectators enjoying the Indians' sport.

On the pretext of retrieving their errant ball, the Indian men rushed inside the fort. Arming themselves with hatchets and spears the women had hidden beneath their blankets, they quickly overpowered the fort's garrison of about forty soldiers. According to eyewitnesses, the Indians killed and scalped sixteen soldiers and executed five more later. They took everyone else in the fort prisoner, except for the French fur traders who lived there. One English trader, who survived the attack by hiding in the home of one of the Frenchmen, claimed to have seen the Indian warriors "drinking the blood" of their victims, "scooped up in the hollow of joined hands, and quaffed amid shouts of rage and victory."[1]

The attack on Fort Michilimackinac was part of a wider intercultural conflict known as Pontiac's War (1763–5), which was itself an episode in a sixty-year struggle by Eastern Woodland Indians in the Great Lakes region to resist European intrusions on their homelands. The so-called Sixty Years' War (1754–1814) involved many other military engagements of far greater consequence, but the story of the lacrosse ball at Fort Michilimackinac is retold so often because it encapsulates perfectly the stereotypical depiction of

---

1 Alexander Henry, *Travels and Adventures in Canada and the Indian Territories between the Years 1760 and 1776* (1809; Boston, 1901), 81. See also Gregory Evans Dowd, *War under Heaven: Pontiac, the Indian Nations, and the British Empire* (Baltimore, 2002), 126.

Indian warfare in early America.[2] The Ojibwa and Sauk warriors succeeded by springing a vicious trap on an enemy they had lulled into a false sense of security. Their ruse helped them overwhelm an unprepared garrison, and they terrorized the survivors by looting stores, taking scalps, and executing prisoners. This, in a nutshell, was the Indians' "skulking way of war," an indigenous version of *la petite guerre* that observed no conventional rules of European warfare; drew no distinction between soldier and civilian; and outlawed no acts of cruelty, mutilation, or cannibalism against prisoners.

By the time of the attack on Fort Michilimackinac, Europeans were already familiar with the skulking way of war, and they had adopted a variety of strategies and tactics for countering it. During the seventeenth century, colonists learned from hard experience to alter their conceptions, objectives, and methods of warfare when fighting Native Americans. Colonial forces engaged in their own irregular warfare, conducting scorched-earth campaigns against Indian towns, killing their inhabitants without regard to age or sex, and dispersing the survivors by selling them into slavery. The speed and effectiveness with which Europeans adapted to warfare in North America varied considerably from one place to the next, but regardless of location or circumstance, change in the colonists' military culture was an inescapable by-product of their encounter with Indians.[3]

The same, of course, held true on the other side of the cultural divide. Like their European counterparts, the Indians' traditional objectives and methods of warfare experienced profound stress in the crucible of colonization. European firearms and artillery necessitated changes in tactics, while other dimensions of contact with the newcomers – such as trade, disease exchange, and missionary work – challenged the social and cultural

---

2 For a brief introduction to the Sixty Years' War, see David Curtis Skaggs, "The Sixty Years' War for the Great Lakes, 1754–1814: An Overview," in *The Sixty Years' War for the Great Lakes, 1754–1814*, ed. David Curtis Skaggs and Larry L. Nelson (East Lansing, Michigan, 2001), 1–20. Other works that address the contest for the trans-Allegheny West from a native perspective include Richard White, *The Middle Ground: Indians, Empires, and Republics in the Great Lakes Region, 1650–1815* (Cambridge, U.K., 1991), and Gregory Evans Dowd, *A Spirited Resistance: The North American Indian Struggle for Unity, 1745–1815* (Baltimore, 1992). For other recent depictions of the lacrosse ball ruse at Fort Michilimackinac, see David Dixon, *Never Come to Peace Again: Pontiac's Uprising and the Fate of the British Empire in North America* (Norman, Oklahoma, 2005), 122–4; William R. Nester, *"Haughty Conquerors": Amherst and the Great Indian Uprising of 1763* (Westport, Connecticut, 2000), 96–7.

3 For studies of European warfare in Early America, see John Grenier, *The First Way of War: American War Making on the Frontier, 1607–1814* (Cambridge, U.K., 2005); Fred Anderson and Andrew Cayton, *Dominion of War: Empire and Liberty in North America, 1500–2000* (New York, 2005), 1–159; Armstrong Starkey, *European and Native American Warfare, 1675–1815* (Norman, Oklahoma, 1998); and Ian K. Steele, *Warpaths: Invasions of North America* (New York, 1994). For a more focused regional study that questions the degree to which colonists adapted their methods of warfare to New World realities, see Guy Chet, *Conquering the American Wilderness: The Triumph of European Warfare in the Colonial Northeast* (Amherst, Massachusetts, 2003).

assumptions behind Native American warfare. Military historians have long studied the impact Indians had on European warfare, but only within the last generation or so have they used ethnohistorical methods to ask what impact Europeans had on Indian warfare. Not surprisingly, they have found that Indians experienced a military revolution of their own during their long struggle to resist the European invasion of North America.[4]

Recognizing that Native Americans experienced a military revolution does not imply that they experienced it at the same time or in the same manner as Europeans, only that the cultural impact of the European-Indian encounter was a two-way street. This observation is important to bear in mind when examining the Indians' military experience during the age of revolutions. Although historians have found plenty of evidence of an eighteenth-century European military revolution associated with the creation and use of large standing armies, applying that same conclusion to Native Americans is problematic.[5] The Indians' Sixty Years' War did intertwine with several transatlantic conflicts that brought Indians into contact with Europe's emerging modern art of war. However, during the same period, Native Americans clung tenaciously to methods of warfare that had served them well in the past and that, for the most part, continued to do so. The skulking way of war, itself a product of the Indians' seventeenth-century military revolution, proved resistant to the challenges posed by the new style of warfare Europeans brought to North America after 1754. The Eastern Woodlands Indians' political fate may have been profoundly affected by the exportation of Europe's military revolution to North America, but their military culture was not.

THE INDIANS' MILITARY REVOLUTION: THE SKULKING WAY OF WAR

In 1609, Samuel de Champlain and two other Frenchmen from Quebec accompanied a party of about sixty Montagnais and Huron warriors traveling south from the St. Lawrence River into the region surrounding what is now called Lake Champlain. Champlain's Indian allies were entering the country of their traditional enemy, the five Iroquois nations (from east to

---

4 Colin G. Calloway, *New Worlds for All: Indians, Europeans, and the Remaking of Early America* (Baltimore, 1997), 92–114, and James Axtell, *The European and the Indian: Essays in the Ethnohistory of Colonial North America* (New York, 1981), 259–65.

5 European military historians debate the exact chronology and contours of the military revolution in early modern Europe, but they generally agree that the eighteenth century witnessed profound change in how Europeans made war. See the essays collected in Jeremy Black, ed., *European Warfare, 1453–1815* (New York, 1999), and Jeremy Black, ed., *War in the Early Modern World* (Boulder, Colorado, 1999). See also Roger Chickering's introduction to this volume. For a brief statement of these changes, see Starkey, *European and Native American Warfare*, 37–56.

west, the Mohawk, Oneida, Onondaga, Cayuga, and Seneca). Near the southern end of the lake, the members of Champlain's party found what they were looking for: a group of about two hundred Mohawks, prepared for war. The two sides greeted each other, confirmed their intentions to fight, and then spent the night in their respective camps, preparing for battle with songs and ceremonies. In the morning, the two sides marched on each other in massed formations, using war clubs, stone hatchets, and bows and arrows for weapons. Some wore body armor made from woven bark, reeds, and leather. Champlain and his fellow Frenchmen marched behind their Indian allies, hiding themselves and their loaded muskets from the Mohawks. When they were within firing range, the Hurons and Montagnais parted and Champlain discharged his musket directly into the enemy's ranks. Three of the Mohawk leaders fell, and the rest of the Mohawks panicked. After one of Champlain's companions discharged a second musket, the battle turned into a rout and the Mohawks fled the field.[6]

This brief encounter at the outset of the seventeenth century foreshadowed the impact European firearms would have on Native American ways of making war. Before their immersion in the transatlantic fur trade, Eastern Woodlands Indians made war with traditional weapons and for traditional reasons. War was a highly ritualized affair knit into the fabric of their culture. Along with diplomacy and trade, it offered a system for dealing with outsiders. It also served several important functions within the community, as a rite of passage and source of social distinction for young men and as a means of channeling potentially disruptive emotions and behaviors outside the community. As evidenced by Champlain's engagement with the Mohawk, Europeans and their weapons upset the equilibrium in this type of warfare. Firearms had an immediate impact, but other, more subtle changes were put in motion by the Indians' contact with Europeans. Over the course of the seventeenth century, these changes produced what Europeans called the skulking way of war, a collection of tactics and objectives they considered uniquely Native American for their bloodlust and treachery.[7]

At the time of European contact, warfare among Eastern Woodland Indians followed the cultural rules and precedents of what anthropologists call the mourning war complex. Within a native community, war was a means of dealing with feelings of grief and vengeance stirred by the

---

6 Steele, *Warpaths*, 64–5. On the ramifications of Champlain's encounter with Indian warfare, see Anderson and Cayton, *Dominion of War*, 1–53.

7 Francis Jennings, *The Invasion of America: Indians, Colonialism, and the Cant of Conquest* (Chapel Hill, North Carolina, 1975), 146–70, and Patrick M. Malone, *The Skulking Way of War: Technology and Tactics among the New England Indians* (Lanham, Maryland, 1991).

unexpected or violent death of one of its members. If such feelings could not be assuaged through other avenues of mourning, village elders and clan matrons deliberated on going to war. War chiefs recognized for their bravery and skill in battle organized war parties, and young male warriors joined them for any number of reasons: the goading of their kin, the pursuit of personal honor, a desire for plunder or vengeance. A successful war party brought back enemy captives to take the place of the deceased, as well as scalps and other war trophies taken by the warriors as individual marks of their prowess in battle. The fate of captives often depended on their sex and age. Young children and women of childbearing age were likely to be adopted into a family, raised up in the place of deceased kin. Adult male captives, in contrast, represented a threat to the internal security of the community. They were likely to be tortured, executed, and cannibalized in ritual death feasts that allowed for a communal venting of rage against the enemy. Ideally, a war party brought back numerous captives but few if any casualties of its own. It channeled the expression of destructive emotions and behaviors away from the community, while at the same time strengthening its solidarity through the communal adoption or execution of captives. When practiced alongside diplomacy, this type of warfare provided a means of ordering the community's relations with the outside world, dividing it into friends with whom to trade and enemies with whom to fight.[8]

European firearms changed the methods of warfare but not its overall role in Eastern Woodlands cultures. Those Indians who acquired muskets from European allies gained a decisive advantage in battle over those who did not. Although bows and arrows were more accurate and much quieter than muskets, they were not as lethal, nor did they convey the psychological advantage of the musket's noise and smoke. Trade with Europeans also brought other substitutes for traditional weapons – iron knives and hatchets in place of their stone and bone equivalents – that made the Indians' combat more deadly. Armor made from organic materials was of little use against such weapons, nor were the closely packed frontal assaults witnessed by Champlain. In keeping with the mourning war's objective of limited casualties, warriors employed surprise whenever possible, spread out when engaging the enemy, and retreated quickly if the tide of battle turned against them. The skulking way of war, described by many European commentators

---

8 For explanations of the mourning war complex, see Daniel K. Richter, "War and Culture: The Iroquois Experience," *William and Mary Quarterly*, 3rd ser., 40 (1983): 529–37, and José António Brandão, *"Your fyre shall burn no more": Iroquois Policy toward New France and Its Native Allies to 1701* (Lincoln, Nebraska, 1997), 31–44.

as a natural expression of the Indians' innate savagery, was in fact an adaptive response to the European-Indian encounter.[9]

Other factors related to European colonization contributed to this transformation. The staggering impact of Old World diseases on Indian communities increased the importance of the mourning war in replenishing native populations. Captives became an important source of demographic recovery for Indians ravaged by smallpox and other diseases.[10] Competition among Europeans for furs sparked an arms race among Native Americans that intensified their wars. Once the Dutch began supplying arms to the Iroquois at Fort Orange (modern Albany) in the 1620s, French traders began doing the same with their allies in the St. Lawrence Valley. Indians anxious to acquire furs to trade for arms and ammunition plundered one another's trading parties along the St. Lawrence and Great Lakes borderlands, contributing to a cycle of raid and reprisal that lasted throughout the seventeenth century. Catholic and Protestant missionaries expressed moral indignation at the methods of Indian warfare, especially the torture and cannibalization of captives, yet they encouraged their converts to war against religious enemies, native or colonial, in other regions. Some Christian Indians altered their treatment of captives according to the wishes of their spiritual mentors, but they retained their autonomy in deciding when to go to war and still used the occasion to acquire plunder and captives for adoption. Market forces introduced by Europeans also affected Indian warfare. Scalps, traditionally valued by warriors as personal marks of distinction, became commodities when colonial governments offered bounties on them. Likewise, a new incentive for taking captives emerged when colonial governments began paying ransoms for their return. Some Indians found profit in selling captives taken in intertribal conflicts to slave traders who supplied markets in the South and the Caribbean.[11]

French and English colonists in northeastern America responded in different ways to the skulking way of war. In seventeenth-century Canada, whenever the French sent large armies of conquest into Iroquois country, they found that their quarry simply abandoned their village sites and returned to fight another day. French militia and *troupes de la marine* fought much more effectively by adopting the methods of their Indian allies and joining them in surprise winter raids on frontier settlements in New York and New England. In the English colonies, a similar reliance on the methods

---

9 Jennings, *Invasion of America*, 160–8.   10 See Richter, "War and Culture," 537–51.
11 See Axtell, *European and the Indian*, 262–5; Ian K. Steele, *Betrayals: Fort William Henry and the "Massacre"* (New York, 1990), 14–15; and Alan Gallay, *The Indian Slave Trade: The Rise of the English Empire in the American South, 1670–1717* (New Haven, Connecticut, 2002), 288–314.

of irregular warfare emerged during the seventeenth century. Very few British soldiers were posted in North America before 1755, leaving colonial militias to fight hostile Indians. In New England, colonists used total war tactics in the Pequot War (1636–7) and King Philip's War (1675–6). During these conflicts, militias conducted search-and-destroy missions against Indian towns, destroying their crops and food stores, killing the enemy without regard to age or sex, and selling survivors into slavery.[12] As the Iroquois did when faced with invading French armies, Indians fighting the English learned to anticipate these tactics, and if faced with a large, well-armed force, temporarily withdrew into inaccessible forests and swamps.[13] Such defensive measures were another aspect of the skulking way of war, but like the adoption of European firearms, they did not fundamentally alter the cultural role warfare played in Indian society.

THE MODERN ART OF WAR IN NATIVE NORTH AMERICA

The face of American warfare changed forever when General Edward Braddock landed in Virginia with two regiments of British regulars in early 1755. Until that point, European armies had played a negligible role in the contest for empire in North America. In French Canada, royal officials relied most heavily on Indian allies, supplemented by militia and *troupes de la marine* commanded by colonial officers to defend the colony. The British colonies, more often at odds than at peace with neighboring Indians, relied almost exclusively on their militias. When European wars spilled over into northeastern America, they were characterized by raids and reprisals in the style of *petite guerre* carried out across frontier borderlands. Attempts by British colonial administrators to invade Canada with large intercolonial expeditionary forces failed miserably in 1690 and 1711, though it is worth noting that naval expeditions launched from New England against Port Royal (1690) and Louisbourg in Nova Scotia (1745) succeeded.[14]

Braddock's arrival changed the European approach to warfare in colonial America. He brought with him a European way of war hitherto unseen

---

12 For intercultural violence in New England's Indian wars, see Ronald Dale Karr, "'Why Should You Be So Ferocious?' The Violence of the Pequot War," *Journal of American History* 85 (1998): 876–909, and Jill Lepore, *The Name of War: King Philip's War and the Origins of American Identity* (New York, 1998), 71–96. For the broader evolution of European-Indian warfare in the era between 1609 and 1750, see Steele, *Warpaths*, 59–109, and John E. Ferling, *A Wilderness of Miseries: War and Warriors in Early America* (Westport, Connecticut, 1980), 29–54.
13 Wayne E. Lee, "Fortify, Fight, or Flee: Tuscarora and Cherokee Defensive Warfare and Military Culture Adaptation," *Journal of Military History* 68 (2004): 713–70.
14 See Steele, *Warpaths*, 142–5, 155–9.

in the colonies, one that employed thousands of regular troops, made use of military engineering on a grand scale to build roads and forts in the continent's interior, and required transoceanic naval support to maintain supplies and troop strength. This was the modern art of war as practiced in eighteenth-century Europe, inspired by Enlightenment principles of scientific rationality, bureaucratic specialization and efficiency, and aristocratic notions of honor and glory.[15] It was a war of forts and sieges, of uniformed soldiers in linear formations fighting far removed from civilian populations, of intricate rules and customs governing truces, parleys, and negotiated surrenders. It contrasted sharply with the hybrid European-Indian warfare that had defined intercultural conflicts in North America up to that time.

On July 9, 1755, these two methods of warfare clashed spectacularly on the banks of the Monongahela River in western Pennsylvania. Braddock's army of 2,200 men, lugging artillery but bereft of Indian auxiliaries, had cut a road through the forest to lay siege to Fort Duquesne, the French post on the Forks of the Ohio (modern Pittsburgh). A few miles from their objective, Braddock's advance column came under attack by a force of about 650 Indians and 250 Frenchmen. Although this engagement is often called an ambush, it is more properly described as a collision, as the French and Indians rushing from the fort met Braddock's troops earlier than anticipated. In the initial exchanges of musket fire, the British killed the commanding officer of the French and seemed on the verge of dispersing the enemy force. The Indians, however, outflanked the British troops, captured the high ground, and used the natural cover of the forest to their advantage. Braddock's officers attempted to mount a counterattack, but the withering fire from an unseen enemy decimated their ranks and led to a pell-mell retreat.[16]

Braddock's Defeat was the most devastating loss a European army ever suffered at the hands of Native Americans, and contemporaries (and historians ever since) judged it a triumph of the Indians' native methods of warfare over conventional European tactics. It contributed in a large part to the fearsome reputation Indian warriors earned among European soldiers during the Sixty Years' War. However, Indians were equally successful in using their traditional tactic of prudent withdrawal when dealing with regular troops, whether as allies or enemies. In this manner, they retained their

---

15 Starkey, *European and Native American Warfare*, 37–56, and Peter Wilson, "European Warfare, 1450–1815," in Black, *War in the Early Modern World*, 177–206.

16 Fred Anderson, *Crucible of War: The Seven Years' War and the Fate of Empire in British North America, 1754–1766* (New York, 2000), 97–107, and Leroy V. Eid, "'A Kind of Running Fight': Indian Battlefield Tactics in the Late Eighteenth Century," *Western Pennsylvania Historical Magazine* 71 (1988): 160–6.

autonomy in military affairs and proved remarkably resilient in the face of the modern art of war.

Indian military victories during the Sixty Years' War fell into two broad categories: small-scale raids on isolated frontier populations and surprise attacks on militia or regular troops. Both operated according to the same methods used during the colonial wars that predated 1754. During the Seven Years' War in North America (1754–60), a protracted period of frontier raiding occurred in western Virginia and Pennsylvania. The withdrawal of the remnants of Braddock's army to winter quarters in Philadelphia – in August! – left the mid-Atlantic frontier exposed to Delaware, Shawnee, and Seneca raiding parties outfitted at Fort Duquesne. The colonial governments of Pennsylvania and Virginia responded by building an arc of fortified posts stretching from the Susquehanna River to the Shenandoah Valley, but the garrisons were too dispersed and undermanned to be of much use against Indians and Frenchmen who moved quickly through the wilderness, unencumbered by supplies or artillery. These war parties excelled at *petite guerre*. They terrorized settlers by burning homesteads, stealing or destroying livestock, and leaving mutilated corpses in their wake. They interrupted communications between frontier posts and looted supply trains moving between them. During the three years following Braddock's Defeat, they took captives numbering in the hundreds, perhaps as many as two thousand, and caused a panic that led to the almost complete depopulation of backcountry communities.[17]

A similar pattern of frontier raiding occurred during subsequent conflicts associated with the Sixty Years' War. The backcountry communities of Pennsylvania and Virginia had only five years to repopulate before facing the same enemy during Pontiac's War. During the American Revolution (1775–83), the attacks shifted to the northern Susquehanna frontier of New York and Pennsylvania and Virginia's Kentucky settlements, while the Ohio Indian War (1789–1795) brought such raiding to pioneer settlements along the northern and southern banks of the Ohio River. By the time of the War of 1812 (1812–14), the theater of conflict had shifted to northwestern Ohio, Michigan, and Indiana, but the results were the same: panicked settlers, abandoned communities, and civilians carried into captivity. In each conflict, militias and regular troops garrisoned in frontier posts proved incapable of stopping Indian incursions.

---

17 Matthew C. Ward, *Breaking the Backcountry: The Seven Years' War in Virginia and Pennsylvania, 1754–1765* (Pittsburgh, 2003), 45–58. Ward argues that, during this period, the Indians' mutilation of corpses, scalp taking, and other tactics of "psychological warfare" represented a "new response to European contact" (55), but all such actions had precedents in earlier colonial wars.

Yet the methods of *petite guerre* failed in the long run to secure the Indians' homelands. With each war, the theater of conflict moved farther west, as did European pretensions to Indian territory. Regular armies presented several challenges that Native Americans simply could not overcome. Their supply of soldiers and fresh recruits seemed endless. Their warships and artillery provided a tactical advantage unmatched by anything in the Indians' arsenal, and although both sides relied on flintlock muskets as their most common firearm, the Indians lacked the ability to manufacture or repair these weapons or supply them with ammunition and gunpowder independently. Regular armies could also sustain themselves from one campaign season to the next by availing themselves of the resources of local populations. Thus, while Indian warriors may have enjoyed tactical advantages over regular troops in any given engagement, those same troops had long-term advantages in manpower and materiel in North America that the Indians could not match.

Of course, concluding that the Indians' method of warfare failed them during the Sixty Years' War assumes that Indian warriors held a single, unified political objective – stopping the tide of European settlement in their homelands – higher than any number of other cultural motivations they had for making war, such as the personal pursuit of distinction, revenge, plunder, or captives. In the case of these other objectives, *la petite guerre* continued to serve the purposes of individual warriors. It is also important to note that the march of European arms during this era was far from steady. Across the trans-Allegheny frontier, one step forward usually led to two steps back for the armies of Great Britain and then the United States. Over the course of the Sixty Years' War, a pattern emerged in which Indian military resistance forced British and American armies to reconquer territory they thought they had already won in a previous war. Pontiac's War was such a backlash to British pretensions after the fall of New France in 1760, as was the Ohio Indian War to American pretensions to the Ohio Country after the Revolution, as was the Black Hawk War (1832) an epilogue to the War of 1812.[18]

The other category of Indian military victories during the Sixty Years' War involved successful ambushes of enemy troops. At the Battle of Lake George, which occurred only two months after Braddock's Defeat, a combined force of Caughnawaga and other French-allied Indians, Canadian militia, and French regulars commanded by Jean-Armand, Baron de

---

18 For treatment of these conflicts from an Indian perspective, see R. Douglas Hurt, *The Indian Frontier, 1763–1846* (Albuquerque, 2002), 3–11, 103–36, 164–88.

Dieskau, surprised British-allied Mohawks and New England provincial troops marching on a military road. Their fire devastated the Mohawks and provincial ranks and sent the survivors in a panic-stricken flight back to their camp. Dieskau marred the success of this engagement by deciding to follow it up with a frontal assault on the camp, which was fortified with artillery and barricades. His Indian allies thought better of the plan and wisely headed home rather than face the British cannon.[19] Several years later, during Pontiac's War, a force of about three hundred Senecas ambushed and looted a supply convoy traveling the portage road around Niagara Falls; when eighty redcoats from Fort Niagara rushed to assist the convoy, they received the same treatment. It was the worst defeat the British regulars suffered during Pontiac's War.[20]

During the Revolutionary era, American troops proved to be just as slow as their British cousins in learning to defend themselves from Indian ambushes. At the Battle of Oriskany near modern Rome, New York, in August 1777, British-allied Seneca and Mohawk warriors surprised an army of one thousand patriot militiamen as they were marching west to relieve the besieged garrison at Fort Stanwix. In an exceptionally bloody fight, the patriots sustained more than five hundred killed, wounded, or captured.[21] The shock of Oriskany was merely prelude to the humiliation suffered by the United States fourteen years later during the Ohio Indian War. In fall 1791, General Arthur St. Clair led an army of more than two thousand men into western Ohio against the Miami and their allied nations, who had defeated a similar expedition commanded by General Josiah Harmar a year earlier. In a dawn raid on November 4, warriors led by the Shawnee war chief Blue Jacket overran St. Clair's poorly defended camp, picked off his officers and artillerymen with well-aimed fire, and terrorized the rank-and-file and camp followers in hand-to-hand combat. The army's order melted away almost immediately, and retreating survivors left more than six hundred dead and hundreds of wounded in the hands of the enemy. It was the single worst military defeat the United States suffered in its Indian wars.[22] During the War of 1812, Blue Jacket's successor in leading the Shawnee resistance, Tecumseh, successfully ambushed more than one hundred American troops with a force only one-fifth the size as they crossed a creek near Brownstown,

---

19 Steele, *Betrayals*, 28–56.   20 Dowd, *War under Heaven*, 137–8.
21 Barbara Graymont, *The Iroquois and the American Revolution* (Syracuse, New York, 1972), 130–8.
22 John Sugden, *Blue Jacket: Warrior of the Shawnees* (Lincoln, Nebraska, 2000), 99–108, 113–27. See also Wiley Sword, *President Washington's Indian War: The Struggle for the Old Northwest, 1790–1795* (Norman, Oklahoma, 1985), 101–16, 171–91, and R. Douglas Hurt, *The Ohio Frontier: Crucible of the Old Northwest, 1720–1830* (Bloomington, Indiana, 1996), 105–19.

Michigan. Although a minor victory when compared to Oriskany or
St. Clair's defeat, this engagement testified to the enduring effectiveness
of the skulking way of war among Eastern Woodland Indians.[23]

Successful ambushes that gave way to routs of regular troops tended to
overshadow other, more cautious victories Indians won in the Sixty Years'
War. If, as the old song claims, "the secret to a long life is knowing when it's
time to go," then the reason why it took European armies so long to wrestle
the trans-Allegheny West from Indian hands is obvious: sometimes Indians
chose to withdraw rather than fight, and in this manner, they avoided battles
that may have resulted in their annihilation. This strategy was so commonly
employed by Indians that it was a constant frustration to European commanders, whether they were allies or enemies. Dieskau's experience at Lake
George, when his Indian auxiliaries abandoned him rather than face British
cannon, was repeated at Fort Niagara in 1759. Iroquois warriors allied
with the British troops laying siege to the fort conducted their own truce
with French-allied Iroquois inside the fort and thus avoided spilling one
another's blood. In 1764, the British general Thomas Gage sent two coordinated expeditions into the Ohio Country under Colonels John Bradstreet
and Henry Bouquet to deal a decisive blow to the Shawnees, Delawares,
Senecas, and other nations involved in Pontiac's War. Neither of these
heavily armed forays brought Gage a meaningful victory because the Ohio
Indians refused to engage them and sued for peace instead. During the
Revolution, the Continental Army's only major campaign against Native
Americans, the Sullivan-Clinton expedition in 1779, missed its best chance
for a decisive engagement against the Iroquois when warriors abandoned
the field near Newtown, New York, after their planned ambush had been
discovered. For the balance of the campaign, the only Indians encountered by the Continentals were stragglers in deserted Cayuga and Seneca
villages.[24] While such retreats struck European officers as proof of the
Indians' cowardliness, they made perfect sense in a native military culture
that embraced *petite guerre* and avoided heavy casualties at all costs.

Over the course of the Sixty Years' War, European commanders of
North American armies learned that Indians made for dangerous enemies

---

23 For the Harmar and St. Clair defeats and the Battle of Brownstown, see R. David Edmunds, *Tecumseh
and the Quest for Indian Leadership* (New York, 1984), 173–5.
24 For Niagara, see Francis Jennings, *Empire of Fortune: Crowns, Colonies, and Tribes in the Seven Years War
in America* (New York, 1988), 414–19; for the Bradstreet and Bouquet expeditions, see Dowd, *War
under Heaven*, 153–68. For the Clinton-Sullivan expedition and the aborted Battle of Newtown, see
Joseph R. Fischer, *A Well-Executed Failure: The Sullivan Campaign against the Iroquois, July–September
1779* (Columbia, South Carolina, 1997), 86–101, and Graymont, *Iroquois in the American Revolution*,
192–222.

and fickle allies. Efforts to recruit Indians as auxiliaries for the regular armies that fought in the Seven Years' War, American Revolution, and War of 1812 inevitably led to disappointment for the civilian and military officers who undertook them, because they could not coerce Indian warriors in the same way as their own foot soldiers. Indians were notoriously impatient with the siege craft brought to America by Braddock and other European generals during the 1750s, nor could they fit aristocratic notions of the honors of war into their cultural framework for making war and peace. They abandoned the French cause in the Seven Years' War after General Louise-Joseph de Montcalm negotiated a surrender at Fort William Henry in 1757 without regard to their desire for captives, scalps, and plunder. The following year, the British general John Forbes could not keep allied Cherokees in the field because they tired of his slow, methodical progress through the forests of Pennsylvania toward Fort Duquesne.[25] The European soldiers who worked most effectively with Indian allies – the Canadian militia and *troupes de la marine* of the Seven Years' War, the loyalist rangers of the American Revolution, British General Isaac Brock of the Detroit campaign in 1812 – imitated and encouraged their small, highly mobile surprise raids and ambushes. Arguably, the military revolution that occurred in northeastern America between 1754 and 1814 resulted from the impact Native Americans had on the European way of war, rather than the other way around.[26] As one British officer wrote of his experience during the Seven Years' War: "The art of War is much changed and improved here ... by the end of the summer it will have undergone a total Revolution. .... Swords and sashes are degraded, and many have taken up the Hatchet and wear Tomahawks."[27]

THE POSSIBILITIES AND LIMITS OF NATIVE AMERICAN INNOVATION

On the morning of October 10, 1774, about three hundred warriors led by the Shawnee chief Cornstalk engaged an army of one thousand Virginia militiamen encamped near Point Pleasant (in modern West Virginia), where the Kanawha Creek empties into the Ohio River. The Virginians were part of a larger expeditionary force raised by the royal governor of Virginia, Lord Dunmore, to attack Shawnee towns in the Ohio Country in retaliation for raids they had conducted on the Virginia frontier. Cornstalk knew the Virginians were on their way and that they would soon join with an

---

25 Anderson, *Crucible of War*, 195–200, 267–8.
26 See Stephen Brumwell, *Redcoats: The British Soldier and War in the Americas, 1755–1763* (Cambridge, U.K., 2002), 162–226, and Grenier, *First Way of War*, 115–45.
27 Cited in Steele, *Warpaths*, 209.

even larger force Lord Dunmore was raising in Pittsburgh. He saw two options. The first, which he preferred, had worked ten years earlier when the armies of Bradstreet and Bouquet had marched into the Ohio Country: sue for peace in an effort to preserve the Shawnee towns from destruction. Cornstalk's warriors preferred the second option: strike the Virginians at Point Pleasant and hope that a decisive victory would cause Dunmore to abort the entire campaign before it proceeded any further.

Cornstalk conceded to the warriors and organized a predawn attack on the Virginians' camp. They lost the element of surprise when shots exchanged between some Indian scouts and hunters from the camp alerted the sleeping militiamen to the enemy's approach and allowed them the time necessary to take defensive positions. In the battle that followed, each side took cover along the riverbank and poured fire into the other. The Indians tried direct assaults on the Virginians' line, "often running up to the very muzzles of our guns," and Cornstalk and other chiefs rallied their warriors throughout the day by running along their lines and urging them to "lye close" and "shoot well." By nightfall, the Indians had run short of ammunition, and they withdrew under cover of darkness across the river. Militia officer William Fleming, wounded three times, wrote afterward, "Never did Indians stick closer to it, nor behave bolder" than on this day.[28] The Shawnees, now on the defensive, had no choice but to seek peace with Dunmore. He extracted from them in return the cession of all their land claims in Kentucky.

Lord Dunmore's War (1774) was a small chapter in the Sixty Years' War. Nevertheless, its only major engagement, the Battle of Point Pleasant, offers important lessons about how Indians adopted their military culture to the changing nature of North American warfare. Between 1774 and 1794, intercultural warfare was endemic on the "dark and bloody ground" of the trans-Allegheny frontier, and Indian society became more militarized.[29] Leaders emerged who challenged the power of traditional chiefs by uniting large numbers of warriors in intertribal confederacies to resist European aggression. War chiefs such as Pontiac, Cornstalk, Blue Jacket, and Tecumseh led a multigenerational pan-Indian movement in the Great Lakes region. Their innovations as military leaders included the recruitment of large intertribal forces, the use of siege tactics, and as witnessed at Point

---

28 Reuben Gold Thwaites and Louise Phelps Kellogg, eds., *Documentary History of Dunmore's War, 1774* (Madison, Wisconsin, 1905), 256, 264. See also Sugden, *Blue Jacket*, 43–5.
29 See Colin G. Calloway, "The Continuing Revolution in Indian Country," in *Native Americans and the Early Republic*, ed. Frederick E. Hoxie, Ronald Hoffman, and Peter J. Albert (Charlottesville, Virginia, 1999), 3–33.

Pleasant, frontal assaults on enemy positions. Unfortunately, their success was hindered by their continuing material dependence on European trade and the limitations of the skulking way of war in conducting protracted campaigns against well-supplied armies.

During the Seven Years' War, the Indians' experience with siege craft had been overwhelmingly negative. The intensive and dangerous labor that went into conducting a siege on a well-fortified position had no appeal to them, nor did they enjoy the waiting game that a successful siege entailed. Eighteenth-century armies were marching Petri dishes of communicable diseases, and any Indians who traveled with them risked infection. Worst of all, sieges between European armies that ended in negotiated surrenders and the granting of the honors of war to the vanquished – allowing them to retain their arms, baggage, and personal freedom – had no meaning in the context of Indian military culture, which regarded scalps, plunder, and captives as the just rewards of victory.[30]

Nevertheless, Indians from the Ohio and Great Lakes regions conducted sieges of their own against British posts during Pontiac's War. At the outbreak of hostilities in late spring 1763, a number of isolated British forts and blockhouses fell quickly to Indians using traditional tactics of ruse, surprise, and fire to force their surrender (Michilimackinac was among the initial casualties of the war). The three largest western posts – Forts Niagara, Pitt, and Detroit – presented a different problem. All were comparatively well armed, supplied, and fortified. In May, the Ottawa war chief Pontiac initiated a siege of Detroit that continued through the summer months and involved hundreds of Ottawas and other western Great Lakes Indians. Seneca warriors did the same at Niagara, as did Delaware and Shawnee warriors at Fort Pitt. For these sieges, the Indians imitated the European modern art of war in several ways. They played a prolonged waiting game, trying to starve out the soldiers and civilians inside the forts. They conducted periodic diplomatic councils and prisoner exchanges under a flag of truce. They tried to intercept supply convoys and reinforcements headed for the forts.

The Indians lacked two key elements of European siege craft, artillery and large watercraft. While they did build some defensive works outside of Detroit to protect themselves from the garrison's fire and sorties, they did not dig trenches to approach the fort because they had no artillery to protect their advance or to breach the fort's walls. Likewise, they had no watercraft large enough to ferry the supplies necessary to sustain

30 Steele, *Betrayals*, 78–128.

long-term siege operations in the Great Lakes region. The British were able to hold out against these sieges in part because they never lost control of naval operations on Lakes Ontario and Erie. During the siege of Detroit, Indians intercepted shipping headed for the fort, but they did not possess the skill or technology necessary to turn captured British vessels to their long-term advantage. None of the Indians' sieges during Pontiac's War ended in surrender. Rather, the garrisons awaited relief while the Indians' own supplies dwindled and the winter hunting season approached.[31]

During the Sixty Years' War, Indian warriors also became more accustomed to prolonged engagements with European regulars and militias, even if those forces were prepared for attack. Indians never did develop the same tolerance for frontal assaults on well-entrenched positions that European military commanders possessed, but as their familiarity with the modern art of war increased, they did become more willing to engage in battle along traditional European lines. At the Battle of Bushy Run in August 1763, Delaware, Shawnee, and other Ohio Country Indians fought a bloody struggle with five hundred British regulars marching with a supply train to relieve the besieged Fort Pitt. The engagement began in the manner typical of the skulking way of war: under cover of the forest, the Indians fired on the unsuspecting column. This time, however, the troops' commander Henry Bouquet executed a careful retreat to higher ground, where he was able to use flour bags from the convoy's packhorses to build a makeshift defensive enclosure. The Indians continued to fire from cover on Bouquet's troops, but whenever they approached close enough, the regulars responded with bayonet charges to send them back. Despite having lost the element of surprise and the high ground to Bouquet, the Indians did not withdraw overnight. They tried at several points the next morning to overrun Bouquet's camp but were repelled each time by musket fire and bayonets. To draw the Indians into a decisive engagement, Bouquet feigned a retreat. When the warriors rushed in, Bouquet's troops outflanked them and sent them fleeing from the field under heavy fire. Bouquet's troops had suffered considerable casualties over the two-day battle, but they had also inflicted high losses on the Indians.[32]

Defeat at Bushy Run did not prevent Indians from trying frontal assaults on enemy lines again when they thought conditions favorable. During

31 See Dowd, *War under Heaven*, 114–47; Dixon, *Never Come to Peace Again*, 101–70; and Anderson, *Crucible of War*, 535–46.
32 See Dixon, *Never Come to Peace Again*, 185–95. For Bouquet's influence on British tactics in Native American warfare, see Charles E. Brodine, "Henry Bouquet and British Infantry Tactics on the Ohio Frontier, 1758–1764," in Skaggs, *Sixty Years' War*, 43–61.

the climatic campaign of the Ohio Indian War in 1794, a force of one thousand Indians ambushed a supply convoy leaving Fort Recovery in western Ohio but then rashly decided to capitalize on their success by storming the fort itself. Artillery and musket fire inflicted heavy losses on the attackers and forced them to abandon the field. Several weeks later, General Anthony Wayne led his well-trained regulars against an Indian force at the Battle of Fallen Timbers. This time, the Indians were on the defensive, occupying a mile-long battle line, using trees felled by a tornado as their breastworks. Wayne's numerically superior force made short work of them with cavalry and bayonet charges.[33] Perhaps the most significant battlefield defeat the Indians suffered during the Sixty Years' War occurred at Tippecanoe Creek in the Indiana Territory on November 7, 1811. A force of several hundred warriors attempted a preemptive strike on General William Henry Harrison's army before it moved against Prophetstown, the seat of the Indians' resistance. In a turn of events reminiscent of the Battle of Point Pleasant, the Indians lost the element of surprise when sentries alerted the sleeping camp to the attack. The soldiers stood their ground and exacted a heavy toll from the Indians, whose intertribal cooperation never fully recovered from the defeat.[34]

Engagements such as Point Pleasant, Bushy Run, and Tippecanoe often involved just as many casualties for the European forces as they did for the Native American ones, but the Indians could ill afford such warfare by attrition. The Europeans' modern art of war did not flinch at casualties; plenty of surplus population existed in the cities of Europe and the United States to refill the ranks. Native American societies could not match such a demographic advantage. Charismatic war chiefs recruited large intertribal contingents of warriors to their cause, and this success may have encouraged the sort of tactical innovations witnessed at Point Pleasant, Bushy Run, and Tippecanoe. But manpower alone could not win sieges against well-fortified posts or withstand bayonet charges by disciplined regulars. Such large intertribal forces were also impossible to keep at arms for more than several months at a time. Intertribal confederacies were always politically fragile, a weakness European enemies exploited by conducting divide-and-conquer diplomacy, and war chiefs possessed no coercive powers to compel the service of Indian warriors once their alliances had shifted. Domestic responsibilities also called warriors back home, to provide for their families with seasonal hunting, fishing, and trading. Unlike their European

---

33 Sword, *President Washington's Indian War*, 272–311.
34 R. David Edmunds, *The Shawnee Prophet* (Lincoln, Nebraska, 1983), 110–16.

counterparts, Eastern Woodlands Indians never came to regard war as a specialized, year-round profession. Rather, it was an activity in which they expected all adult men to participate but also to abandon as circumstances demanded.

Indian warfare did change over the course of the Sixty Years' War but not in a way profound enough to achieve parity with the modern art of war. With no industrial capacity of their own, Indians lacked the ability to manufacture the materiel necessary for modern European warfare. Only in those conflicts in which they were supplied by European allies were they able to sustain a war effort that lasted for years instead of months. When those supplies were cut off by their allies' surrender, inactivity, or truce with other belligerents, the Indians' resistance invariably collapsed. Indians could afford to imitate the modern art of war only so long as Europeans were footing the bill, as the French did in the Seven Years' War and the British did in the American Revolution, the Ohio War, and the War of 1812. Otherwise, their military culture remained grounded in traditional values, methods, and objectives.

INDIAN WAR AND TOTAL WAR

A British regular serving in the Great Lakes theater of the War of 1812 would have encountered a kind of Indian warfare not that much different from what a New England militiaman experienced during King Philip's War almost 150 years earlier. In the early nineteenth century, Eastern Woodland Indians still used the skulking way of war to fight their enemy, and they still relied on weapons (iron knives and hatchets, flintlock muskets) they acquired from Europeans. Indian warriors still fought for their own culturally sanctioned reasons, such as the pursuit of distinction, revenge, and captives, and they still came and went as they pleased, giving their support and alliance to whomever they chose. War chiefs still relied on their reputation and powers of persuasion to recruit warriors, and the intertribal alliances they knit together to resist European power remained fragile creations subject to the vicissitudes of war and politics. Of course, some change in Indian warfare would have been evident between New England in 1675 and the Great Lakes in 1812. Indians in the latter conflict were more likely to travel great distances to fight a common enemy. They sometimes assembled in forces numbering one thousand or more to do battle and used siege tactics adapted from European armies. Nevertheless, their military culture remained rooted in the methods and objectives of the mourning war practiced by generations of their forebearers.

There were exceptions to the rule, especially among Indians who exhibited a high degree of acculturation to white society. The Stockbridge Indians were a polyglot community inhabiting the last missionary community or "praying town" in colonial Massachusetts. Males from the community served as scouts for British forces in the Seven Years' War and enlisted in the militia and Continental Army during the Revolution. The Loyal Shawnee, an Ohio community led by the accommodationist chief Black Hoof, served as scouts for the U.S. Army during the War of 1812. As the nineteenth century progressed, this pattern among acculturated Indians continued. During the American Civil War, Iroquois and Cherokees enlisted in the Union and Confederate armies, respectively. After 1890, a young Indian male seeking to distinguish himself was more likely to join the U.S. Army than to fight it. Indians who served in World War I and World War II often found themselves segregated into special units and stereotyped as scouts by their commanders, but the modern military also acted an engine of assimilation, taking Indians off the reservation and encouraging them to agitate for their civil and political liberties as U.S. citizens.[35]

In retrospect, total war as Europeans came to understand it during the age of revolutions appears to have been something that was done to Indians rather than by them. Like other indigenous peoples around the globe, they found themselves on the wrong end of Europe's expanding military power. The violence Europeans visited upon Indian communities in the early nineteenth century did not differ substantially from that practiced two hundred years earlier: it still included the assassination of Indian leaders, attacks on undefended noncombatants, the burning of crops and homes, and the forced dispersal of the vanquished from their homelands. During the Sixty Years' War, however, this violence increased in intensity and frequency. Anglo-American society became more tolerant of acts of brutality committed against Indian communities, celebrating some such as Robert Rogers's raid on the Abenaki community of St. Francis in 1759 as great moral victories over the forces of savagery, while turning a blind eye to others that defied whitewashing, such as the systematic murder of

---

35 For the Stockbridge Indians, see Colin Calloway, *The American Revolution in Indian Country* (Cambridge, U.K., 1995), 85–107. For the Loyal Shawnee, see R. David Edmunds, "'A Watchful Safeguard to Our Habitations': Black Hoof and the Loyal Shawnees," in Hoxie, Hoffman, and Albert, *Native Americans and the Early Republic*, 162–99. For the Iroquois and Cherokee during the Civil War, see Laurence M. Hauptman, *The Iroquois in the Civil War: From Battlefield to Reservation* (Syracuse, New York, 1993), and W. Craig Gaines, *The Confederate Cherokees: John Drew's Regiment of Mounted Rifles* (Baton Rouge, Louisiana, 1989), respectively. For Indian military service in the twentieth century, see Michael L. Tate, "From Scout to Doughboy: The National Debate over Integrating Indians into the Military, 1891–1918," *Western Historical Quarterly* 17 (1986): 417–37, and Peter Iverson, *"We Are Still Here": American Indians in the Twentieth Century* (Wheeling, Illinois, 1998), 49–52, 105–10.

nearly one hundred unarmed Delaware converts at the mission village of Gnadenhutten in 1782.[36] Such attacks were the outward manifestation of a racist rhetoric of Indian hating that pervaded the American frontier in the early national era, tarring all Indians as irredeemable savages fit only for ethnic cleansing from the new nation.[37]

Indians responded to this provocation with their own kind of racialized militancy. In the mid-eighteenth century, a nativist movement emerged in the Ohio Country that rejected accommodation to Europeans and preached a message of "separate creations" for white and red.[38] Many warriors involved in Pontiac's War, the most significant intertribal resistance to European expansion since King Philip's War, were inspired by Neolin, a Delaware prophet who believed that Indians had to follow a separate path to salvation than whites and that they would find security and prosperity again only when they had rejected Christianity, alcohol, and other white ways. Purification rituals associated with Neolin's message, such as the communal consumption of the emetic "black drink," became an important means for war chiefs of recruiting and uniting warriors from different nations during the Sixty Years' War.[39] During the decade before the War of 1812, Tecumseh's brother, Tenskwatawa (also known as the Shawnee Prophet), attracted warriors from throughout the Great Lakes to the militants' cause by assuring them that his medicine and rituals would render them invincible to their enemies.[40]

The messianic visions of Neolin, Tenskwatawa, and other prophets inspired among the Eastern Woodlands Indians a total war of their own, one fought on a spiritual plane. This was a struggle to save the Indians' soul from Christianity, to wrestle Indian communities free from the perils of alcohol and its attendant violence, to restore integrity to their traditional customs and beliefs, and ultimately to preserve their way of life from

---

36 For the raid on St. Francis, see Stephen Brumwell, *White Devil: A True Story of War, Savagery, and Vengeance in Colonial America* (Cambridge, Massachusetts, 2005), 183–205. For the attack on Gnadenhutten, see Leonard Sadosky, "Rethinking the Gnadenhutten Massacre: The Contest for Power in the Public World of the Revolutionary Frontier," in Skaggs and Nelson, *Sixty Years' War*, 187–214.

37 On the rise of Indian hating along the trans-Allegheny frontier, see White, *Middle Ground*, 366–412. Two works that draw a parallel between Indian hating and modern episodes of ethnic cleansing are Daniel K. Richter, *Facing East from Indian Country: A Native History of Early America* (Cambridge, Massachusetts, 2001), 235–6, and John Mack Faragher, "'More Motley than Mackinaw': From Ethnic Mixing to Ethnic Cleansing on the Frontier of the Lower Missouri, 1783–1833," in *Contact Points: American Frontiers from the Mohawk Valley to the Mississippi, 1750–1830*, ed. Andrew R. L. Cayton and Fredrika J. Teute (Chapel Hill, North Carolina, 1998), 304–26.

38 See Richter, *Facing East from Indian Country*, 189–236.

39 See Dowd, *War under Heaven*, 94–105, and *A Spirited Resistance*, 23–46.

40 R. David Edmunds, *Shawnee Prophet*, 28–116. For revivalist movements of the early national era, also see Anthony F. C. Wallace, *Death and Rebirth of the Seneca* (New York, 1969).

the ruinous impact of European contact. Unfortunately, it was also a war ill suited to withstand the onslaught of its enemy's superior numbers and firepower. The same tragedy that unfolded on the trans-Allegheny frontier between 1754 and 1814 repeated itself west of the Mississippi, culminating with the Ghost Dance movement and the massacre at Wounded Knee in 1890. The dire consequences of the Sixty Years' War for Native Americans should not obscure the fundamental appeal of the nativist message to the warriors who fought and died for it. For them, warfare had long served as a means of preserving community solidarity and strength. It should come as no surprise, then, that their response to the European way of war was the revitalization, rather than the abandonment, of their own.

8

The American Militias

"The Garnish of a Table"?

MATTHEW C. WARD

In October 1780, after more than five years of fighting in the Revolutionary War, George Washington, commander in chief of the Continental Army, wrote to the governors of all the American states begging them to abandon their reliance upon the militia. He lamented, "Tis time we should get rid of an error which the experience of all mankind has exploded, and which our own experience has dearly taught us to reject; the carrying on a War with Militia." He warned, "If we continue in the infatuation, we shall deserve to lose the object we are contending for."[1] Just a few weeks later, General Nathanael Greene, commander of the Southern Department of the Continental Army, wrote to one of his militia commanders, General Thomas Sumter, echoing Washington's words. He urged Sumter not to place faith in the militia, which, he argued, was capable of winning only minor victories and harassing the enemy, but no more. He concluded that "the salvation of this Country don't depend upon little strokes; nor should this great business of establishing a permanent army be neglected to pursue them. Partizan strokes in war are like the garnish of a table, they give splendor to the Army ... but they afford no substantial national security."[2]

Greene's and Washington's comments are typical of those made by most American commanders during the American Revolutionary War, yet in many ways they are surprising. Although both Washington and Greene had good grounds for disparaging the militia's performance in regular combat during the war, both commanders played an important role in transforming

---

1 Washington, Circular to the States, Oct. 18, 1780, in *The Writings of George Washington from the Original Manuscript Sources, 1745–1799*, ed. John Fitzpatrick 39 vols. (Washington, D.C., 1931–44), 20:209.
2 Greene to General Thomas Sumter, Jan. 8, 1781, in *The Papers of General Nathanael Greene*, ed. Richard K. Showman and Dennis Michael Conrad, 13 vols. (Chapel Hill, North Carolina, 1976–2005), 7:74–5.

the role and function of the militia, particularly in irregular combat and partisan warfare. Indeed, Greene's dismissal of partisan warfare is particularly
surprising, as he exploited those "little strokes" to wear down Cornwallis's army. During the course of the war, both commanders fashioned the
militia into a more radical military institution that played a central role in
the American victory and crafted new patterns of warfare. Indeed, some
historians have even compared the performance of the American militia to
the guerrilla and partisan warfare of revolutionaries such as Mao Tse-tung.[3]

For the first 150 years of their existence, the British North American
colonies had relied almost exclusively on their militias for their defense.
Before the Seven Years' War, few regular British troops had been posted in
North America, and each colony, with the notable exception of Quaker-
dominated Pennsylvania, had developed its own militia. In theory, the militia consisted of all adult males in the colony, but in most colonies African
Americans were excluded from service, and increasing numbers of exemptions were provided for those such as schoolmasters, overseers, and those
who could simply afford to pay a fine.[4] When the Seven Years' War broke
out in North America, the limitations of the militia soon became apparent.
Militiamen refused to leave their homes when exposed to Indian attacks
and refused to serve for more than a few weeks. During the first major
raid on the Virginia frontier in October 1755, one Virginia militia commander bluntly refused to summon his troops, maintaining that "his Wife,
Family and Corn were at Stake, so were those of his Soldiers, therefore it
was not possible for him to come."[5] Over the course of the Seven Years'
War, colonial governors and officials realized the limitations of the militia
in offensive operations and created provincial regiments for that purpose.
The units served for limited periods, sometimes three years but often only
one campaign in the case of many of the New England regiments, and were
outside the direct command structure of the regular British Army. However,
they were professional units and very different in nature from the provincial
militias.[6]

3 See, e.g., John Morgan Dederer, "Making Bricks without Straw: Nathanael Greene's Southern
  Campaigns and Mao Tse-Tung's Mobile War," *Military Affairs* 47 (1983): 115–21.
4 Lawrence Delbert Cress, *Citizens in Arms: The Army and the Militia in American Society to the War
  of 1812* (Chapel Hill, North Carolina, 1982), 3–11; William L. Shea, *The Virginia Militia in the
  Seventeenth Century* (Baton Rouge, Louisiana, 1975); John Shy, *A People Numerous and Armed*, rev. ed.
  (Ann Arbor, Michigan, 1990), 31–40.
5 Washington to Dinwiddie, Oct. 11, 1755, in *The Official Records of Robert Dinwiddie, Lieutenant-
  Governor of the Colony of Virginia, 1751–1758*, ed. R. A. Brock, 2 vols. (Richmond, Virginia, 1883),
  2:239.
6 Fred Anderson, *A People's Army: Massachusetts Soldiers and Society in the Seven Years' War* (Chapel Hill,
  North Carolina, 1984); Matthew C. Ward, *Breaking the Backcountry: The Seven Years' War in Virginia
  and Pennsylvania, 1754–1765* (Pittsburgh, 2003).

As armed conflict between the colonies and Great Britain loomed in the spring of 1775, most Americans expected the militias to take the leading role in military resistance to the British. The forces that skirmished with the British at Lexington and Concord in April 1775 and that then massed around the besieged British garrison in Boston were composed entirely of New England militiamen.[7] Across North America, militia units drilled and mustered and prepared for war. In Virginia, for instance, James Madison reported, "We are very busy at present in raising men and producing the necessaries for defending ourselves. . . . There will . . . be some thousands of well trained High Spirited men ready to meet danger whenever it appears."[8] In the summer and fall of 1775, Americans were well aware of the shortcomings of their militia, especially when facing highly trained regular troops. However, most presumed that the innate virtue of the militia would overcome their weaknesses. Indeed, General Daniel Roberdau of the Pennsylvania militia counseled his men that "the English army derive all their strength from a close attention to discipline, with them it supplies the want of virtue."[9] In the early months of the war, such claims seemed to be justified by the militia's brave performance at the bloody Battle of Bunker Hill.

The militias that began to muster and train during 1775 varied greatly from state to state. New England militiamen tended to have the most military experience at the beginning of the Revolutionary War but may also have been the least disciplined. The New England tradition of the election of officers, which was taken still further in Pennsylvania, was regarded with deep suspicion, and in some cases open hostility, by many more seasoned officers.[10] Even within individual states there were clear distinctions in the nature of militia units. Some units would be called on for only a few days service to defend their localities; others would serve longer periods of time – up to six months – and would be sent as reinforcements to the main armies that often were many miles away. Some militia units might be composed of raw recruits who had never seen battle, and others of seasoned Continental Army veterans. The Virginia militia at the Battle of Camden in August 1780 was composed of inexperienced men and fled

---

7 David Hackett Fischer, *Paul Revere's Ride* (New York, 1994); Merrill Jensen, *The Founding of a Nation: A History of the American Revolution* (New York, 1968), 535–6, 563–7.

8 Madison to William Bradford, Jan. 20, 1775, in *The Papers of James Madison*, ed. Robert J. Brugger, William T. Hutchinson, and William M. E. Rachal, 17 vols. (Chicago, 1962–91), 1:135.

9 Quoted in Charles Royster, *A Revolutionary People at War: The Continental Army and American Character, 1775–1783* (Chapel Hill, North Carolina, 1979), 11.

10 Stephen Rosswurm, *Arms, Country, and Class: The Philadelphia Militia and "Lower Sort" during the American Revolution, 1775–1783* (New Brunswick, New Jersey, 1987); Robert Middlekauff, *The Glorious Cause: The American Revolution, 1763–1789* (New York, 1982), 300.

at the first British charge; the Virginia militia at the Battle of Cowpens in January 1781 was composed of seasoned Continental Army veterans who fought bravely and participated in the rout of the British force.[11]

Differences in the nature of the militia posed problems for American commanders as the caliber of militia units could not be easily gauged. If judging the quality of militia units was difficult, guessing the number of men who would be present on any particular occasion was equally problematic. Washington lamented to his brother John Augustine Washington that the militia was "here today, & gone tomorrow."[12] He soon concluded that "when danger is a little removed from them, they will not turn out at all – When it comes Home to 'em, the well affected instead of flying to Arms to defend themselves, are busily employed in removing their Families & Effects, whilst the disaffected are concerting measures to make their submission & spread terror & dismay all around."[13]

It was not only Washington who encountered problems with militia units deserting or refusing to muster. Even the most experienced militia commanders could face such problems. In February 1781, General Andrew Pickens informed Greene that the Salisbury, North Carolina, militiamen in his service were "continually deserting and no persuasions can prevail with them." He considered them "among the worst Men" he had ever commanded. Greene sanguinely responded that he was "sorry that Militia desert you, but it is the practice of all Militia."[14]

Even when militiamen mustered and remained in service, they were often of limited utility because they lacked basic equipment such as tents and camp equipage or, most importantly, arms. In theory, all militiamen were supposed to provide their own arms. In practice, many did not own, or did not wish to bring, their own guns. When they did posses their own weapons, the guns were of different bores and calibers, making the provision of ammunition difficult. As a result, commanders were forced to provide the militia with most of the equipment that they needed. However, this was not always an advisable decision, for the militia often pilfered supplies

---

11 Washington to John Hancock, Sept. 25, 1776, in, *The Papers of George Washington, Revolutionary War Series*, ed. Philander P. Chase. (Charlottesville, Virginia, 1985–), 6:397; Daniel Morgan to Greene, Jan. 19, 1781, in Showman and Conrad, *Papers of Nathanael Greene*, 7:152–5; John S. Pancake, *This Destructive War: The British Campaign in the Carolinas, 1780–1782* (Tuscaloosa, Alabama, 1985), 104; John Buchanan, *The Road to Guilford Courthouse: The American Revolution in the Carolinas* (New York, 1997), 296.

12 Washington to John Augustine Washington, Feb. 24, 1777, in Chase, *Papers of George Washington*, 8:439.

13 Washington to Hancock, Dec. 5, 1776, in ibid., 7:263.

14 Pickens to Greene, Feb. 20, 1781, and Greene to Pickens, Feb. 21, 1781, in Showman and Conrad, *Papers of Nathanael Greene*, 7:325, 327.

and equipment, especially arms, which were in very short supply. In the autumn of 1780, most of the arms that had been collected in Albany for the use of the Continental Army disappeared, and Washington ordered that in future there be "no more delivered to Militia."[15] When not pilfering, the militia still proved such a drain on precious supplies that, on occasion, both Washington and Greene counseled against mustering it. Indeed, Washington warned Congress, "No magazines can be equal to the demands of an army of Militia, and none ever needed œconomy more than ours."[16]

If recruiting and supplying the militia were not sufficient problems, commanding militia units could be even more challenging. Because the militia represented the locality in which it was raised, and had close ties to that locality, state officials would frequently intervene if army commanders threatened to move their militia elsewhere. In the summer of 1779, for instance, Washington attempted to remove a detachment of the Connecticut militia to cooperate with Continental detachments in operations around New York City, only a few miles away. The local militia refused to cooperate, and soon state officials became embroiled in a bitter dispute with Washington. Eventually, Washington was forced to acquiesce and wrote to the militia commander, reassuring him:

I would not wish by any means to interfere with the intention of the state or to do any thing which may contravene the local purposes for which your party may have been called out; but only to establish such a concert of views between the Continental troops whose object is the same and the militia under your command, as will most effectually promote the service.[17]

Such problems caused all American commanders to be deeply suspicious about the capability of the militia. Such suspicions soon seemed well grounded. Although the militia may have surpassed many people's expectations during the campaigning around Boston in 1775 in the summer and fall of 1776, the militia proved as much a liability as a benefit to Washington as he attempted to halt the British attack on New York and New Jersey. At the Battle of Long Island, Washington's militia-dominated force broke, and perhaps a thousand New York militiamen deserted at the height of the battle. Only good fortune allowed Washington to evacuate his weary and demoralized army from Long Island. In the aftermath of the battle, he informed Congress that "the Militia instead of calling forth their utmost

---

15 Washington to Brig. Gen. James Clinton, Oct. 28, 1780, in Fitzpatrick, *Writings of Washington*, 20:260.
16 Washington to President of Congress, Sept. 15, 1780, in ibid., 20:49.
17 Washington to Maj. Gen. Robert Howe, Aug. 4, 1779, and Washington to Officer Commanding the Militia at Horseneck, Aug. 24, 1779, in ibid., 16:49–50, 163–4.

efforts to a brave & manly opposition in order to repair our Losses, are dismayed, Intractable, and Impatient to return. Great numbers of them have gone off; in some Instances, almost by whole Regiments." He concluded, "All these circumstances fully confirm the opinion I have ever entertained, and which I more than once in my Letters too the liberty of mentioning to Congress, that no dependence could be put in a Militia."[18]

Over the next few weeks and months, the militia did little to gain Washington's trust. On September 15, when the British landed at Kip's Bay on Manhattan, Washington discovered the militia

flying in every direction and in the greatest confusion, notwithstanding the exertions of the General to form them. I used every means in my power to rally them and get them into some order but my attempts were fruitless and ineffectual, and on the appearance of a small party of the Enemy, not more than Sixty or Seventy, their disorder increased and they ran away in the greatest confusion without firing a Single Shot.[19]

Despite its weakness, American commanders had little choice but to use the militia for they lacked the manpower necessary to win the war without the militia's aid. On several occasions, the number of men serving in the Continental Army dwindled to only a few thousand. In January 1777, for instance, the army that Washington assembled at Morristown, New Jersey, contained only about 1,000 Continental troops, while in January 1781, Greene's army in North Carolina contained fewer than 1,500 Continentals. With so few men, the only way the British could be prevented from overrunning the United States was to use the militia wherever and whenever possible.[20]

It was, however, clear from the beginning of the Revolutionary War that the militia did have important uses. In particular, its use as an instrument of state control allowed the Whigs to take and maintain control of the state governments. Initially, the militia enforced the Continental Association – the agreement to boycott all British goods. It then became responsible for enforcing loyalty oaths and ensuring the allegiance of civilians. This role as a police force proved vitally important during the war, for it allowed the Whigs to control all regions not physically occupied by the British Army.

---

18 Washington to John Hancock, Sept. 2, 1776, in Chase, *Papers of George Washington*, 6:199; Don Higginbotham, *The War of American Independence: Military Attitudes, Policies, and Practice, 1763–1789* (New York, 1971), 154–9.

19 Washington to John Hancock, Sept. 16, 1776, in Chase, *Papers of George Washington*, 6:313–14.

20 John S. Pancake, *1777: The Year of the Hangman* (Tuscaloosa, Alabama, 1977), 78; Buchanan, *Road to Guilford Courthouse*, 352.

While the British tried to organize their own Loyalist militia to counter this advantage, the Loyalist militia was rarely as effective as the Whig militia.[21]

There were a number of factors that affected the success or failure of operations that included the militia. The first of these was the extent to which the militia was involved in essentially defensive operations, for the militia was much more suited to defensive rather than offensive operations. Militiamen were also far more prepared to defend their homes and towns than those of the neighboring state or even neighboring county. Thus, a militia unit being used to defend its home county was more likely to muster and remain in service than a militia unit sent to harass a British force in the neighboring state.

The time of year also had a major impact on the willingness of the militia to muster. During planting or harvest time, militiamen would rarely serve for more than a few days even during the most desperate emergency. July and August, often the times of peak campaigning, were particularly bad months for calling out the militia. During General John Burgoyne's invasion in 1777, the New England militia were extremely reluctant to muster throughout July and early August. However, once the harvest was gathered, increasing numbers joined the American cause. Similarly, the militia might turn out for campaigns in the middle of winter, even though such a time was not a usual time for campaigning, because there was little agricultural work that could be done. Indeed, the willingness of the Pennsylvania and New Jersey militia to muster during the winter of 1776–7 allowed Washington to drive the British army from much of New Jersey.[22]

The ability and charisma of the militia's commanders were also important in deciding its success. Charisma was especially important because militia units had to be encouraged to muster and motivated to continue in the service. On occasion, militia units would go so far as to reject commanders they did not like who attempted to take command. Following the fall of Ticonderoga to Burgoyne's army in 1777, for instance, the assembly of New Hampshire attempted to call out the local militia units under the command of General John Stark. Stark was a charismatic local commander

---

21 Joseph S. Tiedemann, "Patriots by Default: Queens County, New York, and the British Army, 1776–1783," *William and Mary Quarterly* 43 (1986): 35–63; Jeffrey J. Crow, "Liberty Men and Loyalists: Disorder and Disaffection in the North Carolina Backcountry," in *An Uncivil War: The Southern Backcountry during the American Revolution*, ed. Ronald Hoffman, Thad W. Tate, and Peter J. Albert (Charlottesville, Virginia, 1985), 125–79.

22 Col. Warner's Circular to Generals of the Militia, July 20, 1777, and Gen. Stark to New Hampshire Council, Aug. 18, 1777, in "Documents in Relation to the Part Taken by Vermont in Resisting the Invasion of Burgoyne in 1777," *Collections of the Vermont Historical Society*, 2 vols. (Montpelier, Vermont, 1870–1), 1189:204–5; David Hackett Fischer, *Washington's Crossing* (New York, 2004), 248.

much beloved by his men. When Congress refused to allow the troops to serve under Stark and instead insisted that they serve under General Philip Schuyler, the men simply refused to muster. Only once Congress had reconsidered did the New Hampshire militia turn out in numbers with the specific "understanding and assurance that they were to serve under 'Gen. Stark.'"[23]

The manner in which the militia was used in combat also determined the extent to which its activities would be successful. If ordered to withstand a bayonet charge from British redcoats, the militia would as often as not turn and run. At the Battle of Camden in 1780, according to one British observer, the American militia, "quickly giving way, threw down their arms and fled."[24] However, if used to harass British flanks and supply lines, the militia could prove very successful. Even in regular combat, the militia could be used effectively if the commander and strategy were correctly chosen. At the Battle of Cowpens, veteran militia commander General Daniel Morgan used the militia to draw Tarleton's seasoned regulars into a trap. He ordered the militia to skirmish with British regulars as they advanced, weakening their lines, and then to fire two volleys at close quarters before withdrawing. He guessed correctly that the withdrawal of the militia would encourage British troops to believe that they had routed the American force and to advance impetuously into his Continentals, held several hundred yards to the rear. So successful were these tactics that Greene consciously copied them at Guilford Courthouse a few months later, though not with the same success.[25]

The militia could also be used to screen regular troops from attack by British regulars. In New Jersey, Washington used a screen of militia to protect his army from direct attack and to alert him of any British movements. In the Carolinas, Greene frequently used a screen of militia to delay British attempts to make river crossings and protect his army. However, the militia soon grew wise to such tactics and increasingly resented being exposed to enemy fire merely to protect the regulars.[26]

---

23 John Stark, "Memoir of General Stark," in *Reminiscences of the French War* (Concord, Massachusetts, 1831), 187, 190, 197.

24 Charles Stedman, *The History of the Origin, Progress, and Termination of the American War*, 2 vols. (London, 1794), 2:209.

25 Morgan to Greene, Jan. 19, 1781, and Greene to Samuel Huntington, Mar. 16, 1781, in Showman and Conrad, *Papers of Nathanael Greene*, 7:152–5, 433–5; Cornwallis to Sir Henry Clinton, Jan. 18, 1781, Charles Ross, *Correspondence of Charles, First Marquis Cornwallis*, 3 vols. (London, 1859), 1:82–4.

26 Showman and Conrad, *Papers of Nathanael Greene*, 7:408n; Mark V. Kwasny, *Washington's Partisan War, 1775–1783* (Kent, Ohio, 1996), 117–18.

It was not only in regular battle that commanders believed that the militia could be used successfully in the war. Washington quickly realized that the militia provided him with an opportunity to sap British strength and slowly undermine the British will to win. From the beginning of 1777 until 1781, he waged in New Jersey what Mark Kwasny has described as a "partisan war."[27] Washington used small mobile parties of militia to launch daily raids against British lines around New York City and on Staten Island and Long Island. He summed up his tactics in a letter to Benedict Arnold in June 1777. He informed Arnold, "I intend by light Bodies of militia, seconded and [e]ncouraged by a few Continental Troops, to harass and diminish their number by continual Skirmishes."[28]

These tactics worked. Captain Johann Ewald of the Leib Jaeger corps reported that "the teasing now occurred daily. . . . Not only did the men have to stay dressed day and night, but they had to be kept together, the horses constantly saddled, and everything packed." Such constant activity sapped British morale and manpower and, more important, made it impossible for British forces to forage for supplies. Ewald continued to lament that as "foraging had to be undertaken, and since the Americans were so close on our necks, we could not procure any forage without shedding blood."[29] British commanders ordered their men to extinguish all lights in camp by eight o'clock to make it difficult for enemy sharpshooters to target the men. Even in relatively secure locations like Long Island, British troops were ordered never to stray more than half a mile from their camps. Continental troops alone would have found such constant activity all but impossible to maintain, but rotating parties of militia, each unit serving for only a few days, could easily continue the "teasing."[30]

Not only did British troops find it difficult to leave the lines to forage, but the militia also effectively intercepted any planters who might have been tempted to sell their produce directly to the British. Here the militia had distinct advantages over regular troops. Rotating parties of militia could remain on constant duty, and the militiamen knew the roads and byways through the woods and could intercept any farmer attempting to sell produce to the British. Even more importantly, the militiamen often came from

---

27 Kwasny, *Washington's Partisan War.*

28 Washington to Arnold, June 17, 1777, in Chase, *Papers of George Washington*, 10:59.

29 Capt. Johann Ewald, *Diary of the American War: A Hessian Journal*, trans. Joseph P. Tustin (New Haven, Connecticut, 1979), 52.

30 Brigade Orders, Jan. 16, 1777, and "British Regiment of Footguards Orderly Book, August 14, 1776–January 28, 1777," in *Early American Orderly Books 1748–1817*, No. 37 (Woodbridge, Virginia, 1977); Brigade Orders, Feb. 18, 1777, and "Brig. Gen Oliver Delancey's Brigade Orderly Book, February 20, 1777–June 29, 1778," in *Early American Orderly Books*, No. 44.

the same communities as those interested in doing business with the British and were thus able to exert not only physical but also psychological pressure on those whose loyalty had been bought by the lure of British gold.[31]

In the southern theater, control of supplies played an even more critical role in the outcome of the war. As Cornwallis advanced into the Carolina backcountry, Greene employed many of his militia units to remove stores, ammunition, and particularly horses. What supplies the militia could not remove they burned. Consequently, Cornwallis had to depend on supplies transported directly overland from Charleston rather than acquired through foraging. However, British supply trains were constantly harassed by the militia's "Daily inroads . . . across the Santee & scarce a public waggons [*sic*] escaped."[32] Lacking a secure supply route, the British army under Cornwallis could move only slowly into the backcountry, encumbered with a large baggage train of supplies. Time and again, Cornwallis attempted to intercept his opponents, but they were able to maneuver out of his reach. Eventually, Cornwallis was forced to destroy his entire baggage train and march into North Carolina with only the supplies that his men carried on their backs. Consequently, although Cornwallis's army finally caught up with Greene's army and defeated him at Guilford Courthouse, it was forced to retreat back to a source of supply at Wilmington, abandoning all of its gains. According to British observer, Charles Stedman, after the battle, "lord Cornwallis was not in a condition either to give immediate pursuit. . . . [A]lthough a victory had been gained, a retreat became necessary."[33]

The role of the militia in controlling supplies was perhaps most decisive in the summer of 1777, when Burgoyne advanced south from Montreal into New York. Burgoyne quickly drove the Continental Army from Fort Ticonderoga and threatened to overrun Albany. American officers reported that "our whole Army is in a very broken situation. . . . [U]nless the enemy be stopped soon and repelled the whole Country will fall into their hands."[34] However, to make his final advance, Burgoyne needed to acquire supplies, particularly fresh horses. He hoped to obtain these from the townships of western Massachusetts and New Hampshire, and he sent out a large

---

31 Washington to Gov. William Livingston, Dec. 16, 1778, in Chase, *Papers of George Washington*, 13:477–8; Washington to Brig. Gen. John Lacey Jr., in Fitzpatrick, *Writings of Washington*, 13: 404–5.

32 Robert Gray, "Col. Robert Gray's Observations on the War in Carolina," *South Carolina Historical and Genealogical Magazine* 11 (1910): 148; Greene to Daniel Morgan, Jan. 8, 1781, and Greene to Thomas Jefferson, Feb. 14, 1781, in Showman and Conrad, *Papers of Nathanael Greene*, 7:72–3, 289.

33 Stedman, *History of the American War*, 2:347; Greene to Samuel Huntington, Jan. 31, 1781, in Showman and Conrad, *Papers of Nathanael Greene*, 7:225; Pancake, *This Destructive War*, 161, 188.

34 Col. Moses Robinson Circular for Aid, July 8, 1777, in "Documents in Relation to Vermont," 175–6.

foraging party of Hessian troops. At Bennington, a substantial party of New England militia surrounded and captured the Hessians and then proceeded to block any possible route of retreat for Burgoyne's army. The activities of the militia, rather than any action of the Continental Army, were thus in many ways responsible for the surrender of Burgoyne's army at Saratoga.[35]

The use of the American militia in this fashion to deprive the British of supplies and intelligence, and to keep British forces on the defensive and constantly fatigued in a war of posts, was an essential part of the American victory. In these ways alone, the militia proved far more than mere garnish. Without the militia's control of supply and constant harassment, the British army would have been able to strike more decisively at the Continental Army. However, in many ways this was simply an extension of accepted patterns of European warfare. Irregular warfare, in particular the use of light infantry and skirmishers, was well established and had been emphasized in military treatises, such as Marshal de Saxe's *Reveries* (1757). The role of irregular warfare had perhaps received its fullest treatment in Jeney's treatise *The Partisan*, which was published just three years later in 1760. Irregular warfare was recognized as distinct from the campaigning of regular armies and was described by the French term *petite guerre*, a term that would later be replaced by the Spanish equivalent, *guerrilla*. Irregular warfare, skirmishing, and keeping the enemy off balance were thus nothing extraordinary in the widely accepted patterns of warfare, although the American militias were particularly well suited to such tasks.[36]

However, what made this irregular combat into a new pattern of warfare, an American way of war, was the manner in which the militias mobilized civilians into the war effort and blurred the boundary between civilian and military. This made it increasingly difficult for both armies to follow the rules of war. Those rules, while not formally encapsulated in any single document, were widely understood by military officers of all nationalities and creeds and had become widely accepted by most European armies.[37] Many armies published codes to guide their officers in military practice. In particular, France's *Code Militaire* was widely consulted by officers of all armies. The codes clearly defined the different rights of civilians and

---

35 Burgoyne to Lord George Germain, Aug. 20, 1777, in *Documents of the American Revolution, 1770–1783*, ed. K. G. Davies, 21 vols. (Dublin, 1972–81), 14:165–7; Bradford S. Sydney, "Lord Francis Napier's Journal of the Burgoyne Campaign," *Maryland Historical Magazine* 57 (1963): 322.

36 Maurice de Saxe, "My Reveries upon the Art of War," in *Roots of Strategy: A Collection of Military Classics*, ed. Maj. Thomas R. Philips (London, 1943), 114; Mr. de Jeney, *The Partisan; or, The Art of Making War in Detachment . . .* (London, 1760); H. C. B Rogers, *The British Army of the Eighteenth Century* (London, 1977), 43; John Grenier, *The First Way of War: American War Making on the Frontier, 1607–1814* (New York, 2005), 1.

37 Hew Strachan, *European Armies and the Conduct of War* (London, 1983), 8–9.

military participants in a conflict. In particular, civilians had to be spared
from the horrors of combat. Armies might campaign across their lands, but
they targeted each other, not the noncombatant population. There were, of
course, exceptions to such rules, and they were honored often as much in
the breach as in their maintenance. Civilians in besieged towns provided an
obvious example; towns that fell following a siege – as opposed to signing
an honorable surrender – could expect the victorious troops to sack and
pillage the town. Yet the sack of a town that refused to surrender and was
taken by storm, horrific though the bloodshed might be, was regarded as a
"legal" aspect of warfare.[38]

Central to this regulation of warfare was the distinction between civilian
and military personnel. Military personnel were supposed to be clearly distinguished from noncombatants by wearing obvious uniforms or insignia.
However, most American militias did not wear such a uniform but campaigned in civilian clothing. In addition, the short term of militia duty meant
that civilians were constantly rotating in and out of the American armies.
One day a farmer could be a civilian; the next day he could be a militiaman sniping at his British opponents. In New Jersey in February 1778, the
British officer Lieutenant John Graves Simcoe "was on horseback, in conversation with Lieutenant Whitlock, and near the out sentinels, [when] a
rifle was fired, and the ball grazed between them." Simcoe sent some of his
men to arrest the perpetrator who could be seen running away. "On being
questioned 'how he presumed to fire in such a manner?' he answered 'that
he had frequently fired at the Hessians, (who a few weeks before had been
there,) and thought that he might as well do so again.'"[39] Was the culprit
to be treated as a brave militiaman carrying out his duty or as a treacherous
civilian contravening the rules of war? Because of their service in the militia,
many Americans saw no difficulty in taking up arms individually and resisting their opponents whenever possible. For the British, this posed an insol-
uble problem: if all civilians whom the British army encountered were
potential enemies, in what fashion was the army to treat them?

The role of the militia in blurring the boundary between civilians and
combatants and in driving a wedge between the British army and the civilian population was a key component of the American victory. The British
had to regain the trust and support of the majority of the civilian population to win the war. Without this, military victories lacked real significance.

38 M. S. Anderson, *War and Society in Europe of the Old Regime* (London, 1988), 190–2.
39 John Graves Simcoe, *Simcoe's Military Journal: History of the Operations of a Partisan Corps . . .* (New
   York, 1844), 39; Fischer, *Washington's Crossing*, 178–9; Peter Wilson, "Warfare in the Old Regime
   1648–1789," in *European Warfare 1453–1815*, ed. Jeremy Black (London, 1999), 69–74.

However, as long as the army and its troops distrusted civilians, such reconciliation was all but impossible. Thus was crafted a distinctive way of war. Some military historians have argued that if there is a distinctive American way of war, then it was crafted on the frontier in warfare against Native Americans. John Ferling, John Dederer, and John Grenier, for instance, have all argued that the nature of frontier warfare shaped the American military experience into a unique American way of war.[40] Yet the Revolutionary War suggests that it was not only the frontier experience that shaped a unique way of war but also the role of the militia in the conflict. The use of the militia blurred the boundary between combatant and noncombatant and paved the way for a drift toward what could be termed *total war*.

Service in the militia served to blur the distinction between civilians and combatants in several ways. Because service in the militia was often of very short duration, perhaps only ten days or two weeks, most adult American men spent some time on active duty but most of their time in civilian life. Militia duties served to arm and train these men in the use of weapons and to encourage them to resist British oppression. It was not surprising that, if a British column should march past, these same men should feel no compunction about grabbing a gun and firing a few shots at the nearest soldiers. Indeed, the very nature of much militia combat and training encouraged individual military prowess. The initial emphasis on the minuteman, quick to muster and armed with his trusty rifle, encouraged an independence of spirit which sat uneasily with eighteenth-century concepts of the rules of war.[41]

The problem was particularly acute because the militia wore no uniforms, which meant, in practical terms, that it was impossible to identify who was serving in the militia and who was not, to distinguish between rebel troops and civilians. On several occasions, officers on both sides mistook friendly militia for the enemy and vice versa. At the Battle of Bennington, for instance, the rebel militia pretended to be Loyalists flocking to join the crown. The commander of the Hessian force, Colonel Baum, sent out orders to his men that the outposts were not to molest the militia as it approached the camp, and indeed some of the pickets were ordered to retire before them to make sure there was no accidental skirmishing. This allowed

40 Grenier, *The First Way of War*; John E. Ferling, *A Wilderness of Miseries: War and Warriors in Early America* (Westport, Connecticut, 1980); John Morgan Dederer, *War in America to 1775: Before Yankee Doodle* (New York, 1990).
41 Michael A. McDonnell, "Popular Mobilization and Political Culture in Revolutionary Virginia: The Failure of the Minutemen and the Revolution from Below," *Journal of American History* 85 (1998): 946–81.

the American militia to advance almost into the Hessian camp and to take up post in the most advantageous positions without a shot being fired.[42]

Because the militia was composed of civilians and not regular troops, both armies had to grapple with the issue of whether militiamen should be treated as civilian traitors and spies or as enemy combatants. Traitors and spies could be executed without trial; enemy combatants had to be respected under the rules of war. When captured by enemy militia, militiamen of either side often faced brutal treatment. Indeed, it was American forces who initially treated Loyalist militia as traitors rather than combatants. After Bennington, General Stark himself reported:

The Hessians were treated with civilities belonging to prisoners of war. The Tories were considered traitors and distinguished as such. They were ordered to be tied in pairs, and those pairs connected by a rope, to which a horse was harnessed with a postillion mounted to lead them away. The ladies of Bennington furnished cords for the purpose, and rendered several other services with the same spirit.[43]

The South Carolina Loyalist Robert Gray claimed:

When ever a Militia Man of our was made a prisoner he was delivered not to the Continentals but to the Rebel Militia, who looked upon him as a State prisoner, as a man who deserved a halter, & therefore treated him with the greatest cruelty. If he was not assassinated after being made a prisoner . . . he was kept a prisoner without friends, money, credit, or perhaps hoped of exchange.[44]

These men were lucky. Not all militiamen who were captured endured only public humiliation.

In the wake of the British defeat at the Battle of King's Mountain in 1780, the Loyalist militia suffered particularly harsh retribution. At the battle, the armies of both sides were composed entirely of militia. Many on both sides had relatives, friends, and neighbors on the opposing side, and personal feelings and animosities ran high. After their victory, the American militiamen plundered the bodies of dead and dying Loyalists. Those who survived the battle sometimes fared little better. As some of the rebel militiamen were local justices of the peace, they began trying the Loyalist militia for treason. Thirty-six men were tried without delay, found guilty, and sentenced to hang. As these were summary trials, the executions were immediate. The condemned men were brought out three at a time, hanged, and left suspended. In all, nine loyalist militiamen were executed before the commander was able to put a stop to the executions. In the wake of the battle, Cornwallis wrote angrily that "the officers and

---

42 Account of the Battle of Bennington, in "Documents in Relation to Vermont," 215–20.
43 Stark, "Memoir of General Stark," 195.   44 Gray, "Observations," 145.

men taken at King's Mountain were treated with an inhumanity scarcely credible."[45] Such behavior, British officers argued, increasingly invalidated the protections offered by the rules of war to American prisoners. Indeed, Loyalists themselves urged the British army to take direct retribution for such actions. Robert Gray argued that in South Carolina, "Nothing will ever be here able to put our Militia here on a proper footing but giving up to them all the rebel Militia when prisoners to be dealt with according to the laws of retaliation."[46]

Such cruelties were not committed only by rebel militia or always in the best interest of their own side. At the Battle of Beattie's Mill in 1781, for instance, the American officer James Dunlop was captured by the British. He was to be held to be exchanged later for some British officers in the hands of the Americans. However, some unknown Loyalist "mountain men" broke into the jail and shot him.[47] Such abuses directly contributed to the breakdown of order and of respect for the rules of war on both sides and particularly enraged British regulars against the civilian population.

In New York and New Jersey, such anger and frustration may well have contributed to the abuses that the British regulars piled on the civilian population and that effectively served to alienate civilians. Property was looted from friend and foe alike, livestock and forage seized from all, and there seem to have been widespread instances of rape.[48] One North Carolina resident considered it fortunate that she was only "plundered of all my horses, dry cattle, horse forage, liquors, and family provisions, and thought I escaped well with my house furniture and milch cattle, when some in this country were stripd of all these things."[49] Despite repeated attempts from British officers to restrain their men, the atrocities continued. As the British army struggled to regain control of the former colonies, increasingly some officers turned to terror tactics in an attempt to crush support for the local militias. In North and South Carolina, when many of those who had formerly sworn allegiance to the crown flocked to join Gates's army in 1780, some British officers argued "that the lenity which had been shewn to them had been abused, and that it was become necessary to restrain their perfidy by examples of severity, and the terrors of punishment."[50] Such feelings hardly

---

45 Cornwallis to Gates, Dec. 1, 1780, in Ross, *Correspondence of Cornwallis*, 1:171; Buchanan, *Road to Guilford Courthouse*, 238–9.

46 Gray, "Observations," 146.   47 Pancake, *This Destructive War*, 190–1.

48 Fischer, *Washington's Crossing*, 178–80.

49 Elizabeth Steele to Ephraim Steele, Apr. 19, 1781, in *The Papers of John Steele*, 2 vols., ed. H. M. Wagstaff, *Publications of the North Carolina Historical Commission* (Raleigh, North Carolina, 1924), 1:9–10.

50 Stedman, *History of the American War*, 2:214.

served to restrain the excesses of pillaging and plundering that regularly took place and certainly served to encourage the excesses committed by officers such as Banastre Tarleton. Indeed, the phrase "Tarleton's quarter" became widely used for the indiscriminate slaughter of prisoners.[51]

The Americans' predilection for the use of the militia may have been rooted in aspects of the Whig ideology of the Revolutionaries. Ideas about the British army as an agent of civil tyranny were used to justify resistance to Britain and the mobilization of the colonial militias. In the state assemblies, perceptions of the military as an agent of political corruption continued to hold great sway during and after the Revolution and encouraged Americans to think of all the citizenry as part of the nation's defense, a belief enshrined in the Second Amendment to the Constitution. The militia rather than any standing army should be the bastion of the republic's defenses.[52] Yet the origins of the reliance on the militia, and an American way of war, may lie not solely in the Anglo-American ideological heritage of the colonists. Britain's American colonists were not alone in using the militia as a principal means of defense and in blurring the distinction between civilian and military. The War of the Conquest in Canada, in particular the years between 1758 and 1760 along the St. Lawrence River, saw the French-Canadian militia also blurring the distinction between combatants and noncombatants and eliciting similar responses from British regulars.[53] This indicates that the lack of a clear distinction between civilians and military personnel may have played an important role in forging an American way of war.

Despite their own misgivings, American commanders were forced by a shortage of manpower to use the militia as part of their struggle. Over the course of the war, American commanders discovered ways in which they could use the militia to wage an effective defensive struggle against the British army. While some aspects of this struggle remained within traditional military practices, such as the use of the militia as skirmishers and partisans, the blurring of the boundary between civilians and combatants to the extent seen during the Revolutionary War was not yet a feature of European warfare. By blurring this boundary, Washington and Greene made it increasingly difficult for the British to develop a military policy to reconquer the colonies and contributed to the final American victory. The

---

51 Russell F. Weigley, *The American Way of War: A History of United States Military Strategy and Policy* (Bloomington, Indiana, 1973), 26.
52 Edward M. Coffman, "The Duality of the American Military Tradition: A Commentary," *Journal of Military History* 64 (2000): 969; Cress, *Citizens in Arms*, 53.
53 Fred Anderson, *Crucible of War: The Seven Years' War and the Fate of Empire in British North America, 1754–1766* (New York, 2000); Matthew C. Ward, *The Battle for Quebec 1759: Britain's Conquest of Canada* (Stroud, U.K., 2005).

use of the militia in this fashion was never a conscious element of American military strategy. There is little evidence to suggest that Greene, Washington, or any other commander tried to use the militia specifically to increase tensions between the British army and civilians. However, by irrevocably blurring the boundary between civilian and combatant, between friend and foe, the use of the militias by both Whigs and Tories fashioned a new and more brutal pattern of warfare, a pattern of almost total war. Although the militia may have been little more than "the garnish of a table" in terms of regular combat, in terms of its role in the final American victory and in the transformation of warfare in North America, the militia was far more central to the American experience of the war.

9

The Logistics of Revolutionary War in France

ALAN FORREST

From Clausewitz and Jomini down to our own day, the focus of military historians in analyzing the wars of Revolutionary France has concentrated on that aspect they identify as most typical of modern warfare – the introduction of a mass army, an army of citizens capable of defending not only the territory of France but also the Revolution itself.[1] They point to the sheer size of the revolutionary armies, their youth, and their identification with the French people from whom they were drawn – a force that could be characterized, as the revolutionaries themselves characterized it, as the nation in arms. This was the image that lived on in popular memory, inspiring future generations of French republicans and of nationalists throughout Europe and beyond. It was the stuff of legend and mythification – a heady mixture of national inclusiveness, spontaneity, and equality that together were taken as constituent elements of French character. And even if the enthusiasm of their engagement is often exaggerated, the sheer achievement of mobilizing a mass army on this scale cannot fail to impress. Their declared aim of having a million men in arms and the notion that every citizen was a soldier – the boldness of the dream dazzled a Europe still accustomed to fight with small professional armies, drilled in complex maneuvers, that could be supplemented in times of crisis by press-gangs and militias. But the task that this implied was a daunting one, and one that had far more to do with the detail of day-to-day administration than with rhetoric or Jacobin ideology. An army of a million men had to be fed and watered, kitted out with uniforms and boots, kept dry in the rains and

---

1 See especially Clausewitz's early essay, "Considérations sur la manière de faire la guerre à la France," quoted in Peter Paret, *Clausewitz and the State* (Princeton, New Jersey, 1985), 80.

I first discussed the problem of army logistics during the French Revolution in the chapter "Providing for the Soldiers," in *The Soldiers of the French Revolution* (Durham, North Carolina, 1990), 125–54.

snows of winter, supplied with drugs and medical services, and, of course, armed for combat. Not only did France have no experience of recruiting large-scale citizen armies, but the revolutionaries soon discovered that they also lacked the logistical backup such an army required. This called for a bureaucracy that far outweighed the normal ambitions of the eighteenth-century state.[2] It also had to be paid for, at a time when inflation and the problems associated with the assignat presented massive problems in their own right.[3]

These implications were, of course, recognized by the political leadership, who were deeply aware of the logistical demands that the war would make. From the outset, they talked of the need for requisitions and set about collecting the statistical information they might need – the numbers of horses and donkeys, carts and carters, for instance – in individual districts and communes.[4] Consider, here, the text of the levée en masse, a document almost as much about the civilian war effort as about active service on the front. It is the young men – those without family responsibilities – who will, in time-honored fashion, march off to the frontiers. As for the rest of the population, they all have their allotted tasks to perform, most of which contribute to military supply – a truly national effort in which everyone has a role to play. Thus "married men will forge arms and transport foodstuffs; women will make tents, and items of clothing, and will serve in the hospitals; children will shred old linen," while old men would have the task of exciting the valor and patriotism of the young.[5] This should not be dismissed as hollow rhetoric; in the critical situation in which France found itself during the summer of 1793, with the *patrie* declared *en danger* and enemy forces massing along the frontiers, national defense was a task in which all were expected to be involved.

The priorities of the politicians at home were reflected in the concerns of the generals on the frontiers, who knew only too well that supply issues affected the morale of an army and determined its physical health and its

2 The most persuasive model for explaining the growth of state bureaucracy – and one that would apply well in this instance – is still Max Weber's *The Theory of Social and Economic Organization* (New York, 1947). A persuasive analysis of his theory is David Beetham, *Max Weber and the Theory of Modern Politics* (London, 1974); see also Stephen Turner, ed., *The Cambridge Companion to Weber* (Cambridge, U.K., 2000), chaps. 7–8.

3 For a discussion of inflation and the problems posed by the introduction of paper currency, see François Crouzet, *La grande inflation: la monnaie en France de Louis XVI à Napoléon* (Paris, 1993), and – rather more polemically – Florin Aftalion, *L'économie de la Révolution Française* (Paris, 1987).

4 The passion for collecting statistics was a feature of the revolutionary period, though it was seldom done innocently, without a desire to control. The topic is addressed by Jean-Claude Perrot and Stuart Woolf, *State and Statistics in France, 1789–1815* (London, 1984).

5 Decree of Aug. 23, 1793, in: *Archives Parlementaire de 1787 à 1860: Recueil complet des débats législatifs & politiques des chambres françaises (1879–)*, 72: 61–2.

potential in battle. Men had to be fed, clothed, and armed, of course, but there was more to it than that. Meat and grain had to be kept at reasonable temperatures to prevent rotting and decay; guns and powder had to be kept dry; and ambulances had to be made available to evacuate the wounded. Shelter had to be found for troops on campaign, and the means of keeping men dry, warm, and at least passably clean to avoid the perils of fevers and infection. None of this was easy to achieve with an army that was moving rapidly from place to place, often in difficult terrain such as the Alps or the Pyrenees. Above all, armies required transport – horses, mules, occasionally even oxen – to ensure that supplies were in the right place when needed. It was an operation that could easily go wrong, as Jean-Paul Bertaud has demonstrated in his study of military transport in the Armée des Pyrénées-Occidentales, where heat and mountainous terrain proved adversaries almost as deadly as the Spaniards, and where living off the land was not an option. Bread and rice rations ran out; excessive heat and oversalted meat led to a high consumption of drink; while wine and alcohol – which were virtual staples in any eighteenth-century army – became so expensive that soldiers had no option but to drink the local water, often stagnant and fetid, at the risk of dysentery and diarrhea. The health of the army, in other words, was undermined and lives lost because of failures of supply. Military efficiency, too, depended on regular and ensured transport in remote mountain areas, as the army required hundreds of kilograms of powder each month for its muskets and large quantities of oil to lubricate its batteries; as soon as the first casualties were suffered, they needed doctors, medical orderlies, and stretcher bearers to evacuate the injured.[6]

The problems the military faced in the Pyrenees were aggravated, of course, by the rugged terrain and the poor quality of local roads, which quickly became dangerous and rutted, transformed by autumn rains into torrents and quagmires. But these were not problems unique to any single region. Armies on every frontier faced supply problems, complained of the lack of competent drivers and of the poor condition of the carts, and pointed to the exhaustion of the draft animals designated to haul them. Dugommier in the Pyrénées-Orientales noted that, in November 1794, men's lives were being put at risk because there were no vehicles on which to evacuate the wounded; by the spring of 1795, he was reporting six-week delays in bringing provisions to the front line.[7] Or else there was no fodder for the

---

6 Jean-Paul Bertaud, "Contribution à l'étude des transports militaires dans les Pyrénées, 1794–95," *Actes du 94e Congrès National des Sociétés Savantes, Pau, 1969*, 2 vols. (Paris, 1971), 1:202–4.
7 Ibid., 212.

animals – a problem almost as great as shortages of rations for the men – with the result that horses and mules were collapsing and dying in their fields, and supply was again put in jeopardy. ("Hunger kills off the horses and mules in the fields; and they devastate the crops."[8]) Far from being a secondary issue, to be addressed only once the more important question of conscription was settled, military supply was recognized as a major priority of government. Besides, there was a political debt to be honored here. Citizen soldiers had the right to regular and efficient supply lines at a time when they were risking their lives for the commonweal. Efficacy and principle both demanded that the challenge of army supply be addressed.

If the authorities were inclined to see shortage and deprivation as the norm for an army on campaign, the young men in the ranks saw things quite differently, as a glance at their correspondence bears out. They complained of hunger so agonizing as to sap their strength, and they craved the familiar flavors of home cooking, the refreshment of wine and beer. When these were unobtainable, they were prone to suspect local farmers or shopkeepers of hoarding or to look for evidence of fraud within the army itself. Some showed more understanding. Alexandre Ladrix, stationed in the Alps, acknowledged that he, like the rest of the army, was hungry. "We are obliged to fast some days," he wrote, and he went on to explain that "the shortage of mules means that we can only get bread in the late afternoon around four or five o'clock, with the consequence that we can only have one meal per day."[9] They talked of the discomfort of sleeping in the open air, condemned to brave the elements because of a lack of tents and mattresses, or of lying in some straw, like the animals, in conditions that encouraged lice and skin diseases, those multifarious and ill-defined diseases that army doctors tended to characterize as "la gale."[10] Some admitted to being dispirited, dejected, and demoralized by the physical hardships they suffered and by the continual state of weariness in which they existed from day to day. "I am in a really critical state," wrote Pierre Girardon from the Army of the Rhine in 1794, his patriotism unabated even as his physical strength was drained by fever and a lack of sleep. But there was no hospital bed available, no way to rest his body until his sickness wore off. "I'm suffering the most dreadful of miseries. A cannon-ball or a bullet would be welcome to finish me off; and I would have no cause to reproach myself. I would have

8 Ibid., 213.
9 Jean Barada, "Lettres d'Alexandre Ladrix, volontaire de l'an II," *Carnet de la Sabretache*, 3rd ser., 9 (1926): 66.
10 Alan Forrest, *Napoleon's Men: The Soldiers of the Revolution and Empire* (London, 2002), 150.

worked as a true republican and I should die gladly with my arms in my hand."[11]

Responsibility for equipping the young soldiers lay with the municipalities that had recruited them, and towns differed greatly in their willingness and ability to provide appropriate funding. Levies generally produced the numbers of men demanded, but equipment was more problematic. Recruits often turned up without shoes or with the wooden clogs they wore on the farm, while uniforms might consist of little more than a loosely patched-up garment, something that would keep out the worst of the cold and might approximate the national blue in color. Firearms, too, could be homespun affairs, as likely to be defective hunting rifles as weapons of war. Examples abound of young men marching forth from their villages wearing threadbare shirts and armed with makeshift weaponry. Reports from around the country in the autumn of 1793 show how desperate some of the solutions turned out to be. In the district of Sainte-Ménehoulde, for instance, the council organized a collection of hunting rifles from the local peasantry; and in La Rochelle they sent off their recruits armed only with sticks.[12] Even once they arrived at their regiments, there was no guarantee that soldiers would be properly armed, as the army itself did not have sufficient stocks of serviceable firearms. Against a well-armed enemy, a soldier armed only with a pike could feel cruelly exposed.

Yet it is difficult not to have some sympathy with the revolutionary authorities. They had no precedent they could turn to for supplying a military machine of this size, and the structures they inherited from the ancien régime did not offer much help. During most of the eighteenth century, and most recently between 1785 and 1788, supply had been left to contractors, the War Ministry contracting with private entrepreneurs to provide subsistence for the army at a price agreed to with the government. But in the last months before the Revolution, this system had collapsed, and the War Council had responded by devolving responsibility for contracts for grain, fodder, uniforms, and equipment of all kinds to the administrative council of each regiment – an exercise in decentralized decision making that led to serious supply shortages and a failure of quality control.[13] As a result, the early revolutionary assemblies had little option but to return to the use of private contractors, whom they often disguised as government agents,

---

11 Eugène Maury, ed., *Lettres de volontaires républicains, 1791–94* (Troyes, 1901), 26–7.
12 Jean-Paul Bertaud, *La Révolution armée. Les soldats-citoyens de la Révolution Française* (Paris, 1979), 239–40.
13 Howard G. Brown, *War, Revolution and the Bureaucratic State: Politics and Army Administration in France, 1791–99* (Oxford, 1995), 99–100.

though this double role confused both the status of the companies and their bookkeeping practice. In the summer of 1791, controls were at a minimum – all price controls on bread and meat had been removed, inflation was rampant, and there were no mechanisms to guarantee the quality of the goods purchased. Indeed, the whole system soon suffocated in abuse; by the time the war broke out, private contracting had been largely enveloped within state-incorporated bureaucracies, whose operating conditions were defined by law and regulated by the minister of war. When war was declared the following year, it surprised no one that the scope of corruption was shockingly widespread.[14] The way was open for further centralization of military supply under the Republic – something that was seen as necessary not only to stamp out fraud but also to improve discipline and morale in the ranks.

It fell to the Jacobins to dismantle the system of private contracting and to assume greater public control of the market. This fit well with their wider economic policy, moving away from the free market economy of the earlier Revolution to regulate the grain trade in May 1793 and introduce the law of the maximum – to control essential commodity prices – in September.[15] Government contractors had little choice but to charge prescribed prices and to accept payment in paper currency. Requisitions and compulsory purchases soon followed, a process that was usually limited to departments adjacent to the war zone, where peasants were forced to sell a proportion of their crop for the exclusive use of the troops. The effectiveness of these measures was, however, uneven, depending on such variables as the passage of deputies on mission from the Convention and the stubbornness of local peasants in maintaining their traditional customs and markets. But what is not in doubt is the will to control, shown most clearly in the bodies they set up to oversee supply – the Commission du Commerce et des Approvisionnements to ensure supplies of food and basic equipment, the Commission des Transports to ensure sufficient carts for army convoys. Both resorted to seizures and requisitions, though the Commission des Transports also bought in the services of carters and paid local firms to take on army contracts.[16] Such latitude was essential if crises were to be averted in individual armies; the government could not afford to be too inflexible in its commercial dealings.

14 Ibid., 103.
15 For a discussion of the more egalitarian reasoning behind Jacobin economic reforms, see Jean-Pierre Gross, *Fair Shares for All: Jacobin Egalitarianism in Practice* (Cambridge, U.K., 1997).
16 Marc Bouloiseau, "L'approvisionnement de l'Armée de l'Ouest en l'an II, d'après les registres du commissaire ordonnateur Lenoble," *Actes du 93e Congrès National des Sociétés Savantes, Tours, 1968*, 2 vols. (Paris, 1971), 1:403–4.

The growth of a controlled economy did, of course, suit the army well, and when, after Thermidor, the controls were relaxed, the degree of the army's dependence on them became clear. Inflation and the freeing of food prices hit the supply administration hard; it did not have the resources to buy in a free market and had little option but to pay in paper currency, whose value diminished almost by the day. Spiraling grain prices, coupled with the freeing of markets, meant that peasants could again sell to the highest bidder, which left the armies exposed and vulnerable. With their funds draining away, they continued to look to price controls , and where they could not enforce controls, they became more and more dependent on requisitions. This, is turn, drove a wedge between the troops and the civilian population. In 1792, notes Robert Werner, soldiers still basked in popular support, to the extent that the people of Wissembourg, on their own initiative, raised funds to improve day-to-day living conditions in the Army of the Rhine; but three years later, that enthusiasm had been squandered by the army's heavy-handed approach to requisitioning. A spirit of cooperation had given way to a sense of resentment and disillusionment.[17]

When armies were stationed on French soil, the full weight of military requisitions fell on local people – a burden that was deemed more intolerable in that agricultural output was already suffering in most French provinces because of the loss of able-bodied young workers to the armies. Requisitions were imposed on all sorts of foodstuffs – straw and hay, wine, cattle, and sheep – but first and foremost they affected cereals, to the point that locally they could totally distort the market in grain. By 1793–4, supplies for the army took precedence over all others, and the authorities knew only too well that their demands were likely to be resisted. This did not encourage a light touch. "I recommend and order you to use the right of preemption," a military inspector wrote to the district of Chalon-sur-Saône, "that is to say to require that all the grain that you come across be transferred to the army. Always work on the principle that the army must be given preference over other citizens, and seize all the wheat you can find." And, he added reassuringly, "Have recourse if necessary to the armed force which you have at your disposal to obtain both wheat and fodder."[18] He knew that the sight of armed soldiers entering their community to impose requisitions would help to concentrate the minds of recalcitrant villagers.

---

17 Robert Werner, *L'approvisionnement en pain de la population du Bas-Rhin et de l'Armée du Rhin pendant la Révolution, 1789–97* (Strasbourg, 1951), 600.
18 Marguerite Rebouillat, "Les réquisitions pour la subsistance des armées et des villes à Sercy (district de Chalon-sur-Saône) pendant la Révolution," *Actes du 93e Congrès National*, 1:392.

Requisitioning fell very unevenly, often on only a handful of departments, and this could place an untenable strain on the tolerance of local people, who might legitimately feel that they were being asked to shoulder an unacceptably large part of the military burden. This was especially true of frontier areas – of the departments of Flanders and Picardy, Lorraine and Alsace, which suffered long months of military activity with the presence of two armies (the Nord and the Rhine); of Savoy and the Alpine departments in the catchment of the Army of the Alps; and of Roussillon, the Béarn and the Pays Basque, which had to support the armies of the eastern and western Pyrenees. Inequities were not always the product of deliberation. In the east, where the Army of the Rhine drew on the grain of seven departments, requisitions tended to be concentrated on the immediate war zone because of a chronic shortage of transport.[19] The Roussillon – the new department of Pyrénées-Orientales – was subjected to heavy demands, especially after the Spaniards invaded and Perpignan fell into enemy hands. But even a French military presence proved difficult to bear, because at any one time there might be between 10,000 and 40,000 soldiers for a resident population of only 125,000, an incursion that was increasingly resented by local people as repeated requisitions came close to destroying the precarious balance of their agricultural economy.[20] So in the Alpes-Maritimes – a small department with fewer than ninety thousand inhabitants before 1792 – the French placed a resident garrison of ten thousand men, while in the period up to the summer of 1794, the landscape was constantly trampled by both French and Piedmontese, certain operations involving as many as thirty thousand soldiers (or one for every three inhabitants).[21] Animals were requisitioned and herds decimated. These losses could not be quickly repaired. In 1806, the prefect of the Alpes-Maritimes noted how cattle disease had inflated the impact of requisitions, with the consequence that herds remained depleted, while wheat yields were poor and olive production had fallen badly as a result of the war.[22]

With the outbreak of civil war in the Vendée, it was the turn of the western departments to feel the brunt of requisitions. Lenoble, charged with requisitions in Saumur, responded to government demands in Messidor II

---

19 Werner, *L'approvisionnement*, 597.
20 Michel Brunet, "Les armées de la Révolution et la population roussillonnaise, 1791–94," *Annales du Midi* 83 (1971): 226.
21 Alain Ruggiero, "La présence de l'armée et ses conséquences dans le département des Alpes-Maritimes de l'an II l'an X," in *La Révolution française: la guerre et la frontière*, ed. Monique Cubells (Paris, 2000), 156.
22 "Situation du département des Alpes-Maritimes en 1806," quoted in Ruggiero, "La présence de l'armée," 166.

by purchasing, at the prices laid down by the maximum, a wide range of commodities for the use of the army, ranging from red wine to oil and honey. His activity soon brought him into conflict with those of his colleagues who were tasked with requisitioning for the civilian population, particularly for the towns. He warned one of them to expect intrigue and denunciation and urged him to defend his rights against importunate civilians. "You know well enough," he added, "their animosity towards the military."[23] He knew, too, the conflicting interests that divided producers and consumers, peasants and townspeople, interests that made agents of the supply administration a target ripe for denunciation.

Lenoble was a *commissaire des subsistances*, one of a number of carefully selected administrators entrusted with the task of ensuring that the armies were properly and promptly supplied. The post was not a new one; there had been *commissaires des guerres* under the ancien régime, too, but the scale of the Revolutionary wars meant that their powers were repeatedly reviewed, while political considerations, combined with the fear of abuse, led to a purge of those who had worked in the service of the Bourbons. As a *mémoire* of Year II rather pointedly put it, "During the reign of the despots, when the armies were the property of kings and the regiments of their courtiers, these courtiers were sufficiently adroit to appoint as *commissaires* their secretaries, stewards and other creatures," who stole from the army on their masters' behalf and depressed the lot of the ordinary soldier.[24] The 390 *commissaires* whom the Convention appointed in April 1793 were to have different interests and priorities, men with relevant military experience who also knew something of administration or accounting. They needed this range of experience, as their authority stretched from arranging food purchases to imposing quality controls, from requisitioning carters to organizing the billeting of new influxes of soldiers. It was their job to keep the army happy, to prevent mutiny – the revolutionaries never forgot that it was problems of supply that, more than anything, had caused the wave of mutinies in Nancy and the east in 1790[25] – and to ensure that the men were not compelled to loot and pillage from the local peasantry.[26] In the Sambre-et-Meuse, studied by Peter Wetzler, all those appointed were former soldiers, and many of them had been supply quartermasters or had worked in military transport before their appointment. Some of the older men had served in the line, but most were taken from the revolutionary battalions or from the National Guard

23 Bouloiseau, "L'approvisionnement de l'Armée de l'Ouest," 410.
24 Archives Nationales (hereafter AN), AD-VI 45, *mémoire* on *commissaires des guerres*, 10 Brumaire II.
25 S. F. Scott, *The Response of the Royal Army to the French Revolution* (Oxford, 1978), 46–80.
26 AN, AD-VI 45, decree on *commissaires des guerres*, Apr. 16, 1793.

(in Rennes, Nantes, Nancy, and Dunkerque – the catchment was wide ranging). Most were in their twenties or thirties, though a few were much older. They were often talented and well read: there were students among them, young men with a grounding in the law and a broad knowledge of foreign languages. Occasionally, they appointed much older candidates, but only when they brought relevant skills: Jacques-Joseph Tamboise was appointed at the age of fifty-one after twelve years as an army chaplain, while Pierre Nadaud, age forty-four, had been secretary to the intendances of Limoges and Tours, in charge of military issues, for more than twenty years before becoming a battalion quartermaster in the Armée des Alpes.[27]

Astute and talented they may have been, but it is difficult to avoid the impression that theirs was a largely thankless task, a job in which it was difficult to succeed and even harder to please one's political masters. There were so many potential conflicts in which a *commissaire* could become embroiled, whether with peasants angry at the removal of their crops, local authorities facing their own internal subsistence crisis, or *commissaires* from other regiments trawling in the same waters for limited supplies of clothing. Military-civilian relations, as Ute Planert points out elsewhere in this volume, were dominated by issues of supply and requisition.[28] Each *commissaire* received hundreds of pleas and petitions, yet he would himself be the subject of gossip and denunciation, which at the height of the Terror could make his task dangerous as well as politically sensitive.[29] The Robespierrist paper, *L'Antifédéraliste*, claimed that the whole supply administration was riddled with corruption, contaminated by "a band of brigands who had previously spent their time in the antechambers and the stables of Versailles and in the brothels of the Palais Royal." In the political climate of 1794, this scarcely made for cheering reading. More threatening still was a charge leveled by Saint-Just in October 1793, when he claimed that the Republic was being undermined by its own officials, by hangers-on "who corrupt it, battle against it, and bleed it of resources." This was a particularly damaging accusation, coming as it did from a man who had recently returned from a mission to the Army of the Rhine and who had taken a particular interest in pillage, self-aggrandizement, and corruption, especially in matters of army contracting and supply.[30] Saint-Just saw virtue in the volunteer offering his blood for the Republic; those working in the wings, in the offices of the

---

27 Peter Wetzler, *War and Subsistence: The Sambre and Meuse Army in 1794* (New York, 1985), 269–93.
28 See Ute Planert, "Innovation or Evolution? The French Wars in Military History" in this volume.
29 Forrest, *Soldiers of the French Revolution*, 134.
30 Robert Devleeshouwer, *L'arrondissement du Brabant sous l'occupation française, 1794–95* (Brussels, 1964), 143–4.

supply administration, he tended to dismiss as self-interested, pampered, and corrupt.

Indeed, there is no reason to believe that the supply administrators were trusted by the Jacobins any more than were the generals themselves; by 1793, the deputies sent out from the Convention on mission, like Saint-Just, were inspecting their performance every bit as closely as the record of the military high command. There were to be three deputies on mission with each army, given overall direction of the military – though not, it must be stressed, of executing tactical maneuvers (Saint-Just was quite specific in drawing this distinction). The law invested them with unlimited powers, and both civil and military agents owed them total obedience. In return, they had to implement measures of public safety, arrest suspects, oversee propaganda in the regiments, and where necessary, call up units of the National Guard to increase numbers. In the last months of Jacobin rule, they even had the power to issue decrees on their own authority.[31] The point was yet again driven home that the military did not constitute a world apart from society, with its own customs and values, its autonomous or traditional practices. The army and those who worked for it were answerable for their actions just like any other body of citizens.

When the French armies moved abroad, the supply problem did not disappear; it was simply exported, imposing on others the obligations that previously had been borne by the French. But what obligations? Were Germans or Belgians to be treated in the same way as the population of a French province and made to furnish requisitions or pay war indemnities? Were they to be treated as friendly populations, welcoming of the liberty that the French had brought them, or as enemies, the inhabitants of conquered territories that had resisted and lost? In principle, of course, the revolutionaries had renounced wars of conquest, declaring in May 1790 their repugnance at any action that would deprive others of their liberty.[32] They had assimilated current thinking on what constituted a just war, and their ideas were rooted in the theories of Grotius, Vattel, and Pufendorf: rape, pillage and marauding at the expense of local people stood condemned as the Assembly dreamed of liberating the rest of Europe from the tyranny of church and king. Yet within months, French generals were seeking to establish natural frontiers along the Rhine, a traditional and unrevolutionary war aim, while logistical demands made it necessary to impose taxes and feed the armies from the economies of the conquered territories. As Jacques

31 Jacques Godechot, *Les commissaires aux armées sous le Directoire* (Paris, 1937), 26–7, 32.
32 Declaration of May 22, 1790, in: *Archives Parlementaires de 1787 à 1860*, 15: 661–2.

Godechot rightly observed, the revolutionaries had, within twelve months, reverted to the practice of the ancien régime, exporting the material cost of the war by living off the land wherever they campaigned and even, by 1796, seeking to improve French finances by the full-scale exploitation of occupied lands. The *commissaires'* first duty was not to the peoples of Europe but to the army and to France; the message they repeatedly received from Paris was the need to "nourrir la guerre par la guerre, faire vivre l'armée sur le pays."[33]

The implication was unambiguous: the first priority of the occupier was to the army, not to local people. Supply must always have precedence. In Nice, occupied by the French in 1792 to be turned into a base for supplying the armies in Italy, the authorities requisitioned the flour mills and, in periods of drought, demanded the exclusive use of water, needed to work the hydraulic mechanism on which milling depended, so that they could maintain the supply of bread to the military.[34] They then added insult to injury by requisitioning local transport to ensure that the bread was delivered where it was required. By 1793, even the Jacobins had given up any pretense that occupation of foreign territory could translate into liberation for its inhabitants. Occupation was a policy founded in pragmatism, and because French agriculture was patently incapable of feeding all the men fighting in the armies, the Committee of Public Safety had no choice but to order its generals to procure their stocks of food, fodder, boots, clothing, and transport from the people of the territories they occupied. Within days of entering Brabant, for instance, orders were issued to impose requisitions on the peasantry and to levy customs duties on municipalities. The aim was simply to raise money, and money that could be converted into foreign exchange to pay for much-needed imports. Indeed, it is ironic that, at the very moment when they were imposing the worthless assignat on the Belgians, the French also demanded that taxes and requisitions due to them should be paid in metal – metal drawn from municipal treasuries, hard currency that had an assured value.[35] And this was only the beginning. In the six months from October 1794, the French extracted requisitions worth more than 27 million livres, and in Year III, the *commissaire-ordonnateur général* in charge of Belgium, Sabin-Bourcier, ruled that half of all the grain produced in the country should be requisitioned to support the French

---

33 Jacques Godechot, "Les variations de la politique française à l'égard des pays occupés, 1792–1815," in *Occupants, occupés, 1792–1815. Colloque de Bruxelles, 29–30 janvier 1968* (Brussels, 1969), 22–25.
34 René Tresse, "La mouture des grains à Nice, 1792–1800," *Actes du 93e Congrès National*, 1:424–6.
35 Devleeshouwer, *L'arrondissement du Brabant*, 75–6.

army.[36] The Belgians, like others after them, were paying the costs of their own army of occupation.

Sabin-Bourcier's demands demonstrate two things. First, they show the huge costs incurred by keeping an army of this size in the field, season after season, campaign after campaign. The geographical scope of the fighting merely compounded the problem, as armies were constantly on the move and it became increasingly difficult to organize fixed lines of supply. It would have been impossible, logistically, to supply regiments fighting in Germany or Poland from metropolitan France; living off the land was inevitable. But it brought with it terrible risks. Requisitioning alienated local people and led to resistance from peasants who felt they were being cheated or bullied out of their just rewards. It was difficult to organize, creating a second army of clerks and bureaucrats whose sole purpose was to administer supply. And it could go terribly wrong, as the armies were led to depend on supplies that were not there: the Moscow campaign would end in disaster largely – though not entirely – because of Napoleon's failure to manage logistics, his armies consuming the crops on the way out that they needed for survival during their long, desperate retreat.[37] Second, the demands point to a new kind of warfare, providing a foretaste of the Directory's imperialistic approach to occupation, the sense of the deliberate policy of annexation to extort food and resources from the occupied territories and to sustain the army without cost to the French treasury. War was coming to be waged to maximize requisitions; the logistics of the army had become, to that degree, both the motor of warfare and the raison d'être for further invasion. Of course, the peoples who suffered invasion at French hands were unlikely to detect much difference between requisitions and pillage at the hands of the state, especially as the goods requisitioned were not restricted to the needs of the army. Occupation also meant income generation, as the occupier, here in the Rhineland, requisitioned "arms, cereals, goods and merchandise of all kinds, and carried off to France many works of art."[38] Only some of the goods would be used for the army and can be explained as part of a coherent logistical policy. By 1795, military requisitioning blended seamlessly into a wider policy of economic exploitation.

For the armies in the field, however, these were questions for others. For them, the basic purpose of requisitioning remained unchanged, the eternal issue of providing those day-to-day essentials without which life became

36 Ibid., 126.
37 Charles Esdaile, *The Wars of Napoleon* (London, 1995), 260–1.
38 Walter Grab, "La Rhénanie face à l'occupation par les armées révolutionnaires françaises, 1792–99," in *Occupants, occupés*, 133.

impossible, made all the more urgent by the fact that France had created a mass citizen army of the sort that would characterize modern nations without first having in place that other characteristic of modernity, a developed industrial base. Food supplies were only one part of a much wider problem; more serious in the long term was the need to find sufficient arms and uniforms. The full shock was, of course, felt in 1793, when the men mobilized by the levée en masse had to be equipped, though clothing proved a persistent problem – one that still bedeviled the supply administration when conscription was decreed six years later. When there was not a mechanized textile industry, where was the army to obtain uniforms and clothing on the scale that was demanded? Local businesses were, of course, invited to bid for their share in the military market, but some were reluctant: they had other customers, raw materials were difficult to find, or they were deterred by the government's reputation for defaulting on payment. Locating sources of regular supply was, in any case, a long-term solution to the problem; in the short term, they looked to find seamstresses wherever they were available, and for political reasons, they preferred to channel work to the public workshops that had been set up in the Paris sections, with sectional *commissaires* ensuring that every seamstress who registered with the section was allocated her share of the available work. It was a political solution, one that appealed to the more egalitarian instincts of the sections and to the predilections of the war minister of the moment, the ultra-Jacobin Bouchotte. But it could not guarantee steady deliveries to the armies; nor, if the complaints of rough cloth and shoddy workmanship are to be believed, did it do much to ensure that the troops were kept warm and well clad.[39]

Just as damaging was the shortage of footwear, especially, again, in 1793–4, when the supply administration was suddenly faced with the prospect of finding boots for several hundred thousand raw recruits. Again, the structure of the shoemaking industry did them few favors, as this was a traditional artisanal activity, the preserve of family firms and individual cobblers, established in a local neighborhood and serving a neighborhood clientele. It was not easily adaptable to the needs of the military or to the organization of large-scale production. And because the *commissaires* could not restructure the boot-making industry overnight, they had little choice but to appeal to the patriotism and good will of *cordonniers* across the country and to urge them to work hard and quickly for the national cause. It did not help that leather was in short supply, or that the government obliged them to pay for all orders in devalued paper currency. In the course of the long

---

39 General Herlaut, *Le colonel Bouchotte, ministre de la guerre en l'an II*, 2 vols. (Paris, 1946), 1:142–67.

marches the armies were forced to endure, boots wore out quickly, and such supplies as were held in stores did not suffice for long. Carnot was obliged in 1794 to admit that there was no immediate solution to the shortage, even suggesting that troops in the Armée du Nord be asked to wear wooden clogs, as traditionally worn by the peasantry in many parts of the country, until new supplies of boots arrived.[40] Some had a long and arduous wait; in Ventôse II, one of the deputies on mission with the army, Cellier, was still complaining that boots had not arrived and drew attention to the anger that this caused among the men. "Most of them still go barefoot," he reported. "They do not even have clogs; there are angry murmurs in the ranks, and they are afraid that they will still be in this state when the campaigning season begins."[41]

Even those to whom footwear was issued had reason for complaint. They were often badly made, of poor quality and ill fitting, and they let in water. Philoxène Leulier, in a report to the minister of war, recognized that the soldiers had solid grounds for complaint. "The shape of the sole, square instead of being cut to the shape of the foot, and the badly-designed heel both impeded walking and caused continual injuries," while the weight of the buckle resulted in bruised and calloused feet. Army doctors agreed. In 1795, one *officier de santé*, Lavallète, reported that the boots were so uncomfortable and so ill suited to the troops' grueling routine that the soldiers preferred to go without them, many of them taking the opportunity to sell them to peddlers or passersby. The tone of his report is factual; the soldiers were ridding themselves of an encumbrance, and Lavallète clearly sees nothing in their behavior to merit reproach.[42] Even when there were no shortages, the supply administration was not above criticism.

And what of weaponry, on whose availability and quality every soldier's life depended? Before the Revolution, the infantry had been issued a standard musket, the so-called *fusil de munition* that had been introduced in 1777 and that would remain in service throughout the Revolution and into the Consulate. It had its weaknesses, among them a rather labored loading mechanism and the need to give the barrel a complete clean after every thirty or forty shots fired, and its accuracy was highly flawed.[43] But it did, at least, provide soldiers with firepower in battle and a means of self-defense, and those who had the musket were grateful for it. But many did not. Unfortunately, the arsenals that the Revolution inherited, while adequate

---

40 Albert Soboul, *Les soldats de l'an II* (Paris, 1959), 157.
41 Ibid., 159.
42 Jean-Paul Bertaud, *La vie quotidienne des soldats de la Révolution, 1789–99* (Paris, 1985), 74.
43 Ibid., 79–80.

to the needs of the royal regiments of the 1780s, were unequipped to deal
with the new mass armies, and the problem was made worse by the effects
of the early defeats. The armories tended to be sited along the frontiers,
and several were lost to the enemy, including Maubeuge and Charleville,
while the federalist revolt in Lyon in 1793 temporarily put the major arms
manufacture at Saint-Étienne out of action. Once again, the government
responded with a series of emergency measures to raise arms production,
in effect nationalizing the arms industry in France. It set up a score of new
armories in provincial towns, constructed open-air forges along the Seine
and in many of the squares of the capital – an activity immortalized in the
gouaches of Le Sueur[44] – and drew on the organizing capacities of clubs
and sections.[45] The Committee of Public Safety itself took charge of arms
manufacture.

Yet still there were not enough guns to go around, even taking account
of the thousands of shotguns and hunting rifles that municipalities supplied
along with the men of their contingent. Weapons that were damaged in
action or that had exploded through overuse had to be repaired or replaced;
around the frontiers, indeed, the *commissaires'* most urgent work was often
to requisition armorers to mend discarded rifles, a burden that once more
fell on the towns closest to the area of engagement.[46] In February 1794, the
armies were still reporting substantial shortfalls – ten thousand in the Armée
du Nord, twelve thousand in the Alps and the Rhine, twenty thousand in
the Pyrénées-Orientales.[47] Being a soldier did not provide any guarantee
that one would have access to firepower. Troops were issued with bayonets
and urged to charge the enemy, a form of fighting that many claimed to be
better suited to the fiery, impetuous, undisciplined character of the French
soldier. By 1793, the sans-culottes had identified the *arme blanche* as the most
effective as well as the most Gallic form of combat, playing down the value
of powder and praising the virtues of hand-to-hand fighting. The pike was
turned into a symbol of both courage and élan; it was, in the view of the
sectional radicals, the preferred weapon of patriots. Its virtues were praised
by the Commune and the Jacobin Club, in the pages of the radical press,
and in many of the *feuilles volantes* that circulated in the capital, whipping
up popular support for one faction or another. Among the popular figures
who appealed to Parisian patriotism were such military heroes as Va-de-
Bon-Coeur and the significantly named Général La-Pique, whose faith
in the *arme blanche* was unconditional.[48] But we should not be deceived

44 Musée Carnavalet, Paris.   45 Soboul, *Les soldats*, 144–53.
46 Forrest, *Soldiers of the French Revolution*, 138.   47 Bertaud, *La vie quotidienne*, 83–4.
48 Ouzi Elyada, *Presse populaire et feuilles volantes de la Révolution à Paris, 1789–92* (Paris, 1991), iv.

by the power of such rhetoric or by the easy theatrical style of popular pamphlets. The pike was often the only weapon available to the troops, and the revolutionaries' reliance on it cost many young lives.

If supplying and repairing weapons posed a serious logistical challenge for the armies, so did ensuring sufficient supplies of gunpowder for the artillery and for those in the infantry who did have muskets in working order. This required a major effort to locate and treat saltpeter, and because it was no longer possible to import supplies, the powers of the *régie* responsible for munitions were greatly increased and the soil of the whole country placed at its disposal. New deposits were uncovered, and householders were urged to search in their cellars and outhouses – once again the Republic turned to a civilian mobilization, to the levée en masse of the whole community in the war effort. They relied heavily on the patriotism of Paris and of the sansculotte militants who organized themselves to search cellars and separate saltpeter from the damp and rotting earth to which it clung. In all, Albert Soboul concludes, about sixty sectional workshops were set up, and they produced fifty thousand pounds of saltpeter every ten days, permitting the armies to overcome what would have been a major logistical crisis.[49] But it was a short-term solution, dependent on goodwill and popular enthusiasm. It could not survive the destruction of sectional power that followed the ninth of Thermidor.

The treatment of the sick and wounded is a subject in its own right, part of a broader history of medicine in this period, but military medicine, more than its civilian counterpart, depended heavily on rapidity of movement and logistical support. Again, the sheer scale of the war presented massive problems. Beds had to be found close to war zones that were constantly moving from town to town and from valley to valley. Doctors and surgeons had to be recruited for the *service de santé* in numbers that far exceeded the requirements of peacetime. And the state had to train more students in medicine, to provide more places in *écoles de médecine* and *de chirurgerie* if medical expertise were to be learned and applied. In theory, the National Assembly was prepared to fulfill all these commitments, agreeing in 1791 that the debt owed to the troops represented the "most sacred" of obligations, and that it was the government's duty to provide the best medical care for all those of its citizens who were wounded in action – as well as pensions for those too badly wounded to continue their service.[50] A further decree of April 1792, once war had been declared, laid down that

49 Soboul, *Les soldats*, xx.
50 AN, AD-VI 613, *Projet de décret soumis par le Comité de Guerre et le Comité des Secours Publics*, 1791.

wherever there were troop concentrations, military hospitals should be set up, both fixed hospitals behind the lines and *hôpitaux ambulants* that could accompany the men to the battlefield. In practice, however, the problems were seemingly endless.[51] If military hospitals on French soil were often relatively well equipped and supplied – the hospital at Limoges lost only one patient during three months of Year IV – many of those closest to battle zones were sorely neglected.[52] The hospitals had often been hastily set up in commandeered buildings; were dirty, overcrowded, and poorly supplied; and were regarded with suspicion as sources of infection by both troops and local civilians. There were serious shortages of linen and medicines as well as of straw and mattresses, which led to sick soldiers being turned away; and if they were transferred to civil hospitals in local towns, their presence there was often resented, because they were viewed as a drain on supplies and – very often – as an outrage to morals and public decency.[53]

The shortage of medical staff was never completely resolved, but it was eased by a series of pragmatic reforms: it was decided to exempt *officiers de santé* from a military service that was keeping them away from their patients, for instance, and more pupils were to be prepared for the army by offering instruction in the *hôpitaux militaires* of Lille, Metz, Strasbourg, and Toulon. More significant, a decree of August 1793 allowed the minister to requisition all *officiers de santé*, chemists, surgeons and doctors between the ages of eighteen and forty for service with the army.[54] By such drastic measures the staffing crisis began to be resolved. But not everything could be cured by legislation. Fevers, vomiting, and diarrhea still killed as many men in hospital beds as did enemy fire in battle.[55] A chronic lack of medicines and the onset of gangrene led to prolonged and agonizing suffering, so that when soldiers talked of hospitals, they did so with fear and trepidation. Too many were left to die on the battlefield itself, though the introduction of Larrey's *ambulances volantes* did help to reduce the suffering of the wounded and speed the journey to the surgeon's table. The lot of sick and injured soldiers, like so much else in the army, would be determined by logistics – by

51 Albert Fabre, ed., *Histoire de la médecine aux armées*, 3 vols. (Paris, 1984), 2:5.
52 A.D. Haute-Vienne, L 375, report on the state of the military hospital in Limoges, 9 Vendémiaire V; Alan Forrest, *The French Revolution and the Poor* (Oxford, 1981), 66–8.
53 A.D. Rhône, 1L903, report of the *comité militaire* in Lyon, June 2, 1793.
54 Fabre, *Histoire de la médecine*, 2:10–13.
55 A doctor's account of the ailments brought on by heat and long marches in the Egyptian campaign is "Notes sur les maladies qui ont régné en frimaire an VII, recueillies dans l'hôpital militaire du vieux Caire," by B. Barbès, "médecin ordinaire de l'armée d'Orient," in René-Nicolas Desgenettes, *Histoire médicale de l'Armée d'Orient* (Paris, 1835), 303–12.

the availability of *infirmiers* and stretcher bearers, the provision of clean water and bed linen, efforts to keep roads and tracks open in bad weather, and the arrival of rations and of fodder for the horses and mules. These were vital to the survival of the army and to maintaining morale and cementing men's loyalty to the Republic, and they could not be guaranteed by political will alone.

10

Revolt and Repression in Napoleonic Italy, 1796–1814

MICHAEL BROERS

The *epoca francese*, as the period of Napoleonic occupation is known in Italian historiography, is generally and correctly credited with the introduction of the fundamental elements of the modern nation-state into Italian society. It was, without doubt, the period when a public sphere centered on the institutions of the French Revolutionary state was injected into the territories of the former states of the old order, witnessing the establishment of the Napoleonic Code and the prefectorial system of administration into the entire peninsula. The Napoleonic occupation also brought about the most comprehensive territorial reorganization Italy had undergone since Roman times, giving it a degree of political unity hitherto unknown, and not witnessed again, until unification in 1859. Under Napoleonic hegemony, the peninsula was divided into three units: the Kingdoms of Naples (minus Sicily), the Kingdom of Italy (to which Venetia was added in 1807, having been seized from the Austrian Empire), and the imperial departments – the *départements réunis* – that eventually came to embrace the mainland possessions of the House of Savoy, Liguria, Tuscany, the Papal States, and the Duchy of Parma-Piacenza. All this took place well behind the lines of the major campaigns of the Napoleonic Wars after 1800.

Although the peninsula saw fierce fighting between 1796 and 1800, during the first and second Italian campaigns, it did not experience any major military operations again until 1814, save for some counterinsurgency operations in the northeastern Alps in 1809, in the wake of the Wagram campaign and Hofer's Tyrolean revolt. This picture is very misleading, however. The first impression is of a region in a rare and enviable state of peace in a largely war-torn continent, receiving its apprenticeship in a long-overdue process of state building, albeit under foreign tutelage. In these years, the foundations of the Risorgimento were laid. Although not in itself untrue, this view has been corrected and refined by much recent historiography. The experience of Napoleonic occupation was not only unwelcome and resented by Italian reformers for its authoritarianism and the disappointment of initial Jacobin hopes, it was a traumatic experience for the Italian masses, particularly for the communities of its mountainous hinterlands, and that trauma often expressed itself in violent revolt long after the great risings attendant on the first Italian campaign of 1796–7 and the short-lived but bloody French retreat of 1799. The story of the *epoca francese* is neither tranquil nor reassuring for the future of the modern state in Italy.

The history of the anti-French revolts in Napoleonic Italy divides into three distinct but related phases, each of which will be considered in the successive sections of this chapter. Only one was precise in time and can be accounted as *évenmentielle*, as it were: the almost instinctive popular resistance that followed the initial French invasion of 1796–7, culminating in the truly massive, pan-peninsular revolts of 1799 that accompanied – and in some cases, actually preceded – French military reverses at the hands of the forces of the Second Coalition in 1799. The second comprises the localized, if ferocious, revolts that immediately followed the reoccupation and annexation of the individual Italian states to the empire; they follow sequentially, the process of the creation of the *départements réunis*: Piedmont witnessed peasant revolts in Aosta and its Alpine valleys in 1800–1; Liguria and Parma-Piacenza experienced a short, if bitter, revolt in the Piacentino in the winter of 1805–6; Tuscany saw serious uprisings in the Aretino and Maremma, in the south, and near Pistoia, in the north, in 1808. Only the Papal States did not follow this pattern, as resistance there took the singular form of a mass campaign of passive resistance to the deposition of Pius VII and annexation to France.[1] Thus, the second phase of revolt actually spreads itself across the years 1800–8, as a series of successive waves. This chronology was punctuated by the fifth phenomenon: the two great rebellions in the kingdom of Italy in 1809: the revolt of the Apennine valleys of central Italy, now the Emilia-Romagna, and that of the uplands of Venetia, connected to the Tyrolean revolt of Andreas Hofer, and the Calabrian brigand war of 1810–11, perhaps the closest the Italian peninsula came to emulating the Spanish guerrilla. Finally, the sixth type of revolt is generic, in that it is best understood not as individual events, but as occurrences connected to one another by circumstances, causes, and character. These are the hordes of microrevolts provoked by the enforcement of conscription, of the alien religious reforms of the Napoleonic concordat or simply by the conduct of

---

1 See Michael Broers, *Politics and Religion in Napoleonic Italy, 1802–1814: The War against God* (London, 2002), 146–60.

French gendarmes and civilian administrators, up and down the peninsula, from the Piedmontese Alps to Calabria.

All of them cast long shadows over the *epoca francese*; that of 1799 has gone down in liberal Italian historiography as *l'anno nero* – the black year – better known for the sufferings of pro-French Italian collaborators, the *giacobini* or *patriotti*, than for the mass participation of so many Italian peasantries and even urban populations. *L'anno nero* has attained the status of a *folklorique* for successive generations of the progressive chattering classes. Yet the inchoate revolts that followed each annexation – often directly linked to those of 1799 – and, perhaps even more, the microrisings, often little more than riots, that rumbled on under French rule, might provide the most revealing insights on the impact of modernity and the machinery of war on Italian society. The link between war and the process of state building in the *epoca francese* is not direct, but it is emphatic, and it exposes the deep-rooted, enduring trauma of the militarization throughout societies and communities where war and strong armies had been virtually unknown for generations. This emerges in three distinct ways in the Italian case. The most obvious and well-studied incursion of the Napoleonic Wars into these societies was the imposition of conscription, which provoked violent resistance and demanded constant policing, and the introduction of a rural paramilitary police force, the gendarmerie, to do so. The second ramification of militarization was the need for constant, not intermittent, repression and coercion in regions that had never known a strong or permanent state presence before. The third, and most pervasive, consequence of state incursion, if also the most diffuse, was the suspicion and hatred the whole panoply of the new regime embedded in Italian society. These elements, taken collectively, produced widespread trauma among the vast majority of Italians and engendered a tradition of antistatism – still prospering under the adage of the acknowledged gap between the *paese reale* and the *paese civile* (the real and the official country). It has its most tangible historical roots in the bringing of Italians into the Napoleonic war effort that lay at the heart of the *epoca francese*.

THE FIRST FRENCH INVASION, 1796–99

The invasion route from France to Italy has always run through Piedmont. Geography makes it impossible to do otherwise, and throughout the early modern period, from the point the two kingdoms became established neighbors, the Piedmontese had been ready for the French. Savoy and Nice, on the wrong side of the Alpine watershed, as it were, fell quickly, passing to

Revolutionary France in 1790. It was very different on the other side of the Alps, however. There, a long tradition of resistance to French incursions had evolved, expressed through the regular provincial militias and in the illegal activities of the *barbetti*, smuggler-bandits who, in times of crisis throughout the late seventeenth and eighteenth centuries, rallied to the same crown that harassed them in peace time. In 1796–7, they defended the passes of the southern Alps, around Cuneo and Mondovì, with the same ferocity they normally fought authority. One of the striking paradoxes of Piedmontese resistance in those years was the ferocious loyalty to the monarchy displayed by the most unruly provinces and social elements in Piedmont. Mondovì had been subjected to a virtual military campaign and ruthless punishment a century earlier, the so-called Salt Wars, as the government set about vainly trying to extirpate smuggling. In the succeeding decades, neither attitudes nor behavior altered much on either side. Yet during the War of the Polish Succession, in the 1730s, Mondovì and Cuneo had fought the French bitterly. It was no different when Napoleon launched himself into Italy. The seismic ideological shifts from the ancien régime were nothing to the people of these valleys, nurtured on a folk memory of French hating, an outlook sharpened by cross-border skirmishes connected with smuggling. Indeed, although the Army of Italy swept all before it in the field, as it moved into the valley of the Po and on to Milan, the *barbetti* continued to harass the French rear throughout the period 1796–9, and they were able to initiate attacks on it, as it fell back over the passes, in 1799. This stood in striking contrast to the capitulation of many major provincial centers to the French, the town of Mondovì among them. The bishop and the royal intendant actually dissuaded the peasant militias from investing the town in their intent to stiffen its resistance to the oncoming French. Instead, the authorities and townspeople alike preferred capitulation and occupation to an alliance with the peasantry. The same pattern reproduced itself along the line of towns at the heads of all the major Alpine passes in the summer of 1797, where the urban elites opened their gates to the French when faced with the prospect of rural revolt. Indeed, it was in such places and circumstances that collaboration flourished.[2]

Although the metamorphosis of the Piedmontese uplands from violent lawlessness to ferocious loyalty is seemingly incongruous, it was a behavioral norm rooted in recent experience. It was to be expected, even if it is not readily explicable. The Piedmontese were, indeed, the front line. However, as the French advanced into the rest of Italy, into areas devoid of any military

---

2 Blythe Alice Raviola, "Le rivolte del luglio 1797 nel Piemonte," *Studi Storici* 39 (1998): 401–47.

tradition, still less a tradition of direct contact with a hated French other, the same pattern emerged. The French swept across the northern Italian lowlands, initially occupying the large cities with little or no resistance, a course of events that was repeated when they crossed the Po south into the Papal Legations, Tuscany and, by 1798, the Kingdom of Naples. The helplessness of the cities and lowlands did not betoken sympathy for the French, however, at least not for long. However, where urban revolt took place, it was not initiated within the city but came from the surrounding countryside. The first major example of this was the revolt of Pavia, in eastern Lombardy, in May 1797. When the peasantry of the surrounding area concentrated itself for an assault on the French-occupied city, centuries of urban-rural antagonism were momentarily swept aside as a considerable proportion of the townspeople sided with the peasant rebels driven to revolt by heavy French requisitioning against the French garrison. This was bolstered by the traditionally pro-Habsburg politics of Pavia, which had always lived in the shadow of Milan and looked to the imperial center for protection.[3] In the Papal Legations, the municipalities of Bologna and Ferrara – long resentful of rule from Rome – initially sided with the French, but as the price of the occupation mounted, popular resentment grew. The trigger, however, came from the smaller town of Lugo, which revolted first against Ferrara's attempts to foist the bulk of requisitions on it, and then against the French. As in Pavia, however, the revolt of Lugo found a popular echo in Ferrara itself. The smaller centers of Faenza, Ravenna, and Cesena underwent the same process of rural revolt, finding ready support among the urban popular classes. The truly great regional centers of Milan and Bologna, by contrast, were able to absorb the impact of the costs of occupation.[4] In each of these cases, the French suppressed the urban revolts with considerable cruelty. The two striking exceptions to this rule were the great ports of Genoa and Naples. Unlike Milan, Bologna, Turin, and even Rome, they followed the pattern more common in subordinate regional cities like Ferrara and Pavia. Genoa had a long tradition of resisting foreign occupations, and it was resurrected in 1798, when the townspeople rose to open the gates to the peasant militias of the valleys of the Apennine hinterlands and almost ejected the French. The Neapolitan *lazzaroni* were more successful when they joined forces with Cardinal Ruffo's provincial army of the San Fedisti and virtually drove the French and their indigenous

---

3 J. Felix-Bouvier, "La révolte de Pavie," *Revue Historique de la Révolution Française* 2 (1911): 519–39.
4 For an overview, see Carlo Zaghi, *La Rivoluzione Francese e l'Italia* (Naples, 1966), 129–67.

supporters into the sea in 1799.[5] These were true capital cities, with powerful allegiances to their respective ancien régime states, one a kingdom of long territorial standing – if not always of dynastic stability – and the other an ancient oligarchic republic.

In all of these cases, however, several significant common strands emerge. The first was the inability large urban centers to initiate resistance; the new regime would have little trouble in usurping the traditional loci of the state. The second and most important for the future of the Napoleonic occupation of Italy post-1800 was their ability to revolt when able to connect with nearby rural revolts, or successful risings in smaller towns and cities. Although in Genoa and Naples this represented an atavistic response to invasion, it was anything but the norm in most other cases. In Pavia, Ferrara, and even the smaller towns of southern Piedmont, the unity of town and country – to say nothing of the propensity of the town to open its gates to the rural hordes – betokened a shattering of a millennium of mutual suspicion, urban exploitation of the hinterland, and general mutual suspicion. Finally, it revealed the real, if only semipublic, ties that bound elements of the cities to the hinterlands: anti-French resistance in the countryside was generally triggered by the economic harshness of the occupation, as well as French anticlericalism, as will be explored below. However, urban elites – mainly the landowning nobility – were often able to activate their ties to the peasantry during 1796–9, thus creating an organizing link between urban rural revolt that might otherwise have made widespread resistance impossible. This was especially true in Genoa and Ferrara. Everywhere, the clergy proved another vital link in the counterrevolutionary chain: Ruffo was a known quantity to the Neapolitan masses even if his forces were not; the rural clergy provided crucial leadership in the storming of Pavia; at Ravenna, the archbishop invoked the peasantry to attack the town and galvanized urban support for them. This was a potential nexus of resistance the French would always have to fear, even after their return in 1800. Finally, the events of 1796–9 exposed the deep divisions within many Italian urban elites, now compounded by the collaboration of some with the French and, above all, the central fact that only the weakest, most marginal elements of the urban elites had sided with them. The Italian "patriots" – the *giacobini* – were an embattled minority in the cities as well as in the smaller rural centers, and a terrible revenge was taken on them in 1799, during the brief

---

5 John Davis, "1799: The 'Sanfede' and the Crisis of the 'Ancien Régime' in Southern Italy," in *Society and Politics in the Age of the Risorgimento*, ed. John Davis and Paul Ginsborg (Cambridge, U.K., 1991), 1–25

restoration of the old order, in all the Italian states – a revenge not initiated by the returning regimes but usually spontaneous and local in character. Its most spectacular manifestation was the bloodbath at Naples, but equally vicious reprisals took place in Pavia and Siena, in Tuscany, long before the restored rulers instigated institutionalized witch hunts.[6]

Above all, the revolts of the *triennio* originated in the countryside and the smaller urban centers; the revolts drove those of the cities, and the French were generally unable to crush them, certainly not with anything like the ease they displayed in Pavia or Ferrara. Moreover, the revolts were spontaneous, self-sustaining, and determined.[7] They were usually characterized by a remarkable capacity for organization and class unity, if all too often only on a very localized scale. Seldom did they await or even require external motivation or even military support from the Austro-Russian armies in 1799. Ironically, too, the same peripheral communities that rose so ferociously for the old order were almost always traditionally the most insubordinate parts of the state. None of this boded well for the longer-term occupation of Italy, and so the anatomy of the 1799 revolts is essential to understanding the nature of future Napoleonic repression.

Counterrevolution was strongest – that is, best placed to resist the French and the patriots – in environments where traditions of local independence were strongest. The will to resist was certainly there in subordinate urban centers like Ferrara and Lugo, but the French had the ability to suppress it in such circumstances. In the small towns of the valleys and foothills of the Apennines and Alps, topography bound the way to the will. However, there was something else to reckon with. In the hinterlands, traditions of local leadership and independence were still the reality of the public sphere; that sphere was severely atomized, but it was vibrant and able to provide leadership in the unprecedented crisis of the French invasion. At the risk of a seeming contradiction, it is possible to discern a wide pattern in this series of widespread revolts so avowedly particularist in aim and character, though this ought not to confound the rebels' conscious motives with their coincidental manifestation. The rural model depends on the relative autonomy that prevailed under the ancien régime; this was the case in the Piedmontese province of Mondovì, as has been seen; in the fishing

---

6 On Pavia, see Renato Sóriga, "La reazione dei tredici mesi in Pavia e le sue vittime politiche," *Bollettino della Società Pavese di Storia Patria* 16 (1916): 5–52. On Siena, see E. A. Brigidi, *Giacobini e realisti, o Viva Maria: storia del 1799 in Toscana* (Siena, 1882).

7 For an overview of the revolts that stresses their economic causes, see Vittorio Scotti Douglas, "Le insorgense antinapoleoniche in Italia: controrivoluzione ideologica o sommosse di affamati?" in *L'Europa Scopre Napoleone 1793–1804*, ed. Vittorio Scotti Douglas, 2 vols. (Turin, 1999), 2:557–75.

communities of the Puglian coast;[8] in the Neapolitan provinces of the Abruzzi – where resistance was ferocious but in the hands of forty-two local militias (*masse*) in the province of L'Aquila alone in 1799;[9] and in the papal province of Tolfa.[10] In these areas, and in many others like them, the success of the revolts could be striking when the local elites were integrated into the popular reactions to invasion. No one was more aware of this than Cardinal Ruffo, the most successful counterrevolutionary leader to emerge in 1799. His *sanfediste* forces in Calabria stand out as one of largest and most sustained challenges to Franco-patriot rule, for Ruffo somehow kept the semblance of an army together on the long march up Calabria to Naples. Particularism was both a strength and a weakness. On the one hand, Ruffo found a province already in arms against the French and knew his main role was to coordinate local resistance, not incite it. On the other, he had to extend their range and hold them together long enough to take the capital.[11]

In all these instances, from the Puglian coast to the Piedmontese Alps, the essential prerequisite for the emergence of successful resistance was the survival of an indigenous elite in autonomous communities, unshaken by any and all attempts at reform from the center. This state of affairs constituted, precisely, the political order they were all prepared to defend, and once set in this context, the metamorphosis from recalcitrant periphery to bastion of loyalty to throne and altar becomes more explicable, if no less complex. None of this boded well for the new regime that swept across Italy after 1800.

THE SECOND FRENCH INVASION, 1800–9

The French reoccupation of Italy was a gradual process, governed increasingly by the shifting circumstances of war and diplomacy and the workable demands of the continental blockade. The mainland territories of the House of Savoy were reoccupied in 1800 and finally annexed to France in 1802; those of the former Cisalpine Republic were reconstituted quickly in 1800 as the new Republic of Italy (kingdom in 1805); the lands of the Republic

---

8 Francesco Calabellese, ed., *In Terra di bari dal 1799 al 1806* (Trani, 1900). Saverio La Sorsa, *I moti rivoluzionari a Molfetta nel primi mesi del 1799* (Trani, 1903).

9 Niccolo Rodolico, *Il Popolo agli inizi del Risorgimento nell'Italia Meridionale, 1799–1801* (Florence, 1925), 57. See also Luigi Coppa-Zuccari, *L'Invasione francese negli Abruzzi, 1798–1810*, 4 vols. (L'Aquila, 1927).

10 Ottorina Morra, *L'insorgenza antifrancese di Tolfa durante la Repubblica Romana del 1798–1799* (Rome, 1942).

11 Gaetano Cingari, *Giacobini e Sanfedisti in Calabria* (Reggio, 1978).

of St. George (Genoa) were converted into a sister republic – the Ligurian – also in 1800. Most of the rest of the peninsula was left alone politically, although the central duchies and the Papal States received large French garrisons. The next, and most extensive, wave of expansion came in 1805 in the wake of the War of the Third Coalition and brought with it the annexations of Liguria and Parma-Piacenza to France and the seizure of the mainland of the Kingdom of Naples, with first Joseph Bonaparte and then Joachim Murat replacing the Bourbons on the throne. In the same year, the Habsburgs were deposed in Tuscany, and the archduchy became the short-lived Kingdom of Etruria under the Spanish Bourbons. The year 1806 saw the incorporation of the lands of the Republic of Venice – Austrian provinces since 1797 – into the Kingdom of Italy. In 1808, Napoleon annexed Tuscany to France; the Papal States followed in 1810.

Such was the military power of the Napoleonic state that resistance of the kind shown in urban centers like Lugo or Pavia, during the more chaotic *triennio*, proved impossible to replicate; consequently, the reconstruction of the Italian republic proved relatively easy for the French. However, whenever the French annexed a given part of Italy – whether directly or as a satellite kingdom – they were soon confronted with a resurgence of revolts in the hinterlands. Despite the staggered timing of their absorption of the territories of mainland Italy, the reactions they provoked were remarkably similar, as were their efforts to repress them. In Piedmont, the crushing military triumph of the Battle of Marengo was matched by a fresh outbreak of mass peasant revolt in the Val d'Aosta, identical to that of 1799, and repeated the following year. The same years saw an upsurge in banditry along the Ligurian border, which was not fully quelled until 1807. The annexations of Liguria and Parma-Piacenza were followed by a short-lived but well-supported peasant rising in the Piacentino, the Apennine border country between the two former states. Tuscany saw two major revolts in 1808, in the mountains around Pistoia, in the north, and in the Aretino, in the south, areas where both the ducal regime and the French had faced unrest in the 1790s and earlier. They year 1806 saw another series of local revolts in the Abruzzi.

The geographic pattern of revolt, thus recounted, takes on almost the hallmarks of tradition, and it certainly clarifies a geography of discontent and danger that the French carried in their minds at all times. Nevertheless, the French presence in Italy post-1800 was of a very different order to that of the *triennio*. Whereas their presence in the 1790s had been driven by war and the havoc they caused arose from campaigning, requisitioning, and supporting their collaborators, after 1800, they came to rule, to establish the institutions and mores of the Napoleonic state, and most traumatically for the Italian masses, to impose conscription and taxation on a scale hitherto unimaginable for the communities of the hinterlands. If no longer torn by war directly, the peoples of Italy were designated by their new masters to become the fodder of the Napoleonic war machine. These isolated, supposedly backward communities showed their awareness of these momentous changes through revolt; the French, in their turn, unleashed the institutional and organizational prowess of the Napoleonic state on the Italian peripheries. The battlegrounds were the same, as were the protagonists, but the nature of the repression – and the consequences for the vanquished – were of a magnitude different from the transient horrors of the *triennio*. Absorption into the Napoleonic state, and so into its war effort, spelled the end of a way of life and of a particular political culture. Each postannexation revolt was marked by this mutual awareness, if also driven by fresh memories of the reciprocal atrocities of 1796–9.

With the exception of the banditry on the Piedmontese-Ligurian frontier and on the border between the former Papal States and the Kingdom of Naples, all the postannexation revolts were put down with a minimum of regular troops and were of short duration, facts that enhance rather than diminish their significance. Piedmont had been a particularly war torn and relatively militarized state in the late 1790s, and its brigandage was linked intimately to salt and cattle smuggling under a determined mercantilist old order. Even after 1800, this combination of circumstances forged a link between a social banditry like that Hobsbawm described and a quasi-counterrevolutionary guerrilla akin to that discerned in Provence in the same period.[12] Nevertheless, its defeat by 1807 proved definitive, and the French learned many powerful lessons in counterinsurgency in the course of subduing southern Piedmont that were simultaneously applied to Liguria and Parma-Piacenza in 1805–6; subsequently to Tuscany; and, with less success, to the Papal States and the Kingdom of Naples. The revolt of the Piacentino came as bolt from the blue for the French, for the region had never shown a capacity for collective, large-scale revolt during the *triennio*, although it had seen much localized resistance to both French and Russian marauding. In late 1805, however, whole villages across several valleys rose at once, in well-organized fashion, to attack local officials. introduction of conscription was certainly the trigger, but the rebels' petitions and proclamations pointed equally to the new, unprecedented

---

12 Eric Hobsbawm, *Bandits* (London, 1969); Gwyenne Lewis, "Political Brigandage and Popular Disaffection in the South-East of France, 1795–1804," in *Beyond the Terror*, ed. Gwynne Lewis and Colin Lucas (Cambridge, U.K., 1983), 195–231.

forms of taxation; to the disruption of religious life; and to the requisitioning of their mules. That last point was, in their eyes, far from trivial or transient: the rebels saw it not just as economically ruinous in the short term but as part of a more pervasive policy of destroying the haulage trade of the smuggler-bandits. The valleys were quickly overrun by the rebels, but a coordinated assault from Liguria and Piacenza broke them by the first weeks of 1806. This had been accomplished mainly by gendarmes and the reserve companies; regular troops arrived in force only in the final stages of resistance. Napoleon was infuriated that such an uprising had broken out at all in a region so far from the front line. But the real lesson was, in fact, the power of his state: a rebel force estimated at a hard core of seven thousand to eight thousand and able to muster several times that number on occasion had been destroyed by virtually the last line of the regime's coercive forces. On the annexation of Tuscany in 1808, the twin pillars of resistance in 1799 – the Aretino in the south and the hills around Pisa and Pistoia in the north – sprang to life. The presence of the gendarmerie was enough to prevent them from taking the major cities of Siena and Pistoia, in contrast to 1799, although in Tuscany, it needed a considerable influx of regular troops to push the Aretino rebels back into the swamps of the Maremma. In all these cases, mass revolt would not rear its head again, but the French perceived a need for constant vigilance.[13] They had learned that the end of collective resistance did not equate to true pacification. A long, if atomized, bandit guerrilla war awaited them.

The long wars of the 1790s, the internal struggle against counterrevolution in the Vendée-Militaire and the Midi included, had created a reserve of experienced soldiers in the French war machine from which its gendarmerie and departmental reserve companies could be drawn, even if the men seconded to these corps seldom met the high standards set for them in theory.[14] Nevertheless, the Napoleonic state had ready reserves of men to staff these paramilitary units at will, and so it was able to follow up its initial military conquests of new territories, first with the ability to crush large peasant revolts and then, perhaps more important, to consolidate those successes by establishing the gendarmerie as a permanent presence in the Italian hinterlands. Each canton received a six-man brigade of either foot or horse, depending on the terrain, and the state ensured that at least four members of each brigade were always French veterans, who were usually housed in barracks apart from the communities they served and paid by

---

13 Based on the primary research in Michael Broers, *The Napoleonic Empire in Italy, 1796–1814: Cultural Imperialism in a European Context?* (Basingstoke, U.K., 2005), esp. 41–6, 83–9.
14 Clive Emsley, *Gendarmes and the State in Nineteenth Century Europe* (Oxford, 1999).

the central government. Most of the Italians who made up the remainder
of the corps were Piedmontese veterans. In this fundamental, often brutal
manner, the Revolutionary state was brought deep into the Italian periphery; hitherto isolated, autonomous communities were now under the eye
of a remote, imperial center. On a general level, this was how conquest
was made lasting and complete; in the particular, this was how conscription
was enforced. When the French imposed their conscription quotas on the
imperial departments or on those of the Republic/Kingdom of Italy, it had
the coercive force to make them a reality. Smuggler banditry could be continuously and persistently harassed in areas where it was well entrenched,
as in the Apennine communities of the Piacentino between Liguria and
Parma. Those who had been the ringleaders and linchpins of the initial
revolts against annexation were gradually weeded out and hunted down.
This was the hard reality of the new order. As often as four times a year,
the prefects toured their entire departments, accompanied by the reserve
company. In each cantonal seat, they worked with the local gendarmerie
brigade and the justices of the peace – men who had usually been collaborators during the *triennio* – to ensure that those conscripted were rounded
up, by force if required. The operations often provoked conflict and armed
resistance almost everywhere – administrative success should not be interpreted as acquiescence – but the new state won such confrontations, at least
on the functional level of extracting most of the conscripts it demanded.
The process of conscription fostered banditry in areas where it had not been
especially rife before, as in Tuscany, and often broadened its scope where it
was deeply rooted, as in southern Piedmont and the Papal States, where the
bands became rallying points and nuclei for young men trying to evade
the gendarmerie.[15] However, unlike any coercive power before them, the
French returned and returned, sweeping collective, open resistance aside and
usually driving the bandits to the margins of their communities. This pattern was far from universal, as shall be seen, but it was successful enough
often enough to make the power and permanent presence of the state very
real where it had never dared venture before.

The initial revolts always led to pure military justice through short-
lived extraordinary military commissions. Composed wholly of soldiers, the
commissions administered martial law in the wake of widespread disorder.
This was to be expected, in the light of French conduct during the *triennio*, as

15 Alexander Grab, "Army, State and Society: Conscription and Desertion in Napoleonic Italy (1802–
    1814)," *Journal of Modern History* 67 (1995): 25–54. Michael Broers, *Napoleonic Imperialism and the
    Savoyard Monarchy, 1773–1821: State Building in Piedmont* (Lampter, U.K., 1997), 318–25.

was the harsh military repression that preceded and served them. However, the real power of the new state and its ability to establish a permanent system of repression emerged in what followed the early cycles of revolt and repression, not in those immediate, impetuous, often bloodthirsty shows of military force. It is in the later, less dramatic but equally determined, phases of their occupation that the replacement of the ideal "well-ordered police state" of the old order, defined by Marc Raeff, with that of the more entrenched, pervasive "security state" delineated by Howard Brown in the case of Revolutionary France, emerges as the foundation of the Napoleonic regime in Italy.[16]

This policing apparatus was supported by the French judicial hierarchy and its legal codes, which were imported verbatim into the imperial departments, and in essence, into the two satellite kingdoms of Italy and Naples. Under the old order, one of the few common strands in the highly diverse legal systems of the Italian states had been a penchant for arbitrational justice, as practiced between the center and the communities of the hinterlands. It was the result of a combination of practical experience and the intrinsic weakness of the central governments – even that of the House of Savoy – and their common inability to establish any reliable, permanent coercive force on their peripheries. As a result, the magistracy – the *togati* – won what respect it held by its ability to achieve acceptable compromise between the state and these communities, and between warring factions within them. The arrival of the French swept this away and replaced it with a legal system laid down at the center, which was meant to be enforced and obeyed, and also to shape the character of the society it administered. The new legal mores were introduced literally overnight, and where resistance to them was deemed likely, the French had evolved a more militarized version of their system; this was the version applied to Italy. The criminal courts of the imperial departments, like those of the Vendée-Militaire and many departments of the Midi throughout the Consulate and the Empire, were composed of a combination of military judges – usually drawn from the higher echelons of the regional gendarmerie – and civilian magistrates, almost all of them French or, later, Piedmontese. Juries were never accorded to any of the tribunals of the imperial departments in Italy. Above all, virtually all the public prosecutors of all the courts, at every level,

16 Marc Raeff, *The Well Ordered Police State* (New Haven, Connecticut, 1988). Howard G. Brown, "From Organic Society to Security State: The War on Brigandage in France, 1797–1802," *Journal of Modern History* 69 (1997): 661–95.

were French or Piedmontese: this important office in the administration of justice, particularly in criminal cases, was never let out of the hands of the occupiers.[17] Likewise, most of the prefects and even the subprefects of the imperial departments were French. Although the civil administration and the magistracy were less French dominated in the two kingdoms, the composition and command of their gendarmeries remained mainly in French hands, despite the emergence of an Italian officer corps in their regular armies. The essence of the Napoleonic state in Italy reflected the deep-seated fears of the French, stemming from the traumas of the *triennio*, which were reenforced by the revolts attendant on annexation after 1800. They and their *administrés* remained all too aware of what their success depended upon. The great revolts that punctuated the *epoca francese* after definitive occupation provide evidence that this pessimism was not entirely without foundation.

THE GREAT REVOLTS: THE VENETO, CALABRIA, AND EMILIA-ROMAGNA

Two of the three great revolts that punctuated Italy after the final consolidation of Napoleonic hegemony with the annexation of the Papal States in 1809 were peripheral in the geopolitical sense. That of the Veneto was an aftershock from the Tyrolean rebellion of 1809, just over the Alpine watershed. The Calabrian disturbances, which reached their height in 1810–11, derived their intensity, if not their origins, from the British presence in Sicily. Set in this perspective, they serve to show how isolated most of Italy actually was from direct involvement in the major stages of the Napoleonic Wars in that only the furthest extremities of the peninsula could achieve such levels of overt, collective resistance to the occupation.

The Venetian revolts centered on the Alpine valleys that had formed the hinterland of the former Republic of Venice, and they originated in those valleys closest to the Tyrol and to the Kingdom of Italy. Two such valleys, the Vallentina and the Valcamonica, had seen minor revolts immediately after their annexation of the Kingdom of Italy in 1806. They shared much in common with the revolts that accompanied annexation elsewhere in Italy, both in their location and in the grievances the rebels articulated, which amounted to a wish to return to a more archaic political order. The proclamation of the rebels of Schio, issued at the height of the revolts in July 1809, encapsulated this outlook and echoes those issued by the *vallegiani* of

---

17 Broers, *Napoleonic Empire in Italy*, 118–21, 175–207.

the Piacentino in 1806 in its essentials. In the words of the historian of the revolt:

When the musket fire ceased, they hoisted the flag of St Mark (that of the Republic of Venice); they proclaimed the return of the old laws and (thus) they would establish a form of government after their own fashion, publishing decrees on the circulation of money, on the abolition of tolls and conscription and, above all, on the restoration of Religion and Finances.[18]

What marked them out from other annexationalist revolts, such as the Piacentino or the Aretino, was less their fundamental character or the composition of their participants than their proximity to the war zone in Austria and thus their ability to revive resistance. Although the risings were sparked by the much more orchestrated revolt in the Tyrol and never achieved much coherence above village or valley level; in contrast to Hofer's better-known rebellion, they outlasted the Tyroleans.[19] Another vital difference with revolts elsewhere was that they actually proved a threat to major urban centers and routes as they broke out of the hinterland and into the Po Valley, something even Hofer did not achieve. Order was not restored in the high valleys until November 1809, and isolated attacks on government officials and acts of arson against government buildings continued into 1810 on the outskirts of the major centers of Vicenza, Verona, and Belluno. As the revolts spread out of the valleys, there was a widespread breakdown of law and order in the countryside of the Po Valley that enabled an eight-thousand-strong force of highland peasants to besiege Vicenza for almost two weeks. Once established as a presence in the lowlands, the rebels attracted to their ranks large numbers of deserters as well as men from the cities now able to avoid conscription in the general disorder. Most of the large urban centers stood with the French against the rebels, driven by atavistic fear of the hinterland, newly awakened by the criminality that the revolts provoked. However, initially at least, they were supported by several urban centers in the Po Delta, notably Este and Rovigo, which rose in their support expressly to restore the republic. Broadly, those cities whose hinterlands were the Alpine valleys, and thus the centers of revolt, fought the rebels – Vicenza, Treviso, Feltre – while those further away from the valleys, which had little direct contact with the rebels' communities, joined them. Once the French were able to reassert their military superiority, the rebels dispersed into small bands and turned to banditry in the lowlands. As the revolts subsided, nine military

18 Carlo Bullo, "Dei movimenti insurrezionali del Veneto sotto il dominio napoleonico, e specialmente del brigantaggio politico del 1809," *Nuovo Archivio Veneto* 17 (1899): 66–101.
19 F. Gunther Eyck, *Loyal Rebels: Andreas Hofer and the Tyrolean Uprising of 1809* (New York, 1986).

commissions were created and hundreds of executions followed. The commission's arrests and inquiries revealed that the debris of the rising – the small brigand bands – were often a fusion of the original rebels and lowland or urban deserters. The Veneto rebellions were just that, a series of revolts rather than one huge explosion, as in the Tyrol. They represent, however, a potent series of chain reactions that could only be produced by their geographic proximity to the Tyrol and the major campaigning of 1809. The Wagram campaign spawned the Tyrol; the Tyrol gave impetus to the revolts in the valleys, and they, in turn, provided a rallying point for more disjointed discontent in the Po Valley. The rebels had a political goal that was clear – the restoration of the Republic of St. Mark; even if naive, they believed the Austrians would help them achieve it. Many of these characteristics were present in the Calabrian unrest of 1810–11, although they emerged in very different social conditions.

Calabria had always been a backward, convulsed region where the authority of Naples, under whatever dynasty, paled into insignificance beside the power wielded by a powerful feudal baronage. Brigandage was as deeply rooted and diffuse in Calabria as in the rest of the Apennine spine, but here it owed its existence and survival to circumstances very different from elsewhere. Whereas the activities of the bandits of the Piacentino or the Piedmontese-Ligurian border, or of the Alpine valleys of the Veneto centered on smuggling, making them the linchpins of the local economy, the Calabrian brigands had no economic function other than as agents of the barons. They were, in effect, private armies there to coerce and control the peasantry and to intimidate the only viable rivals to the baronage for local power, the rural bourgeoisie.[20] Some mobilized behind Ruffo in 1799; some did not, according to their masters' allegiances or their own local interests, and it proved the same when French hegemony was definitively asserted over the kingdom, in 1806.[21] Thus, the Napoleonic occupation did not create instability in Calabria, nor did Calabria's proximity to British occupied Sicily particularly change its character. Rather, the fact that Calabria was a war zone, at the front line of the war between the empire and Britain, perpetuated its chronic unrest and hamstrung all French attempts to pacify the region. Whether such efforts would have borne the same fruit as, say, in southern Piedmont, is a counterfactual question.[22] There were signs amid

---

20 In a vast literature, Pasquale Villani, *Mezzogiorno tra riforme e rivoluzione* (Rome, 1973). Gaetano Cingari, *Brigantaggio, proprietari e contadini nel sud* (Bari, 1976).
21 Gaetano Cingari, *Giacobini e sanfedisti in Calabria nel 1799* (Messina, 1957).
22 For the view that Murat might have broken these patterns, see Angela Valente, *Giacomo Murat e l'Italia Meridionale* (Turin, 1965).

the continuous upheavals that many sections of the peasantry, the rural bourgeoisie, and even the baronage were amenable to collaboration with Murat's regime, if it led to a semblance of social peace, but the British remained as an alternative source of patronage for the bandits, whenever their traditional retainers wavered or turned on them. Naval raids from Sicily were only occasional, as resources were diverted to the war on the Iberian Peninsula, but the flow of gold from Palermo to whomever would unsettle Murat's rule was constant. As his attempts from 1808 onward to destroy feudalism encroached on the traditional foundations of their power, most barons looked to the exiled court in Palermo for support. When Murat attempted to extend conscription to the province in 1809, banditry was given a new impetus and a new dimension. As in 1799, in contrast to the norm in the region, the bandits found something of a common cause in many rural communities. Murat's response was twofold and unique. On the one hand, conscription was suspended, a retreat made nowhere else in Italy, save in the dying days of French rule in Tuscany and the Papal States. On the other, he launched a series of ferocious paramilitary campaigns in the region under General Manhès in 1810–11 that captured and killed scores of bandits, intimidated many barons, and appeared to win the confidence of the rural bourgeoisie and other elements that there was now a central government strong enough to provide order. Even this high tide of Napoleonic power was achieved in ways different from elsewhere, however. Manhès's gendarmerie was never deployed over the countryside in permanent brigades, as happened almost elsewhere in Italy; instead, it operated in mobile columns, sweeping out the major towns and returning to them afterward.[23] The incursions were periodic, but the state did not implant itself in the heart of brigand country; consequently, Calabria never evolved from the first phase of French occupation to the second. Local conditions would undoubtedly have made such a transformation problematic, but it was at this point that Calabria's proximity to Sicily became, if hardly decisive, then powerfully influential for the course of pacification. The anticonscription revolts of 1809, which widened the scope of disorder in new ways, provided the impetus for increased British intervention, which offered the bandits more independence and latitude from the barons and, in turn, drove the nobles to renew their ties with them, fearing a loss of control either to them or to a central authority whose power could only increase at their expense. In this way, the old patterns reasserted themselves, and the limited British interest in the region – centered on disruption rather than reconquest, as in

23 Umberto Caldora, *Calabria Napoleonica* (Naples, 1960).

Spain – fostered a state of permanent unrest without the promise of external regulation of any kind that continued well after the end of the wars. Spain has sometimes been described as the Vietnam of the Napoleonic Wars. If so, then Calabria was the Cambodia.

Perhaps the revolts that swept through central Italy in 1809, which originated in the Apennine valleys of the Emilia-Romagna, were the most unsettling of all for Napoleonic imperialists. They exploded unheralded by any prehistory of marked recalcitrance to authority under the old order, and they were not inspired or sustained by external support long after Napoleonic rule had become established, as in the Veneto or Calabria. They anteceded the Wagram campaign and the revolts in the Veneto, and they were far from the fighting. In their aftermath, the authorities of the Kingdom of Italy searched in vain for the presence of Austrian agents or a British hand behind them. These risings – first localized, then widespread – had no external connections; the rebels needed no one to agitate or instigate revolt on their behalf, nor did they have resident brigands to create a nucleus of resistance for them. The revolts of 1809 in central Italy represent a spontaneous, sui generis outburst of hatred at the demands of the new state, demands that were driven by war. As such, they are manifestations of the instability the Napoleonic war effort induced, in contrast to the permanent order its exigencies could create in other parts of Italy in the same years. This, perhaps, is what gives them their major historical importance. In contrast to the revolts in Calabria and the Veneto, those of Emilia-Romagna seem devoid of explicit political content; they did not aim at a papal restoration but were provoked by the growing burdens of taxation. The first risings in the Apennine valleys near Bologna in July 1809 were triggered by taxes on basic necessities and, particularly, on the use of flour mills.[24] However, as Alexander Grab has emphasized, the revolt took place in the wider context of resentment against conscription, which provided its fuel if not its spark. When the rebels entered the plains, as in the Veneto, their ranks were swelled by deserters, who became a considerable presence in their midst. Indeed, if the rebels possessed any constant organizing element, it was probably the deserters who provided it and enabled the revolt to continue once it spread beyond the valleys. Of the one thousand rebels brought before the special military commission in Bologna, more than half were deserters.[25] Early in the revolt, they besieged Bologna, but when they

---

24 Mario Leonardi, "L'insorgenza del 1809 nel regno d'Italia," *Annunario dell'Istituto per l'Età Moderna e Contemporanea* 31–2 (1979–80): 435–57; Alexander Grab, "State Power, Brigandage and Rural Resistance in Napoleonic Italy," *European History Quarterly* 25 (1995): 39–70.
25 Luciano Valente, *La Corte Speciale per i delitti di Stato del dipartimento del Reno (1809–1811)* (Tesì di Laurea, Bologna, 1973), 29, 36n2.

failed to gain support in the town, the revolt turned on the surrounding countryside. The rebellion swept through the lowlands, where the rebels targeted public buildings that housed tax and conscription records, but again as in the Veneto, as the authorities fought back from the cities, the rebellion quickly dissipated into localized brigandage led by deserters.[26] Indeed, banditry did not shrink back to what were considered normal proportions until May 1810, when the armed police columns were finally ended. Only after ten months did the disturbances cease to resemble revolt. They were a warning of what could happen when the workings of conscription broke down and the ingredients of an army slipped the lead in a countryside already ill disposed to the unprecedented demands of a centralized state. If the mechanisms of control failed or were successfully thwarted, however briefly, the chaos of early modern warfare was not far away.

In the course of the revolt and afterward, *fragility* was a term often used by the Italian prefects to describe their position, seeing resistance to the new state at every level of society. Despite the firmness of the cities of Bologna and Ferrara in the face of the rebels, they were more concerned by the propensity of the great landowners to let the revolts run their course, as they were not its targets. The revolts brought to the surface a sense of unease long present among the administrators of the new state. Henceforth, increasing stress was placed on increasing the powers of the prefects and all the state's mechanisms of social control, because, as Livio Antonielli has discerned, they saw in social control the only feasible way to consolidate Napoleonic rule at the local level in the long term.[27] For contemporaries, these seemingly anarchic, shapeless revolts had a heightened significance belied by their courses. There were not simply outbursts against conscription and taxation: they signaled a determined rejection of the modern state itself. Napoleonic administrators saw instantly this dangerous abyss between the state and its *administrés*, but they could see little to bridge it in the face of the unrelenting demands of war, save coercion.

STATO REALE E STATO CIVILE: A GRAMSCIAN VISION?

Napoleonic rule in Italy met with collective armed resistance and so had to begin with concerted acts of repression: this marked its character henceforth. However, the need to harness Italy's resources – its male population, to be precise; the need to enforce mass conscription for the war effort; and the effective coercive powers of the Revolutionary–Napoleonic state together

---

26 Grab, "State Power."
27 Livio Antonielli, *I preffetti dell'Italia napoleonica* (Bologna, 1983), 507.

ensured that the process of internal conquest was continuous. Revolt and repression were woven into the fabric of the relationship between the state and the citizen, and the essential question during the Napoleonic occupation was which of the two would predominate in any given region. In Piedmont and most of Lombardy and central Italy, repression was effective and gave way to a lasting social peace, at least in the context of basic law and order. In Calabria, the Abruzzi, and much of the southern Papal States, it proved the reverse. Napoleonic repression sharpened the divide between north and south in terms of the state's presence in society and thus redrew the map of Italy along lines still evident today. From the perspective of the state – whoever controlled it – the borders between Piedmont and Liguria, and between Liguria and the Piacentino, had been as lawless as much of the Mezzogiorno before the Revolutionary wars; after Napoleonic rule, that was no longer the case. The Apennine spine was no longer a red thread of unpoliced, largely autonomous hinterlands that defined almost all the states of the peninsula. It now had a scission through it, somewhere in central Italy: the mass revolt of 1809 in Emilia-Romagna had been quelled; the vicious banditry of Calabria had not, and each time the tenure of the Bourbon dynasty was threatened again in the early nineteenth century, it would be accepted into the fold of political weaponry by the state and given a new lease of life, notably in 1849 and 1860 – a course of policy unthinkable in the north.

The heavy-handed character of Napoleonic rule belongs in wider contexts than that of revolt and repression, for it was the baptism by fire for most parts of Italy, as regards the modern state, and the mores and institutions of that state were generally alien to Italian soil. The military campaigning that brought about the occupation was itself an alien experience to most of Italy, a region of Europe that had managed to avoid direct involvement in the great wars of the eighteenth century. The second phase of the occupation implanted the gendarmerie in the heart of the Italian hinterlands, bringing with it not just external interference but also the permanent presence of state power to independent communities. It did so primarily to tax and conscript: other benefits in terms of protection of persons and property that might accrue from its work were incidental. In the north, the secondary benefits came to be appreciated; in much of the Mezzogiorno, they remained stillborn. What mattered most, however, was the very presence of a state possessed of such coercive force and, above all, the perception of that force as both alien and malign when it arrived. Finally, the new state brought with it a new ethos and a new vision of society. A state at war made militarism into a virtue; it conceived its duty to Italians of all classes as that of instilling martial spirit and, with it, patriotism and a sense of social discipline in them. As one French official put the view of the rulers, "Their youth turns to brigandage, whereas long ago in France, it turned to soldiering."[28] It was a falsehood of the most self-deluding kind, but no matter in such powerful hands. The ultimate result of repression in the cause of the war effort was to be a cultural and social revolution – the regeneration of Italian society through military service. Rebelliousness was to be converted into military valor; repression was meant to convert not just to cow Italians. It would be an understatement to say that this philosophy fell on stony ground in Italy. Yet the essence of this vision was seized on by Mazzini and incarnated by Garibaldi, and later refined by Crispi. The Gramscian concept of Italian popular culture as derivative, as a bastard child of elite hegemony, might also be applied to much of its official Risorgimento-inspired ideology when its Napoleonic parentage is recalled. By contrast, Italian suspicion of the state has much more spontaneous origins.

28 Archives Nationales de Paris, F7 (Police-Générale) 8889 (Rome) Director General of Police to Minister, Police-Générale, Sept. 20, 1812.

11

Naval Power in the Revolutionary Era

JEREMY BLACK

⎮Discussion about military modernization and revolution and total warfare in the period 1775–1815 focuses on land conflict in Europe and generally ignores or underrates the importance of naval developments⎮ This is unfortunate because, on the world scale, it was as naval powers that the European states were particularly important. Indeed, there was a Western naval exceptionalism that rewards attention. On land, of course, the capability of Western powers was readily apparent from the Ohio River to Sri Lanka and Sumatra. The newly independent Americans made important gains to the west of the Appalachians, the French conquered Egypt in 1798, the Russians defeated both Turks and Persians, and the British made important gains in South Asia. Each was impressive but also needs to be placed in perspective. Aside from the defeat of attacking Western forces at the hands of non-European powers, such as the British in Egypt in 1807, these latter powers also campaigned actively on land and with important consequences. These consequences included the consolidation of Vietnam in the 1790s and 1800s, the replacement of the Hausa states by the Sokoto caliphate in West Africa, major campaigns by Burma and Siam, and the development of de facto independent Egyptian power under Mehmet Ali. Ranging more widely chronologically, the Qianlong emperor in China (reigned 1736–98) ended the challenge from the Dzungars in the 1750s.

These campaigns deserve attention, not least as the steppes of Central Asia and the Sahel of West Africa can be considered as land-seas that had certain similarities to the oceans. The Chinese advances might not seem as impressive as Western transoceanic campaigns, but they were formidable achievements. China under the Manchu emperors successfully solved the logistical problems central in managing steppe warfare, which was considered the supreme strategic threat by all Chinese dynasties. In the 1750s, the Chinese established two chains of magazine posts along the main roads on which they advanced. Supplies were transported for thousands of miles, while the Mongolian homelands controlled by their eastern Mongol allies provided the horses and fodder. These improvements in logistics – partly due to a desire to keep the troops from alienating the populace – ensured that the invading Chinese armies did not disintegrate as Napoleon's did in Russia in 1812, and the comparison is instructive. To wage war with the Dzungars, there was a massive transfer of resources from eastern to western China: the application to military purposes of the great demographic and agricultural expansion in China during the century.[1] There was a parallel with the British navy, with organizational factors proving a crucial precondition for campaign success.

If Western powers shared land capability with non-Western counterparts, the situation was different at sea. It was not that the Westerners alone had naval forces. Other states also did. These included the North African powers, the Ottoman (Turkish) empire, Kamehameha I of Hawaii, and a number of others, but the literature devoted to them is limited and certainly far less than that on Western navies. It would be mistaken to lump non-Western navies all together, as there were major differences in fighting styles and environments. For example, the Ottomans were capable of fleet engagements, while the North African powers – Morocco, Algiers, Tunis, and Tripoli, essentially deployed privateering forces appropriate for commerce raiding. The Ottomans and the North Africans used essentially the same maritime technology (galleys and square-riggers) as Western Europeans.

Most non-Western naval forces, however, were not deep sea. Instead, particularly along the African coasts, there were polities that controlled flotillas operating in inshore estuarine, deltaic, and riverine waters. These boats were shallow in draft, and therefore enjoyed a local range denied European warships. Their crews usually fought with missile weapons, which in the eighteenth century increasingly meant muskets, and some canoes also carried cannon. Similar technology was also employed in the Pacific, in New Zealand, and in Pacific North America. As with land warfare in some non-Western societies, and in marked contrast to the situation in the West, the divide between conflict between humans and the hunting of animals was not too great at this level of weapon technology and military organization. At the same time, non-Western naval and amphibious forces not only were hunters or raiders but also could achieve operational goals. This was seen in the conflict among the New Zealand Maori in the early nineteenth

---

1 I am most grateful to Jan Glete and Richard Harding for their comments on an earlier draft. C. Perdue, "Culture, History and Imperial Chinese Strategy: Legacies of the Qing Conquests," in *Warfare in Chinese History*, ed. H. van de Ven (Leiden, 2000), 277.

century and, even more clearly, in the earlier unification of the Hawaiian archipelago. By 1789, Kamehameha I was using a swivel gun secured to a platform on the hulls of a big double canoe. Soon after, he had a large double canoe mounting two cannon and rigged like a European schooner. Such boats helped him as he expanded his power across the archipelago. Kamehameha won dominance of the island of Hawaii in 1791 and of the islands of Maui and Oahu in 1795. In 1796 and 1809, the difficult waters between Oahu and Kauai, and outbreaks of disease, ended his plans to invade Kauai, but in 1810, Kaumualii, the ruler of the islands of Kauai and Niihau, agreed to serve as a client king.[2]

None of this stands comparison with Western navies, but instead of considering a single standard of capability, it is necessary to note the diversity of goals and the variety of best practices. For example, the Barbary, Omani, and Maratha ships were commerce raiders whose emphasis was on speed and maneuverability,[3] whereas the heavy, slow ships of the line of European navies were designed for battle and emphasized battering power.

There was no revolution in Western naval capability vis-à-vis non-Western powers in this period. The strength of Western battle fleets was already apparent in the early sixteenth century, with successive victories in the Indian Ocean, and the balance of battle advantage remained with the West, increasingly so in conflict with the Ottomans in the Mediterranean and, later, in the Black Sea. It would be mistaken to see this advantage simply in terms of firepower. The most dramatic Western naval victory over non-Western forces – at Çeşme off Chios in 1770 – was primarily due to the effective use of fireships against the closely moored Ottoman fleet by the Russians; both the method and the result were highly unusual. About eleven thousand Turks were killed, although the Russians totally failed in their attempt to exploit the situation by driving the Ottomans from the Aegean.

In part because the Western powers devoted so much of their effort between 1775 and 1815 to fighting one another, there was no focus on naval action with non-Westerners. This was just as well, as there was no increase in relative Western capability. Such an increase, indeed, was not to occur until the application of steam power, and this bore no relationship to the American and French revolutions. In 1813, the American Robert Fulton drew up plans for a powerful steam-propelled frigate, significantly

---

2 R. Tregaksis, *The Warrior King: Hawaii's Kamehameha the Great* (New York, 1973).
3 See also H. Moyse-Bartlett, *The Pirates of Trucial Oman* (London, 1966) and L. R. Wright, "Piracy in the Southeast Asian Archipelago," *Journal of Oriental Studies* 14 (1976): 23–33; B. Sandin, *The Sea Dayaks of Borneo: Before White Rajah Rule* (London, 1967).

named *Demologos* (Voice of the People), but such developments still lay in the future.[4]

Indeed, the early history of the steamship was a hesitant one. In 1707, Denis Papin, professor of mathematics at Marburg, demonstrated the first working steamship, the *Retort*, at Kassel, only to have the boat speedily demolished by rivermen who feared competition. It was not until 1783, on the river Saône near Lyons, that the Marquis Jouffroy d'Abbans conducted the next successful demonstration of a workable steamboat.[5]

Early steamships suffered from slow speed, a high rate of coal consumption, and the problems posed by side and paddle wheels, but steam power replaced dependence on the wind and increased the maneuverability of ships, making it easier to sound inshore and hazardous waters and to attack opposing fleets in anchorage. This was demonstrated in the First Burmese War of 1824–6 when the sixty-horsepower engine of the East India Company's steamer *Diana*, a hundred-ton paddle tug built in India in 1823, allowed her to operate on the swiftly flowing Irrawaddy River. The *Diana* towed sailing ships; destroyed the Burmese war boats; and was crucial to the successful British advance four hundred miles upriver, which led the Burmese to negotiate and accept British terms. In 1830, the HMS *Dee*, the first British purpose-built steam warship entered service. Steamships showed their ability to operate inshore when the British bombarded Acre in 1840, and they played a major role in the Opium War of 1839–42 with China. By 1842, the British had deployed twelve thousand troops, twenty-five sail-powered warships, and fourteen steamers, and the last played a key role in permitting an advance on Nanjing up the Yangtze River. New naval technology transformed the situation in inshore and, even more, in riverine waters, providing a greatly enhanced capability to amphibious power. Indeed, as far as rivers such as the Nile and the Niger, the Yangtze and the Yellow were concerned, the military revolution was a nineteenth-century one.[6]

The absence of earlier deep-sea naval conflict not involving Western fleets in the eighteenth century draws attention to Western exceptionalism and to the interacting roles of military goals, strategic cultures, and interest groups.

4 C. O. Philip, *Robert Fulton* (New York, 1985), 302.
5 P. P. Bernard, "How Not to Invent the Steamship," *East European Quarterly* 14 (1980): 1–8.
6 P. Hore, "Lord Melville, the Admiralty and the Coming of Steam Navigation," *Mariner's Mirror* 86 (2000): 157–72; A. Lambert, "'Within Cannon Shot of Deep Water': The Syrian Campaign of 1840," in *Seapower Ashore: 200 Years of Royal Navy Operations on Land*, ed. Hore (London, 2001), 153–62; R. V. Kubicek, "The Colonial Steamer and the Occupation of West Africa by the Victorian State, 1840–1900," *Journal of Imperial and Commonwealth History* 18 (1990): 9–32, and "The Role of Shallow-Draft Steamboats in the Expansion of the British Empire, 1820–1914," *International Journal of Maritime History* 6 (1994): 86–106.

There was no inherent reasons why major non-Western powers, especially those of East Asia, should not deploy substantial fleets, and some had done so in the past, such as the Chinese in the early fifteenth century and the Japanese and Koreans in the 1590s.[7] That they no longer did so is a subject that, by its nature, is difficult to probe. Aside from the conceptual problem of assessing why something did not occur, there are major difficulties in researching the subject. It is instructive, however, to consider the emphasis in recent study on European naval developments, particularly by Jan Glete and Nicholas Rodger,[8] on the cooperation of states and mercantile elites, and in particular on the openness of the first to advice from the latter, and on an ability to derive mutual profit from naval requirements and financial resources. Oceanic naval power depended on a maritime economy to supply resources in depth: demand from governments alone would not generate sustainable maritime infrastructure. It required both a strong state infrastructure and a strong maritime economy, and that was quite rare.

The situation was certainly different in the rest of Eurasia because, although Asian merchants remained important in long-distance trade,[9] the mercantile elites were generally separated from rulers by ethnic or religious divides. Linked to this, the relationship between port cities and states was often uneasy and was nothing like that represented by the role of London. Jews, Greeks, and Armenians did not have close relations with the Ottoman Turks, while China after the Manchu conquest was very much dominated by an elite whose values were not maritime. The same was true of the Mughals in India and of the rulers who succeeded the Safavids in Persia. Close attention reveals, however, that, whatever the political and governmental system outside Europe, there were generally more accommodation, compromise, and pressure from short-term exigencies than concern with formal structures might suggest. Provincial notables holding public office acted in an autonomous fashion. Looked at differently, this was an aspect of the flexibility of provincial administration.[10] This process left plentiful spaces for maritime activity.

7 L. Levathes, *When China Ruled the Seas: The Treasure Fleet of the Dragon Throne, 1405–1433* (New York, 1995); S. Turnbull, *Samurai Invasion* (London, 2002); K. M. Swope, "Crouching Tigers, Secret Weapons: Military Technology Employed during the Sino-Japanese-Korean War, 1592–1598," *Journal of Military History* 69 (2005): 31–4.

8 J. Glete, *Warfare at Sea, 1500–1650* (London, 2000) and *War and the State in Early Modern Europe* (London, 2002); N. A. M. Rodger, *The Safeguard of the Sea* (London, 1997) and *The Command of the Ocean* (London, 2004).

9 S. Chaudhury and M. Morineau, eds , *Merchants, Companies and Trade: Europe and Asia in the Early Modern Era* (Cambridge, U.K., 1999).

10 D. Crecelius, "Egypt in the Eighteenth Century," in *The Cambridge History of Egypt, II. Modern Egypt,* ed. M. W. Daly (Cambridge, U.K., 1998), 60; J. Hathaway, *The Politics of Households in Ottoman Egypt: The Rise of the Qazdaglis* (Cambridge, U.K., 1997).

As the newly independent United States of America showed, however, such activity was not synonymous with naval strength, certainly of the battle-fleet type with its focus on ship killing rather than self-financing commerce raiding. As a consequence, attention has to return to the state level, because the organization of such forces was a formidable task. Many states lacked the requisite stability, and their government by ruler-generals accentuated the focus on land forces and campaigning, as was amply seen in eighteenth-century Burma, Persia, and Siam. China and Japan had greater governmental continuity, but this did not lead to a focus on naval forces. Japan was very much an insular state, and if the term *strategic culture* means much, then it certainly pertains to the inward-looking governing elite. As a sign of widespread conservatism, most political, economic, cultural, and intellectual efforts were directed at the preservation and strengthening of established arrangements, but by the end of the century, there was greater interest in new political, economic, and cultural forms.[11] The formidable bureaucratic culture that was a legacy of the Chinese past maintained by the Manchu was not open to mercantile influences, and certainly not in comparison to Western Europe.

Furthermore, policy goals (themselves set in the context of sociopolitical assumptions and strategic cultures) did not lend themselves to naval development. Having vanquished the Dzungars and occupied Kashgar in the 1750s, China did not move into a military quiescence comparable to that of Japan. Instead, there were a series of wars, unsuccessful against Burma in 1765–9, and Tongkin (northern Vietnam) in 1788–9, and successful against Nepal in 1792. None of these required long-range naval activity: Burma was attacked overland, not by sea. With its settlement colonies on its landward frontiers,[12] China's ambitions focused on near China, not on distant seas. Its international relations were based on Chinese hegemony, and the offer of tributes by neighbors sufficed. Taiwan had been brought under control in 1683; there was no drive to conquer Japan, as the Mongols had sought to do in the thirteenth century; and the frontier with Russia fixed in 1685 and 1729, which excluded Russia from the Amur Valley, was considered acceptable. Vietnamese, Thai, and Burmese actions and ambitions similarly focused on landward activities, and despite the earlier interests of the Maratha Angria family and, to a lesser extent, the rulers of Mysore, this was also true of Indian counterparts.[13] Persian rulers claimed hegemony

---

11 C. Totman, *Early Modern Japan* (Berkeley, California, 1994).

12 J. A. Millward, *Beyond the Pass: Economy, Ethnicity and Empire in Qing Central Asia, 1759–1864* (Stanford, California, 1998).

13 M. Malgonkar, *Kanhoji Angrey, Maratha Admiral* (Bombay, 1959).

over the Persian Gulf, and Nadir Shah had sent a force to Oman,[14] but Persian warfare focused on conflict on landward frontiers to east, north, and west: with Indian rulers, the Uzbeks, Russia, and the Ottomans.

As a consequence, insofar as the development of modern naval power by non-Western powers constituted a naval revolution, it needs to be dated to the late nineteenth century. At the turn of the seventeenth and eighteenth centuries, the Ottomans had abandoned their traditional dependence on galleys and built a new fleet of sail-powered galleons that carried more cannon, as a result checking a largely Venetian fleet off Cerigo in 1718. The Ottomans continued their borrowing, employing French experts on ship construction in the mid-1780s. No comparable response to Western naval power occurred in the Orient until the late nineteenth century.

Even in the case of the New World, where European control largely collapsed in 1775–1826, naval power in terms of significant specialized fleets did not develop until the second half of that century. The new states focused their military activity on armies, militia ideas proved far more conducive to land than sea capability, and considerable reliance was placed on the support of European navies or unofficial support: by the Americans on France in 1778–83, and by the Latin Americans on British support.[15] In the United States, the Department of the Navy was established in 1798, and the governing Federalists revived the navy, first to fight the Barbary States and then to engage France in the Quasi-War of 1798–1800. the French sank or captured more than three hundred American merchantmen in response to the American role in maintaining British trade routes: France did not accept that neutral ships should carry British goods. Clashes between warships from the summer of 1798 were largely won by the Americans.[16]

The Federalist plan to build up the navy was stopped when Jefferson and the Republicans gained power after the election of 1800. Jefferson favored coastal gunboats rather than the more expensive frigates with oceanic range built in the 1790s. The emphasis on gunboats conformed to the militia tradition of American republicanism, and militia could use gunboats to defend the coastal fortifications being built. Based in New Orleans, American gunboats operated against French and Spanish privateers off the Mississippi Delta in 1806–10, while others played a valuable role against Britain in the War of

---

14 L. Lockhart, "Nadir Shah's Campaigns in Oman, 1734–1744," *Bulletin of the School of Oriental and African Studies* 8 (1935–7): 157–73.

15 B. Vale, *A War betwixt Englishmen: Brazil against Argentina on the River Plate, 1825–1830* (London, 2000).

16 A. DeConde, *The Quasi-War: The Politics and Diplomacy of the Undeclared War with France, 1797–1801* (New York, 1966).

1812.[17] Nevertheless, although thanks to the expansion of their merchant marine the Americans had an abundance of trained seamen to man their fleets, and the most powerful frigates of the age, which they were adept at handling in ship-to-ship actions, they had no ships of the line, and their total navy at the outset comprised only seventeen ships. They thus lacked the capacity for fleet action. This reflected the force structure and doctrine developed under Jefferson's agrarian republicanism. It was very different in its military results to the large battle fleets developed and sustained by the mercantile republics of the United Provinces and Commonwealth England in the seventeenth century.

The focus in naval power is therefore resolutely European. Although European warships (and merchantmen) found it difficult to operate in tropical estuary, delta, and river waters,[18] there was no naval balance, nor any frontier of capability and control between European and non-European powers on the oceans of the world. The absence of any challenge to Western naval power on the oceans was dramatically demonstrated in the 1770s, 1780s, and 1790s, as European warships under naval commanders explored the waters and shores of the Pacific, charting and (re-)naming the world, and established European trading bases and colonies in Australasia and along the west coast of North America (the latter process had started earlier).[19] There was still much of the world's land surface where European military strength and models were unknown, but the warships that showed their flags and ran out their guns around the globe were the forceful edge of a European integration of the world. This, however, was not new, having begun in the late fifteenth century.[20]

If this was not a revolution, there was still an important buildup of naval strength within the existing technological constraints. There was a major European naval race in the 1780s. Britain, France, and Spain all launched a formidable amount of tonnage. These huge naval forces dwarfed those of non-European powers far more decisively than they had when Christopher Columbus and Vasco da Gama sailed forth in the 1490s. Some other powers also greatly expanded their navies in the 1780s. This was particularly true of Russia and the Dutch, which became the fourth- and fifth-largest naval

---

17 S. C. Tucker, *The Jeffersonian Gunboat Navy* (Columbia, South Carolina, 1993); C. L. Symonds, *Navalists and Antinavalists: The Naval Policy Debate in the United States, 1785–1827* (Newark, Delaware, 1980).

18 A. Deshpande, "Limitations of Military Technology: Naval Warfare on the West Coast, 1650–1800," *Economic and Political Weekly* 25 (1992): 902–3.

19 J. C. Beaglehole, *The Exploration of the Pacific*, 3rd ed. (Stanford, California, 1966).

20 G. V. Scammell, *The World Encompassed: The First European Maritime Empires, c. 800–1650* (London, 1981).

powers. Denmark, Sweden, Naples, Portugal, and the Ottoman Empire all increased the size of their navies. The total displacement of European navies rose from 750,000 tons in 1770 to 1 million tons by 1760 and 1.7 million tons in 1790.[21] Alongside new shipping, there was the continual effort required to maintain and repair ships, an effort that stemmed, in part, from the vulnerability of ships' organic properties, especially wood and canvas.[22] As the specifications of warships changed relatively little, ships could be kept in the line for decades as long as they were kept seaworthy.

Programs of naval construction and enhancement registered not only the growing resources of European governments but also the capability of their military-industrial complexes and the ability of their administrative systems to plan and implement changes. Fleets of warships were powerful and sophisticated military systems, sustained by mighty industrial and logistical resources based in dockyards that were among the largest industrial plants, employers of labor, and groups of buildings in the world, for example, Portsmouth, Plymouth, Brest, Toulon, Cádiz, and Karlskrona.[23] These dockyards were supported by massive storehouses, such as the vast Lands Zeemagazijn in Amsterdam, which was destroyed by fire in 1791. Naval bases also required considerable investment. As soon as the Russians had seized a Black Sea coastline and the Crimea in 1783, they began to develop bases there, particularly at Kherson, Sevastopol, and Odessa. These threatened a direct attack on Constantinople, providing the Russians with a strategy different to that of a land advance across the eastern Balkans. As a result, Sevastopol was to play a key role in allied goals during the Crimean War (1854–6). Catherine II took the visiting Joseph II to visit Sevastopol in 1787.

The establishment of military-industrial complexes also demonstrated a more widespread capacity to stimulate change. There were numerous innovations, which were put to good use. As an instance of the importance of incremental improvements, British cannon fire proved particularly effective in the British victory over the French off the Îles des Saintes on April 12, 1782. These improvements, including in flintlocks, tin tubes, flannel cartridges, wedges to absorb recoil, and steel compression springs, increased the ease of serving cannon, of firing them instantaneously, and the possible angles of training. The location of the battle, south of Guadeloupe, was a

---

21 J. Glete, *Navies and Nations: Warships, Navies and State Building in Europe and America, 1500–1860*, 2 vols. (Stockholm, 1993), 1:313.

22 E.g., J. E. Talbot, *The Pen and Ink Sailor: Charles Middleton and the King's Navy, 1778–1813* (London, 1998).

23 R. Morriss, *The Royal Dockyards during the Revolutionary and Napoleonic Wars* (Leicester, 1983); C. Wilkinson, *The British Navy and the State in the Eighteenth Century* (Woodbridge, 2004).

testimony to the importance of transoceanic operations: in 1759, in contrast, the key battles had been fought in European waters, as the central issue was the threat of a French invasion to Britain.

During the century, improvements in seaworthiness, stemming in part from the abandonment of earlier top-heavy and clumsy designs, increased the capability of warships, both to take part in all-weather blockades and to operate across the oceans. In the case of Britain, George, Lord Anson, First Lord of the Admiralty, in 1751–62, and the outstanding designer Sir Thomas Slade were responsible for valuable innovations in warship design. The old ship types with eighty, seventy, and sixty guns were abandoned in favor of seventy-four gunners and sixty-four gunners; the fifty-gun ship was discarded as a ship of the line but retained in limited number as a heavy cruiser; the small two-deck cruisers of forty-four guns were abandoned in favor of the single-decked frigate; and better three-deckers were designed. These changes helped increase the operational effectiveness of the navy.

During the War of American Independence (1775–83), the British navy responded to the crisis both by arranging a major program of construction and by technological advances. Copper sheathing reduced the difficulties caused by barnacles, weeds, and the teredo worm, and the consequent loss of speed, and made refits easier. It was pressed forward from February 1779 by Sir Charles Middleton, comptroller of the navy from 1778 to 1790. In 1780, forty-two ships of the line were given copper sheathing. Politicians noted a sense of new potential, and the Marquess of Rockingham claimed in 1781, "The copper bottoms occasioning our ships to sail so much better enables us either to go and attack if we should see an inferior fleet or to decline the attempt if we should see a superior fleet." The value of copper sheathing can be questioned, but the administrative achievement was considerable. The introduction of the carronade, a new, light, short-barreled gun that was very effective at close quarters, adopted by Britain in 1779, was also important: it was used with effect at the Îles des Saintes.[24] After the War of American Independence, the French adopted recent British naval innovations, such as copper sheathing. Standardization, furthermore, was increasingly apparent prior to the changes brought by steam power and amour plating; in 1786, the French adopted standard ships designs for their fleet.

---

24 Rockingham to Earl of Hardwicke, *c.* Ap. 1781, Sheffield, City Archive, Wentworth Woodhouse Mss. R1–1962; J. E. Talbott, "Copper, Salt, and the Worm," *Naval History*, 3 (1989), 53, and "The Rise and Fall of the Carronade," *History Today* 39, no. 8 (1989), 24–30; R. J. W. Knight, "The Royal Navy's Recovery after the Early Phase of the American Revolutionary War," in *The Aftermath of Defeat: Societies, Armed Forces, and the Challenge of Recovery*, ed. G. J. Andreopoulos and H. E. Selesky (New Haven, Connecticut, 1994), 10–25.

More generally, progress in British metallurgy improved their gunnery toward the end of the century. Britain had an advantage in technology and benefited from superior seamanship and well-drilled gun crews. This had an impact on effectiveness. The impact of British naval gunfire on enemy hulls and crews markedly increased during the war period 1793–1815, when enemy ships were reduced to wrecks in a comparatively short time. This need helped drive the growth of the iron industry.

The incremental process of naval improvement continued in the last decades of sail, but with hindsight provided by subsequent technological developments, it is possible to see the period in terms of the use of yet greater resources of people, materiel, and funds to pursue familiar military courses. The American and French revolutions certainly did not bring changes in naval warfare comparable to those on land. Instead, the long-term growing stress on naval firepower continued to affect fleet structures. Whereas in 1720 there were only two warships displacing more than three thousand tons, by 1815, nearly a fifth of the naval strength greater than five hundred tons was in this category. In 1800 – fifteen ships of 2,500–3,000 tons achieved greater importance, whereas those of 2,000–2,500 and 1,500–2,000 tons declined in number. These bigger ships were able to carry heavier guns. Whereas the average ship of the line in 1720 had sixty guns and was armed with twelve- and twenty-four-pounders, that of 1815 had seventy-four guns with thirty-two- and thirty-six-pounders on the lower deck. Nevertheless, this greater firepower did not lead to dramatic changes in naval warfare and it did not begin in the Revolutionary-Napoleonic period.[25]

There were other improvements. Better signaling from the 1790s onward helped to enhance the potential for tactical control. The invention of a system of ship construction using diagonal bracing to strengthen hulls and to prevent the arching of keels, was to increase the resilience of ships, and thus their sea- and battle-worthiness, and to permit the building of longer two-deckers armed with eighty or ninety guns. These improvements helped make earlier ships appear redundant, certainly for the line of battle, but, although Seppings experimented in the 1800s at Plymouth and Chatham, the first ship built entirely on this principle, HMS *Howe*, was not launched until 1815. Diagonal framing was mainly significant after the introduction of steam made it important to build longer ships. It was also possible to fit at least some diagonal framing in older ships when they were repaired

---

25 Glete, *Navies*, 402, 405. Glete employs a different system of measurement from those traditionally used, and the tonnages are therefore higher by 500–750 tons than normally given.

so that they did not become obsolete. Older and smaller battleships were made obsolete after 1815 by improved gun foundry (and possibly improved gunpowder), which made the traditional smoothbore guns considerably more powerful and devastating. Because of advances in metallurgy, the British navy already had more powerful guns in the period 1793–1815.

Europeans also took their naval military-industrial capability abroad, developing major shipyards at colonial bases such as Havana and Halifax. The growing British naval and mercantile presence in the Indian Ocean owed much to shipyards in India, where merchantmen averaging six hundred to eight hundred tons and capable of carrying very large cargoes were constructed, as well as naval vessels, including several ships of the line.

Logistical limitations, however, along with disease and climate, substantially circumscribed European power projection outside European waters. Notwithstanding Halifax, Bermuda, and Jamaica, the British navy lacked the requisite support bases to mount an effective blockade of the east coast of North America, either in 1775–83 or in 1812–14, although it could inflict considerable damage on the American economy.[26] Indeed, the course of the War of Independence indicated the limitations of naval and amphibious power. The campaigns that led to the British relief of Quebec in 1776 and their capture of New York (1776), Philadelphia (1777), Savannah (1778), and Charleston (1780), and to the Franco-American concentration against the British in Yorktown in 1781, each reflected, at least in part, the amphibious capability stemming from naval strength.

Nevertheless, in each case, the exploitation of this capability was dependent on the campaigning on land. More generally, British naval strength could not ensure a decisive victory over the main American field army.[27] This factor, and the consequences of French entry for British amphibious capability, were important, whereas American experimentation with new naval technology in the shape of the submarine had no effect. The first known description of a viable submarine was published by the English mathematician William Bourne in 1578, but an American, David Bushnell (1740–1824), constructed the first operational machine. In 1774, he began to experiment with a submersible that would plant gunpowder beneath a ship; the following year, a prototype was ready for testing and a way had been found to detonate a charge underwater. The wooden submarine, in effect an underwater minelayer, contained a tractor screw operated by hand and pedals, a surfacing screw, a drill for securing the explosive charge, fitted

---

26 R. Buel Jr., *In Irons: Britain's Naval Supremacy and the American Revolutionary Economy* (New Haven, Connecticut, 1999).
27 D. Syrett, *The Royal Navy in American Waters, 1775–1783* (Aldershot, U.K., 1989).

with a time fuse, to the hull of the target, a depth pressure gauge, a rudder with a control bar, bellows with tubes for ventilation, ballast water tanks, fixed lead ballast, detachable ballast for rapid surfacing, and a sounding line. The same year, Joseph Belton of Groton presented to the Pennsylvania Committee of Safety his plan for a submersible, which was expected to hole warships below their water line. The boat was designed, unlike Bushnell's, to carry one or more cannon.

These ideas were genuinely revolutionary and offered a mode of warfare against which the British had no defense. Bushnell's *Turtle* could attack only ships at anchor, but even so the anchorages of the British fleet provided obvious targets. However, successful execution was a different matter. The *Turtle* was first employed against HMS *Eagle* in New York Harbor on September 6, 1776, but Bushnell encountered serious problems with navigating in the face of the currents and could not attach the charge, which went off harmlessly in the water. The second attempt, against HMS *Phoenix* on October 5, 1776, also failed: the *Turtle* was spotted, Bushnell's depth measurer failed, and he lost his target. George Washington pointed out the difficulty of operating the machine satisfactorily, and it is not surprising that Bushnell received scant support from the hard-pressed government while Belton had no success.

French entry into the war in 1778, followed by that of Spain in 1779 and the Dutch in 1780, totally altered the maritime situation, leading to a worldwide naval conflict, at once more extensive and in some spheres, such as the Bay of Bengal, intensive than previous maritime wars between Western powers. British warships were redeployed as Britain responded to the integration of the American conflict into a wider struggle in which the naval balance in American waters was interrelated with that in European and, more obviously, Caribbean waters. By 1780, thanks to shipbuilding since 1763, France and Spain had a combined quantitative superiority over Britain of about 25 percent, and, partly as a result, Britain gained control of neither European nor American waters, and was unable to repeat its success in the Seven Years' War of 1756–63.

The War of American Independence posed serious problems of naval strategy for Britain and France, although there was no revolution in strategy, nor a different scale permitting the use of the term *total*. For Britain, the problem of numbers of warships interacted with disputes over strategy, as the desirability of blockading French ports, for which there were arguably too few ships, clashed with the prudent argument of John, Fourth Earl of Sandwich, the First Lord of the Admiralty, that naval strength should be concentrated in home waters not only to deter invasion but also to permit a serious challenge to the main French fleet, which was based at Brest, and thus to gain a position of naval dominance. This goal would be compromised by dispersing much of the fleet among distant stations, where it could support amphibious operations and protect trade, but not materially affect the struggle for naval dominance. Because of the state of communications technology, a situation that was not to change radically until the use of radio, the commanders of those distant stations were difficult to control effectively and they jealously guarded their autonomy and resources, producing an inflexibility that was ill suited to the need to react to French initiatives.[28]

Despite grave strategic and organizational problems, the French were also more successful at sea than in the Seven Years' War (1756–63), in part thanks to a determined and effective leadership.[29] Indeed, the role of the latter, a factor that is difficult to discuss or categorize in terms of the debate over military revolutions, emerges clearly in the French war effort. There is a ready contrast between the able and energetic Admiral Pierre André Suffren, who proved a persistent, redoubtable, and brave opponent to the British in the Bay of Bengal and off Sri Lanka in 1782–3, and Admiral Louis-Guillouet, Comte d'Orvilliers, commander of the attempt to invade England in 1779. This was thwarted by disease and poor organization, rather than British naval action, for despite the hopes of George III, the outnumbered Western Squadron under Admiral Charles Hardy failed to mount an effective response.

The battles of the period also indicated the difficulty of achieving a sweeping naval victory, which the British were not to gain until 1782. Lacking, by modern standards, deep keels, sailing vessels suffered from limited seaworthiness, while the operational problems of working sailing ships for combat were very different from those that steam-powered vessels were to encounter. The optimal conditions for sailing ships were to come from windward in a force 4–6 wind across a sea that was relatively flat; it was more difficult to range guns in a swell. Limitations on maneuverability ensured that ships were deployed in line to maximize their firepower, and skill in handling ships entailed getting wind behind the topsails. Line tactics and fighting instructions were designed to encourage an organizational cohesion that permitted more effective firepower. The nature of conflict at sea made it difficult, however, to maintain cohesion once ships became closely engaged. John Blankett, Fourth Lieutenant on Admiral Augustus Keppel's

28 N. A. M. Rodger, *The Insatiable Earl: A Life of John Montagu, 4th Earl of Sandwich* (London, 1993), 365–77.

29 J. R. Dull, *The French Navy and American Independence: A Study of Arms and Diplomacy, 1774–1787* (Princeton, New Jersey, 1975).

flagship HMS *Victory*, underscored the dependence on the wind in his report on of the battle with the French Brest fleet off Ushant on July 27, 1778:

Your Lordship will recollect that the forcing a fleet to action, equal in force, and with the advantage of the wind must always be done with great risk, and our fleet was not equal to that manoeuvre, but chance, which determines many events, put it out of the Admiral's power to choose his disposition.... The French behaved more like seamen, and more officerlike than was imagined they would do.... [T]he truth is, unless two fleets of equal force are equally determined for battle, whoever attacks must do it with infinite risk, but a fleet to leeward attacking one to windward is a dangerous manoeuvre indeed.[30]

Three years later, Admiral Thomas Graves failed to defeat the French off the Virginia capes, an indecisive battle in terms of the damage inflicted, but, as it prevented British relief of Cornwallis's encircled army at Yorktown, an important success for the French. The engagement lasted for just over two hours, neither side having any ships sunk but both suffering considerable damage.

In contrast, the British enjoyed far more sweeping victories in the 1790s and 1800s, particularly Glorious First of June (1794), St. Vincent (1797), the Nile (1798), and Trafalgar (1805). This success reflected fighting ability within a defined military system rather than a quantum leap forward, whether described as revolutionary or not. Well-drilled gun crews, superior seamanship, bold leadership, and effective command were key. In contrast, the French Revolution brought turmoil to the administration and leadership of the French navy.[31]

Thanks to its naval strength, Britain was able during the French Revolutionary and Napoleonic Wars to maintain an effective convoy system that helped them increase their proportion of world mercantile shipping, and to deny access to world markets to the French and their allies. More generally, the strength and nature of British naval power and maritime resources enabled Britain to resist Napoleon's attempt to isolate her commercially from the Continent from 1806. Naval strength also supported the Duke of Wellington's campaigns in the Iberian Peninsula,[32] and permitted amphibious operations, leading to the capture of French and allied overseas bases, which further lessened their ability to challenge the British. Cape

30 Blankett to Earl of Shelburne, July 29, 1778, London, British Library, Bowood Papers 511 folios 9–11.
31 W. S. Cormack, *Revolution and Political Conflict in the French Navy, 1789–1794* (Cambridge, U.K., 1995).
32 D. D. Howard, "British Seapower and Its Influence on the Peninsular War, 1810–18," *Naval War College Review* 21 (1978): 54–71; C. D. Hall, "The Royal Navy and the Peninsular War," *Mariner's Mirror* 79 (1993): 403–18.

Town fell in 1806, Martinique in 1809, Réunion and Mauritius in 1810, and Batavia in 1811. In 1808, Napoleon planned to take over the Spanish overseas empire, not only in the New World but also in the Philippines. These hopes were thwarted by Spanish resistance but would, anyway, have been inhibited by British naval power, just as the French attempt to regain Saint-Domingue (Haiti) had been

Naval operations outside Europe, especially in the Indian Ocean and the Caribbean, remained greatly conditioned by climate and disease. Despite improvements in some spheres, in the British case by the Sick and Hurt Board, the general conditions of service at sea remained bleak. Aside from cramped living conditions and poor sanitation, food supplies could be inadequate and inappropriate, with a lack of fresh food, fruit and vegetables, and thus of vitamin C. The cumulative impact was both to make naval service unattractive and to lead to losses among those already in service. Nevertheless, the administration was good enough to ensure that warships fulfilled their operational role on distant stations.[33]

British naval strength was also crucial in the War of 1812–15 with the United States. At sea, the British suffered initially from overconfidence, inaccurate gunnery, and ships that were simply less powerful and less well prepared than those of their opponents. However, aside from three frigates lost in 1812, the British losses were all of smaller vessels, and British naval effectiveness improved during the war, both in Atlantic waters and on the Great Lakes. Naval blockade, which became effective from 1813, hit the American economy; amphibious forces were able to approach Baltimore and burn Washington; and it was possible to send reinforcements to Canada to resist successfully poorly led and uncoordinated American attacks. The American plan in May 1813 and May 1814 for a small squadron to cruise off Nova Scotia and the St. Lawrence to intercept British supply ships failed in large part because of the British blockade. To operate in North America, the British were dependent both on routes across the Atlantic and on an ability to act in coastal waters.[34]

British naval power rested on a sophisticated and well-financed administrative structure, a large fleet drawing on the manpower of a substantial mercantile marine and fishing fleet (although there were never enough sailors), and an ability to win engagements that reflected widely diffused

33 C. Crewe, *Yellow Jack and the Worm: British Naval Administration in the West Indies, 1739–1748* (Liverpool, U.K., 1993).

34 L. Maloney, "The War of 1812: What Role for Sea Power?" in *This People's Navy: The Making of American Sea Power*, ed. K. J. Hagan (New York, 1991), 46–62; R. Morriss, *Cockburn and the British Navy in Transition: Admiral Sir George Cockburn, 1772–1853* (Exeter, U.K., 1997), 83–120.

qualities of seamanship and gunnery, a skilled and determined corps of captains, and able leadership. This was true not only of command at sea, as with Nelson's innovative tactics, but also of effective institutional leadership that developed organizational efficiency. In turn, this rested on the unique European experience of creating a global network of empire and trade, which was based on a distinctive type of interaction between economy, technology and state formation, and on the specific strength of the liberal political systems, which were notably successful in eliciting the cooperation of their own and other capitalists, producing a symbiosis of government and the private sector that proved both effective and, especially, valuable for developing naval strength. In contrast, China, Korea, and Japan could build large ships and manufacture guns, their states were relatively centralized, and their economies and levels of culture were not clearly weaker than those of contemporary European states. However, there was hardly any interaction in the three states among economy, technology, and state formation aimed at creating maritime effectiveness.

The potential of Western naval power was still far less than it was to be within 105 years of the close of the period. First submarines and subsequently aircraft carriers led to a transformation in the relationship between warships and the environment in which they operated. The latter changed the way in which naval forces could press on land powers, as well – more specifically, as their ability to mount successful amphibious assaults. This was to be continued with submarine-launched cruise missiles.

In contrast, naval power in the period under consideration was not able to have comparable impact. This was made clear by the course of the French Revolutionary and Napoleonic wars. Successive naval victories protected Britain from invasion and enabled it to risk amphibious operations, but neither those victories nor such operations, even if successful, could determine the course of conflict on land. After Trafalgar, in which nineteen French and Spanish ships of the line were captured or destroyed, the British enjoyed a clear superiority in ships of the line, but Napoleon's victories over Austria, Prussia, and Russia in 1805–7 ensured that the War of the Third Coalition ended with France in an even stronger position in Europe. The British could not overthrow Napoleon without the help of powerful land allies. This repeated the failure to coerce Russia into returning conquests from Sweden and the Ottomans, in 1720–1 and 1791, respectively.

Victory in battle certainly had a strategic impact as far as the war at sea was concerned. The first British naval victory of the war, the Glorious First of June in 1794, helped deter France from plans drawn up a year earlier to build up a major fleet, reduced the French naval threat in home waters, and therefore helped free more of the British navy for operations further afield. The fate of battle partly explains the contrast between the first two years of this war, in which France lost twenty-two ships, and the first four years in the Anglo-French stage of the War of American Independence, in which France lost only four warships.[35] Four years later, the Battle of the Nile, followed by the capture of Seringapatam in Mysore in 1799 and by victory over the French army in Egypt in 1801, made it clear that France would not be able to project its power successfully along the Egypt-India axis.

War with Britain prevented France from enjoying the benefits of the European hegemony it grasped. The colonial empires of her European allies were outside her (and their) control, and the resources that Napoleon deployed could not be used to project French power. This was a failure that was not inherent in France's position but one that reflected the relatively low priority of maritime as opposed to continental activities, and the successes of the British navy. Like Louis XIV, Napoleon wanted colonies and a strong navy, but under pressure, the army came first.

Yet victory at sea could not prevent the French from trying to build up their navy, not least after Trafalgar. By 1809, the Toulon fleet was nearly as large as the British blockaders. French naval strength, however, had been badly battered by losses of sailors in successive defeats, and in 1808, Napoleon also lost the support of the Spanish navy.

Britain's military capability was effective in the crucial period of Napoleonic decline, 1812–14, but as part of an international league in which the major blows against France were struck on land and by Britain's allies. Furthermore, some amphibious expeditions, such as those against Buenos Aires and Egypt in 1807 were eventually unsuccessful, in the former case leading to the surrender of the British force. The same year, the Turks refused to yield to naval intimidation when a fleet under Vice Admiral Sir John Duckworth forced the Dardanelles, destroying a squadron of Turkish frigates. His return through the Dardanelles proved far more difficult.

Naval battles between Britain and France and her allies – Spain, the Dutch, and the Danes – tend to dominate attention, but the strength and weaknesses of naval power also emerge clearly from a consideration of other aspects of naval activity. Blockade was particularly important, with British squadrons policing the seas of Europe and, to a lesser extent, the oceans of the world. The history of these squadrons was often that of storms and

---

35 C. Ware, "The Glorious First of June: The British Strategic Perspective," in *The Glorious First of June 1794: A Naval Battle and Its Aftermath*, ed. M. Duffy and R. Morriss (Exeter, U.K., 2001), 38–40.

of disappointed hopes of engaging the French. There were different types of blockade. Close blockade was designed to stop an enemy naval force emerging, while open blockade was intended to catch an enemy naval force emerging, and maritime to stop maritime commerce and have a direct economic impact on the opponent's society, an aspect that can be related to notions of total war. These different forms of blockade had variable success rates.

Blockade was not easy: blockading squadrons could be driven off station by wind and weather.[36] Blockading Toulon was particularly difficult.[37] The small watching squadron off Toulon was blown off station when the French sailed in May 1798. The exposure of warships to the constant battering of wind and wave placed a major strain on an increasingly aging fleet. The Channel fleet, for example, was dispersed by a strong gale on January 3, 1804, and the blockade of Le Havre lifted, although that of Brest was swiftly resumed. The weather claimed and damaged more ships than the French: out of the 317 warships lost in 1803–15, 223 were wrecked or foundered, including, in December 1811, HMS *St. George*, a ninety-eight-gunner, with the loss of all bar 12 of the crew of 850, and HMS *Defence* when they were driven onto the Danish coast in a storm. Tropical stations could be particularly dangerous and in 1807 Trowbridge and HMS *Blenheim* disappeared in a storm off Madagascar.

Fog was also a problem, particularly for blockaders. It could cover French movements, as when the Brest fleet sailed in April 1798, and once a fleet had sailed, it was impossible to know where it had gone: in this case, the British were unsure of whether the French would head for Ireland or the Mediterranean. In January 1808, the French Rochefort squadron evaded the British blockaders in bad weather and poor visibility and sailed to Toulon, making a concentration of French warships there more serious. Fog was also a hazard to British warships. HMS *Venerable*, part of the squadron covering Brest, sank on the Devon coast in 1804 after running ashore in a thick fog. The poorly charted nature of inshore waters was a problem that led to ships frequently running aground. Nearly four hundred men drowned in March 1801 when HMS *Invincible* ran aground near Great Yarmouth. It was particularly easy to do so when enforcing blockades, and shoals were also a problem when attacking enemy warships sheltering in coastal waters. Once aground, ships were vulnerable to attack and weather.

36 R. Morriss, ed., *The Channel Fleet and the Blockade of Brest, 1792–1801* (Aldershot, U.K., 2001).
37 P. Mackesy, *The War in the Mediterranean, 1803–1810* (London, 1957); P. Krajeski, *In the Shadow of Nelson: The Naval Leadership of Admiral Sir Charles Cotton, 1753–1812* (Westport, Connecticut, 2000).

Wind-powered warships were dependent both tactically and strategically on the weather. Ships could only sail up to a certain angle to the wind. Too much or insufficient wind were serious problems. Reliance on the wind alone made inshore naval operations very chancy. French ships could leave their major Atlantic port – Brest – only with an easterly wind. This was not all that prevalent, and that helped the British blockaders. There were also serious limitations in the surveillance and command and control capabilities of naval power. These made it very difficult to see or control in any strategic sense, and they certainly limited the value of any blockade. It was generally possible for a lookout to see only about fifteen miles from the top of the main mast in fine weather.

Yet the operational limitations were tested by skill and developments. Specialized sailing ships, in particular bomb ketches, were designed with coastal operations in shallow waters during the sailing era foremost in mind. It is also possible to adduce examples of successful campaigns in precisely such waters, for example the Chesapeake campaign of 1814.

Despite its difficulties, naval power permitted a great increase in maritime strength. This was important to the global expansion of British commerce. British commercial penetration of South and Southeast Asia and the Far East was aided by naval strength: occupation, as of Java in 1811–16, was important. Her dominant position served to ensure that Britain took the leading role in exploration, trade, and the assembly of knowledge about the world. This left its mark on the imperial capital where there was a major expansion in shipping and docks: the London Dock was excavated in 1801, followed by the West India Docks in 1802, the East India Docks in 1805, and the start of work on the Surrey Commercial Docks in 1807, all important developments in the commercial infrastructure of the empire. Elsewhere in Britain, the war led to an expansion of shipbuilding, both for the navy and for trade. Naval power was a condition as well as a product of economic growth. As the Industrial Revolution was crucial to British and subsequently global modernization, so the ability of the British navy, operating effectively within existing constraints, to foster British trade was central to what was a nonmilitary revolution. This industrial revolution was to have fundamental implications for the ability in the nineteenth century to develop and sustain new-model navies with totally different tactical, operational, and eventually strategic capabilities to those hitherto.

This provides a way to consider issues of military revolution, modernity, modernization, and total warfare that play a major role in the literature. If a technology-driven account of warfare is employed, then the naval capability of the period certainly does not deserve discussion in terms of naval revolution. Indeed, the case of the submarine demonstrated that an awareness of the difficulties posed by introducing new developments helped ensure reluctance in adopting them. An American, Robert Fulton, produced one in 1797, but found neither France nor Britain greatly interested in its acquisition. His experiments for the French in 1800–1 included the testing of a system of compressed air in a portable container and the successful destruction of a vessel by an underwater explosion. Fulton also proposed the use of steamships for an invasion of England, but in 1803, the French Academy of Sciences rejected the idea. In Britain, in 1804–6, Fulton worked on mines. They were used, with scant effect, for an attack on French shipping in Boulogne in 1804, but in trials in 1805, he became the first to sink a large ship with a mine. British interest, however, declined after Trafalgar, while Fulton was held back in his experiments with torpedoes from 1807 by his failure to devise an effective firing device. During the Anglo-American War of 1812–15, Fulton played a role in unsuccessful American experiments with a submarine, mines, and underwater guns. He was not alone. In 1807–10, Ivan Fistum, a Russian, made advances in electrical detonation and the use of floating mines for harbor defenses, while in 1809, Napoleon authorized a French company to build a submarine.[38]

Yet a focus on technology is of limited value. Instead, it is more helpful to consider multidefinitional approaches to capability, effectiveness, and development.[39] In that context, a key element was the ability to operate at reasonable effectiveness within existing constraints, and this was and is easier in contexts in which there are not radical shifts in technological potential – in other words, periods such as 1775–1815; as opposed, for example, to World War I. As far as the former period is considered, the key element in operating at such effectiveness tends to be institutional, a product of administrative skill, financial support, and governmental stability. All three criteria found Britain at an advantage, both before and after the French Revolution.[40] It would indeed be possible to argue that the British navy of the period 1793–1815 was so much ahead of all other navies that it could be described as a modern navy while other navies still were early modern, although such vocabulary also introduces a problematic teleology that needs to be considered in terms of contemporary strategic cultures and the related concept of fitness for purpose in terms of specific force structures and

---

38 A. Roland, *Underwater Warfare in the Age of Sail* (Bloomington, Indiana, 1978); W. S. Hutcheon, *Robert Fulton, Pioneer of Undersea Warfare* (Annapolis, Maryland, 1981); G. L. Pesce, *La Navigation sous-marine* (Paris, 1906), 227.

39 J. Black, *Rethinking Military History* (London, 2004).

40 J. Pritchard, *Louis XV's Navy, 1748–1762: A Study of Organisation and Administration* (Montreal, 1987); Cormack, *Revolution and Political.*

investment patterns. Nevertheless, to return to the concept of the British navy as modern, it was not warship technology that was different (British warships for most of the period were, on average, older than those of the French), but British advances in gun foundry, gunnery methods (flintlocks), food supply and methods for storing food on ships, naval medicine and surgery, and the quality of sails and ropes were all considerable in 1793–1815, while they were largely absent in other navies, which, to some extent, actually went backward and were deskilled.

Furthermore, the British navy was able to achieve the contemporary goals of naval power. As yet, the ability to act against a continental state that was to stem from airpower and, subsequently, missiles was not conceivable, no more than the earlier shifts arising from steam power, shell guns, and iron ships, or, subsequently, radio. These paradigm shifts in capability were revolutionary as far as ship killing, ship control, and power projection were concerned, and indeed in 1806, Fulton had argued, "It does not require much depth of thought to trace that science by discovering gunpowder changed the whole art of war by land and sea; and by future combination may sweep military mines from the ocean."[41]

It is far from clear, however, that these shifts in capability led to as total an experience of naval conflict as that experienced during the French Revolutionary and Napoleonic wars. The length of large-scale, deep-sea naval conflict then has never been matched since, the nearest equivalent being the American-Japanese war in the Pacific during World War II. It is therefore paradoxical to adopt a definition of total war that excludes the warfare of 1793–1815, while the standard linear concepts of development lead to the paradoxical conclusion that it was but a stage to a superior subsequent situation, which is not really a helpful account of naval conflict in the following decades. The naval warfare of 1894–1905 (the Sino-Japanese, Spanish-American, and Russo-Japanese wars) was to be different in character to that of 1816–93, but in none of those conflicts was it necessary to sustain a long-term naval struggle.

Linearity therefore is unhelpful. Because of circumstances stemming from the period 1775–1815, particularly the sustaining of Britain's maritime strength and ability to thwart invasion, there was no parity subsequently but rather a naval hegemony resting on industrial strength and strategic culture, which ensured that shifts in technological potential occurred within the existing hierarchy of naval power rather than overthrowing it. This remained

---

41 Fulton to William, Lord Grenville, British Prime Minister, Sept. 2, 1806, British Library, Additional Mss., vol. 71593, folio 134.

true even of the major challenge from Germany, a major industrial power willing to invest in naval strength, and the assault it mounted with both surface warships and submarines during World War I. The subsequent shift to American naval hegemony, accomplished by 1945, was achieved without conflict between Britain and the United States; and even Germany and Japan in cooperation were not able to thwart this transformation. In terms of linearity, Britain versus France can therefore be viewed as part of a sequence of challenges, not as a limited form of warfare that subsequently became total or more total.

12

Partisan Warfare in Spain and Total War

JOHN LAWRENCE TONE

Spain's war against Napoleon began with a revolutionary act. On May 2, 1808, the people of Madrid rose up against the French occupation, inaugurating six years of warfare that turned Spain into a quagmire from which Napoleon could not extricate himself.[1] The Dos de Mayo failed, but it inspired people all across Spain to sweep old municipal elites aside and form revolutionary juntas committed to resisting the French. The juntas raised new armies, and in the countryside, civilians formed partisan bands and fought a guerrilla war that shocked Europe. The extent of this partisan activity made the war in Spain unique, as many contemporaries readily acknowledged.[2] But was it a case of total war? Before tackling this question, it will be useful to review the literature on the Spanish partisans in the War of Independence.

PATRIOTS, FANATICS, AND BANDITS

Spaniards who lived through the War of Independence depicted their resistance as a "spontaneous" and "organic" outgrowth of "the people."[3] Manuel Quintana, poet and editor of the *Semanario Patriótico*, argued that the Spanish insurgency signaled something new in the world – the creation of

---

1 Napoléon confessed on St. Helena, "All the circumstances of my disasters are bound up in that fatal knot," a reference to the Spanish quagmire. Emmanuel Las Cases, *Mémorial de Sainte Hélène*, 2 vols. (Paris, 1861), 1:609–10.
2 On the influence of the Spanish war on Austrian and German national movements, see Walter Consuelo Langsam, *The Napoleonic Wars and German Nationalism in Austria* (New York, 1930), 51, 70–1, 114; and F. Gunther Eyck, *Loyal Rebels: Andreas Hofer and the Tyrolean Uprising of 1809* (Lanham, Maryland, 1986), 57, 101. On the war's influence in Russia see Carlos Ibañez Ibero, *Episodios de la Guerra de la Independencia* (Madrid, 1963), 31.
3 Patriotic proclamations affirming the unanimity of the Spanish nation against the French may be found in the Archivo Histórico Nacional, Madrid, Estado, legs. 12–13.

243

a real nation, unlike the shapeless and shallow-rooted nations of Europe that excluded the masses and were, therefore, unable to resist French domination.[4] José María Toreno, one of the leaders of the revolution of 1808, rhapsodized that "women and children, youths and old men, overcome with patriotic ardor, filled with rage and anger, called unanimously and simultaneously for a quick, noble, and tremendous revenge."[5] Most scholars of Spanish history, until quite recently, continued to echo Toreno, emphasizing the spontaneity and unanimity of the struggle. They characterized the war as a people's war, ubiquitous and uniform across the map of Spain, that mobilized virtually everyone behind God, king, and country.[6] Whether the war was in any way a case of total war, one could certainly make the case that the patriotic rhetoric was totalizing.

The French occupiers, in contrast, initially viewed the partisans as bandits, the movement of a few malcontents.[7] But as the partisan war expanded to involve tens of thousands of Spanish civilians, this interpretation quickly became untenable. By 1809, the French had reversed themselves. They began to see partisans everywhere. Marshall Nicolas Soult thought he was fighting against "the entire nation: all the inhabitants, men, women, children, old men, and priests, are in arms, the villages abandoned, the defiles guarded."[8] Another French officer agreed and added that the only way to victory in Spain would be to fight a "war of extermination."[9] Ironically, this ugly language echoed the Spanish propaganda, except that where the Spanish saw a nation of heroes, the French saw a countryside filled with fanatics. This interpretation of the insurgency in Spain revived the French Republic's discourse about the Vendée rebellion of 1793. And as in the

---

4 *El Semanario Patriótico*, Oct. 27, 1808.
5 José María Toreno, *Historia del levantamiento, guerra, y revolución de España*, 3 vols. (Paris, 1851), 1:186. For interesting observations on Spanish romanticism and the people's war, see José Luis Abellán, *Liberalismo y romanticismo* (Madrid, 1984), chaps. 4–7.
6 For declarations on the national character of the war, see José Gómez de Arteche y Moro, *La Guerra de la Independencia*, 5 vols. (Madrid, 1868), 1:9–12, 20; Enrique Rodríguez-Solís, *Los guerrilleros de 1808, historia popular de la guerra de la independencia*, 2 vols. (Madrid, 1887), 2:27; Antonio Ramos Oliveira, *Politics, Economics, and Men of Modern Spain* (New York, 1972), 21–5; María Cruz Figueroa Lalinde, *La Guerra de la Independencia en Galicia* (Vigo, 1993), 36, 159. This tendency to view the resistance as unanimous, spontaneous, and organic is not limited to Spanish scholars. See, e.g., Anthony James Joes, *Guerrilla Conflict before the Cold War* (Westport, Connecticut, 1996), 93. The exception to this rule was Juan Mercader Riba in *José Bonaparte, Rey de España* (Madrid, 1971), and *Barcelona durante la ocupación francesa* (Madrid, 1949).
7 The French Senate thought the insurgents were bandits in the pay of the British and said so in the pages of the *Moniteur*. Their words were reprinted and ridiculed in the *Semanario Patriótico*, Oct. 13, 1810.
8 Jean Nicolas Soult, *Mémoires du Maréchal Soult. Espagne et Portugal* (Paris, 1955), 68.
9 Louis Florimand Fantain des Odoards, *Journal du Général Fantin des Odoards; étapes d'un officier de la grande armée, 1800–1830* (Paris, 1895), 211.

Vendée, the genocidal French rhetoric served to justify the liberal use of terror against civilians.[10]

To explain the roots of the widespread hostility they encountered in Spain, French combatants ascribed certain characteristics to the entire population. Spaniards were an inferior and ignorant people directed by priests and incapable of realizing that the French occupation was in Spain's best interest.[11] This viewpoint came to dominate the French historiography. Thus, the underlying problem for the French occupation, according to Maximilién Foy, was that Spaniards were so backward. "One can't bring progress to nations against their will," Foy argued, for the attempt will only turn fanatics into partisans.[12] Geoffroy de Grandmaison related the partisan movement to "customs, climate, and fanaticism," which combined to make Spaniards pitiless at the same time they were antimodern.[13] Even quite recently, Jean-Louis Reynaud recapitulated this old argument when he characterized the Spanish partisan war as "the insurrection of an entire people, a veritable crusade," by "a people of twelve million souls, made fanatical by its clergy."[14]

British combatants held a very different view of partisan warfare in Spain. They saw partisans as bandits and malingerers. George Gleig reported that the guerrillas he saw were "vile" and went around boasting of their deeds in an "ungentlemanly" manner, when everyone knew that it was the British who delivered Spain from Napoleon.[15] William Napier likened the guerrillas to "livid blotches" that had appeared on the body of Spain in its weakened state, and he asserted that the insurgents were militarily detrimental.[16]

The explanation for this peculiar British perspective is not hard to find. The British who fought with Wellington thought they, and not the Spanish, deserved the laurels of victory. And they had reasons for thinking that way. The Spanish regulars who fought alongside the British did not perform well, and the British had little contact with any important centers of guerrilla warfare until the very end of the conflict. The guerrilla forces they encountered in western Spain were small and had little military value.

10 Raynald Secher, *Le Genocide Franco-Français: la Vendée Vengée* (Paris, 1986).
11 General Duhesme, "Résumé des Opérations," Archives de l'Armée de Terre, Vincennes (hereafter AAT), C8, 7. See also Napoleon's reflections in Las Cases, *Mémorial*, 2:774, 777, 779.
12 Maximilién Sébastien Foy, *Histoire de la guerre de la péninsule*, 4 vols. (Paris, 1827), 4:25.
13 Charles Alexandre Geoffroy de Grandmaison, *L'Espagne et Napoleon*, 3 vols. (Paris, 1925–31), 3:215.
14 Jean-Louis Reynaud, *Contre-Guerrilla En Espagne (1808–1814). Suchet pacifie l'Aragon* (Paris, 1992), 31–2. For further examples of this sort of literature, see Jean Thiry, *La Guerre d'Espagne* (Paris, 1965); Georges Roux, *Napoléon et le Guêpier Espagnole* (Paris, 1970), Jean-René Aymes, *La Guerre d'Independence Espagnole, 1808–1814* (Paris, 1973).
15 George Robert Gleig, *The Subaltern* (London, 1825), 369.
16 William Napier, *History of the War in the Peninsula and the South of France*, 5 vols. (New York, 1882), 1:iv; 2:127–9, 331, 349; 3:269.

Often they were deserters or mere bandits. The British, with few exceptions, like the poet Southey, had little doubt that partisans deserved no credit for Spain's liberation.

This perspective became enshrined in British historiography with the work of Charles Oman, who, relying primarily on accounts by British officers, concluded that combat outside Wellington's theater of operations counted for very little.[17] This British tradition of disdain for the Spanish partisans has been revived recently by Charles Esdaile, who gives credit for victory to Wellington while discounting the partisans as bandits who hurt the allied cause.[18]

The problem with all of these interpretations is that they rely almost exclusively on the memoirs and correspondence of officers and politicians. But French, English, and Spanish elites had little direct knowledge of the partisans and ample reason to view them either as paragons of virtue (the Spanish liberal viewpoint) or as objects of suspicion, fear, and hatred (the viewpoint of most officers and political figures). The bandit thesis associated with Esdaile is particularly unsustainable, based, as it is, on the opinions of men who, because of their class and profession, saw irregulars as a threat. In fact, testimony from such quarters is useless except as a way to address the question of what elites thought of armed civilians. That they thought of them as good-for-nothing bandits is not really very surprising or illuminating. In guerrilla war, partisans seize produce destined for the market. They attack collaborators, who are often men of substance. They place illegal levies on towns deemed too friendly to the enemy. Such activities may appear superficially to be banditry, but this is an illusion easily dispelled by going beyond the testimony of officers and politicians to see what sort of people the partisans really were.

RESTATING THE PROBLEM: THE VARIETIES OF RESISTANCE

It is difficult to generalize about the various partisan movements in Spain. Factors present in Seville did not operate in Madrid. The urban rising in Zaragoza was not like that in Valencia. And the guerrilla war in the Basque Country was different from that in La Mancha. Nevertheless, we will hazard and then test two generalizations about the partisans.

17 Charles Oman, *The History of the Peninsular War*, 7 vols. (London, 1903–30), 2:1, 3:461.
18 Charles Esdaile, *The Wars of Napoleon* (London, 1995), 139. See also his *The Spanish Army in the Peninsular War* (Manchester, U.K., 1988), 125, 141–3, *The Duke of Wellington and the Command of the Spanish Army* (London, 1990), 117–18, and *Fighting Napoleon: Guerrillas, Bandits and Adventurers in Spain, 1808–1814* (New Haven, Connecticut, 2004), 130, 176, 200.

First, urban movements were quite distinct from the guerrilla war in the countryside. The resistance in cities sometimes began in a spontaneous manner, but it always fell under elite control. It was often overtly ideological, with the defense of God, king, and country supplying at least part of the motivation. In contrast, the guerrilla movement in the countryside was more spontaneous and organic, with leadership supplied by local landowning peasants and artisans, but it is hard to find evidence that the guerrillas were fighting for God, king, or country.

Second, although partisans were active in many corners of Spain during at least part of the conflict, really effective resistance did not occur everywhere. For one thing, cities could not sustain partisan warfare against the overwhelming forces Napoleon placed in Spain. The same can be said, in fact, for much of the countryside. Indeed, the areas that gave birth to successful guerrilla movements tended to lay in a band of territory across northern Spain, from Catalonia to Galicia, and they shared some fundamental social characteristics that can be identified and analyzed. There is, in other words, a human geography to the guerrilla war that serves to explain it better than any of the traditional theories about patriots, fanatics, or bandits.

The following section looks at three cases of urban resistance: the rising of Aranjuez, the Dos de Mayo in Madrid, and the revolution and resistance in Zaragoza. I then examine the two most important cases of guerrilla warfare: Galicia and Navarre. The purpose will be to test my two generalizations en route to answering the following additional questions: Who were the partisans? Why did they fight? How successful were they? And, finally, can the Spanish Revolution of 1808 and War of Independence be considered in any way an example of total war as we understand that concept today?

URBAN RESISTANCE MOVEMENTS

Aranjuez

On March 18, 1808, an uprising at Aranjuez, the royal retreat south of Madrid, toppled the Spanish monarchy and set in motion a train of events that made war between France and Spain all but inevitable. However, the rising at Aranjuez was anything but spontaneous and organic. Rather, it was inspired and organized by a reactionary political faction opposed to the Bourbon government.

King Charles IV, Queen Luisa, and the man behind the throne, Manuel Godoy, had, over a number of years, alienated a significant segment of the Spanish population. Godoy had carried out important agrarian and ecclesiastic reforms in the tradition of Bourbon enlightened absolutism, but this alarmed the clergy and the towns whose entailed property he seized. Naval defeat at Trafalgar made people restless and dissatisfied with the pro-French posture of the government. Luisa's rumored sexual affair with Godoy, a commoner, inspired loathing among Spanish elites jealous of his influence. And a series of bad harvests and epidemics created enemies of thousands of people who did not know who else to blame if not the unholy trinity of Charles, Luisa, and Godoy. These disgruntled elements rallied around the figure of Prince Ferdinand, whose resulting conspiratorial behavior led to his house arrest in the fall of 1807.[19]

Meanwhile, by the Treaty of Fontainebleau, signed on October 27, 1807, Godoy allowed Napoleon to send thousands of troops across Spanish territory to drive the English from Portugal. That achieved, however, the French continued to pour across the Pyrenees, so that by February 1808, one hundred thousand French troops occupied the Iberian Peninsula, most of them stationed in Spain. Napoleon, being Napoleon, could not resist using these forces. On February 16, General D'Armagnac seized Pamplona's great citadel. Two weeks later, General Duhesme occupied the fortress at Montjuich in Barcelona. A week later, General Thouvenot installed himself in San Sebastián, and two weeks after that the border fortress of Figueras came under French control. Thus, without ever declaring open hostilities, the French became masters of Spain's key fortresses.

The initial reaction among the populace to these machinations was hostile. In Pamplona, a crowd directed by students and joined by peasants from the surrounding countryside occupied the streets. Incidents also occurred in Barcelona, Valladolid, and elsewhere. All of these events appear to have been the result of local initiatives. There was no overall direction to the movement. On February 18, the Council of Castile, in a passing fit of bravery, sent a secret agent to foment an uprising in Pamplona, but it was already too late with the French ensconced in the citadel. On March 16, King Charles gave up any chance he may have had to provide direction to the incipient resistance when he mendaciously proclaimed that the emperor had occupied Spain to protect it from the English.[20]

For the enemies of Charles and Godoy, this was too much. On March 18, members of Ferdinand's inner circle engineered a riot in Aranjuez. The

19 See Richard Herr, "Good, Evil, and Spain's Rising against Napoleon," in *Ideas in History: Essays Presented to Louis Gottschalk*, ed. Richard Herr and Harold T. Parker (Durham, North Carolina, 1965), 157–81.
20 These events are reconstructed from documents and correspondence in the AAT, C8, 4, 5, and from Andrés Martín, *Historia de los sucesos militares de la División de Navarra, y demás acontecimientos de este Reyno durante la última guerra contra el Tírano Napoleón*, 2 vols. (Pamplona, 1953), 1:5.

crowd invaded the royal palace and forced Charles to abdicate in favor of Ferdinand. When news of the coup at Aranjuez spread, it produced euphoria among people who assumed that Ferdinand, now dubbed *el deseado* (the desired one), would finally stand up to the French. Although it was possible to rig an enthusiastic reception for Murat's triumphal entry into Madrid in late March, the real mood of the country quickly became evident in the explosion of anti-French violence. Overnight, partisans began to attack French stragglers along the highways. In some areas, it was as if war had been openly declared. Incidentally, the evident relation between these hostilities and the political events at Aranjuez is one of many pieces of evidence against the bandit thesis associated with Esdaile, who makes the astonishing argument that the partisans were motivated primarily by greed, when in fact their resistance was directly related to the great (though false) hope Ferdinand gave them that it might be possible to do something about the humiliating and damaging informal French occupation of the country since early 1808.[21]

The irony is that the coup at Aranjuez elevated to the throne a man no less submissive to Napoleon than his father and Godoy had been. Against the wishes of his advisers, Ferdinand ignored calls to organize resistance to the French occupation. Instead, and again despite warnings from his counselors, Ferdinand decided to accept Napoleon's invitation to a conference at Bayonne. He arrived on April 20, was immediately placed under arrest, and shortly thereafter forced to abdicate in favor of Napoleon's elder brother Joseph.[22]

The Dos de Mayo

News of Aranjuez caused a wave of violence in Madrid. On March 25, Spanish troops killed a French soldier and wounded two others in a fight over who had the right to use a particular brothel. In early April, devout worshipers beat a French soldier who refused to take his hat off during a religious procession. News of Ferdinand's arrest in late April triggered a new crescendo of violence. On April 26, three French soldiers killed and

---

21 On Aranjuez, see Juan Antonio Llorente (pseud. Juan Nellerto), *Memoria para la historia de la Revolución española* (Paris, 1814), 16–20. Esdaile, *Fighting Napoleon*, 191.

22 The description of events in Bayonne is based on correspondence between Ferdinand and his brother Antonio dated April 28, 1808 in AAT, C8, 5, on Pedro Cevallos, *Exposición de los hechos y maquinaciones que han preparado la usurpación de la corona de España y los medios que el emperador de los franceses ha puesto en obra para realizarla* (Cádiz, 1808); and Juan Escoiquiz, *Idea sencilla de las razones que motivaron el viage del Rey Fernando VII a Bayona en el mes de abril de 1808, dada al públilco de España y de Europa* (Madrid, 1814).

robbed a civilian, and one of Murat's aides murdered another. The next day a shopkeeper stabbed a French soldier, and a mob of civilians attacked seven others, leaving three of them gravely wounded.[23]

On April 30, Joachim Murat, the military governor of Madrid, ordered the exile of Francisco de Paula, the last Bourbon heir left in Spain. A group of Ferdinand's supporters made certain that the populace knew about the departure of the prince scheduled for nine in the morning on May 2. Just after daybreak on May 2, a crowd of men and women gathered in front of the royal palace. They destroyed the carriage waiting to transport Francisco de Paula. Then, to shouts of "Death to the French!" the crowd surged through the streets looking for victims.

A few unfortunate French soldiers fell, but Murat and General Emmanuel Grouchy, who commanded the garrison, responded with overwhelming force. Armed with scissors, knives, and stones, the partisans had no chance. Only in the artillery park, where a group of soldiers joined the civilians did the resistance last more than a few minutes, and by early afternoon, even that had ended. Grouchy estimated that he killed between four hundred and five hundred Spanish in the fray, including those executed afterward, while the French, again according to Grouchy, suffered fourteen deaths, almost all during the assault on the regular Spanish troops at the artillery park.

Zaragoza

The Dos de Mayo failed, but it inspired others. Information about the catastrophe, combined with news of Ferdinand's humiliation at Bayonne, triggered uprisings in a number of other Spanish cities in late May and early June.[24] One of these occurred in the city of Zaragoza, which happened to be the home of several of Ferdinand's closest collaborators.

The uprising at Zaragoza started with a miracle in the cathedral. On May 17 during the noon Mass, a crown surrounded by palm fronds appeared

---

23 For events in Madrid, I employ the following sources: the reports and correspondence of Murat and Grouchy, AAT, C8, 5, 6, and 381; Gómez de Arteche, *Guerra de la Independencia*, 1:322–35, 356; Juan Pérez Guzmán, *El 2 de Mayo de 1808* (Madrid, 1908); Joaquín Ezquerra del Bayo, *Guerra de la Independencia, Retratos* (Madrid, 1935); Cayetano Alcázar, "El Madrid del Dos de Mayo," in *Itinerario de Madrid* (Madrid, 1952); Carlos E. Corona, "Precedentes ideológicos de la Guerra de la Independencia," in *IIº Congreso histórico internacional de la Guerra de la Independencia y su época*, 2 vols. (Zaragoza, 1959), 1:5–24; and Jesusmaría Alía y Plana, "El primer lunes de Mayo de 1808 en Madrid," in *Madrid, el 2 de Mayo de 1808, viaje a un día den la historia de España* (Madrid, 1992), 105–38.

24 On Bayonne and its relationship to Dos de Mayo, see the material in the Archivo Histórico Nacional (AHN), Madrid, Estado, leg. 28, no. 34; Pierre Conard, *La constitución de Bayonne* (Lyon, 1909); and Juan Priego López, *La Guerra de la Independencia*, 4 vols. (Madrid, 1972), 2:140–53.

above the altar to the Virgin Mary with the inscription: "God supports Ferdinand." Clergy marched through the city proclaiming that the miracle was a sign that people should rise in favor of Ferdinand. They said that the city's patron, the Virgin of the Pillar, had authorized a hundred years off any time spent in purgatory for individuals wounded fighting against the French, while anyone killed could, like the Savior himself, count on being reborn in paradise after only three days.[25]

A few days later, a mob led by students and clergy seized an arsenal of twenty-five thousand muskets and eighty cannon, marched to the home of prominent resident and supporter of Ferdinand, General José Palafox y Melci, and gave him command of what had become an armed militia. On May 29, 4,500 regulars added their numbers to the defense of the city, and Palafox began to drill both regulars and militia in preparation for a French attack.

The French response came on June 15, when General Lefebvre-Desnöettes attacked the city with six thousand troops. He expected a quick surrender, but Zaragoza had achieved something that actually approximated the much-abused image of the people in arms. Behind walls and trenches, from their homes and churches, fighting at times with knives and bare hands, citizens of Zaragoza fought and repelled a French assault. The French sent more troops but again failed to take the city. A final grand assault by fifteen thousand men on August 4 was likewise turned back. The French withdrew and did not return until November, but even then could not take the city until the following February.

These three examples of partisan warfare in urban settings exhibit certain common characteristics. First, the leadership role of traditional elites is obvious. A cabal of men around Ferdinand engineered Aranjuez. The Dos de Mayo, while much more spontaneous, also required leadership from Ferdinand's friends to alert Madrileños to the impending departure of Francisco de Paula. And only the efforts of officers and troops at the artillery park produced even a small measure of success. The resistance of Zaragoza was led from the first by clergy and the capable José Palafox, and Zaragoza also made use of thousands of regular troops.

Second, in all three cases, partisans fought, at least in part, for overtly ideological causes. In Aranjuez, they fought to overthrow one monarch for

25 For events in Zaragoza, I use AAT, C8, 6, 7; José de Rebolledo Palafox y Melci, *Autobiografía*, ed. J. García Mercadal (Madrid, 1966); Toreno, *Historia del levantamiento*, 1:56–81; Agustín Alcaide Ibieca, *Historia de los dos sitios que pusieron a Zaragoza en los años de 1808 y 1809* (Madrid, 1830); Mariano de Pano y Ruata, *La Condesa de Bureta* (Zaragoza, 1908); and Oman, *History of the Peninsular War*, 1:140–62.

another whom they mistakenly thought would be more capable of resisting the French. In Madrid, the uprising was explicitly royalist, beginning around the person of a Bourbon prince, Francisco de Paula. In Zaragoza, the revolutionary movement was clearly both religious and royalist in inspiration.

The old saying that the Spanish fought for God, king, and country seems apt, therefore, as a description of these three examples of partisan warfare in urban settings. The point should not be exaggerated. In Madrid, the presence in and around the city of thirty-six thousand French soldiers may have been enough of an irritant to trigger some kind of uprising regardless. Nevertheless, the notion that "Spain" rose up against the French for religious and patriotic reasons may not be entirely wrong where some of the urban risings are concerned. However, the image of spontaneous and organic enthusiasm for Ferdinand and the church should give way before evidence that the clergy and Ferdinand's supporters played an important role in fomenting this supposed spontaneity.

The urban revolutions and resistance movements of 1808 ultimately failed, and this distinguishes them from the guerrilla war fought in the countryside. The efforts of dozens of cities, from Seville and Valencia to Madrid and Zaragoza, helped to liberate most of Spain for a few months in the fall of 1808. But then Napoleon sent new armies to Spain. Following a series of sharp victories, the French expelled the English, who could not return for several years. Spain's makeshift armies disintegrated before the renewed onslaught. And Spain's cities fell one after another. By 1810, most of Spain had been pacified.

But the French could not subject all of Spain. In some rural areas, a new sort of conflict, dubbed guerrilla warfare, grew in importance. The following section discusses guerrilla warfare in two regions, Galicia and Navarre, and identifies the factors that made the guerrillas in these two provinces so successful.

GUERRILLA WARFARE

Galicia

In 1809, Galicia became the site of the first important guerrilla insurgency in Spain. In the summer of 1808, popular risings in Galicia handed power to a revolutionary junta, which raised and trained a small army. On July 14, the French destroyed this force at Medina de Río Seco. Those who escaped died later or were dispersed during the disastrous fall offensive. Thus, in

January 1809, when Marshall Soult invaded Galicia, he found an exhausted and demoralized people. He also found many collaborators in cities like La Coruña, El Ferrol, Santiago de Compostela, and Vigo. Indeed, noble, clerical, and bourgeois elites in these cities opened their arms to Soult, just as their counterparts in Madrid, Barcelona, Seville, and other cities were doing.[26]

In the countryside, however, the resistance was just beginning. From February to June 1809, almost fifty-six thousand peasants fought a guerrilla campaign against Soult's forty thousand men, who were joined by an additional eighteen thousand troops under Marshall Michel Ney. The Galician irregulars sniped but did not often engage the French in open combat. When the French approached villages, they found them deserted and the livestock gone. French officials likened their passage through Galicia to "the progress of a ship on the high seas: it cuts through the waves, but these close behind, and all evidence of its passing quickly vanishes."[27]

Napoleon had tasked Soult to invade Portugal from the north, but when he finally did, he had only twenty-two thousand men. The rest, thirty-seven thousand troops, were busy trying to occupy Galicia. As a result, in May, the British expeditionary force under Arthur Wellesley, the future Duke of Wellington, had superior numbers at Oporto and succeeded in forcing Soult out of Portugal. Meanwhile, the forces Soult had left behind under Ney had lost control of Galicia. They evacuated Vigo in March, Tuy in April, Santiago in May, and La Coruña and El Ferrol after the disastrous French defeat at the battle of Puente San Payo in June. That summer, the French abandoned Galicia, never to return.

The uprising of Galicia has often been cited as an example of a spontaneous and unanimous people's war in defense of religion and country. But this is not strictly true. Galicia mobilized as a result of several factors that had little to do with king and country and even less to do with God. In the winter of 1808–9, the region had suffered from the continuous presence of Spanish, English, and French armies. In December 1808, shoeless, starving, and thoroughly whipped Spanish forces under General Blake sacked and looted with abandon, so that Blake had to start shooting his men to restore order. On Blake's heels came the English under General Moore, and

---

26 This account of events in Galicia is based on materials in Gómez de Arteche, *Guerra de la Independencia*, 6:92–102; Manuel Pardo de Andrade, *Los guerrilleros gallegos de 1809* (La Coruña, 1892); Andrés Martínez Salazar, *De la Guerra de la Independencia en Galicia* (Buenos Aires, 1908); Ramón de Artaza Malvarez, *Reconquista de Santiago en 1809* (Madrid, 1909); Priego López, *Guerra de la Independencia*, vol. 4; Oman, *History of the Peninsular War*, vol. 2; Gabriel Lovett, *Napoleon and the Birth of Modern Spain*, 2 vols. (New York, 1965), vol. 1; and Figueroa Lalinde, *Guerra de la Independencia*.

27 D. J. Goodspeed, *The British Campaigns in the Peninsula* (Ottawa, 1958), 72.

they, by all accounts, behaved even worse. When the French arrived, the province had been devastated, so that Soult had great difficulty extracting food for his troops. Normal stores were gone, so the French had to send small requisition parties from village to village to force the peasants to give up their food. This is what produced the necessary conditions for guerrilla warfare, as small requisition parties provided perfect targets for partisans. And these partisans were none other than the peasants who were being robbed. In other words, they were defending their property.[28]

On February 9, the priest of Couto, Marcelino Troncoso, brought together a small band of peasants that became the nucleus of the so-called Division of the Miño. Troncoso did not mobilize these men by appeals to nation or religion, priest though he was. Rather, he called on them to resist a new requisition of horses and twenty thousand rations to be collected from the towns of Crecente and Alveos. These towns had little choice but to agree to the new tax to avoid being sacked, but Troncoso blockaded the towns, so that none of the peasants in the area delivered any goods to market. As a result, Crecente and Alveos could not supply the French with the promised goods and were duly punished for it, ensuring local resentment of the occupation. Troncoso then enlisted the aggrieved young men of Crecente and Alveos. That very day, his enlarged force attacked another French requisition party, killing fifteen soldiers and capturing another fifty-one. During the following few weeks, Troncoso undertook a classic guerrilla campaign, preventing goods from entering cities and towns, obliging Soult and Ney to send requisition parties to every village, and ambushing them when they did. By the end of February, Troncoso had eight thousand men under arms, and by April, this number had risen to sixteen thousand, though it never operated at any one time with anything close to these numbers.

This short account of the guerrilla war in Galicia illustrates a number of points. The function of guerrillas is first and foremost to control the countryside and prevent towns from obtaining produce and livestock. Guerrilla warfare by its very nature always contains elements of a rural–urban conflict. An occupying power might take control of cities and towns, the natural site of collaboration, but if these are cut off from peaceful contact with the countryside, they cannot supply the occupation's needs. This forces the occupier to send out requisition parties to acquire food, fodder, and fuel, among other things. In a region like Galicia, characterized by tiny properties, known as *minifundia*, leased or owned by peasant farmers, this meant

---

28 The correspondence related to Blake's experience in Galicia is located in AHN, Estado, leg. 42, nos. 155–60.

that numerous small requisition parties had to be sent out to hundreds of villages and isolated farms. This, in turn, allowed guerrillas to achieve some measure of military success engaging small French detachments. Each small victory produced a cache of weapons. These in turn allowed recruitment to proceed.

The events that followed the French withdrawal from Galicia also give us clues about the nature of the guerrillas there. When Ney and Soult withdrew to León and Castile, the Galician irregulars did not pursue. They dissolved. Their object had never been the liberation of Spain. At most, they dreamed of liberating Galicia. With this objective met and with the French gone, Galicians demobilized and never again played a significant part during the rest of the war.[29]

A later event, in January 1810, also provides clues about the nature of the Galician insurgency. For a brief time, a new French invasion of Galicia appeared in the offing, and twenty thousand Galicians volunteered to oppose it. But the menace passed, and this army also dissolved. The Spanish government in Cádiz sent agents to reenlist the men into regular units of the Spanish army. To avoid this fate, thousands fled Galicia to Lisbon and Oporto. The Spanish consul in Oporto appealed to the patriotism of these expatriates, but in trying to convince them to return to Spain to fight the French, the language he used left no doubt that he understood well the limits of patriotism. He declared: "The defense of king, country, and religion, irresistibly calls all Galicians able to take arms to return and join their compatriots in order to drive the cruel invaders from their country (in case it should be newly invaded), and defend with their last efforts their homes and families."[30] The key to understanding this appeal lies in the phrase, "in case it should be newly invaded," for it can have applied only to Galicia, not to Spain, given that most of Spain was at the time occupied. Indeed, attempts to recruit these Galician men to fight for Spain failed miserably. The government tried paying them. This met with a sort of success: 150 volunteers accepted the proffered bounty to join the Spanish army, but word got out that they were to be marched south to Cádiz not north to Galicia, and two-thirds of them deserted.

The case of Galicia warns us against making any simplistic assumptions about the Spanish guerrillas. Attempts to see them as symbols of Spanish nationalism and piety founder on the facts. This is not to say that Gallegos were bad Catholics or bad Spaniards. In the early nineteenth century, the

---

29 Galician forces always resisted taking part in actions outside the province, even in 1808. See AHN, Estado, leg. 28, no. 23, and leg. 42, no. 102.
30 Figueroa Lalinde, *Guerra de la Independencia*, 136.

nation was still rudimentary, distant, unknown, and unloved, not just for
Spaniards but for most people the world over. Nor were the church and the
king as desired as propaganda portrayed them. Galicians fought against the
French occupation in the spring of 1809 and helped liberate Europe from
Napoleon because they had no choice. They did it to survive. When given
a choice, they stayed home, something characteristic of guerrilla fighters
not just in Spain but in other times and other wars.

Navarre

In Navarre, partisan warfare began in earnest in the fall of 1808, when
a number of small bands began to attack French stragglers, agents, and
collaborators, even gaining control of several mountain towns and valleys.
In August 1809, a student named Javier Mina took command of the largest
of these bands, the seven hundred men of the so-called Land Pirates. The
French captured Mina in March 1810, but his relation, Francisco Espoz y
Mina, succeeded him and consolidated all the guerrilla forces in the province
under his rule. Two years later Espoz's Division of Navarre numbered seven
thousand men, growing to eleven thousand by the end of the war.[31]

Good data from military records, tax rolls, land surveys, and other sources
allows us to speak with great authority about the men in the Division of
Navarre.[32] We know, for example, that 80 percent of them came from
the northern, mountainous part of the province, the Montaña, while only
10 percent came from the southern half of the province, the Ribera. The
remainder came from outside Navarre.[33] This preponderance of Montañeros
suggests an important question. What was it about the Montaña that produced guerrillas, and what was it about the Ribera that did not? By addressing this question, we can also address three others: Who were the partisans
in Navarre? Why did they fight? How successful were they?

The Ribera of southern Navarre is defined by the flat and relatively arid
valley floor of the Ebro River. Ribereños lived in a handful of large cities
and towns. Few of them owned homes or land. Almost every man worked
for a wage, usually in agriculture. The typical Ribereño lived from hand to
mouth in a rented dwelling located in a city and owned next to nothing.
This basic social reality had important implications. Ribereños had little

31 This account of the war in Navarre is based on my books *The Fatal Knot* and *La guerrilla española*.
32 The archives of Navarre may be the best in Spain. Especially useful are the Archivo General de
   Navarra (AGN), especially the Sección Estadística, legs. 6, 16, 20, 25, 31, and the Archivos de
   Protocolos Notariales (APN), which contain detailed information about local businesses, land sales,
   political disputes, criminal records, and more.
33 Percentages are based on numbers reported in AGN, Guerra, legs. 18–21.

motive to resent French requisitions and taxes, which did not affect them directly but fell on their landlords and employers. Neither did they have the means to fight the French, living, as they did, in cities easily dominated by garrisons and lacking any resources, including weapons, with which to fight. It is not surprising, therefore, that few Navarrese partisans came from the Ribera.

The Montaña presents a stark contrast with the Ribera. As in Galicia, Montañeros lived in small villages, hamlets, and homesteads scattered over the countryside. There were more than seven hundred villages in the Montaña, and the French could manage a permanent presence in only a few of them. Three-quarters of all families in the Montaña owned the land they worked, and most of the others leased sizable parcels. These facts meant that peasants had both motive and means to resist the French. The motive was the protection of private property, and the means were their resources, including livestock and weapons. To access the wealth of the Montaña, the French had to send requisition parties to hundreds of villages to extort goods from independent farmers. It was an impossible situation.

We know that most of the guerrillas were peasant proprietors – or the sons of proprietors – from the Montaña. Espoz and all of the other officials attached to the Division of Navarre were, without exception, owners of sizable estates. Espoz's second in command was a minor nobleman. When the French police investigated the backgrounds of known guerrillas in the valley of Echauri, they discovered that all were proprietors and one a wealthy estate owner. All available data point to the same conclusion: as in Galicia, the partisans were men of substance, not bandits.

The notion that the partisans were fanatics fighting for the church is likewise difficult to credit where the Navarrese guerrillas are concerned. The French certainly persecuted the clergy of Navarre as if they were the enemy. Parish priests were popular and populist figures in the Montaña, so it is not unreasonable to assume that their suffering may have induced some peasants to take up arms. But it needs to be reiterated that this remains conjecture. There is no real evidence for it, nor is there any data suggesting a causal link between the ideals of nation and king and the willingness of the Navarrese to fight. The only ideological content in the sources – and there is little of this – relates to the defense of regional customs and privileges, property rights, and the "manly" independence of the Navarrese people, a notion called simply "the idea" by its adherents.

How successful were the guerrillas of Navarre? They fought many small engagements during the war almost always successfully, because they usually chose the ground and the circumstances under which they engaged the

French. The French lost 17,000 men killed and captured to Espoz and another 325 to Javier Mina. This is a significant number, and it does not count men lost to other insurgents operating in Navarre in 1808 and 1809. Nor does it count sick and wounded, a high figure judging from the fact that the hospital in Pamplona was always filled to capacity with French soldiers. Casualties aside, the French dedicated tens of thousands of troops to the occupation of Navarre, troops that could have been dedicated to other tasks, such as the defeat of Wellington.

Nevertheless, it needs to be stated clearly that the guerrillas could not have liberated Navarre on their own. They could not fight large-scale battles: doing so, they would have run out of ammunition and faced annihilation. Just as the guerrilla army in Galicia required the help of regular forces, most notably, of course, the intervention of the British at Oporto, to free Galicia, Espoz needed help from British, Portuguese, and Spanish regulars to drive the French from Navarre. But openly challenging the French in battle was not the guerrillas' primary purpose. Rather, they focused most of their efforts on isolating the French from the resources of the countryside and punishing collaborators – activities, incidentally, that are easily mistaken for banditry. In these tasks they succeeded. By 1812, few outside Pamplona were willing to risk the wrath of Espoz, preferring instead to go into hiding at the approach of French requisition parties, which were lucky if they made it back to Pamplona with their skins, much less any resources. The French starved, shivered, and sickened inside Pamplona, while Espoz became unofficial king of Navarre. It was not necessary to fight the French when one could starve them. The Navarrese partisans denied the French and their collaborators peaceful access to the manpower and resources of a province that was and still is one of the richest in Spain. This was their victory.

PARTISANS AND TOTAL WAR

The evidence presented here suggests that partisan warfare in urban areas differed markedly from the guerrilla war in rural Spain. In cities, the partisans were attached to local elites and seemed to have overtly ideological motives, corresponding to some degree with the old image of a people fighting for God, king, and country. They also ultimately failed.

The guerrilla movements in Galicia and Navarre were successful. They were not mobilized by the government, the high clergy, the nobles, or any other elites. Indeed, in both Galicia and Navarre, official attempts to raise guerrilla parties failed. Instead, the guerrillas were led and mobilized

in Galicia by a parish priest and in Navarre by a cadre of peasant proprietors. Love of God, king, and country were not obvious motives in either
Galicia or Navarre, and in neither province does the bandit thesis hold any
explanatory value. Instead, the war was fought by small and middling peasant proprietors and leaseholders to defend their property and the property
of their neighbors. What happened in Galicia and Navarre repeated itself
with some variations in Upper Aragon, the Basque Provinces, Western
Catalonia, and northern Old Castile. All were regions characterized by
peasant landholding, small, dispersed settlement, the continued strength of
the church, and most of the other features present in Galicia and Navarre.

This way of viewing the Spanish insurgency takes us some distance from
a conventional definition of total war. Total war normally involves at least
the two following things: a majority of the civilian population must be
involved in combat and/or wartime occupations in support of the military
effort. Second, a majority of the resources of the country must be redirected
toward the war. By both of these measures, the Spanish Revolution of 1808
and the War of Independence do not measure up. Although the Peninsular
War in Spain probably involved more civilians in combat than any other
Napoleonic campaign, it was never a majority of the population as wartime
propaganda claimed. Even in guerrilla country, resistance was undertaken by
a small minority of the people. And in most of Spain, civilians remained on
the sidelines. Moreover, few civilians worked in wartime industry because
the economic mobilization of the country was nil. The partisans fought
with what they had at hand, what they captured, and what the English
supplied. Spain never mobilized its resources in the manner of any of the
belligerents in the two world wars in the twentieth century or, for that
matter, of France or England in the Napoleonic period. Indeed, it was not
even remotely possible for Spain to fight a total war between 1808 and 1814.
After all, most of the country's resources were in the hands of the French:
the government had been overthrown, and the revolutionary movements
that stepped into the bresch controlled very little of the national territory.
Mobilizing the nation for war was, therefore, impossible. The remarkable
thing about the Spanish war and what impressed contemporaries was that,
with their government overthrown, Spaniards found a way nonetheless to
mount an effective campaign against Napoleon.

PART III

Civil Institutions and the Growing Scope of War

13

Where Have All the People Gone?

Reflections on Popular Political Mobilization on the Eve of American Independence

T. H. BREEN

Large-scale political mobilization accompanied by partisan violence has not sparked much curiosity in recent years among historians of the American Revolution. The explanation for this lack of interest is clear enough. The dominant questions that drive the field reflect the general culture in which history is produced. And at the start of the twenty-first century, people in the United States have chosen to remember the American Revolution as an event or series of events defined chiefly around the activities of the Founding Fathers. Evidence for this claim is not hard to find. A near obsession with the lives of the great revolutionary leaders sustains a burgeoning market for popular biographies, many of which appear regularly on best-seller lists.[1]

Because I want to advance a different perspective, one that is less centered on the Founding Fathers, it seems worthwhile at the beginning to revisit the revolutionary story that modern Americans are so eager to hear. They are drawn to a tale of selfless gentlemen – planters, merchants, and lawyers – who at the moment of imperial crisis articulated the sources of political discontent so effectively and so reasonably that other, more ordinary Americans followed along without serious second thought. Indeed, as the controversy with Parliament grew more threatening, these gifted leaders came forward like ancient Romans and, drawing upon a language of liberty and virtue, produced documents that energized popular resistance to Great Britain, then the most powerful military empire the world had ever seen. This comfortable narrative recounts how the Founding Fathers traveled during

---

1 Two extremely readable examples of the recent wave of Founding Father biographies are David G. McCullough, *John Adams* (New York, 2001), and Joseph J. Ellis, *His Excellency: George Washington* (New York, 2004).

The author would like to thank Professor Hermann Wellenreuther of the University of Göttingen for his help in locating and interpreting the records of many revolutionary Committees of Safety and Observation. Christopher Hodson and Patrick Griffin also provided valuable criticism.

the late summer of 1774 from Boston and Williamsburg, New York and Charleston, to Philadelphia, where they revealed even more impressively than they had at the local level an extraordinary strength of character and intellectual breadth. As delegates to the Continental Congress, they championed an enduring republican ideology. Perhaps it is because leadership of this sort seems so thin on the ground today that this particular rendering of the nation's revolutionary past resonates so positively with the current generation. Americans may now be flocking once again to the likes of George Washington, Thomas Jefferson, and John Adams for political inspiration.

Largely absent from this story are the ordinary people who presumably also made major sacrifices for the revolutionary cause. Insomuch as they appear in the familiar narratives of resistance, they are assigned shadowy, often unflattering roles. They roam the streets of Boston and New York City as members of a faceless mob, employing violence in ways that set them apart from the more enlightened Founding Fathers, who condemned such excess. Or, in other accounts, the people seem hapless figures unable to comprehend the larger issues of political protest. Much like traditional peasants, they seem in the pages of history to be waiting patiently for their social betters to explain the tenets of republican theory.

One could readily understand why during the run-up to revolution Tories described the people in such dismissive terms. Peter Oliver is a case in point. Appointed chief justice of the Superior Court of Massachusetts Bay, Oliver constructed a successful career around royal patronage, and not surprisingly, he was driven from Boston for his support of the empire. In an account of the coming of independence, Oliver insisted, "Such was the Frenzy of Anarchy, that every Man was jealous of his Neighbour, & seemed to wait his Turn of Destruction; & such was the political Enthusiasm, that the Minds of the most pious Men seemed to be wholly absorbed in the Temper of Riot."[2] Curiously, even leaders identified with the patriot cause expressed similar sentiments about the people. Gouverneur Morris of New York, for example, surveyed a crowd gathered below his balcony and concluded, "The mob begins to think and reason. Poor reptiles! It is with them a vernal morning; they are struggling to cast off their winter's slough, they bask in the sunshine, and ere noon they will bite, depend on it."[3] Other well-to-do Americans avoided comparisons to serpents, but like Morris, they too feared the rabble might transform liberty into anarchy.

2 Peter Oliver, *Origin and Progress of the American Revolution: A Tory View*, ed. Douglass Adair and John A. Schutz (Stanford, California, 1961), 53.
3 Peter Force, ed., *American Archives*, 4th ser., 9 vols. (Washington, D.C., 1837–53), 1:342–3.

Later American historians expressed no more enthusiasm about popular participation in the Revolution than had the Founding Fathers. During the nineteenth century, George Bancroft's books reached a huge audience. In his writings, the actual people who threw off the yoke of British rule disappear in a Hegelian mist, for as Bancroft explained, "The hour of the American Revolution was come. The people of the continent obeyed one general impulse, as the earth in spring listens to the command of nature and without the appearance of effort bursts into life."[4] A hundred years later, the so-called progressive historians, a group that included Carl Becker, invited the people back into the revolutionary story. They returned not as colonial liberators but as members of a largely urban lower class eager to seize power from an entrenched ruling elite. No doubt, colonial artisans probably had had their fill of strutting would-be provincial aristocrats. Turning the breakdown of British authority into a tale of class conflict, however, does not provide much insight into why ordinary Americans, most of them rural farmers, became insurgents in a war against a European empire.[5]

In more recent times, historians have transformed the American Revolution into a defining moment in the development of political ideas that originated in Renaissance Italy. In these accounts, the people again go missing. Nowhere in the analysis of revolutionary ideology is it made clear whether ordinary men and women shared the views found in the formal pamphlets, and the most violent act that one encounters in such intellectual history is a clash between republican and liberal discourses.[6] On the level of abstract political theory, observes one historian, "a new generation of historians rediscovered the constitutional and conservative character of the Revolution and carried the intellectual interpretation of the Revolution to new heights of sophistication." For him and for others of his persuasion, the focus on abstract ideas is a positive development. Such an approach frees the historian from worrying over much about why the slaves did not become free, Native Americans not genuine citizens, women not full participants in civil society, and the people not partakers of real economic equality.[7]

Whatever the rationale for marginalizing the people in the story of the American Revolution, their absence surely makes it a lot harder to explain

---

4 George Bancroft, *History of the United States of America* (New York, 1883–5), 4:3–4, cited in Bernard Bailyn, *The Origins of American Politics* (New York, 1968), 6.
5 The weaknesses of the progressive argument are discussed in Edmund S. Morgan, "The American Revolution: Revisions in Need of Revising," *William and Mary Quarterly*, 3rd ser., 14 (1957). 3–15.
6 For example, Bernard Bailyn, *The Ideological Origins of the American Revolution* (Cambridge, Massachusetts, 1967), and J. G. A. Pocock, *The Machiavellian Moment: Florentine Political Thought and the Atlantic Republican Tradition* (Princeton, New Jersey, 1975).
7 Gordon Wood, *The American Revolution: A History* (New York, 2002), xxiv.

popular mobilization. It also reduces discussion of popular ideology to the status of nonstarter, for if rank-and-file colonists were either empty-headed followers or crazed members of mobs, then their ideas about the republic's future are of little significance. That is not the interpretive path we shall take. However much historians may want to turn their backs on these unwelcome guests, the ordinary men and women of late colonial America refuse to disappear. At the end of the day, narratives of resistance must account for the sacrifices that families made sending sons into harm's way, for shifting political identities at the grassroots level, and for unprecedented participation on committees and militias.[8] And, of course, so long as the American Revolution is seen as involving only a contest between different bundles of ideas, it will defy thoughtful comparative history, for a tale celebrating the intellectual virtuosity of the Founding Fathers will not do much to advance our understanding of the popular violence and community rituals that defined revolutionary movements in other places at other times.

A more inclusive explanation for popular mobilization on the eve of independence would necessarily be a messier history, one that breaks with the currently orthodox intellectual interpretation of the origins of revolution and replaces its analytic lexicon with harsher words and phrases such as *insurgency, vigilantes, fear, intimidation, outrage, betrayal, revenge, censorship, extralegal organizations,* and *rituals of popular violence.*[9] The goal is not to romanticize the people. They had plenty of faults, and some of what they did in the name of colonial liberation defied patriotic hagiography. Ordinary people demand attention not as agents of class unrest but as rebels against an empire they deemed oppressive. They made decisions that forced their leaders to rethink the meaning of a common cause.

While we can imagine a history of the American Revolution without Founding Fathers, we find it hard to accept one that excludes those colonists who actually risked their lives in a political movement that they understood as fully as did the gentlemen who served in the Continental Congress. Matthew Patten of Bedford, New Hampshire was such a person. The day (May 21, 1776) he learned that his son John had been killed in battle – two months before publication of the Declaration of Independence – Matthew wrote in his diary, John "was shot through his left arm at Bunker Hill fight and now was lead after suffering much fategue to the place where he now

---

8 On the need to restore violence to our understanding of the Revolution, see Allan Kulikoff, "Revolutionary Violence and the Origins of American Democracy," *Journal of the Historical Society* 2 (2002): 229–60.
9 T. H. Breen, "Moments of Decision: Popular Mobilization on the Eve of the American Revolution," Society of the Cincinnati Lecture 2005–2006, University of Richmond, February 16, 2006.

lyes in defending the just Rights of America to whose end he came in the prime of life by means of that wicked Tyrannical Brute (Nea worse than Brute) of Great Britan. He was 24 years and 31 days old."[10] In the presence of such pain, we sense that we are moving closer to the core of the people's revolution.

In a more populist interpretation of the American Revolution, the ordinary colonists properly enter the story sometime during the summer of 1774. By that time royal authority in the countryside, especially in New England, had dissolved, and fully two years before the passage of the Declaration of Independence, huge regions had taken major steps toward self-government. A chain of actions and reactions that accelerated the collapse of the empire began with the destruction in Boston Harbor of a cargo of tea owned by the East India Company. The details of this event are less important for our purposes than are the bundle of punitive statutes collectively known in the colonies as the Coercive Acts that Parliament passed during the spring of 1774. Communities throughout New England moved quickly to halt consumption of tea. They also recommended with increasing stridency a halt to the importation of all British manufactures. By midsummer, crown officials who lived outside Boston found their situation untenable. Large crowds of country people visited their homes, demanding resignation and public apology. It would be incorrect to label these groups, often numbering three or four thousand, as mobs. They bore witness against oppressive rule. They seldom abused private property. But the threat of massive popular resistance sent the king's appointees running to Boston and the safety provided by a British army occupying Boston.[11]

More to the point, Committees of Correspondence and a well-developed commercial press reported these local confrontations to men and women scattered over a very large area.[12] Communication amplified the power of popular protest. Newspapers spoke for an imagined force called public opinion. The pressure that ordinary people put on royal officials also put pressure on the leading spokesmen for the American cause. The activities of the crowds in the Massachusetts countryside reduced the space available for negotiations with Parliament. Compromise with Great Britain was still possible in mid-1774, of course, but incidents of widening popular participation in the protest movement made compromise a moving target. After

---

10 *The Diary of Matthew Patten of Bedford, N.H. from 1754 to 1788* (Camden, Maine, 1993), 361.
11 T. H. Breen, *The Marketplace of Revolution: How Consumer Politics Shaped American Independence* (New York, 2004), 294–332.
12 Richard D. Brown, *Revolutionary Politics in Massachusetts: The Boston Committee of Correspondence and the Towns, 1772–1774* (Cambridge, Massachusetts, 1970).

so many royal appointees had been sent packing, it was no longer realistic to claim that mere cosmetic reforms could restore the empire.

The most dramatic restructuring of the popular political culture occurred in America during the months following the meeting of the First Continental Congress. The delegates who journeyed to Philadelphia in September 1774 concluded that the most promising way to force the king and his ministers to back down from the Coercive Acts would be to institute a massive boycott of all British imports. They argued that a commercial disruption of this magnitude might throw thousands of English laborers out of work and drive Atlantic merchants to the edge of bankruptcy. To accomplish that end, Congress created the Association, a vast network of local committees charged with monitoring trade with the mother country. The key provision appeared in the eleventh section. Congress authorized "a committee be chosen in every county, city, and town by those who are qualified to vote for representatives in the legislature, whose business it shall be attentively to observe the conduct of all persons touching this Association." The local committees were authorized to expose publicly anyone found guilty of violating the regulations. When the majority of a committee discovered evidence of noncompliance, it was ordered to "forthwith cause the truth of the case to be published in the gazette; to the end that all such foes to the rights of British America may be publicly known, and universally condemned as the enemies of American liberty." The Association possessed a real bite. Those who thought that they might continue to trade with England were warned "thenceforth we respectively will break off all dealings with him or her."[13]

Like radical seeds sowed on fertile political ground, committees sprung up throughout America. They took different names. Often, the older Committees of Correspondence simply added monitoring trade to their responsibilities for gathering intelligence. In some towns, the members of groups charged with policing public political behavior called themselves Committees of Observation, Committees of Inspection, or Committees of Safety. Local committees frequently formed county committees. The committees of observation were generally composed of the wealthier and more prominent men of their towns. Widespread implementation of the Association, however, represented more than another chapter in the story of the Founding Fathers. Between November 1774 and April 1775, the committees recruited large numbers of new people into the political culture. The very

---

13 The Association of the First Continental Congress, Oct. 20, 1774, in *American Colonial Documents to 1776*, ed. Merrill Jensen (New York, 1969), 815.

size of the committees suggests the stunning dimensions of change. One committee operating on the frontier of Maryland, for example, where presumably one would not have encountered many British merchants, listed more than 150 persons. The results in other colonies were similar. Virginians established fifty-four committees, averaging twenty-one members each. Approximately 160 local committees sprang up in Massachusetts. Over time, the size of the committees tended to expand, so that by the end of 1775, the number of people enforcing the Association from Georgia to New Hampshire reached several thousand. Most of these men had had no political experience – except perhaps as voters – in the old colonial system. And by listing their names in the newspapers, they publicly broadcast their personal allegiance, a highly risky move during this period.[14]

Precisely where the pressure for broader participation originated is hard to discern. One Marylander reported early in 1775 that committee size expanded because "it would Engage the Country People more warmly if gratified in a more Numerous Appointment amongst them." The members of the Harford County Committee in Maryland held meetings in different locations because they deemed it "Necessary that the good People of this County be Informed of the Proceedings of their Deputies in Committee."[15] It should be noted that, at the same time that the committees were taking control over local affairs, communities throughout America dismissed militia officers who had been appointed by royal governors and replaced them with men elected by the ordinary soldiers. If we include militia elections as a legitimate expression of political mobilization – and such a move seems unobjectionable – we begin to appreciate better the role of the "Country People" in making their own revolution.

Crown officials comprehended quite early the serious threat that the committees posed to imperial rule. British authorities could deal with isolated pockets of resistance. But a massive network of insurgency escalated the danger. The Association provided colonial rebels with an infrastructure, a means of communication and enforcement that modern historians have often taken for granted. However important abstract republican ideas may have been in bringing about national independence, they could not alone sustain a revolutionary movement. The committees were sites where ordinary people translated principle into action, reimagined political identity,

---

14 The fullest study of the activities of the various committees is David Ammerman, *In the Common Cause: American Response to the Coercive Acts of 1774* (Charlottesville, Virginia, 1974). For the expansion of the size of the committees, see chapter 7.

15 Ibid., 108. Also valuable is Hermann Wellenreuther, "Associations, the People, Committees of Observation and the Culture of Rights, 1774–1776," a conference paper presented at "The Languages of Rights," Northwestern University, Evanston, Illinois, May 2004.

and drew hard boundaries between friends and enemies. The political harvest of the committees was plain to see. A letter published in the *New York Gazette*, an aggressively pro-British newspaper, complained in April 1775 of

the prevailing rage of the present time for people of all ranks, orders, and professions to form Associations, and erect themselves into what they call Congresses and Committees of various denominations; who, under pretext of redressing grievances and reforming church and State, have made most audacious and iniquitous resolves, tending to the subversion of all order and good government and the total abolition of law and justice.[16]

This assessment made good sense to William Franklin, royal governor of New Jersey. In mid-1775, he reported to Lord Dartmouth, the British secretary of state, "All legal Authority and government seems to be drawing to an End here, and that of Congresses, Conventions, and Committees establishing in their Place."[17] Lord Dunmore, the royal governor of Virginia, had already reached a similar conclusion. In December 1774, he informed Dartmouth that the committees

are now enforcing throughout this country with the greatest rigor. . . . [T]he Committee assumes an authority to inspect the books, invoices, and all other secrets of the trade and correspondence of Merchants; to watch the conduct of every inhabitant, without distinction, and to send for all such as come under their suspicion into their presence; to interrogate them respecting all matters which, at their pleasure, they think fit objects of their inquiry.

Dunmore believed that extralegal bodies invited "the vengeance of an outrageous mob," but in fact, just the opposite occurred.[18] By energetically enforcing the will of the Continental Congress, the Virginia committees effectively preserved the order of local society.

The open, fluid composition of the various committees draws our attention to a perennial interpretive problem confronting historians of the American Revolution. The literature of this field often organizes itself around terms meant to reflect accurately the political identities of the colonists who supported or opposed resistance to Great Britain. One learns, for example, that colonists sorted themselves out into clearly defined groups bearing names such as Whig and Tory, radical and conservative, or patriot

---

16 Force, *American Archives*, 2:284–5.

17 Cited in Larry R. Gerlach, *Prologue to Independence: New Jersey in the Coming of the American Revolution* (New Brunswick, New Jersey, 1976), 263.

18 Lord Dunmore to the Earl of Dartmouth, Dec. 24, 1774, in *The Committees of Safety of Westmoreland and Fincastle: Proceedings of the County Committees, 1774–1776*, ed. Richard B. Harwell (Richmond, Virginia, 1956), 19.

and loyalist. But when we examine political mobilization on the local level, we discover that these labels obscure contingency and process over time. In other words, patriots and loyalists were not monolithic groups. Political identity grew out of an ongoing conversation with friends and neighbors who espoused different opinions about rights and empire.[19]

Few men who served on the committees before the end of 1775 saw the goal of resistance as national independence. Many colonists simply wanted Parliament to respect the political institutions that had developed in America over the course of centuries. The loyalists in the local communities also appreciated the need for reform. But once the committees began to interrogate their opponents, defining some publicly as "Enemies of America," the loyalist position hardened. To be classified as a friend of George III meant something quite different in 1775 from what it had meant at the close of 1773. The same observation could be made of those who protested British policy. Each new crisis – the destruction of the tea, the passage of the Coercive Acts, the meeting of the Continental Congress, the Battles of Lexington and Concord – set off a new round of debate on the local level. What the Committees of Observation did was make it a lot harder for ordinary people to remain neutral. In fact, efforts to enforce the Association thus simultaneously created new allies and new enemies.

Events that took place in the small farming community of Eastham, Massachusetts, early in 1775 reveal how local conversations over allegiance evolved. The town had elected a Committee of Correspondence, and even though its members gave only guarded support to the radical calls for resistance coming from Boston, it claimed to reflect public opinion in Eastham. As the full impact of the Coercive Acts became apparent throughout New England, however, a large body of residents challenged the legitimacy of their own Committee of Correspondence. In a statement dated February 24, 1775, ninety-three men declared, "It appears to us that a number of men in this town have been and still are using their influence and power in opposition to the measures adopted by the Americans to recover, preserve, and maintain those rights and privileges which our illustrious ancestors so nobly contended for." The problem was not that their neighbors were incorrigible Tories. Rather, they had dragged their feet; they had not kept up with what it meant to be a patriot. "Now, in order to free ourselves as much as possible from the embarrassments of those men and convince their

---

19 Ethan H. Shagan presents historians of the American Revolution with an extremely useful model for understanding the open, fluid character of political identity during times of rapid change in *Popular Politics and the English Reformation* (Cambridge, U.K., 2003).

American brethren of their noble efforts to throw off the yoke of tyranny,"
announced the protesters, "we think it highly expedient to form ourselves
into an Association." They pledged "to each other" to enforce the resolves
of "the Continental, our Provincial, and this County Congresses" for the
express purpose of "recovering, securing, and maintaining our just rights
and privileges."[20] In the Eastham case, external events triggered a debate,
which crystallized political identities. Allegiance became a matter of public
record.

The committees had lives of their own. Charged with policing trade, they
looked at first primarily for suspicious cargoes of goods. In urban ports such
as Philadelphia, the work was demanding, and committeemen held regular
meetings to interrogate recently arrived ship captains, dodgy merchants, tea
drinkers, and individuals who refused to accept the local colonial currency.
But the committees soon expanded their spheres of authority. During the
early months of 1775, members of these local enforcement bodies questioned people about whom they had heard reports of disloyalty. Often the
evidence of wrongdoing amounted to little more than gossip. Procedu-
rally less amorphous in these extralegal tribunals were published statements,
which seemed in the eyes of the committeemen to undermine the authority
of the Continental Congress and to suggest that the colonists were not fully
united in support of American liberty.

One obtains a sense of the temper of the local committees from an
exchange that occurred in New Jersey. In July 1775, the Somerset County
Committee instructed local committees of observation that they should
expose those "who shall, either by word or deed, endeavor to destroy
our unanimity in opposing the arbitrary and cruel measures of the British
Ministry" in ways that "shall seem most conducive to prevent any injury
to the glorious cause of American freedom." Two months later, the Sussex
County Committee revealed how far it was prepared to go to stifle political
dissent. It announced that anyone who "Shall hereafter Asperse any of the
friends of Liberty in this County on Account of their Political Sentiments,
or Shall Speak Contemptuously or Disrespectfully of the Continental or
Provincial Congress or any of the Committees for the Public good &
Safety" shall be brought up before the committee with the assistance of the
local militia and be "dealt with according to his or their Deserts."[21]

From a comparative perspective, the activities of the various committees
may seem rather tame. After all, they did not authorize the burning of manor
houses or the hanging of notorious Tories from the nearest tree. But, as in

---

20 Force, *American Archives*, 2:1051–3.   21 Gerlach, *Prologue*, 275.

so many early modern societies, the Americans did not aim to destroy their enemies. They developed carefully choreographed rituals of shame and humiliation, and the desired end was not to administer physical suffering or death. Rather, the committees wanted to extract public confession. Acts of contrition served to reaffirm the justice of American resistance. Apologies appeared in the newspapers. Of course, if the accused refused to admit to political crimes, he or she faced more serious sanctions. The committees ordered all patriotic Americans to cut off normal contact with known enemies. For small merchants, punishment of this sort threatened their livelihoods. They became nonpersons, an intolerable status in small, intimate communities. It is not surprising that so many people who had been ostracized from local society soon had second thoughts about political allegiance and rated confession as preferable to isolation.

The process of shaming neighbors varied from place to place. Some committees initiated private conversations before administering full sanctions. One town developed extraordinary rules for dealing with persons caught violating the Association. A committee in Sutton, Massachusetts, decided that one could converse with an enemy if

it shall appear to the Committee that such person did no more than to help in case of absolute sickness or some casualty, in which a Building or the Life of some person or creature was in danger of immediately perishing, or spake nothing other to the offender than to demand, or pay a debt or Tax, or about the Things of the Eternal World, or to convince him or her of his or their error in transgressing as above, or if he only spake a word inadvertently, and desisted upon being reminded of the state of such Offended.[22]

Perhaps such political casuistry had a special appeal in a small Calvinist community. Whatever the townspeople may have thought, they revealed the seriousness that committees brought to the task.

In other rural areas throughout the colonies, Committees of Observation and Iinspection served not only to identify political enemies but also to compel friends of America to come forward and to declare openly their hostility to Great Britain's colonial policies.[23] Small groups of people in villages such as Sutton should therefore be seen as a key element in sustaining revolutionary mobilization. Several examples provide a better sense of how the local committees went about their business. The Accomack County Committee in Virginia, for example, found a creative means to join rituals

---

22 William A. Benedict and Hiram A. Tracy, *History of the Town of Sutton, Massachusetts, from 1704 to 1876* (Worcester, Massachusetts, 1878), 93–4.
23 "Minutes of the Committee Safety of Bucks County, Pennsylvania, 1774–1776," *Pennsylvania Magazine of History and Biography* 15 (1891): 265–66.

of patriotic affirmation with tough-minded punishment of a supporter of the king. On June 27, 1775, the committee learned that John Sherlock "has expressed himself in such a manner as to prove him an enemy to the liberties of this Country." He was immediately called before the committee. At that moment, Sherlock made a terrible mistake. Instead of appearing as requested, he sent the committeemen "an abusive and insulting letter." This provocation persuaded the committee to redouble its efforts. Witnesses were called; testimony recorded. It soon became apparent that Sherlock had run his mouth on a number of occasions. Neighbors remembered him saying, "Such people as oppose the Ministerial measures with America are rebels, that he shall be employed hereafter in hanging them, and that if no hemp can be got, he has plenty of flax growing." Not surprisingly, the committee announced that henceforth Sherlock should be held in "public contempt." That decision did not end the affair. "After the Committee had proceeded against him agreeable to the rules of the Association," recounted a Virginia newspaper, "part of the Independent [militia] Company of this County went to his house, took, and carried him to the Court House and after a solemn trial received from him under the Liberty Pole, his recantation." The incident could have ended more violently. After Sherlock spotted the solders marching to his house, he ran to the second floor carrying "two loaded guns." With wonderful understatement, the journal observed that at the moment of confrontation with the militia, Sherlock "was prudent enough to decline making use of them."[24]

Sherlock probably never represented a serious threat to Accomack. But that is not the point. By the time Sherlock returned home, a large number of ordinary people had demonstrated – as members of the committee, as militiamen, and as spectators in the crowd around the Liberty Pole – that they endorsed the liberty of a country that would, of course, not come into existence for more than a year. The committee later published Sherlock's recantation. He admitted to having uttered many "idle and foolish words." And, whether out of fear or new political conviction, he announced, "I most heartily wish success to this my native Country in her present honest struggle for liberty with the Mother Country and do here promise to do all in my power to retrieve my character with my countrymen."[25]

During the summer of 1774, the very notion that committees could act in the name of the people sparked a major controversy in Worcester, Massachusetts. A group of local men fearful that various committees throughout the colony had pushed resistance to the Coercive Acts too far

24 Force, *American Archives*, 2:1112–13.   25 Ibid.

took control of the town meeting. Whether they kept to the strict letter of the law was not clear. Later challenges claimed that they had packed the assembly with people who did not actually live in Worcester. Whatever the case may have been, more than fifty individuals clearly of a loyalist persuasion passed a resolution that Clark Chandler, the town clerk, carefully entered into the official records. In their statement, these people announced that "each of us declare and protest . . . that the Committees of Correspondence in the several towns in this Province, being creatures of modern invention, and constituted as they be, are a legal grievance, having no legal foundation, contrived by a junta to serve particular designs and purposes of their own, and that they . . . are a nuisance."[26]

The loyalists badly miscalculated public opinion. The opposition swept into the next town meeting, demanding a complete reversal of everything that had happened at the previous session. As the new group declared, "There is a malignity cast upon the Committees of Correspondence in general throughout the continent, and in particular against the committee chosen by this town." Such disrespect could not be tolerated. After all, Chandler and his allies "have endeavored to insinuate into the minds of the public, that the men of which Committees of Correspondence are composed through the Province are a parcel of unprincipled knaves." The defenders of the American cause forced Chandler before a large audience to "obliterate, erase, or otherwise deface the said recorded protest, and the names thereto subscribed, so that it may become utterly illegible and unintelligible." He obeyed the order, or so he thought. In the eyes of the committeemen, Chandler needed to do a better job. The people who attended the meeting forced him to dip his fingers in ink and draw them over the offending words several times. As Sherlock learned in Accomack, the committees did not regard apology before the members of the local community as a sufficient demonstration of contrition. The loyalists had called into question Worcester's patriotism. On September 5, 1774 – the day that the First Continental Congress convened in Philadelphia – several newspapers in Massachusetts carried a public announcement signed by forty-two people from Worcester: "we acknowledge we have cast cruel aspersions upon the town of Worcester and upon the Committee of Correspondence for said town, and upon all Committees of Correspondence throughout the Province, for which we are sorry, and take this opportunity publicly to manifest it."[27]

26 Albert A. Lovell, *Worcester in the War of the Revolution* (Worcester, Massachusetts, 1876), 35–6.
27 Ibid., 37–8, 41–2.

A schoolteacher with an unlikely name goaded a Committee of Safety in Westmoreland County, Virginia, to exercise its political muscle. As in the Worcester example, the committee itself forced people to declare precisely where they stood on the question of resistance to Great Britain. It was a catalyst for mobilization. The trouble in Westmoreland began quite innocently. David Wardrobe, the local schoolmaster, wrote a letter to a friend in Scotland. Believing that he could express his political opinions freely in such private correspondence, Wardrobe suggested that patriots of Virginia lacked genuine revolutionary resolve. "In the country of Richmond, about ten days ago, I saw an elegant effigy of Lord North hanged and burned in the midst of a vast concourse of people. I was particularly attentive to the countenances of the spectators, and was really pleased to see so few express any outward signs of approbation on the occasion." As for talk of a boycott of British imports, Wardrobe did not think Virginians had the stomach for consumer sacrifice. If the Coercive Acts continued, he concluded, "their resolutions will soon fail them, for I am convinced that the disadvantage they must labor under by adopting such a [nonimportation] plan will be so great that had it been imposed upon them, they would think it the greatest evil that ever befell them since they were a colony."[28]

After several months, Wardrobe discovered that his letter had been published in the *Glasgow Journal*. It was there that the sharp-eyed members of the Westmoreland Committee of Safety spotted it. They were not amused. They informed Wardrobe that they wanted to talk to him about "a letter, false, scandalous, and inimical to America . . . said to be written by a gentleman from Westmoreland County." It did not take long to tie the document to Wardrobe, and although he seemed contrite, the committee "seriously considering the fatal consequences that will infallibly be derived to the dearest rights and just liberties of America, if such enemies are suffered to proceed in this manner, of giving false and mischievous accounts to Great Britain" decided to punish Wardrobe. It ordered parents to remove immediately their children from the school. The Committee of Safety reminded those affected by the closing that he was "regarded as a wicked enemy to America, and be treated as such."[29] The local vestry, which had allowed him a room for teaching, reneged on its agreement.

When the committeemen asked Wardrobe if he had second thoughts, he penned a note, described in the Westmoreland records as "insulting." Finally, the committee obtained the result that it had desired all alone. Wardrobe offered a public apology "for so gross an offence." In the *Virginia*

---

28 Harwell, *Committees of Safety*, 35.   29 Ibid., 32–3.

Gazette, he begged "most heartily and willingly, on my knees, [and] implore the forgiveness of the country for so ungrateful a return for the advantages I have received from it, and the bread I have earned in it, and hope, from this contrition for my offence, I shall be at least admitted to subsist amongst the people I greatly esteem."[30] Sincerity is not at issue. Wardrobe offered no threat to the security of Westmoreland. His indiscretion, however, served spectacularly to accelerate the political mobilization of this community; people associated with the vestry and parents with school-age children had learned a sobering lesson from Wardrobe.

Freedom of the press presented an extremely difficult challenge for the committees of inspection. To be sure, most Americans who expressed sympathy for the patriotic cause regarded newspapers as absolutely essential in sustaining broad popular mobilization. In a highly literate society, the journals generated large readership, and almost all the committees published local resolutions and decisions about those deemed "Enemies of the Country" in the provincial gazettes. The members of these bodies probably did not perceive communication of political news as blatant propaganda. Indeed, aggressive editors, such as Isaiah Thomas, who produced the *Massachusetts Spy, or, American Oracle of Liberty*, were convinced that their papers countered the lies broadcast by the representatives of a thoroughly corrupt British ministry. And there was the rub. The men who served on committees of inspection defended only the free circulation of news that supported their own political aims. The loyalist gazettes were another matter.

None irritated the extralegal committees more than James Rivington's *New-York Gazetteer*. On March 1, 1775, the Newport, Rhode Island, Committee for Inspection reached the limit of its modest tolerance for dissent. Opening a public declaration on the subject with a fulsome reminder that a free press was "of the utmost importance to civil society," the authors spoke of the value of uncensored expression in advancing "truth, science, morality and arts in general, in its diffusion of liberal sentiments on the administration of government, its ready communication of thoughts between subjects, and its consequential promotion of union among them, whereby oppressive officers are shamed or intimidated into more honorable and just modes of conducting affairs." When that "noble pillar" of public inquiry no longer promoted "beneficial purposes," however, it had to be silenced. Although the Rhode Islanders could not smash Rivington's presses – that job fell to a group of vigilantes in New York – the members of the committee could protect local readers from dangerous "falsehoods." Their actions did not

30 Ibid., 34.

compromise notions of a free press, because, as was commonly known, the Tory publisher "impelled by the love of sordid pelf, and haughty domineering spirit hath for a long time in the dirty *Gazetteer*, and in pamphlets, if possible still more dirty, uniformly persisted in publishing every falsehood which his own wicked imagination . . . could suggest and fabricate."[31] The committee turned to the *Newport Mercury*, where it recommended that every person in the colony immediately drop Rivington's newspaper. The opposition journal suddenly became in this community a marker of allegiance. Of course, not all those men and women who rejected the *New-York Gazetteer* could be counted as fervent patriots, but that is not the point. The local committee had found a means to push popular mobilization forward, a way to force ordinary people to demonstrate visible, public support for resistance.

In Freehold, New Jersey, censorship played out in a strikingly different way. On March 6, 1775, the members of the local Committee of Observation and Inspection explained that "a number of their constituents" had presented before a public meeting a pamphlet recently published by Rivington. The people present closely analyzed the essay, and after "mature deliberation unanimously declared [it] to be a performance of the most pernicious and malignant tendency." However shocked the committee may have been by what it had read, it did not quite know what to do. The "people" did. They "immediately bestowed upon it a suit of tar and turkey-buzzard's feathers, one of the persons concerned in the operation, justly observing that although the feathers were plucked from the most stinking fowl in creation, he thought they fell far short of being a proper emblem of the author's odiousness to every advocate for true freedom." Everyone marched out into the courtyard. "The pamphlet was then, in its gorgeous attire, nailed up firmly to the pillory-post, there to remain as a monument to the indignation of a free and loyal people against the author and vendor of a publication so evidently tending both to subvert the liberties of America and the Constitution of the British Empire."[32] In other New Jersey and Hudson Valley townships, the local hangman burned the same offending pamphlet in a complex community ritual of unity and rejection.

Some committees refused to allow ordinary Americans to remain anonymous. It was highly probable, of course, that the parents who took their children out of Wardrobe's school or the Newport residents who cancelled subscriptions to the *New-York Gazetteer* sympathized with the resistance movement. But one could never be sure what the individual believed. As

31 Force, *American Archives*, 2:12–13.   32 Ibid., 35.

a spectator to the destruction of a pamphlet, for example, an individual could drift, observing the Association while at the same time keeping his or her political options open. By mid-1775, various committees dealt with neutrals and trimmers by demanding that every male of a certain age sign a public document pledging to support the American cause. Committeemen literally carried the rebellion to the people, going door-to-door with their forms. On May 15, 1775, the members of the Newburg, New York, Committee of Correspondence and Observation decided that it was time to identify inequitably political friends and enemies. They announced that "the bloody measures of a wicked ministry" – a reference to the recent Battles of Lexington and Concord – had persuaded them of "the great utility of a General Association being fully signed by every male person from the age of sixteen and upwards in this Province." They would have preferred to take a less intrusive course, but they had received troubling intelligence that "a number of persons . . . are so lost to the preservation of themselves and their country that they refuse or neglect to sign the Association with the rest of their neighbors, fellow-suffers, and countrymen." The committeemen resolved, therefore, to "wait on such person or persons who have neglected and refused to sign the said Association and in the most friendly manner to invite them to sign the same."[33] One wonders just how friendly this invitation could have been. Those men who refused to sign the list before the end of the month became "enemies to their Country." The committee also sent their names to the local newspaper so that patriots living in nearby towns would isolate these people from civil society.

Committees operating in other parts of America followed the same basic pattern. In Wilmington, North Carolina, a committee voted to "go in a body and wait on all the Householders in Town . . . and request their signing it, or declare their reasons for refusing, that such Enemies to their Country may be set forth to public view and treated with the contempt they merit."[34] The yield apparently justified the time it took to visit so many residents. A list published in the local gazette contained the names of a doctor, a planter, two tailors, and seven merchants living in Wilmington who did not recognize the authority of the Continental Congress.

The Committee of Inspection in Fairfield, Connecticut also urged every person in the community to sign an Association oath. Individuals were free to ignore the request, but if they did so, they knew that the committee would "take down in writing the names of all those enemies of their

---

33 Ibid., 606. For Sheffield, Massachusetts, see also ibid., 545.
34 Cited in Ammerman, *Common Cause*, 118.

Country...who refuse to subscribe." Like many other committees throughout America, the Fairfield group drafted a statement of political principle, which each signer presumably read at the moment he added his name to the public list. A supporter of the common cause agreed that "the British Administration have long been plotting against the liberties of America, and [have] finally stepped forth and openly avowed their wicked system, and are now pursuing measures, which, if successful, will terminate in the total destruction of American liberty." Signers promised to obey the Continental Congress and declared that they were "firmly persuaded of the justice of their cause, and that resistance is indispensable, [and] committing their cause to Heaven, [they] have opposed force to force, and are determined to die or be free." The patriots of Fairfield identified themselves "as men, Christians, and freemen." The local tally was impressive by any standard. The community poll contained 1,855 names. Only seventy men defied the committee, a brave decision for which they undoubtedly paid a heavy price.[35]

The activities of the committees, which energized revolutionary mobilization on the local level, raise a vexing problem about popular ideology. One might argue that these organizations simply bullied their communities – radical cadres using intimidation to gain their own political goals during a time of social instability – and that the ordinary people were either led by the nose or, if they were of a Tory turn of mind, silenced. The evidence, however, does not sustain such a conclusion. A broad electorate selected most committeemen. And, over time, as the number of persons serving on these bodies escalated, the committees became a legitimate voice for the towns and villages where they operated. Matthew Patten, the New Hampshire farmer whose son was wounded at Bunker Hill, had served on at least one local committee before John took up arms against the empire.[36] The Bedford, New Hampshire, committee did not force either Matthew or John Patten to become revolutionaries. Quite to the contrary, the committee channeled the popular conviction that George III and his ministers had betrayed America into focused acts such as gathering weapons and gunpowder, communicating with other like-minded villages, and passing resolutions in support of the Continental Congress and the Association.

Therefore, the question is, Exactly what did the ordinary colonists believe? Historians have had a ready answer. A close reading of several score of learned pamphlets published during the decade before independence suggests that the leading spokesmen for American resistance had a coherent

35 Force, *American Archives*, 1:141–2. 36 *Diary of Matthew Patten*, 331–62.

political ideology.[37] Although this body of ideas presents itself under several different names, it is fair to describe it simply as classical republicanism, a theory of political obligation with a very long genealogy. The central elements of ideology are well known. Within civil society, power engages in an unceasing and ferocious contest with liberty. Officeholders must be watched all the time. The only safeguard against despotism is the vigilance of virtuous men, usually independent property holders whose landed wealth preserves them from insidious forms of bribery and corruption. But even a Cincinnatus had reason to be uneasy. The Sirens of tyranny lured virtuous republicans onto the shoals of luxury and effeminacy. Once the guardians of liberty had surrendered virtue, they lost their ability to resist the designs of power. That Americans on the eve of independence found this a credible ideology, one that helped them explain to themselves what had gone so very wrong in Great Britain, is certainly true. The learned pamphlets that historians now regard as comprising the canon of late-eighteenth-century American political thought most certainly spoke of evil conspiracies and enervating consumer luxury.

At issue, however, is the relation between the ideas of the great planters and learned lawyers and the popular beliefs that sustained popular mobilization during the last years of the empire in America. The interpretive problem turns on whether the leading figures in the traditional narrative of revolution – in other words, the Founding Fathers – spoke for or to the ordinary colonists who empowered the local committees. It must be confessed immediately that one can never get into the heads of the ordinary people who favored resistance over accommodation. Their secret thoughts remain secret. But such an admission hardly closes off analysis. It would be difficult to marshal a persuasive argument that the pamphlet writers ever intended to speak to the populace. Quite to the contrary, the Founding Fathers seemed far more interested in impressing other Founding Fathers – in solidifying elite opinion over a huge geographic area – than in educating ordinary people about the need to defy parliamentary policy. One might even observe that the leading pamphlet writers appeared more eager to enter into a conversation with British thinkers about the balanced constitution and the proper character of representative government than they did in addressing their own constituents. On the level of an Atlantic or Enlightenment discourse, of course, these pieces were reflective, erudite, even profound productions.

37 For example, see Bailyn, *Ideological Origins*.

By turning the problem of revolutionary ideology on its head, one is compelled to confront the possibility that the Founding Fathers spoke for the ordinary people. Such an interpretive move would force a more serious discussion of the bundle of political ideas encountered at the committee level. Instead of viewing the men and women who actually energized the resistance movement as an uncomprehending audience for notions broadcast by the leading lawyers and planters, we might ask what political ideas were circulating on the community level, and then move to the question of how these local beliefs and principles filtered up to the Founding Fathers, who felt it necessary in an Atlantic forum to organize and polish a rough set of ideas that may have justified John Patten's sacrifice to his family and his community. The central elements of a popular ideology were a strongly religious belief that God sanctioned resistance to tyranny; that people unwilling to defend the rights and property inherited from previous generations of independent Americans did not deserve liberty; that the British ministry really had conspired to reduce free, white colonists to slavery; that ordinary people possessed rights that no ruling authority could take away; and finally, that any claim to imperial power that smacked of special privilege ran counter to the fundamental equality of free colonists.[38]

Perhaps aspects of this popular ideology picked up strands of a republican tradition. But to interrogate the resolutions of local committees for references to European political philosophers or opposition writers who flourished in mid-eighteenth-century London misses the point. The emotional power of popular ideology is discovered not in intellectual genealogy but in the rhetoric of frightened men attempting to explain to themselves armed resistance to Great Britain. In early June 1775, the members of a committee in Tryon County, New York wrestled with these issues. In slightly apologetic tones, they explained that they had been slower to act than had many other American communities. But the crisis of empire could no longer be ignored. "Was it any longer a doubt that we are oppressed by the Mother Country and that it is the avowed design of the Ministers to enslave us," the Tryon farmers announced, "we might perhaps, be induced to use argument to point out in what particulars we conceive that it is the birthright of English subjects to be exempted from all taxes." The hour was late, however, and Parliament had ignored honest colonial petitions. And so, faced with a British army in America and treated with contempt by Parliament, "we have been appointed to consult methods to contribute

---

38 T. H. Breen, *The Lockean Moment: The Language of Rights on the Eve of the American Revolution* (Oxford, U.K., 2001).

what little lies in our power to save our devoted country from ruin and devastation."[39]

At the moment when real violence touched their lives, the people of Farmington, Connecticut, situated their own sacrifice within a vast satanic conspiracy. They declared in dramatic language that the British ministry had been "instigated by the devil, and led on by their wicked and corrupt hearts." Writing in the shadow of the Battles of Lexington and Concord, they bravely insisted, "We scorn the chains of slavery; we despise every attempt to rivet them upon us; we are the sons of freedom, and resolved, that, till time shall be no more, that god-like virtue shall blazon our hemisphere."[40] The members of the local committee in Hanover County, Virginia, avoided hyperbolic language of this sort. They admitted that they were a little isolated from the events tearing the empire apart. "The sphere of life in which we move," they confessed, "has not afforded us light sufficient to determine with certainty concerning those things from which the troubles at Boston originated." Whatever had originally sparked resistance, however, the people of Hanover without once mentioning either the liberal tradition of John Locke or the republican heritage of Niccolò Machiavelli asserted, "But this we know, that the parliament by their proceedings have made us and all North America parties in the present dispute, and deeply interested in the event of it; insomuch, that if our sister Colony of Massachusetts Bay is enslaved, we cannot long remain free."[41]

A history of revolution that focuses not so much on the doings of the delegates to the Continental Congress but on the operation of hundreds of local communities restores the people to the story of national independence. The Founding Fathers still have a central role in this narrative. And well they should. If, however, we want to escape anodyne accounts that depict popular mobilization as somehow inevitable – like the earth in spring listening to the command of nature – or as a failure of ordinary people to comprehend abstract philosophic constructs, then we must take onboard the violence, censorship, and intimidation, as well as the wonder of resisting an empire in the name of rights and liberty. Without the likes of John and Matthew Patten, the Revolution would have died aborning, remembered today only as a curious debate among provincial planters and lawyers that never resonated positively for a popular audience.

39 Force, *American Archives*, 2:879.
40 *Essex Gazette* (Salem, Massachusetts), May 17–24, 1774.
41 Force, *American Archives*, 1:616.

14

Achilles' Heel

Slavery and War in the American Revolution

JÖRG NAGLER

In June 1775, after the creation of the Continental Army, James Madison expressed a concern shared by many of the revolutionaries throughout the colonies. "It is imagined our Governor has been tampering with the slaves & that he has it in contemplation to make great Use of them in case of a civil war in this province," he wrote. "To say the truth, that is the only part in which this Colony is vulnerable; & if we should be subdued, we shall fall like Achilles by the hand of one that knows that secret."[1] That secret – which was anything but – was the presence of five hundred thousand unfree African Americans in the colonies, 20 percent of the entire population. The possibility that war might spark slave resistance and that Britain might exploit this Achilles' heel was to haunt the patriots through the course of the Revolution.[2]

Benjamin Quarles, one of the most knowledgeable students of African Americans in the era of the American Revolution, has argued that the Revolution constituted the first large-scale slave rebellion.[3] The fact that some one hundred thousand African Americans gained their freedom in the context of the Revolutionary War, whether through liberation or

---

1 James Madison to William Bradford, June 19, 1775, cited in William T. Hutchinson and William M. E. Rachal, eds., *The Papers of James Madison*, 10 vols. (Chicago, 1962–76) 1:153.
2 Benjamin Quarles, "The Revolutionary War as a Black Declaration of Independence," in *Slavery and Freedom in the Age of the American Revolution*, ed. Ira Berlin and Ronald Hoffman (Charlottesville, Virginia, 1983), 283–301; Benjamin Quarles, *The Negro in the American Revolution* (Chapel Hill, North Carolina, 1996); Herbert Aptheker, *The Negro in the American Revolution* (New York, 1940); Philip S. Foner, *Blacks in the American Revolution* (Westport, Connecticut, 1975); Sylvia R. Frey, *Water from the Rock: Black Resistance in a Revolutionary Age* (Princeton, New Jersey, 1991); Robert Ewell Greene, *Black Courage, 1775–1783: Documentation of Black Participation in the American Revolution* (Washington, D.C., 1984); Woody Holton, "'Rebel against Rebel': Enslaved Virginians and the Coming of the American Revolution," *Virginia Magazine of History and Biography* 105 (1997): 157–92; David Brion Davis, *The Problem of Slavery in the Age of Revolution, 1770–1823* (Ithaca, New York, 1975); Jeffrey J. Crow, *The Black Experience in Revolutionary North Carolina* (Raleigh, North Carolina, 1989).
3 Quarles, "Revolutionary War," 284.

self–liberation, marked the American Revolution as a social transformation.[4] One could argue further that slave resistance and the desire of slaves for emancipation in the decade before the American Revolution were linked to social and cultural processes that culminated in the Revolution.[5]

The fear of insurrection and conspiracy inhered in the institution of slavery, and it was accompanied by anxiety that rebellious slaves would ally with other social outcasts, such as Native Americans or members of the white underclass.[6] Only by coercion and the threat of punishment could the slave system function. But the dread of slave resistance was oriented not only toward the internal menace.[7] The nightmare of slave insurrections instigated by an external foe had also haunted the colonies ever since the introduction of slavery. Armed slaves had figured in wars, revolutions, and insurrections throughout world history.[8] The military role of North American slaves in the wars with Spain and France compounded the fear.[9]

The British had, in fact, developed a strategic scenario in which slaves would be encouraged, with the promise of freedom, to join the British side in the war in the American colonies. The rebellious colonists would thus be forced to control or suppress their own "troublesome property" on the home front, and that effort would reduce their ability to wage war. There was an economic warfare component in this strategy, too: by withdrawing slave manpower, the British aimed to undermine the plantation economy that was financing the war.[10] The British were well aware of slave resistance – or, to put it in positive terms, of the slaves' longing for freedom – and its potential as a military asset. British strategy encompassed psychological

---

4 Ronald Hoffman and Peter Albert, eds., *The Transforming Hand of Revolution: Reconsidering the American Revolution as a Social Movement* (Charlottesville, Virginia, 1995).

5 Peter H. Wood, "'Liberty Is Sweet': African-American Freedom Struggles in the Years before White Independence," in *Beyond the American Revolution: Explorations in the History of American Radicalism*, ed. Alfred F. Young (De Kalb, Illinois, 1993), 168–9; Peter H. Wood, "The Dream Deferred: Black Freedom Struggles on the Eve of White Independence," in *Resistance: Studies in African, Caribbean, and Afro-American History*, ed. Gary Y. Okihiro (Amherst, Massachusetts, 1986), 166–87.

6 Merton L. Dillon, *Slavery Attacked: Southern Slaves and Their Allies, 1619–1865* (Baton Rouge, Louisiana, 1990), 25.

7 Gerald W. Mullin, *Flight and Rebellion: Slave Resistance in Eighteenth-Century Virginia* (New York, 1972); Jörg Nagler, "Afroamerikanischer Widerstand im Herrschaftssystem der Sklaverei von der Amerikanischen Revolution bis zum Bürgerkrieg," in *Nationale und Internationale Perspektiven amerikanischer Geschichte. Eine Festschrift für Peter Schäfer*, ed. Jörg Nagler (Frankfurt, 2002), 33–57; Okihiro, *Resistance*; James Sidbury, *Ploughshares into Swords: Race, Rebellion, and Identity in Gabriel's Virginia, 1730–1810* (New York, 1997).

8 Christopher Leslie Brown and Philip D. Morgan, eds., *Arming Slaves: From Classical Times to the Modern Age* (New Haven, Connecticut, 2006).

9 Peter H. Wood, *Black Majority: Blacks in Colonial South Carolina from 1670 through the Stono Rebellion* (New York, 1974), 305; Dillon, *Slavery Attacked*, 23–7.

10 F. Nwabveze Okoye, "Chattel Slavery as the Nightmare of the American Revolutionaries" *William and Mary Quarterly* 37 (1980): 3–28.

warfare as well, for the threat that the British might instigate slave revolts would demoralize the rebellious colonists.[11] Even without the strategic calculations of the British, most runaway slaves would have joined the British side because the prospect of freedom was more enticing than remaining with revolutionary slaveholders.

As in other colonial wars, the British sought local loyal elites as a fifth column, but they incorporated the slaves of Tories as well as revolutionaries into their strategy. The mobilization of slaves gave a transatlantic dimension to questions of race. While the British confronted the subject of race as they planned use of African Americans as auxiliaries in the fight against white colonists, the Americans stressed the "uncivilized" and "barbarous" character of Britain's tactics in hopes of convincing France to join the revolutionary side.[12]

Because they commanded insufficient manpower, the Americans, too, were forced to include African Americans in their strategic planning. Military necessity on both sides thus created a paradoxical situation. With the promise of liberation, unfree African Americans were to participate in a war to maintain the institution of slavery, which neither the American side nor the British side intended to abolish in case of victory. In other words, in a conflict between two white belligerents, African Americans became, voluntarily or involuntary, part of what Sylvia Frey has called the "triagonal" War for Independence.[13]

Before the hostilities began, the revolutionary discourse on freedom and tyranny had taken shape in a charged environment in which the presence of a half million enslaved African Americans stood in stark contrast to the revolutionaries' rhetoric of liberty. Many revolutionaries were aware of the contradiction between their rhetoric and reality, while others – consciously or unconsciously – constructed a liberal ideology that linked freedom to individual choice. The revolutionary slogan "liberty or death" was transposed onto slaves, who theoretically had the option of liberating themselves from bondage.[14] "Liberty," as chanted by the white protesters against the Stamp Act, had already gained a different meaning for African Americans: it

---

11 Carl Berger, *Broadsides and Bayonets: The Propaganda War of the American Revolution* (Philadelphia, 1961); Patricia Bradley, *Slavery, Propaganda, and the American Revolution* (Jackson, Mississippi, 1998).
12 Gary Nash, *Race and Revolution* (Madison, Wisconsin, 1990); Robert Glenn Parkinson, "Enemies of the People: The Revolutionary War and Race in the New American Nation" (Ph.D. diss., University of Virginia, 2005).
13 Frey, *Black Resistance*, 45, 63; Douglas R. Egerton, *Rebels, Reformers, and Revolutionaries: Collected Essays and Second Thoughts* (New York, 2002), 7; Gary B. Nash, *The Unknown Revolution: The Unruly Birth of Democracy and the Struggle to Create America* (New York, 2005), 331.
14 François Furstenberg, "Beyond Freedom and Slavery: Autonomy, Virtue, and Resistance in Early American Political Discourse," *Journal of American History* 89 (2003): 1295–330.

had transcended the political and metaphorical dimension by aiming at the physical chains that prevented them from gaining freedom.[15] For the white revolutionary population, slavery had ceased to be a metaphor for British mistreatment by 1775 and had become instead a military problem.[16]

The concentration of slaves in the southern colonies shaped strategic planning in London. William Knox, one of the undersecretaries of state for the colonies, recommended that Britain begin its campaign in the south by inciting slave revolts.[17] In the same spirit, Lord North informed King George III in October 1775 that three of the American colonies were in a "perilous situation" on account of their large slave populations.[18] In a debate in the House of Commons, the southern colonies were described as the weak links in the American chain on account of the large numbers of slaves, who would rebel and "imbrue their hands in the blood of their masters." British strategy thus included an element of counterrevolution, insofar as loyalists and slaves would unite to bring the rebellious colonists "back to their senses."[19]

In a speech in the House of Commons, Edmund Burke, who was the colony agent of New York, suggested in 1775 that, a "general enfranchisement" of the slaves should be declared to reduce the revolutionaries in Virginia and the Carolinas. Although Burke's proposal failed, it amplified suspicions among the revolutionary colonists that slaves would be turned loose on their masters in the event of war with the mother country. Although he thought the presence of large numbers of slaves in the colonies could be exploited to Britain's advantage, Burke saw slavery as a source of strength for the patriots. Domination over a "vast multitude of slaves" had fortified the colonists' proud "spirit of liberty" to a degree, Burke thought, that "renders it invincible." Furthermore, Burke argued, slavery had produced attachments and loyalties among the slaves and they might be mobilized in the service of armed rebellion against Britain. Would slaves not, he asked, "suspect the offer of freedom from that very nation which has sold them to their present masters"?[20]

Burke's assessment of the situation in the colonies did not, however, represent a preponderance of opinion in London on the eve of the war. Although numerous strategic considerations of how to use slavery as an

15 Dillon, *Slavery Attacked*, 29.   16 Bradley, *Slavery*, 134.

17 David Waldstreicher, *Runaway America: Benjamin Franklin, Slavery, and the American Revolution* (New York, 2004), 210.

18 Cited in Quarles, *Negro*, 113.

19 Cited in Carl Berger, *Broadsides and Bayonets: The Propaganda War of the American Revolution* (Philadelphia, 1961), 84.

20 Cited in Waldstreicher, *Runaway*, 210–11.

instrument of war were discussed in the House of Commons, the majority hesitated to do so directly. Nevertheless, Lord Dunmore, the royal governor of Virginia, proclaimed on November 14, 1775, that all slaves who "willing to bear Arms" and to join "His Majesty's Troops, as soon as may be, for the more speedily reducing this Colony to a proper Sense of their Duty, to His Majesty's Crown and Dignity" would gain their freedom.[21] With this proclamation, the revolutionaries' nightmare of armed slaves seemed to be realized. Indeed, only a few weeks later, Dunmore established the so-called Ethiopian Regiment of three hundred fugitive slaves and slaves turned over by fleeing loyalist masters. They made up half of Dunmore's troops. They wore an insignia proclaiming "Liberty to Slaves," and they soon did battle with the revolutionary troops.[22] The total number of blacks who joined with Dunmore's forces has been estimated at between eight hundred and one thousand, suggesting that his proclamation was widely seen as a beacon of hope among slaves. Many African Americans thus regarded Dunmore, who was himself a slaveholder, as a liberator, despite the fact that he and the British command offered emancipation for military rather than humanitarian reasons.[23] The fact that it became possible to view Dunmore as either a liberator or a despot (as white colonists did) reflected the ambiguous character of the social revolution brought about by the war.[24] For many African Americans, the call to arms held deep symbolic significance. Serving in uniform as members of an organized regiment and confronting their onetime masters as equals on the battlefield raised former slaves to a new status and challenged the master-slave relationship.[25] The Ethiopian Regiment remained an anomaly during the war, however, for the British seldom turned fugitive slaves into combat soldiers. Instead, they used them as military laborers.[26]

Allegiances were, however, divided in slave communities, as they were, for different reasons, among white Americans. Dunmore's proclamation posed an existential question for slaves. Should they remain – and perhaps fight – with their masters, demonstrating their loyalty, or should they show their allegiance to the imperial authorities? In the end, the decision rested on calculations of where the greater chance for obtaining freedom lay. A

21 Bradley, *Slavery*, 134–8; Gerald W. Mullin, *Flight and Rebellion: Slave Resistance in Eighteenth-Century Virginia* (New York, 1972), 130–3.
22 John E. Selby, *The Revolution in Virginia, 1775–1783* (Williamsburg, Virginia, 1988), 66–7; Sidney Kaplan, *The Black Presence in the Era of the American Revolution, 1770–1800* (New York, 1973), 62.
23 See Benjamin Quarles, "Lord Dunmore as Liberator," *William and Mary Quarterly*, 15 (1958): 494–507.
24 Quarles, "Dunmore," 507. 25 Bradley, *Slavery*, 140.
26 Charles P. Neimeyer, *America Goes to War: A Social History of the Continental Army* (New York, 1996), 65–88; Wood, "Dream," 166–87.

substantial number of African Americans decided to take their chances with
the British even though the family members they left behind were often
subject to retaliation.[27]

Dunmore's strategy initially appeared to work. The threat of slave rebellion caused upheaval in Virginia. The colonists found their ability to
raise troops hampered, for they had to use soldiers constantly to patrol
regions with large slave populations.[28] Nor were only Virginians affected.
Dunmore's proclamation was published in all major American newspapers.[29]
Revolutionaries foresaw severe military consequences in all the colonies. In
December 1775, George Washington wrote from his camp in Massachusetts
that Dunmore "should be instantly crushed, if it takes the force of the whole
colony to do it." "But that which renders the measure indispensably necessary," he continued, "is the negroes. For if he [the Negro] gets formidable,
numbers will be tempted to join, who will be afraid to do it without."
Washington concluded with a grim forecast: "like a snow Ball in rolling, his
army will get size."[30] Edmund Pendleton reported with alarm to Richard
Lee, "Letters mention that slaves flock to him [Dunmore] in abundance; but
I hope it is magnified."[31] In December 1775, Dunmore was the subject of
debate in the Virginia General Convention, which condemned his proclamation. It "hath offered freedom to such able-bodied slaves as are willing to
join him, and take up arms, against the good people of this colony, giving
thereby encouragement to a general insurrection." The Convention then
threatened to inflict "the severest punishments" on fugitive slaves, those
"unhappy people," who are "already deluded by his [Dunmore] base and
insidious arts." Slaves who did not return to the American side within ten
days faced the death penalty.[32]

The widespread alarm among the patriots testifies to the effectiveness
of Dunmore's strategy. It was reported that slaves were meeting to plan
action against their owners, whom they perceived as obstacles to freedom.
The colonists responded with counterpropaganda and published warnings to
slaves that Dunmore was himself a slaveholder who would sell fugitive slaves
as soon as the British army had no further need of them. In general, however,
the colonists regarded this kind of racial warfare as unnatural, barbarous, and

---

27 Bradley, *Slavery*, 134; Mullin, *Flight*, 134–5.
28 David K. Wilson, *The Southern Strategy: Britain's Conquest of South Carolina and Georgia, 1775–1780*
   (Columbia, South Carolina, 2005), 3.
29 Neimeyer, *America*, 69–71.
30 Washington to Lt. Joseph Reed, Dec. 15, 1775, *George Washington, 1732–1799: The Writings of George
   Washington from the Original Manuscript Sources*, Electronic Text Center, University of Virginia, 4:164.
31 Pendleton to Lee, Nov. 27, 1775, quoted in Mullin, *Flight*, 131.
32 http://collections.ic.gc.ca/blackloyalists/documents/official/dunmore.htm.

uncivilized. According to Benjamin Franklin, Dunmore's proclamation was meant "to excite the domestic slaves . . . to cut their [masters'] throat." The result would make "War like Nations who never had been Friends, and never wish to be such while the World stands."[33]

The British mobilization of slaves was a doubled-edged sword. Dunmore had called only on the slaves of patriots to join his troops. There was, however, the danger that the slaves of loyalists would do the same. The resulting property losses among the loyalists might spur resistance to the British cause in these circles. More important was the effect of Dunmore's proclamation on the great portion of moderate, undecided colonists, particularly because the revolutionaries quickly sensed the propaganda value of the proclamation. They depicted Dunmore as a despot who aimed to radicalize the war. The military advantage of the proclamation to the British was thus counterbalanced by the revolutionaries' use of it to conjure up the specter of slave insurrection. It mattered not whether the British had orchestrated insurrection; in revolutionary propaganda, the design was depicted as a "diabolical scheme." "Instigated insurrections" became a code that minimized regional political differences.[34]

Reports and instances of resistance among slaves confronted plantation owners with a new dimension in the problem of control that challenged their confidence in white hegemony.[35] As the Declaration of Independence was ratified, newspapers throughout the colonies carried numerous reports of escaping slaves, resistance activity, open support by slaves for the British side, and marooned communities of white colonists in the south.[36] The declaration itself blamed the British king for exciting "domestic insurrections amongst us" – a reference to slave rebellions.[37] News of slave conspiracies, rebellions, and African Americans' offers to fight for the British had previously been withheld from the public in the hope of preventing panic among whites.[38] Such information was to be "concealed as well suppressed," as Madison suggested to his friend William Bradford Jr.[39] Nevertheless, rumors had spread rapidly. By 1778, the same rumors became the objects of propaganda, complements to continuously published reports of British encouragement to insurrection among the slaves.

---

33 Carl van Doren, ed., *Benjamin Franklin's Autobiographical Writings* (New York, 1945), 408–9.
34 Bradley, *Slavery*, 134.
35 Frey, *Black Resistance*, 56–62; Bradley, *Slavery*, 134.
36 Richard S. Dunn, *Sugar and Slaves* (Chapel Hill, North Carolina, 1972), 38.
37 Sidney Kaplan, "The Domestic Insurrections of the Declaration of Independence," *Journal of Negro History* 61 (1976): 243–55.
38 Bradley, *Slavery*, 132–3.   39 Ibid., 132.

The newspapers also warned African Americans not to join the British side, which suggests, first, that slaves were among the papers' readers and, second, that they, like white colonists, were aware of the enticements the British were offering. African Americans also maintained their own sophisticated communication networks, which often adopted the methods of the committees of correspondence. As John Adams noted in his diary, news such as Dunmore's proclamation could "run hundreds of miles in a week or fortnight" among the slaves.[40] Slaveholders attempted to exploit this communications system for their own purposes. They spread their own propaganda about the British among African Americans, claiming, for example, that the British would sell slaves to Caribbean masters in the event of an American defeat.[41]

Soon after the Americans declared their independence, an internal discourse began over whether the colonists should mobilize their unfree population for the war effort.[42] The Americans' shortage of manpower created a paradoxical situation: while an army of liberation fought the British, it also defended the institution of slavery.

Ethnic and racial divisions posed a real challenge to the colonists. Irish and German immigrants enlisted in the Continental Army to change their status in colonial society, as did, to an extent not yet sufficiently appreciated by historians, African Americans.[43] The manpower shortage provoked a range of proposals, depending on the importance of slavery to a given region and the place of slavery in the regional political culture and economy. In the South, anxieties about slave conspiracies and rebellions lent central importance to fears of losing this "troubled property." Consequently, the proposal to arm slaves, whether for the British or for the American cause, provoked visions of rebellion and sexual violence committed by African American men against white women.

In June 1775, the Continental Congress called for the recruitment of eighty-eight regiments totaling sixty-three thousand men to serve as the core of the Continental Army. The thirteen colonies did not fulfill the quotas, in

---

40 Cited in L. H. Butterfield, ed., *The Adams Papers: Diary and Autobiography of John Adams*, 4 vols. (New York, 1961), 2:182–3.

41 Quarles, "Dunmore," 499.

42 Pete Maslowski, "National Policy toward the Use of Black Troops in the Revolution," *South Carolina Historical Magazine* 73 (1972): 1–17; Billy G. Smith, "Runaway Slaves in the Mid-Atlantic Region during the Revolutionary Era," in *The Transforming Hand of Revolution: Reconsidering the American Revolution as a Social Movement*, ed. Ronald Hoffman and Peter Albert (Charlottesville, Virginia, 1995), 199–230.

43 Neimeyer, *America*, 27–64; cf. Arthur Marwick, *War and Social Change in the Twentieth Century* (London, 1974), 11–13.

part because there was no central executive power to compel them to do so. It was recommended by the Continental Congress that the colonies mobilize their militias to meet the required numbers.[44] The Continental Congress initially decided not to recruit African Americans because such a policy was "inconsistent with the principles that are to be supported." African Americans nevertheless served in large numbers in most of the regiments.[45] Slaves were given the promise of liberation in return for their service. They were heavily recruited for service in Cambridge, Massachusetts, and other areas. The need for manpower overrode reservations both in the army command and Congress about the propriety of using enslaved or free African Americans. The soldiers fought for wages, enlisted for longer periods of service than their white counterparts, and took their chances to become free.[46] For a short time, until November 23, 1775, Congress thus supported the enlistment of African Americans. It then reversed policy and required the discharge of blacks from the Continental Army. By the time the Declaration of Independence was signed the following summer, some states, particularly in New England, where the numbers of slaves were limited and there was little fear of slave revolts, were defying this decision and enlisting African Americans.

Early in 1777, Massachusetts made African Americans eligible for the draft. In February 1778, the legislature of Rhode Island voted to raise two battalions of former slaves. The substitute system encouraged the enlistment of African Americans, for hiring a slave was easier and less expensive than finding a white substitute. In New England, proportionately more African Americans enlisted than whites. In Massachusetts, where 4,500 free African Americans lived, 500 (12 percent) volunteered for military service.[47] In Connecticut, three hundred African-American soldiers joined the Continental Army.[48] The difficulty of mobilizing white manpower led to a change of attitude in Virginia and Maryland toward the prospect of black soldiers, especially after the South became the main theater of the war.[49] By the third year of the war, the fear of arming slaves had receded generally outside the South, as some commentators argued that recruiting African Americans made them easier to control.[50] Congress, however, which was bound by the need to conciliate the South, refused to sanction the enlistment of blacks anywhere.

44 See Matthew Ward, "The American Militias: 'The garnish of a table'?" in this volume.
45 Neimeyer, *America*, 65–88.   46 Maslowski, "National Policy," 16–7.
47 Philip S. Foner, *Blacks in the American Revolution* (Westport, Connecticut, 1975), 68.
48 David O. White, *Connecticut's Black Soldiers* (Chester, U.K., 1973), 8.
49 Quarles, *Negro*, xxviii.   50 Ibid., xxvi.

Approximately five thousand African Americans served in the Continental Army as soldiers and military auxiliaries. They have been compared to the "hordes of Irish and German immigrants" who also served in the Continental Army.[51] African Americans represented a small segment of the army — one out of every sixty soldiers — but they tended to serve longer than their white counterparts: four and a half years, on average, as compared to a year and a half. The length of their service increased the presence of African Americans in the Continental Army.[52] Black soldiers were often depicted in paintings of the Revolutionary era — usually as soldiers rather than military laborers.[53]

After the British shifted military operations to the South in 1778, they systematically exploited potential slave resistance. In December 1778, they captured Savannah, whereupon they used African American manpower to fortify the city. As they increased their manpower with fugitive slaves, they withdrew essential human resources from the plantation economy. Some fifty thousand slaves sought freedom through self-liberation or were stranded in war zones, where the British treated them as contraband. Whereas escaped slaves had represented a small stream ever since the introduction of slavery in the South, they became a flood with the approach British troops. Thomas Jefferson reported that in Virginia as many as thirty thousand slaves escaped to the British in 1778.[54] Although the accuracy of this estimate is open to question, the losses due to runaway slaves were undoubtedly severe. In South Carolina, a quarter of the slave population escaped to the British between 1779 and 1781.[55] According to the Lutheran minister Henry Melchior Muhlenberg, slave communities were convinced that a British victory would bring emancipation.[56] That more did not escape in view of this prospect was because of the precautions that the Americans had taken after the Dunmore proclamation to prevent the flight of slaves to the British. Those precautions, which were organized by military commanders and civilian officials, claimed military and economic resources. Militia companies; Committees of Correspondence, Inspection, and Safety; or Councils of Safety were all occupied with capturing fugitive slaves.[57]

51 Ibid., ix; Neimeyer, *America*, 85.
52 Robert Ewell Greene, *Black Courage, 1775–1783: Documentation of Black Participation in the American Revolution* (Washington, D.C., 1984), 2; Neimeyer, *America*, 82.
53 Ibid., 84.
54 Cassandra Pybus, "Jefferson's Faulty Math: The Question of Slave Defections in the American Revolution," *William and Mary Quarterly* 62 (2005): 243.
55 Frey, *Black Resistance*, 174, 211n; Nash, *Race*, 60–1.
56 Quarles, *Negro*, 115.   57 Ibid., 124, 135.

Although the British themselves relied heavily on slave manpower in their military operations, Sir Henry Clinton, the British commander in chief, criticized the revolutionaries for using slaves as military personnel. As a countermeasure against this "practice of enrolling Negroes Among their Troops," he announced in June 1779 that each African American soldier or auxiliary whom the British captured from the Americans would be sold or forced to work or fight on the British side. The British general-provost had already appointed an agent to organize the capture of slaves and their transfer to British military service. Slaves who escaped from their rebel masters, however, were to be offered refuge, shelter, freedom, and employment. Altogether, Clinton employed five thousand African Americans in his operations.[58] He also supported economic warfare against rebel slave owners. He was no abolitionist, however; he ordered that the runaway slaves of loyalists be returned to their masters, insisting, though, that they not be punished.

Clinton announced these policies in the so-called Philipsburg Proclamation, which also urged slaves to run away from their masters.[59] Unlike Dunmore's proclamation, Clinton's appeal to slaves drew almost no reaction from the revolutionaries. One of the reasons was that American generals were themselves employing African Americans on a large scale by that time; Clinton's proclamation thus could not be exploited for propaganda at home or in Europe. Both sides were by then seeking military advantage by using slaves. Nonetheless, Clinton's proclamation antagonized the colonists and, in many cases, created sympathy for the Revolution. The revolutionaries responded by liberating the captured slaves of loyalists; in the tumult of war, however, both sides also sold captured slaves for profit. The War of Independence was thus even more complex than the word *triagonal* suggests. Not only were two sets of white belligerents fighting each other, but also the colonists' camp was split between loyalists and patriots while the slave population was split between the two belligerent sides.[60]

The rebellion thus turned into a fierce civil war, particularly in the South. It transformed South Carolina's once-thriving plantation economy into a wasteland as rival armies gained and lost ground. When Georgia became the theater of war, the British again seized slaves extensively. Slaves again escaped to the British lines on their own initiative, while American commanders again attempted to recapture slaves from the British. Slaves were integral to the operational and logistical planning of both sides. The

58 Ibid., 135, 138.
59 Frey, *Black Resistance*, 108, 113–14, 118–19, 121, 141, 175, 192.
60 Ibid., 45.

British had to deal with so many runaway slaves in the South that they faced difficulties in feeding, clothing, and controlling them. When Charleston fell to the British in May 1780, the large numbers of slaves who came over to the British prompted General Charles Cornwallis to discourage them.[61] Nevertheless, more than five thousand slaves accompanied the British when they evacuated Savannah.[62] When the British army left South Carolina on its way to Yorktown in the winter of 1781, numerous African Americans followed it across North Carolina, where they were assigned to collect provisions.[63] Because they feared losing control over these slaves, British officers normally chose not to arm them. In February 1781, Cornwallis decreed that African Americans should be allowed under no circumstances to carry firearms.[64]

In 1781, Lord Dunmore returned from England to Charleston. He still believed in recruiting and mobilizing slaves on a large scale. Doing so, he declared on his arrival, would solve Britain's military problems in the South. His commissioner thereupon developed a detailed plan to recruit ten thousand African American troops. Dunmore advised Clinton to compensate loyalist owners for the loss of their slaves and to offer freedom to African American soldiers.[65] Although there were strong advocates of this policy on his staff, Clinton himself hesitated to support Dunmore and postponed a decision. Dunmore's renewed attempt to mobilize slaves, like his plans to establish refuges for loyalists in New Orleans and western Florida with the help of black troops, thus came to nothing.[66] The course of the war then put a stop to further plans to employ blacks as an auxiliary force.

Overall, the Americans profited from the British hesitancy to take full strategic advantage of slavery. Only in certain regions and contexts did the British use slaves as troops effectively or inflict an economic burden on the rebellious colonists by depriving the plantation economy of slave manpower. One reason the British did not apply a full-fledged slavery strategy was that they themselves harbored racial prejudices. Another was the difficulty of managing the influx of runaway slaves. In addition, the arrival of thirty thousand Hessian mercenaries eased Britain's manpower problems and made the recruitment of African Americans less urgent. More significantly, the systematic countermeasures enacted by Southern slaveholders prevented a mass flight of slaves to the British side — at the cost, though, of tying up

---

61 Quarles, *Negro*, 132.
62 Frey, *Black Resistance*, 174, 211n; Nash, *Race*, 60–1.
63 Quarles, *Negro*, 140.   64 Ibid., 141, 148.
65 Ibid., 150–1.
66 J. Leitch Wright Jr., "Lord Dunmore's Loyalist Asylum in the Floridas," *Florida Historical Quarterly* 49 (1971): 379; Bradley, *Slavery*, 139.

manpower and military recourses. In the end, the presence of five hundred thousand unfree African Americans did not prove a military Achilles' heel, as the revolutionaries had feared.

The mobilization of slaves on both sides of the American Revolutionary War left a paradoxical legacy. About a hundred thousand slaves gained their freedom during or immediately after the war by either liberation or self-liberation. That was one of the revolutionary consequences of the war. Their liberation challenged white hegemony and provoked increased anxieties among white Americans in the South. The central paradox of the American Revolution lay in the simultaneous struggle of white and black Americans for freedom. The struggle paved the way to emancipation in the northern states while it cemented slavery in the South – now with harsher rules and a new kind of racism. In the northern states, black soldiers who had served in the Revolutionary armies were rewarded with freedom and, in some cases, land grants as slavery was gradually abolished after the war.[67] In the South, by contrast, there had been bitter resistance to the recruitment of African American soldiers. In South Carolina and Georgia, only the British, not the rebellious white colonists, used black soldiers. Southern slaveholders never were well aware that in times of crisis they could not depend on the loyalties and gratitude of their slaves.

The participation of African American soldiers on both sides during the Revolution anticipated the 186,000 black troops who fought for the Union during the second American revolution, the Civil War. In that later conflict, the military mobilization of African Americans contributed to the destruction of slavery.[68]

---

67 John W. Shy, *A People Numerous and Armed: Reflections on the Military Struggle for American Independence* (Ann Arbor, Michigan, 1990), 124, 257; Quarles, *Negro*, xxix; Waldstreicher, *Runaway*, x.
68 Joseph Glatthaar, "African-Americans and the Mobilization for Civil War," in *On the Road to Total War: The American Civil War and the German Wars of Unification, 1861–1871*, ed. Stig Förster and Jörg Nagler (New York, 1997), 199–215.

15

Revolutionary France and the Meanings of Levée en Masse

WOLFGANG KRUSE

The levée en masse is often regarded as the beginning of a most powerful political and social institution, universal conscription. When the National Convention announced it in August 1793, the term *levée en masse* evoked the double sense of the word *levée* – "levying" and "uprising." This is not to deny that universal conscription was an invention of the French Revolution.[1] In 1789, the military reformer Edmond Dubois-Crancé and other revolutionaries, calling for radical change, proposed that the French military be based on the citizen-soldiers of the newly created National Guard. But when universal conscription was finally inaugurated in September 1798, it did not put the ideas of 1789 into practice. The relationship between the revolutionary citizens and the military had in the meantime undergone a fundamental change: no longer relying on the eagerness of committed citizens to defend their revolution, the newly emerged professional military of the late 1790s advocated universal conscription to fill the ranks of the army and to subjugate the young citizens under its rule. The levée en masse of 1793 was a pivotal moment in this change in the conception of revolutionary military service, but it also had its own revolutionary meaning as well. It rallied the French people as whole to take up arms against the enemies threatening the Revolution both from outside France and within.

The term *levée en masse* implied different conceptions of this mobilization – an armed revolutionary uprising of the people, on the one hand,

---

1 See Jean-Paul Bertaud, *The Army of the French Revolution: From Citizen-Soldiers to Instrument of Power* (Princeton, New Jersey, 1988); Alan Forrest, *Soldiers of the French Revolution* (Durham, North Carolina, 1990); Wolfgang Kruse, *Die Erfindung des modernen Militarismus: Krieg, Militär und bürgerliche Gesellschaft im politischen Diskurs der Französischen Revolution 1789–1799* (Munich, 2003).

My thanks to Roger Chickering, Beatrice Heuser, David Lazar, Jean-Clément Martin, and Thomas Sokoll for their help and critique.

and, on the other, the centralized organization of a society for war. The object of this essay is to distinguish among the stages in the development of this term and among the projects that it implied. These projects not only entailed different conceptions of the military but also had lasting effects on the development of modern society. It is thus necessary to examine the idea of the citizen-soldier as well as the new idea of war that emerged during the French Revolution – the revolutionary civil war.

When Dubois-Crancé first suggested the idea of a citizen-soldier to the French National Assembly in December 1789, he was not thinking of a system of compulsory military service – of forcing the citizens to serve in a military organization separated from civil society. Rather, he saw it as the logical response of an armed popular revolution that found itself confronted by powerful enemies abroad and, most threateningly, at home. Dubois envisaged a military organization that would be suitable for a "nation bound to be free but surrounded by powerful neighbor states and infiltrated by secret and dangerous factions." The royal army, which was "governed by a despotic regime," seemed to pose a particular threat. Therefore, Dubois declared, "In France every citizen has to be a soldier and every soldier a citizen, or we will never have a Constitution."[2]

Dubois' remedy was a fundamental reorganization of the French armed forces. Its foundation was to be the National Guard, the force created spontaneously by the insurgent residents of France's cities and towns to defend their revolution against the imminent threat of a military-based counterrevolutionary assault against the National Assembly. Foreign war was not at issue in these days, for the revolutionaries insisted that the new state and society they were creating would be committed to peace. The domestic enemies of the revolution appeared to pose a more immediate threat, and their most dangerous incarnation was the army of the absolutist state. The National Assembly's Military Committee thus considered ways to bind the armed forces to the new order. The aim was to create an army "able to defend France against foreign enemies... without ever being able to threaten its inner freedom," as the committee's leading figure, Alexandre Lameth, put it.[3] Dubois-Crancé's proposal to base the military in civil society was the most radical expression of this. It was rooted in a revolutionary discourse that was directed against the traditional military. As early as August 1789, the newspaper *Révolutions de Paris* distinguished between armed revolutionary

---

2 *Archives Parlementaire de 1787 à 1860: Recueil complet des débats législatifs & politiques des chambres françaises, première série* (1787–1799) (Nendeln, 1969) (hereafter AP), 10:519–21, 611.

3 AP 11:521. See Samuel A. Covington, "The Comité Militaire and the Legislative Reform of the French Army 1789–1791," Ph.D. diss., University of Arkansas, 1976.

citizens and traditional soldiers: "Have you forgotten that a man is a citizen who carries his arms only to defend himself, while a soldier sells his liberty to become the slave of those who pay for him? . . . We don't need to build up regiments, only a civil guard; we don't need to create soldiers, only free persons, citizens." Dubois adopted this concept of a military based on the civilian National Guard, which was to be "the armed nation itself; in truth, it is not an institution, but the natural condition of men in society, the place of a free people."[4]

The moderate majority in the Military Committee did not accept these ideas. These liberals did not want to oblige all their fellow citizens to military service. They also felt that an army based primarily on self-organized citizens would be not only unprofessional but also dangerous, insofar as it gave armed power to the people. Instead, the moderates in the Military Committee and in the National Assembly voted for a professional army. At the same time, they also tried to strengthen the rights of common soldiers and to exercise civilian control over the military. But this approach lost its persuasiveness once foreign war became the order of the day. Waging war against powerful monarchies with an army that had been roused by the Revolution but was controlled by an officer corps whose loyalty to the Revolution was doubtful was, revolutionary leaders realized, a worrisome prospect. The revolutionary remedy was mass mobilization of loyal volunteers, mainly from the National Guard. It began in June 1791, when the flight of the king first confronted the revolutionaries with the prospect of war. Further calls for volunteers were issued in 1792, as the nation found itself engaged in a war that was going badly. Increasingly based on volunteers in self-organized units, the armies of Revolutionary France increasingly came to resemble the citizen army Dubois-Crancé had envisioned in 1789.[5] The new revolutionary army was successful both politically and militarily. With the élan of its volunteers, it was able to achieve victory, and the loyalty of the citizen-soldiers to the Revolution deterred ambitious generals from trying to lead their forces against Paris.

The Revolution had to contend with more than foreign enemies and suspect generals. The loyalty of social and political elites to the Revolution was in doubt. Those close to the crown, which was thought to be interested in exploiting military defeat to regain its absolutist power with the support of foreign monarchs, were a particular concern. This link between the

---

4 *Révolutions de Paris*, July 26–August 1, 1789.
5 See Jean-Paul Bertaud, *Valmy: La démocratie en armes* (Paris, 1989); Samuel F. Scott, *The Response of the Royal Army to the French Revolution: The Role and Development of the Line Army 1789–1793* (Oxford, 1978).

foreign and domestic enemies of the Revolution was the key element in a revolutionary discourse that prompted the revolutionaries to abandon pacifism for bellicosity in the winter of 1791–2.[6] They felt threatened by French émigrés, who were building armed legions in western Germany and agitating for an invasion of France by the armies of the Holy Roman Empire. Meanwhile, a so-called Austrian committee at the French court conspired with Emperor Leopold II, the brother of Marie Antoinette, who sought to strengthen the position of Louis XVI by threatening military measures. In response, the revolutionaries tried to force the king to take a stand against all foreign threats to the sovereignty of the French people – or to expose himself as an enemy of the Revolution. "War! War! It will be the touchstone of executive power," the Jacobin Pierre Manuel declared. "If he is perfidious again, it will be for the last time."[7]

The war conceived by the revolutionaries thus took on a different, a revolutionary character. They not only envisaged a war of liberation; they transported conflicts within revolutionary France into the international arena – and international conflicts into France.[8] The war that the Jacobin majority called for was a war of the people against their oppressors. It would transcend borders and be fought within every state and every society. In the minds of the revolutionaries (and their political enemies, too), a revolutionary civil war pitted the Revolution against the ancien régime, revolution against counterrevolution, inside and outside France. It was in such terms that the Jacobins discussed war in the winter of 1791. "The demarcation line is now drawn between the societies and their governments," Jacques Pierre Brissot remarked. Pierre Louis Roederer regarded the coming war as something different from both traditional civil wars and wars between states. "This is a war of Frenchman against Frenchman, brother against brother, combined with the war of prince against nation; it is a civil war combined with foreign war," he wrote. "This is a war of the nobility against equality, a war of privileges against the common good, a war of all the vices against public and private morality, of all tyrannies against all liberties and against personal security."[9]

The revolutionaries' stance was initially defensive, but they quickly developed the more aggressive idea of the war of liberation. This new type of war set the French Revolution and its citizen-soldiers against the French

---

6 See Frank Attar, *1792: La Révolution française déclare la guerre à l'Europe* (Brussels, 1992); Timothy C. W. Blanning, *The Origins of the French Revolutionary Wars* (London, 1986).

7 "Discourse prononcée aux amis de la Constitution," *Patriote Français*, Jan. 5, 1792.

8 See Marc Belissa, *Fraternité universelle et intérêt national (1713–1795): Les cosmopolitiques du droit des gens* (Paris, 1998); Jean-Clément Martin, *Contre-Révolution, Révolution et Nation en France 1789–1799* (Paris, 1998), 128–37.

9 "Discourse prononcée aux amis de la Constitution," *Patriote Français*, Dec. 28, 1791.

king and his court, who were evidently allied with the Revolution's foreign enemies. The idea of a revolutionary civil war, which combined defensive and offensive elements, pushed the French revolutionaries toward the concept of the levée en masse, designed primarily to defend Revolutionary France by revolutionary means. The term *levée en masse* began to be used several weeks after the war began, as foreign invasion became likely for the first time. It soon became clear that many leading officers in the French army, like the king and his court, did not wish the French troops to be victorious. Faced with the prospect of defeat in a revolutionary civil war, the leadership of the National Assembly issued the first call for a levée en masse. The term meant a revolutionary mobilization of the entire French people, especially all the armed citizen-soldiers in the National Guard. The effort was to be directed against foreign troops and their allies within France itself, notably the royal head of state.

On May 28, 1792, the Girondist minister of war Joseph Servan asked the National Assembly to declare "that the whole nation has the duty to rise up."[10] Several days earlier the Girondist deputy Alba Lasource had declared that "the French people must rise up, but *en masse*" against foreign military aggression, as well as against counterrevolutionary forces within France. It soon became clear the revolutionaries meant the king and his court when they spoke of the enemy within. The Girondists' call for a levée en masse – this was the most radical phase of Girondist politics – implied the overthrow of the monarchy as part of a revolutionary civil war. The Parisian Jacobins declared that "the source of all our problems, brothers and friends, lies in this Austrian committee, the born enemy of the French nation.... Awaken, citizens, the whole nation has to rise up.... Prepare within France our means of defense."[11]

Although the moderate majority was reluctant to resort to extreme measures, the decisions reached by the National Assembly derived from the Girondist and Jacobin project. The Assembly decided to ask all French departments to send armed representatives to Paris. A *camp des fédérés*, a camp of armed revolutionary citizens from all parts of France, was to protect the capital against the advancing troops of the Duke of Brunswick and to deal with the French counterrevolutionary forces. In the words of Jean Debry, the purpose of the camp was "foreign defense and internal protection."[12] It was to "stand against the foreign enemies and intimidate those within the country," as the radical Cordeliers Club put it.[13]

---

10 AP 44:188; AP 43:560.
11 Circular of the Parisian Jacobin Club to the affiliated societies, 6.6.1792, *Annales Patriotiques*, 13.6.1792, supplément.
12 AP 44:644.   13 *Patriote français*, June 14, 1792.

The camp was set up despite the king's veto of the enabling legislation. The so-called *fédérés* thereupon became the vanguard of the revolutionary upheaval of August 10, 1792, destroying the French monarchy before leaving for the front. The essential prelude to these events was the National Assembly's declaration of "la patrie en danger" in July 1792. "The nation awaited only this terrible cry before it rose up," emphasized Jean-Baptiste Louvet.[14] Brissot explained the purpose of the declaration: "Our Fatherland is in danger . . . because its forces are paralyzed. And who has paralyzed them? It is only one person, the same person whom the Constitution calls its head. . . . You are told to fear the kings of Hungary and Prussia; but I tell you that the main force of these kings is the French court, and it is primarily here where we have first to defeat them."[15]

Consequently, the revolutionaries conceived the overthrow of the monarchy, which was carried out on August 10, 1792, as an integral part of the war effort: the enemy within had to be destroyed in order to strengthen the fighting spirit of the revolutionary nation. This interpretation was confirmed when the French troops gained their first military victory some weeks later at Valmy and halted the invasion of France. The defenders of the Revolution struck a second blow against the counterrevolutionary forces in France – or what was thought to be – during the so-called September Massacres in the prisons of Paris and other towns. In acts of "people's justice," agitated crowds killed the prisoners, calling them partisans of counterrevolution who were ready to destroy the Revolution once its defenders had left for the front. The revolutionary leaders were ashamed about these acts of violence, but the radicals interpreted the slaughter "as essentially bound to August 10, for it has contributed no less to save the Republic."[16]

In many respects, the levée en masse of 1793 was the child of this first wave of revolutionary mass mobilization and spontaneous acts of terror, which discursively linked the overthrow of the monarchy to victory in a foreign war. But there were also important differences. In 1792, the first of the levées was the common project of bourgeois revolutionaries and more radical popular activists to destroy the monarchy and save the revolution. By 1793, the situation had changed fundamentally, and there was no longer a common revolutionary project. Two new, independent conceptions of the levée en masse emerged. One was put forward by the radical forces in the

---

14 *La Sentinelle*, July 8, 1792.   15 AP 46:264.

16 Circular of the Parisian Jacobin Club to the affiliated societies, Nov. 30, 1792, François Victor Alphonse Aulard, ed., *La Société des Jacobins. Recueil de documents pour l'histoire du Club des Jacobins de Paris*, 6 vols. (Paris, 1889–97), 4:538.

Parisian clubs and sections, and the other by the bourgeois revolutionary leadership.

There was much overlap between these two visions of the levée en masse but also one crucial difference. Both rested on the assumption that foreign war and counterrevolutionary insurrection were two dimensions of the same challenge. Both called for merciless struggle against counterrevolution at home and abroad. Both accepted terror as a legitimate political tool. Politically, however, the two visions aimed at very different ends. For the Parisian sans-culottes and their leaders, the levée en masse was synonymous with the revolutionary uprising of the sovereign people, with direct democracy and social revolution by the poor against the rich. Confronted with this radical agenda, the leaders of the National Convention tried – successfully – to transform the call to arm the nation. As they conceived it, the levée en masse would be the organization of society from above for total war.

The war went well for the revolutionaries in the fall of 1792. French troops invaded foreign territories and for the first time had to confront the practical problems of exporting revolution. Success did not last long, however. In the spring of 1793, the first anti-French coalition took shape and the new French regime, which was threatened by counterrevolutionary uprisings in the Vendée and elsewhere, again faced military defeat. This situation encouraged the radicalization of the Revolution, again in the name of revolutionary civil war and on the initiative of the radical forces in the Parisian sections. The levée en masse seemed again to provide the solution, but now it was associated with political and social terror.

The idea of terror captured the political imagination of the most radical revolutionaries and the Parisian masses during the spring of 1793. "Rise up, yes, let us all rise up!" proclaimed the Parisian Jacobins under the presidency of Jean-Paul Marat in April 1793. "We must annihilate without pity all the conspirators if we don't want to be annihilated ourselves."[17] A month later, the Jacobin activist Louis Châles called for an uprising "of all of us together, three or four million men."[18] This general uprising, too, was to be directed against not only foreign troops but also against counterrevolutionary forces in France. The leader of the most radical *enragés*, Jacques Roux, proclaimed that at the "moment when Paris is lying between the iron of the Austrians and the fire of the rebels," it was necessary "to rise up in large numbers to

---

17 Circular of the Parisian Jacobin Club to the affiliated societies, April 5, 1793, ibid., 5:127.
18 *Journal des débats et de la corresponcance de la Société des amis de la Constitution, séanté aux Jacobins à Paris,* May 12, 1793.

defend the frontiers and to destroy the rebels."[19] The Revolution's domestic enemies were to be placed at the front line of battle, where they would fight or die as the shield of republican forces "in enemy fire, or rather from the iron of the assassins whom they themselves have recruited."[20]

The term *enemy* thus lost its specific referents and expanded to include all suspected of opposing the Revolution. The aristocrats who had staffed the French officer corps came under growing suspicion after the "Jacobin general" Charles Dumouriez tried to overthrow the Convention and fled to the enemy in March 1793. The Parisian sans-culottes called for draconian measures. The dependents of all those who were thought to oppose the Revolution, they argued, should be taken hostage. A delegation of the Parisian sections demanded that the wives and children of traitors be slaughtered.[21]

The calls for a general revolutionary uprising were tied up with social terror as well as political terror. The people of Paris were starving in 1793. They embraced the idea of a revolution of the poor against the rich. Their fury was now directed toward not only former aristocrats but also wealthy bourgeois. The sansculottes associated wealth, hoarding, and profiteering with counterrevolution and support for the foreign enemy, and they conceived of social revolution as an integral part of revolutionary civil war. "The rich have always betrayed you," declared Roux. "They always will betray you; during the war they will carry your armies to the slaughterhouse, in the capital they will sell the rights of the people; in the temple of law they will sacrifice the innocent. In a word, there is no kind of crime that the thirst for gold and riches has not committed; republicans, it is your task to wreak just revenge for the scourges that the rich have brought to the nation."[22]

The revolutionary activists in the sections demanded political measures such as taxes and price ceilings (the famous maximum), and they cast the rich as the domestic enemy undermining the Revolution. "Legistators," the Cordeliers Club and the Club of Republican Women proclaimed in May 1793,

beat up the speculators, the profiteers, the egotistical merchants. There is a cruel conspiracy to make people die of hunger by imposing outrageous prices on food. At

19 "Discours sur les moyens de sauver la France et la liberte," in *Jacques Roux: Scripta et Acta*, ed. Walter Markov (East Berlin, 1969), 73; cf. Markow, *Die Freiheiten des Priester Roux* (East Berlin, 1967).
20 "Le Publiciste de la République française, par l'ombre de Marat, 3.8.1793," in Markov, *Jacques Roux*, 210–4.
21 AP 61:279–80.
22 "Sur les causes des malheurs de la République," in Markov, *Jacques Roux*, 131. See generally Albert Soboul, *Les Sans-Culottes parisiens en l'an II. Mouvement populaire et gouvernement révolutionnaire, 2 juin 1793 – 9 thermidor an II* (Paris, 1958).

the head of this conspiracy stands the mercantile aristocracy of a class without mercy, which wants to become like royalty and accumulate all the wealth.... Annihilate all these scoundrels; the fatherland will be rich enough if it is left with only the sansculottes and their virtues.[23]

Through the levée en masse, social revolution became a dimension of war. All the nation's resources were to be mobilized, including its citizens. "How can we set in motion millions of men at once, how can we arm them and provision them?" asked the Hébertist Père Duchesne. Social terror against the rich was his answer: "It will be necessary first to requisition all the supplies in the republic."[24] Because these were mainly "in the hands of counterrevolutionaries," the fight against the rich was an appropriate means to save the Republic from foreign invasion. "We have to rise up en masse," was Roux's conclusion. We must "rush to the frontiers and, to benefit the volunteers, confiscate the property of those who refuse to fight."[25] Fighting against the rich was now militarized; it was the counterpart to combat at the front. It was to be carried out by armed units of sans-culottes, the so-called *armées révolutionnaires*.[26]

These bellicose ideas underlay the revolutionary levée en masse announced by the Parisian Commune in early July 1793. It was initially restricted to the capital until the delegates of the electoral assemblies asked the National Convention to extend it to the nation as a whole. These delegates had come to Paris bearing the results of the referendum on the new constitution. Like the *fédérés* in 1792, they became an important revolutionary force in the sections of Paris. But this time they postulated not only a self-organized form of mass mobilization but also political and social terror. Their speaker, Charles Royer, urged them to

issue a call to the people to rise up en masse; only the people can annihilate so many enemies; only the people can secure the triumph of freedom.... [I]t is necessary that in our hands the aristocracy become the instrument of its own destruction. We ask you to decree solemnly that all suspects will be arrested and sent to the frontiers, pursued by the terrible mass of all the sansculottes in the republic.

"Legislators," he concluded, "be terrible, but save our freedom; surround us with the almighty power of the people who have risen en masse."[27]

---

23 Aulard, *Société*, 5:198–9.   24 *Père Duchesne*, No. 274.

25 Roux, "Sur les causes des malheures de la République," in Markov, *Jacques Roux*, 132.

26 See Richard Cobb, *The Peoples Armies. The Armées Révolutionnaires, Instrument of the Terror in the Departments April 1793 to Floréal Year II* (New Haven, Connecticut, 1987).

27 AP 72:101; cf. Wolfgang Kruse, "Massenmobilisierung und Terror in der Französischen Revolution: Eine Quelleninterpretation zum Verständnis der revolutionären Radikalisierung des Jahres 1793," *Geschichte in Wissenschaft und Unterricht* 52 (2001):111–21. For a contrary view, see Mona Ozouf, "War and Terror in French Revolutionary Discourse," *Journal of Modern History* 56 (1984):579–97.

The republican elite in the National Convention did not rejoice at the prospect of these radical projects. In the view of these leaders, the general mobilization of the French people was dangerous militarily and politically. It seemed to provide for a chaotic and inefficient form of military mass mobilization, and it posed a threat to their representative form of political rule. Although they ended up agreeing to the levée en masse under intense pressure from the sections, their conception of the project was not the same as the radicals'. The leading figures in the Convention, Georges Danton and Maximilien Robespierre, took up the levée en masse on August 12, 1793. At the same time, they made it clear that the measure was to be carried out "in an orderly fashion."[28] The revolutionary authorities were to organize the fighting masses, and the terror was to be guided by revolutionary justice.

When the National Convention announced the levée en masse eleven days later, it made no mention of a revolutionary uprising. Orders were to come from above. The famous decree of August 23, 1793, which Bertrand Barère and Lazare Carnot formulated, declared that all the French people, soldiers as well as civilians, were liable for military service:

From now on, until the complete expulsion of all our enemies from the territory of the Republic, all French people are subject to military service. The young men will march to the battlefield, the married men will forge the arms and transport supplies, the women will produce tents and clothes and serve in the hospitals, the children will make dressing material from old linen, the old men will be carried to public places to encourage the warriors and to preach hatred of kings and the unity of the Republic.[29]

This was not the revolutionary levée en masse that the radical sectioneers had envisaged. They reacted at once, demanding the introduction of the terror by the National Convention. In their view, the terror was not only inseparably connected with the levée en masse; it was also a metaphor for revolution, an instrument of revolutionary upheaval from below. It was "the only means to awaken the people and force them to save themselves," as Royer explained to the Jacobins.[30] Once again, the representatives gave in when the Parisian sections marched on the Convention in early September 1793 and forced it to proclaim terror "the order of the day" and to establish the *armées révolutionnaires*.[31] And once again, the outcome was different from what the radicals had anticipated. The Convention's action did not

28 AP 72:102–3.   29 Ibid., 688.
30 Aulard, *Société*, 5:383.
31 See Jacques Guilhaumou, "La formation d'un mot d'ordre: 'Plaçons la terreur à l'ordre du jour' (13 juillet 1792 – 5 septembre 1793)," *Bulletin du Centre d'Analyse du Discours* 5 (1981):149–96.

bring permanent revolution from below, nor did it transform "the whole of France into a general committee that is occupied exclusively with the welfare of the people," as Royer and his followers had hoped.[32] Rather, the representatives made the terror an instrument of political leadership and inaugurated revolutionary dictatorship from above. In much the same way, they saw the levée en masse as a means for the state to undertake total war.

The term *total war* was not coined during the French Revolution. It is of twentieth-century origin and associated with the potential of industrial warfare.[33] However, Clausewitz did use the term *absolute war* to characterize Revolutionary and Napoleonic warfare.[34] The Revolution's struggle for survival in 1793–4 prompted strong "totalizing" tendencies in war, both at the front and within French society. "The Republic is now nothing but a large town in a state of siege," Bertrand Barère argued in support of the levée en masse. "It is necessary that all of France become nothing but a vast military camp; houses of the nation and the empty houses of the émigrés will be transformed into barracks, public places into workshops."[35]

It was not a big ideological step from revolutionary war to total war. From the beginning, the French revolutionaries conceived of a war of antagonistic principles that would end in the destruction of one side. When it became clear that France had to fight not only monarchs and their mercenary armies but also hostile peoples, the revolutionaries broadened their idea of war to encompass war of annihilation, particularly with respect to the domestic enemy.[36] The "besieged Republic" resolved to fight a war à outrance, and the Vendée became an early theater.[37] In theory, all French people were to participate voluntarily in this struggle for survival – or to be treated as enemies. In practice, participation was strong and enthusiastic at first. But as the number of volunteers later declined, a revolutionary government

---

32 Aulard, *Société*, 5:364.
33 See Raymond Aron, *The Century of Total War* (Garden City, New York, 1954); Ian F. W. Beckett, "Total War", in *Total War and Historical Change: Europe 1914–1955*, ed. Arthur Marwick, Clive Emsley, and Wendy Simpson (Philadelphia, 2001), 24–41; Roger Chickering, "Total War: The Use and Abuse of a Concept," in *Anticipating Total War: The German and American Experiences, 1871–1914*, ed. Manfred A. Boemecke, Roger Chickering, and Stig Förster (Cambridge, U.K., 1999), 13–28.
34 Carl v. Clausewitz, *On War* (Princeton, New Jersey, 1976); see also Peter Paret, *Understanding War: Essays on Clausewitz and the History of Military Power* (Princeton, New Jersey, 1992).
35 AP 72:678.
36 Jean-Yves Guiomar, *L'invention de la guerre totale* (Paris, 2004). David A. Bell, *The First Total War* (Boston, 2007) gives an exaggerated picture because it ignores the importance of the industrialized state and society for the concept of total war.
37 See Reynald Sécher, *A French Genocide: La Vendée* (Notre Dame, Indiana, 2003); Jean-Clément Martin, *La Vendée et la France* (Paris, 1987). For the brutalizing effects of civil war see Arno J. Mayer, *The Furies: Violence and Terror in the French and Russian Revolutions* (Princeton, New Jersey, 2000); Jean-Clément Martin, *Violence et Révolution. Essai sur la naissance d'un mythe national* (Paris, 2006).

vested with increasingly unrestrained powers began to organize popular participation by force.[38]

This change was evident in the recruitment of soldiers. In 1791–2, the armies of revolutionary France comprised volunteers who were eager to fight for the defense of the Revolution. Their units were later amalgamated with those of the regular army. As the need for soldiers increased in 1793, the National Convention moved toward forcible recruitment. All French departments had to provide a fixed number of soldiers, be they volunteers or conscripts. As a consequence, young men were under increasing pressure to serve in the army; those who refused were persecuted as deserters and enemies of the Revolution.[39] The government intensified this practice in the summer of 1793, declaring that all unmarried young men aged twenty to twenty-five years were obligated to do military service. The decree of the levée en masse provided that all French people were liable for military service, and it enabled the government to use force in imposing this obligation. Nevertheless, the levée en masse did not bring universal conscription in the current understanding of the term. Although the levée en masse applied to the entire French nation, it was an emergency measure limited to fulfilling a concrete goal, the liberation of French territory from foreign troops and counterrevolutionary insurgents. There was no plan to institutionalize it permanently.

The revolutionary government saw the levée en masse as a key element in the state's effort to organize French society for war. All of society's resources were to be placed under state control – goods, the means of production, and people. The government established a machinery of production, requisition, and distribution to supply the armed forces. The result was something like a mixed economy that combined governmental control and private enterprise.[40] The common people in particular were subject to authoritarian rule. As the sansculottes had demanded, the National Convention imposed price controls on basic foodstuffs and essentials, but it added ceilings on loans as well. The government also developed a form of industrial conscription. The decree on the levée en masse provided that

the Committee of Public Safety is charged with taking all measures necessary to set up without delay the extraordinary production of all sorts of arms that correspond

38 See Alan Forrest, "La patrie en danger: The French Revolution and the First *Levée en masse*," in *The People in Arms: Military Myth and National Mobilization since the French Revolution*, ed. Daniel Moran and Arthur Waldron (Cambridge, U.K., 2003), 8–32.
39 See Alan Forrest, *Conscripts and Deserters: The Army and French Society during the Revolution and Empire* (New York, 1989).
40 See Howard G. Brown, *Politics and Army Administration in France, 1791–1799* (Oxford, 1995), 98–123; Marc Bouloiseau, *La République jacobine: 10 août 1792 – 9 thermidor an II* (Paris, 1972), 113–24.

to the resolve and energy of the French People. Hence, it is entitled to set up all the establishments, factories, workshops, and plants that are necessary for the carrying out of this work, as well as to conscript throughout the Republic all the artisans and workers who can contribute to its success.[41]

Like soldiers at the front, workers in the factories that produced arms and military supplies were increasingly subject to forced labor. Many men were interested in jobs in the growing war industries, which carried exemption from military service, but they faced heavy workloads and gave up their civil rights. They were not allowed to leave their employment. They had to accept conditions of labor decreed by the government, and they were subject to military discipline. Unions and strikes were generally prohibited in revolutionary France, and those who engaged in such actions were branded as military deserters and faced revolutionary justice. The Committee of Public Safety decreed that "coalitions or meetings of any kind are forbidden. . . . In no case are workers allowed to meet in order to express their complaints; meetings will be dispersed, instigators and ringleaders will be arrested and punished according to the law."[42]

The claims of the revolutionary state on its citizens became total. In practice, civil war and counterrevolutionary resistance prevented the state from exerting those claims to their full extent, but the concept of organizing society by dictatorship from above to wage total war was born under the aegis of the levée en masse. The instrument to impose total war on a reluctant society was state-organized terror. In 1793–4, the Terror hit not only the declared enemies of the Revolution but also anyone who appeared troublesome or even neutral. The Terror then turned against its original advocates in the Parisian sections and clubs as the state came to see their revolutionary aspirations as a threat to domestic unity and support for the war. Already in the autumn of 1793, the National Convention suppressed the *enragés* and the Club of Republican Women. Early in 1794, it eliminated the Parisian *armée révolutionnaire* and brought the Cordeliers Club, which again threatened to provoke a revolutionary uprising, under state control. With the elimination of the factions in the spring of 1794, the Revolution eventually froze, as Saint-Just observed; but the terror continued, forcing a politically paralyzed nation to support its armies. When victory came in the early summer of 1794, the levée en masse and the government's rule by terror lost their basic rationale and came to an end.

41 AP 72:689.
42 François Victor Alphonse Aulard, ed., *Recueil des Actes du Comité de Salut Publique, avec la correspondance officielle des représentants en mission et le registre du conseil exécutif,* 25 vols. (Paris, 1889–1918), 9:347–51.

When universal conscription was finally decreed in September 1798, it was presented as a levée en masse. This levée inaugurated a "levée en masse of youth," and it was to be "a permanent institution," as General Jean-Baptiste Jourdan, its initiator, declared.[43] It signified neither armed revolutionary uprising by the people nor total war organized by the revolutionary government. Nor did it have much in common with Dubois-Crancé's early proposal to anchor the military in civilian society by recruiting armed citizen soldiers. Instead, universal conscription was designed to provide the manpower for a military that had developed its own claim to social and political power. Increasingly distanced from civilian society, the soldiers of the Revolution no longer saw themselves as the armed spearhead of a civilian revolution. In their eyes, the military had become the guardian of revolutionary values; it was destined, they believed, to rebuild civilian society, which had fallen prey to private interests. The soldiers had long called for "forcing insolent youth to rally to the flag of glory."[44] When the French Republic was threatened with collapse in 1799, this project implied the complete and lasting militarization of civil society. "Our incessant wars show the French people that they must become a militarized people," argued the military planners. "For this nation, it will not suffice to look war-like whenever it takes up arms. It is necessary more than ever to be prepared for war at any time."[45] With the military coup of Brumaire in 1799, Bonaparte took up this challenge.

---

43 *Moniteur universel*, 29:348.   44 *Journal militaire*, Jan. 20, 1796.
45 *Mon Contingent de civisme pour la crise présente. Par le citoyen Picauld-Desdorides, ancien général*, 19. Flor. VII/8.5.1799. Archives de guerre, Château Vincennes, Série mémoires et reconnaissances, 1161, No. 53. See Jean-Paul Bertaud, *Bonaparte prend le pouvoir: La République, meurt-elle assassinée?* (Brussels, 1987).

16

Religion in a Time of War

The Case of Lower Alsace, 1789–1794

DONATUS DÜSTERHAUS

"The word revolution has become a terrible term among us and our contemporaries. It is a sister or companion, or rather a mother of this bloodthirsty war."[1] These words, uttered by a Protestant pastor during a funeral oration in the Alsatian town of Brumath in 1809, testified to how interconnected the terms *religion, revolution*, and *war* had become in that border region during the upheavals after 1789. As the historian Georges Livet has written, "the cross-border revolutionary war was crucial for the process of the Revolution in Alsace."[2] Given its location and its political ties to both to Germany and France, Alsace was affected by events to both the west and the east. Before the Revolution, the region's multiplicity of religious and political structures had made it a microcosm of the Holy Roman Empire even though it was under the rule of the French monarch. Lutherans, Calvinists, Anabaptists, and Jews lived side by side with Roman Catholics — a situation that was unique in France.

This essay addresses the attitudes of Catholics, Lutherans, and Jews toward the French Revolution and the Revolutionary wars. It concentrates on events in the department of the Lower Rhine, which was the most religiously diverse part of the region, and on the period 1789–94, when religious life in Alsace was most immediately affected by revolutionary policies and when warfare occurred in Alsace.

It was less the war that affected the population of Alsace and provoked popular resistance than the antireligious measures the revolutionary

---

1 "Todten-Feyer zur Ehre der gefallenen Krieger gehalten in der protestantischen Kirche zu Brumath den 17ten Christenmonath 1809," *Miscellanea Protestantica Alsatica*, 5 vols. (Strasbourg, 1810), 4:15. This essay draws upon the author's book *Die Revolution als Schwester des Krieges: Deutungen und Wahrnehmungen von Lutheraner in Elsaß in der Zeit der französischen Revolution und napoleonischen Empires (1789–1815)* (Münster, 2009).

2 Georges Livet, "Conclusion: L'Alsace au coeur de l'Europe révolutionnaire," *Revue d'Alsace* 116 (1989–90): 402.

government enacted in connection with it. The war, which directly touched northern Alsace only for a few weeks in the fall of 1793, is of special pertinence to the topic of revolutionary religious policy. The approach of war heightened fears among the revolutionaries and their supporters that defeat would bring not only retaliation but also the restoration of the old order. The opponents of the Revolution, especially the faithful, associated the prospect of a successful invasion by the Austrian-Prussian coalition and the army led by the prince of Condé with the restoration of traditional religious practices in both private and public life. The Revolution's efforts to suppress established religious worship took place against the background of the permanent threat of war in the border province of Alsace. This played an important role in how the population there viewed the period from 1789–94. The sources left by contemporaries attest to the decisive role of the Revolution's antireligious struggle. This chapter traces the interaction of religion, revolutionary ideology, and war from the beginning of the Revolution to the Terror.

Alsace was a comparatively recent addition to the kingdom of France at the time of the Revolution. The province of Alsace comprised the region around Belfort in the south and the city of Landau in the north. Except in a few spots, the Rhine constituted the political and military frontier between France and the Holy Roman Empire, and a customs frontier ran along the crest of the Vosges.[3]

In 1698, the Conseil Souverain d'Alsace (Sovereign Council of Alsace) was established in Colmar as the successor to the Austrian provincial government. The French king was represented in Alsace by an intendant, who was the head of the provincial administration. The king's presence was embodied by royal legislation and the army – in particular the fortresses and the garrison cities of Landau, Fort St. Louis, and Huningue – and by the internal revenue department. Royal taxes amounted to fourteen livres plus one sou per head, which was about the average in the rest of France.[4]

After 1680, all the Alsatian princely and aristocratic territories of the Holy Roman Empire came under French rule. In exchange for their recognition of the king's supremacy, the princes and other lords received guarantees that their special rights and privileges would remain intact. They were allowed to exercise their powers of local government and to accept oaths of allegiance from their Alsatian subjects. In addition, they could maintain their own seats

3 Bernard Vogler, *Histoire politique de l'Alsace: de la Révolution à nos jours, un panorama des passions alsaciennes* (Strasbourg, 1995), 13.
4 Klaus-Jürgen Matz, "Das Elsaß als Teil der französischen Monarchie," in *Das Elsaß: Historische Landschaft im Wandel der Zeit*, ed. Michael Erbe (Stuttgart, 2002), 92.

of administration and fief chambers (*Lehnskammern*), exercise jurisdiction, and nominate heads of villages and members of local courts.[5] The princes were also exempt from taxation. As a result, many received considerable income from Alsace until the end of the ancien régime, and they remained closely bound to their Alsatian territories. These arrangements also held for the ecclesiastical territories. Thus, a territorial mosaic of local jurisdictions prevailed in Alsace until the French Revolution.

In 1787, a provincial assembly was established in Alsace. The work of this assembly reflected a desire for reform, particularly of public administration and the administration of taxes, along with hopes for improvements in the province's infrastructure. The minutes of the assembly's meetings also make clear that members had a distinct regional consciousness.

Nonetheless, the province of Alsace retained the legacy of its earlier membership in the Holy Roman Empire. The province's administrative integration within France was not as successful as the government in Versailles had hoped. While the language of the administration was French, most of the population in Alsace continued to speak German. Elsewhere in France, the province was generally regarded as foreign.[6]

In 1789, there were 440,000 Catholics in Alsace, organized into five dioceses (Basel, Besançon, Metz, Speyer, and Strasbourg). The bishopric of Strasbourg was also an ecclesiastical principality. Its bishops exercised jurisdiction on both banks of the Rhine. The Protestant city of Strasbourg had become a target of Catholic missionary work after surrendering to Louis XIV in 1681, and by the eve of the Revolution, its Catholic residents were in the majority. According to Claude Muller, eighteenth-century Alsace was a focus of religious vocations.[7] Religious orders attracted increasing numbers of novices. The province was different in this respect from the rest of France and other parts of Europe, where male religious houses complained of a lack of vocations. In 1790, there were 1,065 members of religious orders, 584 of whom lived in the northern part of Alsace. The majority of the Catholic clergy, about 80 percent, comprised parish priests, while the rest were members of monastic orders. Their age structure was well balanced.[8]

The Catholic Church was hostile to the other denominations in Alsace. During the Counterreformation, the church had tried, under the leadership of the Jesuits, to expand in Alsace at the expense of the Protestants.

5 Ibid.
6 Roland Marx: "De la Pré-Révolution à la Restauration," in *Histoire de l'Alsace; Univers de la France et des pays francophones; Histoire des provinces*, ed. Philippe Dollinger, 2 vols. (Toulouse, 1970), 1: 356–8.
7 Claude Muller, "La suppression des ordres religieux masculins en Alsace" *Revue d'Alsace* 116 (1989–90), 246–7.
8 Ibid.

Regulations such as the prohibition of mixed marriages survived to anchor discrimination against practicing Protestants. Major administrative positions were reserved for Catholics. In 1789, the official letters of complaint (*cahiers des doléances*) from the Catholic clergy showed little tolerance toward Protestants or Jews.[9] The clergy in the districts of Sélestat and Colmar demanded the demolition of two Protestant churches in Strasbourg and Ribeauvillé. These letters of complaint were directed against Protestant administrative equality, including the right of Protestants to hold public office. Alsace sent two Protestants and one Jew to Paris for the Estates General in 1789 – along with twenty-four Roman Catholics.

Territorial changes at the conclusion of the Thirty Years' War had put the Protestants of Alsace under the jurisdiction of the Catholic kings of France. Special clauses in the peace treaties, however, protected Protestants against arbitrary acts by the French crown. Because Alsace had been politically part of the Holy Roman Empire until 1648, the Protestant territorial churches survived with all their constitutional and liturgical prerogatives.

The 220,000 Lutherans living in Alsace in 1789 made up about a third of province's population.[10] They were organized into 146 congregations served by 220 ministers. The majority lived in northern Alsace (later designated as the Department of the Lower Rhine [Département du Bas-Rhin] and the cities of Strasbourg and Colmar (Department of the Upper Rhine [Département du Haut-Rhin]).[11] The Lutherans made up a wealthy and influential minority. They were disproportionately engaged in trade and industry, and they were barred from holding administrative offices. Restrictive legislation also forbade them to settle in exclusively Catholic areas.

Strasbourg's Protestant university was a great asset and an object of pride to Alsatian Protestants.[12] It was the intellectual basis of the church of the Augsburg Confession in the city and surrounding countryside, and it engaged in lively exchanges with universities in the Holy Roman Empire. The university retained its independence under the "most Christian" French kings and became the leading school for diplomats of the eighteenth century. Although Protestants had not been entitled to write letters of complaint in 1789, some of their communities responded to charges against them in

---

9 Robert Steegmann, "Les cahiers de doléances en Alsace," *Revue d'Alsace* 116 (1989–90), 23–34.
10 Marcel Scheidhauer, *Les églises luthériennes en France 1800–1815, Alsace-Montbéliard-Paris* (Strasbourg, 1975), 20.
11 See Claude Muller, "Wir haben den selben Herrgott. Luthériens et catholiques en Alsace au XVIII siècle," in *Terres d'Alsace: Chemins d'Europe; mélanges offerts à Bernard Vogler*, ed. Dominique Dinet et François Igersheim (Strasbourg, 2003), 423–45.
12 See Jürgen Voss, *Universität, Geschichtswissenschaft und Diplomatie im Zeitalter der Aufklärung: Johann Daniel Schöpflin (1694–1771)* (Munich, 1979).

letters from Catholics.[13] They called for religious tolerance for the denominations, more political influence for them, particularly in the cities, and access to public office.

Many Alsatian Calvinists, who numbered about twelve thousand in the late 1690s, were descended from Huguenots expelled from France.[14] They had been required in the eighteenth century to baptize their children as Catholics; their churches were forbidden to have spires, bells, or other external features of religious significance. The law of toleration of 1787 improved their situation only slightly.[15] Lutherans, too, showed a deep aversion to Calvinists, whose faith was officially forbidden in Strasbourg, although it could be practiced in the neighboring town of Wolfisheim, where 1,528 Calvinists lived in 1697. Important centers of Calvinism lay also in Bischwiller in Lower Alsace, in Sainte-Marie-aux-Mines,[16] and in Mulhouse in Upper Alsace. There were also sixty-two Anabaptist families in Alsace in 1700, which comprised 496 people. They were predominantly farmers who raised cattle in the valleys of the Vosges, but some were active as tradesmen.[17]

In 1789, about twenty thousand Jews, more than half of all Jews in France, resided in Alsace.[18] Like the Jews of Lorraine, the Alsatian Jews were Ashkenazim, which was unusual in France, if not in the Holy Roman Empire. The majority of Alsatian Jews lived in the religiously diverse Lower Alsace, and they benefited from their rights of residence. They were organized in five rabbinates. Most were poor and could be characterized as country Jews.[19] They were not allowed to farm, though, and repeatedly suffered discrimination and waves of persecution. The letters of protection (*lettres patentes*) of 1784 failed to improve their situation significantly.[20] Only a small upper class enjoyed economic success and public recognition.

As the Revolution spread from parliament into the streets of Paris, dissatisfied citizens in Alsace took the offensive. On July 19–20, 1789, unrest broke out in Strasbourg and Hagenau in Lower Alsace, where urban dwellers

13 Rodolphe Reuss, *Les églises protestantes d'Alsace: Esquisse historique* (Paris, 1906), 23.
14 Michel-Edmond Richard, *La vie des protestants français de l'Edit de Nantes à la Révolution 1789–1802* (Paris, 1994), 219.
15 Johannes Schneider, *Geschichte der evangelischen Kirche in der Zeit der französischen Revolution 1789–1802* (Strasbourg, 1890), 14.
16 See Rebecca McCoy, "The Société Populaire at Sainte-Marie-aux-Mines: Local Culture and National Identity in an Alsatian Community during the French Revolution," *European History Quarterly* 27 (1997): 435–74.
17 Richard, *La vie des protestants*, 219.
18 Georges Weill, "La société juive à la veille de la Révolution," in *Histoire des Juifs en France*, ed. Bernhard Blumenkranz (Toulouse, 1972), 166.
19 Ibid.
20 Paul Assall, *Juden im Elsaß* (Bühl-Moss, 1984), 149–50.

demonstrated against the local administration. On July 20, a mob ransacked the municipal archives in Strasbourg's city hall.[21] Riots also occurred in rural Lower Alsace directed against the monasteries. Farmers attacked the abbeys of Andlau and Marmoutier, and the Benedictine monks of the Abbey of Saint-Jean fled to Saverne, the residence of the bishop of Strasbourg. The riots then spread to Saverne, where farmers invaded the properties of the bishop on July 31 and unsuccessfully tried to loot them.[22]

The National Assembly's abolition of the privileges on August 4–5, 1789, did not fully remove the causes of unrest in Alsace. The property-owning nobility and clergy from the Holy Roman Empire insisted on retaining the privileges that had been guaranteed in 1648. The troubles decreased in northern Alsace after the middle of August, but tax evasion and attacks by local farmers on territorial institutions continued until October. The lingering unrest and the attacks on the clergy were motivated less by religious reasons than economic: taxes remained high, and the harvest was bad. As Fernand L'Huillier has noted, there was no open hostility toward the Catholic Church.[23]

The Jews, too, were victims of rampaging farmers in the summer of 1789, again more for economic than religious reasons. Especially in the Sundgau and Upper Alsace, in Durmenach, Hagenthal, and Hegenheim, the houses of Jews were plundered.[24] In response to these attacks, Alsatian Jews commissioned David Sintzheim and Joseph Brunschwig to take letters of complaint to Paris. These letters demanded an end to the discrimination that Jews faced, in particular the tax burdens they bore and the limits that were placed on their professional activities.[25]

The situation of the clergy changed fundamentally in the summer of 1790, when the National Assembly in Paris abolished the contemplative orders, nationalized monastic property, and introduced the Civil Constitution of the Clergy. The clergy in Lower Alsace immediately rejected the provisions of the Civil Constitution. Cardinal Rohan of Strasbourg mobilized almost all the Catholic priests in Lower Alsace in opposition.[26] Particularly objectionable to Alsatian Catholics were the provisions that

21 René Epp, "De la Révolution à l'annexion," in *Histoire du diocèse de Strasbourg*, ed. Francis Rapp (Paris, 1982), 173.
22 Daniel Peter, "Les Manifestations paysannes en Alsace du Nord durant l'été 1789," *Revue d'Alsace* 116 (1989–90): 44.
23 Fernand L'Huillier, "L'Eglise d'Alsace pendant la Révolution," *Saisons d'Alsace* 9 (1964): 44.
24 Claude Muller, "Religion et Révolution en Alsace," *Annales Historiques de la Révolution Française* 337 (2004): 70.
25 See Jean Daltroff and Robert Weyl, "Le cahier des doléances des juifs d'Alsace," *Revue d'Alsace* 116 (1989–90): 173–86.
26 Epp, "De la Révolution à l'annexion," 172.

made priests employees of the state and introduced electoral assemblies into the church. In the view of the historian René Epp, the Gallican goals of the Civil Constitution provoked the resistance of the ultramontane clergy in Lower Alsace.[27]

Another provocation was the introduction of an obligatory oath of loyalty to the Civil Constitution. Priests who refused to take it were removed from office. In the summer of 1790, Rohan fled across the Rhine to Ettenheim, never to return. From Ettenheim, which was part of his diocese, he organized resistance against the Revolution.[28] The result of his efforts was that nearly one thousand parish priests, about 80 percent of the secular clergy in Alsace, refused to swear the oath. Many emigrated into the Holy Roman Empire or the Swiss Confederation. In March 1791, Pope Pius VI spoke out against the Civil Constitution in his encyclical *Quod aliquantum*. All the "constitutional" priests who had sworn loyalty to the Civil Constitution, the pope declared, were schismatics.

Only 34 of the 412 priests in the Lower Rhine department – fewer than 8 percent – swore the oath to the Civil Constitution.[29] That was the lowest regional percentage in France. One of the reasons for this opposition lay in institutional reforms that, by establishing a single diocese in each French department, brought about the religious separation of Alsace from the Holy Roman Empire. The diocese of Strasbourg lost its territory on the right bank of the Rhine, while the bishop of Speyer lost his Alsatian lands.

Bishop Rohan's refusal to swear the oath of allegiance made it necessary to elect a new bishop for the department of the Lower Rhine. In an electoral assembly, where Protestants were also present, the only candidate, François-Antoine Brendel (1735–1800), received a majority of the votes and was consecrated in Paris on March 25, 1791.[30] Catholic professors at the University of Strasbourg voiced their displeasure over the events, and the students who were studying for the priesthood announced their continued loyalty to Rohan, whom they regarded as the legitimate bishop. The resistance of the clergy to the Civil Constitution was reflected in the growing shortage of parish priests. Vacancies could be filled only by inviting priests from central France or the Holy Roman Empire.[31] The closure of

27 René Epp, "Le Bas-Rhin, département français au pourcentage de prêtres le plus faible," *Revue d'Alsace* 116 (1989–90): 237–44.
28 See Frédéric-Charles Heitz, *La Contre-Révolution en Alsace 1789–1793: Pièces et documents relatifs à cette époque* (Strasbourg, 1862), 52–60.
29 Claude Muller, "Religion et Révolution," 67.
30 Rodolphe Reuss, *La constitution civile du clergé et la crise religieuse en Alsace (1790–1795)*, 2 vols. (Strasbourg, 1922), 1: 136–8.
31 See Louis Kammerer, "Les prêtres allemands dans le clergé constitutionnel en Alsace," *Revue d'Alsace* 116 (1989–90): 285–94.

the monasteries in 1791 and the convents in the fall of 1792 aggravated the situation, as hundreds of members of religious orders went into exile.

Protestants were at first undecided about the new religious laws. In the summer of 1790, the National Assembly exempted the properties of the Protestant churches from sale or nationalization, so Protestants initially felt secure. The Declaration of the Rights of Man guaranteed them freedom of conscience, and a decree of December 24, 1789, gave them access to civil and military office.[32] In the larger towns of Lower Alsace, such as Saverne, Hagenau, and Strasbourg, so-called Societies of the Friends of the Revolution (Sociétés des Amis de la Constitution) attracted many Protestants.[33] These political clubs were home to both radical and moderate supporters of the Revolution, and they served as a forum for lively discussions about the legal position of Protestants and Protestant church properties. The majority of Protestants opposed the proposal that the government sell those properties. In December 1790, the National Assembly reaffirmed the exemption of Protestant religious possessions from public sales of church property. Another issue was the Civil Constitution. On the one hand, many Protestant ideas were embedded in this document; on the other hand, Alsatian Protestants feared that the special rights and traditions of their congregations would not be protected.[34] A single state Protestant church, they feared, would blur the distinctions among the Protestant denominations. A commission of Alsatian Protestant clergy and theologians was established in Strasbourg to draft proposals for constitutional protections for denominational rights. Its recommendations were, however, rejected by the local friends of the constitution. Meanwhile, the National Assembly was too preoccupied with Catholic affairs to consider reorganizing the Protestant churches in Alsace.

The initial phase of the Revolution was thus on the whole favorable to Alsatian Protestants. The new laws looked promising and gave Protestants legal protections that they had long desired. In April 1791, the secular authorities in the district demanded that Alsatian Lutheran and Calvinist ministers, professors, and teachers take the constitutional oath. The Protestant ministers in Strasbourg demonstrated their patriotism and swore the oath unanimously.[35] Most of the Lutheran and Calvinist clergy elsewhere in Lower Alsace followed their example. Those who refused did so for

---

32 Reuss, *Les églises protestantes*, 320.
33 See Daniel Schönpflug, *Der Weg in die Terreur: Radikalisierung und Konflikte im Straßburger Jakobinerklub (1790–1795)* (Munich, 2002).
34 Henri Strohl, *Le protestantisme en Alsace* (Strasbourg, 1950), 312.
35 Voeltzel, "Les protestants d'Alsace," *Saisons d'Alsace* 9 (1964): 61.

political rather than religious reasons, above all because the Revolution had threatened regional identities. The clergy who refused included ministers in regions that had once belonged to Hanau-Lichtenberg and Pfalz-Zweibrücken.[36] Clergy in those regions continued to say prayers for their former rulers.[37]

The enthusiasm of Alsatian Lutherans for the Revolution was also evident in the establishment of newspapers such as the *Wöchentliche Nachrichten* and the *Straßburgische Zeitung*.[38] Another indication was that voluntary donations to the state – so-called *dons patriotiques* – were higher in Protestant than in Catholic areas in the years 1790–2. Protestants also participated in larger proportions in elections than did Catholics. Young Protestants expressed their patriotism by joining the newly formed voluntary battalions in greater numbers than Catholics.[39] Many rural Protestant congregations celebrated the acceptance of the new French constitution by the king in 1791.

Strasbourg's Protestant mayor, Friedrich Dietrich, and the leading Protestant theologian, Johann Lorenz Blessig, showed great enthusiasm for the Revolution.[40] Some Catholics charged that Protestant enthusiasm for the Revolution was spurred by the opportunities created by the nationalization of Catholic ecclesiastic properties, but that accusation was overstated. Recent studies have shown that Protestants and Catholics alike purchased secularized church property.[41]

The position of Alsatian Jews was more complicated. In January 1790, the National Assembly granted civil rights to Jews in Bordeaux, Bayonne, and Avignon. These rights did not, however, extend to Jews in Alsace. The prospect of Jewish emancipation was not met with enthusiasm in Alsace, where Catholics and Lutherans feared the consequences. Discriminatory measures enacted under the ancien régime thus remained in force.[42] Jews' rights of residence were limited. At least in Strasbourg, however, Jews nonetheless greeted the Revolution.[43] Max Berr, for example, was accepted into the National Guard and the Society of Friends of the Constitution in February 1790. The emancipation of the Alsatian Jews finally took place in September 1791.

---

36 Schneider, *Geschichte der evangelischen Kirche*, 64.
37 Reuss, *Les églises protestantes*, 106.
38 See Susanne Lachenicht, *Information und Propaganda: Die Presse der Jakobiner im Elsaß (1791–1800)* (Munich, 2004).
39 Marc Lienhardt, "Les protestants," in *Catholiques, protestants et juifs en Alsace*, ed. François Georges Dreyfus (Mulhouse, 1992), 118.
40 Muller, "Religion et Révolution," 69.   41 Ibid.
42 See Rodolphe Reuss, "L'antisémitisme dans le Bas-Rhin pendant la Révolution (1790–1793). Nouveaux documents inédits," *Revue des Études Juives* 78 (1914): 246–63.
43 Muller, "Religion et Révolution," 70.

It was the overthrow of the monarchy and the outbreak of war that ultimately radicalized politics in Alsace. The new political climate was captured in "La Marseillaise," which its composer, Colonel Claude Joseph Rouget de Lisle, sang for the first time on April 25, 1792, in the home of Strasbourg mayor Friedrich Dietrich.[44] Many Alsatians were to have distinguished careers in the army, notably François-Étienne Christophe Kellermann, Jean-Baptiste Kléber, and Jean Rapp.

The Jacobins, who emerged as the leading political faction in Paris after the toppling of the monarchy on August 10, 1792, nonetheless regarded the Alsatians as unpatriotic. So-called *commissionaires* or *représentants en mission* (representatives on mission) were sent to Alsace with special powers to keep the region under Paris's control.[45] Aided by a network of local informants, revolutionary authorities soon dismissed many leading functionaries, such as Mayor Dietrich, from their posts. A number of institutions were dissolved or staffed with functionaries who were loyal to the Revolution.

After the French army's victory at Valmy (1792) and advance into the Palatinate, the Austrian army under General Dagobert-Sigismund von Wurmser successfully launched a counter-offensive in the fall of 1793 with the support of an antirevolutionary French army led by the prince of Condé and Prussian troops under the command of the Duke of Brunswick. Coalition forces scored a victory at Wissembourg on October 13, 1793, that opened the way to Strasbourg and Hagenau.[46] Opponents of the Revolution greeted this victory as a divine signal, as a victory of religion over the "godless" revolutionary forces. On the morning of the battle, numerous witnesses later reported, there was a cloud formation in the sky in the shape of a cross (Figure 1).[47]

In response to the coalition's advance to Hagenau, which was captured also in October 1793, revolutionary authorities launched the Terror in Alsace in October 1793. The religious policies of the national government became more severe, while anti-Alsatian hysteria broke out in Strasbourg among Jacobins who had come to the city from the French interior. They debated whether to forbid the use of German in Alsace as well as the wearing of traditional Alsatian clothing.[48]

---

44 Vogler, *Histoire politique*, 26.
45 See Jörg Monar, *Saint-Just: Sohn, Denker und Protagonist der Revolution* (Bonn, 1993).
46 See Arthur Chuquet, Les guerres de la révolution, 5th ed., 11 vols. (Paris, 1925).
47 On this battle, see Raymond Oberle, ed., *Batailles d'Alsace du Moyen-Age à 1870* (Strasbourg, 1987), 235.
48 Bernard Vogler, *Histoire culturelle de l'Alsace: Du Moyen-Age à nos jours: les très riches heures d'une région frontière* (Strasbourg, 1994), 190.

ÉVÉNEMENT REMARQUABLE

arrivé le 13 Octobre 1793, jour de la prise des lignes.
de Weilenbourg

à Sept heures et un quart du matin, pendant que l'armée combinée, sous les ordres de M.r le Comte de Wurmser, attaquoit la fameuse redoute de Steinfeld, on apperçut dans le ciel le plus azuré, une Croix blanche, distinctement formée par les deux seuls nuages, qui fussent alors sur l'horison ; elle dura environ une demie heure, ensuite se dissipa .

Ce fait vraiment extraordinaire fut remarqué, et frappa toute l'armée, Signe miraculeux du triomphe de la Religion, il fut sans doute le présage heureux de la victoire complette, que l'armée combinée remporta sur les régicides ; ils furent totalement mis en déroute dans cette journée, et chassés des redoutables Lignes de la Lauter .

Ce fait a été attesté par la Signature de tous les officiers Généraux et d'une foule de témoins oculaires .

Figure 1. "Remarkable event that occurred on October 13, 1793 . . .": a contemporary report of the Battle of Wissembourg. Illustration courtesy of the Bibliothèque Nationale Universitaire de Strasbourg.

323

The coalition army that had nearly reached Strasbourg in the fall of 1793 was unable to hold its situation. The position of the Catholics in the region, who had welcomed the Austrians as liberators, became increasingly precarious. Toward the end of 1793, after the coalition troops had withdrawn, they began to fear reprisals from the advancing revolutionary army. Some twenty thousand Catholics fled from Alsace, particularly the Department of the Lower Rhine, into the Holy Roman Empire, and many were to remain there for years.[49] Two nonjuring Catholic priests from Hagenau were arrested in flight by soldiers and guillotined in Strasbourg in late December 1793. A third priest died of typhoid as he was making his way to the empire.[50] The antireligious agitation by the revolutionaries and their supporters during the Army of the Rhine's advance through Alsace was recorded by the nonjuring priest Sebastian Krummeich of Reichshofen. He relates that the local church was ransacked by radical supporters of the Revolution for several days after the Austrian retreat. The tabernacle was broken up; the chalices were stolen; and the hooligans dressed up in vestments. The altar was destroyed, and pictures and statues of saints were publicly derided and later burned to ashes.[51]

The reprisals that befell the Catholics who remained had been anticipated in a series of measures enacted at the end of 1791 against nonjuring priests. Highly frequented places of worship, such as the pilgrimage church of Marienthal, were finally closed in 1793.[52] Conflicts raged between local priests who had and had not sworn the oath to the Civil Constitution and their adherents.

When a new oath for priests was imposed in 1793, the first priests to refuse it were arrested. Many Alsatian priests then escaped into the Holy Roman Empire. The political situation in Alsace worsened in the course of the year as the result of the antagonism between radical Jacobins and the rural Catholic population, who increasingly resisted the Revolution. War aggravated the hostility between supporters and opponents of the Revolution. In the Catholic town of Molsheim, an uproar occurred when

---

49 Rodolphe Reuss, *La grande fuite de décembre 1793 et la situation politique et religieuse du Bas-Rhin de 1794 à 1799* (Strasbourg, 1924); Wilhelm Kreutz, "Das Elsaß zwischen Französischer Revolution und Reichsgründung," in *Das Elsaß*, 107.

50 Joseph Klélé, *Hagenau zur Zeit der Revolution 1787–1797 (18.brumaire VIII)* (Strasbourg, 1885), 183–4.

51 Sebastian Krummeich, *Erlebnisse eines elsässischen Priesters zur Zeit der französischen Revolution. 1789–1798* (Strasbourg, 1902), 34.

52 André Marcel Burg, *Histoire du couvent et du pèlerinage sous les guillelmites, les jésuites et le clergé séculier* (Phalsbourg, 1959), 190–1.

some five hundred people demonstrated in front of the recruitment office and voiced their loyalty to both the French Crown and the Holy Roman Empire. Soon afterward, three men paid with their lives for participating in this demonstration.[53]

Local revolutionary policy on religion in Alsace was also shaped by Eulogius Schneider, a former Franciscan monk and so-called German Jacobin.[54] Schneider was appointed public prosecutor for the department of the Lower Rhine in February 1793. He thereupon toured the department with a mobile guillotine and spread terror with his tribunals. Schneider concentrated on the nonjuring priests and their supporters. Outward signs of religious devotion, such as crosses and statues, were removed from churches and chapels. Churches were stripped of all but one bell apiece, and seized bells were taken to Strasbourg to be melted down. In September 1793, all the churches in Alsace were closed. The buildings were leased, sold, or like the cathedral in Strasbourg, transformed into "temples of reason." Although the revolutionaries refrained from destroying the cathedral, they took out all the statues of saints and crowned the spire with a copper Jacobin hat, a symbol of the Revolution.[55] Places that were associated with Christian saints were renamed, and religious references were purged from the public realm. In the summer of 1793, a total of twenty-seven church bells from Alsace were melted down in Strasbourg and made into cannon. The leaden ornamental fittings from coffins in cemeteries and churches in Strasbourg were likewise confiscated and melted down.[56] The government's list of enemies of the Revolution grew ever longer and came to include – along with foreign military enemies – émigrés, speculators, Rohan's supporters, and supporters of nonjuring clergy.[57]

Antireligious policy reached its high point in Alsace in the months between September 1793 and Robespierre's downfall in July 1794. Priests who belonged to the constitutional church were called on to renounce their faith publicly. About 113, fewer than one-third of the priests in Lower Alsace who by that time had sworn the oath, obeyed this demand. Fifty-three married after leaving office.[58] During the most intense phase of the

53 Reuss, *La constitution civile du clergé*, 2:179.
54 See Claude Betzinger, *Vie et mort d'Euloge Schneider, ci-devant fransicain. Des lumières à la Terreur, 1756–1794* (Strasbourg, 1997).
55 Schönpflug, *Der Weg in die Terreur*, 237.
56 Zoltan-Etienne Harsany, *La vie à Strasbourg sous la Révolution* (Strasbourg, 1975), 247.
57 Ibid., 236.
58 Claude Muller and Dominique Varry, *Hommes de Dieu et Révolution en Alsace* (Turnhout, 1993), 179.

Terror and official efforts to suppress Christianity in France, two thousand people were arrested in Alsace for purportedly counterrevolutionary offenses. Of the ninety-three subsequently sentenced to the guillotine, twenty-five had been condemned for religious reasons – nineteen laypersons and six priests.[59] Alsace was spared the large-scale massacres of priests like those that occurred in the Vendée and elsewhere, primarily because proximity to the Holy Roman Empire and the Swiss Confederation offered the chance to flee. Most Alsatian priests chose exile, but a small number remained with their parishioners or went into hiding.

By July 1794, 285 of the priests still in Alsace, including many too infirm to flee, had been arrested. They were first held as prisoners in the seminary in Strasbourg; most were later taken to Besançon. From Besançon, they were to be deported to Cayenne, in what is now French New Guinea, but the British navy blocked the way. Instead many were sent to the Île d'Aix near La Rochelle.[60]

The policy of dechristianization was anything but a success in Alsace. Although the Christian churches had been officially closed, the new cult of reason won little support among the people. Catholic worship continued in private. Alsatians held Sunday services even during the worst persecutions.[61]

In contrast to the Catholic majority, Alsace's Protestants retained a positive attitude toward the Revolution during 1791 and 1792. They became model citizens, distinguishing themselves by their lack of political extremism and their support for public order.[62] The Civil Constitution of the Clergy caused few problems for them, and their ministers cooperated with the local administration and obeyed the law. Consequently, Protestants, in contrast to Alsatian Catholics and Jews, did not find themselves the subject of polemical pamphlets during the early years of the Revolution.

The Protestants' attitude toward war is of special interest. When war was declared in April 1792, it was mostly in Protestant communities that volunteer battalions were formed in Alsace. According to Rodolphe Reuss, many more Catholics than Protestants later deserted these units.[63] In March 1792, the Protestant congregations of Alsace voluntarily handed over surplus church bells to the local administration. These congregations also prayed for the French army. One of the few surviving sources documenting a Protestant clergyman's attitude toward the war is a speech that Pastor Johann-Friedrich

59 Ibid.
60 Muller and Varry, *Hommes de Dieu et Révolution en Alsace*, 158.
61 See Claude Muller, *Dieu est catholique et alsacien: La vitalité du diocèse de Strasbourg au XIXe siècle: 1802–1914*, 2 vols. (Lille, 1987).
62 Vogler, *Histoire politique*, 25.   63 Reuss, *Les églises protestantes*, 119.

Oberlin delivered to volunteers in his congregation in the Ban-de-la-Roche area in the Vosges on August 5, 1792:

Act, dear friends, act in all spheres of life in such a way that our sermons and the grace of God can rest in you. When you enter a hostile country, remember that we are not enemies of the people; we have sworn this. The French princes, the deserters, the emigrants, the King of Prussia, the German Emperor are our enemies and not their subjects. Show compassion for them, helpfulness to everybody.... [A]nd if one of you were to find his grave far from here he will see that the countries where God and our duties lead us to are the closest to heaven.[64]

It is interesting that this document also contains the slogan "War on the palaces, peace to the huts" and that the topic of death for the fatherland is vividly discussed.

Amid the continuing radicalization, some Protestants turned hostile to the Revolution. Pastor Jean-Jacques Fischer of Dorlisheim was the most striking example.[65] Although he had become an official in the local administration, he criticized the persecution of the nonjuring priests and the sale of church property. After publicly expressing his joy about the advance of the coalition army, he was arrested by the local revolutionary committee. On November 24, 1793, he was sentenced to death and guillotined. Fischer was the only Protestant minister in Alsace to fall victim to the Revolution in this manner.

Protestants could not accept the execution of Louis XVI and thus broke with the Revolution in early 1793.[66] As Protestants withdrew their support for the Revolution, they became targets of revolutionary criticism and repression. Eulogius Schneider's paper *Argos*, for example, increasingly attacked them.[67] The Jacobins regarded Protestants as aristocrats and traitors. In the fall of 1793, the Revolution's antireligious policies were extended to Protestants, too. Their services were forbidden and churches closed. The Lutheran Temple Neuf in Strasbourg was turned into a warehouse for animal fodder and then used as a pigsty. The Lutheran churches of St. William and Young St. Peter became barns, St. Thomas a military depot, and St. Nicolas a pigsty and then a warehouse for clothing.[68] Religious ornaments were confiscated from Protestant churches, as they had been from Catholic churches. Alsatian Protestant and Catholic clergy were now incarcerated

---

64 "Exhortation faite par le Sieur Oberlin Ministre de Waldersbach au Ban de la Roche, aux Volontaires de sa paroisse, avant leur départ dimanche 5 aout 1792." Archives Municipales de Strasbourg (Fonds Oberlin 77Z.323).
65 Michel Erbe and Claude Muller, "Les vicissitudes du culte sous la Révolution à Dorlisheim," *Annuaire d'Histoire et d'Archéologie de Molsheim et Environs* 24 (1983): 113.
66 Bernard Vogler, "Les protestants et la Révolution," *Revue d'Alsace* 116 (1989–90): 200–2.
67 Ibid.   68 Ibid., 75.

together in the former seminary in Strasbourg. During his imprisonment, a second Protestant minister, Jean-Michel Lobstein, died of ill health. Twelve Protestant ministers were quickly transported to Besançon for deportation to Cayenne. Another twenty Lutheran ministers (out of 220) left office during the Reign of Terror.[69]

On the whole, however, Protestants were less affected than Catholics by dechristianization. They continued to worship, often in schools or private homes. Dechristianization was aimed primarily at the sacraments, so Catholics were more affected. The well-known Lutheran pastor Johann-Friedrich Oberlin reportedly characterized the Terror as a temporary period of disorder, which would have salutary effects:

What is taking place right now can be compared to a Saturday: everything is being cleaned for Sunday. The furniture is carried outside, everything is to be dusted. People sweep, wipe, scrub, and disorder becomes unavoidable. A large cloud of dust arises, which prevents us from breathing and seeing clearly. Some arms and feet become disjointed, pieces of furniture are occasionally damaged in such an intensive cleanup. People mend and repair everything and get the impression that everything looks better than before. After the parlor has been scrubbed, the furniture is put back, piece by piece. Order and cleanliness follow disorder, the result of the terrible disorder that reigned before. On Sunday, then, everything looks beautiful and is sparkling clean. The head of the household, who was absent on Saturday, returns, and it looks as if he, without saying so, finds his home in a better state than on Friday.[70]

The emancipation of the Alsatian Jews ended the legal discrimination against them, but social discrimination continued. Few could turn to agriculture. Most continued their traditional activities as small traders. In one area, the head tax for Jews was abolished, but elsewhere Jews were ordered to pay back taxes.[71] Most Jews were spared direct attack until the beginning of the Terror, but they sometimes became targets of anti-Revolutionary propaganda. Toward the end of 1792, attacks occurred in several places. In Barr, the houses of the towns' Jewish residents were plundered following rumors implicating them in the persecution of nonjuring priests. The district administration attempted to punish those responsible for spreading the rumor.[72]

Government officials in Alsace denied the repeated requests from Jews serving in the National Guard to be allowed to arrange for substitutes on

69 Reuss, *Les églises protestantes*, 135.
70 Octavie de Berckheim, *Souvenirs d'Alace: Correspondane des Demoiselles de Berckheim et de leurs amis précédée d'un extrait du Journal de Mlle Octavie de Berckheim*, 2 vols. (Paris, 1895) 1:110–11.
71 See Rodolphe Reuss, "L'antisémitisme dans le Bas-Rhin," 246–63.
72 Ibid., 259.

the Sabbath. These requests were denied on the grounds that Jews now had the full obligations as well as the full rights of French citizenship. At the beginning of 1793, newspapers in Alsace, above all in Strasbourg, stepped up their attacks on the Jews. One notable exception was Schneider's *Argos*, which, citing the equality of all men and freedom of religion, defended the Jews.

After a decree of November 9, 1793, had closed all religious buildings in Alsace, the district administration in Strasbourg proceeded against the Jews. The synagogue and Jewish butcher shops were closed. Circumcision was outlawed, as was the wearing of full beards and tall black hats.[73] The Jacobins began to brand Jews as bad citizens, and the authorities ordered the burning of books in Hebrew, including the Talmud.[74] Prominent members of Jewish communities – for example, the cantors and butchers in Selestat and Colmar – were imprisoned. Religious objects were confiscated from synagogues and melted down. In the spring of 1794, the Jacobin club in Strasbourg debated whether the Jews should be expelled from Alsace or, indeed, all of France. Like many Catholics and Protestants in Alsace, Jews continued to practice their faith in secret despite the measures enacted to suppress religious worship.

Religious persecution was relaxed after moderate revolutionaries seized power in Paris in the wake of Robespierre's fall. A decree issued in February 1795 granted freedom of worship. Churches reopened shortly thereafter, and many émigré priests were able to return to Alsace without having to swear the oath. After Brendel had resigned from office, the episcopal chair in Strasbourg remained vacant until the reign of Napoleon.[75]

The first Revolutionary war was an ideological matter, an attempt to realize principles that stood in contrast to the tradition and religion of the people in Alsace. These new ideological principles were to be forced on the population, regardless of regional or denominational traditions and privileges. The war led to radicalization, the replacement of the Revolution's original ideas with totalitarian concepts. The radical Weltanschauung that claimed the mantle of pure reason assaulted freedom of religion and of conscience. The repudiation of the basic rights of man, which had been enunciated earlier in the Revolution, drove people from their homes. Alsatians fled their homes en masse less to escape war and its attendant violence than to avoid the reprisals they feared the revolutionary regime would inflict on

73 Muller and Varry, *Hommes de Dieu*, 165.
74 See Geneviève Herberich-Marx and Freddy Raphael, "L'imagerie religieuse durant la Révolution en Alsace, L'œuvre au noir," *Revue d'Alsace* 116 (1989–90): 339–40.
75 Epp, "De la Révolution à l'Annexion," 185.

those who had resisted it. As explained earlier, civilians in Alsace were more affected by the political consequences of the war than by warfare. It was above all the collateral effects of the war in Alsace like the ideological struggles over religion that touched the faithful. In this exposed border region, which was endangered by the threat of war and invasion, the ideological fights took place behind the lines. One can talk of a double war experience. On the one hand, people were confronted with the state's demands for men, money, and supplies for the army. On the other, there were the ideological conflicts prompted by the Revolution's increasingly radical religious policy. In this context, the Lutheran theologian Johann Lorenz Blessig of Strasbourg talked of a war against inner and outer enemies that the people had suffered: "We survived a double war, an inner war against oppressors, an outer war against hostile enemies."[76] Describing, however, the situation he and his coreligionists in Strasbourg faced in 1793, Blessig wrote: "[A]nd throughout the most terrible acts of war which took place only one hour away from us, did we not act as if we were living in a totally different part of the world? You heard the war, you saw it, but you didn't experience it. God in his great mercy received you in his home on the day of fear."[77] This quotation makes evident that the war, at least from a Strasbourg perspective, only played a secondary role in the perception of the people. In the years after 1792, the Revolution's antireligious policies went hand in hand with the diverse measures enacted to mobilize the nation for war.[78] It was in particular the devoutly religious population of Alsace who were affected by those measures. As the Revolutionary war effort approached something like total war and infringed increasingly on religious life, more and more Alsatians rejected the Revolution and all it represented.

Given the variety of religious denominations and traditions in Alsace, the Revolution's abstract political philosophy could be implemented there only with great difficulty and against dogged resistance. The kinds of state-controlled religious institutions associated with the term *Gallicanism* were as unimaginable in Alsace as was the idea of a state religion based on reason. In Alsace, regional consciousness was inseparable from denominational variety and the coexistence of confessions.

---

76 Predigt bey dem Ernste-Herbst und Friedens-Fest den XXIV. Trinit. 1801 in der Neuen Kirche gesprochen von D. Johann Lorenz Blessig. Voran gehet eine Rede über Ordnung, nebst einem Gebet um den Frieden bey einem feyerlichen Anlasse gesprochen (BNUS M104377), 33.

77 Ibid., 28.

78 See also Roland Marx: "De la Pré-Révolution à la Restauration," in *Histoire de l'Alsace; Univers de la France et des pays francophones; Histoire des provinces*, ed. Philippe Dollinger, 2 vols. (Toulouse, 1970), 1: 356–8.

17

The Military and Masculinity

Gendering the History of the Revolutionary and Napoleonic Wars, 1792–1815

KAREN HAGEMANN

"Who is a Man?" asked the well-known political writer Ernst Moritz Arndt in a poem that first appeared in February 1813 in the appendix to the *Kurzer Katechismus für Deutsche Soldaten* (Brief Catechism for German Soldiers). This question occupied not only him but also his contemporaries to a degree scarcely imaginable nowadays. Diverse images of masculinity developed in the period of the Napoleonic Wars. Arndt, for example, formulated one in his poem:

> He is a man prepared to fight,
> For his wife and his dear child;
> For a cold breast lacks will and might,
> And its deeds will be as wind.
>
> He is a man prepared to die,
> For God and fatherland,
> Until the grave he'll carry on
> With heart and voice and hand.
>
> He is a man prepared to die,
> For liberty, duty, and right:
> A God-fearing heart knows all is well,
> His step is ever light.
>
> So, German man, so free man,
> With God your lord to the foe!
> For God alone can aid your cause,
> And luck and victory bestow.[1]

1 Ernst-Moritz Arndt, *Kurzer Katechismus* (n.p., 1813).

The fourth Section of this chapter (346–51) is based on an article that Stefan Dudink and I wrote together (see *infra* note 4). I would like to thank him for the ongoing cooperation in our research on masculinity during the age of democratic revolutions. I would also like to thank Alan Forrest and Laurence Hare for their comments on an earlier version of this paper, and Pamela E. Selwyn for her support with the translation.

The *Kurzer Katechismus* was one of the most widely disseminated propaganda texts during the wars of 1813–14. The Prussian army printed and distributed an estimated eighty thousand copies. In it, Arndt campaigned on behalf of general conscription without proxies or exemption, as he tried to mobilize Prussian and German men for the war against Napoleon.[2] In this poem, as in others in the *Kurzer Katechismus*, he entreated German men to recall their core virtues. Along with military valor, these included love of liberty and country, piety, strength, and courage – manly virtues, he asserted, that their Germanic forefathers had demonstrated. At the center of this model of masculinity was the inseparable equation of masculinity (*Männlichkeit*); military valor (*Wehrhaftigkeit*), a man's willingness to defend his family, home, and fatherland; and patriotism (*Vaterlandsliebe*), understood as the unconditional, self-sacrificing love of fatherland.[3]

This relationship among military valor, patriotism, and masculinity played a central role in contemporary political discourses far beyond Prussia's borders, but it has long been overlooked in historical scholarship on the Revolutionary and Napoleonic Wars. For many historians, this relationship appears to be so self-evident that it is not worth mentioning. Politics and war have become the seemingly natural provinces of masculinity – a masculinity that has sometimes been explicit but more often masked by the equation of *man* with *human* and *mankind*, terms that conceal masculinity within discourses of general interest and universality.[4]

If we want to gender the history of the French Wars, we need to deconstruct these discourses.[5] To this end, it is not enough to focus on women as historical agents or to analyze concepts of femininity. Rather, gender research needs to become more open to the study of men and masculinities. The concept of gender as introduced by Joan Scott is the most productive one for this purpose. She defines *gender* as the knowledge about sexual differences produced by culture and society. This knowledge is neither absolute nor true; it is always relative and manufactured within complex discursive contexts. It is a manner of ordering the world hierarchically and

2 Karl-Heinz Schäfer, *Ernst Moritz Arndt als politischer Publizist. Studien zu Publizistik, Pressepolitik und kollektivem Bewußtsein im frühen 19. Jahrhundert* (Bonn, 1974), 174ff.
3 Karen Hagemann, *"Mannlicher Muth und Teutsche Ehre": Nation, Militär und Geschlecht zur Zeit der Antinapoleonischen Kriege Preußens* (Paderborn, 2002), 271–350; Hagemann, "Of 'Manly Valor' and 'German Honor': Nation, War and Masculinity in the Age of the Prussian Uprising against Napoleon," *Central European History* 30 (1997): 187–220.
4 Stefan Dudink and Karen Hagemann, "Masculinity in Politics and War in the Age of Democratic Revolutions, 1750–1850," in *Masculinities in Politics and War: Gendering Modern History*, ed. Stefan Dudink, Karen Hagemann, and John Tosh (Manchester, U.K., 2004), 3–21.
5 Charles Esdaile, *The French Wars, 1792–1815* (London, 2001).

asymmetrically that is linked with political and social organization.[6] Such a concept of gender makes it possible to analyze as gendered even those subjects previously conceived of as gender neutral and universal, and thus to deconstruct their internal or implicit value judgments and hierarchies.

This deconstruction should also be the main object of an analysis of the interactions among gender, politics, and war in the period of the Revolutionary and Napoleonic Wars. Such a gendered analysis shows that an either-or approach for the analysis of this period (e.g., its interpretation as revolutionary or anti- or nonrevolutionary, modern or traditional, national or indifferent, reform or restoration) does not help us grasp the ambiguities and paradoxes of this time of accelerated change. The sometimes sudden and dramatic transformations in the economy, politics, the military, and society not only occurred unevenly across Europe but also accompanied stagnation and the persistence of tradition in other areas of work and life, particularly in the culture of everyday life. This paradox, the concurrence of nonsimultaneity (*Gleichzeitigkeit von Ungleichzeitigkeiten*), was one of the chief characteristics of this period.[7] Contemporaries therefore perceived it as an "unstable" and "insecure" time of "rapid transition" and "upheaval."[8] They had to cope with the paradox of accelerated change and cultural persistence. The mentality and thinking of people changed profoundly and lastingly in this period. Alongside the French Revolution, the experiences of the wars between 1792 and 1815 seem to have played an important part here.[9]

As a key category of difference during this period, gender played a critical new role at both the structural level and the levels of experience, practice, and discourse.[10] In interaction with other categories of difference such as class, race, ethnicity, religion, age, and familial status,

---

6 Joan W. Scott, "Gender: A Useful Category of Historical Analysis," *American Historical Review* 98 (1986), 1053–75; see also John Tosh, "Hegemonic Masculinity and the History of Gender," in Dudink et al., *Masculinities*, 41–60.

7 Michael Broers, *Europe under Napoleon, 1799–1815* (London, 1996); Philip Dwyer ed., *Napoleon and Europe* (London, 2001); Michael Rowe, ed., *Collaboration and Resistance in Napoleonic Europe: State Formation in an Age of Upheaval, c. 1800–1815* (Basingstoke, U.K., 2003).

8 Quotations from the German-national writers and publishers Friedrich Perthes and Ernst Moritz Arndt in Hagemann, *Muth*, 186; see also Ernst Wolfgang Becker, *Zeit der Revolution! – Revolution der Zeit? Zeiterfahrungen in Deutschland in der Ära der Revolutionen 1789–1848/49* (Göttingen, 1999).

9 Werner K. Blessing, "Umbruchkrise und 'Verstörung'. Die 'Napoleonische' Erschütterung und ihre sozialpsychologische Bedeutung (Bayern als Beispiel)," *Zeitschrift für Bayerische Landesgeschichte* 42 (1979): 75–106; Bernd v. Münchow-Pohl, *Zwischen Reform und Krieg. Untersuchungen zur Bewußtseinslage in Preußen 1809–1812* (Göttingen, 1987); John E. Cookson, *British Society and the French Wars, 1793–1815* (Oxford, 1985); Simon Burrows, *Culture and Misperception: The Law and the Press in the Outbreak of War in 1803* (Cambridge, U.K., 1996).

10 As an example for the gender differences in war experiences and memories: Karen Hagemann, "Reconstructing 'Front' and 'Home'; Gendered Experiences and Memories of the German Wars against Napoleon – A Case Study," *War in History* 16 (2009):25–50.

gender helped to create order by constructing distinctions, asymmetries, and hierarchies. For the analysis of this period of war, as for others, gender is therefore an important marker of the changes and continuities, the ambiguities and paradoxes in war, society, and culture. It is a central indicator of the intensity and totality of war because it marks most strongly the blurring of the lines constructed between the military and civilian realms.[11] By focusing on gender, we can identify one of the most important changes in European societies and cultures during the Revolutionary and Napoleonic wars. For the first time, the military and civil society alike were mobilized all over Europe for war on a hitherto-unknown scale. These were the first modern wars, if not, as David Bell recently argued, the first total wars.[12] Because the historiography of the Revolutionary and Napoleonic wars has often focused exclusively either on the military or on politics, civilian society, or culture and in general has ignored the gender dimension, the modern character of these wars has tended to be overlooked.[13]

This chapter emphasizes the importance of culture and gender to an analysis of this period. It compares the debates on universal military service and citizenship, their gendered meanings, and their cultural representations in France and Prussia – two different societies and political systems. In both cases, the essay focuses on the moment when civic duties and rights became associated with military service. To situate these debates in their historical context, the analysis begins with some thoughts on the character of the

11 The erasure of the lines separating the military and civilian realms is defined as one of the chief characteristics of any total war that results from the interplay among the four ideal-typical elements of a total war: the totality of war aims, methods, mobilization, and control. See Stig Förster, "Das Zeitalter des totalen Krieges, 1861–1945," *Mittelweg* 36, no. 8 (1999), 12–29.

12 David A. Bell, *The First Total War: Napoleon's Europe and the Birth of Warfare as We Know It* (Boston, 2007).

13 See, most recently, "Gender, War and the Nation in the Period of the Revolutionary and Napoleonic Wars – European Perspectives," ed. Katherine Aaslestad, Karen Hagemann, and Judith Miller, special issue, *European History Quarterly* 37, no. 4 (2007); and Karen Hagemann, Gisela Mettele, and Jane Rendall, eds., *Gender, War, and Politics: Transatlantic Perspectives, 1775–1830* (forthcoming); Linda Colley, *Britons: Forging the Nation, 1707–1837* (New Haven, Connecticut, 1992); Hagemann, *Muth*; Dirk Reder, *Frauenbewegung und Nation: Patriotische Frauenvereine in Deutschland im frühen 19. Jahrhundert (1813–1830)* (Cologne, 1998). Claudia Opitz, "Der Bürger wird Soldat und die Bürgerin? Die Revolution, der Krieg und die Stellung der Frauen nach 1789," in *Sklavin oder Bürgerin. Französische Revolution und neue Weiblichkeit 1760–1830*, ed. Viktoria Schmidt-Linsenhoff (Marburg, 1989), 38–54; Karen Hagemann, "A Valorous Volk Family: The Nation, the Military, and the Gender Order in Prussia in the Time of the Anti-Napoleonic Wars, 1806–15," in *Gendered Nations: Nationalisms and Gender Order in the Long Nineteenth Century*, ed. Ida Blom, Karen Hagemann, and Christine Hall. (Oxford, 2000), 179–205; Karen Hagemann, "Female Patriots: Women, War and the Nation in the Period of the Prussian-German Anti-Napoleonic Wars," *Gender and History* 16, no. 3 (2004), 396–424; Patricia Y. C. E. Lin, "Citizenship, Military, Families and the Creation of a New Definition of 'Deserving Poor' in Britain, 1793–1815," *Social Politics* 7 (2000), 5–46; Emma Vincent Macleod, "Women at War: British Women and the Debate on the Wars against Revolutionary France in the 1790s," *Enlightenment and Dissent* 15 (1996), 3–32; John Lawrence Tone, "Spanish Women in the Resistance to Napoleon, 1808–1814," in *Constructing Spanish Womanhood: Female Identity in Modern Spain*, ed. Victoria Lorée Enders and Pamela Beth (New York, 1999), 259–82.

Revolutionary and Napoleonic wars and their effects on the gender order. It then presents visual representations of this wartime gender order. Finally, it contrasts them in an analysis of the notions of masculinity, conscription, and citizenship that were produced in the French and Prussian discourses.

MASS ARMIES, NATIONAL WARS, AND THE GENDER ORDER

No period between the Thirty Years' War and the First World War influenced European history more profoundly or lastingly than the era of the Revolutionary and Napoleonic wars. These first modern wars extended well beyond Europe's shores and lasted more than twenty years.[14] They were the first to be conducted as national wars, with mass armies legitimized through patriotic-national propaganda.[15] France introduced the levée en masse in 1793, followed by a conscription system with proxies and exemptions in 1798. The number of soldiers mobilized surpassed anything previously seen in Europe. More than 2 million Frenchmen – 7 percent of the male population – served between 1792 and 1813. Half of them never returned home.[16] Conscripts from annexed and neighboring regions added another 1 million soldiers. The Grande Armée thus reached enormous proportions. Napoleon is said to have marched on Russia with some 650,000 men in 1812, more than half of them provided by France's allies.[17]

To face this massive force, France's enemies also had to introduce forms of mass recruitment. Austria, for example, introduced a militia in 1808 and mustered some 150,000 militiamen to fight alongside its standing army

14 See Stig Förster, "Der Weltkrieg, 1792 bis 1815: Bewaffnete Konflikte und Revolutionen in der Weltgeschichte," in *Kriegsbereitschaft und Friedensordnung in Deutschland 1800–1814*, ed. Jost Dülffer (Münster, 1995), 17–38; Paul Fregosi, *Dreams of Empire: Napoleon and the First World War, 1792–1815* (London, 1989).

15 The term *patriotic-national* indicates the ambiguous character of the discourse, which mixed old an new elements of political rhetoric; see Miroslav Hroch, "From National Movement to the Fully-Formed Nation: The Nation-Building Process in Europe," in *Becoming National: A Reader*, ed. Geoff Eley and Ronald G. Suny (New York, 1996), 60–77, 62. On the importance of war propaganda, see Alan Forrest, "'La patrie en danger': The French Revolution and the First Levée en masse," in *The People in Arms: Military Myth and National Mobilization since the French Revolution*, ed. Daniel Moran and Arthur Waldron (Cambridge, U.K., 2003), 8–32; Hagemann, *Muth*, 105–68; Hagemann, "Francophobia and Patriotism: Images of Napoleon and 'the French' in Prussia and Northern Germany at the Period of the Anti-Napoleonic Wars, 1806–1815," *French History* 18, no. 4 (2004), 1–22; Emma Vincent Macleod, *A War of Ideas: British Attitudes to the Wars against Revolutionary France, 1792–1802* (Brookfield, Vermont, 1998); Ernst Zehetbauer, *Landwehr gegen Napoleon. Österreichs erste Miliz und der Nationalkrieg von 1809* (Vienna, 1999), 220–52.

16 Alan Forrest, *Conscripts and Deserters: The Army and French Society during the Revolution and Empire* (New York, 1989), 20; Forrest, *The Soldiers of the French Revolution* (Durham, 1990); Forrest, *Napoleon's Men: The Soldiers of the Revolution and Empire* (London, 2002); Alain Pigeard, *La conscription au temps de Napoléon* (Paris, 2003).

17 Stuart Woolf, *Napoleon's Integration of Europe* (New York, 1991), 172–5; Geoffrey Ellis, *The Napoleonic Empire* (Basingstoke, U.K., 2003), 61–3.

against Napoleon during the Austro-French war of 1809.[18] Prussia introduced universal conscription without proxy or exemptions in March 1813. The following month, the Prussian field army grew to about 250,000 men, 46 percent of whom were militiamen and 8 percent volunteers. In 1813, more than 10 percent of the Prussian male population was mobilized for war; in 1806, the figure had been 2 percent.[19] Russia, too, recruited an impressive army through a traditional conscription system, and 240,000 men – mainly conscripts – marched against Napoleon in 1812.[20] The prerequisite for an efficient deployment of these mass armies was reform of the military system. The states of the ancien régime had to adapt their methods of warfare to those of the French foe to adopt a more offensive strategy.[21]

Conducting war on this scale required broad popular support. Military mobilization of this extent could not have been based on coercion alone.[22] as in many other states, In France and Prussia, it was preceded and accompanied by intense patriotic propaganda. Bourgeois men in particular, who had previously been exempt from military service and often felt considerable antipathy toward it, had to be motivated to take up arms.[23] War was legitimized as national war. It was no longer the exclusive province of governments and armies. With the French Revolution, war became, as Carl von Clausewitz observed, "the affair of a people numbering thirty million, every one of whom regarded himself as a citizen."[24] In France in 1792–3, as in Prussia in 1813, propaganda revolved around the idea that men were duty-bound as citizens, fathers, and brothers to defend their families,

---

18 Zehetbauer, *Landwehr*.   19 Hagemann, *Muth*, 36–40.
20 Alexander Martin, "The Russian Empire and the Napoleonic Wars," in Dwyer, *Napoleon*, 243–63, 258.
21 Horst Carl, "Der Mythos des Befreiungskrieges – Krieg und martialische Nation im Zeitalter der Revolutions- und Befreiungskriege 1792–1815," in *Föderative Nation – Zeitgenössische Vorstellungen vom 16. bis zum 19. Jahrhundert*, ed. Dieter Langewiesche and Georg Schmidt (Munich, 2000), 63–82; Jean-Paul Bertraud, *La Révolution armée: les soldats-citoyens et la Révolution Française* (Paris, 1979); Cookson, *Armed Nation*; Hagemann, *Muth*, 73–104; Dierk Walter, *Preußische Heeresreformen 1807–1870. Militärische Innovation und der Mythos der "Roonschen Reform"* (Paderborn, 2003), 235–324.
22 Forrest, *Conscripts*; Josef Smets, "Von der 'Dorfidylle' zur preußischen Nation. Sozialdisziplinierung der linksrheinischen Bevölkerung durch die Franzosen am Beispiel der allgemeinen Wehrpflicht (1802–1814)," *Historische Zeitschrift* 262 (1996), 695–738; Hagemann, *Muth*, 397–404.
23 Wolfgang Kruse, *Die Erfindung des modernen Militarismus. Krieg, Militär und bürgerliche Gesellschaft im politischen Diskurs der Französischen Revolution 1789–1799* (Munich, 2003), 129–266; Isser Woloch, "The Napoleonic Regime and French Society," Dwyer, *Napoleon*, 60–78; Hagemann, *Muth*, 396–426; Zehetbauer, *Landwehr*; Martin "Russian Empire"; Janet Harteley, "The Patriotism of the Russian Army in the 'Patriotic' or 'Fatherland' War of 1812," in *Popular Resistance in the French Wars: Patriots, Partisans and Land Pirates*, ed. Chares J. Esdaile (London, 2005), 181–200; John L. Tone, "The Peninsular War," in Dwyer, *Napoleon*, 225–42; Cookson, *Society*; Clive Emsley, *British Society and the French Wars 1793–1815* (London, 1979).
24 Carl von Clausewitz, *Vom Kriege. Hinterlassenes Werk* (Berlin, 1999), 667.

homes, and country. In this way, the willingness to fight was intertwined with masculinity. The hero's death was now open for the first time to every man; it was deemed the highest form of patriotism. The man who was a fatherland-loving citizen, who was willing to fight and die for his nation, and who demanded representation in the government became the new masculine ideal for the society of citizens.[25]

From the Greeks through the Renaissance city-states, republicanism had been tied to the notion of a self-governing community of men under arms. Its hallmark was the citizen militia rather than an army commanded by aristocrats and staffed by mercenaries. No experiment in republican or democratic self-government before the French Revolution had, however, resorted to universal military service and linked it to political rights – even if those rights were restricted to men of property and education. Accordingly, the forms of mobilization introduced in different countries during the wars between 1792 and 1815 dramatically altered eligibility for military service, and they required a new rhetoric to legitimate this change as they induced men to fight.[26]

The new form of warfare had two far-reaching consequences. One was a sharp rise in casualties. At some 5 million, the number of war dead (including civilians) between 1792 and 1815 approached the dimensions of the First World War, calculated in terms of victims per population.[27] Only a minority of the victims were soldiers who died in battle, however. Most perished because of injuries, disease, and epidemics that also affected the civilian population. The Russian campaign was the most lethal. Only 25,000 of the 650,000 men in the Grande Armée who marched on Russia returned home.[28] Families all over Europe lost fathers, brothers, and sons. Thousands more soldiers returned home disabled and faced the prospect of trying to survive without adequate state support.

The other consequence of the new form of warfare was that military engagements, troop movements, occupation, and annexation affected civil society more deeply than during any of the eighteenth-century wars.[29] The costs of the new mass warfare were paid primarily by civilians. Old systems of supply through state repositories had to be replaced by new

25 Hagemann, "Of 'Manly' Valor," 218–19; Hagemann, "German Heroes: The Cult of the Death for the Fatherland in Nineteenth-Century Germany," in Dudink et al., *Masculinities*, 116–34; George Mosse, *Gefallen für das Vaterland: Nationales Heldentum und namenloses Sterben* (Stuttgart, 1993).
26 Joan B. Landes, *Visualizing the Nation: Gender, Representation, and Revolution in Eighteenth-Century France* (Ithaca, New York, 2001), 106–7.
27 David Gates, *The Napoleonic Wars, 1803–1815* (London, 1997), 272.
28 Martin, "Russian Empire," 260.
29 Blessing, "Umbruchkrise," 75–106; Woolf, *Napoleon's Integration*, 156–64; Emsley, *Society*.

requisitions systems. The lands that mass armies crossed had to feed them. In this respect, these armies did not distinguish between friend and foe. The civilian population therefore had to finance the wars not only by means of higher taxes and tariffs but also by providing all kinds of goods – not just weapons and uniforms but also other clothes and food, animals, and carts. In the occupied regions, they also had to make contributions.[30] An additional factor was the harsh economic effects of war. Most disruptive in this respect was the Continental System, which devastated the economy after 1806, particularly in the French-occupied territories of northern Germany.[31]

The new form of mass war could only be fought successfully if the civilian population – men and women alike – was mobilized as well. They had to support the war financially and practically. The levée en masse in August 1793 set out a clear wartime gender order for France: young men of military age were to become soldiers, and old men were to support the war effort with material and ideas. Women, by contrast, were to ensure that the warriors were equipped with tents and uniforms, to care for sick and wounded soldiers, and to bolster the men's fighting resolve. They should become "republican mothers."[32] Political differences notwithstanding, the same principles informed the Prussian propaganda that accompanied the introduction of universal military service. For without the support of substantial parts of the civilian population, monarchical Prussia could not have launched the wars of liberation against France. The national emergency of the wars of 1813 thus opened opportunities for noble and middle-class women in arenas of public life that had previously been closed to them. They were allowed – it was said – to expand their "motherly duties" beyond their families because the "fatherland was in danger." Some 420 patriotic women's associations were active during the wars of 1813–15 in Prussia alone. They collected money and material, and they organized wartime nursing and relief work.[33] Although most of these associations ceased their activities after the wars, they remained an important model for the middle-class women's movement that emerged later in the century. Recent research suggests that similar developments took place in other European countries during the Napoleonic Wars.[34]

---

30 Alexander Grab, "State, Society and Tax Policy in Napoleonic Europe," in Dwyer, *Napoleon*, 168–86.
31 François Crouzet and Eric Aerts, eds., *Economic Effects of the French Revolutionary and Napoleonic Wars* (Louvain, 1990); Woolf, *Napoleon's Integration*, 133–84; Broers, *Europe*, 144–233.
32 Opitz "Bürgerinnen"; Harriet B. Applewhite and Darline G. Levy, "Women and Militant Citizenship in Revolutionary Paris," in *Rebel Daughters: Women and the French Revolution*, ed. Sara E. Melzer and Leslie W. Kabine (New York, 1992), 79–101.
33 Reder, *Frauenbewegung*; Hagemann, "Female Patriots."
34 Colley, *Britons*, 237–82; Macleod, "Women"; Lin, "Citizenship."

The new demands that national mass wars placed on both men and women rested on changes in ideas about the gender order that had been introduced in the second half of the eighteenth century. Traditional Christian and corporatist legitimations of gender difference came under attack during the Enlightenment and were replaced by an anthropological mode of explanation. Gender differences were now generally regarded as rooted in men's and women's different physiology and natures. This proposition assigned men and women tasks in the state, military, economy, and society that were defined as complementary.[35] The reigning notions of the bourgeois gender order assigned – to quote a German writer of the time – "man the public and woman the domestic sphere, man the universal and woman the particular, man the business of the world and woman the affairs of the family."[36] These attributions hardened in the context of continuing warfare after 1792, as universal conscription in principle assigned all men the duty to defend family, home, and country.[37] At the same time, women not only were excluded from state affairs but were also assigned the primary task of being housewives and mothers, regardless of social distinctions. As Ernst Moritz Arndt put it in his *Basic Outlines of a German Military Order* in 1813:

> And if man does not bear arms,
> And woman does not tend to the hearth,
> In the long run all must go awry,
> And house and empire be ruined at last.[38]

Arndt not only accorded the gender order a central role in the proper functioning of the state order but also described its collapse as a cause of national division and decline.

VISUAL REPRESENTATIONS OF WARTIME GENDER ORDERS

The existing scholarship suggests that between 1792 and 1815 war was as important for recasting gender relations as gender images were for mobilizing men and women. At first sight, moreover, the basic structures of the gender order of wartime society in France and Prussia were similar,

---

35 Claudia Honegger, *Die Ordnung der Geschlechter. Die Wissenschaft vom Menschen und das Weib 1750–1850* (Frankfurt, 1991), 186–99; Karin Hausen, "Family and Role Division: The Polarisation of Sexual Stereotypes in the Nineteenth Century – An Aspect of the Dissociation of Work and Family," in *The German Family: Essays on the Social History of the Family in Nineteenth- and Twentieth-Century Germany*, ed. Richard J. Evans and W. R. Lee (London, 1981), 51–83.
36 Friedrich Ehrenberg, *Der Charakter und die Bestimmung des Mannes*, 2nd ed. (Elberfeld, 1822), 11–12.
37 Karen Hagemann, "Of 'Manly' Valor," 187–220; Hagemann, "A Valorous Volk Family."
38 Ernst Moritz Arndt, *Grundlinien einer teutschen Kriegsordnung* (n.p., [1813]).

despite their political differences. The visual representations of this gender order in the two enemy states confirm this impression.

A central motif was the departure of the volunteer, who was portrayed as the embodiment of the heroic masculine ideal. In both France and Prussia, the early images that accompanied the introduction of the levée en masse or universal compulsory service displayed similar pictorial features. These features were captured in an oil painting of 1792 by Francois Louis Joseph Watteau de Lille titled *The Departure of the Volunteer*, which was widely disseminated as an engraving (Figure 1). The volunteer's mother looks worried, his father determined, and his young wife fearful. This gender- and age-specific division of emotional labor can also be found in Jacques-Louis David's well-known painting *The Oath of the Horatii* (1784), which invoked the republican tradition of heroic masculinity and its feminine counterpart (Figure 2).[39] In the context of the levée en masse, however, this division of labor was democratized. The scene shifted to the present, for every man, as a citizen, now had both the right and the duty to defend family and country. Similar pictorial language was common in Prussia in 1813. The print by Johann Heinrich Jügel, *Two Riflemen Bid Farewell to Their Parents*, was widely reprinted (Figure 3). It shows two young volunteers, presumably brothers, saying good-bye to their family. Their father offers encouragement, their mother and sister look concerned, and their younger brother looks disgruntled because he is too young to go to war.[40]

In a similar historical situation the patriotic discourse of the two enemy states invoked the nation as a *Volk* family, in which every member was assigned a patriotic duty suitable to his or her status, age, and sex. At the center of this *Volk* family stood the volunteer or conscript who was protecting the family and the fatherland according to his autonomous, free, and manly will.[41] Images of the nation as a *Volk* family are evident in both French and Prussian pictorial representations.[42] On closer examination, however, dissimilarities reflect differences in the two social and political systems: whereas the French imagery is grounded in the Enlightenment

---

39 Joan B. Landes, "Republican Citizenship and Heterosocial Desire: Concepts of Masculinity in Revolutionary France," in Dudink et al., *Masculinity*, 96–116, 108–9; Alex Potts, "Beautiful Bodies and Dying Heroes," *History Workshop* 30 (1990), 1–21; Abigail Solomon-Godeau, *Male Trouble: A Crisis in Representation* (London, 1997).

40 Karen Hagemann, "Gendered Images of the German Nation: The Romantic Painter Friedrich Kersting and the Patriotic-national Discourse during the Wars of Liberation," *Nations and Nationalism* 12 (2006): 653–79.

41 Hagemann, *Muth*.

42 Lynn Hunt, *The Family Romance of the French Revolution* (Berkeley, California, 1992); Hagemann, "Volk Family," and *Muth*, 350–94.

Figure 1. François Louis Joseph Watteau de Lille, *The Departure of the Volunteer*, 1792 (Paris, Musée de la Ville de Paris [Musée Carnavalet]).

and classical antiquity, and rejects a religious idiom, traditional Christian views of the family unit dominate the Prussian imagery.

A French example of this contrast an oil painting of 1799 by Guillaume Guillon-Lethière, *The Fatherland Is in Danger*, which was exhibited with

Figure 2. Jacques-Louis David, *The Oath of the Horatii*, 1784 (Paris, Musée du Louvre).

great success at the Paris Salon and later disseminated as a print (Figure 4). The composition revolves around two groups. At the center is a mass of recruits who salute the seated statue of La Patrie – the Republic – with swords raised. La Patrie holds smaller figures of Liberty and Equality in one hand; her other hand rests on the fasces, which symbolize Liberty and Unity. One of the soldiers, about to take the oath, is captured at the moment of a passionate farewell kiss. To the left, a young woman holds up a child as if to sacrifice it to the fatherland, while on the right another woman steps forward with an armload of weapons. Whereas previous images of soldiers leaving for war – like the 1792 painting by Watteau de Lille – had generally portrayed feminine anxiety and grief as counterpoints to male courage and duty, this image depicts shared sacrifice willingly borne. Women, not just the state, send men to war, as the obligations to defend family and fatherland merge.[43]

A characteristic example of German patriotic imagery is the popular broadside *The Cultural Progress of the Human Race* by Johann Nußbiegel

43 Forrest, "La patrie," 23; see also Landes "Citizenship," 109–10.

Figure 3. Johann Heinrich Jügel, *Two Riflemen Bid Farewell to Their Parents*, 1813 (Staatliches Museum Schwerin)

Figure 4. Guillaume Guillon-Lethière, *The Fatherland is in Danger*, 1799 (Paris, Musée du Louvre).

(1815; Figure 5).[44] It, too, offers a representation of the gender order of national war. With the blessing of their father and mother, the sons go off to war as volunteers to "sacrifice themselves on the altar of the fatherland." Images of religious and military leaders on the wall point to the glorious tradition of this patriotic sacrifice. The daughters are sewing the soldiers' kit in the background, but the accompanying text praises their activity as being of equal value to the son's military service. Referring to the twofold victory over Napoleon, the poem asks:

> But who accomplished this splendid deed?
> Twice destroying the world-conqueror's power?
> Your people, O Herman! For the sacred sign
> Of the Cross consecrates the sons, who resemble you,
> And adorns your daughters, no sword-bearing
> Battling Amazons they,
> But, more womanly, tend the quiet household altar
> On behalf of the warrior host.
> Has there ever flourished in any corner of the earth
> A fatherland so rich in noble women?
> For God and them, and the honor of Germany's peoples,
> The young lads assemble to form an army,
> Enflamed by paternal blessings they go forth
> From mother's kiss to face a hero's death.
> The Lord's word accompanies them to war,
> But his hand and German courage to victory.[45]

Guillon-Lethière's painting and Nußbiegel's broadside share many motifs, but they also illustrate national differences. To be sure, an underlying structure transcended national differences in the gender-specific division of labor in wartime society. Even during the First and Second World Wars, propaganda invoked this structure, which was based on so-called universal, anthropologically legitimated gender differences. But this gender order was also charged in nationally specific terms, for it was linked to collective images of the self, the other, and the enemy. Contemporary notions of national character were gendered, while notions of gender-specific character were nationalized; in fact, these notions referred to each other across the frontlines.[46] The two pictures render political differences visible. The pictorial language of Guillon-Lethière's painting reflects the political tradition of the republic. The struggle is for liberty, equality, and unity. Christian symbolism is absent. Nußbiegel's broadside, by contrast, emphasizes the

---

44 Schmidt-Linsenhoff, *Sklavin*, 601–2.   45 Ibid., 601.
46 Schmidt-Linsenhoff, "Male Alterity in the French Revolution – Two Paintings by Anne-Louis Girodet at the Salon of 1898," in Blom et al., *Gendered Nations*, 81–106; Hagemann, *Muth*, 206–70.

Figure 5. Johann Nußbiegel, *The Cultural Progress of the Human Race*, 1813–14 (Germanisches Nationalmuseum Nuremberg).

Christian tradition. As the text accompanying the images explains, the struggle here is a "holy war" for liberation from the "world-conqueror" Napoleon.

The visual images employed in Revolutionary France and monarchical Prussia were in many ways similar. In both countries, imagery appealed to military valor, love of country and liberty, strength, and courage. But a closer look reveals differences. The French representations are more liberal and secular. They dwell less on the past, because the new political order has made a clean break, rejecting the central embodiments of the past, the king and the church. Although French Revolutionary artists added devotion to the Revolution to love of *la patrie* and *liberté*, much of the imagery they employed was traditional – the cult of antiquity and classical male heroism, the appeal to forgo personal interests for the common good, the idealization of heroic sacrifice as the supreme act of male independence and liberty. These themes were all present during the last years of the ancien régime before the French Revolutionaries adapted them.[47] The Prussian representations, too, praised male heroism and idealized heroic sacrifice as the supreme patriotic act, but unlike their French counterparts, they were informed by the Christian tradition and Prussia's military glory in the eighteenth century. Furthermore, Prussian patriots, artists, and writers propagated these values within the context of a traditional, hierarchical political order. They therefore incorporated crown and church in their representations.

UNIVERSAL MILITARY SERVICE AND MALE CITIZENSHIP

The political differences in these models of military values, citizenship, and masculinity become clearer in texts of the period addressing universal military service and male citizenship. The French model of the citizen-soldier stands in contrast here to the Prussian model of the burgher as national warrior.

When "the people" entered the stage in France, war and politics not only became connected with the Revolution; their relationship with each other changed as well. From 1789 onward, the revolutionaries introduced a new politics that drew on established ideas about republican masculinity but also profoundly changed them. "All men are citizens," the leaders of the French Revolution proclaimed. As France became ever more frequently entangled in war after 1792, the proposition that all men were equal citizens led to a corollary: because all men are citizens, all men should be soldiers.

---

47 Landes, "Citizenship"; Potts, "Beautiful Bodies."

Universal male citizenship was defined in the discourse of the French Revolution above all by freedom of opinion and assembly, the right to be represented in government, and general conscription.[48] Sexual difference became a prime criterion of citizenship, as women were excluded from those rights and military duties. Revolutionary institutions attributed masculinity, and the rights and duties it conferred on the individual, to all men. Sexual difference surpassed class, regional, religious, and racial distinctions. Universal male suffrage made it possible for men to interact as equals with men who had previously been their social superiors or inferiors. At the same time, the conflation of male citizenship with military service compounded the "virile aspects" of masculinity, distinguishing it ever more from femininity.[49] This conflation was born of specific political and military circumstances and drew upon a variety of cultural elements. The new male condition was thus defined contextually despite the language of nature that was invoked to legitimize sexual difference. A closer look at the histories of French and Prussian citizenship and conscription in this era shows how much the new masculinity differed in the two countries, the universalizing logic of political and military institutions and the ideologies of natural sexual difference notwithstanding. Both French revolutionaries and Prussian reformers were impressed by the military powers unleashed in the American War of Independence.[50] After their unpleasant encounters with the French Revolutionary armies, the Prussians had every reason to think of France as both an adversary and a model. Nevertheless, the bond of nation and military took on different forms on the two sides of the Rhine, as did the masculinities produced in the process.

In France, the Revolutionary governments tried to recruit soldiers by means ranging from calling for volunteers to the levée en masse of 1793, but the hunger for new recruits could not be satisfied by these means alone. In 1798, the second Directory introduced conscription as a permanent institution for all unmarried men between the ages of twenty and twenty-five. This system remained in force, with minor adjustments, throughout the Napoleonic years.[51] The Declaration of the Rights of Man and Citizen thus stood at the beginning of the road toward the forced integration of male citizens into the military. It opened the state to the nation's male citizens on an unprecedented scale. Political and civil rights therefore preceded military duties in France. Large groups of men nevertheless remained excluded from the full enjoyment of these rights, and Revolutionary governments after

48 Forrest, "Citizenship."
49 André Rauch, Crise de l'identité masculine, 1789–1914 (Paris, 2000), 4.
50 Geoffrey Best, War and Society in Revolutionary Europe, 1770–1870 (London, 1982), 54.
51 Forrest, Conscripts, 58–88.

1793 became less generous in this respect. Still, both the pervasive ideological presence and the legal reality of political and civil rights profoundly
affected the introduction of general military service. They gave birth to the
idea of the citizen-soldier, the male citizen who was willing to fight and
sacrifice for the political community of which he was a full member.

The history of draft evasion and desertion from the Revolutionary and
Napoleonic armies reveals that soldiering was by no means entirely voluntary, as does the history of state repression that followed attempts to escape
conscription.[52] Nevertheless, many French men subscribed to the revolutionary ideals of fighting voluntarily as a citizen of a republic. It was a strong
ideological tool that the revolutionaries used to legitimize conscription, as
they described men who had been drafted as volunteers.[53]

The French discourse of the citizen-soldier revolved around a powerful
new notion of masculinity. This was a masculinity of radical citizenship. It
was defined by identification with the revolutionary state, which was itself
the embodiment of this masculinity.[54] The citizen whom the revolutionaries created was male, and so was public life. Not all male citizens had
the same rights, nor were they allowed to exercise citizenship in the same
way. Poor men and those categorized as *citoyens passifs* were, like women,
excluded from active participation in the so-called public sphere.[55] Nevertheless, like women, these men had to fulfill their patriotic duties. After the
declaration of war in 1792, military service was one of them.[56] For these
men, fulfilling this patriotic duty was a precondition for exercising more
active political rights. Because of this linkage, in 1792–3, some revolutionary women demanded the right to bear arms and to protect the endangered
fatherland and thereby to become full citizens. The Revolutionary government rejected this demand.[57]

A different masculinity emerged in Prussia in the interactions among
the state leadership, the military reformers, and the educated male patriots
who dominated public discourse. Political differences notwithstanding, the

---

52 Ibid.   53 Ibid., 67.
54 Norman Bryson, "Géricault and 'Masculinity'," in *Visual Culture: Images and Interpretations*, ed.
    Norman Bryson, Michael Ann Holly, and Keith Moxey (Hanover, New Hampshire, 1994),
    247.
55 Joan B. Landes, ed., *Feminism, the Public and the Private* (Oxford, 1998).
56 Forrest, "La patrie"; Forrest, "Citizenship and Military Service," in *The French Revolution and
    the Meaning of Citizenship*, ed. Renée Waldinger, Philip Dawson, and Isser Woloch (Westport,
    Connecticut, 1993), 153–65; Kruse, *Erfindung*; Kruse, "Bürger und Soldat. Die Entstehung des
    modernen Militarismus in der Französischen Revolution," in *Der Bürger als Soldat. Die Militarisierung
    der europäischen Gesellschaft im langen 19. Jahrhundert: Ein internationaler Vergleich*, ed. Christian Jansen
    (Essen, 2004), 47–67.
57 Opitz, "Der Bürger "; Applewhite and Levy, "Women".

three groups shared a single aim: to take revenge on Napoleonic France for the dramatic defeat of the Prussian-Saxon army in 1806–7. They agreed that this objective could be realized only in a people's war (*Volkskrieg*). Despite considerable disagreement on the details, the central project was thus the introduction of universal conscription. The defeat had so shaken the foundations of the Prussian state and military system that the king and ruling elites were forced, if they wished to recover both, to call for fundamental change.[58]

Universal wartime conscription was introduced in Prussia by decrees enacted in February and March 1813. The institution was extended to peacetime in September 1814. From then on, Prussian men between the ages of seventeen and forty were to serve in the army or the militia. The result was the most radical system of conscription in Europe. While French conscription laws allowed for proxies, the Prussian regulations did not.[59]

The universal nature of conscription in Prussia introduced equality among conscripts from different social and confessional backgrounds, which contradicted the hierarchical nature of Prussian state and society. For the first time all men – independent of their social status – were treated equally, at least under military law. To mobilize men for war who had previously been exempt, the propaganda promised political rights to all men who fulfilled their military duties and liberated Prussia and German nation. By linking military duty and political rights rhetorically, which was necessary to mobilize for war, the Prussian government reluctantly imported radical policies into a traditional political and social order.[60] The military reformers who pressed for universal conscription were aware of the dangers, but they were also clear about their priorities. For them, conscription and the modernization of the army were military undertakings aimed at increasing the military might of the Prussian monarchy. The reformers regarded the promise of expanded political rights at best as an expedient for organizing the kind of people's war that they knew was necessary to defeat France's mass army.[61]

While male citizens entered both politics and the military in France, which fostered their identification with the state, Prussian males were integrated into the military alone. This innovation did not make them citizens

58 Hagemann, *Muth*, 73–105 and 204–349; Hagemann, "Of 'Manly' Valor."
59 Hagemann, *Muth*, 75–91; Walter, *Heeresreformen*, 281–316; see also Dierk Walter, "Reluctant Reformers, Observant Disciples: The Prussian Military Reforms, 1808–14" in this volume.
60 Ute Frevert, "Das Jakobinische Modell: Allgemeine Wehrpflicht und Nationsbildung in Preußen-Deutschland," in *Militär und Gesellschaft im 19. und 20. Jahrhundert* (Stuttgart, 1997), 17–47.
61 Hagemann, *Muth*, 75–91.

(*Staatsbürger*). Instead, it reinforced their status as duty-bound subjects of the king. They became *Bürger* (burgher) of the culturally constructed Prussian and German nation, not *Staatsbürger* (citizens) of the Prussian territorial state. They had to fulfill their military duties as conscripts without first acquiring political rights.[62] Only after they had performed their military duties and demonstrated their willingness to die for the fatherland (a term that was used in contemporary discourse synonymously with *nation*) could they become citizens (*Staatsbürger*) of the territorial state but with rights limited according to their income. The realm into which they were welcomed as conscripts was thus the culturally defined nation. In the official war propaganda, however, the term could refer both to both the Prussian territorial state and to the German nation as a whole. Prussia was regarded as a monarchical nation that stood above the various ethnic groups in the population of the territorial state and formed the heart of the German cultural nation (*Kulturnation*).[63] The idea of a German nation-state was still far from a fully developed political concept, but the Prussian discourse on military, war, and masculinity were to play an important role in turning it into one. A masculinity of duty, loyal service, and sacrifice helped to shape a vision of the monarchical nation for Germany, which was ultimately embodied in the emperor.[64]

Alternative constructions of masculinity also developed within the context of the contemporary discourse on patriotism, valor, and manhood, and they contested the hegemonic concept of war propaganda. The army reformers were not the only advocates of a revival of martial spirit among German men. Civilians contributed to this discourse as well. In the view of the so-called patriots, most of whom were educated civil servants, teachers, and writers, the valorous masculinity they propagated was to be institutionalized not in the regular army but in militias — civil forms of military organization. Presenting the war against France as a people's war as well, these men defined the German nation too as a *Kulturnation*, but they also aimed to establish a nation state in the form of a confederation of German territorial states with a constitution and basic political rights.[65] And although they continued to think of this confederation as a monarchy, they called far more vehemently for the extension of political and civil rights to deserving males in both the territorial states and the German Confederation. They

62 For more, see Hagemann, "The First Citizen of his State: Paternal Masculinity, Patriotism and Citizenship in Early Nineteenth Century Prussia," in *Representing Masculinity: Citizenship in Modern Western Political Culture*, ed. Stefan Dudink, Karen Hagemann, and Anna Clark (Houndsmills, U.K., 2007).

63 Cf. Hagemann, *Muth*, 271–303; Hagen Schulze, *Staat und Nation in der Europäischen Geschichte* (Munich, 1994), 126–49 and 172–88.

64 Hagemann, "On 'Manly' Valor."   65 Hagemann, *Muth*, 289–303.

wanted to become equal *Staatsbürger* in both. But at the same time most patriots agreed that only educated and propertied Christian men of full age deserve equal political rights, because "ordinary" men, such as workers and peasants, or non-Christian men, like Jews, were in their view not capable of becoming *Staatsbürger*. The phrase that they used for this concept of valorous, civic masculinity was "citizen as national warrior" (*Staatsbürger als Nationalkrieger*), who took up arms only when the "fatherland was in danger."[66] After the final victory over Napoleon in 1815, however, this concept was increasingly marginalized in the patriotic-national discourse. It nevertheless remained a feature of Prussian and German political memory and became the heart of struggles to extend political rights to wider circles of educated and propertied men.[67]

CONCLUSION: GENDER, WAR, AND THE MILITARY

Changes in the conduct of warfare and in political culture have repeatedly intersected with the history of gender and masculinity. The years of the Revolutionary and Napoleonic wars were a key period in the construction of hegemonic concepts of nineteenth-century masculinities.[68] It is tempting to conclude that citizenship was masculinized and that masculinity was militarized in the years from 1789 to 1815 and, in turn, to characterize this constellation of masculinity, politics, and war as a central gender structure of modern Western society. To a certain degree, these conclusions are also valid. Democratic revolutions withheld full citizenship from women and established political equality among men. Conscription became the dominant model of military recruitment, and conscription and the right to citizenship were often connected – if only ideologically. We must not, however, ignore the fact that citizenship rights had, for the most part, been restricted to men even before the French Revolution and that they were democratized after 1789. Following the Declaration of the Rights of Man and Citizen, groups of both men and women who had been excluded from political rights began to demand equal citizenship. Moreover, we should not ignore the different ways in which men were integrated into states, militaries, and nations, or the divergent masculinities that were deployed and produced in the process.

To claim that the masculinization of citizenship and the militarization of masculinity were crucial structural features of the history of gender in the modern era is also to project the French historical trajectory onto other

---

66 Ibid.
67 Hagemann, "German Heroes" and "The First Citizen."
68 Robert W. Connell, *Masculinities* (Cambridge, 1995), 192.

countries. With its rigid conscription system and absence of political rights, Prussia represents a different trajectory as well as another construction of masculinity in politics and war. Claims concerning the simultaneous masculinization of citizenship and militarization of masculinity also reproduce the ideological work of contested concepts of masculinity in discourses of universal citizenship and general conscription. The construction of masculinity as a universal category, as a biological given that transcended differences of class, religion, and region, was a powerful ideological asset in political and military projects that aimed at mass mobilization. But masculinity's ideological influence in such projects should not be confused with their outcomes. Citizenship was not masculinized to the same extent and in the same way everywhere, and the same holds true for the militarization of masculinity. We must contextualize and thereby historicize the relationship between the military and masculinity, and ask whether politics or war, or both together, formed the specific relationship during the period of the Revolutionary and Napoleonic Wars. What other factors played a role? What other changes took place? What lasting effects did they have?

Equally important is the fact that women, despite all the male rhetoric, were part of political discourses and practices – in Revolutionary France, wartime Prussia, and elsewhere – albeit not to the same degree or in the same ways as men. Women were excluded from military duties, citizenship rights, and the centers of power, but not from politics and the military altogether. They played important roles in national wars and nation building. They did so not only because they were defined as men's complements in the *Volk* family, but also because they were involved in patriotic movements. A gendered analysis of the military, war, and politics thus needs not only to historicize discourses and practices. It must also distinguish between the state and the nation. The fascinating question is, How can we explain the similarities in representations of gender and military service despite the many economic, political, and cultural differences?

18

A Tale of Two Cities

Washington and Baltimore during the War of 1812

MARION BREUNIG

The War of 1812 was certainly the strangest war the United States ever fought. It was declared after the ostensible cause – the British Orders in Council – had been removed, and it concluded, after a series of embarrassing defeats, with a notable American victory in a battle fought weeks after the Treaty of Ghent had formally brought the war to an end. After two years of war, both sides were content to confirm the status quo.

The War of 1812 was a by-product of the major European conflict, and it took the young nation nearly ten years to decide whether it was worth challenging the old mother country, which still treated it with the utmost contempt in hampering its trade and impressing its seamen into the Royal Navy. Politically, the United States was deeply divided between the Federalists and the Republicans in 1812. The question of how to handle British provocations soon became the subject of a bitter partisan struggle. While the Federalists considered good relations with Great Britain of paramount importance, the Republicans stressed national honor and invoked old resentments. On a more tangible level, the Republican war hawks represented the growing western interest and entertained aggressive designs on Canada, whereas the Federalists represented the old maritime elite who eyed the young nation's rapid western expansion with growing suspicion.

Between these poles the question how to deal with the European and maritime situation was decided. But neither side offered conclusive reasons why the war was inevitable. Little wonder that attempts to get down to the causes of the war were heavily disputed. The competing interpretations are summed up in the labels "Mr. Madison's War" and the "Second War for American Independence." The most philosophical comment was made by

353

Woodrow Wilson in his *History of the American People*: "The grounds of the war were singularly uncertain."[1]

This curious war would probably have been all but entirely forgotten had it not been for two events that were to become part of America's national memory: the humiliating capture and burning of Washington by British troops in August 1814 and the successful defense of Baltimore, which Francis Scott Key commemorated in the poem "The Defence of Fort McHenry," better known today as the song "The Star-Spangled Banner." These two events, which took place within a fortnight of each other, are symptomatic of the weakness and the strength of the U.S. military establishment in the republic's early years. As one historian has noted of this period: "American military success was in an inverse ratio to the scale of the federal government's involvement."[2]

Nearly a decade of continual discussion of the pros and cons of going to war did not result in appropriate preparations to confront the greatest naval power of the Western Hemisphere. The U.S. Navy commanded only sixteen vessels, as opposed to more than six hundred that the British had in active service.[3] But because of the British forces' preoccupation with Napoleon, the threat to America's Atlantic coastline seemed only hypothetical. In addition, the Americans – always great proponents of private enterprise – relied on hundreds of privateers who were only too eager to conduct a waterborne guerrilla war with Great Britain along the Atlantic and Pacific trade routes. The Madison administration concentrated its war efforts mainly toward the northern and western frontiers, seeing war as an opportunity to seize territory in Canada and to put an end to British cooperation with Indian tribes in the west.

Why were American political and military leaders so blind to the dangers of Britain's naval power? What conclusions can be drawn about the efficiency of the federal government when the nation's capital was abandoned with little resistance whereas Baltimore was successfully defended mainly by local militia? The answers historians have offered so far are not entirely convincing: misplaced optimism and bad leadership in the Madison administration are frequently invoked in explaining the Washington

---

1 Woodrow Wilson, *A History of the American People*, 5 vols. (New York, 1902), 3:212.
2 Joseph A. Whitehorne, *The Battle for Baltimore, 1814* (Baltimore, 1997), x.
3 Harry L. Coles, *The War of 1812* (Chicago, 1965), 71.
4 For a discussion of the strategic plans of the Madison government, see Peter J. Kastor, "'Towards the Maritime War Only': The Question of Naval Mobilisation, 1811–1812," *Journal of Military History* 61 (1997): 455–80.

debacle, while Baltimore's militia leader Samuel Smith is highly praised for his circumspection and foresight.[5]

But there seem to have been more fundamental problems. The American federal military system did not prove adequate to the threat posed by the British tactic of flexible amphibious warfare. In the long war against France, the British military establishment had learned to adapt its strategy to exploit the perceived vulnerabilities of republican governments. The British operations in the Chesapeake Bay area served political, or rather psychological, ends by trying to convince the populace of Britain's military superiority and the futility of resistance. Lieutenant George Gleig, a participant in Britain's Chesapeake and New Orleans campaigns, stated this idea concisely, arguing that

in absolute monarchies, where war is more properly the pastime of kings, than the desire of subjects, non combatants ought to be dealt with as humanely as possible. Not so, however, in States governed by popular assemblies. By compelling the constituents to experience the real hardships and miseries of warfare, you will soon compel the representatives to a vote of peace.[6]

Considered in the light of this strategy of psychological warfare, Washington, the new unfinished but highly symbolic national capital, was an ideal target. Baltimore, by contrast, was an obvious target for a more traditional operation. It was thus easier to anticipate and prepare for a British attack. Before looking for shortcomings on the part of the American military and political leadership, it is important to consider the structural differences between the two cities.

THE CHESAPEAKE BAY IN BRITISH AND AMERICAN STRATEGY

The British government was genuinely surprised by America's declaration of war. Giving priority to the European war, the Admiralty pursued a defensive strategy and considered the eighty ships already operating in American waters more than adequate to protect British interests. Assuming that the war had come about from a failure of communication, British leaders hoped that the United States would soon be willing to negotiate a peace once it learned of the repeal of the Orders in Council. They not only found themselves mistaken but also had to suffer a series of embarrassing defeats at

5 See, e.g., Frank A. Cassell, "Baltimore in 1813: A Study of Urban Defense in the War of 1812," *Military Affairs* 33 (1969): 349–61.
6 George R. Gleig, *A Narrative of the Campaigns of the British Army at Washington and New Orleans*, 2nd ed. (London, 1826).

the hands of the small but highly motivated American navy. Only with the decline of Napoleon was Britain able to adopt a more offensive stance. In February 1813, Admiral John Warren, the new commander of the North Atlantic station, ordered a blockade on the Delaware River and Chesapeake Bay. The blockade was soon extended from New York to the mouth of the Mississippi. By excluding New England, the stronghold of the Federalists, the British sought to foment internal division. Leaving New England's ports open also served Britain's needs because its troops in both Canada and Europe depended on the American trade for most of their provisions.[7] But the day after signing a peace treaty with the restored Bourbon government on May 30, 1814, Britain put the entire Atlantic coast of the United States under blockade.

While Britain slowly tightened the noose, U.S. political and military leaders did little to prepare a defense. They also seem to have been hampered by a serious lack of communication. Although President Madison had claimed in November 1811 that the nation's maritime frontier was well defended,[8] Secretary of the Navy Paul Hamilton acknowledged to a congressional inquiry a few weeks later that "the protection which . . . we should be able to afford to our coasting trade, would obviously be very imperfect."[9]

Within the U.S. government there existed an astonishing disregard for the dangers of Britain's naval power. Madison planned the war as a short inexpensive land operation against Canada mainly that would be conducted with militia forces. Secretary of State James Monroe also saw no use for the navy, believing "that the best disposition which could be made of our little navy would be to keep it in a body in a sa[f]e port."[10] When it dawned on Congress that a war that had grown out of a maritime conflict could not be conducted solely as a land war, it authorized the building of ten new vessels.[11] That planned increase in naval forces was partially offset, however, when William Jones, the new secretary of the navy, ordered a dramatic reduction in the number of gunboats to cut costs. Gunboats were

---

7 Robert S. Quimby, *The U.S. Army in the War of 1812: An Operational and Command Study*, 3 vols. (East Lansing, Michigan, 1997), 3:642.

8 James P. Richardson, *A Compilation of the Messages and Papers of the Presidents, 1789–1897*, 10 vols. (Washington 1896–9), 1:493.

9 Secretary of the Navy, Hamilton to Congressman Langdon Cheves, Dec. 3, 1811, in *American State Papers: Documents, Legislative and Executive, of the Congress of the United States*, Class VI, Naval Affairs (Washington, D.C., 1832–61), 248.

10 James Monroe to Thomas Jefferson, June 16, 1813, in Kastor, "Maritime War Only," 462.

11 William S. Dudley and Michael J. Crawford, eds., *The Naval War of 1812: A Documentary History*, 3 vols. (Washington, D.C., 1985–2002), 2:43.

small armed vessels designed to operate in shallow coastal waters and to protect small harbors and settlements without proper fortifications. In Jones's opinion, they were "scattered about in every creek and corner as recepticles of idleness and objects of waste and extravagance without utility."[12] Many local commanders could not make sense of the order. The commander of the naval station at Wilmington, North Carolina, for example, complained to his superior, "I then shall sit down in sullen retirement and view the Boats in the mud and . . . reflect on the situation of my state not a single armed vessel allotted for her defense."[13]

Given the deficiencies of naval protection, coastal areas had to rely on forts, batteries, and other fortifications. These fell under the responsibility of Secretary of War John Armstrong, whose preoccupation with the demands of the army made him even less receptive to the vulnerability of the coastal areas. Armstrong tried to encourage local self-defense by placing the militia of the maritime regions on the federal payroll and offering arms and advice.[14] But with federal funds scarce, only a few prominent seaports profited. Most of the vast coastal frontier of the United States had to rely almost entirely on the ability of local militia leaders to mobilize men and money.

The British Admiralty, meanwhile, became exasperated with Admiral Warren's slack conduct of the blockade and the growing number of American naval victories – many of which were won by privateers. In an attempt to take the offensive, it sent reinforcement to the Chesapeake Bay under the command of the more energetic Rear Admiral George Cockburn. He was under orders to take aggressive action in the bay area to divert American troops from Canada and to take retaliation on unprotected coastal towns there for Baltimore privateers' attacks on British shipping. Upon arrival, Cockburn also realized that it would be possible to reprovision the fleet by raids on the prosperous towns and farms on the Chesapeake's shores. He lost no time pointing out to Warren that, with the impending arrival of British ground troops, "the whole of the Shores and Towns within this vast Bay, not excepting the Capital itself will be wholly at your mercy."[15] In the interim, Cockburn and Warren were limited to harassing smaller settlements and reconnoitering the shoal-ridden waters of the Chesapeake and its numerous estuaries in preparation for a major offensive.

---

12 Jones to his brother Lloyd Jones, Feb. 27, 1813, in ibid., 2:52.
13 Thomas N. Gauthier to Capt. John H. Dent, Mar. 29, 1813, in Dudley and Crawford, *Naval War*, 2:60.
14 Cassell, "Baltimore in 1813."
15 George Cockburn to John Warren, Mar. 13, 1813, in Dudley and Crawford, *Naval War*, 2:322.

Between March 1813 and June 1814, the British navy conducted an amphibious guerrilla war in the Chesapeake that spread terror throughout the unprotected towns along its shores. Cockburn's policy was to spare towns that did not offer resistance and to lay waste those that did. Among the towns that suffered for putting up a fight were Havre de Grace and Hampton. Baltimore was threatened twice, but each time the British navy drew back fearing heavy losses.

British naval operations under Warren and Cockburn in 1813 can be described only as a complete failure. The Admiralty had sought to "effect a diversion on the Coast of the United States of America in favor of Upper and Lower Canada."[16] American strategy nonetheless remained single-mindedly directed against Canada. The second British objective, to use terror and destruction to undercut American popular support for the war, also fell far short of the mark. People were terrified and suffered severe economic losses, but, contrary to British hopes, this experience united Republicans and Federalists. The sole benefit the British derived from the operations under Warren and Cockburn was the experience gained in navigating the waters of the Chesapeake and its tributaries. They were thus able to develop plans for exploiting the region's vulnerabilities once sufficient forces became available.[17]

It must have been clear to all participants that the activities of the Royal Navy in 1813 were only a prelude should the war continue.

AMERICAN DEFENSE PLANS

The attempt to understand the contrasting fates of Washington and Baltimore in the fall of 1814 must start with the question how the authorities of both cities reacted to the crisis of 1813. When the Royal Navy sailed up the Potomac in July 1813, Armstrong, Jones, and Monroe took turns inspecting defenses along the river, and all three cabinet members declared them sufficient to repel an invasion.[18] This confidence can be interpreted only as wishful thinking, because the capital's only fortification was Fort Washington, located ten miles below the city on the Maryland side of the Potomac. The fort – in fact, hardly more than a battery – was open on the landside and thus useless in the event of an amphibious attack.[19]

---

16 Earl Bathurst to Colonel Thomas Beckwith, Mar. 20, 1813, in Dudley and Crawford, *Naval War*, 2:325.

17 Whitehorne, *Baltimore*, 85.   18 See Whitehorne, *Baltimore*, 77.

19 Robert S. Quimby, *U.S. Army 1812*, 3:650–2.

Federal officials surpassed one other in complacency. When General Steuart of Maryland tabled a motion in the House of Representatives to arm the citizens of the District of Columbia, it was passed on to the military affairs committee, which declared the following day that it was satisfied that the preparations made to receive the enemy were "in every way adequate to the emergency."[20] The commander of Washington's militia, Major General Van Ness, did not share this happy-go-lucky attitude. An eminent banker and one of the city's wealthiest men, he had far more at stake than most government officials, who very often had neither families nor property in Washington to worry about. Van Ness later complained that the secretary of war had several times declared his concurrence when approached on the subject of the city's need for proper fortifications, declaring that he would have them executed as soon as the best sites were selected.[21] This answer obviously had been Armstrong's standard response to tedious inquiries. Armstrong later justified his inaction by pointing to the expense that would have been incurred in erecting field works.[22]

The astonishing complacency of Washington's political and military leaders cannot be explained solely by financial worries, however. If they wanted to avoid expenditure on Washington's defense, it was because they considered it unnecessary. Assuming that the British would concentrate on more accessible and richer targets along the Chesapeake Bay, they completely neglected the psychological impact that an attack on the nation's capital would have on both sides of the Atlantic.

The awareness that it was a prime target was one of the main factors behind Baltimore's deliverance. Baltimore's residents were aware from the outset of the war of the threat to their city, which was not only a major commercial center but also the home port of hundreds of privateers. As early as February 1813, when the arrival of the British fleet in the Chesapeake was first reported, Baltimore businessmen asked Secretary of the Navy Jones for financial assistance for the city's defense, reminding him of the federal government's constitutional responsibility to protect American commerce.[23] Jones, pointing to the limited funds at his disposal, responded that Baltimore would have to depend on "the voluntary local force, whose interests &

20 John S. Williams, *History of the Invasion and Capture of Washington* (New York, 1857), 16–18.
21 Quimby, *U.S. Army 1812*, 3:651.
22 Armstrong to the Congressional Investigating Committee, Oct. 17, 1814, *American State Papers, Military Affairs*, 1:538–40.
23 Committee of Underwriters of Baltimore to Secretary of Navy Jones, Feb. 1813, in Dudley and Crawford, *Naval War*, 2:329–30.

feelings are directly assailed."[24] The residents of Baltimore thus knew that the fate of their city rested entirely on their own abilities and resources.

Baltimore, like Washington, was protected on the waterfront by only one fort. Fort McHenry had last been strengthened in the 1790s, and it was manned with about fifty regulars. It was thus fortunate for Baltimore that it had a political and military leader who not only realized the threat confronting the city but also was able to mobilize the men and resources needed to defend against it. Major General Samuel Smith, commander of Maryland's Third Militia Division, was a distinguished veteran of the Revolutionary War and one of Baltimore's wealthiest merchants. He sat on the boards of several banks and real estate firms, and he could also look back on twenty years of service in Congress, first in the House of Representatives and later in the Senate.[25] With his military, political, and financial expertise, Smith was the ideal person to orchestrate Baltimore's defense preparations and was well positioned to secure maximum support from state and federal officials. When Smith complained to Maryland Governor Levin Winder in March 1813 that not even fifty regular army troops manned Fort McHenry and just one gunboat protected the harbor, Winder evasively authorized him to make "the necessary arrangements of the militia for the defense of the Port of Baltimore."[26] Not one to shy away from responsibility, Smith interpreted this vague order in the broadest way possible: as a commission to take overall command of the city.

Smith's most pressing problem was not finding men to mobilize but rather arming, feeding, and paying them. His pleas to the federal government for funds were partially fulfilled when Armstrong assented to pay and supply two thousand state militia as well as Smith's own city brigade. Smith tried to make the best use of his force by frequently rotating the troops, thereby training as many men as possible at a minimum of expense. That Smith was able to secure federal assistance at all was due more to his political influence than to the secretary of war's concern for Baltimore. Armstrong, who had proclaimed Washington to be too insignificant to attract the British, now reversed his arguments and claimed that Baltimore was too big a bait for them.[27]

Smith's ties to Baltimore's financial elite proved even more important than his political connections in Washington. When the members of Baltimore's city council realized how slow and insignificant federal aid would be, they

24 Jones to Committee of Underwriters of Baltimore, Feb. 16, 1813, in Dudley and Crawford, *Naval War*, 2:330–1.
25 Cassell, "Baltimore in 1813," 350.   26 Ibid., 351.
27 Ibid., 354.

created the Committee of Public Supply, which consisted of the city's most influential merchants and bankers. All were friends and business associates of Smith's. With almost unlimited funds now at his disposal, the general could equip his troops, hire additional laborers to hasten work on fortifications, and build additional gunboats to supplement the single vessel the federal government had provided. He even created a special unit, the Marine Fencibles, made up of unemployed sailors to serve as crew in guard boats and the water battery of Fort McHenry.[28]

When the British twice declined to attack Baltimore in 1813 after taking measure of its defenses, Armstrong and Smith could each consider himself justified. Cockburn had not dared to challenge the city with the limited number of ground troops at his disposal. When the British returned in 1814 with a larger ground force, Baltimore could rely on a well-trained although untested militia. And even more important, it had developed a network of organizations through which the citizens could be mobilized in the shortest possible time. Looking back on the events of 1813–14 a couple of years later, Smith observed, "The preparations made in 1813 enabled us to meet the enemy when he attacked us by land in 1814. The city was saved by the preparations of 1813."[29]

WASHINGTON AND BALTIMORE IN 1814

It is difficult to understand why Washington's defenses were so totally neglected during two years of war, especially after the lessons of the first British raids along the shores of the Chesapeake in 1813. Historical scholarship on the War of 1812 shares the general opinion that "the man most at fault was the secretary of war."[30] As evidence, an alleged remark of Armstrong's is often cited. When Van Ness expressed his fears of an invasion, Armstrong is supposed to have replied, "By God they would not come with such a fleet without meaning to strike somewhere. But they certainly will not come here! What the devil will they do here? No! No! Baltimore is the place, Sir. That is of so much more consequence."[31] But it was not Armstrong's indolence alone that was responsible for the total neglect of the capital's safety, for his cabinet members, the Congress, and President Madison supported his views. As numerous letters show, most

28 Whitehorne, *Baltimore*, 354.
29 Smith to George Graham, Dec. 30, 1816, quoted in Cassell, "Baltimore in 1813," 360.
30 Anthony S. Pitch, *The Burning of Washington: The British Invasion of 1814* (Annapolis, 1998), 40.
31 Van Ness to Congressional Investigating Committee, Nov. 23, 1814, *American State Papers*, 1:581.

military leaders also shared the belief that Washington was safe.[32] It was only men involved in city government like Mayor James Blake and General Van Ness who challenged that view.

Where did this certainty come from? Why was it that the appeals of the inhabitants of the District of Columbia had so little effect? And why did they not resort to self-defense like their neighbors in Baltimore? Van Ness, after all, was no less eager than Smith to prepare for the emergency. The answer becomes clear in comparing the two cities.

Baltimore, home to more than fifty thousand inhabitants, was the third-largest city in the United States in 1812. A thriving port and manufacturing center, the city had seen its population triple since the first national census in 1790. Its large multinational communities set it apart from Maryland's other maritime towns, which were dominated by the state's old planter elite.[33] Baltimore's commercial elite were solidly Republican, in contrast to the state's predominantly Federalist ruling class, and had long clamorously urged war with Britain. The fact that many city leaders were self-made merchants or manufacturers accustomed to relying on their own resources added greatly to the dynamism of Baltimore's defense preparations.

Washington, by contrast, was "a city only in name" that was being built "for the ages" rather than for the immediate comfort of its residents, as First Lady Abigail Adams had complained to her daughter in 1800 after getting lost in dense woods on her way to join her husband at the still unfinished White House.[34] Fourteen years later, the city was still "a meagre village," according to Attorney General Richard Rush, "a place with a few bad houses and extensive swamps."[35] In 1810, the city had 8,208 residents, of whom 5,904 were white and the remainder free blacks and slaves.[36] Although Washington had almost twice the population of nearby Georgetown, federal employees and diplomats were not taken by the new capital. The problem was that Pierre L'Enfant had planned the capital on a grand scale, placing government buildings far apart and connecting them with commanding avenues on the optimistic assumption that the space in between would be filled by private enterprises. But it would be decades before Washington developed the bustling commercial center the Founding Fathers had confidently envisioned. Apart from boardinghouses and hotels

32 For example, see Gen. Wadsworth to Armstrong, May 28, 1813, in Pitch, *Burning of Washington*, 154; Secretary of the Navy Jones to Com. Rodgers, Aug. 19, 1814, in Dudley and Crawford, *Naval War*, 3:199.
33 Whitehorne, *Baltimore*, 12.
34 Phyllis L. Levin, *Abigail Adams* (New York, 1987), 388.
35 Attorney General Richard Rush to John Adams, Sept. 5, 1814, in Pitch, *Burning of Washington*, 29.
36 Pitch, *Burning of Washington*, 29.

for members and employees of government and diplomats, Washington's main place of business was its impressive Navy Yard. And it was the ships and supplies of the shipyard that many inhabitants thought would be the main attraction for a British attack.[37]

Washington's problem seems to have been that the officials in charge of the defense had such little regard for the town and thought it so insignificant that the idea of its being a possible target did not enter their heads. Moreover, most Congressmen and employees of the federal government lived in boardinghouses, generally without their families, while Congress was in session and did not own property in the city. They could thus take a rather detached view of the situation. They had much less to fear than the inhabitants of Baltimore, who were well aware that their lives and livelihoods were at stake.

THE BURNING OF WASHINGTON

The year 1814 did not bode well for the Americans. The Admiralty at last had withdrawn the lethargic Warren from the North American station and replaced him with Sir Alexander Cochrane. His orders were to conduct the war more aggressively, and, prompted by both duty and inclination, he did so. Having lost his brother at Yorktown, Cochrane had no hesitations about conducting a vigorous retaliatory war.[38] His first act after taking over the command on April 1, 1814, was to issue a proclamation urging slaves to leave their masters.[39] Only a year earlier, the British secretary of state for war had emphatically forbidden utilizing the slaves, claiming moral scruples but being actually moved by more worldly reasons like the difficulty to maintain and transport them.[40] Cochrane complemented his proclamation with an order to his captains to "destroy and lay waste such towns and districts upon the coast as you may find available."[41]

The British war effort gained momentum following the French capitulation in March 1814. By June, an army of 2,500 well-trained veterans of Wellington's peninsular campaign was on its way to America. These were not the twenty thousand soldiers Cochrane had hoped for, but he and Cockburn spent the better part of the summer discussing possible targets among

37 Secretary of the Navy Jones to Congressman Richard Johnson, Oct. 3, 1814, in Dudley and Crawford, *Naval War*, 3:314–15.
38 Dudley and Crawford, *Naval War*, 3:38.
39 Cochrane's Proclamation, Apr. 2, 1814, in Dudley and Crawford, *Naval War*, 3:60.
40 Earl Bathurst to Col. Beckwith, Mar. 20, 1813, in Dudley and Crawford, *Naval War*, 3:325–6.
41 Quoted in Whitehorne, *Baltimore*, 88.

Rhode Island, Philadelphia, Baltimore, Annapolis, and Washington.[42] It was
Cockburn who persuaded the vacillating commander in chief of the advantage of moving against the capital first and then proceeding to Baltimore
from its less fortified landside.[43]

It was only when the storm was already gathering that federal officials began to contemplate a defensive strategy for Washington. Madison
ordered the mobilization of approximately fifteen thousand militia troops
from Maryland, Virginia, and Pennsylvania; fewer than half that many men
had been mustered by the time the invasion was under way.[44] Adding to the
confusion, Madison and his cabinet created a new military district on July 1
that encompassed the District of Columbia, Maryland, and part of Virginia.
The district was put under the command of General William Winder, a
recently released prisoner of war with little military experience who had
been chosen for the position because he was a nephew of Maryland's Federalist governor Levin Winder. If Madison had hoped that General Winder's
family ties would speed up the mobilization of the Maryland militia, he
had deceived himself. By August 20, when the British landed about forty
miles south of Washington in Benedict, Maryland, Governor Winder had
sent only 250 men. Governor Simon Snyder of Pennsylvania shrugged off
the request with the explanation that he had no legal authority to call out
the militia: the state legislature had, inconveniently, decided on a complete reorganization of the state's militia but had adjourned before taking
action.[45] General Winder's army was thus drawn largely from the District
of Columbia and Virginia militias, supplemented by about one thousand
army regulars and four hundred seamen from Baltimore's gunboat flotilla
under Commodore Joshua Barney. Winder's most reliable militia force was
the Baltimore militia levied by Smith and commanded by General Tobias
Stansbury.

When the armies finally met on August 24 at Bladenburg – only three
miles from the capital – Winder's 5,000 men outnumbered the 4,500 invasion troops under General Robert Ross.[46] But even entrenched behind
a narrow bridge they could not hold off the experienced British veterans. Ross and Cockburn needed only their advance troops to send the
Americans into blind retreat. The untrained militia troops were especially
unnerved by the British force's use of Congreve rockets. This new weapon

42 Cochrane to Cockburn, July 1, 1814; Cochrane to First Lord of the Admiralty Melville, July 17,
   1814; Cockburn to Cochrane, July 17, 1814, in Dudley and Crawford, *Naval War*, 3:129–39.
43 Cockburn to Cochrane, July 17, 1814, in Dudley and Crawford, *Naval War*, 3:138.
44 Quimby, *U.S. Army 1812*, 657.   45 Ibid., 659.
46 Pitch, *Burning of Washington*, 659.

could not be aimed very accurately, but it was easier to transport than conventional artillery and quite effective, zooming in almost horizontally into the enemy's lines.[47]

With the American defeat at Bladenburg, the British had an open road to Washington. Having staked everything on one horse, Winder had not fixed an assembly point where his troops should regroup, nor had he made plans for the evacuation of the capital. Many militiamen therefore just went home to look after their families.[48] Left to their own resources, Washingtonians had to decide whether to leave the city or stay and try to protect their property. First Lady Dolley Madison had just ordered dinner for the cabinet and the senior officers when the alarm was given. Saving only a copy of the Declaration of Independence and a portrait of George Washington, she fled the capital and took refuge at a friend's home in the countryside.[49]

It has often been said that the British intended to lay Washington under contribution – that is, they would spare public property in exchange for a sum of money. This account originated with Lieutenant George Gleig, who wrote that the decision to burn the city was made only after the emissaries entering the town with a flag of truce to negotiate the deal were fired on.[50] But Gleig's otherwise very reliable report cannot be trusted here. Neither of the commanding officers, Ross or Cockburn, mentioned the intention to demand a ransom in their reports to Cochrane or Earl Bathurst, the secretary of state for war. To the contrary, Ross explicitly called the destruction of the public buildings the "object of the expedition."[51] The whole reason for the operation in the Chesapeake was to take the war home to the Americans – or, in the words of Admiral Cochrane, "to give them a complete drubbing before Peace is made."[52] To go to such lengths as the British had done just for a ransom of a couple of thousand dollars seems most unlikely, and there is no evidence that the thought ever entered the minds of the British military leaders. The burning of Washington was a highly symbolic act, the British revenge not only for the American declaration of war and the

47 There are many eyewitness accounts of the Battle of Bladenburg. The most comprehensible is by British Lieutenant George Gleig, in his *Narrative*, 115–17. The effect of the rockets is described in Admiral Cockburn's report to Admiral Cochrane, Aug. 27, 1814, in Dudley and Crawford, *Naval War*, 3:221.

48 Report of Gen. Walter Smith, Oct. 6, 1814, *American State Papers*, 1:565.

49 For a vivid account of the chaotic conditions in Washington after the Battle of Bladenburg, see Pitch, *Burning of Washington*, 86–98.

50 Gleig, *Narrative*, 124–5. Gleig's story is still repeated in recent publications. See, e.g., Coles, *War of 1812*, 181, Quimby, *U.S. Army 1812*, 2:693, or Whitehorne, *Baltimore*, 135.

51 Cockburn to Cochrane, Aug. 27, 1814, and Ross to Bathurst, Aug. 30, 1814, in Dudley and Crawford, *Naval War*, 3:220–2.

52 Cochrane to Bathurst, July 14, 1814, *Naval War*, 3:131.

depredations in Canada but also for Yorktown and the loss of the North American colonies.

The British paid scrupulous attention that they destroy only public property in Washington. Starting at the Capitol, they continued with the White House – or President's Palace, as it was then called – where they first helped themselves to the dinner the first lady had ordered only a short while earlier.[53] Prior to departing the next morning, they set fire to the Treasury and the Departments of State and War. The Patent Office was spared after a clerk there protested that the patents housed there were private property.[54] The invaders did not need to destroy the Navy Yard: Secretary of the Navy Jones had given the commandant of the Navy Yard, Commodore Thomas Tingey, orders to set it ablaze if the British entered the city.[55]

Ross and Cockburn decided to withdraw their small force after only twenty-four hours in Washington, fearing that Winder's regrouped army might cut off their retreat. They need not have worried. The only serious obstacle they had to face was a hurricane, which killed thirty British soldiers and threw the army into confusion. After just nine days, the invasion force reembarked at Benedict. Ross had dismissed the idea of continuing the march north from Washington to Baltimore as Cockburn had been urging.

It was obvious to Ross and his officers that a coup like the capture of Washington could not be easily repeated. While the commanding officers sent their self-congratulating reports to London, Lieutenant Gleig soberly observed:

[T]he truth is, that this capture was brought about more by the extreme folly of the American government, and their absurd confidence that it would never be attempted, than by any other cause. Had the emergency been contemplated, and in a proper manner provided against . . . the design . . . would have been either abandoned immediately, or must have ended in the total destruction of the invaders.[56]

THE DEFENSE OF BALTIMORE

The withdrawal of British land troops from Washington did not mean the end of the threat to the region. A British fleet under Captain James Gordon had sailed up the Potomac intending to attack Fort Washington on August 27. But hardly had the British fired the first shot than the nervous American commander, who obviously had a very low opinion of the fort's strength and his men's dedication, decided to blow up the fort and evacuate his

---

53 Gleig, *Narrative*, 128–30.   54 Pitch, *Burning of Washington*, 99–144.
55 Tingey to Secretary of the Navy Jones, Oct. 18, 1814, in Dudley and Crawford, *Naval War*, 3:318–19.
56 Gleig, *Narrative*, 133.

troops without firing a single shot. The astonished invaders proceeded to Alexandria, forcing the city council of the defenseless town to surrender the ships docked there and the contents of its warehouses.[57]

The political consequences of these military defeats for the Madison administration were disastrous. Many coastal towns had opposed Madison and the Republicans from the outset of war and had become openly defiant of the federal government. Officials in Alexandria refused to raise the American flag for several days after the British fleet had withdrawn, and leading Georgetown citizens made it clear that they would follow Alexandria's example.[58] Madison tried to regain the initiative by replacing Armstrong, by then the most hated man in the capital, with James Monroe. He also issued a proclamation denouncing British vandalism and urging the Americans to defend the independence won by their fathers.[59]

Residents of Baltimore and other communities along the Chesapeake faced a difficult decision. Should they make a stand against the British in support of a government that had led them into war without providing for their protection, or should they try to come to terms with the enemy? Leading militia officers were convinced that Baltimore would not have fought if the British had proceeded there immediately after the attack on Washington. John Nicholson, a prominent lawyer and commander of a volunteer company, described the general mood in Baltimore to Secretary of the Navy Jones: "there has been a deliberate plan to surrender [Baltimore] without a struggle, and if General Ross had marched to this place instead of to Patuxent he would have been master of our city with even less trouble than he had at Washington."[60]

The British, however, vacillated once again. Cochrane was frustrated that Ross refused to carry out his concept of retaliatory warfare. But instead of confronting the general directly, he intimated to the Admiralty that "some hint ought to be given to General Ross."[61] Cochrane wanted to leave the Chesapeake during malaria season and continue the raids to the north. Cockburn seems to have pressed for an attack on Baltimore. Ross was initially undecided but was eventually won over by Cockburn. They then joined forces to persuade Cochrane to move against Baltimore – a target that in the end was too tempting to resist.[62]

---

57 Capt. Gordon to Cochrane, Sept. 9, 1814, in Dudley and Crawford, *Naval War*, 3:238–40, and Jones to Com. Rodgers, Aug. 29, 1814, in ibid., 243–4.
58 Pitch, *Burning of Washington*, 166 and 179.
59 Madison's Proclamation, Sept. 3, 1814, quoted in Pitch, *Burning of Washington*, 166.
60 Joseph Nicholson to Jones, Aug. 28, 1814, in Pitch, *Burning of Washington*, 181.
61 Cochrane to Melville, Sept. 2, 1814, in Dudley and Crawford, *Naval War*, 3:269.
62 Adm. Codrington to Jane Codrington, Sept. 5, 1814, in Dudley and Crawford, *Naval War*, 3:271.

In the two weeks the British needed to make up their minds, American public opinion underwent a complete change. The shock at the burning of Washington ebbed and defeatism gave way to resolve to fight. By September 4, fifteen thousand militia troops from Maryland and the neighboring states had assembled in Baltimore.[63] As in 1813, Baltimore's city council did not rely on outside help. The new Committee of Vigilance and Safety reactivated the organizations established the year before and began to coordinate the city's defense. It raised $600,000 in a few days and arranged logistic support to maintain the huge militia force. The city council once again asked Samuel Smith to take command of the city's defense. That decision drew from General Winder, who, on his arrival from Washington, claimed the assignment for himself. Weary of these rivalries about rank and seniority, Smith referred the dispute to Governor Winder, who was not only General Winder's uncle but also a political opponent of Smith. Recognizing Smith's outstanding achievements and merits, the governor decided in his favor and his nephew subordinated himself to the militia commander and did what he was told. This incident alone indicates the new spirit that had transformed the American forces.[64]

Smith's great military experience was evident when he correctly anticipated the exact approach the British invasion force would take. He had his troops prepare to oppose a landing at North Point, some fourteen miles east of Baltimore, and concentrated on fortifying the eastern side of the city. Fort McHenry and its two auxiliary batteries were also readied to expect a naval attack. The inner harbor was made impassable by sinking ship hulks, thus protecting the city from being fired on from the seafront. Knowing that the British had no intention to lay the city under a prolonged siege, Smith planned to fortify Baltimore to such an extent as to deter attack altogether. Unlike General Winder at Bladenburg, Smith did not intend to rely solely on a single line of defense. He planned to harass the British forces from the moment they landed and, if necessary, to continue harassing them all the way into Baltimore. He even went so far as to order that the city's new cathedral be converted into a fort.[65]

Lieutenant Gleig, elated by the British forces' recent triumph, mistook the activity along the Chesapeake's shores as manifestations of panic. "Wherever a lighthouse or signal station was erected, alarm-guns were fired, and beacons lighted. In a word, all the horrors of doubt and apprehension

---

63 Commodore Rodgers to Com. Murray, Sept. 4, 1814, in Dudley and Crawford, *Naval War*, 3:263.
64 Quimby, *U.S. Army 1812*, 2:716; Whitehorne, *Baltimore*, 163.
65 Whitehorne, *Baltimore*, 170–2.

seemed to oppress the inhabitants of this devoted district."[66] As Smith had anticipated, Cochrane and Ross intended to take the city by a coup de main and provisioned their army for three days only. As the ground troops approached Baltimore from the east, the fleet was to destroy the harbor defenses.[67] The plan began to go awry only hours after disembarkation when the charismatic commander Ross was killed in a skirmish. His successor, Colonel Arthur Brooke, managed to dislodge the American defenders from North Point but only at the cost of sustaining more losses than it inflicted. Unlike at Bladenburg, the American militia did not scatter in chaos but retreated behind newly erected earthwork defenses. After assessing those strong fortifications, Brooke informed Cochrane that a frontal attack would result in too-heavy losses and could be risked only with the assistance of the fleet. The success of the operation would therefore depend on the ability of the fleet to get past Fort McHenry. When Fort McHenry still gave no sign of surrender after twenty-four hours of bombardment, Cochrane decided to abandon the attack and to save his troops – if not his reputation – for the already-planned New Orleans expedition.[68]

While Francis Scott Key, held hostage on a British ship, started to put his feelings into the famous poem that, decades later, would become the text of the national anthem, the victorious defenders of Fort McHenry were not in a poetic mood. The fort's commander, Major Armistead, was so exhausted by the bombardment that he needed two weeks before he was able to write his report to Secretary of War Monroe. Amazingly, he had to report only 4 soldiers killed and 24 wounded at the fort, while General Smith reported a total of 24 killed, 139 wounded, and 50 taken prisoner.[69]

Historians have generally given Smith the lion's share of the credit for the successful defense of Baltimore. It is true that he was the central figure who coordinated the efforts of the military and the citizenry and did so with great competence – a quality not often found among American political and military leaders during that war. But Smith could not have succeeded had not the whole atmosphere changed after the destruction of Washington. For the first time, American leaders did not allow party loyalties or professional rivalries guide their actions. The two-week respite that British indecision had provided was sufficient to transform even the staunchest Federalists into ardent patriots. Baltimore, where the announcement of the declaration of

66 Gleig, *Narrative*, 165.
67 Ibid.; Cochrane to Crocker, Sept. 17, 1814, in Dudley and Crawford, *Naval War*, 3:286.
68 Cochrane to First Secretary of the Admiralty Croker, Sept. 17, 1814, in ibid., 3:286–8.
69 Armistead to Monroe, Sept. 24, 1814, in Dudley and Crawford, *Naval War*, 3:302–4; Smith to Monroe, in ibid., 293–8.

war in 1812 had been accompanied by mob actions against the Federalist minority and riots bordering on civil war,[70] was united two years later in a common cause. Whatever the British might have sought to achieve in the Chesapeake, their attacks on the region's two main cities – the national capital and the great commercial center – ultimately accomplished what blundering American national officials had tried in vain to do: they excited a sense of patriotism, reminiscent of old revolutionary times, that had long been thought lost to sectionalism and party strife.

CONCLUSION

The British offensive in the Chesapeake ended in a stalemate, which mirrored the situation in the other war theaters and contributed to the confirmation of the status quo in the Treaty of Ghent. It is doubtful whether a British success at Baltimore would have had any other result than solacing the revengeful spirit of British merchants suffering from American privateers. More important were the lessons the British offensive carried for the Americans.

The events leading to the burning of Washington showed dramatically the defects of the federal military system. The idea of keeping a large regular army was not popular among Republican leaders who still preferred to rely on militia troops. The militias were, however, under the control of the states according to the Constitution. The inadequate response to Madison's request for fifteen thousand state militia in July 1814, the appointment of General Winder as commander of the Tenth Military District in the hope of securing the cooperation of his uncle the governor, the inability of Pennsylvania's governor to call out the militia as a result of the state legislature's negligence – all of these failures originated in the structural weakness of the federal government in military matters, not blunders on the part of individuals. The District of Columbia, unlike the states, had to rely on outside help in case of emergency. If assistance was not granted or – as was the case in 1814 – was requested too late, the outcome could easily be predicted. The citizens of Washington lacked the resources Baltimore's populace could muster. That does not mean that Washington's fall in August 1814 was inevitable. It was an act of self-deception on John Armstrong's part to proclaim the

70 Frank A. Cassell, "The Great Baltimore Riot of 1812," *Maryland Historical Magazine* 70 (1975): 241–95.

city safe and then do nothing to bolster its defenses, and that he was able to do so also throws an unfavorable light on Madison's way of managing his cabinet.[71]

Another problem was the commissioning of officers on the basis of seniority and political connections rather than professional experience and expertise. It was only after the war, in reducing the army to a peacetime level, that Madison ordered an evaluation of the officer's corps.[72] The blunders and failures of the war thus served to help lay the foundations for the professionalization of the American military.

While the example of Washington provides a case study on the defects of the U.S. military establishment in the early republic, Baltimore highlights its strengths. Given time and good leadership, militia forces could hold their ground against any regular army, especially in a defensive operation. General Smith had provided both. When the long-anticipated British attack came, every officer and private knew his task. Fortifications had been built that even the British were forced to admire.[73] Smith also resisted the temptation to enhance his military reputation by harassing the retreating enemy, but he kept his troops on the defensive.

It is difficult to assess British military strategy in the Chesapeake Bay region, and it is hardly surprising that most studies dealing with the naval war end with a narrative epilogue rather than struggle with the problems of evaluation. The original design behind the British maritime activities along the United States' Atlantic coast was to enforce a blockade and impede American commerce. This blockade was very effective, as was immediately evident in the inflation of prices for commodities of all kinds.

As the war continued, the objective of the Chesapeake campaign was expanded. The British sought to tie down American troops intended for Canada. The British hoped that pressure on noncombatants would encourage Federalist antiwar sentiments, assuming that the harassed populace would blame the federal government that could not protect them rather than the aggressors. This strategy implied a high level of discipline on the side of the British troops. But with captains eager for prize money and soldiers hungry for plunder, the necessary distinction between public

---

71 C. Edward Skeen, "Monroe and Armstrong: A Study in Political Rivalry," *New York Historical Society Quarterly* 57 (1973): 121–46.

72 William B. Skelton, "High Army Leadership in the Era of the War of 1812: The Making and Remaking of the Officer's Corps," *William and Mary Quarterly*, 3rd ser., 51 (1994): 243–74, and 272.

73 Gleig, *Narrative*, 198.

and private property, or inimical and sympathetic inhabitants, was seldom scrupulously made.[74]

The problem was that British military leaders never developed a clear strategy how this psychological warfare should be conducted. Characteristically, neither the Admiralty nor the War Office gave the naval commanders of the North American station specific orders. Warren and Cochrane received identical instructions to employ their forces in any way that "may be found most expedient for . . . the annoyance of the Enemy."[75] At the same time the ministry was clamorous for results. British naval commanders were left to conduct the war according to their own gusto but were forced to report substantial victories to appease the home front. The result was the chaotic hit-and-run tactics a British general derisively called a "species of milito-nautico-guerilla-plundering warfare."[76]

The idea of staging raids along the Atlantic coast to divert American forces from Canada does not seem to have been well devised. To begin with, it did not work because the U.S. government refused to accept the imminent danger and diverted few forces to avert it. But even more important, the British wasted their best troops in a strategically peripheral guerilla war, while their own reinforcements could have been far better employed in Canada. Even the most memorable success of the campaign – the burning of Washington – did not achieve any military objective. To the contrary, it promoted popular support and national unity – exactly the effects British strategy wanted to prevent.

The indecisive outcome of the Chesapeake campaign in 1814 can thus be seen as a focal point for an altogether indecisive war. As thirty years earlier, the British were unable to find the vulnerable spot in the vastness of the North American continent.

---

74 *Barbarities of the Enemy: Report of the Committee Appointed to Enquire into the Spirit and Manner in Which the War Has Been Waged by the Enemy* (Troy, New York, 1813). Adm. Codrington to Captains, Aug. 24, 1814, in Dudley and Crawford, *Naval War*, 3:229–31.
75 First Secretary of the Admiralty Crocker to Cochrane, in Dudley and Crawford, *Naval War*, 3:70–1.
76 Sir Harry Smith, in Coles, *War of 1812*, 264.

19

Lost Neutrality and Economic Warfare

Napoleonic Warfare in Northern Europe, 1795–1815

KATHERINE B. AASLESTAD

In 1813, an anonymous pamphlet appeared in Sweden and Britain depicting the disastrous consequences of the Continental System on northern Europe. *An Appeal to the Nations of Europe against the Continental System* described the steady impoverishment of Holland after 1795, the destruction of Hanseatic commerce after 1806, and the dismal fate of Bonaparte's ally Denmark. The pamphlet strongly indicted Napoleon as "the author of all evils" and defended Britain's maritime policies, in particular its position toward neutrals and its treatment of Denmark.[1] The pamphlet touched on precisely the themes that most decisively characterized the experience of northern European states during the Napoleonic Wars: the violation of neutrality, expanded commercial warfare, the economic deterioration associated with the Continental System, and an exploitative military occupation. The pamphlet highlighted the importance of the often-overlooked northern European front during the Napoleonic Wars. The wartime experience of these states demonstrates both the rapid intensification of commercial warfare and the expansion of the naval conflict between Britain and Napoleon beyond the struggle to control the seas. In fact, they sought to destroy completely the enemy's economy. In this contest, small states lost all chance for neutrality and saw their peoples and economies become pawns in the great power conflict.

This chapter explores the wartime experiences of three northern European coastal regions: the United Provinces of the Netherlands (referred to

---

1 *An Appeal to the Nations of Europe against the Continental System, published in Stockhold by the Authority of Bernadotte in March 1813* (London, 1813). It appears to be a close replication of *The Continental System and Its Relations with Sweden*, trans. August Wilhelm Schlegel (London, 1813).

The author would like to thank sincerely Paul W. Schroeder and John P. Lambertson for insightful comments that strengthened this article, and the West Virginia Humanities Council for research support.

as Holland – one of its' most significant provinces – by most sources), the northern German Hanseatic cities, and the conglomerate kingdom of Denmark (comprising Zealand, Jutland, Fyn and the smaller islands, the duchies of Schleswig and Holstein, and Norway as well as its northern Atlantic territories and colonial holdings in the East and West Indies). Located on the periphery of the empire, each region had a different relationship with imperial France: Holland occupied in 1795, ruled by Bonaparte's brother after 1806 and annexed in July 1810, the Hanseatic cities occupied in 1806 and annexed in December 1810, and Denmark neutral until 1807 and allied with Napoleon until 1814. Regardless of these distinctions, each region shared common war experiences. As small neutral states, they had no desire to engage in international hostilities but were engulfed or coerced into the growing conflict as helpless targets of great-power competition in which both British and French policies were equally menacing. If the British were notorious for the ruthless exploitation of their naval superiority, Bonaparte's Continental System ultimately inflamed popular hostility as it ruined the coastal economies. Material distress and hardships combined with imperial occupation alienated the populations of northern Europe against Napoleon's empire by 1813, leading to revolts in north Germany and Holland. Rapid economic deterioration in Denmark, associated with its alliance with France, even prompted the kingdom briefly to join the coalition against Bonaparte. The case of northern Europe illustrates salient aspects of the radicalization of international warfare during the Revolutionary and Napoleonic era: the impossibility of neutrality for smaller states, economic warfare on a new scale manifest in the Continental System, and ceaseless mobilization of men and material to support French expansion.

THE PROBLEMS OF EIGHTEENTH-CENTURY NEUTRALITY

The northern European maritime states benefitted from a dramatic growth in North Sea and Baltic trade during the eighteenth century. Based on foreign trade and the expansion and reliability of seaborne transport, the late-eighteenth-century European economy revolved around such shipping and commercial centers as Amsterdam, Rotterdam, Bremen, Hamburg, Lübeck, and Copenhagen. Dutch, Hanseatic, and Danish ships transported goods from the Baltic to the Mediterranean and participated in the colonial trade in Asia, Africa, and the West Indies. Port cities with industrial hinterlands were particularly prosperous. Regional distribution of colonial goods and expansion of European trade, in fact, helped revive the Dutch economy after its relative decline from the late seventeenth century.[2] The expansion of international trade within and beyond Europe led to increased competition and rivalry among European powers. When rivalry gave way to war, neutral powers often stood to profit. Their ability to exploit new trade routes and markets opened by war depended, however, on their ability to defend their neutrality.

Conflicts between major powers, like the Seven Years' War, created a huge demand for neutral tonnage and generated vast fortunes in continental and colonial trade. Holland controlled a large share of colonial commerce and provided shipping services to other nations with its huge merchant fleet. Other small powers like Denmark tried to avoid armed conflict and benefit from the expansion of trade and shipping during times of war.[3] Yet, neutral shipping undermined Britain's efforts to use its unrivaled naval power to conduct economic warfare. Thus, the expansion of the global economy that made seafaring neutrals wealthy also increased their vulnerability as economic warfare gained increasing importance. Increased Dutch participation in the West Indies and North American trade during the American Revolutionary War prompted Britain to declare hostilities against Holland in 1780 (the Fourth Anglo-Dutch War) and seize Dutch shipping and colonies to offset its own losses and restore its prestige. Trade and shipping under neutral flags generated huge profits. During the Seven Years' War and, to an even greater extent, the American Revolutionary War, Denmark successfully exploited the vast commercial opportunities available in neutral trading states as it simultaneously avoided conflict.

There were, however, inherent problems in eighteenth-century neutrality and neutral trade. There was no international consensus on the principles of neutrality, especially the rights and obligations of belligerents toward neutrals.[5] Defending the principle of "free ships, free goods," Holland, Denmark, and the Hanseatic cities claimed the right as neutrals to trade with nations at war and their colonies as well as to transport goods belonging to belligerents. They defined contraband narrowly as war materials (munitions and armaments) and contended that merchant vessels in neutral

2 Jan de Vries and Ad van der Woude, *The First Modern Economy: Success, Failure, and Perseverance of the Dutch Economy, 1500–1815* (Cambridge, U.K., 1997), 683–4.
3 Ole Feldbaek, *Denmark and the Armed Neutrality, 1800–1801: Small Power Policy in a World War* (Copenhagen, 1980), 18.
4 H. S. K. Kent, *War and Trade in Northern Seas: Anglo-Scandinavian Economic Relations in the Mid-Eighteenth Century* (Cambridge, U.K., 1973).
5 W. Allison Phillips, *Neutrality, Its History, Economics and Law*, vol. 2, *The Napoleonic Period* (New York, 1936), 11.

convoys should be free from search and seizure on the high seas. Britain, in contrast, took a far more restrictive view of neutrality and disputed the claim that neutral cargo was inviolable. The British defined contraband broadly as any article destined for the enemy that would be useful in its war effort. They asserted that belligerents had the right to visit and search all neutral vessels to inspect their cargos and papers, and that blockades applied to enemy and neutral shipping alike. These different interpretations of neutrality and contraband often pitted small neutral powers in an unequal contest against Britain and its navy. Denmark, though it continued to argue for neutrals' rights, had to adapt its practice of neutral shipping to avoid open conflict with Britain or still worse restriction of Danish trade.[6] The League of Armed Neutrality sponsored by Russia in 1780 might have served to promote the neutrality principles supported by the Dutch, Danes, Swedes, and Prussians, but it manifested international opposition to Britain rather than a genuine league of states defending neutral rights. Catherine II herself would renounce the principles of 1780 thirteen years later during the second partition of Poland. Neutral rights had no champions with teeth, so that small powers were forced into a pragmatic policy of exploiting opportunities open to neutrals wherever possible without expecting international recognition for the principles of free ships and free trade.

The outbreak of war in Europe in 1792 generated new opportunities for neutral trade and shipping that were welcomed and exploited by Denmark, Sweden, the Hanseatic cities, and the United States. In what has been called the golden age of neutral trade, the volume of colonial trade carried on in Hamburg, Bremen, Copenhagen, and Wismar – coffee and sugar from Central and South America, and tobacco and cotton from North America – increased substantially during the 1790s.[7] Neutral port cites amassed remarkable wealth during the decade. Hamburg dominated continental wholesale trade, as the Elbe became the gateway for distributing English and American goods on the continent. The French conquest of the Low Countries in 1795 limited Holland's direct participation but contributed to economic expansion in the Hanseatic cities and Denmark at Dutch expense. Dutch shipping continued, however, until 1806 under flags of convenience and in close collaboration with the neutral American fleet. The Batavian Republic of 1795, a French satellite and pawn, faced severe

---

6 Ole Tuxen, "Principle and Priority: Danish View of Neutrality during the Colonial Wars," *Scandinavian Journal of History* 13, no. 3 (1988): 207–32.

7 Silvia Marzagalli, "Port Cities in the French Wars: The Responses of Merchants in Bordeaux, Hamburg, and Livorno to Napoleon's Continental Blockade, 1806–1813," *The Northern Mariner/Le Marin du Nord* 6, no. 4 (1996): 65–73, here 66; Sam A. Mustafa, *Merchants and Migrations, Germans and Americans in Connection, 1776–1835* (Aldershot, U.K., 2001), 117–30.

economic losses in overseas trade, shipbuilding, industry, and fishing as a result of war with Britain and privateers. French economic intervention also ended Amsterdam's major role in international finance. Dutch colonies in Suriname, Curaçao, southern India, Dutch Ceylon, South Africa, and eventually Java all fell to Britain. Aside from a brief interlude following the Peace of Amiens, Holland's East Indian trade was severely disrupted. The dockyards and wharfs of the United East India Company closed in 1803.[8] Colonial and local commerce persisted, however, through smuggling and trade in neutral bottoms. Napoleon's exasperation with the Dutch government's inability to enforce economic embargoes against Britain or to raise troops and money for France finally led him to disband the republic in 1806 and make Holland a monarchy ruled by his brother Louis.

With France, and by extension Holland, at war with Britain, Denmark assumed a crucial role in international and colonial commerce, transporting huge stocks of coffee, sugar, and spices from Asia under neutral colors. The Copenhagen merchant and war speculator Frédéric de Coninck carried on the Dutch China trade in Danish ships. A fleet of ships carrying more than 185,000 tons discharged a total of 350 Asian cargos in Copenhagen, bringing great wealth in the form of profits, custom duties, and employment to the Danish economy until 1807.[9] Following the death of Foreign Minister A. P. Bernstorff, the architect of Denmark's pragmatic neutrality, the Danes adopted a policy of offensive neutrality in 1797 in response to growing problems with French privateers.[10] This shift in policy, which entailed the reintroduction of the convoy system, ultimately provoked the British. After a series of incidents in which Danish convoys refused to allow search by British squadrons, the British demanded that the Danes cease convoying in 1800. An appeal to Russia and other neutrals to support the principles of maritime neutrality, including the inviolability of convoys, unwittingly landed the Danes in the morass of Anglo-Russian hostility that arose from the collapse of the Second Coalition (Russia, Great Britain, and Austria) against France. Czar Paul I, Catherine's successor, promoted among Denmark, Sweden, and Prussia a second League of Armed Neutrality, the Nordic League, largely as an anti-British weapon. Dependent on Russia to support its territorial integrity against Swedish designs on Norway, Denmark was

---

8 Simon Schama, *Patriots and Liberators, Revolution in the Netherlands, 1780–1813* (New York, 1992), 370–3; Jonathan Israel, *The Dutch Republic, Its Rise, Greatness and Fall, 1477–1806*, (Oxford, 1995), 1127; de Vries, *Dutch Economy*, 685.

9 Ole Feldbaek, "The Danish Asia Trade, 1620–1807," *Scandinavian Economic History Review* 39 (1991): 3–27.

10 On defensive and offensive neutrality, see Ole Feldbaek, *The Battle of Copenhagen, Nelson and the Danes*, trans. Tony Wedgewood (Annapolis, Maryland, 2002), 14–23.

compelled to take far stronger measures than it had originally intended. On Russia's instructions, it occupied Hamburg in 1801 and embargoed British trade. Denmark and Sweden thus became pawns in an Anglo-Russian conflict.

Britain responded forcefully. After imposing naval blockades on all neutral shipping in January 1801, it moved first against the Danes in the West Indies by occupying the Danish Virgin Islands and then against Danish outposts in India. In late March, a British fleet of more than fifty ships approached Copenhagen. On April 2, a squadron led by Admiral Horatio Nelson quickly neutralized the Danish line of ships protecting the city, which thereupon became vulnerable to bombardment. After six days of negotiation, the Danes signed an armistice, under the terms of which they agreed to leave the Nordic League and suspend all naval activity for fourteen weeks. The punishment was an effective lesson to Denmark and its neutral neighbors of the threat that unrestrained great powers posed to small states.[11] Clearly, the expanding scope of great-power conflict made the kind of neutrality Denmark had previously maintained impossible.[12] Following the British attack, the Danes kept a low profile in their relations with the British and the French, abandoned offensive neutrality and commercial exploitation of their neutral status, and built up their naval defenses against a possible attack by Sweden. But the attempt to hide from the consequences of great-power war proved unsuccessful. Following the brief Peace of Amiens in 1802, Denmark would remain vulnerable to Anglo-French economic warfare. The war of the Third Coalition (Great Britain, Russia, and Austria against Napoleon's empire and his German, Spanish, and Italian satellites), in particular the battles of Trafalgar and Austerlitz in late 1805, sealed Britain's supremacy on the sea and Napoleon's on land and heightened the economic war between Britain and France. French expansion into northern Germany in 1806 in the conquest of Prussia put Denmark directly at risk and increased the chances that it might fall victim to the Anglo-French conflict, as indeed it did in 1807.

Like Denmark, the Hanseatic cities Hamburg, Bremen, and Lübeck sought to avoid war and exploit wartime commercial opportunities under neutral flags. Following the flight of capital and trade from Holland to northern Germany, Hamburg was central to Britain's continental commerce after

---

11 This conflict was resolved at any rate following the murder of Czar Paul and the reversal of his policies by his son Alexander.

12 Paul W. Schroeder, *The Transformation of European Politics, 1763–1848* (Oxford, 1994), 221–2; Ole Feldbaek, "Denmark and Britain, 1720–1864," in *In Quest of Trade and Security: The Baltic in Power Politics, 1500–1990*, ed. G. Rystad, K.-R. Böhme, and W. Carlgren I (Lund, 1994), 277.

1795.[13] Hamburg and Bremen became Europe's most important commercial centers for colonial goods and products from the United States.[14] Traffic through Hamburg's port increased dramatically. The bulk of the city's trade was carried in foreign bottoms, Dutch above all (until 1795) but also British, Danish, and American. The wars that provided commercial opportunity, however, also threatened Hanseatic sovereignty, as became evident in 1795, when Hanoverian and British troops temporarily occupied Bremen. Later that year, representatives from the three cities convened in Hamburg to draft a common neutrality program. The resulting document presented Hanseatic independence and neutrality as serving the trade, banking, transportation, and communication interests of all nations.[15] Aware that those with power determined the rights of neutrals, Hanseatic statesmen sought to convince France and Great Britain that it was in French and British interests to support Hanseatic neutrality.[16] Hamburg and Bremen also sought to purchase French support, but years of negotiations and the expenditure of huge sums in so-called gifts and contributions failed to secure Paris's recognition of Hanseatic neutrality.[17]

Napoleon's success at Austerlitz against the Austro-Russian armies, the establishment of the French-sponsored Confederation of the Rhine, and the demise of the Holy Roman Empire made it imperative for the Hanseatic cities to formalize their sovereignty and neutrality. Aware that they could not survive independently and drawing on their common commercial and republican traditions, Hamburg, Bremen, and Lübeck formed a regional neutral free-trade zone in 1806 in an attempt to preserve their independence and safeguard their commercial interests.[18] In November 1806, less than a

13 Import trade between Britain and Hamburg increased from 21.8 million francs in 1798 to 96.9 million francs in 1799, and export trade skyrocketed from 42 million francs in 1789 to 224.1 million francs in 1799. Burghart Schmidt, *Hamburg im Zeitalter der Französischen Revolution und Napoleons (1789–1813)* (Hamburg, 1998), 232–4; Eli F. Heckscher, *The Continental System: An Economic Interpretation* (Oxford, 1922), 96; Phillips, *Neutrality*, 2:271.

14 Schmidt, *Hamburg*, 234; Mustafa, *Merchants*, 117–30.

15 Schmidt, *Hamburg*, 148–54; Ernst Wilmanns, "Der Gedanke einer Neutralisierung der Hansestädte 1795–1803," *Hansische Geschichtsblätter* 49 (1924): 1–43; Hans Wiedemann, *Die Außenpolitik Bremens im Zeitalter der Französischen Revolution, 1794–1803* (Bremen, 1960), 39–43.

16 Johann Georg Büsch, *Über die durch den jetzigen Krieg veranlaßte Zerrüttung des Seehandels und deren insbesondere für den deutschen Handel zu befürchtende bösen Folgen* (Hamburg, 1793); Büsch, *Unparteiische Erörterung der wichtigen Frage, was hat Deutschland in Ansehung seines Land-und Seehandels von den so nahen Friedens-Unterhandlungen zu erwarten?* (Hamburg, 1795); Büsch, *Die politische Wichtigkeit der Freiheit Hamburgs und ihrer Schwesterstädte Lübeck und Bremen für das ganze handelnde Euroepa in ein neues Licht gestellt* (Hamburg, 1797).

17 Burghart Schmidt, "Pot-de-vin und Staaträson: Ein Beitrag zur deutsch-französischen Diplomatiegeschichte Ende des 18. und Anfang des 19. Jahrhunderts im Zeichen von Erpressung und Korruption," *Prague Papers on History of Intenational Relations* (1999): 173–94, here 180–5.

18 Bremen Staatarchiv (hereafter cited as BSt) Gutachten der im September und October zu Lübeck zusammengetretenen Hanseatischen Deputation. 2. B. 5.e. 3. Katherine Aaslestad, *Place and Politics:*

month after the three cities proclaimed a Hanseatic federation, the French attacked and occupied Lübeck as they pursued the collapsing Prussian army in the wake of the Battle of Jena. Hamburg and Bremen surrendered to French forces two weeks later. It was clear that the fate of the Hanseatic cites, like that of other small neutral states, was beyond their own control.

Napoleon's victories over the third and fourth coalitions only further undermined neutral rights. No great power supported neutrality. Neither Britain nor France recognized neutral rights on the high seas. Britain sought to prevent French commerce in neutral bottoms and forced neutrals to accept British goods in defiance of the French campaign to exclude British trade with the Continent.[19] The French exploited neutrality as a weapon against the British and a means to exhort increasing financial demands from desperate small states like the Hanseatic cities. Indeed, both great powers used small powers in trying to retaliate against each other. Britain's blockades of the Elbe, Weser, and Eider in response to France's temporary occupation of Hanover and Ritzbüttel underscored the growing pattern of great-power reprisal by targeting small neutral states. As the war progressed, relentless commercial warfare with virtually no recognition of neutral commercial rights characterized the conflict between Britain and France.

THE CONTINENTAL SYSTEM, 1806–1812

As noted, Napoleon's victory against Prussia in October 1806 extended imperial military might into northern Germany and made Denmark, Sweden, and Russia frontline states in the ongoing international conflict. The military campaign in north Germany – the "forgotten front," as one recent scholar dubbed it – put an end to any lingering hope for the neutral states that they might escape involvement in the international conflict.[20] With his Berlin Decrees (November 1806), Napoleon set out to subjugate and reshape the continent's economies to serve France. If the origins of Napoleon's decision to establish a continental blockade – the Continental System – remain contested, it is clear the Berlin Decrees marked an intensification of economic warfare.[21] Not content merely to deprive Britain

---

Local Identity, Civic Culture, and German Nationalism in North Germany during the Revolutionary Era (Leiden, 2005), 203–44; Paul W. Schroeder, "Making a Necessity of Virtue: The Smaller State as Intermediary Body," *Austrian History Yearbook* 29 (1998): 1–18.

19 Phillips, *Neutrality*, 2:9; Heckscher, *Continental System*, 55–8, 82.

20 Christer Jörgensen, *The Anglo-Swedish Alliance against Napoleonic France* (London, 2004), 41.

21 Scholars have contended that the Berlin decrees represent an extension of traditional Anglo-French commercial warfare dating from 1660–1786 as well as a legacy from the 1793 French Navigation Acts. Heckscher, *Continental*, 13–29; Frank Edgar Melvin, *Napoleon's Navigation System, A Study*

of its trade with the continent, Napoleon wanted to destroy his enemy's economy. Under the emperor's dictate, all trade, traffic, and correspondence between Britain and the Continent were to be immediately halted, British nationals imprisoned, and all British property, merchandise, and correspondence confiscated. Britain's Orders in Council and Napoleon's 1807 Milan Decrees extended the war to neutral shipping and broadened economic warfare throughout the Atlantic. The blockade against British goods and communication, however, was but one part of Napoleon's economic campaign. Described by the historian Albert Sorel as a "two-trigger engine," the blockade had both a destructive and a constructive purpose. It was intended, on the one hand, to disrupt Britain's economy and thereby reduce its capacity to wage war. On the other, it also sought to redirect continental trade according to a new "market design" that would establish French industrial and commercial hegemony on the continent.[22] The blockade imposed in 1806 thus had far-reaching goals beyond subduing Britain; the real target of French economic restructuring was the Continent.[23]

The escalation of economic warfare thus went hand in hand with French military and political expansion across Europe. The blockade against Britain could succeed only if the empire could successfully control the entire European coastline. In 1806, Napoleon installed his brother Louis as the king of Holland and occupied northern Germany.[24] The obvious movement of illicit goods from Friesland to Zeeland and the presence of smuggled British goods in Dutch shops frustrated Napoleon, who had charged Louis with enforcing the blockade and raising troops, money, and material for French expansion. In 1810, Louis's failure to fulfill either duty led to the demise of the Dutch Kingdom. Napoleon annexed the entire North Sea coastline, including Holland and northern German territories. The three Hanseatic cities, the duchies of Lauenburg and Oldenburg and northwestern Hanover, were merged into the three Hanseatic departments to form the Empire's Thirty-second Military District.

French expansion also had drastic consequences for Scandinavia. Denmark again endured naval attack by Britain. Following the disaster of 1801, Denmark had sought to ensure its neutrality by deploying a new fleet of gunboats and brigs to protect its coasts and stationing the bulk

of Trade Control During the Continental Blockade (New York, 1919), 7–10; Schroeder, *Transformation*, 307–9; Philip Dwyer, "Napoleon and the Drive for Glory: Reflections of the Making of French Foreign Policy," in *Napoleon and Europe*, ed. Philip Dwyer (London, 2001), 118–35, here 123–4.

22 Geoffrey Ellis, *The Napoleonic Empire* (Basingstoke, U.K., 2003), 111.

23 Schroeder, *Transformation*, 308–9.

24 The military occupation of northern Germany in 1806 preceded even further military expansion across southern Europe and eventually widespread territorial annexation into the empire.

of it army in Holstein. It withdrew those troops in 1806 to avoid clashes with the French as they expanded their military operations into northern Germany. The Franco-Russian Treaty of Tilsit (1807) and the specter of Russo-French cooperation, however, thrust Denmark unwillingly into the thick of the international conflict. At Tilsit, Napoleon required Alexander to agree to force the northern neutral states of Denmark and Sweden to adhere to the Continental System; in compensation, he offered the czar a free hand in Swedish Finland. Fearful that the strategically situated Denmark and its navy might fall under French control, Britain issued an ultimatum to Denmark, with the intent to give a clear warning to Russia against allying with France.[25] It summoned the Danes under threat of war either to enter into alliance with Britain and place their navy at Britain's disposal or to hand over their fleet to Britain as an assurance of Danish neutrality. Meanwhile, Napoleon's forces appeared ready to invade Holstein and Schleswig, threatening the integrity of Danish sovereignty, which might lead to the loss of Norway. The French likewise issued an ultimatum to Denmark: join the Continental System and the war against Britain or expect hostilities from France. Prince Frederik, in Holstein with the army, rejected the British ultimatum. In late August 1807, British troops invaded Zeeland, dispersed the Danish peasant militia, and bombarded Copenhagen to force him to reconsider his position. The attack from land and sea culminated in a three-day bombardment of Copenhagen. The attack and ensuing fires destroyed more than a third of the city.[26] The Danes capitulated and surrendered their entire navy to Britain: fifteen ships of the line, fifteen frigates, seven gunboats, many smaller vessels, and 2 million pounds of naval stores. The British soon decided on military grounds to evacuate Danish territory except for the island of Helgoland at the mouth of the Elbe and Denmark's West Indian and Indian colonies.[27]

Denmark responded to the British attack by allying itself with Napoleon in October 1807; the French emperor was the only ruler willing to guarantee Danish territorial integrity, recognize its claim to Norway, and promise

---

25 London feared impeded traffic through the Baltic as British Isles. Britain depended on grain and naval stores imports and colonial exports to finance the war. Feldbaek, "Denmark," 279.

26 Scholars have regarded this attack as the first terror bombing of a civilian target in a modern war; see ibid, 278. For recent assessments, see: Bård Frydenlund and Rasmus Glenthøj, eds., *1807 og Denmark-Norge, På vei mot atskillelsen* (Oslo, 2009); Thomas Munch-Peterson, *Defying Napoleon: How Britain bombarded Copenhagen and seized the Danish Fleet in 1807*, (Stroud, 2007), Peter Henningsen, ed., *Københaven 1807: belejring og bombardement*, (Copenhagen, 2007), and Rasmus Glenthøj and Jens Rahbek Rasmussen, eds., *Det venskabelige bombardement: Københaven 1807 som historisk begivenhend og national myte*, (Copenhagen, 2007).

27 Ole Feldbaek, "Denmark in the Napoleonic Wars," *Scandinavian Journal of History* 26 (2001): 89–101, here 92.

to return the Danish fleet. The price was high, as Napoleon obliged Denmark to enforce the Continental System and help pressure Sweden to join. Hatred for Britain as well as fear of French occupation prompted the government in Copenhagen to support Napoleon's system. During the following seven years, the Danes did everything possible to damage British shipping in the Danish straits, and they captured seven British brigs.[28] But as former beneficiaries of neutral trade, Denmark applied Napoleon's blockade inconsistently. It became an active partner in the Continental System only in 1808, and even then it continued to trade with Britain through licenses and false papers. Continuing to trade with Britain was a pragmatic not a political decision: the Danes wanted to salvage what they could of their maritime economy. In fact, the bulk of the Danish population, even state officials, worked to circumvent their state's official Francophile policies because they damaged the economy and caused material hardships.

French economic warfare reached a new level with the Fontainebleau, Trianon, and Saint Cloud Decrees issued in 1810. Napoleon sought to increase pressure on Britain by clamping down on the smuggling of British goods into continental markets, to strengthen the already-privileged position of French industry and commerce by raising imperial tariffs, and to turn smuggling to the advantage of the French treasury by requiring special licenses for agricultural exports and imports. Along the recently annexed North Sea coastline, he enforced the blockade by deploying growing numbers of customs officials and imperial troops. Smugglers caught in the act were punished brutally. French authorities gave public display of their intention to end smuggling by staging bonfires of seized British goods in late 1810 and early 1811. Dutch and northern German merchants initially hoped that, as new members of the Empire and its preferential market zone, they might benefit from imperial reforms and trade with France on equal terms. To their bitter disappointment, tariff barriers remained as the expansion of the empire sought to meet short-term logistical and military needs, not the equitable integration of new territories into France. Napoleon and his minister of commerce intended to control strictly all trade in foreign goods through import licenses and to enrich privileged French ports at the expense of those in the annexed territories. The consequences of this policy were catastrophic for annexed regions where shipping and manufacturing were central to the local economy.

---

28 Roland Ruppenthal, "Denmark and the Continental System," *Journal of Modern History* 15 (1943): 7–23, here, 12; Hertel P. Rasmussen, "Dansk Udenrigspolitik, 1812–1813," *Historisk Tidsskrift* 77 (1977): 65–84.

THE CONSEQUENCES OF THE CONTINENTAL SYSTEM
IN NORTHERN EUROPE

Across northern Europe, the Continental System shattered economies, caused material and social hardships, and eventually stoked popular hostility toward France. Port cities – Amsterdam, Rotterdam, Bremen, and Hamburg – experienced immediate commercial and industrial decline as they were blocked from trade with Britain and deprived of continental markets as a result of Napoleon's export restrictions. French political and military power, however, could ensure neither consistent nor adequate enforcement of the blockade until 1810. Economic stagnation and decline with short-term fluctuations in illicit trade characterized the first four years of the blockade. In 1807 and the first half of 1808, for example, shipping nearly ended on the coast of the North Sea, but by midyear, British merchandise and colonial goods passed through holes in the blockade into European markets. In fact, the visibility of colonial goods with Anglo-Dutch origins led Napoleon to seal France from all Dutch products in September 1808.[29] The war against Austria in 1809, temporarily distracting Napoleon from the commercial-naval war with Britain, provided some relief to northern European ports, and northern Germany reemerged as the most important destination of British exports, receiving 12 percent of its exports.[30] Such fluctuations and the porous nature of the blockade along the North Sea coastline ceased dramatically after 1810. Although some illicit trade based on falsified documents continued, imperial reinforcement of the blockade with arbitrary nocturnal arrests, extensive searches, and seizures combined with the eastward shift of contraband to Sweden and the Baltic had eradicated most large-scale smuggling operations by 1812.

Between 1806 and 1810, as traditional trade, shipping, and manufactures declined, Dutch, North German, and Danish merchants adapted to the French blockade by turning to "alternative trade routes," fraud, bribery, and above all, smuggling.[31] Shipping on Dutch rivers, the Vlie, Maas, and Goeree, fell by more than 60 percent from prewar levels. Between 1806 and 1809, however, the Dutch were the third-best customers of British manufactured and colonial exports following Denmark and Russia. In fact, 16 percent of British colonial reexports arrived in Holland.[32]

29 Schama, *Patriots*, 569.
30 Burghart Schmidt, "Die ostfriesischen Inseln zu Beginn des 19. Jahrhunderts," *Emder Jahrbuch für Historische Landeskunde Ostfreislands* 78 (1999): 188–231, here 191.
31 Schama, *Patriots*, 568–72; Marzagalli, "Port Cities," 65–73; Mustafa, *Merchants*, 205–14.
32 Schama, *Patriots*, 561–9.

Smuggling contraband cargoes to Amsterdam via the Ems from Emden or overland through Friesland and to Hamburg via Danish Tönning and Helgoland accounted for this alternative economy. Coastal geography supported smuggling, as river deltas, mudflats, marshes, coastal islands, and sand dunes were particularly difficult to monitor and secure.[33] In 1807, Britain seized the Danish island of Helgoland, which served as a key transit station for smugglers and emerged as the "warehouse of Europe."[34] By autumn 1808, warehouses on the island were stocked with colonial goods valued at roughly 1 million pounds sterling, including coffee, sugar, spices, indigo, cotton, English-manufactured stoneware, muslin, and cotton textiles. A British naval squadron protected the small island and the three hundred to four hundred ships that visited it daily.[35]

Thrown out of work by the continental blockade and new export tariffs, the unemployed turned to smuggling as a means to feed their families. Fishermen and farmers transported illegal cargoes of British and American goods. Smuggling was profitable; farmers earned more transporting smuggled goods than through agriculture.[36] It was also dangerous and developed into a guerilla war against imperial toll inspectors and custom agents.[37] Small-scale smuggling, pervasive at city gates, relied largely on women, youth, and servants, who concealed bags of coffee beans, sugar, pepper, and syrup in their clothing, stockings, boots, and hats. One pound of coffee slipped into Hamburg from Altona could bring the equivalent of a day's wages.[38] Authorities in Hamburg estimated that some six thousand to ten thousand people smuggled goods between Hamburg and Altona each day, and the distance between the two cities was so short that smugglers could make ten to twelve trips a day. French authorities confiscated no more than 5 percent of this contraband.[39] Hard numbers on the value of illicit trade between 1806 and 1810 are difficult to determine, as most of it remained unrecorded in official ledgers. Judging from the value of confiscated goods,

---

33 See French military assessments cited in Schmidt, "Ostfriesischen Inseln," 204–31; K. J. Kuipers, *Een Groninger Zeeman in Napoleontische Tijd, Kleine Handelsvaart contra Continentaal Stelsel* (Zutphen, 1980).

34 Wernher Mohrhenn, *Helgoland zur Zeit der Kontinentalsperre* (Berlin, 1926), 46; Schmidt, *Hamburg*, 299–302.

35 Detlef Zunker, Hamburg in der Franzosenzeit 1806–1814: Volkskultur und Volksprotest in einer besetzten Stadt (Hamburg, 1983), 43.

36 Dieter Kienitz, *Der Kosaken winter in Schleswig-Holstein 1813–1814* (Heide, 2000), 27.

37 Jean Mistler, "Hambourg sous l'occupation Françaose: Observations au sujet du Blocus continental," *Francia, Forschungen zur westeuropäischen Geschichte* 1 (1973): 451–66, here 452.

38 Walther Vogel, *Die Hansestädte und die Kontinentalsperre* (Munich, 1913), 52. Zunker, *Franzosenzeit*, 39–40; [Johann Georg Rist], *Johann Georg Rist in Hamburg aus seinen Lebenserinnerungen* (Hamburg, 1913), 96.

39 Schmidt, *Hamburg*, 307; Stuart Woolf, *Napoleon's Integration of Europe* (New York, 1991), 152.

however, it was clearly significant. For example, in Holland, toll officials estimated that 3 million guilders' worth of goods entered Holland between Rotterdam and Amsterdam during a three-week period in 1809.[40]

Corruption among French administrators, soldiers, and even customs agents also undermined the imperial blockade against Britain. Merchants often succeeded in passing English merchandise under the cover of false certificates that attested their origin in Denmark, Sweden, America, or Russia. In Holland, the enforcement apparatus was both inefficient and corrupt. Walking among the dunes along the Dutch coast, ruminating about her pitiful life, Queen Hortense could spot English vessels on the horizon "doubtless engaged in some smuggling trade."[41] Confusion and competition among officials prevented effective enforcement, and corruption among officials at all levels, including government administrators, soldiers and army commanders, coast guard, and even Louis's advisers, ensured that pockets would be lined when British manufactured and colonial goods reached Leiden, Amsterdam, and Rotterdam.[42] The extent of corruption and smuggling is evident in the 1809 case of Zeeland merchant Cornelis Cats, who slipped a toll official forty thousand guilders and promised him a commission on the profits of further business transactions.[43] Recognizing the crucial role of commerce in the Dutch economy, even King Louis turned a blind eye to illicit commerce, temporarily reopened Dutch ports, and granted royal licenses for trade with Britain. Similarly, the corrupt French military administration in Hamburg benefited from commerce with Britain. The city spent 1.5 million francs in early 1807 to encourage the new French authorities to overlook trade on the Elbe.[44] That year a French police report stated, "Trade with English goods in the city continues as prior to the decree."[45]

This atmosphere changed abruptly following the October 1810 Fontainebleau Decree. Designed to reinforce the Continental System, the decree ordered that all confiscated British goods be publicly burned. Within two months, fifty-six bonfires took place at forty-five locations throughout the continent.[46] On November 16, 1810, the French confiscated more than eight hundred thousand francs' worth of English goods in Hamburg. They

40 Johan Joor, *De Adelaar en het Lam. Onrust, opruiing en onwilligheid in Nederland ten tijde van het Koninkrijk Holland en de Inlijving bij het Franse Keizerrijk, 1806–1813* (Amsterdam, 2000), 429.
41 Jean Hanoteau, ed., *The Memoirs of Queen Hortense*, trans. Arthur Griggs (New York, 1927), 203.
42 Schama, *Patriots*, 569–609.   43 Joor, *Adelaar*, 429.
44 Marzagalli, "Port Cities," 68; Schmidt, "Pot-de-vin," 186–92.
45 Cited in Schmidt, *Hamburg*, 275.
46 Roger Dufraisse, "Blocus Continental," in *Dictionnaire Napoléon*, ed. Jean Tulard (Paris, 1987), 232.

resold the most valuable goods and burned those of lesser value with great fanfare outside the city gates. Similar bonfires along the Elbe and in Bremen and Lübeck signaled an abrupt hardening of French efforts to seal the continent to Britain and to intensify economic warfare. In November 1810, the American businessman John Greene Proud characterized North Sea and Baltic trade as "dead for the present."[47] Writing of Hamburg, another contemporary observed, "All traces of wealth have slowly vanished. There is no mention of trade."[48] As the imperial forces established control over northern European rivers and coastal mudflats, transporting colonial goods through the "black market Eldorado" of Helgoland became too risky, and the island lost its prominence as a smuggling emporium.[49] No ships entered Lübeck's harbor in 1811, and by March 1812, river traffic on the Elbe was limited to the transport of food, travelers, and soldiers.[50] Blockade enforcement, high taxes, and arbitrary fees caused many north German wholesale merchants to relocate to London, St. Petersburg, Göteborg, or Kiel, and midsized firms, no longer able to bribe the French and to secure their existence with false papers, failed in record numbers.[51] As illicit commerce retreated east toward Sweden and the Baltic, so, too, did investments and finance.[52] Unable to import raw materials or to sell in export markets, Hamburg's sugar, textile, and tobacco industries collapsed, resulting in mass unemployment. Economic warfare left poverty in its wake. As one contemporary recorded, "Everyone, even those who do not hear the resounding drums of war, feel themselves oppressed, half numb, hopeless, and brought to desperation."[53] Even Danish Altona and Flensburg, port cities that prospered on black

---

47 Cited in Daniel A. Rabuzzi, "Cutting out the Middleman? American Trade in Northern Europe, 1783–1815," in *Merchant Organization and Maritime Trade in the North Atlantic, 1660–1815*, ed. Olaf Uwe Janzen (Newfoundland, 1998), 175–97, here 176.

48 Heinrich Reincke, "Aus dem Briefwechsel von Karl und Diederich Gries 1796 bis 1819," *Zeitschrift für Hamburgische Geschichte* 25 (1924): here 257.

49 Any local contact with Helgoland was regarded as an act of espionage, and should any ship be proved to have stopped there, the vessel would be confiscated and its captain punished with death. Schmidt, *Hamburg*, 636–67.

50 Franklin Koptizsch, "Das 18. Jahrhundert: Vielseitigkeit und Leben," in *Lübeckische Geschichte*, ed. Antjekatrin Grassmann (Lübeck, 1989); Archives Nationales, Paris France (hereafter cited as AN) dossier F⁷3060, Report, Mar. 8, 1812.

51 On mercantile losses, see Percy Ernst Schramm, *Neun Generationen: Dreihundert Jahre deutscher "Kulturgeschichte" im Lichte der Schicksale einer Hamburger Bürgerfamilie (1648–1948)* (Göttingen, 1963), 1:364–6.

52 Jörgensen, *Anglo-Swedish*, 184–5; Leos Müller, *Consuls, Corsairs, and Commerce: The Swedish Consular Service and Long Distance Shipping, 1720–1815* (Uppsala, 2004). On privateering in Christianssand see, Finn-Einar Eliassen, "Kriegen og de norske byene Militarisering, folketap og en overklasse foran undergangen," in Frydenlund and Glenthøj, *1807*, 69–72.

53 [Johann Albrecht Heinrich Reimarus], *Klagen der Völker des Continents von Europa die Handelsperre* (Hamburg, 1809), 12.

market trade, faced severe economic crisis after 1810.[54] In fact, the abrupt termination of sugar and tobacco production in Flensburg left enduring economic problems into the 1820s.[55] In Holland, the sudden contraction of smuggling destroyed the contraband-driven illicit economy, bringing poverty to fishermen, pilots, warehouse keepers, and others. The arbitrary conduct of Imperial customs officials in their constant search for contraband also alienated Danes.[56]

Annexation into the empire, combined with enforcement of the blockade, made living conditions in northern Europe worse not better. The final years of the Continental System were a time of pauperization and depopulation in the North Sea port cities. Dock laborers, ship carpenters, sail makers, artisans, cigar rollers, oil pressers, and brewers faced destitution. In the long term, black market trade could not replace steady employment for the mass of the coastal population; urban laborers emigrated, resorted to begging, or stole.[57] Amsterdam lost 10 percent of its population; in Lübeck, outward migration left two hundred homes empty.[58] Unstable market prices and rampant inflation further impoverished the unemployed; only soup kitchens and the distribution of free fuel prevented complete destitution in urban Holland.[59] In Leiden, Amsterdam, Hamburg, and Bremen, growing numbers of inhabitants lived off public welfare services, which struggled to cope with rising indigence.[60] Entire towns faced devastation. For example, in Gouda, where the bulk of the working population depended on the pipe industry, the loss of traditional markets as a result of imperial tariffs had catastrophic economic consequences.[61] Ultimately, even Denmark found its economy ruined and at the mercy of Napoleonic mercantilist policies applied to enemy and ally alike. Although allied with France, it resorted to privateering and smuggling, as legitimate business remained impossible. Schleswig-Holstein continued to profit from illicit trade until 1811, when income from tolls as well as smuggling ceased and contributed

54 Rolf Gehrmann, "Handeleskonjunkturen in Schleswig-Holstein zur Zeit der Kontinentalsperre, 1807–1813," in *Wirtschaftliche Wechsellagen in Schleswig-Holstein vom Mittelalter biz zur Gegenwart*, ed. Jürgen Brockstedt (Neumünster, 1991), 145–74.
55 Ulrike Albrecht, "Wirtschaftliche Wechsellagen Flensburgs vom ausgehenden 18. Jahrhundert bis 1864," in *Wirtschaftliche Wechsellagen*, 99–120, here 111–12.
56 Ruppenthal, "Denmark," 16.
57 Erik Buyst and Joel Mokyr, "Dutch Manufacturing and Trade During the French Period," in *Economic Effects of the French Revolutionary and Napoleonic Wars*, ed. Erik Aerts and Francois Crouzet (Leuven, 1990), 66–71.
58 de Vries, *Dutch Economy*, 686; Vogel, *Hansestädte*, 51.
59 Buyst and Mokyr, "Dutch," 69; Joor, *Adelaar*, 60–3.
60 Schama, *Patriots*, 581–9; Mary Lindemann, *Patriots and Paupers, Hamburg, 1712–1830*, (Oxford, 1990), 183–6.
61 Schama, *Patriots*, 580.

to state bankruptcy.[62] Deteriorating economic conditions combined with troop movements led to a drastic rise in prostitution, illegitimate births, and abandoned babies.[63]

To measure the full impact of the Continental System on northern Europe, the cost of imperial occupation must also be taken into account. Dutch military obligations, including the cost of supporting the twenty-five thousand French troops in Holland, consumed 80 percent of ordinary revenues.[64] Military occupation in 1806 brought a variety of transient Dutch, Spanish, and French officers and soldiers, who lodged with the native population in the Hanseatic cities. In Hamburg, residents were obliged to provide the occupying troops with daily rations of meat, bread, vegetables, rice, beer, and brandy; in addition, they also had to pay monetary allowances to officers.[65] As the number of soldiers increased, so, too, did the financial demands on the local populations. The French military requisitioned private and public buildings as barracks in 1807 and obliged the Hanseatic cities to procure coats, boots, shirts, and medical supplies for imperial troops.[66] Expecting the cities to finance his wars, Napoleon demanded in October 1807 that the Hanseatic cities pay 400,000 francs monthly in salary for his troops at a time when occupation costs alone had risen to more than 10 million francs.[67] Quartering soldiers posed a severe burden on small towns. Krempe, near Glückstadt, with a population of one thousand inhabitants and two hundred homes, housed and fed more than two thousand soldiers.[68] Similarly, Altengamme and Bergedorf outside of Hamburg supported numerous imperial troops and their horses as the local agrarian economy declined.[69] Denmark also faced burdens associated with requisitioning and billeting imperial troops in 1807 and 1808

62 Rolf Gehrmann, "Handelskonjunkturen in Schleswig-Holstein zur Zeit der Kontinentalsperre, 1807–1813," in *Wirtschaftliche Wechsellagen*, 145–74.

63 Rist, *Lebenserinnerungen*, 39–40; Heide Soltau, "Verteufelt, verschwiegen und reglementiert: Über den Umgang der Hanseaten mit der Prostitution," in *Hamburg im Zeitalter der Aufklärung*, ed. Inge Stephen and Hans-Gerd Winter (Hamburg, 1989), 373–97; Schmidt, *Hamburg*, 530–31; Joor, *Adelaar*, 69.

64 Schama, *Patriots*, 478.

65 "Auszug aus dem Tagesbefehl des 8 Corps der großen Armee aus dem Hauptquartier zu Hamburg, den 22. November 1806," *Wöchentliche gemeinnützige Nachrichten von und für Hamburg*, November 26, 1806.

66 "Publicandum," *Wöchentliche gemeinnützige Nachrichten von und für Hamburg*, Sept. 2, 1807.

67 BSt Apr. 22, 1810, letter from Senator Smidt to Syndic Schöne, Senator Dr. Gonslehr, Senator Vollmers, and Senator Gröning in Hamburg and Lübeck, 2-B.5e.5. Schmidt, *Hamburg*, 362–4, 366–7; Gerhard Ahrens, "Staatsschuld und Anleihepolitik der hanseatischen Stadtrepubliken im frühen 19. Jahrhundert," *Blätter für deutsche Landesgeschichte* (1998): 361–406; Helmut Stubbe da Luz, *Okkupanten und Okkupierte, Napoleons Staatthalterregimes in den Hansestädten*, vol. 2 (Munich, 2005).

68 Kienitz, *Kosakenwinter*, 99.   69 Schmidt, *Hamburg*, 557–66.

during preparations for an invasion of Sweden. Compelled to house, feed, equip, and pay French, Spanish, and Dutch troops, the Danes felt less like French allies than occupied subjects.[70] Military expenses generated huge community expenditures. Hadersleben in Holstein, which averaged eleven thousand rigsdaler in incoming revenue, faced twenty thousand rigsdaler in expenses to support foreign troops.[71] Regardless their economic capacity, French allies and occupied territories alike had to meet increasing requisitions of equipment and supplies.

Ruined state finances and enormous debt were the natural consequences of subsidizing Napoleonic campaigns. The new tax system that Holland established to increase revenue proved incapable of keeping up with rising military expenditure. Moreover, with between 30 and 40 percent of Amsterdam's population on poor relief and the Dutch fishing fleets confined to the harbor, increased taxation added to material hardships associated with French rule.[72] The demands of military expansion also dictated Hamburg's civic expenditure; by 1811, the city directed one-third of its finances to outfitting and arming Napoleon's army.[73] In Denmark, the deep economic crisis that had emerged in 1807 worsened in 1811. Prices rose 50 to 100 percent during the first years of the war and by 300 percent during the last years.[74] Despite efforts by the government to fix prices, inflation spiraled out of control and bankruptcies proliferated. At the height of the economic crisis, money lost its value and Copenhagen declared state bankruptcy in January 1813.

1813: ANTI-FRENCH HOSTILITY AND POPULAR UPRISINGS

When measuring the impact of the Continental System, historians have tended to consider such long-term consequences as structural transformations based on institutional and administrative reforms or the geographical shift in trade inland from the Atlantic seaboard to the heartland of Western Europe.[75] Recent studies emphasize that the economic impact of the

---

70 Kienitz, *Kosakenwinter*, 24; Feldbaek, "Napoleonic," 96.
71 Henrick Fangel, "Wirtschaftliche Konjunkturen in Hadersleben im 19. Jahrhundert," in *Wirtschaftliche Wechsellagen*, 121–44, here 122–3.
72 Schama, *Patriots*, 501–3; Joor, *Adelaar*, 67.
73 Frank Hatje, *Repräsentationen der Staatsgewalt: Herrschaftsstrukturen und Selbstdarstellung in Hamburg, 1700–1900* (Basel, 1997), 257.
74 Lars Lindeberg, *De sa det ske Englandskriegene 1801–1814* (Copenhagen, 1974), 204. See also Frydenlund and Glenthøj, *1807* and Glenthøj and Rasmussen, *Det venskabelige, bombardement*.
75 For an overview, see Wolfram Fischer, "Wirtschaft und Wirtschaftspolitik in Deutschland unter den Bedingungen der Britisch-Französischen Blockade und Gegenblockade (1797–1812)," in *Historismus und Modern Geschichtsweissenchaft*, ed. Karl Otmar von Aretin (Stuttgart, 1987), 243–54.

blockade and Napoleon's economic strategies were far from uniform on the continent and must be examined on a regional basis.[76] Despite their different relationships with France, the experiences of Holland, Denmark, and the Hanseatic cities were similar: loss of neutrality and commerce, economic devastation, military requisitioning, and a growing hostility toward the empire. By 1813, the deterioration of livelihoods brought on by imperial commercial warfare and exploitation generated an ever-growing anti-French sentiment that would become increasingly explosive.

The Dutch, Hanseatics, and Danes understood by 1811 the basic principle of Napoleonic rule: administrative directives were designed to strengthen imperial control over occupied territories and allies alike. Popular resistance, expressed in smuggling, forgery, or open revolt against Napoleonic rule, grew from frustration born of declining living standards and unceasing exploitation associated with warfare. Of all French officials, the toll agents and custom police were most hated, as they were associated with all the negative aspects of the Continental System. Even French administrators in Holland complained about their compatriots' ill treatment and abuse of the Dutch population: violations of law, brutal house searches, corruption, extortion, and racketeering by gendarmes and toll inspectors.[77]

Following Napoleon's retreat from Russia, foreign newspapers, pamphlets, broadsheets, and private letters inundated the North Sea coastline with detailed accounts of the French military disaster.[78] Across northern Europe, anti-Napoleonic pamphlets, posters, graffiti, and songs openly expressed popular dissatisfaction with French rule as imperial police reported to Paris.[79] Yet there was no immediate popular rising; the population in the Hanseatic cities remained remarkably calm, awaiting liberation by the Russians. In Hamburg, however, the arrest of several petty smugglers by French officials in front of an impoverished crowd on February 24, 1813, touched off a spontaneous popular revolt that quickly spread across the city. Unemployed workers, women, and children attacked and destroyed palisades, customs houses, and watch houses. Angry throngs stoned the

76 For emphasis on region, see Ellis, *Empire*; Michael Broers, *Europe under Napoleon* (London, 1996); Alexander Grab, *Napoleon and the Transformation of Europe* (Basingstoke, U.K., 2003).

77 Schama, *Patriots*, 620–1.

78 See, e.g., *Einzig vollständiger authentischer Bericht über den Rückzug der französischen Armee von Moskau im Oktober und November 1812* (Stockholm, 1813); *Rückzug der Franzosen, nebst einer Liste der gefangenen Generale* (St. Petersburg, 1813). See also AN dossier F[7]6349, Bulletins Particuliers, January–February 1813.

79 Burghart Schmidt, "Die französische Polizei in Norddeutschland: Die Berichte des Generalpolizeidirektors D'Aubignosc aus den Jahren 1811–1814," *Francia* 26 (1999): 92–114; Schama, *Patriots*, 626.

despised French officials and threw many of them into the canals.[80] Gaining strength in numbers, protesters tore down French flags, signs, and imperial eagles. More concerned with dispensing "natural justice" than with driving the French from Hamburg, they focused their hostility on the hated tax collectors, customs agents, and police rather than on the imperial army or individual French families.[81] The French authorities attempted to forestall any further rebellion through harsh reprisals and rapid executions, but the brutal tactics misfired. Hostility toward the French intensified. Although the revolt was short lived, it triggered subsequent insurrections in the neighboring cities of Harburg, Lübeck, Stade, and Lüneburg, as well as in towns along the Elbe, and it also contributed to a mass desertion of northern Germans from the Grande Armée.

Triggered by hostility toward the Continental System and conscription, small-scale riots, mass desertions, and other forms of public unrest became increasingly violent in Holland. Protests were most intense in impoverished western Holland.[82] Riots in rural villages between Dordrecht and Rotterdam spread, and a rebellion in Leiden lasted three days in April 1813, illustrating the inability of French to control popular hostility and frustration. French authorities responded brutally to popular uprisings with public executions by firing squads in Zaandam, The Hague, and Rotterdam; as in Hamburg, this tactic backfired. As the French situation worsened in the fall of 1813, serious rebellion against imperial rule broke out across Holland. Cossacks were welcomed as liberators. The Dutch reserve army defected en bloc, and violent riots and attacks on customs posts and gendarmeries became commonplace.[83] In early November, imperial authority collapsed in Holland. Wagons filled with families and belongings of French officials crowded roads from Amsterdam, Utrecht, The Hague, and Rotterdam on their way to Antwerp.

Popular unrest against the empire, even when violent, was very symbolic. Protestors attacked tollhouses, administrative buildings, conscription registers, and imperial ensigns – in short, representations of French authority. In both Holland and northern Germany, burning customhouses and

---

80 "Volks-Aufstand zu Hamburg, an 24 Februar," *Politische Journal* (March 1813); Rist, *Lebenserinnerungen*, 208–11; Aaslestad, *Place*, 266–72; Burghart Schmidt, *Norddeutsche Unterschichten im Spannungsfeld von Krieg, Okkupation und Fremdherrschaft* (Hamburg, 2004), 72–84.

81 The French also recognized that public hostility was directed against the toll agents, not the French generally. AN dossier F73649, Bulletin Particulier, Mar. 1, 1813.

82 Joor, *Adelaar*, 685.

83 Schama, *Patriots*, 630; Joor, *Adelaar*, 665–73; Mark van Hattem, *Kozakkendag, de bevrijding van Utrecht in 1813* (Utrecht, 1993).

targeting officials like toll collectors and police illustrated the source of local grievances and popular hostility. The French were hated and despised because their rule brought war, poverty, and misery. If such protests vented hostility against poverty and war tied to French rule, protesters openly associated peace with trade and prosperity. In Hamburg, publicists urging recruitment for local militias celebrated the collective memory of a prosperous Hanseatic past to project a Hansa tradition of safeguarding home and trade.[84] During the November revolt in Amsterdam, revelers carried the banner "For Peace and Trade" through the streets.[85] By 1813, the scale of economic dislocation, unemployment and poverty, combined with material and manpower mobilization against Napoleon's wars, dramatically revealed the home front as a war zone.

Even in Denmark, Napoleon's ally, anti-French sentiment grew in the duchies and southern Jutland as a result of the unpopularity of the war and the kingdom's deteriorating economy. Danish cities were bankrupt and inundated with refugees. The countryside was overrun and plundered by foreign soldiers. In Danish Altona, inhabitants threw stones and excrement at French soldiers, compelling Danish forces to patrol the streets to prevent public riots.[86] Despite their ongoing enmity toward the British who dominated Danish waters, seized half of the Danish merchant marine, and attacked Danish privateers, the Danish government sought to abandon France and join the Quadruple Alliance during the spring of 1813. Danish soldiers even fought with Russians against the French in May. The Danes insisted only that the allies guarantee that Norway remain Danish. Unfortunately, Britain had promised Norway to Sweden in negotiating the Anglo-Swedish alliance. That promise ruined any chance of the Danes joining the allied coalition and thrust them back into Napoleon's camp.[87] Denmark emerged from the Napoleonic Wars a genuine loser, with Norway gone, its state finances in utter disorder, and its crippled merchant marine half its former size.[88] Following the war, the drop in grain prices and loss of Norway as a domestic market generated an agricultural crisis that lasted through the 1820s.

---

84 [Ferdinand Beneke], *Heer Geräth für die Hanseatisch Legion* (n.p., 1813); "Das deutsche Meer," *Hamburgisches Unterhaltungsblatt*, Apr. 7, 1813; "Zuruf an die Freiwilligen der Hanseatischen Legion," *Orient oder Hamburger Morgenblatt*, Apr. 1, 1813; "Der Hanseatische Bund," *Die neue Biene*, May 25, 1813.
85 Joor, *Adelaar*, 561 and 679.   86 Kienitz, *Kosakenwinter*, 65.
87 Schroeder, *Transformation*, 459; Ole Feldback, "Denmark and the Treaty of Kiel," *Scandinavian Journal of History*, 4, no. 15 (1990): 259–68.
88 Ruppenthal, "Denmark," 23; Kent Zetterberg, "State-Formation, Public Resistance and Nation-Building in Scandinavia in the Era of Revolution and Napoleon, 1789–1815," in *Collaboration and Resistance in Napoleonic Europe*, ed. Michael Rowe (Basingstoke, U.K., 2003), 203–12.

CONCLUSION

If anti-French sentiment and popular uprisings across northern Europe were local in origin and far from coordinated, they shared a common context and developed from common experiences. By the time peace finally came to Holland, northern Germany, and Denmark in 1814, large sections of their populations had been uprooted and impoverished. Along the urban coastline, the war had completely disrupted all levels of economic and social life for a generation. This devastation was the result of a radicalization of economic warfare practiced on a far greater scale than in earlier conflicts. It was a war that did not tolerate neutrality and used new strategies – the intensification and expansion of economic warfare in particular – to mobilize all available material and manpower, subject and ally alike, toward victory. Napoleon's colonialist economic system rested on imperial military power and oppression, and when that structure collapsed, the entire Continental System fell with it.

Economic warfare and exploitative occupations occurred in earlier conflicts during the seventeenth and eighteenth centuries, evidenced in the Thirty Years' War, the Dutch War of Independence (1568 1648), and the conflicts of the 1700s. The tactics of warfare between 1792 and 1815 remained rooted in the past. The scale of traditional combat, however, distinguished the Napoleonic Wars during these decades of transition at the dawn of the nineteenth century. If the constant radicalization in economic warfare from the rejection of neutrality to the enforcement of the Continental System does not correspond with twentieth-century notions of total war, it clearly points to that future. The scale and scope of war experiences that north Europeans faced reveals the diverse and "pluralistic nature of warfare" that comprised economic destruction combined with the day-to-day experience of military occupation, billeting and requisitions, heavy taxation and ruined state finances, and increased poverty.[89] The Continental System brought war into the harbors, warehouses, marketplaces, and homes. It short, it ensured that the home front became a war zone, as there was little distinction between combatant and civil society in the increasing mobilization of economic resources in Napoleonic military exploits and the coalition's countermeasures to halt imperial expansion.

89 Jeremy Black, *Rethinking Military History* (London, 2004), 2–3.

20

War and Everyday Life in Britain

MARY A. FAVRET

Even before the full realization of total war, we can glimpse the emergence of a cultural awareness of war as unbounded, involving not only the military but also the civilian population. Though the wars of the late eighteenth and early nineteenth centuries were indeed conducted on a global scale, this unboundedness was not merely spatial or geographical. The unbounded nature of war was, in that time, represented as occupying minds as well as bodies to such an extent that the conduct of daily life became, for a few key cultural observers, utterly infused with an awareness of global warfare. This awareness was especially acute in Great Britain, a nation that found itself engaged in military conflict almost unceasingly in this period; and yet Britons encountered warfare primarily at a distance. With the exception of the brief uprising in Ireland in 1798, the fighting threatened but never actually came home to the island kingdom during these years. Yet the economic structure of Great Britain, the rise in taxation, repressive government policies, food shortages, and the availability of certain goods were all fundamentally implicated in the escalating struggle with France and its allies. Aiming to represent to themselves the experience of living through distant wars, British writers began to contemplate the routines and habits of everyday life as engaged at almost every turn with the conduct of global war.

This chapter considers representative passages from four poems written in this period to demonstrate the ways war infiltrated, even determined, the representation of everyday life. What becomes clear in this decisively new type of poetry is not only that the effects of war pervaded the most common level of life on the home front but also that war was understood to condition habits and thought itself. To say that war conditions not only how people live but also how they think is not to say that the era of total war has begun. Yet it might begin to suggest one measure of the expansiveness and intensiveness of modern warfare.

READING IN WARTIME

To understand the historical distinctiveness of this turn in the poetry, we might recall the relatively new phenomenon of a wartime mediated to an unprecedented degree by print culture. For the British, more insulated from the fighting than their Continental neighbors, the experience of war came primarily as an experience of reading or spectatorship: the literate population read periodical accounts, navy lists, letters from family members and friends in the far-flung military; they watched plays and viewed spectacles that celebrated British victories abroad; they viewed paintings and bought engravings depicting foreign scenes of battle.[1] Plays and spectacles offered a shared, public sense of being at war; but newspaper and letter reading molded a more private experience of the conflict. Benedict Anderson's influential account in *Imagined Communities* argues for the creation of nationalism in the eighteenth century through the proliferation of specific reading practices, especially the "extraordinary mass ceremony" of reading the morning paper:

At the same time, the newspaper reader, observing exact replicas of his own paper being consumed by his . . . residential neighbors, is continually reassured that the imagined world [of the nation] is visibly rooted in everyday life. . . . [Q]uietly and continuously, [newspaper reading is] creating that remarkable confidence of community in anonymity that is the hallmark of the modern nation.[2]

Anderson neglects to explain in his account why the newspaper reader needs to be reassured of the viability of the nation, but the dramatic upturn in the number of newspapers and newspaper readers at the turn of the eighteenth century offers one rationale: war threatened the nation. For the wars with Revolutionary and Napoleonic France were not simply territorial wars; they were also ideological, aimed at preserving (or destroying) political systems, value systems, ways of life. In this way, even as it reinforced a sense of everydayness, newspaper reading became for the literate public in Britain a mode – however attenuated – of national defense, a daily shoring up of the idea of the nation even as it was under attack.

The very notion of a pervasive "modern wartime," Jerome Christensen has recently argued in an extension of Anderson's argument, arose in Britain in this period as a function of the periodical press.[3] The news produced a new experience of time; with its punctuated but regular rhythms, it

1 See Gillian Russell, *The Theaters of War: Performance, Politics and Society, 1793–1815* (Oxford, 1995).
2 Benedict Anderson, *Imagined Communities: Reflections on the Origin and Spread of Nationalism*, rev. ed. (London, 1991), 35–6.
3 Jerome Christensen, *Romanticism at the End of History* (Baltimore, 2000) 4–5.

organized the home front into a wartime to be experienced by the group Samuel Taylor Coleridge (1772–1834) identified as "spectators and non-combatants."[4] Christensen elaborates in ways that point to the internalized effect of war reporting: "in wartime reported incidents of conflict acquire a pronounced episodic structure that, in the reporting[,] . . . effectively implicates the noncombatant auditor or reader in its narrative unfolding."[5] Readers experience the war as something read, read according to an everyday routine, and read along with a sense of anticipation or suspense. In this way, though sponsoring a shared collective sense of the nation in time of war, newspaper reading also made this experience something "performed in silent privacy," as Anderson puts it, "in the lair of the skull."[6]

We should be cautious in taking this internalization as a diminishment or restriction of the scope and scale of far-flung warfare. The internalizing of news did bring the distant war home, domesticating it in a way that we now recognize as closely linked to literary developments of the period, namely the early romantic movement in Britain. But that movement could also be said to have opened up an entirely new front, introducing new pains and strife to supplement the violence abroad. Coleridge, the wartime editor and journalist who doubled as poet and philosopher, provides a representative version of this turn. His poem "Fears in Solitude, Written in April 1798 during the Alarm of Invasion" neatly maps out what is, in fact, a historical shift in the apprehension of war. Coleridge begins the poem by painting a scene of calm security, set within local, tenable boundaries, the "small and silent dell" (2) into which intrudes the noise of distant "uproar" and "strife" (34). For Coleridge, the noise arises less from cannon and trumpets than from public discourse (debates and sermons) and the daily newspapers that, after a long jeremiad, Coleridge rejects.[7]

> Secure from actual warfare, we have loved
> To swell the war-whoop, passionate for war!
> Alas! . . .
> We, this whole people, have been clamorous
> For war and bloodshed; animating sports,
> The which we pay for as a thing to talk of,
> Spectators and not combatants. . . .
> We send our mandates for the certain death

---

4 Samuel Taylor Coleridge, "Fears in Solitude, Written in April 1798, during the Alarm of an Invasion," in *Selected Poetry and Prose of Coleridge*, ed. Donald A. Stauffer (New York, 1951), 64–70: here, line 96 (references hereafter to line numbers).

5 Christensen, *End of History*, 5.   6 Anderson, *Imagined Communities*, 35.

7 See also Mark Jones, "Alarmism, Public Sphere Performatives, and the Lyric Turn; or, What Is 'Fears In Solitude' Afraid Of?" *Boundary 2*, no. 30 (2003): 67–105.

> Of thousands and ten thousands! Boys and girls,
> And women, that would groan to see a child
> Pull off an insect's wing, all read of war,
> The best amusement for our morning meal! (88–90, 93–6, 104–8)

Coleridge sees the newspaper as amusement and "a thing to talk of," not quiet enough for his purposes. The poem thus proceeds to reorient the thrust of the news and his response to the threat of invasion by turning deliberately homeward and inward. The poem ends by calling upon "my intellectual life, / All sweet sensations, all ennobling thoughts" as witness to his patriotism, and by turning from the world at war back to the "small and silent dell" that stands in for little England but also for the poet's "private lair of the skull":

> O green and silent dell!
> . . . [I am] grateful, that by nature's quietness
> And solitary musings, all my heart
> Is softened, and made worthy to indulge
> Love, and the thoughts that yearn for human kind. (228–42)

Though at first glance Coleridge seems to muddy Anderson's and Christensen's assessment of the role of the newspaper in producing a quietly private, nationalizing practice, the effect of the poem actually clarifies and extends their point: news had to be made into a private rather than a public medium; the public houses that Coleridge derides had to be replaced by the meditations of the solitary reader. From reading the newspaper and the public debate about war (and invasion), the poet is prompted to cultivate an internalized sort of patriotism, a defense of his country based on "solitary musings," "thoughts that yearn for human kind," and ultimately a poetry forged in response to the news. Typically, and very deliberately, Coleridge turns the matter of war away from external and empirically verifiable events, to metaphysical and moral considerations. Though this move may at first appear a narrowing of concerns into a tiny circumference – that dell or lair – it can also be taken as introducing modern warfare into new terrain, allowing it to invade and shape the workings of the mind.

STILLNESS AND ROUTINE

"Fears in Solitude" displays very neatly this translation of war in the Napoleonic era into a new vocabulary and range of significance. In this poem, Coleridge in fact refines a strategy laid earlier, if less aggressively, by his older contemporary, William Cowper (1731–1800), who was writing in the tense period of the American War of Independence and the colonial wars in India (often seen as failed wars of independence). Cowper may seem an unlikely candidate for a discussion of war, total or otherwise. Arguably the most influential poet of the late eighteenth century, Cowper was celebrated for his epic-length hymn to domestic retirement, *The Task*, written between 1783 and 1785. Catherine Hall and Lenora Davidoff have shown in detail how pivotal Cowper was for the construction of nineteenth-century middle-class sensibilities, organized around a new but quickly mainstreamed image of private life removed from the turmoil of the world.[8] In a famous passage from book 4 of *The Task*, "The Winter's Evening," for instance, Cowper describes his habit of reading the evening newspaper with its record of pain and violence:

> . . . I behold
> The tumult and am still. The sound of war
> Has lost its terrors 'ere it reaches me;
> Grieves but alarms me not. (4:99–102)[9]

Shut away from the cold and dark of the outside world, Cowper deliberately focuses on everyday routine. He gives elaborate descriptions of his anticipation of the coming of the post boy every evening; the setting of the teakettle on the fire; the cozy recourse to "intimate delights, fireside enjoyments, home-born happiness / And all the comforts of . . . undisturb'd retirement" (4:139–42). Moments such as these encouraged contemporary readers, such as Francis Jeffrey of the *Edinburgh Review*, to cherish the poem's "minute and correct painting of those home-scenes and private feelings with which everyone is internally familiar."[10] "By inspiring a feeling of intimacy, a kind of domestic confidence in his readers," wrote a later nineteenth-century assessment, "[Cowper] made his works 'household words'" – even as he seemed to make the household a world unto itself.[11] In this very explicit celebration of the pleasures of everyday activities "internally familiar" to his readers, Cowper announces what would emerge as romantic sensibility in the writing of his acolytes in the next generation, among them William Wordsworth, Jane Austen, and Coleridge himself.

8 Leonore Davidoff and Catherine Hall, *Family Fortunes: Men and Women of the English Middle Class, 1780–1850* (Chicago, 1987), 158–67. "In celebrating domesticity," they write, "[Cowper] crossed political, religious and economic divisions and established himself as the most beloved writer of the period" (158).

9 William Cowper, *The Task and Selected Other Poems*, ed. James Sambrook (London, 1994).

10 Francis Jeffrey, "Hayley's Life of Cowper," *Edinburgh Review* 2 (1803): 64–86, 84.

11 George Godfrey Cunningham, ed. *Lives of Eminent and Illustrious Englishmen*, 8 vols. (Glasgow, 1838), 6:327.

What these responses neglect to mention, however, are the conditions motivating Cowper's retirement from the world via everyday routine.[12] Careful attention to the language of *The Task* reveals the powerful and nearly unremitting dialectic the poet establishes between his version of the everyday and his consciousness of the surrounding winter of global conflict. In fact, a closer reading of Cowper's influential *The Task* suggests that the emergence of this private, domestic ideal at the end of the eighteenth century was conditioned by a new awareness of global war, also emerging in this period. The poet's attention seems to be torn equally between the inner circle of the domestic hearth and the world he absorbs through his reading of the newspaper. In "The Winter's Evening," in particular, consciousness of a world variously at war underwrites, even informs, the sense of privacy and retirement with which, supposedly, all readers are internally familiar.

Cowper begins his scene of retirement by announcing the advent of the post boy:

> Hark! 'tis the twanging horn! O'er yonder bridge . . .
> He comes, the herald of a noisy world,
> With spatter'd boots, strapp'd waist, frozen locks,
> News from all nations lumb'ring at his back, . . .
> He whistles as he goes, light-hearted wretch,
> Cold and yet cheerful: messenger of grief
> Perhaps to thousands, and of joy to some,
> To him indiff'rent whether grief or joy. . . . (4:1, 3–5, 12–15)

Cowper depicts the post boy's coming mockingly as a pseudomilitary charge, all the while reminding his reader of the wartime atmosphere that surrounds this daily event, "usher'd in / With such heart-shaking music" (4:23–4). This atmosphere agitates his own impatience: "What are its [the newspaper's] tidings?" he wonders:

> . . . have our troops awak'd?
> Or do they still, as if with opium drugg'd
> Snore to the murmurs of the Atlantic wave?
> Is India free? And does she wear her plum'd
> And jewell'd turban with a smile of peace,
> Or do we grind her still? (4:25–30)

Cowper "longs to know" what is happening in the world, specifically what is happening in Britain's military engagements in North America, where

12 The standard explanation for this turn to retirement invokes Cowper's strong evangelical beliefs, as well as his several bouts of depression. Not discounting those explanations, I nonetheless attend to the language of the poem itself and how it produces its own explanations. See Davidoff and Hall, *Family Fortunes*, 162–7; Brian Spiller, ed., *Cowper: Prose and Poetry* (London, 1968); Martin Priestman, *Cowper's Task: Structure and Influence* (Cambridge, U.K. 1983).

recently, and crushingly, its "snoring" troops had been defeated, and in India, where the aggressive and unpopular policies of the East India Company had also led to recent defeats in the Second Mysore War (1781–3). This passage illustrates two strategies Cowper devises to handle his awareness of and helplessness before the fact of wars conducted in his name but beyond his ken. First, he resorts to figurative language to capture (but also distract from) what he cannot know: hence the troops "opium drugg'd" by the Atlantic wave and a personified India's eye-catching turban. The exoticism of the imagery, however, only underscores his desire and inability to know what these wars entail. Second, and this is the larger strategy of the book, Cowper converts the contingency and violence of warfare into a matter of daily routine: he makes it clear that such questions arise every evening at the same time, conditioned by the arrival of the post boy, who dumps his load so that the poet may sit before his fireplace to read "fast-bound in chains of silence" (4:53). The "noisy world" at war is reduced to the silence of habitual reading in the same way that the wintry weather is managed by the warmth of home and hearth. The open questions posed by warfare and furthered by the poet's distance from the action are answered by the assurances of everyday domestic routine. The insecurities of wartime, in other words, produce the poet's recourse to the security of home and the quotidian.

To assume that Cowper has effectively removed himself from the pains and demands of war, however, would be to misread his language. Even when he maintains that, in reading, "I behold the tumult / And am still," the emphasis that falls on that word *still* echoes his earlier questions ("Is India free? . . . / Or do we grind her still?" "Have out troops awak'd? or do they still . . . / Snore?"). In the longer, much-cited passage from which this line is extracted, Cowper's imagery deliberately confuses the separation between home and war. Here the poet describes his nightly reading as a "loop-hole of retreat" through which he "peeps" at the noisy world and hears

> . . . the roar . . .
> At a safe distance, where the dying sound
> Falls a soft murmur on the uninjur'd ear.
> Thus sitting and surveying thus at ease
> The globe and its concerns, I seem'd advanc'd
> To some secure and more than mortal height,
> That lib'rates and exempts me from them all.
> . . . I behold
> The tumult and am still. The sound of war
> Has lost its terrors 'ere it reaches me,
> Grieves but alarms me not. (4:88, 91–7, 99–102)

Yes, "dying sounds" of violence fall softly on the "uninjur'd ear," but they cannot do so without hinting at other dying, other falls, and all the injuries that the uninjur'd have been spared. Similarly, the innocent pleasures of the evening cannot fully escape the world outside Cowper's retreat: a "clear voice" sings "in the charming strife triumphant still"; a needle, a "threaded steel," flies swiftly to its target; Scripture reading recalls "the dangers we have 'scaped . . . / The disappointed foe . . . / life preserved and peace restored" (4:163, 165, 185–7). The distance of war is itself a constructed illusion: whatever promise of refuge they offer, Cowper knows that both *loophole* and *retreat* are fundamentally military terms.[13] A decade later, readers of *The Task* would recognize in the words *terror* and *alarm* the signal terms of their own wartime climate.[14] Intimations of warfare, in other words, seep into and shape the familiar activities of Cowper's "The Winter's Evening." Even the liberation and exemption mentioned here demand that the reader be "bound in chains" of silence: no simple freedom or peace is available. In such moments, *The Task* reveals the everyday not as a zone of peace in contrast to a distant war but as the unspectacular register or correspondent of wartime. For all its internal familiarity and its interiority, Cowper's construction of the individual in retirement must acknowledge even as it tries to organize and buffer his consciousness of distant war. To his devoted readers in the decades of the Revolutionary and Napoleonic wars, as they read of the violence spreading to all corners of the globe, Cowper's poetry appealed because they felt perhaps even more urgently his desire to order the experience of war at a distance, to fashion it into their everyday.

A MILITARIZED SOCIETY

While Cowper absorbed newspaper reading into his poetry, the papers he read had begun absorbing poetry into their columns. By the end of the eighteenth century, thanks to developments in print technology and postal delivery as well as increasing literacy rates, the newspapers themselves

13 On this passage in *The Task* and the question of historical mediation, see Kevis Goodman, "The Loophole in the Retreat: The Culture of News and the Early Life of Romantic Self-Consciousness," *South Atlantic Quarterly* 102 (2003): 25–52. Goodman prefers to read the loophole primarily as a passage or conduit for information, veering away from its first definition (Oxford English Dictionary) as "a narrow vertical opening . . . to allow for the passage of missiles."

14 By 1795, *terror* would be inextricably linked to the violent outcome of the French Revolution, against which the British had declared war in 1793. *Alarm* was the term used by the Pitt administration to rouse British fears of a French invasion. Beginning in 1795, and increasingly in the coming decade, propagandists in Britain would cultivate such alarms to increase public support for an otherwise unpopular war. See Jones, "Alarmism," 67–75; and Mark Rowlinson, "Invasion! Coleridge, the Defense of Britain and the Cultivation of Fear," in *Romantic Wars: Studies in Culture and Conflict, 1793–1822*, ed. Philip Shaw (Aldershot, U.K., 2000), 110–36.

provided a more thoroughgoing rendering of the everydayness of war —
even and especially in their own wartime poetry. Betty T. Bennett's valuable
anthology *British War Poetry in the Age of Romanticism, 1793–1815* collects
the war poems printed in newspapers and periodicals and exhibits, among
many other things, the importance of poetry to the average reader's daily
construction of events abroad.[15] Like letters to the editor, poems were sent
in to the dailies and weeklies, registering in verse the readers' response to the
news and its bearing on their lives. During these years, the poetry columns
would, in general, print at least one poem a day addressing the war.[16]
Popular war poems circulated through the press, appearing in as many
as five periodicals and occasionally reprinted as broadsides or collected
in topical collections such as *The Spirit of the Public Journals*. As early as
1793, war poems were ubiquitous, the product of "every hireling scribbler,"
according to a complaint in the *Analytic Review*.[17] Here stories of widows,
orphans, impressed sailors, and wounded soldiers highlighted effects of the
decades-long war that were visible and felt on the home front. In many of
the poems, characters spoke in emotion-laden voices of their struggle to
survive, suggesting a heightened awareness of the subjective experience of
war on everyday lives. As Bennett notes, poems written for both radical and
conservative periodicals reflected this shift toward articulating stories of the
common man simply and with feeling, in such a way that they too became
"internally familiar."[18] War poems were commissioned from popular poets
of the day; others were merely sent to the editors, often anonymously. Few,
if any, were aimed at posterity; many presented themselves as resolutely tied
to a particular moment, their titles bearing an almost journalistic dateline
(e.g., "The Present State of Spain, Written at Madrid, June 1, 1814," or
Coleridge's extended title "Fears in Solitude, Written in April 1798 during
an Alarm of Invasion"). My point here is not just to call attention to the
reciprocity between journalism and poetry in this period but also to frame
such reciprocity as a daily event of reading about and responding to the
ongoing wars. To an unprecedented degree, amateur and professional poets
in the Revolutionary and Napoleonic era were following Cowper's lead,
reading the newspapers to learn about war, then supplementing, extending,
or revising that everyday practice of reading with the language and structures

15 Betty T. Bennett, ed., *British War Poetry in the Age of Romanticism, 1793–1815* (New York, 1976)
   Bennett's anthology can be found in a digital edition by Orianne Smith, http://www.rc.umd.
   edu/editions/warpoetry.
16 Bennett, *War Poetry*, 7
17 Quoted in Bennett, *War Poetry*, 6; see also 46–8.
18 Bennett, *War Poetry*, 47.

of poetry, which in turn became what other readers found to read in their daily paper, part of each day's experience of wartime.

   The celebration of retirement and domesticity that Cowper fashioned in response to reading the news encouraged women readers to coordinate their experience with the conduct of worldly events; not surprisingly, it also licensed women writers to enter into this public and poetic discourse on the war. Charlotte Smith, Amelia Alderson Opie, Helen Maria Williams, Hannah More, Anne Yearsley – all were sought-after contributors to the poetry columns of the print media, and along with many lesser-known women writers, they found new ways to document their felt experience of the ongoing wars. Perhaps the most successful woman poet working in the periodicals was Mary Robinson, a celebrity in the London press renowned not only for her poetic gifts but also for her beauty, her theater career, and, not least, her former liaison with the Prince of Wales. Increasingly, she has been recognized by critics for having "changed the very nature of the craft of poetry" in this period.[19] Robinson understood as well as any of her contemporaries the complicity between her own celebrity and the power of the press; but for all her games with identity and performance, she was capable of delivering a razor-edged vision of the experience of everyday war.[20] As a woman, and as a barely respectable member of society, Robinson cast a jaundiced eye on the mechanisms of power. In an early newspaper poem, "January 1795," she gave her reading of the wartime climate:

> Pavement slipp'ry; People sneezing;
> Lords in ermine, beggars freezing;
> Nobles, scarce the wretched heeding;
> Gallant soldiers – fighting! – bleeding![21]

Robinson's quatrain with its echoing rhymes calls into question the distance between battlefield and London streets; her sense of the brutal winter weather cannot be easily separated from her sense of a brutal war. Robinson's style in this poem and elsewhere deliberately propels the newspaper reader to ponder the unstated connections between these everyday urban vignettes and the scene of bloodshed.

---

19 Stuart Curran, "Mary Robinson and the New Lyric," *Women's Writing* 9 (2002): 9.
20 See Judith Pascoe's excellent discussion of Robinson in *Romantic Theatricality: Gender, Poetry and Spectatorship* (Ithaca, New York, 1997), 130–83, as well as her introduction to *The Poems of Mary Robinson* (Peterborough, U.K., 2002). On Robinson's influence in the London scene and in subsequent generations of poets, see Curran, "New Lyric," and Tim Fulford, "The Electrifying Mary Robinson," *Women's Writing* 9, no. 1 (2002): 23–36.
21 "January 1795," in Bennett, *War Poetry*, 142–4; first published in the *Morning Post*, Jan. 29, 1795.

Robinson extends this rhetorical strategy in her poem "The Camp," her fullest consideration of a militarized society. First published in the *Morning Post* of 1802, "The Camp" catalogs the social effects of military camps established on English soil in response to the war in America and later expanded during the wars with France. The "military mania" promoted by camp culture is shown by Robinson to work its way into every layer of society – women, men, children, the elderly, husbands, wives, aristocrats, and tradesmen – fashioning habits of sex, consumption, business, and dreaming. I quote only the closing movement of a forty-eight-line poem:

> *Aid-de-camps* and youthful pages,
> Prudes and vestals of all ages!
> Old coquets and matrons surly,
> Sounds of distant hurly-burly!
> Mingled voices, uncouth singing,
> Carts full laden, forage bringing; . . .
> Tradesmen, leaving shops and seeming
> More of *war* than profit dreaming;
> Martial sounds and braying asses,
> Noise that ev'ry noise surpasses!
> All confusion, din and riot,
> Nothing clean – and nothing quiet.[22]

Robinson's finale reads as riposte to Cowper's wartime quiet: this hurly-burly is hardly distant. Her vision of a nation at war – with its proliferating lists, headlong rhythms, and apparently unmotivated conjunctions – emphasizes the meaningless din of a military culture escalating out of bounds. Her verse abandons conventional narrative logic (there are no finite verbs, for instance), displaying a social order that has been shredded even while posing as a plausible inventory (her parody of military culture). In "The Camp," military culture has infiltrated and disrupted the everyday life of the English countryside (one is reminded of Jane Austen's use of the Meryton militia in her *Pride and Prejudice*); this includes not simply the underclass of widows and discharged soldiers, common in other periodical poetry, but also the middling ranks as well as gentry and nobility. In coming home in this way, moreover, the nature of war has itself changed. What war has brought to England is understood as a circumambient "noise" that shapes the drinking of beer and whisky, the longings of maids and matrons, the movement of bodies and goods in and out of any town in England: in the absence of any

---

22 "The Camp," in Bennett, *War Poetry*, 273–4. For more on the "military mania" associated with the camps, see Russell, *Theaters of War*, 33–41.

other logic, war – in its confusion and riot – holds these disparate activities and attitudes together.

A WAR OF THE MIND

A further refinement on the everyday sense of war developing in Great Britain in this period surfaces in the work of William Wordsworth, the major poetic voice of his age and deeply influenced by Cowper. In fact, though following the lead of the newspaper poets in the 1790s in his depiction of a society debilitated by war, Wordsworth – like his friend Coleridge – increasingly adopted Cowper's stance of rural retirement, fashioning there a new, and shockingly prescient, response to global warfare.[23] Wordsworth had actually traveled to France to revel in the initial years of the Revolution but left in 1793 at the outbreak of war, leaving behind his French mistress and their child.[24] His growing disillusionment with the course of the Revolution and his attempt to repair his faith in human nature via the mysteries of nature and the vocation of poetry motivate his two most ambitious works, *The Excursion* (1814) and, more famously, *The Prelude* (1805; 1850). The latter especially announces its debt to Cowper's *The Task*. Commonly taught as a poet of nature, Wordsworth nevertheless trains his attention onto the natural world to register – in often complex and vexed fashion – the drama of his historical moment.[25]

Lyrical Ballads (1798), the book of poetry that gave Wordsworth his initial fame and is still considered one of the foundational texts of modern poetry, was, in the words of his collaborator Samuel Coleridge, designed to re-create the "charm" of the everyday by "awakening the mind's attention from the lethargy of custom, and directing it to the loveliness and the wonders of the world before us."[26] For all its charm, though, the everyday

23 Recent studies on the relationship between Cowper and Wordsworth include David J. Leigh, "Cowper, Wordsworth, and the Sacred Moment of Perception," in *The Fountain Light: Studies in Romanticism and Religion in Honor of John L. Mahoney*, ed. J. Robert Barth (New York, 2002), 54–72; Tim Fulford, "Wordsworth, Cowper and the Language of Eighteenth-Century Politics," in *Early Romantics: Perspectives in British Poetry from Pope to Wordsworth*, ed. Thomas Woodman (Basingstoke, U.K., 1998), 117–33; Karen O'Brien, "'Still at Home': Cowper's Domestic Empires," in Woodman, *Early Romantics*, 134–47.
24 See biographies by Stephen Charles Gill, *William Wordsworth: A Life* (Oxford, 1990); and Kenneth R. Johnston, *The Hidden Wordsworth: Poet, Lover, Rebel, Spy* (New York, 1998).
25 A debate continues over whether Wordsworth represses or records history through his turn to nature, and the matter is not easily resolved. On the side of repression or evasion, see Marjorie Levinson, *Wordsworth's Great Period Poems: Four Essays* (Cambridge, 1986); and Alan Liu, *William Wordsworth: A Sense of History* (Stanford, California, 1989). On the opposite side, see Kenneth Johnston, "The Politics of 'Tintern Abbey,'" *Wordsworth Circle* 14 (1983): 6–14; and Kevis Goodman, *Georgic Modernity and British Romanticism* (Cambridge, 2004), 106–43.
26 Samuel Taylor Coleridge, "Biographia Literaria," in *Poetry and Prose*, 314–15.

in this period of imperial expansion was, as we have seen, simultaneously wedded to an awareness of the impact of war. *Lyrical Ballads* is famously populated by the residue of a violent age: vagrants and paupers, widows and orphans, thoughtless murder and untimely deaths. In a second edition, Wordsworth explained that the "principal object" of the collection had been "to choose incidents and situations from common life, and to relate or describe them, throughout, as far as was possible in a selection of language really used by men," and thereby to investigate "the primary laws of our nature."[27] Despite this apparently universal claim, Wordsworth understood that this turn to common life was governed by his sense of the "present state of the public taste in this country," and furthermore by "the revolutions, not of literature alone, but likewise of society itself."[28] Unlike *The Task*, and much like the newspaper verse, *Lyrical Ballads* attends to the everyday experience of the underclass, those dispossessed by the recent wars and the economic policies supporting them (see, e.g., "The Mad Mother," "The Last of the Flock," "Old Man Traveling," or even the more famous "Rime of the Ancient Mariner," read now as a fable of imperial expansionism).[29] Wordsworth and Coleridge together aimed to make the familiar unfamiliar through their series of charmed, if uncanny, accounts of common men and women; yet their revised version of Cowper's "internally familiar" everyday still offered a temporal and experiential structure for wartime, reiterating on home turf the experience, however distant and haunting, of combat.[30]

For Wordsworth, both the emphasis and the mode of representing the landscape of wartime changed in the coming years, as the war modulated from one against the revolutionary government to an imperial war against the "tyrant" and "genius" Napoleon.[31] A simple example of the transformation can be found in a relatively minor poem on a characteristically romantic topic, "To the Clouds," written in 1808. What began with Cowper as an inscription of warfare into the domestic interior develops here into internalization tout court: The evidence of the external world at war is

---

27 William Wordsworth, "'Preface' to Lyrical Ballads (1800)," in *Prefaces and Prologues to Famous Books*, ed. Charles W. Eliot, vol. 39 (New York, 1909–14), at http://www.bartleby.com/30/36.html.

28 Ibid.

29 For this interpretation of "Rime," see Sonia Hofkosh and Alan Richardson, introduction to *Romanticism, Race and Imperial Culture* (Bloomington, Indiana, 1995), 1–9.

30 Another locus classicus for Wordworth's uncanny handling of the everyday experience of war occurs in his encounter with the discharged soldier in William Wordsworth, *The Prelude: The Four Texts* (1798, 1799, 1805, 1850), ed. Jonathan Wordsworth (London, 1995). See the 1850 version, 4:369 ff.

31 For an extended account of this change for Wordsworth, see Gill, Wordsworth, and Johnston, *Hidden Wordsworth*; for English culture more generally, see Simon Bainbridge, *Napoleon and English Romanticism* (Cambridge, U.K. 1995).

first naturalized, then taken in as the work of the mind. Unlike Cowper questioning the post boy, Wordsworth begins by questioning the skies:

> Army of clouds! Ye winged Host in troops
> Ascending from behind the motionless brow
> Of that tall rock, as from a hidden world,
> Oh whither with such eagerness of speed?[32]

As he watches troops move through the sky, disappear and be replaced, the poet's mind is full of speculation: "Contend ye with each other?" or "post ye over vale and height / To sink upon your mother's lap – and rest?" or "Is your impetuous march the likeness / Of a wide army pressing on to meet / Or overtake some unknown enemy?" But then, "Fancy . . . compares your squadrons to an endless flight of birds." And so on, each image of war – and image of peace – revealed as pure imagining. The poem is never able to settle the matter: What are these troops up to? Is the atmosphere one of war or peace? And are the clouds/armies transient or permanent? In contemplating the susceptibility of clouds to the human imagination, Wordsworth is following the lead of Shakespeare's *Hamlet* and Milton's *Paradise Lost*; but where his predecessors saw animals, he sees the movement of armies in these changing forms. The movement of the lines (of troops as well as of poetry) apparently gives the poet warrant to declare in the end, "My thoughts / Admit no bondage and my words have wings," converting his view of the clouds – and all their military possibility – into evidence of the poet's own liberty, his "thoughts" and "words"(58–9). The progression of thought is itself curious, betraying perhaps an Englishman's justification for military aggression overseas: be it warmongering or peacekeeping, the distant mobilization of troops – a hot political topic in Great Britain in 1808 – secures his own sense of liberty.[33] Yet the immediate political ramifications might distract from more fundamental curiosities. Here Wordsworth locates his thoughts about global war in the everyday fluctuation of the weather;[34] the movement of these nebulous armies, moreover, is conceived as evidence of the motion of the poet's own mind. It is as if war itself were the work of imaginative genius (here the poet betrays his rivalry with Napoleon); and as if war, like weather, took place – to be noticed or not – any day or every day.[35]

---

32 William Wordsworth, *The Poems*, ed. John Hayden, 2 vols. (New Haven, Connecticut, 1981), 1:815.

33 As their allies were quick to point out, the British were generally reluctant to send an expeditionary force to the continent, but in 1808 and against opposition, Castlereagh used the insurrection in Spain to dispatch thirty thousand men, the largest force yet, under the command of Arthur Wellesley. Georges Lefebvre, *Napoleon: From Tilsit to Waterloo, 1807–1815* (New York, 1969), 92–3.

34 See Mary A. Favret, "War in the Air," *Modern Language Quarterly* 65, no. 4 (2005): 531–59.

35 Other male poets aimed to militarize the work of the imagination. See Marlon Ross, *The Contours of Masculine Desire: Romanticism and the Rise of Women's Poetry* (New York, 1989), 40–9; Bainbridge, *Napoleon and Romanticism*, 1–16, 54–94.

Few poems more baldly express the difficulty the British public experienced as it tried to imagine a far-flung war conducted outside and beyond any individual point of view.[36] Few poems reveal better the desire to surmount this difficulty by comprehending global warfare through this aerial and finally abstract point of view. Whereas Cowper incorporated it into the rhythms of his evening rituals, Robinson wove it into the disruptive libido of society at large, and Coleridge converted it into moral musings, Wordsworth's solution here is to elevate distant war into the work of speculation and imagination. The strategy was at work earlier, in 1804; when he first described the power and strength of imagination in his masterpiece, *The Prelude*, Wordsworth famously dressed it in the colors of war, so that it became, in the words of Alan Liu, "the uncanny double of Napoleon": "Imagination!... in such strength / Of usurpation... under such banners militant" (6:592–609).[37]

The poet does not merely enter the world of war imaginatively; he makes the work of imagination consonant with the work of war, and vice versa. If for him the power of imagination doubles and rivals the power of Napoleon, it can do so only if the two operate in comparable arenas; and that arena is both war and the everyday, or what we might call everyday war, understood theoretically or speculatively (and somehow detached from human bodies). Wordsworth's contemporary William Blake, also writing in 1804, performed a similar translation in his epic *Milton*, when he calls rousingly and in words that have served British militancy ever since:

> Bring me my Spear: O clouds unfold!
> Bring me my Chariot of fire!
> I will not cease from mental Fight.[38]

Blake envisions his poetry fighting the forces that "depress Mental & prolong Corporeal war," thereby liberating England from its foes. Like Coleridge and Wordsworth, and even more aggressively, Blake sees war in the romantic age mutating into a moral and psychic affair, fought by the mind with sublime technologies of imagination and language. What for earlier readers and writers could not be fully known because it could not be seen ("Is India

36 After 1798, war reporting was subject to increasing government censorship. On the various acts passed to restrict freedom of the press in England, see R. Fox Bourne, *English Newspapers* (London 1887; reprint, New York, 1966); Arthur Aspinwall, *Politics and the Press, 1780–1850* (London, 1949); and Kevin Gilmartin, *Print Politics: The Press and Radical Opposition in Early Nineteenth-Century England* (Cambridge, U.K. 1996).

37 Alan Liu masterfully explains how Wordsworth maps this crucial passage onto 1804 accounts of Napoléon's crossing of the Alps and later defeat in Egypt. *A Sense of History*, 23–31. See also Bainbridge, *Napoleon and Romanticism*, 89–95.

38 William Blake, preface to "Milton," in: *The Complete Poetry and Prose of William Blake*, ed. David V. Erdman, rev. ed. (Berkeley, California, 1982), 95.

free? . . . or do we grind her still?") has been converted into the very terrain of an active, expansive imagination.

These examples, brief though representative, all indicate an accelerating comprehension of the ideological nature of warfare and its reach far beyond the fields and seas of battle. The celebration of domestic retirement in Cowper, the newspaper stories of individuals suffering through the impersonal mechanisms of far-flung violence, the sense that military culture has leaked out from the army itself to rearrange the fabric and habits of society, the belief in the power and strength of imagination to wage a war of spirit and mind – these methods of registering the effects of global war did themselves multiply and extend the terrain of warfare in the modern era.

Index

411

Lightning Source UK Ltd.
Milton Keynes UK
UKOW05f2307111114

241457UK00001B/63/P